THE EUROPEAN AI ACT

European Union Law Series

This series brings together major works in the field of European Union Law. It features a diverse range of publications, including comprehensive handbooks designed to teach European Union Law, treaties for legal practitioners and academics, monographs on specialised topics and some of the best doctoral dissertations from across Europe. Additionally, it includes publications detailing conference proceedings on topical issues, as well as commentaries on major judgments and decisions handed down by the Court of Justice of the European Union.

P. Durand and A. Gilbert-d'Halluin (eds.), *Directive (EU) 2022/2464 as regards Corporate Sustainability Reporting (CSRD)*, 2024.

G. Marti (ed.), *European Citizenship through the Lens of EU Values*, 2025.

A. Gridel, *Financial Markets and Instruments in Private International Law*, 2025.

THE EUROPEAN AI ACT

SUMMARY, KEY POINTS AND ARTICLE-BY-ARTICLE ANALYSIS

Alain Bensoussan, Jérémy Bensoussan
and Virginie Bensoussan-Brulé

INTERSENTIA
LEFEBVRE GROUP

Intersentia
Lefebvre Belgium SA
Avenue Jean Monnet, 4
1348 Louvain-la-Neuve
Belgium
Email: contact@larcier-intersentia.com

Distribution for the UK, Ireland and
Rest of the World (excl. France, Belgium and Luxembourg)
Ingram Publisher Services UK
1 Deltic Avenue, Rooksley
Milton Keynes MK13 8LD
United Kingdom
Tel: +44 1752 202 301 | Fax: +44 1752 202 331
Email: ipsuk.customercare@ingramcontent.com

Distribution for France and Other Countries (excl. Ireland and the UK)
Interforum Editis
92 avenue de France
75013 Paris
France

Distribution for Belgium and Luxembourg (excl. France, Ireland and the UK)
Larcier-Intersentia
Avenue Jean Monnet, 4
1348 Louvain-la-Neuve
Belgium

The European AI Act. Summary, Key Points and Article-by-Article Analysis

ISBN : 978-1-83970-487-1
D/2025/06040/0489
NUR 820

British Library Cataloguing in Publication Data. A catalogue record for this book is available from the British Library

ACKNOWLEDGMENTS

This book was written by Alain Bensoussan in collaboration with Jérémy Bensoussan and Virginie Bensoussan-Brulé.

The authors would like to thank Marie-Cécile Berthod and Isabelle Buffelan Abu Sbeit for their careful review of the French version of the manuscript, as well as Frédéric Forster and Marilyne Barzun for its translation into English.

TABLE OF CONTENTS

EXECUTIVE SUMMARY

1 GENERAL APPROACH

1.1. Preamble

1. This AI Regulation[1] is the outcome of a more than 5-year process where it was discussed whether the appropriate EU instrument to lay down harmonised rules on AI was a regulation or a directive. The type of legal act eventually chosen—a Regulation—shows that the objective is to guarantee a single market, allowing the development, deployment and use of artificial intelligence systems guaranteeing a high level of protection in the fields of:

- health;[2]
- safety;[3]
- democracy;[4]
- the rule of law;[5]
- fundamental rights;[6]
- the environment.[7]

---

1 AI Act or AIA. Regulation (EU) 2024/1689 of the European Parliament and of the Council of 13 June 2024 laying down harmonised rules on artificial intelligence and amending Regulations (EC) No 300/2008, (EU) No 167/2013, (EU) No 168/2013, (EU) 2018/858, (EU) 2018/1139 and (EU) 2019/2144 and Directives 2014/90/EU, (EU) 2016/797 and (EU) 2020/1828 (Artificial Intelligence Act), [2024] OJ L, 2024/1689, ELI: http://data.europa.eu/eli/reg/2024/1689/oj.

2 Health: Arts. 1, 3, 6, 7, 10, 13, 14, 36, 43, 46, 57.

3 Safety or security:
- safety of property and individuals: Arts. 1, 2, 6, 7, 9, 10, 13, 14, 15, 17, 25, 36, 39, 43, 46, 57, 58, 59.
- security-of-supply: Art. 17.
- product safety: Art. 2.
- national security: Art. 2.
- safety component: Arts. 3 (definition), 6, 25.
- cybersecurity: Arts. 13, 15 (Accuracy, robustness and cybersecurity), 31, 42, 55, 58.

4 Democracy: Arts. 1 and 74.

5 Rule of law: Art. 1.

6 Fundamental rights: Arts. 1, 2, 3, 6, 7, 9, 10, 14, 27 (Fundamental rights impact assessment for high-risk AI systems), 28, 36, 39, 41, 43, 57, 58, 66, 70, 77 (Powers of authorities protecting fundamental rights), 79, 82, 86, 112.

7 Environmental protection: Arts. 1, 3(49), serious incident (d), 46, 59, 95, 112.

2. The aim is to provide a framework for the third digital revolution, after the IT revolution (dematerialisation of media) and the Internet revolution (dematerialisation of relationships). This profound transformation of all human activities can be summed up as follows:

- 'We are about to witness', predicts Jean-François Bonnefon, Director of Research in Cognitive Psychology at the Toulouse School of Economics, 'an upheaval in human culture which, in terms of importance, is the equivalent of the return of the explorers from China at the time of Marco Polo, their arms laden with novelties such as paper money, and the invention of the printing press by Gutenberg... All the great culture shocks of European history will be concentrated in a few years'.[8]

3. This Regulation aligns with the proposals put forward by the European Parliament concerning the regulation of artificial intelligence systems, robotics and related technologies, in the fields of:

- ethics;[9]
- liability;[10]
- intellectual property rights.[11]

4. Notes:

- (1) Unlike the European Parliament's resolutions,[12] the new Regulation only concerns artificial intelligence systems as such, whether or not they are integrated into a robotics package.
- (2) Only intangible systems are concerned by these legal obligations.
- (3) Related technologies such as sensors, the Internet of Things (IoT) and robots, are not taken into account directly, but only through the implementation of elements falling into the category of artificial intelligence systems.
- (4) The Regulation concerning artificial intelligence (AI) is referred to herein as AI Act or AIA.

5. This Executive Summary only describes the general obligations and associated main requirements; detailed presentations, comments or controversies can be found under the relevant Article of the Regulation.

---

8 L. Carpentier, 'L'IA et la culture: les machines sont-elles nos amies?' ['AI and culture: are machines our friends?'], *Le Monde*, 1 October 2023, p. 26 [Translated by the author].

9 European Parliament resolution of 20 October 2020 on a framework of ethical aspects of artificial intelligence, robotics and related technologies, 2020/2012(INL).

10 European Parliament resolution of 20 October 2020 on a civil liability regime for artificial intelligence, 2020/2014(INL).

11 European Parliament resolution of 20 October 2020 on intellectual property rights for the development of artificial intelligence technologies, 2020/2015 (INI).

12 Resolution 'Ethics and Framework for AI', 2020/2012(INL) of 20 October 2020 and Resolution 'Liability for damage caused by AI', 2020/2014(INL) of 20 October 2020.

1.2. History

6. Key dates are listed in the timeline below:

- 1950 Alan Turing (Principles of AI)
- 1956 John McCarty (Definition of AI)
- 1966 Eliza Chatbot
- 1970 Mycin is used to diagnose blood diseases
- 1986 Navlab, the first autonomous driving vehicle
- 1987 Yann Le Cun (thesis on neural network machine learning)[13]
- 1997 World chess champion Garry Kasparov is beaten by Deep Blue (IBM supercomputer)
- 2010 Deep Learning makes its mark on AI technologies
- 2011 Siri virtual assistant is integrated into Apple iPhone handsets
- 2012 ChatGPT takes over the world alongside other generative AIs
- 2016 Chatbots become widespread among the general public
- 2016 World Go champion Lee Sedol is beaten by AlphaGo[14]
- 2017 World Go champion Ke Jie Alpha is beaten by AlphaGo[15]
- 2020 White paper on artificial intelligence
- 2020 Framework on the ethics of AI, robotics and related technologies[16]
- 2022 OpenAI deploys ChatGPT worldwide
- 2023 Open letter from by 60 personalities warning of the risk of AI systems[17]
- 2024 European AI Office is created (24.01)
- 2024 Seoul Declaration for safe, innovative and inclusive AI (21.05)
- 2024 Artificial Intelligence Act (AI Act) (13.06)
- 2024 AI Act is published (12.07)
- 2024 AI Act enters into force (01.08)[18]
- 2024 European AI Office is unveiled (29.05)

---

13 Y. Le Cun, 'Modèles connexionnistes de l'apprentissage' ['Connectionist learning models'], PhD thesis in Computer Science on the automatic learning of neural networks, defended 15 June 1987 at Paris 6 University.

14 AlphaGo: DeepMind algorithm (Google).

15 'L'intelligence artificielle AlphaGo bat une nouvelle fois le champion du monde de go' [Artificial intelligence AlphaGo beats the world go champion once again], *Le Monde*, 25 May 2017.

16 European Parliament resolution of 20 October 2020 with recommendations to the Commission on a framework of ethical aspects of artificial intelligence, robotics and related technologies (2020/2012(INL)) (P9_TA(2020)0275), www.europarl.europa.eu/.

17 L. Alexandre and M. Rameaux, 'Des experts tech du monde entier appellent à une pause dans le développement de l'IA. Mais pouvons-nous nous le permettre' ['Tech experts around the world are calling for a pause in the development of AI. But can we afford it?'], Atlantico.fr, 31 March 2023.

18 For specific application dates, see § Summary table of dates.
Notes:
- (1) The regulations for activities in Section A of Annex I concerning high-risk AI systems are in line with the requirements of the new European legislative framework.
- (2) This is not yet the case for the regulations of the activities corresponding to Section B of Annex I, for which the Commission has been mandated to take into account the AI technologies implemented in these areas.

1.3. *General Architecture of the Regulation*[19]

7. The Regulation is structured as follows:

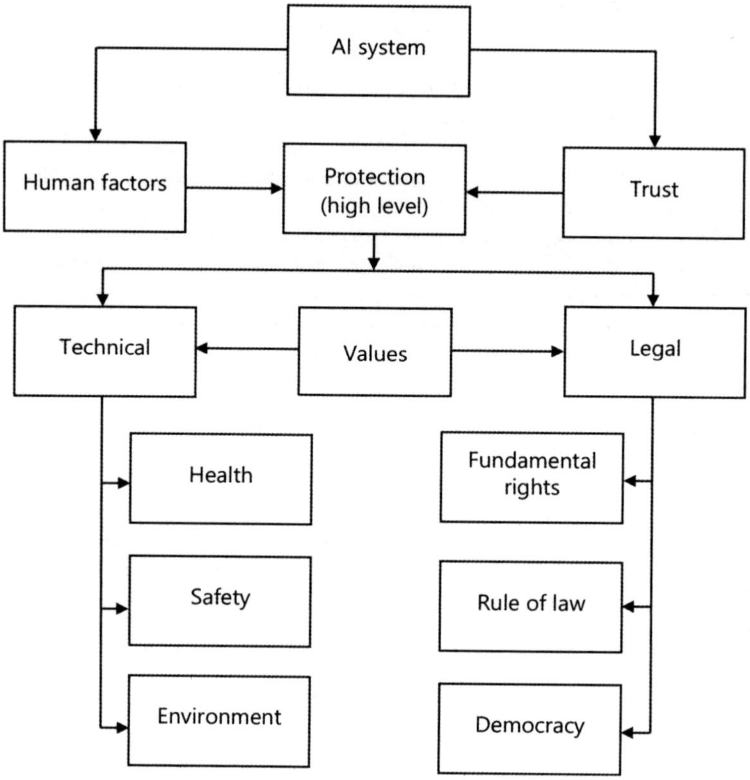

1.4. *Objectives*

8. The objectives are set out below:

- to make the EU a global leader in the development of secure, trustworthy and ethical AI;[20]
- to ensure the protection of ethical principles, as specifically requested by the European Parliament;[21]
- to establish a high level of protection;
- to organise the smooth functioning of the single market by creating the right conditions for the development and use of trustworthy AI in the European Union;

---

[19] AI Act, Art. 1.

[20] AI Act, Rec. 8.

[21] AI Act, Rec. 8.

- to ensure that AI systems are safe and respect law on fundamental rights and European Union values;
- to ensure legal certainty to facilitate investment and innovation in AI;
- to enhance governance and effective enforcement of existing law on fundamental rights and safety requirements applicable to AI systems;
- to facilitate the development of a single market for lawful, safe and trustworthy AI systems and prevent market fragmentation;[22]
- to align EU Regulation with the achievement of the United Nations Sustainable Development Goals (SDGs).

9. The main challenges facing the Regulation can be summarised under the following headings, listed in alphabetical order:

NO.	THEME	CHALLENGES
1.	Creation	Plundering of works during the training phase of large language models[23]
2.	Economic model	Shift from work value to creation value
3.	Employment	Bipolarisation of the market between highly skilled individuals and others, along with associated conflicts
4.	Intelligent divide	Widening of the digital divide
5.	Production	Stereotyped outputs[24] and associated loss of human skills
6.	Technological eugenics	Confrontation between humans, natural humans vs. augmented or enhanced humans
7.	Technological slavery	Dependence on AI systems

1.5. Approach

10. In 2024, regulations concerning AI systems worldwide follow a vertical approach, i.e. they address:

- autonomous cars;
- industrial robots;
- autonomous ships;
- etc.

---

22 Proposal for a Regulation of the European Parliament and of the Council laying down harmonised rules on artificial intelligence (Artificial Intelligence Act) and amending certain union legislative acts {SEC(2021) 167 final} – {SWD(2021) 84 final} – {SWD (2021) 85 final}, explanatory memorandum, p. 3, Brussels, 21 April 2021.

23 AI Act, Art. 51: general-purpose AI system model such as ChatGPT (OpenAI) or Gemini (Google).

24 S. Duranton, 'IA générative et productivité: pour le meilleur et pour le pire' ['Generative AI and productivity: for better or for worse"], *Les Échos*, 3 October 2023.

11. In contrast, the Regulation follows a horizontal approach, by introducing horizontal rules that apply to all AI systems,[25] onto which vertical or sector-specific rules will be added.

12. The framework is based on managing the risks posed by AI systems, which could represent '[a]n extinction risk for humanity'.[26]

13. This approach results from coordinated legal management based on EU values and the risks of harm to those values.[27]

1.6. Values-Based Management

1.6.1 Introduction

14. The purpose of the legal framework is to protect natural persons, undertakings and democracy.[28]

1.6.2 Health

15. The concept of health covers the physical and psychological protection of individuals.

1.6.3 Safety

16. This concept covers:

- the protection of individuals, corporate bodies and property;[29]
- cybersecurity.[30]

1.6.4 Environment

17. Environmental protection is one of three values, along with the rule of law and democracy, that have been included in the latest versions of the new Regulation. The concept of environment is not defined as such.

---

[25] With some exceptions, see below.

[26] Sam Altman, OpenAI CEO, quoted by J. Le Bolzer, in 'Risques, régulation, éthique: état des lieux des enjeux qui questionnent l'IA' ['Risks, regulation, ethics: an overview of the issues surrounding AI'], *Les Échos*, 12 October 2023, p. 32 (paper), 20 September 2023 (online).

[27] C. Crichton, 'Règlement sur l'intelligence artificielle: premiers éléments d'analyse' ['AI Act: Initial points for discussion'], HAL, 23 July 2024.

[28] AI Act, Rec. 1.

[29] The technical aspects of AI technology safety are dealt with in a separate section. See section 6.14 Safety.

[30] AI Act, Art. 15.

18. The expected benefits of AI technologies in this field include:
- environmental monitoring;
- the conservation and restoration of biodiversity;
- climate change mitigation and adaptation.[31]

1.6.5 Fundamental Rights

19. These rights are those referred to in the Charter of Fundamental Rights of the Union.[32]

20. They are taken into account in two ways:
- the obligation to respect the fundamental values of European democracy;[33]
- the need to implement these requirements in such a way that AI systems integrate these imperatives into their 'natural behaviour'.

21. 'The use of AI with its specific characteristics (e.g. opacity, complexity, dependency on data, autonomy) can adversely affect a number of fundamental rights enshrined in the EU Charter of Fundamental Rights.'[34]

22. Notes:
- (1) The requirement of alignment with human intentions is a decisive element in the consideration of fundamental rights.
- (2) This requirement is one of the essential obligations of providers of general-purpose AI models with systemic risk.[35]
- (3) The Regulation does not establish any principles or rules on the methods or type of solutions to achieve such alignment.[36]

1.6.6 Rule of Law

23. AI systems must be framed in such a way as not to lead to dictatorships of a technological nature within the European Union.

---

31 AI Act, Rec. 4.

32 Charter of Fundamental Rights of the European Union (2016), [2016] OJ C202/389, https://eur-lex.europa.eu/eli/treaty/char_2016/oj.

33 Council Decision (EU) 2024/2218 of 28 August 2024 on the signing, on behalf of the European Union, of the Council of Europe Framework Convention on Artificial Intelligence and Human Rights, Democracy and the Rule of Law, http://data.europa.eu/eli/dec/2024/2218/oj.

34 EDPS, Opinion 44/2023 of 23 October 2023 on the Proposal for Artificial Intelligence Act in the light of legislative developments, p. 7.

35 AI Act Annex XI, section 2(2).

36 P. Molga, 'L'intelligence humaine progresse toujours' ['Human intelligence continues to progress'], *Les Échos*, 23 October 2023, p. 13.

24. This would undermine:

- the principle of separation of powers;
- the independence of the judiciary;
- access to rights;
- participation in public debate.

1.6.7 Democracy

25. AI systems may not be designed and implemented throughout their entire lifecycle on a basis that could:

- undermine the integrity of the institutions of the European Union or of individual Member States;
- jeopardise the independence of democratic institutions;
- explicitly or implicitly bias or block democratic processes as a whole.

1.7. Risk-Based Management

1.7.1 Introduction

26. In the Regulation, risks are classified as follows:

NO.	RISK	SPECIFICATION	REFERENCE
1.	Unacceptable	AI systems that contradict EU values	AIA, Art. 5
2.	Systemic	General-purpose AI system	AIA, Art. 51[37]
3.	High	AI systems that can lead to serious consequences	AIA, Art. 6
4.	Specific	Transparency obligation	AIA, Art. 50
5.	Minimal	Optional adherence to a code of practice	AIA, Art. 56
6.	Exclusion	Special cases	AIA, Art. 2

[37] OpenAI's ChatGPT, Google's Gemini, or Anthropic's Claude.

1.7.2 A Product and Risks View

27. The general framework for AI technology 'products' is subject to cross-cutting legislation on market surveillance and product compliance (hereafter referred to as 'MS&PC').[38]

28. However, the main concepts concerning products and risks are much broader.

29. These include:

NO.	THEME	MSR (MS&PC)	AI ACT	COMMENT
1.	Product	Definition None	Definition None	In the AI Act, the term is cited 122 times in connection with AI systems
2.	Operator	Economic operator Regulation (EU) 2019/1020 Art. 3(13)	Economic operator AI Act (EU) 2024/1689 Art. 3(8)	The AI Act integrates deployers and end-users as entities or individuals acting in the course of a professional activity
3.	Product presenting a risk	Regulation (EU) 2019/1020 Art. 3(19)	No definition as such	Concepts relating to protection in the face of risk: • health; • safety; • environment; • fundamental rights; • rule of law; • democracy. AIA, Art. 1(1)
4.	Risk	Regulation (EU) 2019/1020 Art. 3(18)	AI Act (EU) 2024/1689 Art. 3(2)	The notion of risk is more limited in the AIA: 'danger' for one (Reg. 2019/2020) and 'harm' for the other (AIA)

[38] AI Act, Art. 74(1): 'Regulation (EU) 2019/1020 shall apply to AI systems covered by this Regulation. For the purposes of the effective enforcement of this Regulation:
(a) any reference to an economic operator under Regulation (EU) 2019/1020 shall be understood as including all operators identified in Article 2(1) of this Regulation;
(b) any reference to a product under Regulation (EU) 2019/1020 shall be understood as including all AI systems falling within the scope of this Regulation.'

1.8. Values-Based and Risk-Based Management

1.8.1 Introduction

30. This approach is determined by guiding principles.[39] Each of these principles is broken down into specific principles.[40] The principles are the subject of legal obligations. Each legal obligation is then articulated around of technical,[41] organisational[42] or legal[43] requirements.

31. The provider should determine its solution in such a way that it complies with these requirements.

1.8.2 Management Structure

NO.	THEME	SPECIFICATION
1.	Initial phase	Implementation of requirements according to the AI system type and the general-purpose AI model *ex ante*
2.	Compliance phase	Compliance checks for certain high-risk AI systems[44] Self-compliance for others
3.	Market phase	National market surveillance authority Self-surveillance for high-risk AI systems

1.9. Harm

32. This covers both material and immaterial damage,[45] including physical, psychological, societal and economic harm.[46]

39 See section 7.3 Guiding Principles.

40 See section 7.4 Specific Principles.

41 Risk management system for high-risk AI systems. AI Act, Art. 9.

42 Documentation keeping. AI Act, Art. 18.

43 Written mandate for relations between a provider and an authorised representative. AI Act, Art. 22.

44 High-risk AI systems, AI Act, Art. 6(1), Section A of Annex I List of Union harmonisation legislation.

45 AI Act, Rec. 5.

46 See section 6.6 Damage and Harm.

1.10. *Missing Concepts*

33. Many concepts in the sphere of artificial intelligence have not been included in the Regulation. This is the case for the following concepts:

NO.	TECHNOLOGY	SPECIFICATION
1.	Robot	See section 3.8 Robotic Systems below
2.	Sensor	See section 3.8 Robotic Systems below
3.	Algorithm	See section 3.2.3 Algorithm below

2 SCOPES

34. The scopes include:
- the geographical scope;
- the historical scope.

2.1. *Geographical Scope*

2.1.1 Introduction

35. The Regulation applies to:[47]
- providers established within the EU;
- manufacturers of products embedding AI technologies;
- providers established or located in a third country placing on the market or putting into service in the EU;
- providers established or located in a third country, where the output produced by the AI system is used in the EU;
- deployers of AI systems located within the EU;
- deployers established or located in a third country, where the output produced by the AI system is used in the EU;
- affected persons located in the EU.

2.1.2 Extraterritorial Scope

36. The Regulation has an extraterritorial effect through a ripple effect.

[47] AI Act, Art. 2.

37. It applies to:

- providers established in a third country and operating within the EU; and:
- output generated outside the EU and used in the EU.

2.1.3 Global Influence

38. As with the GDPR, the extraterritoriality rules of the Regulation initiate a process of universality that will ultimately lead to a homogenisation of the key principles and general terms of implementation of AI systems around the world.

2.1.4 EU Providers

39. The concept of establishment implies the exercise of activity through stable arrangements. The form of such arrangements may be a body with a legal personality or a mere establishment.

40. Only AI systems operated within the EU are concerned. AI systems intended for export are not subject to these requirements.

41. The activities of providers include either or both of the following:

- the placing on the market;
- the putting into service.

42. Notes:

(1) Design and development activities are not relevant for the scope.

(2) However, these two phases are subject to obligations and associated requirements for high-risk AI systems. These include:
   - o record-keeping;[48]
   - o accuracy, robustness and cybersecurity.[49]

2.1.5 Product Manufacturers

43. Product manufacturers are comparable to providers when they integrate an AI system into a product under their own name or trademark.[50]

44. The status of provider applies when the product is put into service.

---

48 AI Act, Art. 12.

49 AI Act, Art. 15.

50 AI Act, Art. 2(1)(e).

2.1.6 Non-EU Providers

45. Where providers that are not established within the EU operate in one or more Member States, AI systems must comply with all the obligations.

2.1.7 Non-EU Providers of Outputs

46. The use of output produced by AI systems originating from third countries is subject to the Regulation; the main purpose is to protect deployers.

2.1.8 Deployers

47. A deployer is 'a natural or legal person, public authority, agency or other body using an AI system under its authority except where the AI system is used in the course of a personal non-professional activity'.[51]

48. All uses of AI systems located in the EU must comply with the requirements relating to AI technologies. The same applies when these uses are limited to output produced by AI systems from countries outside the EU.

2.1.9 Affected Persons

2.1.9.1 *Introduction*

49. The protection applies to:

- natural persons;
- undertakings.[52]

2.1.9.2 *Natural Persons*

50. They are protected as individuals[53] or as a group of individuals.[54]

---

51 AI Act, Art. 3(4).

52 AI Act, Rec. 2.

53 AI Act, Art. 5(1)(a) referring to 'a person's consciousness'.

54 AI Act, Art. 5(1)(b) referring to groups of vulnerable persons.

51. This applies in particular in the following cases:

NO.	PROTECTION	SPECIFICATION
1.	AI literacy	Awareness-raising and training obligations[55]
2.	Automated decisions	Information on the use of high-risk systems covered by Annex III[56]
3.	Human/AI interface	AI systems subject to a transparency obligation[57]
4.	Testing in real-world conditions	High-risk systems[58]

2.1.9.3 *Undertakings*

52. Focused on competition law,[59] the term 'undertaking' means all entities engaged in an activity, whether natural persons or legal persons governed by private or public law.[60]

2.1.9.4 *Criterion*

53. The affected persons are those 'that are located in the Union'.[61]

2.1.10 Other Actors

54. They are as follows:

NO.	ACTORS	SPECIFICATION
1.	Distributor	'A natural or legal person in the supply chain, other than the provider or the importer, that makes an AI system available on the Union market'[62]
2.	Importer	'A natural or legal person located or established in the Union that places on the market an AI system that bears the name or trademark of a natural or legal person established in a third country'[63]

55 AI Act, Art. 4.
56 AI Act, Arts. 26(11) and 86(1).
57 AI Act, Art. 50(1).
58 AI Act, Art. 60(1).
59 TFEU, Arts. 101 and 102: 'Rules applying to undertakings'.
60 This does not apply to activities in the exercise of public powers, such as those of Member States, local authorities or specific bodies.
61 AI Act, Art. 2(1)(g).
62 AI Act, Art. 3(7).
63 AI Act, Art. 3(6).

NO.	ACTORS	SPECIFICATION
3.	Exporter	No legal rules as such[64]
4.	Authorised representative	'A natural or legal person located or established in the Union who has received and accepted a written mandate from a provider of an AI system or a general-purpose AI model to, respectively, perform and carry out on its behalf the obligations and procedures established by this Regulation'[65]
5.	Operator	'A provider, product manufacturer, deployer, authorised representative, importer or distributor'[66]
6.	Subject	'A natural person who participates in testing in real-world conditions'[67]
7.	Staff (or personnel)	Employees of providers and deployers[68]

2.1.11 Institutions of the European Union

55. The Regulation applies to EU institutions, bodies, offices and agencies when acting as a provider or deployer of an AI system.[69]

2.1.12 Exclusions

56. They are as follows:

NO.	ACTIVITIES	SPECIFICATION	REFERENCE
1.	Personal activity	Deployers that are natural persons who use AI systems in the course of a purely personal non-professional activity[70]	AIA, Art. 2(10)
2.	Scope of the EU	Systems that do not fall within this scope	AIA, Art. 2(4)

64 The terms exporter and export are not used in the AI Act.
65 AI Act, Art. 3(5).
66 AI Act, Art. 3(8).
67 AI Act, Art. 3(58).
68 AI Act, Art. 4
69 AI Act, Rec. 23.
70 The same applies to 'systems that are based on the rules defined solely by natural persons to automatically execute operations' (AI Act, Rec. 12 and 13). These two elements are not really aligned.

NO.	ACTIVITIES	SPECIFICATION	REFERENCE
3.	Design (Phase)	The Regulation does not apply to any research, testing or development activity regarding AI systems or AI models prior to their being placed on the market or put into service: Notes: • (1) This exclusion is distinct from that concerning scientific research as such. • (2) Testing in real-world conditions are excluded	AIA, Rec. 20 AIA, Art. 2(8)
4.	International cooperation	Special agreements	AIA, Art. 2(4)
5.	Provision of intermediary services	Liability system	AIA, Art. 2(5)
6.	Scientific research and development	The Regulation does not apply to AI systems or AI models, including their output, specifically developed and put into service for the sole purpose of scientific research and development	AIA, Art. 2(6) AIA, Rec. 25
7.	Output of AI systems for defence or national security purposes	Use 'in the Union exclusively for military, defence or national security purposes, regardless of the type of entity carrying out those activities'[71]	AIA, Art. 2(3)
8.	AI systems for defence purposes	Purposes exclusive to such purposes As is or with modifications[72]	AIA, Art. 2(3)
9.	AI systems for military purposes	Purposes exclusive to such purposes As is or with modifications[73]	AIA, Art. 2(3)
10.	AI systems for national security purposes	Purposes exclusive to such purposes As is or with modifications[74]	AIA, Art. 2(3)

57. Notes:

- (1) Issues relating to areas in which Member States' have exclusive competence and prohibited practices are examined during the presentation of these practices.

71 Private or public entities.
72 Private or public entities.
73 Private or public entities.
74 Private or public entities.

2.1.13 Coordinated Activities

2.1.13.1 *Introduction*

58. Subject to a reassessment of the situation, in the light of developments in high-risk AI systems by the European Commission, the areas listed below are not subject to the Regulation despite the implementation of AI technologies, in the form of safety components or products.[75]

2.1.13.2 *Modifications*

59. This list of activities is coordinated in Articles 102 to 109.

60. This coordination requires the European Commission to apply the requirements applicable to high-risk AI systems in these areas, which are as follows:

NO.	THEME	REFERENCE
1.	Compliance with the requirements	AIA, Art. 8
2.	Risk management system	AIA, Art. 9
3.	Data and data governance	AIA, Art. 10
4.	Technical documentation	AIA, Art. 11
5.	Record-keeping	AIA, Art. 12
6.	Transparency and provision of information to deployers	AIA, Art. 13
7.	Human oversight	AIA, Art. 14
8.	Accuracy	AIA, Art. 15
9.	Robustness	AIA, Art. 15
10.	Cybersecurity	AIA, Art. 15

2.1.13.3 *List of Activities*

61. It is as follows:

NO.	THEME	SPECIFICATION	REFERENCE
1.	Regulation (EC) No 300/2008	11 March 2008	Common rules in the field of civil aviation security
2.	Regulation (EU) No 168/2013	15 January 2013	Approval and market surveillance of two- or three-wheel vehicles and quadricycles

[75] AI Act, Section B of Annex I.

NO.	THEME	SPECIFICATION	REFERENCE
3.	Regulation (EU) No 167/2013	5 February 2013	Approval and market surveillance of agricultural and forestry vehicles
4.	Directive No 2014/90/EU	23 July 2014	Marine equipment
5.	Directive (EU) No 2016/797	11 May 2016	Interoperability of the rail system within the European Union
6.	Regulation (EU) No 2018/858	30 May 2018	Approval and market surveillance of motor vehicles and their trailers, and of systems, components and separate technical units intended for such vehicles
7.	Regulation (EU) No 2018/1139	4 July 2018	Common rules in the field of civil aviation and establishing a European Union Aviation Safety Agency
8.	Regulation (EU) No 2019/2144	27 November 2019	Type-approval requirements for motor vehicles and their trailers, and systems, components and separate technical units intended for such vehicles, as regards their general safety and the protection of vehicle occupants and vulnerable road users

2.1.13.4 *Architecture*

62. This exclusion list concerns AI technologies relating to high-risk systems. It corresponds to Section B (List of other Union harmonisation legislation of Annex I (List of Union harmonisation legislation).

2.1.13.5 *Special Rules*

63. The areas concerned by the adjustments and referred to in Section B of Annex I are as follows:

NO.	THEME	REFERENCE
1.	Civil aviation	Application of Article 102 amending Regulation (EC) No 300/2008
2.	Agricultural and forestry vehicles	Application of Article 103 amending Regulation (EU) No 167/2013
3.	Two- or three-wheel vehicles and quadricycles	Application of Article 104 amending Regulation (EU) No 168/2013
4.	Marine equipment	Application of Article 105 amending Directive 2014/90/EU

NO.	THEME	REFERENCE
5.	Rail system	Application of Article 106 amending Directive (EU) 2016/797
6.	Motor vehicles and their trailers	Application of Article 107 amending Regulation (EU) No 2018/858
7.	European Union Aviation Safety Agency	Application of Article 108 amending Regulation (EU) No 2018/1139
8.	Motor vehicles and their trailers (approval)	Application of Article 109 amending Regulation (EU) No 2019/2144
9.	Evaluation and review procedure	Trajectory for updating legislation to take into account developments in AI technologies. Application of Article 102
10.	Regulatory sandboxes (Art. 57)	Application if EU harmonisation legislation has taken into account the AI Act requirements for high-risk AI systems
11.	National competent authorities	They are those competent for the aforementioned areas

64. Notes:

- (1) The regulations for activities covered by Section A of Annex I concerning high-risk AI systems are in line with the requirements of the new European legislative framework.[76]
- (2) This is not yet the case for the regulations of the activities covered by Section B of Annex I, for which the European Commission has been mandated to take into account the AI technologies implemented in these areas.

2.2. *Historical Scope*

2.2.1 Introduction

65. The key dates of the Regulation are as follows:

- entry into force: on the twentieth day following that of its publication in the OJEU, i.e. 1 August 2024;[77]
- application: 24 months after entry into force, i.e. 2 August 2026, except in special cases.

66. Within this period, the milestones are set out in the timetable below.

---

76 See section 7.2 Legal Basis of the Union.

77 The twentieth day following that of its publication in the *Official Journal of the European Union* (12 July 2024), i.e. 1 August 2024.

2.2.2 New AI Systems

NO.	SYSTEM	DATE	REFERENCE
1.	Prohibited AI systems	2 February 2025	AIA, Art. 5 AIA, Art. 113(a)
2.	High-risk AI systems covered by Annex III	2 August 2026	AIA, Art. 6(2)
3.	Transparent AI systems	2 August 2026	AIA, Art. 50
4.	High-risk AI systems covered by Annex I	2 August 2027	AIA, Art. 6(1) AIA, Art. 113(c)
5.	High-risk AI systems concerning the public activities referred to in Annex X and placed on the market or put into service before 2 August 2027	By 31 December 2030	AIA, Art. 6 AIA, Art. 111(1)

2.2.3 Old AI Systems

67. The rules are as follows:

NO.	SYSTEM	DATE	REFERENCE
1.	Prohibited AI systems already existing prior to application	2 February 2025	AIA, Art. 113(a)
2.	AI systems existing before 2 August 2027	By 31 December 2030[78]	AIA, Art. 111(1)
3.	High-risk AI systems not concerning public activities and existing before 2 August 2026	• (1) Only if, as from that date, those systems are subject to significant changes in their designs • (2) The actors concerned are operators	AIA, Art. 6 AIA, Art. 111(2)
4.	High-risk AI systems concerning public information activities (Annex X) and existing before 2 August 2026	• (1) Only if, as from that date, those systems are subject to significant changes in their designs • (2) The actors concerned are operators • (3) By 2 August 2030	AIA, Art. 111(2)
5.	Transparent AI system already existing prior to application	2 August 2026	AIA, Art. 50

[78] Providers, authorised representatives, importers, distributors and deployers.

2.2.4 New AI Models

NO.	MODEL	DATE	REFERENCE
1.	General-purpose AI models without systemic risk	2 August 2025	AIA, Art. 113(b)
2.	General-purpose AI models with systemic risk	2 August 2025	AIA, Art. 113(b)

2.2.5 Old AI Models

NO.	MODEL	DATE	REFERENCE
1.	General-purpose AI models placed on the market before 2 August 2025	2 August 2027 Notes: • (1) The actors concerned are providers	AIA, Art. 51 AIA, Art. 111(3)

2.2.6 Evolution

68. New technical developments in AI technologies are taken into account as follows:

NO.	THEME	SPECIFICATION	DATE	REFERENCE
1.	Review	European Commission	By 2 August 2029	
2.	Prohibited practices	Revision of the list	Once a year	AIA, Art. 5
3.	High-risk AI systems	Revision of the list in Annex III	Once a year	AIA, Art. 6(2)
4.	Code of conduct	Effectiveness measurement	2 August 2028 and every three years thereafter	

3 TECHNICAL FRAMEWORK

3.1. Introduction

69. The AI Act is a 'Related Products and Services' regulation[79] which, in certain circumstances, requires CE marking.[80]

70. Conformity obligations concern each AI system as such. This involves creating a mapping of all AI systems and ensuring personalised monitoring of each system throughout its lifecycle.[81]

71. The framework of AI technologies breaks down as follows:[82]

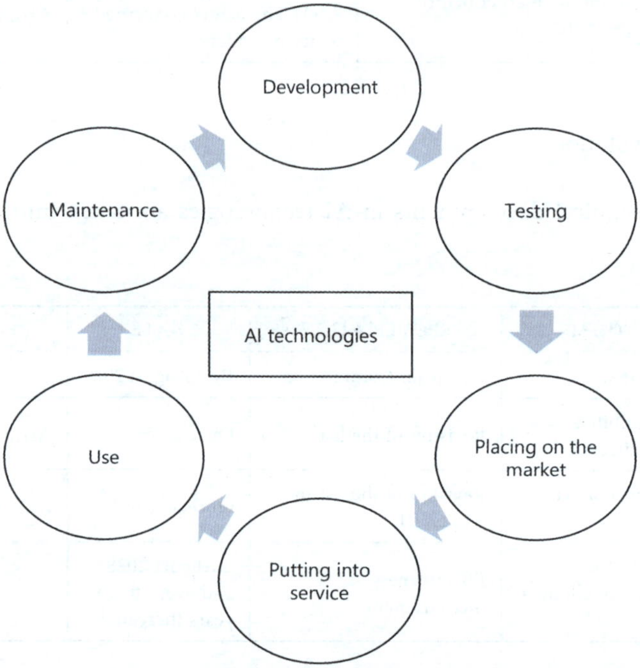

---

79 AI Act, Rec. 3.

80 See AI Act, Arts. 16(h), 23(1)(c), 24(1), 48 CE marking, 83(1)(a) and (b).

81 See AI Act, Arts. 9(2), 15(1), 40(2), 72(2) and point 6 of Annex IV.

82 AI Act, Rec. 1.

3.2. *AI Technologies*

3.2.1 Introduction

72. The deployment of AI systems around the world is the result of a combination of:

- the quality of sensors;
- learning algorithms;
- the computing power;
- the availability of thematic data lakes.

3.2.2 Composition

73. 'AI is a fast evolving family of technologies that contributes to a wide array of economic, environmental and societal benefits across the entire spectrum of industries and social activities.'[83]

74. The final version of the Regulation is based on a generic technical concept. The key terms are:

- AI-related technologies;[84]
- AI technologies;[85]
- AI technologies.[86]

75. In order to maximise the neutrality of the constantly evolving technology, the Regulation does not specifically define the families that make up AI technologies.

76. This generic approach represents an evolution compared to the international regulation of artificial intelligence.

77. The first version of the Regulation defined AI as follows:

- 'software that is developed with one or more of the techniques and approaches listed in Annex I and can, for a given set of human-defined objectives, generate outputs such as content, predictions, recommendations, or decisions influencing the environments they interact with.'[87]

---

83 AI Act, Rec. 4.
84 AI Act, Art. 8.
85 AI Act, Art. 57.
86 AI Act, Art. 72.
87 Proposal for a Regulation on AI COM(2021) 206 of 21 April 2021, Art. 3(1).

78. And, in this context, the AI technologies referred to in the then-current Annex I were broken down as follows:

- (a) machine learning approaches, including supervised, unsupervised and reinforcement learning, using a wide variety of methods including deep learning;
- (b) logic- and knowledge-based approaches, including knowledge representation, inductive (logic) programming, knowledge bases, inference and deductive engines, (symbolic) reasoning and expert systems;
- statistical approaches, Bayesian estimation, search and optimization methods.[88]

79. Notes:

- (1) The technologies referred to in the said then-current Annex I concerned symbolic AI or expert systems and statistical AI, including artificial neural networks.
- (2) This Annex has been deleted and this breakdown between symbolic AI systems and statistical AI systems has not been repeated in the body of the text.
- (3) However, the Recitals state the principle that the AI technologies covered by the Regulation include symbolic AI and statistical AI in the following terms:
    - 'The techniques that enable inference while building an AI system include machine learning approaches that learn from data how to achieve certain objectives, and logic- and knowledge-based approaches that infer from encoded knowledge or symbolic representation of the task to be solved.'[89]
- (4) '[S]ystems that are based on the rules defined solely by natural persons to automatically execute operations' are excluded from the Regulation.[90]

80. From a strictly technical and legal point of view, it should be considered that artificial intelligence is a combination of algorithms and data; just like a song, which is a combination of text and music that is consubstantial with each of the components without being reduced to one of the elements.

88 Ibid, Annex I.
89 AI Act, Rec. 12.
90 Ibid.

81. This combination can be represented as follows:

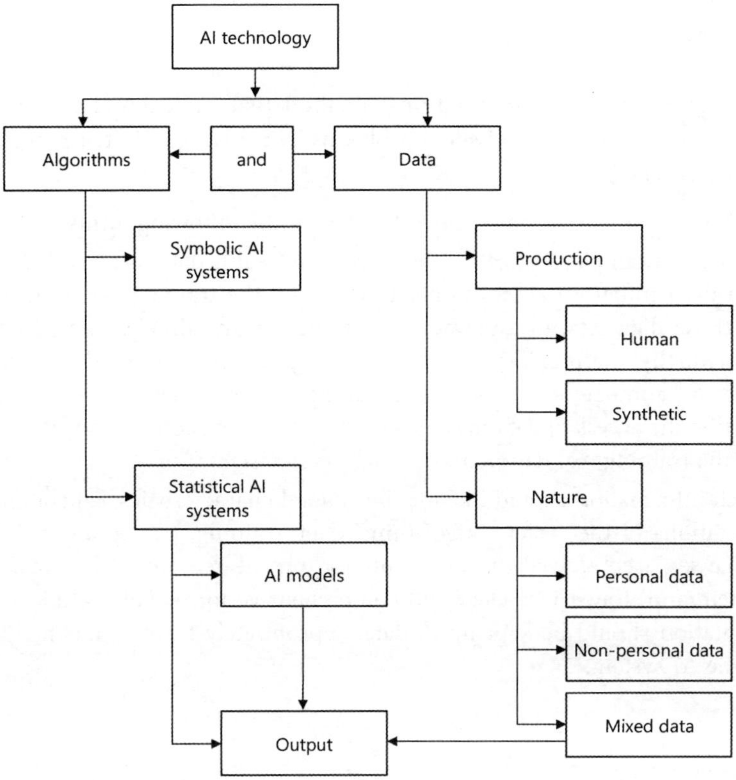

82. For the purposes of the Regulation, the term 'AI technology' legally covers:

- AI systems (strictly speaking);[91]
- high-risk AI systems;[92]
- systems subject to transparency obligations;[93]
- general-purpose AI models;[94]
- general-purpose AI systems.[95]

83. Notes:

- (1) For obligations concerning all types of systems, the expression AI technology helps avoid confusion between the different legal rules.

[91] AI Act, Art. 3(1).
[92] AI Act, Art. 61(1) and (2).
[93] AI Act, Art. 50.
[94] AI Act, Art. 63.
[95] AI Act, Art. 66.

- (2) General-purpose AI models do not fall into the category of AI systems in the strict sense.

3.2.3 Algorithm

84. An algorithm is a 'computational method that indicates the steps to be taken to solve a series of equivalent problems by applying a finite set of rules in a specific order'.[96]

85. This concept is used only in two Recitals in the following terms:

- '[...] For example, in health, the European health data space will facilitate non-discriminatory access to health data and the training of AI algorithms on those data sets, in a privacy-preserving, secure, timely, transparent and trustworthy manner, and with an appropriate institutional governance. Relevant competent authorities, including sectoral ones, providing or supporting the access to data may also support the provision of high-quality data for the training, validation and testing of AI systems';[97]
- 'Such information should include the general characteristics, capabilities and limitations of the system, algorithms, data, training, testing and validation processes used as well as documentation on the relevant risk-management system and drawn in a clear and comprehensive form. The technical documentation should be kept up to date, appropriately throughout the lifetime of the AI system.'[98]

3.3. Data

3.3.1 Introduction

86. AI technologies require huge amounts of data to train systems.

87. Most of these data are of human origin.

3.3.2 Evolution

88. This will not be the case in the coming years.

89. Training is being invaded by artificial production.

90. All sectors will be impacted. For example, in November 2022, a music streaming platform managed to create 'more than a thousand tracks using

[96] Definition by the Académie française dictionary, 9th ed.
[97] AI Act, Rec. 68.
[98] AI Act, Rec. 71.

artificial intelligence. One of them, the track *Today*, has already surpassed 100 million streams…'.[99]

3.3.3 Governance

91. From this perspective, a declaration of the origin for data appears to be a requirement in terms of:

- business ethics;
- control of the training of AI systems;
- respect for authors' rights.

92. The essential themes of this governance are as follows:

NO.	THEME	SPECIFICATION	COMMENT
1.	Committee	Exchange between all business teams using AI systems	Good practice
2.	Presidency	Appointment of an AI manager within the organisation	Good practice
3.	Mapping	Inventory and update of all AI systems	Risk monitoring policy
4.	Framework	IS Policy Specific policy for AI technologies	Policy and procedures[100]

93. The governance of AI technologies concerns two major families:

- symbolic AI systems;
- statistical AI systems.

3.4. Symbolic AI Systems

3.4.1 Introduction

94. Born in the 1950s, symbolic AI was pioneered by Alan Turing[101] and John McCarthy.[102]

---

99 C. Sallé, 'Comment l'IA menace l'industrie de la musique' ['How AI threatens the music industry'], *Le Figaro*, 14 April 2023 (digital version), 15–16 April 2023 (paper version).

100 M. Jasor, 'L'intelligence artificielle générative, nouvelle alliée des DRH?' ['Is generative artificial intelligence the new ally of HRs?'], *Les Échos*, 5 October 2023, p. 11.

101 A.M. Turing, 'Computing machinery and intelligence', (1950) 49(236) *Mind*; I. Berny, '1950 Alan Turing, père de la machine intelligente' [-1950 Alan Turing, father of the intelligent machine'], *Le Figaro*, 21 August 2017.

102 CIGREF, 'Père d'intelligence artificielle… John McCarthy' ['Father of artificial intelligence… John McCarthy'], *Cigref*, 31 May 2014; J. Henno, '1956: et l'intelligence artificielle devint une science' ['1956: And artificial intelligence became a science'], *Les Échos*, 21 August 2017.

95. In the 1970s, these systems developed under the name of 'expert system'.

3.4.2 Composition

96. Symbolic AI systems enable the implementation of reasoning.

97. By combining rules, an output is obtained for which it is possible:

- to trace the logic of the reasoning;
- to measure the relevance or accuracy;
- to demonstrate the stability of the output.

98. These systems can be illustrated as follows:

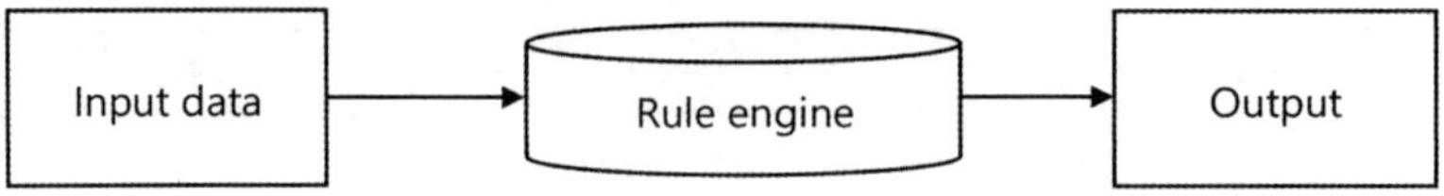

99. The rules engine is made up of knowledge from different sources:

- scientific knowledge;
- state of the art;
- know-how.

100. Knowledge is modelled using specific computer languages such as LISP or Prolog.

3.4.3 Limitations

101. If something changes, the rules have to be changed. There is no machine learning with this technology.

102. Although superseded by artificial neural systems, symbolic systems continue to develop and form hybrid systems with statistical AI systems.

3.5. Statistical AI Systems

3.5.1 Introduction

103. Statistical AI systems are based on learning algorithms that mimic human intelligence.

104. The generic architecture of these systems can be summarised as follows:

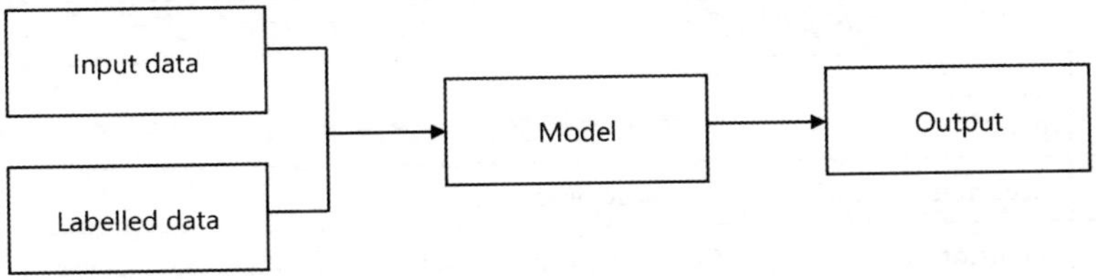

105. The model is trained in such a way as to provide a solution based on examples corresponding to labelled data.

106. The algorithm consists of minimising errors between the expected results and the results produced.

3.5.2 Training

107. There are several types of learning, such as:

NO.	TYPE OF LEARNING	SPECIFICATION
1.	Supervised learning	The model 'learns' from data labelled according to expected outputs. Example: Images depicting a dog or a cat
2.	Unsupervised learning	Exploiting large amounts of unlabelled data to develop rules or models
3.	Reinforcement learning	Learning through a reward mechanism
4.	Learning mode	Instantaneous or continuous

3.5.3 Neural Network

108. Inspired by biological models, neural networks are made up of different layers that enable them to solve complex tasks, such as playing a game of chess or Go, or creating contracts or performing medical diagnoses.

109. There are several categories of neural networks, including the following:

NO.	NEURAL NETWORKS	SPECIFICATION
1.	Convolutional networks	Image processing[103]
2.	Recurrent networks	Language processing
3.	Transformer	Context-sensitive understanding of natural language[104]

3.5.4 Limitations

110. The limitations of neural networks result from:

- the complexity of such systems (more than hundreds of layers and billions of parameters);
- the lack of understanding of the mechanisms for adjusting the hidden layers;
- sensitivity to training data (quality and bias).

111. Notes:

- (1) According to the AI Act, neural networks belong to the category of general-purpose AI systems.[105]

3.5.5 Foundation Models

112. Foundation models are made up of deep neural networks. They allow many functions to be solved in multiple contexts.

113. This is the case with generative artificial intelligences such as ChatGPT,[106] Gemini[107] or Claude 3.[108] In legal terms, they are general-purpose AI models.[109]

[103] Dall-E or Midjourney.
[104] ChatGPT or Gemini.
[105] AI Act, Art. 3(66).
[106] OpenAI.
[107] Google.
[108] Anthropic.
[109] AI Act, Art. 3(63).

3.6. *Technical and Legal Definitions*

114. The main definitions of AI systems are as follows:

NO.	BODY	SPECIFICATION
1.	2018 Montréal Declaration[110]	'Artificial intelligence (AI) refers to the series of techniques which allow a machine to simulate human learning, namely to learn, predict, make decisions and perceive its surroundings. In the case of a computing system, artificial intelligence is applied to digital data'
2.	AI HLEG (High-Level Expert Group on Artificial Intelligence)	'Artificial intelligence (AI) systems are software (and possibly also hardware) systems designed by humans[111] that, given a complex goal, act in the physical or digital dimension by perceiving their environment through data acquisition, interpreting the collected structured or unstructured data, reasoning on the knowledge, or processing the information, derived from this data and deciding the best action(s) to take to achieve the given goal. AI systems can either use symbolic rules or learn a numeric model, and they can also adapt their behaviour by analysing how the environment is affected by their previous actions'[112]
3.	AI Regulation 2024/1689 on IA European Union	'A machine-based system that is designed to operate with varying levels of autonomy and that may exhibit adaptiveness after deployment, and that, for explicit or implicit objectives, infers, from the input it receives, how to generate outputs such as predictions, content, recommendations, or decisions that can influence physical or virtual environments'[113]
4.	CELF (French Language Enrichment Commission)	Theoretical and practical interdisciplinary field whose aim is to understand the mechanisms of cognition and reflection, and to imitate them using hardware and software devices, in order to assist or replace human activities[114]
5.	CNIL (French data protection authority)	Artificial intelligence is a logical, automated process, usually based on an algorithm, which is capable of performing well-defined tasks[115]

110 The Montréal Declaration is a collective work that aims to put AI development at the service of the well-being of all people, and to guide social change by developing recommendations with strong democratic legitimacy: https://declarationmontreal-iaresponsable.com/la-declaration/ and https://declarationmontreal-iaresponsable.com/glossaire/.

111 Humans design AI systems directly, but they may also use AI techniques to optimise their design (notes to the guidelines).

112 AI HLEG (High-Level Expert Group on Artificial Intelligence), 'Ethics Guidelines for Trustworthy AI', European Commission, April 2019, p. 38.

113 AI Act, Art. 3(1).

114 Commission d'enrichissement de la langue française (French Language Enrichment Commission), 'Vocabulaire de l'intelligence artificielle' ['Artificial intelligence vocabulary'], Opinion NOR: CTNR1832601K, *JORF*, n° 0285, 9 December 2018.

115 Definition of the CNIL, https://www.cnil.fr/fr/definition/intelligence-artificielle.

NO.	BODY	SPECIFICATION
6.	CNRS (French National Centre for Scientific Research)	Research into ways of endowing computer systems with intellectual capacities comparable to those of human beings[116]
7.	CoE (Council of Europe)	'A set of sciences, theories and techniques whose purpose is to reproduce by a machine the cognitive abilities of a human being. Current developments aim to be able to entrust a machine with complex tasks previously delegated to a human However, the term artificial intelligence is criticized by experts who distinguish between 'strong' AI (who are able to contextualize very different specialized problems completely independently) and 'weak' or 'moderate' AI (who perform extremely well in their field of training). According to some experts, 'strong' AI would require advances in basic research to be able to model the world as a whole and not just improvements in the performance of existing systems'[117] Similarly, according to the CoE: 'artificial intelligence system' means a machine-based system that for explicit or implicit objectives, infers, from the input it receives, how to generate outputs such as predictions, content, recommendations or decisions that may influence physical or virtual environments. Different artificial intelligence systems vary in their levels of autonomy and adaptiveness after deployment'[118]
8.	ENISA (European Union Agency for Cybersecurity)	'Artificial Intelligence (AI) is an emerging concept facilitating intelligent and automated decision-making and is thus becoming a prerequisite for the deployment of IoT and Industry 4.0 scenarios as well as other application areas'[119]
9.	ISO (International Organization for Standardization)	'Branch of computer science devoted to developing data processing systems that perform functions normally associated with human intelligence, such as reasoning, learning, and self-improvement'[120] 'Capability of a functional unit to perform functions that are generally associated with human intelligence such as reasoning and learning'[121]

116 Dictionary of the Centre National de Ressources Textuelles et Lexicales (CNRTL) (French National Center of Textual and Lexical Resources) created by the CNRS created by the CNRS, http://www.cnrtl.fr/lexicographie/intelligence (point A, § 4: LOG., INFORM. Intelligence artificielle); definition from: La Recherche, January 1979, n° 96, vol. 10, p. 61.

117 Council of Europe glossary: https://www.coe.int/fr/web/artificial-intelligence/glossary#I.

118 Council of Europe Framework Convention on Artificial Intelligence and Human Rights, Democracy and the Rule of Law, CAI, 17 May 2024, https://search.coe.int/cm?i=0900001680afb11f.

119 Emerging Technologies Artificial Intelligence (AI): https://www.enisa.europa.eu/topics/iot-and-smart-infrastructures/artificial_intelligence.

120 ISO 24591-2:2024, Smart water management — Part 2: Data management guidelines, 3.2 [Source: ISO/IEC/IEEE 24765:2017, 3.234], https://www.iso.org/obp/ui/en/#iso:std:iso:24591:-2:ed-1:v1:en.

121 ISO 2382:2015, Information technology — Vocabulary, No 2123770 [Source:ISO-IEC-2382-28 * 1995 * * *] https://www.iso.org/obp/ui/fr/#iso:std:iso-iec:2382:ed-1:v2:en.

NO.	BODY	SPECIFICATION
10.	John McCarthy (1956)	'It is the science and engineering of making intelligent machines, especially intelligent computer programs. It is related to the similar task of using computers to understand human intelligence, but AI does not have to confine itself to methods that are biologically observable'
11.	Marvin Lee Minsky (1956)	'The construction of computer programs that engage in tasks that are, for the time being, more satisfactorily performed by human beings, because they require high level mental processes such as: perceptual learning, memory organization and critical reasoning'[122]
12.	OECD (Organisation for Economic Co-operation and Development)	'Artificial Intelligence (AI) is a general-purpose technology that has the potential to: improve the welfare and well-being of people, contribute to positive sustainable global economic activity, increase innovation and productivity, and help respond to key global challenges. It is deployed in many sectors ranging from production, education, finance and transport to healthcare and security'[123]
13.	OQLF (Quebec Office of the French Language)	Field of study concerned with the artificial reproduction of the cognitive faculties of human intelligence in order to create systems or machines capable of performing functions normally associated with human intelligence[124]
14.	UNESCO (United Nations Educational, Scientific and Cultural Organization)	The Recommendation approaches AI systems as 'systems which have the capacity to process data and information in a way that resembles intelligent behaviour, and typically includes aspects of reasoning, learning, perception, prediction, planning or control'[125]
15.	WIPO (World Intellectual Property Organization)	'Artificial intelligence (AI) refers to the branch of computer science and engineering that focuses on creating systems capable of performing tasks that typically require human intelligence. These tasks include understanding natural language, recognizing images, making decisions and learning from data'[126]

115. These different definitions show that there is a wide variety of approaches to this issue.

---

122 Definition given by one of the pioneers of AI in 1956, Marvin Lee Minsky, See La rédaction Clubic, 'C'est quoi l'intelligence artificielle' ['What's artificial intelligence?'], *Clubic.com*, 16 September 2017.

123 https://legalinstruments.oecd.org/en/instruments/OECD-LEGAL-0449.

124 https://vitrinelinguistique.oqlf.gouv.qc.ca/fiche-gdt/fiche/8385376/intelligence-artificielle.

125 UNESCO, 'Recommendation on the Ethics of Artificial Intelligence', 23 November 2021.

126 WIPO, 'Getting the innovation ecosystem ready for AI – An IP policy toolkit', 2024, p. 7.

116. In summary, and according to these definitions, the main characteristics of AI technologies are as follows:

NO.	BODY	SCHEME	PROCESS	LEARNING	OBJECTIVE	FUNCTION	IMPACT
1.	2018 Montréal Declaration	Set of techniques	Simulation of human intelligence	X	-	Prediction Decision	Environment
2.	AI HLEG	Software Hardware	Reasoning	X	X	Symbolic rules Numerical model	Perception
3.	AI Regulation 2024/1689	Automated systems	Autonomy	Adaptability	X	Prediction Content	Physical Virtual
4.	CELF	Hardware and software device	Mechanisms of cognition and reflection	-	-	-	-
5.	CNIL	Logical and automated process	-	-	-	Defined tasks	
6.	CNRTL	Computer system	Intellectual capacities comparable to those of human beings	-	-	-	-
7.	CoE 2014	Automated system	X	X	X	Prediction Content	Physical Virtual
8.	ENISA	IoT	-	-	-	Decision Intelligent	-
9.	ISO	Data processing system	Functions normally associated with human intelligence	X Self-improvement	-	Reasoning	
10.	John McCarthy (1956)	Smart machine	Understanding human intelligence	-	-	-	-
11.	Marvin Lee Minsky (1956)	Computer programs	Tasks performed by human being	X	-	Critical thinking	-
12.	OECD	General-purpose technology	-	-	-	Improving human well-being Global economic activity	
13.	OQLF	Systems or machines	Artificial reproduction of the cognitive faculties of human intelligence			Functions of human nature	
14.	UNESCO	X	Processes resembling intelligent behaviour	X	-	Reasoning	-
15.	WIPO	IT	Reproduction of human intelligence	X	-	Natural language understanding Image Decision-making	-

3.7. *Machine*

3.7.1 Introduction

117. 'The term "machine-based" refers to the fact that AI systems run on machines.'[127]

118. The French version of the Regulation uses the term '*système automatisé*' [literally, automated system] for AI systems, unlike the English version which uses the term 'machine-based system'.[128]

3.7.2 Typology

119. The terms 'machine', 'machinery', or 'equipment' are used in the following contexts:

NO.	THEME	SPECIFICATION	REFERENCE
1.	CE marking of AI systems	Machine-readable format of output origin	AIA, Rec. 133 AIA, Art. 50(2)
2.	CE marking	Machine-readable code or other electronic means	AIA, Art. 48
3.	Conditions for access to personal data	Terminal equipment	AIA, Rec. 10
4.	Definition of AI systems	'"AI system" means a machine-based system' (English version) The French version uses the term '*système automatisé*' instead of 'machine-based'	AIA, Art. 3(1)
5.	EU Declaration of conformity	Machine readable	AIA, Art. 47
6.	Health	Reference to machinery or medical devices products	AIA, Rec. 64
7.	Implicit reference	Cumulative amount of computation used	AIA, Art. 51(2) AIA, Annex XIII
8.	Interface	Human-machine	AIA, Rec. 14
9.	Machine	Generic term for implementing AI technologies	AIA, Rec. 12
10.	Prohibited practices	Machine-brain interface	AIA, Rec. 45
11.	Readable	Access to EU database by high-risk AI systems Machine-readable	AIA, Rec. 13 AIA, Art. 71(4)

[127] AI Act, Rec. 12.
[128] AI Act, Art. 3(1) and see below section 3.7.2 Typology.

3.8. *Robotic Systems*

3.8.1 Introduction

120. The objective of the European Parliament resolution of 20 October 2020 was to develop a legal framework for 'ethical aspects of artificial intelligence, robotics and related technologies'.[129]

121. This concept of related technologies corresponds to sensors and robots, particularly industrial, service or humanoid robots. It appears under the expression 'related products and services within the internal market'.[130]

3.8.2 Definition

122. Robots are described as follows:

- 'robotics means technologies that enable automatically controlled, reprogrammable, multi-purpose machines to perform actions in the physical world traditionally performed or initiated by human beings, including by way of artificial intelligence or related technologies.'

123. The other elements associated with a robot are understood through the concept of 'related technologies' defined as 'technologies that enable software to control with a partial or full degree of autonomy a physical or virtual process, technologies capable of detecting biometric, genetic or other data, and technologies that copy or otherwise make use of human traits'.

3.8.3 Equipment and Machinery

124. In practice, robotics is taken into account through AI technologies integrated into equipment or technical components.[131]

---

129 Resolution of 20 October 2020 and associated draft regulations.

130 AI Act, Rec. 3.

131 AI Act, Art. 6(1).

125. The various technical components of an AI system can be summarised as follows:

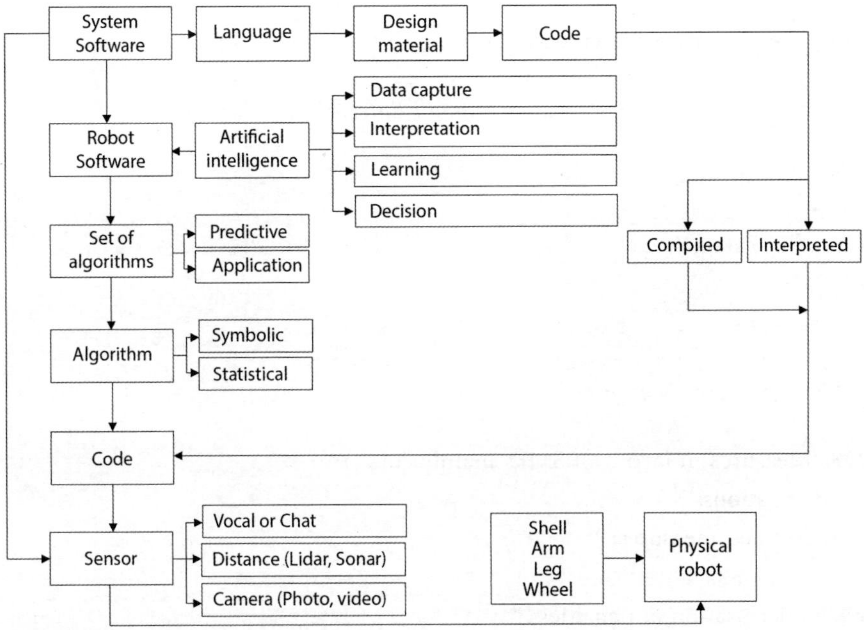

4 ACTORS

4.1. Typology

126. The actors are presented in Section 2.1 Geographical Scope.

4.2. Small Enterprises

4.2.1 Introduction

127. This category covers:

- SMEs;[132]
- start-ups.

4.2.2 Support Measures

128. Measures in favour of SMEs mainly concern:

- derogations;[133]
- dedicated measures;[134]
- special assistance;[135]
- modernisation of penalties.[136]

5 ACTIVITIES

5.1. Introduction

129. They include the following:

- placing on the market;
- putting into service;
- deployment;
- use of outputs.

---

132 Recommendation 2003/361 of 6 May 2003.

133 Exclusion of the design phase (AI Act, Art. 2(8)); the quality management system for high-risk AI systems (AI Act, Art. 17(2)), etc.

134 Support measures from Member States and the AI Office (AI Act, Art. 62).

135 Participation in AI regulatory sandboxes (AI Act, Art. 57(9)(e)).

136 AI Act, Art. 99(1) (definition) and Art. 99(6) (level of financial penalty).

5.2. *Placing on the Market*

130. 'A product is placed on the market when it is made available for the first time on the Union market.'[137]

5.3. *Putting into Service*

131. Putting into service includes:

- installation;
- putting into service in the strict sense;
- use.

132. 'Putting into service takes place at the moment of first use within the Union by the end user for the purposes for which it was intended'.[138]

5.4. *Deployment*

133. Deployment refers to the use of an AI system by a deployer among members of its staff or persons acting on its behalf.[139]

5.5. *Use*

134. Use consists of the operation within private or public organisations by legal or natural persons.

5.6. *Exports*

5.6.1 Introduction

135. The Regulation does not apply to the export of AI systems or models.[140]

5.6.2 Development

136. No prohibitions, essential requirements or technical specifications apply to products intended for export.

---

[137] 'The "Blue Guide" on the implementation of EU product rules 2022' [2022], OJ C 247/1, p. 19.

[138] Ibid., p. 23.

[139] 'Staff' in the broadest sense, including temporary staff, trainees, on-site consultants. The term is used for example in the AI Act, Art. 4 AI literacy.

[140] The terms exporter and export have been left out of the AI Act.

5.6.3 Prohibited Practices

137. They are not prohibited even if they fail to comply with the values of the Union.[141]

138. The Parliament had proposed an amendment in favour of respecting the EU's values when exporting, which was worded as follows:

- 'In order for the Union to be true to its fundamental values, AI systems intended to be used for practices that are considered unacceptable by this Regulation, should equally be deemed to be unacceptable outside the Union because of their particularly harmful effect to fundamental rights as enshrined in the Charter. Therefore it is appropriate to prohibit the export of such AI systems to third countries by providers residing in the Union.'[142]

139. Notes:

- (1) The rules concerning the control of exports of dual-use items apply to such exports;
- (2) AI systems and models are included in the category of software that may be considered as dual-use items.[143]

6 CROSS-CUTTING TECHNICAL ISSUES

6.1. Introduction

140. They include:

- autonomy;
- regulatory sandbox;
- code of practice;
- design;
- damage and harm;
- testing in real-world conditions;
- environment;
- incidents;

---

141 AI Act, Art. 1(1) (Health, Safety, Environment, Fundamental Rights, Rule of Law and Democracy).

142 AI Act, Amendment to Recital 10. Report on the proposal for a regulation of the European Parliament and of the Council of 22 May 2023 on laying down harmonised rules on Artificial Intelligence (Artificial Intelligence Act) and amending certain Union Legislative Acts (A9-0188/2023).

143 Regulation (EU) 2021/821 of the European Parliament and of the Council of 20 May 2021 setting up a Union regime for the control of exports, brokering, technical assistance, transit and transfer of dual-use items (recast), Art. 2(1).

- innovation;
- AI literacy;
- open source;
- research;
- safety;
- dual-use AI systems;
- multi-qualification AI systems.

6.2. *Autonomy of AI Systems*

6.2.1 Introduction

141. This concept is the main key to an AI system.

142. It is presented in the definition of an AI system as follows:

- '"AI system" means a machine-based system that is designed to operate with varying levels of autonomy and that may exhibit adaptiveness after deployment, and that, for explicit or implicit objectives, infers, from the input it receives, how to generate outputs such as predictions, content, recommendations, or decisions that can influence physical or virtual environments.'[144]

6.2.2 Definition

143. In this context, autonomy consists of the AI system performing non-programmed operations in a repetitive sequence.

144. This concept refers to a principle of artificial independence.

145. This autonomy means that AI systems 'have some degree of independence of actions from human involvement and of capabilities to operate without human intervention'.[145]

6.2.3 Risk

146. The level of risk depends on the level of autonomy and the domain in which the AI system operates.

6.2.4 Containment

147. Controlling this autonomy implies managing risks; it leads to a real obligation of containment.

---

[144] AI Act, Art. 3(1).

[145] AI Act, Rec. 12.

148. This control concerns in particular:

NO.	THEME
1.	Quality and risk management
2.	Pre-market testing
3.	Event traceability
4.	Monitoring and alert system
5.	Emergency response
6.	Additional containment measures
7.	Permanent human oversight
8.	Notification of regulatory authorities

6.3. *Regulatory Sandbox*

6.3.1 Introduction

149. A regulatory sandbox is an innovation zone within the regulatory framework where it is possible to access to a range of services and benefit from exemptions to a pre-existing legal framework.

6.3.2 Definition

150. According to the AI Act, AI regulatory sandbox means 'a controlled framework set up by a competent authority which offers providers or prospective providers of AI systems the possibility to develop, train, validate and test, where appropriate in real-world conditions, an innovative AI system, pursuant to a sandbox plan for a limited time under regulatory supervision'.[146]

[146] AI Act, Art. 3(55).

6.3.3 Application

151. The implementation is organised as follows:[147]

NO.	THEME	SPECIFICATION
1.	Geography	Compulsory at national level, with the possibility of local variations
2.	Number	At least one set up by each Member State
3.	Mutualisation	Sandboxes can be grouped together
4.	Composition	Physical, digital or hybrid form[148]
5.	Resources	Administrative, financial and human[149]
6.	Objective	Development of experimentation in a controlled environment[150]
7.	Personal data	Where sensitive data are used, the AI Act provisions regarding AI regulatory sandboxes as such should provide the legal basis for such use[151]

6.3.4 Documentation

152. To participate in a regulatory sandbox, a provider should first submit an application to the national competent authority.

153. This application takes the form of a sandbox plan. A sandbox plan is defined as follows: 'a document agreed between the participating provider and the competent authority describing the objectives, conditions, timeframe, methodology and requirements for the activities carried out within the sandbox'.[152]

6.4. Codes of Best Practice

6.4.1 Introduction

154. In order to promote 'safe, secure, and trustworthy AI',[153] codes of conduct or codes of practice aim to harmonise practices and ensure an ethical-based approach of the risks on a voluntary basis.

147 AI Act, Art. 59.
148 AI Act, Rec. 138.
149 AI Act, Rec. 138.
150 AI Act, Rec. 139.
151 AI Act, Rec. 140.
152 AI Act, Art. 3(54).
153 G7-G20, 'Hiroshima Process International Code of Conduct for Organizations Developing Advanced AI Systems', 30 October 2023.

6.4.2 Requirements

155. Codes of practice may meet all or part of the requirements relating to an AI system or model.

156. The AI Office must encourage and facilitate the voluntary drawing up of such codes.[154]

6.5. Design

6.5.1 Introduction

157. The design phase can be broken down as follows:

- studies;
- algorithm development;
- creation of databases;
- software development;
- testing;
- purposes.

6.5.2 Studies

158. This phase will define:

- the objectives;
- the type of AI technology selected;
- the AI system.

6.5.3 Algorithms

159. The algorithms form the backbone of the future system and are the means for achieving the expected outputs.

6.5.4 Creating Databases

160. Depending on the nature of the training data to be considered, it will be necessary to coordinate the requirements of:

- the AI Act, for governance;[155]
- the GDPR, for protection by design and by default.[156]

---

154 AI Act, Art. 56.
155 AI Act, Art. 10.
156 GDPR, Art. 25(1) and (2).

6.5.5 Software Development

161. One of the key decisions to be made is whether or not to use open-source software.

6.5.6 Testing

162. Testing can be carried out:

- in-house:
- in a regulatory sandbox;
- in real-world conditions.

6.5.7 Formalities

163. Before a product is placed on the market or put into service, a number of steps must be completed, such:

- EU declaration;
- CE marking;
- declarations in records;
- etc.

6.6. *Damage and Harm*

6.6.1 Introduction

164. Compensation for harm is a key element in building trust and minimising the risks associated with the implementation of AI systems.

165. The damage caused may be material or immaterial.[157]

---

157 AI Act, Rec. 5.

6.6.2 Classification

166. It can be summarised as follows:[158]

NO.	THEME	SPECIFICATION
1.	Type	Physical Psychological Reputational Economic Societal
2.	Severity	Minor Low Medium High Major Unbearable
3.	Person	Individual Group Specific population
4.	Geographic scale	Local Regional National EU Group of countries Worldwide
5.	Reversibility	Total Medium Low Possible
6.	Recurrence	No Yes
7.	Timeframe	Short term Medium term Long term

6.6.3 Damage and Liability

167. Compensation for damage resulting from the implementation of an AI system depends on the type of remedy:

- contractual liability;[159]
- tort or non-contractual liability.[160]

---

158 This table is mainly based on: 'Defining AI incidents and related terms', *Artificial Intelligence Papers*, No 16, OECD, 6 May 2024.

159 See section 15.16 Liability.

160 See section 15.16 Liability.

6.7. *Environment*

6.7.1 Introduction

168. The impact (design and use) of AI technologies on the environment is very significant. This issue was only introduced during the trialogue phase.[161]

6.7.2 Guiding Principles

169. Environment is an overarching issue.[162]

170. However, the Regulation does not define essential requirements as such.

171. The principles are based on the following:

- the need to meet environmental targets;[163]
- compliance with ethical principles such as social and environmental well-being;[164]
- environmental protection;[165]
- environmental sustainability;[166]
- codes of conduct;[167]
- environmental crime.[168]

6.8. *Testing in Real-World Conditions*

6.8.1 Introduction

172. Testing in real-world conditions present serious risks when conducted outside the sandbox mechanism. It is subject to strict supervision.

6.8.2 Definition

173. 'Testing in real-world conditions' means 'the temporary testing of an AI system for its intended purpose in real-world conditions outside a laboratory or otherwise simulated environment, with a view to gathering reliable and robust data and to assessing and verifying the conformity of the AI system with the requirements of this Regulation and it does not qualify as placing the AI system

---

161 2023 to 2024.
162 The concept is cited 39 times.
163 AI Act, Rec. 142.
164 AI Act, Rec. 27.
165 AI Act, Rec. 48 and Art. 1.
166 AI Act, Rec. 165.
167 AI Act, Art. 95.
168 AI Act, Art. 5 and Annex II.

on the market or putting it into service within the meaning of this Regulation, provided that all the conditions laid down in Article 57[169] or 60[170] are fulfilled'.[171]

6.8.3 Actors

174. This applies to operators who conduct testing in real-world conditions.

175. Notes:

- (1) Natural persons who participate in testing in real-world conditions are referred to as 'subjects'.[172]

6.8.4 Implementation

176. The testing must be subject to a 'real-world testing plan' defined as follows: 'a document that describes the objectives, methodology, geographical, population and temporal scope, monitoring, organisation and conduct of testing in real-world conditions'.[173]

6.8.5 Testing of High-Risk AI Systems

177. This type of testing is mandatory prior to the placing on the market.

178. When testing is conducting in real-world conditions and outside regulatory sandboxes, the following conditions must be met:[174]

NO.	TESTING	SPECIFICATION
1.	AI systems	Systems covered by Annex III
2.	Actor	Provider on their own or in partnership with deployers
3.	Modality	Real-world testing plan
4.	Date	Before the placing on the market or the implementation
5.	Prerequisites Approval	Ethical review[175] Testing plan must be approved by the market surveillance authority
6.	Duration	6 months, which may be extended once for the same duration

169 AI Act, Art. 57 concerns AI regulatory sandboxes.
170 AI Act, Art. 60 concerns testing of high-risk AI systems in real world conditions outside AI regulatory sandboxes.
171 AI Act, Art. 3(57).
172 AI Act, Art. 3(58).
173 AI Act, Art. 3(53).
174 AI Act, Art. 60(1).
175 AI Act, Art. 60(3).

NO.	TESTING	SPECIFICATION
7.	Subject	Informed consent Protection of vulnerable persons
8.	Supervision	Market surveillance authority

6.9. *Incident*

6.9.1 Introduction

179. The traceability of incidents is essential when developing, deploying and maintaining safe and trustworthy AI.

6.9.2 Traceability

180. The requirements are as follows:

NO.	THEME	INCIDENT	SPECIFICATION	REFERENCE
1.	High-risk AI system	Non-serious	Obligation to record all events, including incidents[176]	AIA, Art. 12(1)
		Serious	Reporting to the market surveillance authority	AIA, Art. 73(1)
2.	General-purpose AI model with systemic risk	Non-serious	Traceability	AIA, Art. 55
		Serious	Reporting to the AI Office and the national competent authorities	AIA, Art. 55(1)(c)
3.	General-purpose AI model without systemic risk	Non-serious	Traceability	AIA, Art. 55
		Serious	Traceability	AIA, Art. 55
4.	General-purpose AI model	Non-serious	Traceability	AIA, Art. 55
		Serious	Traceability	AIA, Art. 55
5.	Transparent AI system	Non-serious	No logs	AIA, Art. 50
		Serious	No logs	AIA, Art. 50
6.	Free AI system Code of conduct option	Non-serious	No logs	AIA, Art. 56
		Serious	Depending on the nature of the risks	AIA, Art. 56

176 AI Act, Art. 12.

6.10. *Innovation*

6.10.1 Introduction

181. Innovation is a key concern and the Regulation should not delay or prevent innovation in an area that is strategic for the EU's economy.

6.10.2 Guiding Principles

182. The guidelines are as follows:

NO.	THEME	SPECIFICATION
1.	Liability	The idea is to promote responsible innovation[177]
2.	Control	As a logical next step, the EU wants to foster innovation that develops in a controlled environment[178]
3.	Support	EU programme to promote trustworthy AI[179]

6.10.3 Support Measures

183. They are organised as follows:

NO.	MEASURE	SPECIFICATION
1.	Actor	SMEs Start-ups[180]
2.	Regulatory sandboxes	Establish at least one regulatory AI regulatory sandbox at national level[181]
3.	AI ecosystem	The aim is to foster ecosystems within the EU that enable innovation to flourish[182]

177 AI Act, Rec. 138.
178 AI Act, Rec. 139.
179 AI Act, Art. 1.
180 AI Act, Art. 1.
181 AI Act, Art. 57.
182 AI Act, Art. 57.

6.11. *AI Literacy*

6.11.1 Introduction

184. Protecting the EU's values in the face of the development of AI technologies and confining risks to a sphere compatible with the benefits expected in a democracy requires that all natural persons have the ability to direct and control AI systems.[183]

6.11.2 Definition

185. The concept of 'AI literacy' means:

- 'skills, knowledge and understanding that allow providers, deployers and affected persons, taking into account their respective rights and obligations in the context of this Regulation, to make an informed deployment of AI systems, as well as to gain awareness about the opportunities and risks of AI and possible harm it can cause'.[184]

6.11.3 Actors

186. The actors concerned by the obligation to AI literacy are the staff of providers and deployers, as well as people with roles that are identical or similar to those of staff members.

6.11.4 Content

187. Awareness-raising and training operations concern:

- operation;
- use.

188. The level of knowledge to be acquired depends on that of the natural persons and the risks involved.

6.12. *Open Source (Free and Open-Source Licences)*

6.12.1 Introduction

189. Open-source AI technologies (AI systems and AI models) benefit from legal derogations.

---

183 AI Act, Art. 4.

184 AI Act, Art. 3(56).

6.12.2 Guiding Principles

190. Open-source systems make it possible to satisfy the following purposes:

NO.	SYSTEM	SPECIFICATION
1.	Dissemination of knowledge	Open source is one of the keys to open science, enabling the exchange of knowledge and the well-being of humanity
2.	Community regulation	Combating prohibitions and bad practices
3.	Transparency	Controlling usage and eliminating voluntary or implicit bias
4.	Free of charge	Exchanges without the constraints of markets

6.12.3 Derogations for AI Models

191. They are as follows:

NO.	THEME	SPECIFICATION	REFERENCE
1.	AI models with systemic risk	No derogation	AIA, Rec. 104 AIA, Art. 53(2)
2.	AI models without systemic risk	Beneficiary: providers Derogations: 'Providers of general-purpose AI models shall: a) draw up and keep up-to-date the technical documentation of the model, including its training and testing process and the results of its evaluation, which shall contain, at a minimum, the information set out in Annex XI for the purpose of providing it, upon request, to the AI Office and the national competent authorities; b) draw up, keep up-to-date and make available information and documentation to providers of AI systems who intend to integrate the general-purpose AI model into their AI systems. Without prejudice to the need to observe and protect intellectual property rights and confidential business information or trade secrets in accordance with Union and national law, the information and documentation shall: (i) enable providers of AI systems to have a good understanding of the capabilities and limitations of the general-purpose AI model and to comply with their obligations pursuant to this Regulation; and (ii) contain, at a minimum, the elements set out in Annex XII.'	AIA, Rec. 102 AIA, Art. 53(1)(a)–(b) AIA, Art. 54(6)

6.12.4 AI System Exclusions

192. The rules are as follows:

NO.	THEME	SPECIFICATION	REFERENCE
1.	AI system	Free and open-source licence Exclusion	AIA, Art. 2(12)
2.	Exception to the exclusion despite the existence of a free and open-source licence	High-risk AI system (AIA, Art. 6)	AIA, Art. 2(12)
		Prohibited AI system that falls under prohibited practices (AIA, Art. 5)	AIA, Art. 2(12)
		AI system subject to a transparency obligation (AIA, Art. 50)	AIA, Art. 2(12)

6.13. Research

6.13.1 Introduction

193. The aim is to ensure that the legal framework for AI technologies is not an obstacle to fundamental research and development activities.

6.13.2 Exception

6.13.2.1 *Field of Research*

194. The Regulation does not apply to AI systems or AI models, including their output, specifically developed and put into service for the sole purpose of scientific research and development.[185]

6.13.2.2 *Research Activities*

195. The Regulation does not apply to any research, testing and development regarding AI systems or AI models prior to their being placed on the market or put into service. Such activities must be conducted in accordance with applicable EU law.[186]

196. Notes:

- (1) Testing in real-world conditions is not covered by that exclusion.[187]

---

185 AI Act, Art. 2(6).
186 AI Act, Art. 2(8).
187 AI Act, Art. 2(8).

6.14. *Safety*

6.14.1 Introduction

197. The concept of safety is considered in the Regulation from the following angles:

- a fundamental protection value: the safety of (natural or legal) persons or property;
- a safety component or a safety product embedding an AI system;
- an essential obligation applicable to AI technologies.

6.14.2 Safety of Persons

6.14.2.1 *Natural Persons*

198. The safety of natural persons includes both physical and psychological safety.

6.14.2.2 *Legal Persons*

199. All organisations are concerned in terms of protection, unlike the GDPR (2016/679)[188] where only the data of natural persons are protected.

6.14.3 Characteristics

200. Unlike the GDPR, security as a set of technical requirements is not subject to specific constaints.[189]

6.14.4 Fraud

201. An initial classification of fraud can be made as follows:

NO.	THEME	SPECIFICATION
1.	Attack	Using the power of AI to commit computer fraud
2.	Counterfeit	Attacks on all types of creations, given the multimodal nature of generative artificial intelligence
3.	Training data	Poisoning Insertion of bias

188 AI Act, Rec. 14.

189 Example: GDPR, Arts 25 and 32.

NO.	THEME	SPECIFICATION
4.	Espionage	Invasion of privacy CEO fraud
5.	Harassment	Illicit and fraudulent threats
6.	Information	False information Conspiracy information Fraudulent sound recordings, videos and documents

202. Notes:

- (1) F. Vallet, 'Sécurité des systèmes d'IA, les gestes qui sauvent' ['AI system security, a first aid guide'], LINC (Laboratoire d'innovation numérique de la CNIL), 21 January 2022.
- (2) ANSSI, 'Security recommendations for a generative AI system', Guide No. ANSSI-PA-102, 29 April 2024.

6.15. Dual-Use AI Systems

6.15.1 Introduction

203. Many AI systems may fall under separate legal frameworks.

6.15.2 Criteria

204. The key is the concept of purpose. This applies in particular to prohibited AI systems:

NO.	THEME	SPECIFICATION	EXAMPLE
1.	Prohibited AI systems	Putting into service for this specific purpose	Predictive policing (AIA, Art. 5(1)(d)) Recognition of emotions (AIA, Art. 5(1)(f))
2.		Law enforcement purposes	Remote biometric identification (AIA, Art. 5(1)(h))

6.16. *Multi-Qualification AI Systems*

6.16.1 Introduction

205. Depending on the purpose and the implementation characteristics, the same AI system (from a technical point of view) may be subject to different legal qualifications.

6.16.2 Criteria

206. The main elements having an impact on legal qualification are as follows:

NO.	CRITERION	SPECIFICATION	COMMENT
1.	Sensitive or protected features	Deduction	Biometric categorisation (AIA, Art. 6(2) Annex III(1)(b))
2.	Consequence	Detrimental Unfavourable Harm	Prohibition of social scoring (AIA, Art. 5(1)(c))
3.	Special data (GDPR, Art. 9)	Deduction	Biometric categorisation (AIA, Art. 5(1)(g))
4.	Function	Emotion recognition	AIA, Art. 6(2) Annex III(1)(c)
5.	Location	Workplace Educational institutions	Emotion detection AIA, Art. 5(1)(f)
6.	Operation (collection)	Scraping	Untargeted scraping of facial images AIA, Art. 5(1)(e)
7.	Operation (predictive)	Assessing the risk of committing a criminal offence	Prohibition of predictive policing except AIA, Art. 5(1)(d)
8.	Technical origin	Internet CCTV footage	Untargeted scraping of facial images AIA, Art. 5(1)(e)

6.16.3 Example

207. For AI systems designed for biometric categorisation, the legal qualification is as follows:

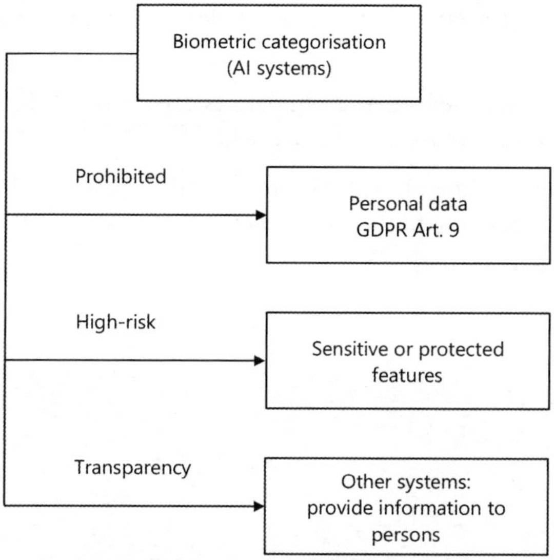

7 GENERAL LEGAL FRAMEWORK FOR AI SYSTEMS

7.1. Hierarchy of European Standards

208. The legal structure is organised as follows:

- the Treaty on European Union (TEU);[190]
- the Treaty on the Functioning of the European Union (TFEU);[191]
- the Charter of Fundamental Rights;[192]
- the Regulation (2024/1689).[193]

---

190 Treaty on European Union, [2016] OJ C202/13/, https://eur-lex.europa.eu/legal-content/EN/TXT/?uri=CELEX%3A02016M%2FTXT-20240901 (consolidated version as of 1 September 2024).

191 Treaty on the Functioning of the European Union, [2016] OJ C202/1, http://data.europa.eu/eli/treaty/tfeu_2016/oj (consolidated version as of 1 March 2020).

192 Charter of Fundamental Rights of the European Union, [2016] OJ C202/389, http://data.europa.eu/eli/treaty/char_2016/oj.

193 Regulation on artificial intelligence (EU) 2024/1689 of 13 June 2024, [2024] OJ L, 2024/1689.

7.2. *Legal Basis of the European Union*

209. The purpose of the Regulation is to organise a 'high level of protection' in order to create a single internal market[194] in relation to artificial intelligence. More generally, the Regulation[195] has been drafted in compliance with Article 2 of the Treaty on European Union[196] and Article 6 of the Charter of Fundamental Rights.[197]

210. Where the data used in AI technologies are personal data, the EU rules specific to such a field must be complied with.[198]

211. The harmonisation of the AI market takes place within the general framework corresponding to the 'New Legislative Cache', which aims to:

- define harmonised rules;
- apply in all sectors.[199]

---

194 TFEU, Art. 114(3): 'The Commission, in its proposals envisaged in paragraph 1 concerning health, safety, environmental protection and consumer protection, will take as a base a high level of protection, taking account in particular of any new development based on scientific facts. Within their respective powers, the European Parliament and the Council will also seek to achieve this objective.'

195 AI Act, Rec. 6.

196 TEU, Art. 2: 'The Union is founded on the values of respect for human dignity, freedom, democracy, equality, the rule of law and respect for human rights, including the rights of persons belonging to minorities. These values are common to the Member States in a society in which pluralism, non-discrimination, tolerance, justice, solidarity and equality between women and men prevail.'

197 Charter of Fundamental Rights, Art. 6: 'Everyone has the right to liberty and security of person.'

198 TFEU, Art. 16(1): 'Everyone has the right to the protection of personal data concerning them.'

199 AI Act, Rec. 9:
Harmonised rules applicable to the placing on the market, the putting into service and the use of high-risk AI systems should be laid down consistently with:

- Regulation (EC) No 765/2008Regulation (EC) No 765/2008 of the European Parliament and of the Council of 9 July 2008 setting out the requirements for accreditation and repealing Regulation (EEC) No 339/93, [2008] OJ L218/30.
- Decision No 768/2008/EC of the European Parliament and of the Council of 9 July 2008 on a common framework for the marketing of products, and repealing Council Decision 93/465/EEC, [2008] OJ L218/ 82.
- Regulation (EU) 2019/1020 of the European Parliament and of the Council of 20 June 2019 on market surveillance and compliance of products and amending Directive 2004/42/EC and Regulations (EC) No 765/2008 and (EU) No 305/2011, [2019] OJ L169/1.

7.2.1 Coordinated Legal Basis

212. The AI Act enshrines 'a human-centric technology',[200] which should 'serve as a tool for people, with the ultimate aim of increasing human well-being'.[201]

213. In this context, the following documents should be taken into account when understanding and interpreting it:[202]

- European Declaration on Digital Rights and Principles for the Digital Decade;[203]
- ethical guidelines for trustworthy AI.[204]

214. Artificial intelligence (AI) systems[205] must be designed on a 'fundamental rights by design' basis[206] or, in short, 'dignity by design'. According to the EU Charter of Fundamental Rights:

- 'Any limitation on the exercise of the rights and freedoms recognised by this Charter must be provided for by law and respect the essence of those rights and freedoms. Subject to the principle of proportionality, limitations may be made only if they are necessary and genuinely meet objectives of general interest recognised by the Union or the need to protect the rights and freedoms of others.'[207]

215. This framework can be summarised as follows:

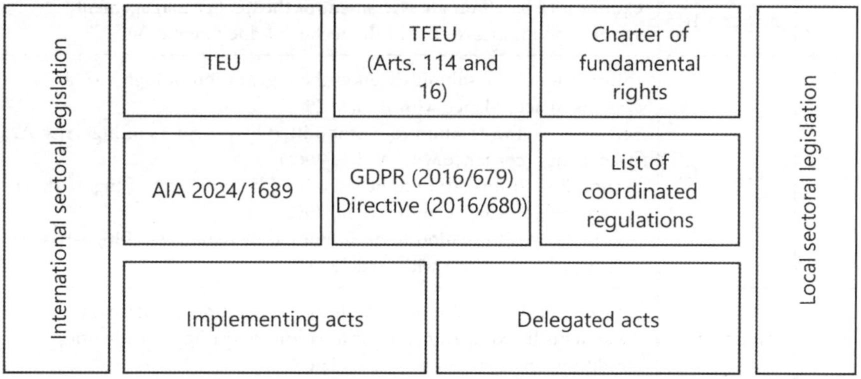

200 AI Act, Rec. 6.
201 Ibid.
202 AI Act, Rec. 7.
203 European Declaration on Digital Rights and Principles for the Digital Decade of 23 January 2023, PUB/2023/89, [2023] OJ C23/1.
204 AI HLEG (High-Level Expert Group on Artificial Intelligence), 'Ethics Guidelines for Trustworthy AI', European Commission, April 2019, 56 p.
205 In this Executive Summary, artificial intelligence systems are referred to as AI systems.
206 Charter of fundamental rights, Art. 1.
207 Charter of fundamental rights, Art. 52(1).

216. The structure of the Regulation comprises:

- 180 recitals;
- 113 articles;
- 13 annexes, which are as follows:

NO.	ANNEX	SPECIFICATION
1.	Annex I	List of Union harmonisation legislation Section A. List of Union harmonisation legislation based on the New Legislative Framework Section B. List of other Union harmonisation legislation Notes: (1) Section B is excluded from the scope of the AI Act pursuant to Article 2, with the exception of Article 112, which defines the principles for assessment and review.[208]
2.	Annex II	List of criminal offences referred to in Article 5(1), first subparagraph, point (h)(iii)
3.	Annex III	High-risk AI systems referred to in Article 6(2)
4.	Annex IV	Technical documentation referred to in Article 11(1)
5.	Annex V	EU declaration of conformity
6.	Annex VI	Conformity assessment procedure based on internal control
7.	Annex VII	Conformity based on an assessment of the quality management system and an assessment of the technical documentation
8.	Annex VIII	Information to be submitted upon the registration of high-risk AI systems in accordance with Article 49 Section A — Information to be submitted by providers of high-risk AI systems in accordance with Article 49(1) Section B — Information to be submitted by providers of high-risk AI systems in accordance with Article 49(2) Section C — Information to be submitted by deployers of high-risk AI systems in accordance with Article 49(3)
9.	Annex IX	Information to be submitted upon the registration of high-risk AI systems listed in Annex III in relation to testing in real world conditions in accordance with Article 60
10.	Annex X	Union legislative acts on large-scale IT systems in the area of Freedom, Security and Justice

[208] This is the case for certain articles relating to sectors such as civil aviation, the automotive industry, the maritime sector and the rail system.

NO.	ANNEX	SPECIFICATION
11.	Annex XI	Technical documentation referred to in Article 53(1), point (a) – technical documentation for providers of general-purpose AI models Section 1: Information to be provided by all providers of general-purpose AI models Section 2: Additional information to be provided by providers of general-purpose AI models with systemic risk
12.	Annex XII	Transparency information referred to in Article 53(1), point (b) – technical documentation for providers of general-purpose AI models to downstream providers that integrate the model into their AI system
13.	Annex XIII	Criteria for the designation of general-purpose AI models with systemic risk referred to in Article 51.

7.2.2 Definition

217. The legal definitions of AI systems have been coupled with technical definitions.[209]

7.3. Guiding Principles

7.3.1 Introduction

218. This new Regulation is both elegant and excellent.

219. Elegant because it bases the regulation of AI systems on the values of the European Union and in particular those referred to in the EU Charter of Fundamental Rights, such as human dignity.[210]

220. Excellent because it seeks a balance between freedom and security of innovation in the field of AI systems.

221. These principles are as follows:

- human sovereignty;
- protection of persons and property;
- AI literacy;
- managing the risks induced by AI technologies.

[209] See section 3.6 Technical and Legal Definitions.

[210] Charter of fundamental rights of the European Union (2016), Art. 1.

7.3.2 The Principle of Human Sovereignty

7.3.2.1 *Introduction*

222. This principle places humans at the centre of AI systems by formulating a principle of sovereignty over artificial intelligence. According to the European Parliament, 'AI technology should be developed in such a way as to put people at its centre, be worthy of public trust and always work in the service of humans; whereas AI systems should have the ultimate guarantee of being designed so that they can always be shut down by a human operator'.[211]

7.3.2.2 *Application*

223. This principle is applied only for high-risk AI systems in the following terms:

- natural persons to whom human oversight is assigned shall be enabled 'to intervene in the operation of the high-risk AI system or interrupt the system through a 'stop' button or a similar procedure'.[212]

224. Notes:

- (1) For other categories of system, the primacy of the human being remains a general ethical principle.
- (2) The 'red button' concept can be considered as good practice in the event of major, systemic or serial risks.

7.3.3 The Principle of Protecting Persons and Property

7.3.3.1 *Introduction*

225. This principle is at the heart of the new horizontal Regulation.

7.3.3.2 *Essential Requirement*

226. All AI systems must comply with the general safety requirements intended to protect persons and property.

227. This obligation must be based on the following architecture:

- ensuring risk minimisation;
- carrying out risk mapping;
- implementing a risk management system;
- conducting an impact assessment of high risks;

---

[211] European Parliament resolution of 6 October 2021 on artificial intelligence in criminal law and its use by the police and judicial authorities in criminal matters (2020/2016(INI)), Rec. E https://www.europarl.europa.eu/doceo/document/TA-9-2021-0405_EN.pdf.

[212] AI Act, Art. 14(4)(e).

- implementing a risk minimisation policy and procedures;
- introducing governance aimed at reducing exposure to risk.

228. Notes:

- (1) According to the European Parliament, 'no AI system used by law enforcement or the judiciary should be enabled to harm the physical integrity of human beings, nor to distribute rights or impose legal obligations on individuals'.[213]

7.3.4 The Principle of AI Literacy

229. It applies to all employers – providers and deployers – in order to enable their staff to know how to operate and use artificial intelligence.[214]

7.3.5 The Principle of Risk Management

7.3.5.1 *Introduction*

230. The European Parliament has called for 'the application of the precautionary principle in all applications of AI in the context of law enforcement'.[215]

231. The precautionary principle does not exist in AI legislation as such. It has been introduced in the form of essential requirements in the context of the implementation of high-risk AI systems.

7.3.5.2 *Essential Requirements*

232. Assessed on the basis of a best efforts obligation, they cover:

- risk mapping;
- risk minimisation;
- information, awareness and training;
- maintenance in operational condition;
- monitoring incidents and adapting situations.

---

213 European Parliament resolution of 6 October 2021 on artificial intelligence in criminal law and its use by the police and judicial authorities in criminal matters (2020/2016(INI)), Rec. 12, https://www.europarl.europa.eu/doceo/document/TA-9-2021-0405_EN.pdf.

214 AI literacy.

215 European Parliament resolution of 6 October 2021 on artificial intelligence in criminal law and its use by the police and judicial authorities in criminal matters (2020/2016(INI)), Rec. 13, https://www.europarl.europa.eu/doceo/document/TA-9-2021-0405_EN.pdf.

7.4. *Specific Principles*

7.4.1 Introduction

233. There are numerous regulations or charters setting out the various principles that should govern artificial intelligence.

7.4.2 Structure

234. Arranged in alphabetical order, in the absence of a hierarchical classification, the structure of the specific principles laid down in the Regulation is as follows:

NO.	THEME	COMMENT
1.	Accuracy	It is mentioned as a requirement for high-risk AI systems.[216] It is not mentioned for AI models
2.	Admissibility	Principle implemented through the conformity mechanisms
3.	Autonomy	This principle has several meanings. In the sense of the integration of persons with disabilities, it is found in the French version of the Charter of Fundamental Rights (the English version uses the term 'independence')[217] It is the major criterion for qualifying an AI system Rejection of technological slavery and recognition of the principle of human autonomy through articles relating to: • AI literacy[218] • human oversight[219]
4.	Common good	No reference
5.	Dignity	In relation to social scoring (prohibited AI system, AIA, Art. 5(1)(c) and Rec. 31)
6.	Diversity	AIA, Art. 1 through the Charter of Fundamental Rights
7.	Environmental sustainability	No reference except through the 'environmental protection'[220] purpose and the Charter of Fundamental Rights.[221]
8.	Equality	In relation to social scoring (prohibited AI system, AIA, Art. 5(1)(c) and Rec. 31)

216 AI Act, Art. 15.
217 Charter of Fundamental Rights of the European Union, Art. 26.
218 AI Act, Art. 4.
219 AI Act, Art. 14.
220 AI Act, Art. 1(1).
221 Charter of Fundamental Rights, Art. 37.

NO.	THEME	COMMENT
9.	Equity	The development of AI must not contribute to increasing social and economic inequalities.[222] It is also referred to in the Recitals. It is not a requirement
10.	Ethics	Testing of high-risk AI systems in real-world conditions outside AI regulatory sandboxes[223] and codes of conduct for voluntary application of specific requirements[224]
11.	Exclusion	No reference as such. Application through the EU Charter of Fundamental Rights
12.	Explainability	This is not a requirement. This concept is included in Recital 27 with regard to the robustness requirements for high-risk AI systems
13.	Governance	Institutions[225] Artificial intelligence[226] Data[227]
14.	Harmlessness	Non-existence as such. Principle implemented through management of the 6 values and 5 risks
15.	Inclusion	No reference[228]
16.	Innovation	Subject matter of the AI Act[229] Standards[230] Threats to innovation[231]
17.	Interoperability	No reference as such
18.	Intimacy	No direct reference except through the prohibition of AI systems deploying subliminal techniques beyond a person's consciousness[232]
19.	Justice	In relation to social scoring and high-risk systems, Annex III[233] (prohibited AI system, AIA, Art. 5(1)(c) and Rec. 31)
20.	Justifiability	See Explainability
21.	Knowledge	Right to knowledge for all induced by generative AI systems

222 2018 Report of the Montréal Declaration for a Responsible Development of Artificial Intelligence, p. 27.
223 AI Act, Art. 60.
224 AI Act, Art. 95.
225 AI Act, Art. 10 and Art. 64.
226 AI Act, Art. 3(47).
227 AI Act, Art. 10.
228 Report of the 2018 Montréal Declaration for a Responsible Development of Artificial Intelligence, p. 32.
229 AI Act, Art. 1.
230 AI Act, Art. 40.
231 AI Act, Arts. 57 ff.
232 AI Act, Art. 5(1)(a)
233 AI Act, Art. 6(2).

NO.	THEME	COMMENT
22.	Life cycle	Application of all steps of AI systems from design to withdrawal
23.	Necessity	Procedure for general-purpose AI models[234]
24.	Non-discrimination	Data sets[235] Powers of authorities protecting fundamental rights[236] In relation to social scoring (prohibited AI system, AIA, Art. 5(1)(c) and Rec. 31)
25.	Personal data	In compliance with the Charter of Fundamental Rights and regulations on personal data[237]
26.	Privacy	Respect of the protection of privacy when using personal data[238]
27.	Proportionality	This principle is of general application within the general framework of EU regulation Rules on certificates[239] Rules on fines[240]
28.	Prudence	Indirect reference through the concept of trust[241]
29.	Reasonable	Prohibited AI systems[242] Risk management system[243] Transparency obligation[244] Serious incidents[245]
30.	Reliability	Principle applied to the results of the conformity assessment activities that the notified bodies conduct[246]
31.	Responsibility/ Liability	Throughout the lifecycle, depending on the role of each actor (e.g. operators)[247]
32.	Safety	Application through the obligation to manage the risks of high-risk AI systems[248] and general-purpose AI models[249]
33.	Solidarity	Through the Charter of Fundamental Rights[250]

234 AI Act, Art. 52.
235 AI Act, Art. 10.
236 AI Act, Art. 77.
237 Charter of Fundamental Rights of the European Union, Art. 7 and AI Act, Art. 1.
238 AI Act, Art. 2.
239 AI Act, Art. 44.
240 AI Act, Art. 101.
241 AI Act, Art. 1(1).
242 AI Act, Art. 5.
243 AI Act, Art. 9.
244 AI Act, Art. 50.
245 AI Act, Art. 73.
246 AI Act, Art. 31.
247 AI Act, Arts. 99 ff.
248 AI Act, Art. 9.
249 AI Act, Art. 51.
250 Charter of Fundamental Rights of the European Union, Chapter IV.

NO.	THEME	COMMENT
34.	Sustainability	In relation to regulatory sandboxes[251] Code of conduct[252]
35.	Well-being	This principle appears in the Charter of Fundamental Rights in relation to the rights of the child. It is also referred to in the Recitals. It is not a requirement[253]

8 PROHIBITED AI SYSTEMS

8.1. Introduction

235. The category of prohibited AI systems includes practices involving the following artificial intelligence technologies:
- subliminal techniques beyond a person's consciousness;
- exploiting the vulnerabilities of a natural person or a group of persons;
- social scoring of natural persons;
- predictive policing;
- facial recognition;
- emotion recognition;
- biometric categorisation;
- real-time remote biometric identification.

8.2. Guiding Principles

236. Prohibited practices cover all activities carried out by means of artificial technologies which correspond to unacceptable risks within the European Union.

237. This protection concerns both adults[254] and minors.[255]

238. The criteria for this category are:
- abusive operations;[256]
- harmful consequences;[257]

---

251 AI Act, Art. 59.
252 AI Act, Art. 95.
253 AI Act, Recs. 6, 27 and 48.
254 AI Act, Rec. 26.
255 AI Act, Rec. 28.
256 AI Act, Rec. 26.
257 AI Act, Rec. 26.

- particularly significant harm.[258]

239. Notes:

- (1) This list is exhaustive. All other uses are permitted subject to the classification based on risk management.

8.3. *AI Systems and a Person's Consciousness*

8.3.1 Introduction

240. The aim is to prohibit the deployment of AI systems[259] whose purpose is to operate beyond a person's consciousness, thereby impairing their freedom to decide.

241. The idea is that AI systems should not be able to implement subliminal techniques that can lead to an alteration of human capacities likely to cause physical, economic and psychological harm.

8.3.2 Prohibition

242. This prohibition relates to the person who is the subject of these techniques and third parties affected by the harmful consequences.

243. Notes:

- (1) It is legitimate to wonder why the prohibition on subliminal techniques is limited to practices resulting from AI systems.
- (2) Its application may be difficult because not all people have the same threshold in this area.

8.3.3 The Moral Element

244. It results from the wording 'purposefully manipulative or deceptive'. The prohibited practice is one that has been 'encoded' so that one of the purposes of the AI technologies implemented is the intention of the provider or deployer to prevent all freedoms allowing individuals to act consciously.

[258] AI Act, Art. 5.

[259] Placing on the market, putting into service and other activities.

8.3.4 A Trend

245. This trend is in line with the need to regulate all forms of control by technologies.[260]

246. Notes:

- (1) Examples of such AI technologies are 'machine-brain interface' currently under development.[261]
- (2) Such a purpose can also be implemented using AI-driven virtual reality or augmented reality techniques.[262]

8.3.5 Neurorights

247. This prohibition implicitly highlights the emergence of a right of consciousness. It is a very topical issue amid the technological development of general-purpose AI systems and the reading and/writing of brain signals.

248. Notes:

- (1) A therapeutic purpose with the patient's consent is not prohibited insofar as the intent is not fraudulent.
- (2) The entire process must be controllable in order to prove the absence of manipulation using AI technologies.

8.4. Manipulating Vulnerable Persons

8.4.1 Introduction

249. AI technologies are all the more unacceptable when they are used on individuals who are not fully capable.[263]

8.4.2 Individuals Concerned

250. They concern natural persons or groups of natural persons.

---

260 A. Piquard, 'Intelligence artificielle: "Demain, faudra-t-il protéger nos "neuro-droits"?"' ['Artificial intelligence: "Will we need to protect our "neuro-rights" tomorrow?"'], *Le Monde*, 26 October 2023, p. 25.

261 AI Act, Rec. 29.

262 AI Act, Rec. 29.

263 AI Act, Art. 5(1)(b).

8.4.3 Modalities

251. They are as follows:

NO.	THEME	SPECIFICATION
1.	Vulnerability	The list is legally restrictive, but in practice it is very broad and includes the following: • age; • disability; • social situation; • economic situation.
2.	Purpose	Distort the behaviour of a person, by impairing their ability to make an informed decision
3.	Measure	Impairment must be very significant, by materially distorting the behaviour of a person or a group of persons
4.	Impact	Causes or is reasonably likely to cause harm
5.	Level	Significant harm to that person or to a third party

8.5. *Social Scoring*

8.5.1 Introduction

252. Social scoring[264] is not prohibited as such.

253. The prohibition is defined in relation to the objectives or purpose of the score.

8.5.2 Actors Concerned

254. Social scoring concerns only natural persons or groups of natural persons to the exclusion of legal persons.

255. The prohibition applies to all operators who may establish a social score, whether they operate in the public or private sector.

256. Notes:

- (1) The initial version of the Regulation prohibited social scoring only 'by public authorities or on their behalf'.[265]

---

264 AI Act, Art. 5(1)(c).

265 Proposal for a Regulation on AI COM(2021) 206 of 21 April 2021, Art. 5(1)(c).

8.5.3 Measurement

257. It relates to:
- evaluation;
- classification.

258. Measurement may result from:
- collection;
- reasoning;
- prediction.

8.5.4 Basis for Measurement

259. It is based on:
- social behaviour;
- personal characteristics;
- personality characteristics.

8.5.5 Purposes

260. Protection is based on the following alternative or cumulative criteria:
- detrimental or unfavourable treatment in social contexts that are unrelated to the contexts in which the data was originally generated or collected;
- detrimental or unfavourable treatment that is unjustified or disproportionate to the natural persons:
  - o social behaviour;
  - o gravity of the social behaviour.

261. Notes:
- (1) Given the criteria, social scoring is possible in the EU as in China, subject to certain specific conditions.
- (2) For example, the prohibition targets social behaviour and not economic or technical behaviour.
- (3) Similarly, social scoring cannot be justified in terms of the legitimate interests of operations, or the social assessment is not really serious, although it is not neutral.
- (4) There are numerous loopholes or potential loopholes that make different forms of social scoring possible; the rating of citizens, taxpayers or customers remains legally eligible for social scoring in the European Union.

8.6. *Predictive Policing*

8.6.1 Introduction

262. The prohibition[266] concerns the detection of a potential commission of an offence, bearing in mind that '[i]n line with the presumption of innocence, natural persons in the Union should always be judged on their actual behaviour'.[267]

8.6.2 Prohibition

8.6.2.1 *Criteria*

263. The prohibition covers detection based on one of the following criteria:
- profiling;
- personality traits;
- characteristics.

8.6.2.2 *Profiling*

264. This concept is defined as follows:
- '"profiling" means profiling as defined in Article 4, point (4), of Regulation (EU) 2016/679.'[268]

265. Under the GDPR, profiling means:
- 'any form of automated processing of personal data consisting of the use of personal data to evaluate certain personal aspects relating to a natural person, in particular to analyse or predict aspects concerning that natural person's performance at work, economic situation, health, personal preferences, interests, reliability, behaviour, location or movements.'

266. Notes:
- (1) The prohibition does not concern the profiling method carried out using AI technology as such; it applies only where the decision is 'based solely on the profiling.'[269]
- (2) Other techniques are possible, such as segmentation using AI systems.

8.6.2.3 *Personality Traits*

267. Detecting the likelihood to commit an offence is a prohibited practice when it is based on the assessment of personality traits.

---

266 AI Act, Art. 5(1)(d).
267 AI Act, Rec. 42.
268 AI Act, Art. 3(52).
269 AI Act, Art. 5(1)(d).

8.6.2.4 *Characteristics*

268. Similarly, it is a prohibited practice to design, place on the market, put into service or use an AI system based on characteristics to predict the commission of an offence, such as:

- nationality;[270]
- place of birth;[271]
- place of residence;[272]
- number of children;[273]
- level of debt;[274]
- type of car;[275]
- type of home.

8.6.3 Derogation

269. The derogation is based on the following:

NO.	THEME	SPECIFICATION
1.	Human assessment	Use of an AI system to prepare the analysis, which will enable a personalised analysis to be carried out manually
2.	Preparatory stage	The purpose of the results is to 'support' the human assessment
3.	Person	The derogation concerns natural persons likely to be involved in a criminal activity
4.	Analysis data	Objective facts Verifiable facts Notes: • (1) objectively and without human assessment[276]

[270] AI Act, Rec. 42.
[271] Ibid.
[272] Ibid.
[273] Ibid.
[274] Ibid.
[275] Ibid.
[276] Ibid.

NO.	THEME	SPECIFICATION
5.	Offence	Directly linked to a criminal activity Notes: • (1) the prohibition does not cover analyses to assess the likelihood of financial fraud by undertakings on the basis of suspicious transactions • (2) AI technologies can be used to predict the localisation of: o narcotics[277] o illicit goods[278]

8.7. *Facial Recognition Databases*

8.7.1 Introduction

270. The creation of facial recognition databases[279] is not prohibited as such, but their use is strictly regulated.

8.7.2 Characteristics

271. The aim is to prohibit the creation of facial recognition databases when they are operated in the following way:

NO.	THEME	SPECIFICATION
1.	Representation	Facial image
2.	Data	Collection Creation
3.	Medium	Photography Video
4.	Modality	Untargeted scraping of facial images
5.	Origin	Internet CCTV footage
6.	Activity	The prohibition concerns the following activities: • placing on the market • putting into service for this specific purpose • use
7.	Exceptions	Medical reasons Safety

277 Ibid.

278 Ibid.

279 AI Act, Art. 5(1)(e).

272. Notes:

- (1) The term 'CCTV footage' should also include facial images from recordings made by video protection systems.
- (2) The prohibition only concerns facial data and not other biometric data.
- (3) The term 'untargeted' seems to open the door to databases of facial images corresponding to specific search criteria.
- (4) The prohibition is justified by the fact that this practice 'adds to the feeling of mass surveillance and can lead to gross violations of fundamental rights, including the right to privacy'.[280]

8.8. *Emotion Recognition*

8.8.1 Introduction

273. The detection of emotions targets specific contexts.[281]

8.8.2 Definition

274. Under the Regulation, an emotion recognition system means 'an AI system for the purpose of identifying or inferring emotions or intentions of natural persons on the basis of their biometric data'.[282]

275. The notion refers to emotions or intentions such as 'happiness, sadness, anger, surprise, disgust, embarrassment, excitement, shame, contempt, satisfaction and amusement'.[283] On the other hand, '[i]t does not include physical states, such as pain or fatigue, including, for example, systems used in detecting the state of fatigue of professional pilots or drivers for the purpose of preventing accidents. This does also not include the mere detection of readily apparent expressions, gestures or movements, unless they are used for identifying or inferring emotions. Those expressions can be basic facial expressions, such as a frown or a smile, or gestures such as the movement of hands, arms or head, or characteristics of a person's voice, such as a raised voice or whispering'.[284]

8.8.3 Protected Persons

276. These are natural persons:

- at their workplace;

---

280 AI Act, Rec. 43.
281 AI Act, Art. 5(1)(f).
282 AI Act, Art. 3(39).
283 AI Act, Rec. 18.
284 Ibid.

- in education institutions.

8.8.4 Derogations

277. There are derogations for:

- medical reasons;
- safety reasons.

278. Notes:

- (1) Emotion recognition in places other than the workplace or education institutions is not prohibited.
- (2) AI technologies may be used in such cases, bearing in mind that there are special rules for:
    - o high-risk AI systems;
    - o AI systems subject to a transparency obligation.

8.9. Biometric Categorisation

279. The prohibited practice concerns the deduction[285] of information from biometric data.

8.9.1 Definition

280. 'Biometric data' means 'personal data resulting from specific technical processing relating to the physical, physiological or behavioural characteristics of a natural person, such as facial images or dactyloscopic data'.[286]

281. 'Biometric identification' means 'the automated recognition of physical, physiological, behavioural, or psychological human features for the purpose of establishing the identity of a natural person by comparing biometric data of that individual to biometric data of individuals stored in a database'.[287]

282. 'Biometric verification' means 'the automated, one-to-one verification, including authentication, of the identity of natural persons by comparing their biometric data to previously provided biometric data'.[288]

283. These include:[289]

- age and sex;
- eye movements and eye colour;

---

285 AI Act, Art. 5(1)(g).
286 AI Act, Art. 3(34).
287 AI Act, Art. 3(35).
288 AI Act, Art. 3(36).
289 AI Act, Rec. 15.

- body shape and tattoos;
- voice and prosody;[290]
- gait and posture;
- heart rate and blood pressure;
- odour.[291]

8.9.2 Inference

284. Biometric categorisation is prohibited for deducing or inferring the following:

- race;
- political opinions;
- trade union membership;
- religious or philosophical beliefs;
- sex life or sexual orientation.

8.9.3 Derogations

285. The derogations are based on the following:

NO.	THEME	SPECIFICATION
1.	Activities	Filtering Labelling
2.	Categorisation	Biometric data of all kinds
3.	Medium	Photography Video
4.	Origin	Lawful data acquisition Law enforcement

286. Notes:

- (1) Cases of biometric categorisation that are not included in the restrictive list of deductions or inferences are not prohibited.

290 Prosody: all the patterns in which verbal expression is modulated (e.g. intonation or rhythm), allowing the meaning, intention or emotion to be nuanced.

291 Comité national pilote d'éthique du numérique (CNPEN), 'Enjeux éthiques des technologies de reconnaissance faciale, posturale et comportementale' ['Ethical issues surrounding facial, postural and behavioural recognition technologies'], Opinion No. 8, 20 November 2023.

8.10. Real-Time Remote Biometric Identification System

8.10.1 Introduction

287. The hazards of biometric systems depend on the context, the purpose and, above all, the scale of use. The indiscriminate surveillance of an entire population at scale presents many risks. In a democracy, the principle of prohibition is one of the keys to protecting privacy. When such surveillance is based on a 'biometric signature' for identification, the risks are multiplied.

8.10.2 Definition

288. 'Remote biometric identification system' means 'an AI system for the purpose of identifying natural persons, without their active involvement, typically at a distance through the comparison of a person's biometric data with the biometric data contained in a reference database.'[292]

289. The notion of 'real-time' means 'without a significant delay'.[293]

8.10.3 Publicly Accessible Spaces

290. A publicly accessible space is characterised by the following criteria:

- a 'publicly or privately owned physical place accessible to an undetermined number of natural persons, regardless of whether certain conditions for access may apply, and regardless of the potential capacity restrictions';[294]
- places accessible to an undetermined number of natural persons;
- places that are privately or publicly owned.

291. Notes:

- (1) Online spaces are not concerned.

8.10.4 Derogations

292. Real-time remote biometric identification in publicly accessible spaces is prohibited, except for law enforcement purposes.[295]

---

[292] AI Act, Art. 3(41).

[293] AI Act, Art. 3(42).

[294] AI Act, Art. 3(44).

[295] European Parliament study, 'Biometric Recognition and Behavioural Detection: Assessing the ethical aspects of biometric recognition and behavioural detection techniques with a focus on their current and future use in public spaces', August 2021.

293. A derogation is introduced for the following purposes:
- the targeted search for potential victims,[296] including minors;[297]
- the prevention of a terrorist attack;[298]
- the prosecution of specific offences.[299]

8.10.5 Exclusion

294. Member States, in the exercise of their exclusive powers, may decide to implement prohibited practices. This applies in particular to activities relating to defence or national security.[300]

9 HIGH-RISK AI SYSTEMS

9.1. Introduction

295. The Regulation defines requirements enabling risk-based management, by providers and deployers,[301] in order to:
- build harmonised legal rules in the EU;
- promote trustworthy artificial intelligence;
- encourage innovation that respects fundamental rights.

9.2. Definition

296. High-risk AI systems are divided into two categories:
- systems falling under the regulations listed in Annex I, corresponding to the list of Union harmonisation legislation; and
- systems covered by the areas listed in Annex III.

297. Notes:
- (1) There are only two categories of high-risk AI systems corresponding to a formal classification.

---

296 AI Act, Art. 5(1)(h), (i).
297 AI Act, Rec. 9.
298 AI Act, Art. 5(1)(h)(ii).
299 AI Act, Art. 5(1)(h)(iii) and Annex II; Council Framework Decision 2002/584/JHA, Art. 2(2).
300 AI Act, Art. 2(3).
301 End users implement AI technologies.

- (2) This 'high risk' classification is independent of the system provider's assessment; this approach is very different from the General Data Protection Regulation.[302]

9.3. *High-Risk AI Systems Covered by Annex I*

9.3.1 Introduction

298. This Annex is divided into two sections:
- Section A is subject to AI legislation;
- Section B is not subject to the AI rules, except in special cases.

9.3.2 High-Risk AI Systems Covered by Section A of Annex I

9.3.2.1 *Criteria*

299. To be considered as high-risk AI systems, two conditions must be met simultaneously:
- the AI system is intended to be used as a safety component of a product, or the AI system is itself a product, covered by the Union harmonisation legislation listed in Annex I; and,
- the product whose safety component is the AI system, or the AI system itself as a product, is required to undergo a third-party conformity assessment, with a view to the placing on the market or the putting into service of that product pursuant to the Union harmonisation legislation listed in Annex I.

300. In this context, a 'safety component' means 'a component of a product or of an AI system which fulfils a safety function for that product or AI system, or the failure or malfunctioning of which endangers the health and safety of persons or property'.[303]

[302] Subjective evaluation of risks and carrying out of an impact assessment, GDPR (EU) 2016/679, Art. 35.
[303] AI Act, Art. 3(14).

9.3.2.2 *List of Legislation*

301. The list of products is as follows:

NO.	THEME	DATE	SPECIFICATION
1.	Directive 2006/42/EC[304]	17 May 2006	Machinery
2.	Directive 2009/48/EC	18 June 2009	Safety of toys
3.	Directive 2013/53/EC	20 November 2013	Recreational craft and personal watercraft
4.	Directive 2014/33/EU	26 February 2014	Lifts and safety components for lifts
5.	Directive 2014/34/EU	26 February 2014	Equipment and protective systems intended for use in potentially explosive atmospheres
6.	Directive 2014/53/EU	16 April 2014	Radio equipment
7.	Directive 2014/68/EU	15 May 2014	Pressure equipment
8.	Regulation (EU) 2016/424	9 March 2016	Cableway installations
9.	Regulation (EU) 2016/425	9 March 2016	Personal protective equipment
10.	Regulation (EU) 2016/426	9 March 2016	Appliances burning gaseous fuels
11.	Regulation (EU) 2017/745	5 April 2017	Medical devices
12.	Regulation (EU) 2017/746	5 April 2017	*In vitro* diagnostic medical devices

9.3.3 High-Risk AI Systems Covered by Section B of Annex I

302. The list of excluded activities is presented in section relating to the geographical scope.[305]

304 This directive, which is still in force, will gradually be replaced by Regulation (EU) 2023/1230 of the European Parliament and of the Council of 14 June 2023 on machinery and repealing Directive 2006/42/EC of the European Parliament and of the Council and Council Directive 73/361/EEC ([2023] OJ L165/1), which will apply from 14 January 2027.

305 See 2.1.12. Exclusions.

9.3.4 High-Risk AI Systems Covered by Annex III

303. The high-risk systems concerned are:

- Biometrics, in so far as their use is permitted under relevant Union or national law:
  (a) remote biometric identification systems;[306]
  (b) AI systems intended to be used for biometric categorisation, according to sensitive or protected attributes or characteristics based on the inference of those attributes or characteristics;
  (c) AI systems intended to be used for emotion recognition.
- Critical infrastructure: AI systems intended to be used as safety components in the management and operation of critical digital infrastructure, road traffic, or in the supply of water, gas, heating or electricity.
- Education and vocational training:
  (a) AI systems intended to be used to determine access or admission or to assign natural persons to educational and vocational training institutions at all levels;
  (b) AI systems intended to be used to evaluate learning outcomes, including when those outcomes are used to steer the learning process of natural persons in educational and vocational training institutions at all levels;
  (c) AI systems intended to be used for the purpose of assessing the appropriate level of education that an individual will receive or will be able to access, in the context of or within educational and vocational training institutions at all levels;
  (d) AI systems intended to be used for monitoring and detecting prohibited behaviour of students during tests in the context of or within educational and vocational training institutions at all levels;
- Employment, workers' management and access to self-employment:
  (a) AI systems intended to be used for the recruitment or selection of natural persons, in particular to place targeted job advertisements, to analyse and filter job applications, and to evaluate candidates;
  (b) AI systems intended to be used to make decisions affecting terms of work-related relationships, the promotion or termination of work-related contractual relationships, to allocate tasks based on individual behaviour or personal traits or characteristics or to monitor and evaluate the performance and behaviour of persons in such relationships.

[306] This shall not include AI systems intended to be used for biometric verification the sole purpose of which is to confirm that a specific natural person is the person he or she claims to be.

- Access to and enjoyment of essential private services and essential public services and benefits:
  (a) AI systems intended to be used by public authorities or on behalf of public authorities to evaluate the eligibility of natural persons for essential public assistance benefits and services, including healthcare services, as well as to grant, reduce, revoke, or reclaim such benefits and services;
  (b) AI systems intended to be used to evaluate the creditworthiness of natural persons or establish their credit score, with the exception of AI systems used for the purpose of detecting financial fraud;
  (c) AI systems intended to be used for risk assessment and pricing in relation to natural persons in the case of life and health insurance;
  (d) AI systems intended to evaluate and classify emergency calls by natural persons or to be used to dispatch, or to establish priority in the dispatching of, emergency first response services, including by police, firefighters and medical aid, as well as of emergency healthcare patient triage systems.
- Law enforcement, in so far as their use is permitted under relevant Union or national law:
  (a) AI systems intended to be used by or on behalf of law enforcement authorities, or by Union institutions, bodies, offices or agencies in support of law enforcement authorities or on their behalf to assess the risk of a natural person becoming the victim of criminal offences;
  (b) AI systems intended to be used by or on behalf of law enforcement authorities or by Union institutions, bodies, offices or agencies in support of law enforcement authorities as polygraphs or similar tools;
  (c) AI systems intended to be used by or on behalf of law enforcement authorities, or by Union institutions, bodies, offices or agencies, in support of law enforcement authorities to evaluate the reliability of evidence in the course of the investigation or prosecution of criminal offences;
  (d) AI systems intended to be used by law enforcement authorities or on their behalf or by Union institutions, bodies, offices or agencies in support of law enforcement authorities for assessing the risk of a natural person offending or re-offending not solely on the basis of the profiling of natural persons as referred to in Article 3(4) of Directive (EU) 2016/680, or to assess personality traits and characteristics or past criminal behaviour of natural persons or groups
  (e) AI systems intended to be used by or on behalf of law enforcement authorities or by Union institutions, bodies, offices or agencies in support of law enforcement authorities for the profiling of natural persons as referred to in Article 3(4) of Directive (EU) 2016/680 in the course of the detection, investigation or prosecution of criminal offences.

- Migration, asylum and border control management, in so far as their use is permitted under relevant Union or national law:
  (a) AI systems intended to be used by or on behalf of competent public authorities or by Union institutions, bodies, offices or agencies as polygraphs or similar tools;
  (b) AI systems intended to be used by or on behalf of competent public authorities or by Union institutions, bodies, offices or agencies to assess a risk, including a security risk, a risk of irregular migration, or a health risk, posed by a natural person who intends to enter or who has entered into the territory of a Member State;
  (c) AI systems intended to be used by or on behalf of competent public authorities or by Union institutions, bodies, offices or agencies to assist competent public authorities for the examination of applications for asylum, visa or residence permits and for associated complaints with regard to the eligibility of the natural persons applying for a status, including related assessments of the reliability of evidence;
  (d) AI systems intended to be used by or on behalf of competent public authorities, or by Union institutions, bodies, offices or agencies, in the context of migration, asylum or border control management, for the purpose of detecting, recognising or identifying natural persons, with the exception of the verification of travel documents.
- Administration of justice and democratic processes:
  (a) AI systems intended to be used by a judicial authority or on their behalf to assist a judicial authority in researching and interpreting facts and the law and in applying the law to a concrete set of facts, or to be used in a similar way in alternative dispute resolution;
  (b) AI systems intended to be used for influencing the outcome of an election or referendum or the voting behaviour of natural persons in the exercise of their vote in elections or referenda. This does not include AI systems to the output of which natural persons are not directly exposed, such as tools used to organise, optimise or structure political campaigns from an administrative or logistical point of view.

9.4. *General Legal Architecture*

304. The legal architecture can be summarised as follows:

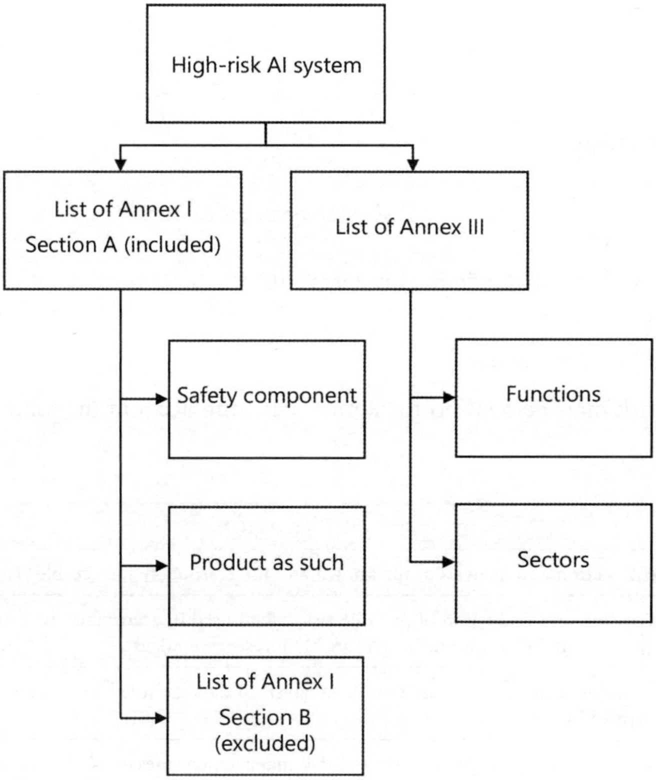

305. Notes:

- (1) The applicable requirements are very similar;[307]
- (2) The main difference is the requirement, for activities covered by Annex III,[308] to identify the provider and the high-risk AI system in the EU database.[309]

9.5. *Requirements*

306. The requirements concern:

- a risk management system (design, use and minimisation of risks);[310]

---

[307] See below.
[308] AI Act, Art. 6(2).
[309] AI Act, Art. 71.
[310] AI Act, Art. 9.

- the data used in AI systems and their governance;[311]
- technical documentation;[312]
- the recording of events as they occur;[313]
- transparency and information for deployers;[314]
- human oversight;[315]
- accuracy;[316]
- robustness;[317]
- cyber security.[318]

9.6. *Risk Management System*

307. Risk assessment[319] is defined in terms of:

- severity;
- probability of occurrence.

308. The risk management protocol must take into account the following main elements:

NO.	SPECIFICATION
1.	Identification and analysis of the known and the reasonably foreseeable risks
2.	Estimation and evaluation of possible risks when used in accordance with intended purpose or under conditions of reasonably foreseeable misuse
3.	Evaluation of other risks based on the analysis of data gathered from the monitoring system (AIA, Art. 72)
4.	Adoption of appropriate and targeted risk management measures

311 AI Act, Art. 10.
312 AI Act, Art. 11.
313 AI Act, Art. 12.
314 AI Act, Art. 13.
315 AI Act, Art. 14.
316 AI Act, Art. 15.
317 Ibid.
318 Ibid.
319 AI Act, Art. 9.

9.7. *Data and Governance*

309. The main categories of data set families are as follows:

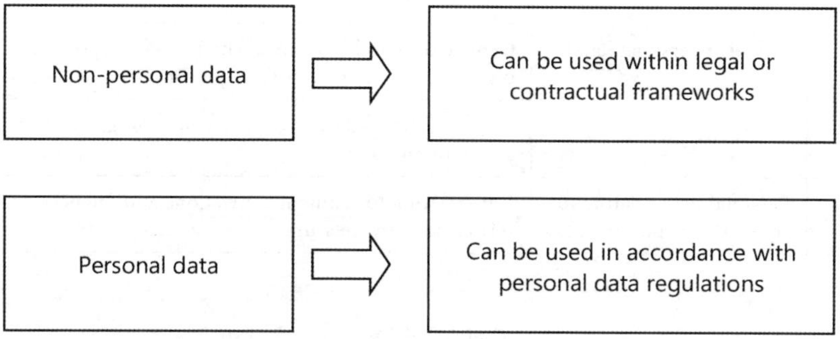

9.8. *Personal Data*

310. For this category, the French data protection authority (CNIL) proposes the following classification:[320]

NO.	DATA	CATEGORY
1.	Common personal data	Identification data (civil status, social security number)
		Data relating to personal life (lifestyle, hobbies, family situation, photos, etc.)
		Data relating to business life (CV, education, professional training, awards, etc.)
		Connection data (IP addresses, connection identifiers, session data, cookies, event logs, etc.)
2.	Data of a highly personal nature	Location data (movements, GPS data, GSM, etc.)
		Data relating to electronic communications
		Economic and financial data (income, financial situation, tax situation, etc.)
		Medical and administrative data (national insurance number, etc.)
3.	Personal data concerning vulnerable data subjects	Identification data, health data, social protection data

[320] Report from LINC, the CNIL's Digital Innovation Lab, 'Sécurité des systèmes d'IA' ['AI system security'], April 2022.

NO.	DATA	CATEGORY
4.	Sensitive personal data	Data revealing racial or ethnic origin, political opinions, religious or philosophical beliefs, or trade union membership
		Genetic data and biometric data for the purpose of uniquely identifying a natural person
		Data concerning health or data concerning sex life or sexual orientation
5.	Personal data relating to convictions and offences	Data relating to criminal convictions and offences or related security measures

9.9. *Technical Documentation*

311. The technical documentation includes elements relating to the following phases:

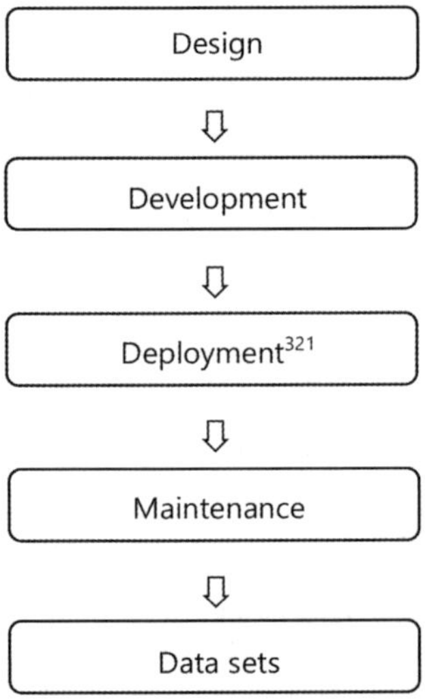

9.10. *Record-Keeping (Logs)*

312. Traceability is a key element of risk-based management.[322]

313. All high-risk AI systems must include automated logs that automatically record the main events over the lifetime of the system.

[321] Placing on the market.
[322] AI Act, Art. 12.

314. The traceability scope includes the following generic elements:

NO.	THEME	SPECIFICATION
1.	Event	History
2.	Measure	Presentation
3.	Monitoring	Modalities

9.11. Transparency and Information

9.11.1 Introduction

315. High-risk AI systems must enable the deployer to:
- understand their outputs;
- use them appropriately.[323]

9.11.2 Requirement

316. To achieve these purposes, instructions for use are required. The instructions for use have the following characteristics:

NO.	THEME	SUB-THEME	SPECIFICATION
1.	Provider	Identity	Contact details and, where applicable, of its authorised representative
2.	Information	Basis	Characteristics, performance and limitations
3.	Metrics	Content	Accuracy Robustness Cybersecurity
4.	Data		Training and testing data sets
5.	Human oversight		Modalities
6.	Duration	Lifetime	Expected lifetime Maintenance information Software updates
7.	Information	Quality	Concise, complete, correct and clear Relevant, accessible and comprehensible
8.	Medium	Format	Digital or paper

[323] AI Act, Art. 13.

9.12. *Human Oversight*

9.12.1 Introduction

317. The beginning of the 21st century marks the era of robotics and the organisation of the Human–Robot mix.[324]

318. In this context, ensuring the predominance of humans when it comes to high-risk AI systems is one of the pillars of trustworthy artificial intelligence.

9.12.2 Objective

319. Human-machine interface tools must enable to:

- minimise risks;
- prevent their occurrence.

320. The risks subject to human oversight are those relating to:

- health;
- safety; and
- fundamental rights.

9.12.3 Design

321. From design to implementation, from production to maintenance, AI systems must include a process where they can be effectively overseen by natural persons.[325]

9.12.4 Process

322. The oversight is built around the following:

- an interface organising the human oversight;
- a documentation allowing the user to remain in control;
- the information and guidance necessary to monitor such systems;
- the integration, in any event, of 'a "stop" button or a similar procedure'.[326]

---

[324] Logical robot (artificial intelligence system) or physical robot (shell with an artificial intelligence system).

[325] AI Act, Art. 14.

[326] AI Act, Art. 14(4)(e).

9.13. *Required Qualities*

323. The consistency and stability of high-risk AI systems are determined according to the following four criteria:

NO.	THEME	SPECIFICATION
1.	Accuracy	Ability to deliver high-quality results
2.	Consistency	Ability to maintain a normal behaviour in accordance with intended purpose
3.	Robustness	Maintaining operational characteristics with regard to purposes
4.	Cybersecurity	Ability to combat fraud

9.14. *Principle of Conformity*

9.14.1 Introduction

324. Echoing the autonomy that characterises AI systems, the conformity principle requires a certification mechanism for high-risk systems.

9.14.2 Intended Purpose

325. The purpose of all the requirements is to confine the AI system to a sphere of trust aligned with the values of the European Union.

9.15. *Persons Concerned*

326. These requirements apply in particular to:
- providers;
- importers;
- distributors;
- deployers.

9.16. *Certification*

327. Certification takes two forms:
- third-party certification for high-risk AI systems that are a safety component or AI systems corresponding to a product listed in Annex I;
- self-certification for other high-risk AI systems.

328. Notes:

- (1) The EDPS underlined that 'insofar as high-risk AI systems require the processing of personal data or process personal data to fulfil their task, the certification of these AI systems in the context of the CE marking should expressly include a verification of compliance, among others, with the data protection by design and by default,[327] given the possible high level of interference of the high-risk AI systems with the fundamental rights to privacy and to the protection of personal data, as well as the need to ensure a high level of trust in the AI system'.[328]
- (2) The foregoing has not been incorporated into the Regulation as such; compliance with the Union's data protection rules is part of the values-based approach set out in Article 16 of the TFEU[329] and Article 8 of the Charter of Fundamental Rights.[330]

9.17. Specific Sectors

329. For high-risk systems of financial institutions, the market surveillance authority is the relevant national financial supervisory authority.[331]

---

327 See EDPB-EDPS Joint Opinion 5/2021 of 18 June 2021, paras. 75 and 76: 'The EP negotiating mandate (Amendments adopted by the European Parliament on 14 June 2023, No TA(2023)0236), under Article 4 a, letter (c), refers to "privacy and data governance" means that AI systems shall be developed and used in compliance with existing privacy and data protection rules, while processing data that meets high standards in terms of quality and integrity', aiming at integrating compliance at the development stage with privacy and data protection. However, this requirement is not explicitly referred to in the context of the certification process of AI systems', Footnote No. 45 in EDPS Opinion 44/2023 of 23 October 2023, para. 27 p. 12.

328 EDPS Opinion 44/2023 of 23 October 2023, para. 27 p. 12.

329 TFEU Art. 16:
'1. Everyone has the right to the protection of personal data concerning them.
2. The European Parliament and the Council, acting in accordance with the ordinary legislative procedure, shall lay down the rules relating to the protection of individuals with regard to the processing of personal data by Union institutions, bodies, offices and agencies, and by the Member States when carrying out activities which fall within the scope of Union law, and the rules relating to the free movement of such data. Compliance with these rules shall be subject to the control of independent authorities.
The rules adopted on the basis of this Article shall be without prejudice to the specific rules laid down in Article 39 of the Treaty on European Union.'

330 Charter of Fundamental Rights of the European Union (2016):
'Art. 8: Protection of personal data
1. Everyone has the right to the protection of personal data concerning him or her.
2. Such data must be processed fairly for specified purposes and on the basis of the consent of the person concerned or some other legitimate basis laid down by law. Everyone has the right of access to data which has been collected concerning him or her, and the right to have it rectified.
3. Compliance with these rules shall be subject to control by an independent authority.'

331 AI Act, Art. 74(6).

330. Member States may derogate from this obligation.[332]

10 GENERAL-PURPOSE AI MODELS

10.1. General Approach

10.1.1 Introduction

331. From a technological point of view, these models are positioned between weak artificial intelligence and artificial general intelligence.[333]

332. They correspond to models with characteristics that allow them to 'competently perform a wide range of distinct tasks'.[334]

333. Notes:

- (1) 'Large generative AI models are a typical example for a general-purpose AI model, given that they allow for flexible generation of content, such as in the form of text, audio, images or video, that can readily accommodate a wide range of distinctive tasks.'[335]

10.1.2 Definition

334. 'General-purpose AI model' means:

- 'an AI model, including where such an AI model is trained with a large amount of data using self-supervision at scale, that displays significant generality and is capable of competently performing a wide range of distinct tasks regardless of the way the model is placed on the market and that can be integrated into a variety of downstream systems or applications, except AI models that are used for research, development or prototyping activities before they are placed on the market.'

332 AI Act, Art. 74(7).
333 Currently in the realm of science fiction.
334 AI Act, Rec. 97.
335 AI Act, Rec. 99.

10.1.3 Classification

335. General-purpose AI models are divided into various categories:

NO.	MODEL	SPECIFICATION	REFERENCES
1.	Category 1	Non-systemic risks	AIA, Art. 51
2.	Category 2	Systemic risks	AIA, Art. 51
3.	Category 3	Exclusion of models that are used for research or prototyping activities before they are placed on the market	AIA, Art. 3(63)

336. Notes:

- (1) A general-purpose AI model shall be presumed to have high impact capabilities when the cumulative amount of computation used for its training measured in floating point operations[336] is greater than 10^{25}.
- (2) 'A compromise was eventually reached between those who, like France, advocated self-regulation, and the others (European Parliament, numerous scientists, etc.) who wanted strict obligations.'[337]

10.1.4 Obligations for Providers

337. The main obligations of providers are as follows:

NO.	OBLIGATION	SPECIFICATION	REFERENCES
1.	Technical documentation	Description of the training and testing process and the results of its evaluation	AIA, Art. 53
2.	Integration documentation	Connector to AI system forms	AIA, Art. 53
3.	Copyright	Policy on complying with law on copyright and related rights	AIA, Art. 53
4.	Training data	Publicly available summary	AIA, Art. 53
5.	Exception	Model under a free and open-source licence unless it presents systemic risks	AIA, Art. 53
6.	Cooperation	Obligation to cooperate with the European Commission and relevant EU organisations regarding the application of the Regulation	AIA, Art. 53

[336] AI Act, Art. 51(2).

[337] F. Schmitt, 'L'UE instaure les premières règles au monde contrôlant l'IA' ['The EU introduces the world's first rules controlling AI'], *Les Échos*, 11 December 2023, p. 26.

338. Notes:

- (1) Authorised representatives of providers of a general-purpose AI model established in a third country shall be designated by written mandate.[338]
- (2) The obligations are similar to those for providers established in the EU.

10.2. General-Purpose AI Models with Systemic Risk

10.2.1 Introduction

339. This classification depends on alternative criteria based on technical or documentary specifications.

10.2.2 Classification

340. The criteria are as follows:

NO.	CRITERION	SPECIFICATION	REFERENCES
1.	High-impact capabilities	'Capabilities that match or exceed the capabilities recorded in the most advanced general-purpose AI models'	AIA, Art. 51(1)(a) AIA, Art. 3(64)
2.	Decision of the European Commission	'decision of the Commission, ex officio or following a qualified alert from the scientific panel"	AIA, Art. 51(1)(b)
3.	Presumption of high-impact capabilities	'when the cumulative amount of computation used for its training measured in floating point operations is greater than 10^{25}'	AIA, Art. 51(2)

10.2.3 Procedure

341. General-purpose AI models with systemic risk are subject to the following main rules:

- notification to the European Commission;
- possibility of requesting an exception to this classification.

338 AI Act, Art. 54.

10.2.4 Obligations of Providers of General-Purpose Models with Systemic Risk

342. The main obligations are as follows:

NO.	THEME	SPECIFICATION	REFERENCES
1.	Information	By the provider to the European Commission	AIA, Art. 52(1)
2.	Deadline	Within two weeks after the requirement is met	AIA, Art. 52(1)
3.	Modalities	List of Article 55	AIA, Art. 55
4.	Obligation of general-purpose AI models	Providers and authorised representatives	AIA, Art. 53 AIA, Art. 54
5.	Systemic risks	Evaluation and mitigation	AIA, Art. 55
6.	Serious incidents	Notification	AIA, Art. 55
7.	Cybersecurity	Ensure an adequate level of cybersecurity protection, including for the physical infrastructure of the model.	AIA, Art. 55

11 GENERAL-PURPOSE AI SYSTEMS

11.1. Introduction

343. This type of system corresponds to ChatGPT (OpenAI),[339] Gemini (Google), Claude (Anthropic) or Mistral (Mistral).

344. There are no specific articles on general-purpose AI systems in the Regulation.

11.2. Definition

345. A general-purpose AI system means 'an AI system which is based on a general-purpose AI model and which has the capability to serve a variety of purposes, both for direct use as well as for integration in other AI systems'.[340]

---

[339] A. Bensoussan, 'ChatGPT dans le monde du droit – La cobotique juridique' ['ChatGPT in the Legal World – Legal Cobotics'], Brussels, Bruylant, 2024.

[340] AI Act, Art. 3(66).

11.3. *Guiding Principles*

346. Such systems belong to one of three objects often determined according to use:

- high-risk AI systems;[341]
- AI systems subject to a transparency obligation;
- systems outside the scope of the AI Act.

11.4. *Requirements*

347. They are primarily focused on general-purpose AI models in the following contexts:

NO.	THEME	SPECIFICATION	REFERENCE
1.	AI Office	Mutual assistance, market surveillance	AIA, Art. 75
2.	Intended purpose	Modification	AIA, Art. 25
3.	Downstream provider	Downstream provider means 'a provider of an AI system, including a general-purpose AI system, which integrates an AI model, regardless of whether the AI model is provided by themselves and vertically integrated or provided by another entity based on contractual relations'	AIA, Art. 3(68)
4.	Scientific panel of independent experts	Advice	AIA, Art. 68
5.	Transparency	Information	AIA, Art. 50

12 AI SYSTEMS AND TRANSPARENCY OBLIGATION

12.1. *Introduction*

348. The transparency of AI systems is one of the foundations of trust.[342] The Regulation lays down general and specific obligations.

[341] AI Act, Rec. 85.
[342] AI Act, Art. 50.

12.2. Typology

349. The AI systems concerned are listed below:

NO.	CATEGORY	SPECIFICATION	REFERENCE
1.	Human-machine relations	Information on the fact that humans are interacting with an AI system	AIA, Art. 50(1)
2.	Contents (Marking)	Marking in a machine-readable format Detectable as artificially generated or manipulated content	AIA, Art. 50(2)
3.	Emotion recognition	Information on how emotion detection and interpretation work	AIA, Art. 50(3)
4.	Biometric categorisation	Information on biometric categorisation unless it is permitted by law to detect, prevent or investigate criminal offences[343]	AIA, Art. 50(3)
5.	Deep fakes	Manipulation of images, videos and sound. A derogation applies for the purposes of detecting, preventing or investigating criminal offences, investigations or in case of editorial control with associated responsibility	AIA, Art. 50(4)

12.3. Main Requirements

350. They are as follows:

NO.	THEME	SPECIFICATION	REFERENCE
1.	Recipient	Natural persons	AIA, Art. 50(5)
2.	Information	Clear	AIA, Art. 50(5)
3.	Identification	Distinguishable	AIA, Art. 50(5)
4.	Period	At the time of the first interaction or exposure	AIA, Art. 50(5)
5.	Transparency (Cumulation)	Obligations that apply in addition to: • the obligations relating to high-risk AI systems when they interface with humans • the transparency obligations laid down in EU or national law for deployers	AIA, Art. 50(6)
6.	AI Office	Identification format Code of practice	AIA, Art. 50(7)

343 AI Act, Art. 59(2).

13 INSTITUTIONAL REGULATION

13.1. Introduction

351. It is supervised and managed by:
- the European Commission;
- the AI Office;
- the European Artificial Intelligence Board;
- the national competent authorities;
- the advisory forum;
- the scientific panel of independent experts;
- specialised or general courts.

13.2. AI Office

352. Within the European Commission, the AI Office develops EU's expertise and capabilities in the field of AI.

13.3. European Artificial Intelligence Board[344]

353. Known as 'AI Board', it is composed of the national supervisory authorities whose tasks are to:
- harmonise application of the Regulation at local level;
- facilitate cooperation between national authorities;
- coordinate guidelines on emerging issues.

13.4. National Competent Authorities[345]

354. Each Member State shall establish or designate as national competent authorities:
- at least one notifying authority; and
- at least one market surveillance authority.

355. Their task is to:
- ensure the application of the Regulation;
- provide guidelines;
- cooperate with the European Commission.

[344] AI Act, Art. 65.
[345] AI Act, Art. 70.

13.5. Advisory Forum

356. The Advisory Forum, made up of stakeholders in the AI technology sector:
- provides technical expertise in the field of AI;
- advises and prepares opinions and recommendations for the AI Board and the European Commission on AI issues.[346]

13.6. Scientific Panel of Independent Experts

357. It consists of independent experts in the field of AI technologies.

13.7. EU's Regulatory Institutions

358. The personal data protection authorities were chosen to regulate AI systems in accordance with the following process:
- designation of the European Data Protection Supervisor to regulate AI systems within the EU;
- declaration of the first G7 Data Protection Authorities.[347]

13.8. Summary Chart

359. The relationship between the different bodies is summarised below:

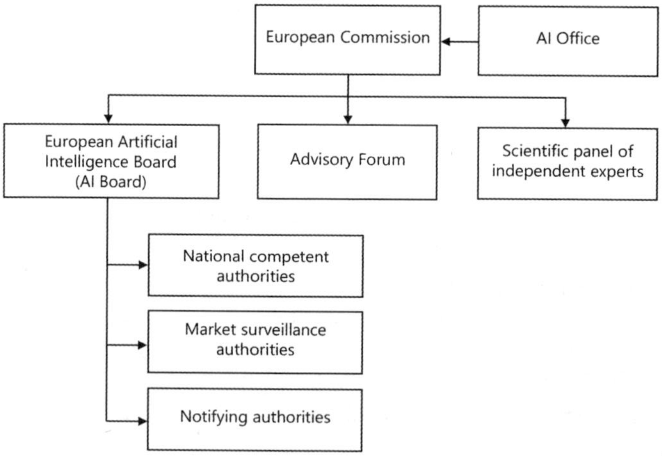

[346] AI Act, Art. 67(1).

[347] CNIL, news of 17 September 2021: 'La coopération dans la régulation du numérique au menu du premier G7 des autorités de protection des données' ['Cooperation on digital regulation on the agenda of the first G7 meeting of data protection authorities'].

14 PENALTIES

14.1. Penalties Relating to AI Systems

14.1.1 Introduction

360. Member States must lay down the legal rules for the implementation of penalties, bearing in mind that the system of administrative fines is subject to a specific framework.

14.1.2 Categories of Fines

361. Administrative fines are divided into three categories as follows:

NO.	OFFENCE	PENALTY
1.	Non-compliance with the prohibition of the AI practices referred to in Article 5	Administrative fine of up to €35,000,000 or, if the offender is an undertaking, up to 7% of its total worldwide annual turnover for the preceding financial year, whichever is higher[348]
2.	Non-compliance with requirements[349]	Administrative fine of up to €15,000,000 or, if the offender is an undertaking, up to 3% of its total worldwide annual turnover for the preceding financial year, whichever is higher[350]
3.	Supply of incorrect, incomplete or misleading information to notified bodies or national competent authorities in reply to a request[351]	Administrative fine of up to €7,500,000 or, if the offender is an undertaking, up to 1% of its total worldwide annual turnover for the preceding financial year, whichever is higher[352]

362. Notes:

- (1) In the case of SMEs, including start-ups, the fine is calculated on a 'whichever is lower' basis.[353]
- (2) Penalties for non-compliance with requirements or failure to supply information fairly to the national competent authorities are independent of the classification of AI systems; they apply indiscriminately to the following AI systems:
    - o high-risk AI systems;

[348] AI Act, Art. 99(3).
[349] All obligations not covered by Article 5 of the AI Act.
[350] AI Act, Art. 99.
[351] AI Act, Arts. 91 and 101.
[352] AI Act, Art. 99(5).
[353] AI Act, Art. 99(6).

  - o general-purpose AI systems;
  - o AI systems subject to a transparency obligation.
- (3) For general-purpose AI models, a special system of penalties is provided for.[354]

14.2. Penalties Relating to General-Purpose AI Models

14.2.1 Introduction

363. The risks involved are such that specific rules are necessary.

14.2.2 Fines

NO.	THEME	SPECIFICATION
1.	Authority	The European Commission
2.	Actor	General-purpose AI model provider
3.	Amount	€15,000,000 or 3% of the annual total worldwide turnover Whichever is higher
4.	Procedure	Adversarial procedure, with the European Commission
5.	AI Office	Information
6.	Failures	Failure to comply with obligations Failure to provide information Failure to comply with a measure requested (AIA, Art. 93) Failure to grant access to the European Commission for evaluation purposes (AIA, Art. 92)
7.	Modalities	Fines must be effective, proportionate and dissuasive
8.	Remedy	Court of Justice of the EU ruling with unlimited jurisdiction

364. Notes:

- (1) Fines are the same for general-purpose AI models with or without systemic risks.

[354] See below AI Act, Art. 101.

14.3. *Penalties Imposed on EU Institutions*

14.3.1 Introduction

365. Such penalties are aimed at:[355]

- EU institutions;
- EU bodies;
- EU offices and agencies.

14.3.2 Fines

366. The guiding principles are as follows:

NO.	THEME	SPECIFICATION	REFERENCE
1.	Jurisdiction	European Data Protection Supervisor	AIA, Art. 100(1)
2.	Fine (1)	Non-compliance with prohibited practices (AIA, Art. 5) €1,500,000	AIA, Art. 100(2)
3.	Fine (2)	Non-compliance of AI systems with requirements €750,000	AIA, Art. 100(3)
4.	Procedure	Adversarial procedure Notes: • (1) complainants, if any, shall be associated closely with the proceedings	AIA, Art. 100(4)
5.	Assessment of fines	Gravity Duration of the infringement Degree of responsibility Actions taken to mitigate the damage Degree of cooperation with EDPS Similar infringement Manner in which the infringement became known Annual budget	AIA, Art. 100(1)

14.3.3 Characteristics

367. Fines must be:

- effective;
- proportionate;
- dissuasive.[356]

---

[355] AI Act, Art. 100.

[356] AI Act, Art. 99(1).

14.3.4 Adjustment

368. These fines must be determined subjectively, taking into account elements including, but not limited to:

- the nature, gravity and duration of the infringement and of its consequences;
- whether administrative fines have already been applied by other market surveillance authorities to the same operator for the same infringement;
- the size and market share of the operator committing the infringement.[357]

14.4. Penalties Imposed on Public Authorities and Bodies

369. Member States are free to lay down rules on to what extent administrative fines may be imposed on public authorities and bodies.

14.5. Summary of Penalties

370. It is as follows:

NO.	AMOUNT	TECHNOLOGY	ACTOR	THEME
1.	€7,500,000 or 1% of turnover	High-risk AI system General-purpose AI system Transparent AI system	Operator	Failure to supply information or supply of incomplete or misleading information
2.	€750,000	All AI technologies	EU institution	Non-compliance
3.	€1,500,000	All AI technologies	EU institution	Non-compliance
4.	€15,000,000 or 3% of turnover	High-risk AI system General-purpose AI system Transparent AI system	Operator	Non-compliance
5.	€15,000,000 or 3% of turnover	General-purpose AI model with or without systemic risk	Provider	Infringement of obligations Failure to supply information Failure to comply with a measure (AIA, Art. 93) Failure to provide access to the European Commission (AIA, Art. 92)
6.	€35,000,000 or 7% of turnover	Prohibited AI system	Operator	Non-compliance

[357] AI Act, Art. 99(7).

15 CROSS-CUTTING LEGAL ISSUES

15.1. Introduction

371. The legal questions that arise concern the following issues in particular:
- AI policy;
- trust;
- consciousness;
- AI officer;
- impact assessments;
- AI system contracts;
- personal data;
- automated decisions;
- creators' rights;
- ethics;
- AI and creation;
- AI and human superiority;
- implementation and deployment;
- economic and social mode of production;
- general regulation;
- liability;
- trade secrets.

15.2. AI Policy

15.2.1 Introduction

372. The AI HLEG[358] has defined seven ethical principles to serve as guidance, namely:
- human agency and oversight;
- technical robustness and safety;
- privacy and data governance;
- transparency;
- diversity, non-discrimination and fairness;
- environmental and societal well-being;
- accountability.

[358] High-Level Expert Group on Artificial Intelligence (AI HLEG) (AI Act, Rec. 7).

15.2.2 Approach

373. The AI Act enables private organisations, i.e. technology companies, companies in the industrial sectors and service providers, or public administrations, public establishments or research bodies, to strengthen protections in order to promote trustworthy AI systems.[359]

15.2.3 Additional Commitments

374. In that context, many companies have adopted such an internal document, which is more general in scope than the requirements of the Regulation.[360]

375. AI can be qualified as ethical if it is:

- privacy-friendly;
- unbiased (it endeavours not to create or reproduce discrimination and favours inclusiveness);
- transparent in its operation (its conclusions can be explained and it is auditable);
- fair in its relations with human beings (it only does what is expected of it and it discloses itself to the user);
- controlled (it remains under the control of humans);
- reliable (it is secure and robust in the face of cyberattacks).[361]

15.3. Trust

15.3.1 Introduction

376. This concept has not been defined. It is one of the key components of the Regulation.

359 Comité national public d'éthique du numérique (CNPEN), 'Ethical issues of generative artificial intelligence systems', Opinion No. 7, 30 June 2023.

360 C. Woitier, 'Le Figaro se dote d'une charte sur l'usage de l'IA générative' ['Le Figaro adopts a charter on the use of generative AI'], *Le Figaro*, 13 December 2023, p. 28; H. de Lestapis, 'Club Med met l'IA sous bonne surveillance' ['Club Med keeps a close eye on AI'], *Les Échos*, 2 October 2023.

361 Numeum, 'Behind the codes and the data: A Pratical Guide to Ethical AI', version 1, September 2021, 72 p.; IBM, 'Everyday ethics for Artificial Intelligence', 11 November 2022, 27 p.

15.3.2 Guiding Principles

377. Trust is associated with the requirement to regulate AI technologies in order to create 'trustworthy' AI.[362]

15.3.3 Components

378. According to the High-Level Expert Group on Artificial Intelligence (AI HLEG), trustworthy AI implies compliance with the following requirements:[363]

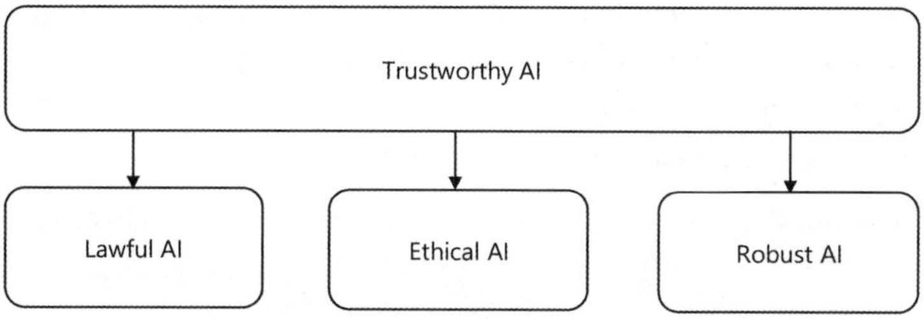

15.4. Consciousness

15.4.1 Introduction

379. This issue is addressed indirectly through prohibited AI systems in the following terms:

- 'the placing on the market, the putting into service or the use of an AI system that deploys subliminal techniques, beyond a person's consciousness.'[364]

15.4.2 Specification

380. This notion is extremely difficult to define and there are many philosophical essays on it.

381. It does, however, coexist with the concept of ipseity, or the ability to perceive one's own existence.[365]

---

362 AI Act, Art. 1 and Art. 95(2)(a).

363 AI HLEG, 'Ethics Guidelines for Trustworthy AI', April 2019, p. 8; AI Act, Rec. 27.

364 Prohibited AI practices include: the placing on the market, the putting into service or the use of an AI system that deploys:
- subliminal techniques beyond a person's consciousness, or
- purposefully manipulative or deceptive techniques. AI Act, Art. 5(1)(a).

365 P. Butlin et al., 'Consciousness in artificial intelligence: Insights from the science of consciousness' (arXiv:2308.08708), 2023.

15.5. AI Officer

15.5.1 Introduction

382. There is no specific obligation to appoint an AI Officer within an organisation. There is no equivalent of the Data Protection Officer (DPO) as in the GDPR.[366]

15.5.2 Best Practices

383. In any event, designating an AI officer or AI champion can enable the implementation of AI technology governance according to:

- the legal requirements; and
- the ethical principles adopted by the company.

384. It is one of the key elements of the compliance accountability process.

15.6. Impact Assessments

15.6.1 Introduction

385. This requirement is not generalised to all AI systems.

15.6.2 Criteria

386. This requirement concerns:

- certain actors;
- specific AI systems.

[366] GDPR (EU) 2016/679, Art. 37.

15.6.3 Classification

387. It is as follows:

NO.	THEME	SPECIFICATION	REFERENCE
1.	Real-time remote biometric identification AI system in publicly accessible spaces	Law enforcement authority Impact on fundamental rights	AIA, Rec. 34 AIA, Art. 5(1)(h)
2.	High-risk AI system	Deployer: • body governed by public law • private entity providing public services • entity that evaluates the creditworthiness of natural persons • insurance (life and health insurance) Impact on fundamental rights	AIA, Rec. 96 AIA, Art. 27 AIA, Annex III 5(b) AIA, Annex III 5(c)

15.6.4 Impact Assessment for High-Risk AI Systems

388. The main elements are as follows:[367]

NO.	THEME	SPECIFICATION
1.	Responsible actor	Deployer
2.	AI system	High-risk AI system
3.	Protection (Values-based approach)	Fundamental rights (Reference: Charter of Fundamental Rights) and rights recognised as such by EU or national law
4.	Process	Description
5.	Period of use	Description of period of time and frequency
6.	Persons concerned	Categories of natural persons or groups
7.	Risks (Description and impact)	Description of harm taking into account providers' transparency obligations (AIA, Art. 13)
8.	Risks (Identification)	Measures to be taken in the case of the materialisation of the risks Internal governance system Internal complaints mechanism

[367] AI Act, Art. 27.

NO.	THEME	SPECIFICATION
9.	Implementation	First use of the system
10.	Notification	Obligation to notify the market surveillance authority using the template developed by the AI Office[368] Derogation: in special cases, with authorisation from the market surveillance authority[369]
11.	Coordination	In the case of an impact assessment of the GDPR[370] type, it is possible to complete the said assessment[371]

15.7. AI System Contracts

15.7.1 Introduction

389. Contractual relationships are not determined as such by the Regulation.

15.7.2 Typology

390. Three main families of contracts emerge in the following technical areas

- licensing of large language models (LLMs) with personalised training services;
- 'AI as a Service' (AIaaS), which provides access to all the major functions such as large language models, customisation and operation;
- AI system design, selection and integration.

15.7.3 Essential Clauses

391. These are as follows:

NO.	CLAUSE	SPECIFICATION
1.	Information	Confidentiality Reservation for the exclusive use of the customer[372]
2.	Conformity	AI Act guarantee

[368] AI Act, Art. 27(5).
[369] AI Act, Art. 27(3).
[370] GDPR, Art. 35.
[371] AI Act, Art. 27(4).
[372] 'AWS promises that Bedrock's customers' data will not be used to train the base models it offers. Customers – and therefore possibly competitors – will not benefit from another customer's data' [Translated by the author], I. Vergara, 'Amazon se lance à son tour dans la course à l'IA générative' ['Amazon takes its turn in the generative AI race'], *Le Figaro*, 14 April 2023 (digital version), 15–16 April 2023 (paper version).

NO.	CLAUSE	SPECIFICATION
3.	Data	Lawfulness of training data
4.	Guarantee	Non-regression Peaceful enjoyment
5.	Neutrality	Do not introduce informational rules such as advertising or guidance recommendations[373]
6.	Service level	Benchmark Scalability
7.	Subject matter	Technical specifications
8.	Price	Definition and conditions of billing strategies
9.	Ownership	Data and documents generated
10.	Responsibility	Best efforts obligation in relation to the results obtained

15.8. *Personal Data and Automated Decisions*

15.8.1 Introduction

392. If personal data are involved when using an AI system, the AI Act should be combined with the GDPR.[374]

393. 'Union law on the protection of personal data, privacy and the confidentiality of communications applies to personal data processed in connection with the rights and obligations laid down in this Regulation',[375] and 'Union legal acts provide the basis for sustainable and responsible data processing, including where data sets include a mix of personal and non-personal data. This Regulation does not seek to affect the application of existing Union law governing the processing of personal data, including the tasks and powers of the independent supervisory authorities competent to monitor compliance with those instruments'.[376]

15.8.2 The Concept of Processing

394. In the GDPR, 'processing' is defined as follows:

- 'any operation or set of operations which is performed on personal data or on sets of personal data, whether or not by automated means, such as collection, recording, organisation, structuring, storage, adaptation or alteration,

373 L. Marchand, 'Comment ChatGPT s'occupe de planifier votre prochain voyage' ['How ChatGPT takes care of planning your next trip'], *Les Échos*, 27 March 2023.

374 General Data Protection Regulation (2016/679) and Law Enforcement Directive (2016/680).

375 AI Act, Art. 2(7).

376 AI Act, Rec. 10.

retrieval, consultation, use, disclosure by transmission, dissemination or otherwise making available, alignment or combination, restriction, erasure or destruction.'[377]

395. Any AI system that uses personal data should therefore be considered to be processing of personal data.

15.8.3 Actors

396. All those involved in the lifecycle of an AI system will have the legal qualification corresponding to their role with regard to personal data:

- controller or joint controller;
- processor;
- recipient;
- authorised third party.

15.8.4 Principle of Lawfulness

397. The processing of personal data by means of AI systems may not be carried out without a legal basis corresponding to one of the following options:

- the data subject has given consent to the processing of his or her personal data for one or more specific purposes;
- processing is necessary for the performance of a contract to which the data subject is party or in order to take steps at the request of the data subject prior to entering into a contract;
- processing is necessary for compliance with a legal obligation to which the controller is subject;
- processing is necessary in order to protect the vital interests of the data subject or of another natural person;
- processing is necessary for the performance of a task carried out in the public interest or in the exercise of official authority vested in the controller;
- processing is necessary for the purposes of the legitimate interests pursued by the controller or by a third party, except where such interests are overridden by the interests or fundamental rights and freedoms of the data subject which require protection of personal data, in particular where the data subject is a child.[378]

---

377 GDPR (2016/679), Art. 4(2).

378 GDPR (2016/679), Art. 6(1).

15.8.5 Data Governance

398. All obligations applicable to high-risk AI systems must be combined with the governance of personal data as enshrined in particular by the application of specific principles.[379]

15.8.6 Purpose Principle

399. The objectives assigned to an AI system correspond to the concept of purpose.

15.8.7 Principle of Minimisation

400. The 'minimisation' requirement is not always easy to determine technically, particularly with general-purpose AI systems.

401. During the design phase, minimisation must be defined with regard to the initial purposes.

---

[379] GDPR (2016/679), Art. 5(1): Personal data shall be:
- processed lawfully, fairly and in a transparent manner in relation to the data subject ('lawfulness, fairness and transparency');
- collected for specified, explicit and legitimate purposes and not further processed in a manner that is incompatible with those purposes; further processing for archiving purposes in the public interest, scientific or historical research purposes or statistical purposes shall, in accordance with Article 89(1), not be considered to be incompatible with the initial purposes ('purpose limitation');
- adequate, relevant and limited to what is necessary in relation to the purposes for which they are processed ('data minimisation');
- accurate and, where necessary, kept up to date; every reasonable step must be taken to ensure that personal data that are inaccurate, having regard to the purposes for which they are processed, are erased or rectified without delay ('accuracy');
- kept in a form which permits identification of data subjects for no longer than is necessary for the purposes for which the personal data are processed; personal data may be stored for longer periods insofar as the personal data will be processed solely for archiving purposes in the public interest, scientific or historical research purposes or statistical purposes in accordance with Article 89(1) subject to implementation of the appropriate technical and organisational measures required by this Regulation in order to safeguard the rights and freedoms of the data subject ('storage limitation');
- processed in a manner that ensures appropriate security of the personal data, including protection against unauthorised or unlawful processing and against accidental loss, destruction or damage, using appropriate technical or organisational measures ('integrity and confidentiality').

15.8.8 Sensitive Information

402. In the fight against bias,[380] it is possible, within a limited framework, to use sensitive information[381] in order to combat bias, particularly in the fight against all forms of discrimination.

403. Notes:

- (1) In terms of accountability, such use must be included in the record of processing activities.[382]

15.8.9 Impact Assessment

404. In most cases, an impact assessment is necessary.

15.8.10 Specific Obligations

405. As such, an AI system that uses personal data during the training phase is subject to all the obligations under the GDPR and local laws on the protection of personal data.

406. These obligations mainly include the following:

NO.	OBLIGATIONS	SPECIFICATION	REFERENCE
1.	Data Protection Officer	Monitoring use of personal data	GDPR, Art. 37
2.	Storage period	According to the purpose	GDPR, Art. 23(f)
3.	Transfers outside the EU	Mapping and supervision	GDPR, Art. 44 GDPR, Art. 45[383] GDPR, Art. 46[384]
4.	Formalities	Informing individuals about AI systems	GDPR, Arts. 12 ff.
5.	Protection by design	Risk-based management of services	GDPR, Art. 25(1) AIA, Rec. 69
6.	Protection by default	Taking security into account	GDPR, Art. 25(1) AIA, Rec. 69
7.	Record	Registration of AI applications	GDPR, Art. 30
8.	Security	General obligation	GDPR, Art. 32

[380] AI Act, Art. 10.
[381] AI Act, Art. 9.
[382] AI Act, Art. 30.
[383] Transfers on the basis of an adequacy decision.
[384] Transfers subject to appropriate safeguards.

15.8.11 Impact of the AI Act on the GDPR

407. The main relations are as follows:

NO.	THEME	SPECIFICATION
1.	Biometrics for law enforcement purposes	The AI Act authorises this type of automated processing within a very specific framework[385]
2.	Data governance	Use of highly personal or regulated sensitive personal data (GDPR, Art. 9) for the purposes of combating bias subject to safeguards for the protection of individuals[386]
3.	Testing	Use of highly personal or regulated sensitive personal data (GDPR, Art. 9) for the purposes of combating bias subject to safeguards for the protection of individuals[387]
4.	Testing in real-world conditions	High-risk AI systems covered by Annex III[388]
5.	Experimentation	Re-use of personal data in regulatory sandboxes[389]

15.8.12 Automated Decision-Making

15.8.12.1 *Guiding Principles*

408. Pursuant to the GDPR, '[t]he data subject shall have the right not to be subject to a decision based solely on automated processing, including profiling, which produces legal effects concerning him or her or similarly significantly affects him or her'.[390]

409. Where the decision is based on AI systems, the two sets of legislation must be coordinated.[391]

385 AI Act, Art. 5(1)(h).
386 AI Act, Art. 10(5).
387 AI Act, Art. 10(6).
388 AI Act, Art. 60.
389 AI Act, Art. 59.
390 GDPR (2016/679), Art. 22.
391 AI Act, Rec. 10.

15.8.12.2 *Profiling*

410. On this subject, the AI Act provides for the following elements to be coordinated with the GDPR:

NO.	THEME	SPECIFICATION	REFERENCE
1.	Assessment	Prohibition of AI-predicted behaviour judgement based on characteristics	AIA, Rec. 42
2.	Offence (detection)	Prohibited to detect offences based on profiling	AIA, Rec. 42
3.	Repeat offence	Prohibited to assess reoffending risk based on personality traits or characteristics	AIA, Rec. 59 AIA, Art. 6 AIA, Annex III
4.	Social score	Special profiling	AIA, Art. 5
5.	High-risk AI system covered by Annex III	Ineligible for exemption from classification as a high-risk system if profiling is performed	AIA, Art. 6(3)

15.9. *Creators' Rights*

15.9.1 Introduction

411. The protection of prior creations, in particular authors' rights, is not directly covered by the regulatory framework.[392]

15.9.2 Training Data

412. Authors should be able to implement their prerogatives on training data through the mechanism of data governance.

413. In this regard, high-risk AI systems are required to specify 'data collection processes and the origin of data, and in the case of personal data, the original purpose of the data collection'.[393]

---

392 A. Bensamoun, 'Report Task Force on the implementation of the European regulation establishing harmonized rules on artificial intelligence ("template")', Conseil supérieur de la propriété littéraire et artistique, Ministère de la culture, 11 December 2024, p. 107.

393 AI Act, Art. 10(2)(b).

414. In that context, authors will be able to check whether and how their works have been used. 'This gives rights holders back control over their content.'[394]

15.9.3 Initial Copy

415. During the training phase, documents are copied for analysis. This falls within the scope of copyright.

15.9.4 Right to Read

416. The right to read is inherent in copyright. In literature, a modification is necessary in order to protect a creation that is commensurate with 'borrowings'.[395]

15.10. Ethics

15.10.1 Introduction

417. In October 2020, the European Parliament placed ethics at the heart of the future regulation.[396] However, in the AI Act, the influence of this concept is more limited.

15.10.2 Application

418. Ethics is a requirement in the following contexts:

NO.	THEME	SPECIFICATION	REFERENCE
1.	Testing	'The testing of high-risk AI systems in real world conditions under this Article shall be without prejudice to any ethical review that is required by Union or national law.'	AIA, Art. 60(3)

394 Statement by Alexandre Lasch, Director General of SNEP (Syndicat national de l'édition phonographique), quoted by M. Alcaraz, in 'L'AI Act ouvre la voie à des négociations pour rémunérer les auteurs' ['The AI Act paves the way for negotiations to remunerate authors'], Les *Échos*, 2 February 2024.

395 G. Koenig, 'Protéger le droit d'auteur à l'ère de l'IA' ['Protecting copyright in the age of AI'], *Les Échos*, 29 November 2023.

396 European Parliament resolution of 20 October 2020 with recommendations to the Commission on a framework of ethical aspects of artificial intelligence, robotics and related technologies (2020/2012(INL, 2020/2012(INL).

NO.	THEME	SPECIFICATION	REFERENCE
2.	Codes of conduct	'The AI Office and the Member States shall facilitate the drawing up of codes of conduct concerning the voluntary application, including by deployers, of specific requirements to all AI systems, on the basis of clear objectives and key performance indicators to measure the achievement of those objectives, including elements such as, but not limited to a) applicable elements provided for in Union ethical guidelines for trustworthy AI;'	AIA, Art. 95(2)(a)
3.	Innovation R&D	'This Regulation should support innovation, should respect freedom of science, and should not undermine research and development activity. […] In any event, any research and development activity should be carried out in accordance with recognised ethical and professional standards for scientific research and should be conducted in accordance with applicable Union law.'	AIA, Rec. 25
4.	Ethics versus risks	'While the risk-based approach is the basis for a proportionate and effective set of binding rules, it is important to recall the 2019 Ethics guidelines for trustworthy AI developed by the independent AI HLEG appointed by the Commission. In those guidelines, the AI HLEG developed seven non-binding ethical principles for AI which are intended to help ensure that AI is trustworthy and ethically sound. The seven principles include human agency and oversight; technical robustness and safety; privacy and data governance; transparency; diversity, non-discrimination and fairness; societal and environmental well-being and accountability […].'	AIA, Rec. 27
5.	Best practice and voluntary standards	'All stakeholders, including industry, academia, civil society and standardisation organisations, are encouraged to take into account, as appropriate, the ethical principles for the development of voluntary best practices and standards.'	AIA, Rec. 27

NO.	THEME	SPECIFICATION	REFERENCE
6.	Providers and deployers	'Providers and, as appropriate, deployers of all AI systems, high-risk or not, and AI models should also be encouraged to apply on a voluntary basis additional requirements related, for example, to the elements of the Union's Ethics Guidelines for Trustworthy AI, environmental sustainability, AI literacy measures, inclusive and diverse design and development of AI systems, including attention to vulnerable persons and accessibility to persons with disability, stakeholders' participation with the involvement, as appropriate, of relevant stakeholders such as business and civil society organisations, academia, research organisations, trade unions and consumer protection organisations in the design and development of AI systems, and diversity of the development teams, including gender balance.'	AIA, Rec. 165

15.10.3 Guidelines

419. Ethics is infra-moral and supra-legal. It is necessary as regulators struggle to keep pace with technological innovation.

420. It is expressed in charters or recommendations issued by regulatory bodies.[397]

15.10.4 Ethical Witnesses and Measures

421. An ethical witness is a measure between a respected legal obligation and a moral value practised by a majority in a democracy oriented towards the fundamental principles of human rights.

422. This can be assessed through the following:

NO.	THEME	SPECIFICATION
1.	Alert	Organise a whistleblowing process
2.	Advantage	Identity the advantages

[397] Comité national public d'éthique du numérique (CNPEN), 'Ethical issues of generative artificial intelligence systems', Opinion No. 7, 30 June 2023.

NO.	THEME	SPECIFICATION
3.	Consent	Need to establish an understanding of the tension in order to allow informed consent and repentance under transparent conditions
4.	Control	Ask contributions from independent personalities
5.	Duration	Set a period for reviewing indicators
6.	Governance	Create a joint committee made up of business experts and external experts
7.	Disadvantage	Identify the disadvantages in a transparent manner
8.	Indications	Qualitative Quantitative
9.	Necessity	Define legitimacy to strengthen the legal framework
10.	Pedagogy	Awareness and training plan
11.	Harm	Assess the material and psychological consequences
12.	Risk	Assess the degree of expertise
13.	Tracing	Provide for the anonymous logging of breaches

423. Notes:

- (1) Following in the footsteps of the EU Parliament, the European Commission is using ethics as a criterion. This is the case, for example, in the pillar for the development of AI in favour of start-ups, with the addition of a specific pillar entitled: 'AI factory pillar for trustworthy and ethical AI.'[398]

15.11. Artificial Intelligence and Creation

15.11.1 Introduction

424. The difficulty of recognising AI authorship for AI-generated works arises from the fact that a creator is defined as a natural person.

425. However, this requirement does not appear as such:

- 'The author of a work of the mind shall enjoy in that work, by the mere fact of its creation, an exclusive incorporeal property right which shall be enforceable against all persons.'[399]

[398] Council Regulation (EU) 2024/1732 of 17 June 2024 amending Regulation (EU) 2021/1173 as regards a EuroHPC initiative for start-ups in order to boost European leadership in trustworthy artificial intelligence, [2024] OJ L.

[399] Art. L.111-1(1) of the French Intellectual property Code.

426. It is deduced from the following rule:

- 'This right shall include attributes of an intellectual and moral nature as well as attributes of an economic nature, as determined by Books I and III of this Code.'[400]

427. It is indeed difficult to grant moral attributes to an AI system.

428. Human authorship as a bedrock requirement of copyright has been cited by American case law for denying such recognition.[401]

429. Notes:

- (1) This decision is open to criticism insofar as, like the photographic work, the digital nature of the photograph leaves the photographer free to make their own artistic choices.
- (2) The prompt is directly at the origin of the creation through a large language model.
- (3) Creation by artificial intelligence is 'deduced' from the command given by the human creator.
- (4) The recognition of a creation is part of a natural right coordinated with the necessary evolution of copyright.

15.11.2 Legal Personality of Robots

430. This would make it possible to move away from the 'author' and 'natural person'[402] debate. It would encourage the emergence of an artificial author.[403]

15.11.3 Uses

431. AI systems, in particular generative AI systems, use millions of documents in the learning phase, including works protected by copyright. Authors and their representatives are opposed to such intellectual plundering.

432. In this context, they demand complete transparency on learning models, in particular on the technical conditions under which the works are used.[404]

---

[400] Art. L.111-1(2) of the French Intellectual property Code.

[401] US district court for the district of Columbia, 18 August 2023, No. 22-1564 (BAH). The claim relates to the creation of an image entitled 'A Recent Entrance to Paradise'.

[402] A. Bensoussan and J. Bensoussan, 'IA robots et droit' ['AI robots and the law'], Théorie et pratique, Brussels, Bruylant, July 2019, 632 p.

[403] D.J. Gervais, 'Pour la cause: la protection par le droit d'auteur des productions des systèmes d'intelligence artificielle' ['For the cause: copyright protection for the products of artificial intelligence systems'], *Les Cahiers de propriété intellectuelle*, January 2023, vol. 35, n° 1, p. 151.

[404] C. Sallé, 'Le cri d'alarme des industries culturelles et créatives face aux "boîtes noires" des IA' ['Cultural and creative industries sound the alarm over AI "black boxes"'], *Le Figaro*, 3 October 2023.

15.11.4 New Right

433. As such, protected works are not copied intellectually. Only physical 'borrowing' takes place during the training phase of large language models.

434. A new right is needed: the right to read in order to build:

- the right to knowledge for all, enshrined in generative AI systems in general;
- the principle of the free flow of ideas, enshrined in copyright law.

435. A recognition of the right to read, as a condition of the right to competition and the right to freedom of conscience in relation to protected works, should help establish a fair balance between human or artificial freedom to read and the economic rights of the authors of the training data.

15.11.5 Right to Opt-Out

436. This right makes it possible to protect intellectual creations by allowing opposition to data mining.[405]

437. Such opt-out right was exercised by Sacem, the French Society of Authors, Composers and Publishers of Music, in 2023.[406]

15.12. Artificial Intelligence and Human Superiority

15.12.1 Introduction

438. Artificial general intelligence (AGI) is still science fiction.

15.12.2 Definition

439. Artificial general intelligence, which should not be confused with general-purpose AI (such as generative AI), has the particular feature of being superior to humans in all the tasks that humans can perform.

440. This is the case for:

- the ability to reason;
- the ability to create;
- the ability to perceive emotions;
- the ability to be self-aware.[407]

---

[405] S. Loignon, 'La Sacem exerce son droit d'opposition face aux outils d'intelligence artificielle' ['Sacem exercises its right to object to artificial intelligence tools'], *Les Échos,* 13 October 2023.

[406] M. Alcaraz, 'La relance de "Plus belle la vie" le pari à 30 millions de TF1' ['The relaunch of "Plus belle la vie", TF1's $30 million gamble'], *Les Échos,* 12 October 2023.

[407] L. Ferry, 'Avec ChatGPT, allons-nous vers l'IA forte?' ['With ChatGPT, are we moving towards strong AI?'], *Le Figaro,* 22 February 2023.

15.12.3 Science Fiction

441. 'Sam Altman, ChatGPT CEO, said that he is convinced that artificial superintelligence will be here before 2030. There's no certainty that we'll get there, but I can see that there are more and more researchers, a large majority in fact, who are now convinced that AI will overtake us in every field.'[408]

15.12.4 Geopolitics

15.12.4.1 *Introduction*

442. Warfare through artificial intelligence is exacerbated in all economic, social and political spheres.[409]

15.12.4.2 *Legal Trajectories*

443. The new regulations are described below in an at-a-glance summary:

NO.	WORLD	SPECIFICATION	COMMENT
1.	Anglo-Saxon	Minimalist regulation and protection for US technology champions	Great Britain USA
2.	European Union	Horizontal regulation at a global level	AIA 2024
3.	China	Political and social regulation at a domestic level	2023 Act
4.	UN	Resolution: 'Seizing the opportunities of safe, secure and trustworthy artificial intelligence systems for sustainable development'	Resolution A/78/L.49 of 11 March 2024

[408] J-O. Martin, 'Laurent Alexandre: "Avec l'IA, la marginalisation de l'espèce humaine est absolument inévitable"' ['Laurent Alexandre: "With AI, the marginalisation of the human species is absolutely inevitable"'], *Le Figaro*, 9 August 2023.

[409] N. Baverez, 'Géopolitique de l'intelligence artificielle' ['The geopolitics of artificial intelligence'], *Le Figaro*, 2 October 2023.

15.13. *Implementation and Deployment*

15.13.1 Introduction

444. Implementing a compliance programme involves the following steps:

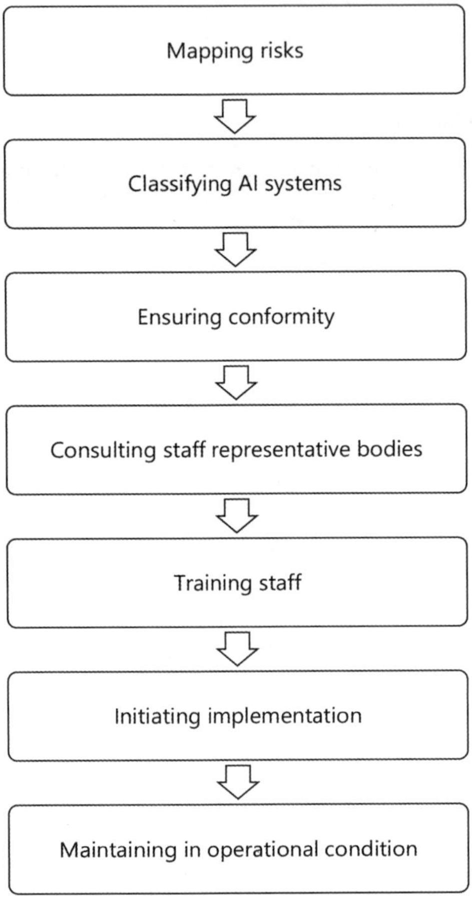

15.13.2 Mapping

445. Mapping is necessary in order to take stock of AI systems and determine compliance actions. This is the case for AI systems,[410] general-purpose AI models[411] and general-purpose AI systems.[412]

410 AI Act, Arts. 5 ff.
411 AI Act, Arts. 51 ff.
412 AI Act, Arts. 50 ff.

15.13.3 Classification

446. Based on the results of the risk mapping, it will be necessary to determine the classification of each AI system.

15.13.4 Conformity

447. Before the placing on the market or the putting into service, it should be checked that the requirements applicable to the class of AI system selected have been met.

15.13.5 Consultation

448. AI systems, general-purpose AI models and general-purpose AI systems affects in particular the company's strategic orientations and social policy, including working conditions.

15.13.6 Training

449. The purpose is to ensure the AI literacy of the staff of providers and deployers who are dealing with AI systems.[413]

15.13.7 Implementation

450. Depending on circumstances, this step includes:

- the placing on the market;
- the putting into service;
- the use.

15.13.8 Maintaining in Operational Condition

451. The obligation to contain risks requires implementing monitoring throughout the entire lifecycle of AI systems and models.

---

[413] AI Act, Art. 4.

15.14. *Economic and Social Mode of Production*

15.14.1 Introduction

452. With the advent of virtual machine tools and the transition from doing to having others do, the traditional economy will be profoundly disrupted.[414]

15.14.2 Value

453. With generative artificial intelligence,[415] the labour value will give way to the creative value.

454. Effort is no longer measured in time spent or crystallized, but in creative contribution.

455. In this mode of production, time is no longer a direct component of the value produced.

15.14.3 Employment

15.14.3.1 *Introduction*

456. According to this trend, new professions will emerge, based on creation rather than the combination of skills and associated experience.[416]

457. These systems will be extensions of every human being.

15.14.3.2 *Market*

458. With the deployment of general-purpose AI systems, the labour market becomes bipolar according to the following breakdown:

- a low added-value market, focused on improving the responses of Artificial Intelligences; a proletarianisation of click-workers;
- a high added-value market, harnessing the concentration of knowledge resulting from large language models.[417]

---

[414] 'I fully embrace using science, technology, and innovation, as long as they are put to the service of the French people. I reject populist rhetoric that recklessly invokes the theory of the "great replacement" to stir fear of technological tools', Stanislas Guerini said during an interview by T. Quinault-Maupoil, in 'Intelligence artificielle le gouvernement lance une vaste expérimentation dans l'administration' ['Artificial intelligence: the government launches a vast experiment in public administration'], *Le Figaro*, 4 October 2023.

[415] Or a general-purpose AI system. AI Act, Art. 3.

[416] Institute for the future, 'The next era of Human-machine partnerships: Emerging technologies' impact on society & work in 2030', *Dell Technologies*, 7 May 2017, 23 p.

[417] M. Bernier, 'Cols bleus, blancs roses: serons-nous tous au chômage à cause de l'IA?' ['Blue, pink and white collars: will we all be out of work because of AI?'], *Les Échos*, 11 August 2023, p. 21.

15.15. *General Regulation*

15.15.1 Introduction

459. The main principles of this regulation are as follows:
- the abandonment of the precautionary principle;
- the application of the ALARA principle;
- the application minimalist framework for the design phase;
- a product regulation;
- the link between product regulations;
- the legal approach of the AI Act (EU) 2024/1689 and the GDPR (EU) 2016/679;
- the absence of legal consequences linked to the concept of autonomy.

460. The Artificial Intelligence package includes:
- the AI Regulation (2024/1689);
- the proposed for a directive on adapting non-contractual civil liability rules to AI;
- the Machinery Regulation;[418]
- the General Product Safety Directive;[419]
- the Coordinated Plan on Artificial Intelligence;[420]
- the AI Pact.

15.15.2 The Precautionary Principle

461. Despite the lack of full risk control, the precautionary principle has not been adopted, notwithstanding pressure from globally renowned researchers and figures.[421]

462. According to Yann Le Cun, '[t]he very idea of wanting to slow down AI research seems to me like a new form of obscurantism. A pause risks hindering the essential progress needed to make these technologies more reliable and able to serve the common good. On the contrary, we need to. On the contrary, we

418 Currently under review.
419 Currently under review.
420 File updated in 2021.
421 Interview with Yoshua Bengio, researcher, by C. Legros, 'Il me semble indispensable de mettre en avant le principe de précaution' ['I believe it is essential to emphasise the precautionary principle'], *Le Monde*, 29 April 2023.

need to speed things up! If I'm not in favour of a pause, it's also because I don't believe in it. It's unrealistic; no one is going to stop AI research for six months'.[422]

15.15.3 ALARA Principle

463. This acronym stands for 'As Low As Reasonably Achievable'.

464. Its application in the context of the AI Act leads to regulation based on:

- risk minimisation;
- the monitoring of the evolution of risks during use;
- the control of AI systems.

15.15.4 A Product Regulation

465. The regulations concerning AI include legal obligations which are broken down into essential requirements.

466. The solution, in terms of implementation, is the responsibility of the operators, who are free to implement it themselves.

467. These regulations are based on the new legislative framework which mainly includes:

- the common framework for the marketing of products;[423]
- market surveillance;[424]
- product compliance;[425]
- conformity accreditation;[426]
- the 'Blue Guide' for implementing all these concepts.[427]

---

422 Interview with Yann Le Cun, Chief AI Scientist at Meta, by C. Legros, 'L'idée même de vouloir ralentir la recherche sur l'IA s'apparente à un nouvel obscurantisme' ['The very idea of wanting to slow down AI research is akin to a new obscurantism'], *Le Monde*, 29 April 2023.

423 Decision No 768/2008/EC of the European Parliament and of the Council of 9 July 2008 on a common framework for the marketing of products, and repealing Council Decision 93/465/EEC, [2008] OJ L218/82.

424 Regulation (EU) 2019/1020 of the European Parliament and of the Council of 20 June 2019 on market surveillance and compliance of products and amending Directive 2004/42/EC and Regulations (EC) No 765/2008 and (EU) No 305/2011, [2019] OJ L169/1.

425 Ibid

426 Regulation (EC) No 765/2008 of the European Parliament and of the Council of 9 July 2008 setting out the requirements for accreditation and repealing Regulation (EEC) No 339/93, [2008] OJ L218/30.

427 'The "Blue Guide" on the implementation of EU product rules 2022', [2022] OJ C247/1.

15.15.5 Coordination Between Product Regulations

468. When a product, in order to be compliant, must comply with several legal acts of Union harmonisation legislation, providers and deployers should 'have flexibility with regard to operational decision to be taken'.[428]

15.15.6 The Legal Approach of the AI Act (EU) 2014/1689 and GDPR (EU) 2016/679

469. The legal approaches are fundamentally different. The GDPR adopts a human rights-based approach (it basically corresponds to the French Data Protection Act[429]), whereas the AI Act is a product-oriented regulation.

470. The references include the following:

NO.	THEME	AI ACT	GDPR
1.	Approach	Product	Human rights
2.	Management	Risk	Protection
3.	Compliance	Notified bodies for certain high-risk AI systems	Self-compliance except in special cases
4.	Market	Monitoring and penalties	Guidance and penalties

15.15.7 AI Act and GDPR Application Matrix

NO.	AI ACT	GDPR
1.	Prohibited AI system (Art. 5)	Application to all systems in so far as the prohibited practices concern natural persons[430]

[428] AI Act, Rec. 46.

[429] Loi n° 78-17 du 6 janvier 1978 relative à l'informatique, aux fichiers et aux libertés, https://www.legifrance.gouv.fr/loda/id/JORFTEXT000000886460.

[430] Not all practices explicitly target natural persons. The references are as follows:
- (1) AI Act, Art. 5(1)(a), 'beyond a person's consciousness';
- (2) AI Act, Art. 5(1)(b), 'vulnerabilities of a natural person';
- (3) AI Act, Art. 5(1)(c), social score of 'natural persons';
- (4) AI Act, Art. 5(1)(d), predictive policing in relation to 'natural persons';
- (5) AI Act, Art. 5(1)(e), 'facial images' only;
- (6) AI Act, Art. 5(1)(f), 'emotions of a natural person';
- (7) AI Act, Art. 5(1)(g), biometric categorisation of 'natural persons';
- (8) AI Act, Art. 5(1)(h), real-time remote biometric identification necessary for (i) the search for 'victims'; (ii) the 'safety of natural persons'; (iii) the 'identification of a person' having committed a criminal offence (Annex II).

NO.	AI ACT	GDPR
2.	High-risk AI system (Art. 6(1) Section A of Annex I)	No personal data Exclusion
		With personal data Application
3.	High-risk AI system (Art. 6(1) Annex I Section B Exclusion)	No personal data Exclusion
		With personal data Application
4.	High-risk AI system (Art. 6(2) Annex III)	No personal data Exclusion
		With personal data Application
5.	Transparent AI system Interface with natural persons (Art. 50(1))	Application
6.	Transparent AI system Contents (Art. 50(2))	No personal data Exclusion
		With personal data Application
7.	Transparent AI system Recognition of emotions of natural persons (Art. 50(3))	Application
8.	Transparent AI system Biometric categorisation of natural persons (Art. 50(3))	Application
9.	AI system with a deep fake (Art. 50(4))	No personal data Exclusion
		With personal data Application
10.	General-purpose AI model (Art. 51)	No personal data Exclusion
		With personal data Application
11.	General-purpose AI system (Art. 3(66))	Depending on the type of AI

471. Or, by way of illustration of the above table:

	AI ACT	GDPR
AI Act	High-risk AI systems without personal data E.g. detection of events involving a more or less urgent level of maintenance for an industrial robot	Transparent AI system E.g. aggressive individuals at a counter to trigger protection from a reception agent.
GDPR	General-purpose AI models with personal data E.g. generative artificial intelligence models such as GPT[431] or Llama[432]	Low-risk AI system with personal data E.g. automatic filing of emails in a digital file

15.15.8 Autonomy

472. This key concept, which allows AI systems to be distinguished from other computer systems, is not subject to a specific legal framework or the definition of a specific legal personality.[433]

15.16. Liability

15.16.1 Introduction

473. The AI Act does not deal with liability obligations as such.[434]

474. This topic is organised as follow:

- contractual liability is governed by the rules of the Member States;
- non-contractual liability is subject to a proposal for a directive.[435]

475. The existence of AI systems' capacity to be autonomous and ability to learn in evolving environments have not been taken into account to justify a no-fault liability system.[436]

---

431 Open AI.

432 Meta.

433 Draft report with recommendations to the Commission on Civil Law Rules on Robotics (2015/2103(INL)): European Parliament, Mady Delvaux-Stehres, 31 May 2016, p. 12; A. Bensoussan and J. Bensoussan, 'IA robots et droit' ['AI robots and the law'], Théorie et pratique, Bruxelles, Bruylant/Larcier, July 2019, 632 p.

434 A. Bretel, 'Rapport sur la mise en pratique de la notion de responsabilité de la Déclaration de Montréal: automne 2023' ['Report on the implementation of the concept of responsibility in the Montreal Declaration: fall 2023'].

435 Proposal for a Directive of the European Parliament and of the Council on adapting non-contractual civil liability rules to artificial intelligence (AI Liability Directive), COM/2022/496 of 28 September 2022; Procedure 2022/0303(COD).

436 See below section 15.16 Liability.

15.16.2 Non-Contractual Liability

15.16.2.1 *Introduction*

476. The proposal for a directive introduces a specific fault mechanism based on the duty of AI systems to comply with the requirements of the AI Act.[437]

477. The aim is to build a compliance obligation for AI systems by means of a set of essential requirements that make it possible to restrict the autonomy of AI systems within a controlled and controllable area.

15.16.2.2 *The Regulation*

478. It is based on a dual obligation:

- the compliance with ex ante requirements;[438]
- the need for ex-post technical risk management.[439]

15.17. Trade Secrets

15.17.1 Introduction

479. Trade secrets are governed by a European directive[440]. In France, it has been transposed into national law through the Commercial Code.[441]

15.17.2 Reservations

480. The obligations of documentation, notification and transparency must not lead to the disclosure of trade secrets.

481. The same applies to the obligations to cooperate between authorities.

---

[437] A. Bensoussan and J. Bensoussan, 'Harmoniser les règles civiles de responsabilité en matière d'IA en Europe' ['Harmonising civil liability rules for AI in Europe'], *RLDI*, 2022, n° 197, pp. 43–46.

[438] Before the placing on the market or putting into service.

[439] Throughout the entire lifecycle of the AI system.

[440] Directive (EU) No 2016/943 of the European Parliament and of the Council of 8 June 2016 on the protection of undisclosed know-how and business information (trade secrets) against their unlawful acquisition, use and disclosure, [2016] OJ L157/1.

[441] French Law of 30 July 2018, Arts. L.151-1 ff. of the Commercial Code.

15.17.3 Modalities

482. The reservations concerning confidential business information and trade secrets are organised as follows:

NO.	THEME	SPECIFICATION	REFERENCE
1.	Intermediary in the AI value chain	Principle of reservations Organisation by contracts using the model terms developed by the AI Office	AIA, Art. 25
2.	Notified body	The personnel of notified bodies are subject to professional secrecy	AIA, Art. 31
3.	General-purpose AI model	Models with systemic risk must be published centrally, subject to protection of trade secrets	AIA, Art. 52
4.	Collaboration between providers of AI models and general-purpose AI systems	Protection of trade secrets The same applies to authorised representatives	AIA, Art. 53 AIA, Art. 54
5.	Confidentiality	As a principle, principle applicable to all regulatory authorities	AIA, Art. 78
6.	Fines and access to high-risk AI systems	Protection of trade secrets	AIA, Annex VII

16 COORDINATION OF REGULATIONS

16.1. Introduction

483. Insofar as the AI Act is a product-oriented horizontal regulation, numerous legislative texts must be coordinated to enable a product to comply with EU and national laws.

16.2. Guiding Principles

484. If there is more than one regulation, all compliance requirements must be met before the product in question is placed on the market.[442]

[442] AI Act, Rec. 46: '[…] the general rule is that more than one legal act of Union harmonisation legislation, such as Regulations (EU) 2017/745 (21) and (EU) 2017/746 (22) of the European Parliament and of the Council or Directive 2006/42/EC of the European Parliament and of the Council (23), may be applicable to one product, since the making available or putting into service can take place only when the product complies with all applicable Union harmonisation legislation.'

16.3. *Application*

485. In the presence of multiple regulations, compliance is determined according to the following elements:

NO.	THEME	SPECIFICATION
1.	Legal compliance strategy	Except in special cases, freely defined by operators at their own risk
2.	Flexibility	Possibility of pooling obligations with the same or similar purpose[443]
3.	Costs	Search for cost minimisation
4.	Administrative burden	Possibility of a reasonable approach so as not to multiply formalities with similar objectives
5.	Regulatory layers	Principle of limitation in order to minimise any restrictions on international trade

17 THE REGULATION AT A GLANCE

486. An at-a-glance view of the new Regulation is presented below, in alphabetical order:

NO.	THEME	SPECIFICATION	REFERENCE
1.	Actor concerned	Natural person Legal person	AIA, Art. 2
2.	Actor cited	Provider Authorised representative Importer Distributor Deployer Subject	AIA, Art. 2
3.	Activity	Development Testing Placing on the market Putting into service Use	AIA, Art. 2

443 AI Act, Rec. 64: 'That flexibility could mean, for example a decision by the provider to integrate a part of the necessary testing and reporting processes, information and documentation required under this Regulation into already existing documentation and procedures required under existing Union harmonisation legislation based on the New Legislative Framework and listed in an annex to this Regulation. This should not, in any way, undermine the obligation of the provider to comply with all the applicable requirements.'

NO.	THEME	SPECIFICATION	REFERENCE
4.	AI system (Typology)	Prohibited High-risk General-purpose Transparent	AIA, Art. 5 AIA, Art. 6 AIA, Art. 51 AIA, Art. 50
5.	AI technology	Symbolic AI Statistic AI	AIA, Rec. 12
6.	Authority	See Body	
7.	Biometric categorisation	Deduction of sensitive information (under GDPR) Prohibited AI system except for labelling or filtering and for law enforcement purposes	AIA, Art. 5(1)(g)
		Deduction of sensitive characteristics High-risk AI systems	AIA, Annex III (1)(b)
		Other use cases Transparent AI systems	AIA, Art. 50(3)
8.	Conformity	Prohibited AI systems Self-assessment	AIA, Art. 5
		High-risk AI system covered by Section A of Annex I Assessment by a notified authority	AIA, Art. 6(1)
		High-risk AI system covered by Section B of Annex I Exclusion	AIA, Art. 2(2)
		General-purpose AI systems According to the type of AI system	AIA, Art. 51
		Transparent AI systems Self-assessment	AIA, Art. 50
		General-purpose AI models Self-assessment	AIA, Art. 51
		Other systems Exclusion	AIA, Art. 2
9.	IA model	General-purpose AI models General-purpose AI models with systemic risk	AIA, Art. 51
10.	Impact assessment	Real-time remote biometric identification AI system in publicly accessible spaces for of law enforcement purposes	AIA, Art. 5(1)(h)
		Specific high-risk AI systems according to the type of actor	AIA, Art. 27 AIA, Annex III 5(b) AIA, Annex III 5(c)

NO.	THEME	SPECIFICATION	REFERENCE
11.	Legal value (Protection)	Fundamental rights Rule of law Democracy	AIA, Art. 1
12.	Market surveillance authority	Designation by Member States	AIA, Art. 70(1)
		High-risk AI system Section A of Annex I: Sectoral authority with the possibility of a derogation	AIA, Art. 74(3) E.g.: For harmonised legislation on medical devices, in France: the National Agency for Medicines and Health Products Safety (ANSM)
		High-risk AI system Financial institutions: Sectoral authority with the possibility of a derogation	AIA, Art. 74(6)
		High-risk AI system covered by Annex III point 1 (Biometrics) for law enforcement purposes, border management and justice and democracy, point 6 (Law enforcement), point 7 (Migration, asylum and border control management), point 8 (Administration of justice and democratic processes): Data protection supervisory authority or specific authorities	AIA, Art. 74(8)
		High-risk AI system covered by Annex III point 1 (Biometrics for purposes other than those referred to above), points 2, 3, 4 and 5: Authority to be designated	AIA, Art. 74(1)
		Transparent AI system: Authority to be designated	AIA, Art. 74(8)
		General-purpose AI model: European Commission and AI Office	AIA, Art. 88
		General-purpose AI system: According to the AI system	See the said AI system
13.	Penalty (AI model provider)	Failure to comply with obligations Failure to provide information Failure to comply with a measure requested (Art. 93) Failure to grant access to the European Commission for evaluation purposes (Art. 92) 3% of turnover or €15,000,000	AIA, Art. 101

NO.	THEME	SPECIFICATION	REFERENCE
14.	Penalty (AI system operator)	Prohibited practices 7% of turnover or €35,000,000	AIA, Art. 99
		Non-compliance[444] 3% of turnover or €15,000,000	AIA, Art. 99
		Failure to cooperate[445] 1% of turnover or €7,500,000	AIA, Art. 99
15.	Penalty (EU institutions, bodies, offices and agencies)	Prohibited practices €1,500,000	AIA, Art. 100
		Non-compliance €750,000	AIA, Art. 100
16.	Regulatory body (EU level)	European Commission AI Office AI Board Advisory forum Scientific panel of independent experts Committee (with the meaning of Regulation (EU) No 182/2011) with the European Commission	AIA, Arts. 64 ff.
17.	Regulatory body (Member State level)	Competition authority Data protection supervisory authority Market surveillance authority Notifying authority Notified body	AIA, Arts. 70 ff.
18.	Risk	Unacceptable Systemic High Reasonable or limited Low	AIA, Art. 2
19.	Sector	Public Private	AIA, Art. 1

[444] AI Act, Arts. 16, 22, 23, 24, 26; Obligations relating to notified bodies (Arts. 31, 33(1), (3) and (4)), Art. 50.

[445] Or incorrect information.

NO.	THEME	SPECIFICATION	REFERENCE
20.	Timeline	1 August 2024: Entry into force	AIA, Art. 113
		2 August 2024 Application	AIA, Art. 113
		2 February 2025: Subject matter	AIA, Art. 1
		2 February 2025: Scope	AIA, Art. 2
		2 February 2025: Definitions	AIA, Art. 3
		2 February 2025: AI literacy	AIA, Art. 4
		2 February 2025: Prohibited AI systems	AIA, Art. 5
		2 February 2025: Notifying authorities and notified bodies	AIA, Arts. 28–39
		2 August 2025: General-purpose AI models	AIA, Arts. 51–56
		2 August 2025: Governance	AIA, Arts. 64–70
		2 August 2025: Penalties	AIA, Arts. 99–101
		2 August 2025: Confidentiality	AIA, Art. 78
		2 August 2025: Designation of national competent authorities	AIA, Art. 70
		2 August 2026: General application with some exceptions	AIA, Art. 113
		2 August 2026: High-risk AI systems (Annex III)	AIA, Art. 6(2)
		2 August 2026: Transparent AI systems	AIA, Art. 50
		2 August 2026: General-purpose AI models (penalties)	AIA, Art. 101
		2 August 2026: General-purpose AI systems except as otherwise provided	AIA, Art. 51
		2 August 2027: High-risk AI systems (Annex I) and associated obligations	AIA, Art. 6(1)
		2 August 2027: General-purpose AI models placed on the market before 2 August 2025	AIA, Art. 111(3)
21.	Technical value (Protection)	Health Safety Environment	AIA, Art. 1
22.	Transparency (Obligation)	High-risk AI system	AIA, Art. 13
		AI system with reasonable risks	AIA, Art. 50

CHAPTER I
GENERAL PROVISIONS

487. **Key takeaways**: General provisions include:

- the subject matter of the Regulation (purposes and protected values of the EU);
- the scope (regulated actors and activities);
- the definitions (68 in total);
- AI literacy, i.e. the obligation for employers, providers and deployers to train their employees.

1 ARTICLE 1. SUBJECT MATTER

1. The purpose of this Regulation is to improve the functioning of the internal market and promote the uptake of human-centric and trustworthy artificial intelligence (AI), while ensuring a high level of protection of health, safety, fundamental rights enshrined in the Charter, including democracy, the rule of law and environmental protection, against the harmful effects of AI systems in the Union and supporting innovation.

2. This Regulation lays down:

(a) harmonised rules for the placing on the market, the putting into service, and the use of AI systems in the Union;

(b) prohibitions of certain AI practices;

(c) specific requirements for high-risk AI systems and obligations for operators of such systems;

(d) harmonised transparency rules for certain AI systems;

(e) harmonised rules for the placing on the market of general-purpose AI models;

(f) rules on market monitoring, market surveillance, governance and enforcement;

(g) measures to support innovation, with a particular focus on SMEs, including start-ups.

1.1. *Recitals*

488. **(1)** The purpose of this Regulation is to improve the functioning of the internal market by laying down a uniform legal framework in particular for the development, the placing on the market, the putting into service and the use of artificial intelligence systems (AI systems) in the Union, in accordance with Union values, to promote the uptake of human centric and trustworthy artificial intelligence (AI) while ensuring a high level of protection of health, safety, fundamental rights as enshrined in the Charter of Fundamental Rights of the European Union (the 'Charter'), including democracy, the rule of law and environmental protection, to protect against the harmful effects of AI systems in the Union, and to support innovation. This Regulation ensures the free movement, cross-border, of AI-based goods and services, thus preventing Member States from imposing restrictions on the development, marketing and use of AI systems, unless explicitly authorised by this Regulation.

489. **(8)** A Union legal framework laying down harmonised rules on AI is therefore needed to foster the development, use and uptake of AI in the internal market that at the same time meets a high level of protection of public interests, such as health and safety and the protection of fundamental rights, including democracy, the rule of law and environmental protection as recognised and protected by Union law. To achieve that objective, rules regulating the placing on the market, the putting into service and the use of certain AI systems should be laid down, thus ensuring the smooth functioning of the internal market and allowing those systems to benefit from the principle of free movement of goods and services. Those rules should be clear and robust in protecting fundamental rights, supportive of new innovative solutions, enabling a European ecosystem of public and private actors creating AI systems in line with Union values and unlocking the potential of the digital transformation across all regions of the Union. By laying down those rules as well as measures in support of innovation with a particular focus on small and medium enterprises (SMEs), including startups, this Regulation supports the objective of promoting the European human-centric approach to AI and being a global leader in the development of secure, trustworthy and ethical AI as stated by the European Council,[1] and it ensures the protection of ethical principles, as specifically requested by the European Parliament.[2]

490. **(9)** Harmonised rules applicable to the placing on the market, the putting into service and the use of high-risk AI systems should be laid down consistently

1 European Council, Special meeting of the European Council (1–2 October 2020) — Conclusions, EUCO 13/20, 2020, p. 6.

2 European Parliament resolution of 20 October 2020 with recommendations to the Commission on a framework of ethical aspects of artificial intelligence, robotics and related technologies, 2020/2012(INL).

with Regulation (EC) No 765/2008 of the European Parliament and of the Council,[3] Decision No 768/2008/EC of the European Parliament and of the Council[4] and Regulation (EU) 2019/1020 of the European Parliament and of the Council[5] (New Legislative Framework). The harmonised rules laid down in this Regulation should apply across sectors and, in line with the New Legislative Framework, should be without prejudice to existing Union law, in particular on data protection, consumer protection, fundamental rights, employment, and protection of workers, and product safety, to which this Regulation is complementary. As a consequence, all rights and remedies provided for by such Union law to consumers, and other persons on whom AI systems may have a negative impact, including as regards the compensation of possible damages pursuant to Council Directive 85/374/EEC[6] remain unaffected and fully applicable. Furthermore, in the context of employment and protection of workers, this Regulation should therefore not affect Union law on social policy and national labour law, in compliance with Union law, concerning employment and working conditions, including health and safety at work and the relationship between employers and workers. This Regulation should also not affect the exercise of fundamental rights as recognised in the Member States and at Union level, including the right or freedom to strike or to take other action covered by the specific industrial relations systems in Member States as well as the right to negotiate, to conclude and enforce collective agreements or to take collective action in accordance with national law. This Regulation should not affect the provisions aiming to improve working conditions in platform work laid down in a Directive of the European Parliament and of the Council on improving working conditions in platform work. Moreover, this Regulation aims to strengthen the effectiveness of such existing rights and remedies by establishing specific requirements and obligations, including in respect of the transparency, technical documentation and record-keeping of AI systems. Furthermore, the obligations placed on various operators involved in the AI value chain under this Regulation should apply without prejudice to national law, in compliance with Union law, having the effect of limiting the use of certain AI systems where such law falls outside the scope of this Regulation or pursues legitimate public

[3] Regulation (EC) No 765/2008 of the European Parliament and of the Council of 9 July 2008 setting out the requirements for accreditation and repealing Regulation (EEC) No 339/93, [2008] OJ L218/30.

[4] Decision No 768/2008/EC of the European Parliament and of the Council of 9 July 2008 on a common framework for the marketing of products, and repealing Council Decision 93/465/EEC, [2008] OJ L218/ 82.

[5] Regulation (EU) 2019/1020 of the European Parliament and of the Council of 20 June 2019 on market surveillance and compliance of products and amending Directive 2004/42/EC and Regulations (EC) No 765/2008 and (EU) No 305/2011, [2019] OJ L169/1.

[6] Council Directive 85/374/EEC of 25 July 1985 on the approximation of the laws, regulations and administrative provisions of the Member States concerning liability for defective products, [1985] OJ L210/29.

interest objectives other than those pursued by this Regulation. For example, national labour law and law on the protection of minors, namely persons below the age of 18, taking into account the UNCRC General Comment No 25 (2021) on children's rights in relation to the digital environment, insofar as they are not specific to AI systems and pursue other legitimate public interest objectives, should not be affected by this Regulation.

491. (144) In order to promote and protect innovation, the AI-on-demand platform, all relevant Union funding programmes and projects, such as Digital Europe Programme, Horizon Europe, implemented by the Commission and the Member States at Union or national level should, as appropriate, contribute to the achievement of the objectives of this Regulation.

492. (176) Since the objective of this Regulation, namely to improve the functioning of the internal market and to promote the uptake of human centric and trustworthy AI, while ensuring a high level of protection of health, safety, fundamental rights enshrined in the Charter, including democracy, the rule of law and environmental protection against harmful effects of AI systems in the Union and supporting innovation, cannot be sufficiently achieved by the Member States and can rather, by reason of the scale or effects of the action, be better achieved at Union level, the Union may adopt measures in accordance with the principle of subsidiarity as set out in Article 5 TEU. In accordance with the principle of proportionality as set out in that Article, this Regulation does not go beyond what is necessary in order to achieve that objective.

1.2. General Approach

1.2.1 Preamble

493. The subject matter of the Regulation concerns:

- the majority of AI systems;
- primarily, the operations related to the placing on the market, putting into service, and use of systems or associated outputs;
- the protection of natural or legal persons in both the public and private sectors;
- boosting innovation and employment.[7]

1.2.2 Guiding Principles

494. The idea is to strike a balance between innovation and regulation.

[7] AI Act, Rec. 2.

495. The regulation of AI systems aims to minimise risks and establish a high level of protection.

496. The Regulation must ensure a high level of protection in the following areas:

NO.	THEME	SPECIFICATION
1.	Technical area	Health[8] Security[9] Environment[10]
2.	Legal area	Fundamental rights[11] Rule of law[12] Democracy[13]

497. Notes:

- (1) The Treaty on the Functioning of the European Union (TFEU) explicitly provides that measures for the approximation of laws concerning health, safety, and environmental protection will take as a base a high level of protection.[14]
- (2) A high level of protection for fundamental rights, the rule of law, and democracy arises from the Regulation applicable to AI systems.

1.3. Guidance

498. The European Parliament had proposed to the European Commission the development of a framework for artificial intelligence based on the ethical aspects raised by these new technologies, in the following terms:

---

8 Health: Arts. 1, 3, 6, 7, 10, 13, 14, 36, 43, 46, 57.

9 Safety or security (public safety, safety of property and individuals): Arts. 1, 2, 6, 7, 9, 10, 13, 14, 15, 17, 25, 36, 39, 43, 46, 57, 58, 59.
- security-of-supply: Art. 17.
- product safety: Art. 2.
- national security: Art. 2.
- safety component: Arts. 3 (definition), 6, 25.
- cybersecurity: Arts. 13, 15 (Accuracy, robustness and cybersecurity), 31, 42, 55, 58.

10 Environmental protection: Arts. 1, 3(49) serious incident (d), 46, 59, 95, 112.

11 Fundamental rights: Arts. 1, 2, 3, 6, 7, 9, 10, 14, 27 (Fundamental rights impact assessment for high-risk AI systems), 28, 36, 39, 41, 43, 57, 58, 66, 70, 77 (Powers of authorities protecting fundamental rights), 79, 82, 86, 112.

12 Rule of law: Art. 1.

13 Democracy: Arts. 1 and 74.

14 TFEU, Art. 114(3) (version of 7 June 2016, updated on 1 March 2020); reference is also made to consumer protection: 'The Commission, in its proposals envisaged in paragraph 1 concerning health, safety, environmental protection and consumer protection, will take as a base a high level of protection, taking account in particular of any new development based on scientific facts. Within their respective powers, the European Parliament and the Council will also seek to achieve this objective.'

'The purpose of this Regulation is to establish a comprehensive and future-proof Union regulatory framework of ethical principles and legal obligations for the development, deployment and use of artificial intelligence, robotics and related technologies in the Union.'[15]

499. The final text acknowledges the necessity of establishing ethics as a principle without formulating it as a legal requirement per se.[16]

500. The scope of the Regulation aligns with the Montréal Declaration for a Responsible Development of Artificial Intelligence, which outlines the following ten principles:

- the well-being principle;
- the respect for autonomy principle;
- the principle of protection of privacy and intimacy;
- the solidarity principle;
- the democratic participation principle;
- the equity principle;
- the diversity inclusion principle;
- the caution principle;
- the responsibility principle;
- the sustainable development principle.[17]

[15] 'Framework of ethical aspects of artificial intelligence, robotics and related technologies', European Parliament resolution of 20 October 2020 with recommendations to the Commission on a framework of ethical aspects of artificial intelligence, robotics and related technologies (2020/2012(INL)): Annex B. Proposal for a Regulation of the European Parliament and of the Council on ethical principles for the development, deployment and use artificial intelligence, robotics and related technologies: Article 1: 'Purpose', [2021] OJ C404/96.

[16] References to this concept are limited to specific references in the Explanatory Memorandum and the Recitals. See in particular Rec. 5 below:
(5) At the same time, depending on the circumstances regarding its specific application, use, and level of technological development, AI may generate risks and cause harm to public interests and fundamental rights that are protected by Union law. Such harm might be material or immaterial, including physical, psychological, societal or economic harm.

[17] The writing of the Montréal Declaration for the responsible development of artificial intelligence is the result of the work of a multidisciplinary and inter-university scientific team that draws on a citizen consultation process and a dialogue with experts and stakeholders of AI development (2018) (Report Montréal Declaration for a Responsible Development of Artificial Intelligence) https://montrealdeclaration-responsibleai.com/.

1.4. *Find Out More*

1.4.1 Toolbox

501. C. de Ganay and D. Gillot, 'Pour une intelligence artificielle maîtrisée, utile et démystifiée' ['For controlled, useful and demystified artificial intelligence'], OPECST Report, no. 4594 *AN* (14th legislature), no. 464 *Sénat* (2016-2017), 15 March 2017.

502. European Commission, 'Communication: The 'Blue Guide' on the implementation of EU product rules 2022', [2022] OJ C247/1.

503. Numeum, 'Behind the codes and the data: A Practical Guide to Ethical AI', version 1, September 2021, 72 p., available in English and in French.

2 ARTICLE 2. SCOPE

1. This Regulation applies to:

(a) providers placing on the market or putting into service AI systems or placing on the market general-purpose AI models in the Union, irrespective of whether those providers are established or located within the Union or in a third country;

(b) deployers of AI systems that have their place of establishment or are located within the Union;

(c) providers and deployers of AI systems that have their place of establishment or are located in a third country, where the output produced by the AI system is used in the Union;

(d) importers and distributors of AI systems;

(e) product manufacturers placing on the market or putting into service an AI system together with their product and under their own name or trademark;

(f) authorised representatives of providers, which are not established in the Union;

(g) affected persons that are located in the Union.

2. For AI systems classified as high-risk AI systems in accordance with Article 6(1) related to products covered by the Union harmonisation legislation listed in Section B of Annex I, only Article 6(1), Articles 102 to 109 and Article 112 apply. Article 57 applies only in so far as the requirements for high-risk AI systems under this Regulation have been integrated in that Union harmonisation legislation.

3. This Regulation does not apply to areas outside the scope of Union law, and shall not, in any event, affect the competences of the Member States concerning national security, regardless of the type of entity entrusted by the Member States with carrying out tasks in relation to those competences.

This Regulation does not apply to AI systems where and in so far they are placed on the market, put into service, or used with or without modification exclusively for military, defence or national security purposes, regardless of the type of entity carrying out those activities.

This Regulation does not apply to AI systems which are not placed on the market or put into service in the Union, where the output is used in the Union exclusively for military, defence or national security purposes, regardless of the type of entity carrying out those activities.

4. This Regulation applies neither to public authorities in a third country nor to international organisations falling within the scope of this Regulation pursuant to paragraph 1, where those authorities or organisations use AI systems in the framework of international cooperation or agreements for law enforcement and judicial cooperation with the Union or with one or more Member States, provided that such a third country or international organisation provides adequate safeguards with respect to the protection of fundamental rights and freedoms of individuals.

5. This Regulation shall not affect the application of the provisions on the liability of providers of intermediary services as set out in Chapter II of Regulation (EU) 2022/2065.

6. This Regulation does not apply to AI systems or AI models, including their output, specifically developed and put into service for the sole purpose of scientific research and development.

7. Union law on the protection of personal data, privacy and the confidentiality of communications applies to personal data processed in connection with the rights and obligations laid down in this Regulation. This Regulation shall not affect Regulation (EU) 2016/679 or (EU) 2018/1725, or Directive 2002/58/EC or (EU) 2016/680, without prejudice to Article 10(5) and Article 59 of this Regulation.

8. This Regulation does not apply to any research, testing or development activity regarding AI systems or AI models prior to their being placed on the market or put into service. Such activities shall be conducted in accordance with applicable Union law. Testing in real world conditions shall not be covered by that exclusion.

9. This Regulation is without prejudice to the rules laid down by other Union legal acts related to consumer protection and product safety.

10. This Regulation does not apply to obligations of deployers who are natural persons using AI systems in the course of a purely personal non-professional activity.

11. This Regulation does not preclude the Union or Member States from maintaining or introducing laws, regulations or administrative provisions which are more favourable to workers in terms of protecting their rights in respect of the use of AI systems by employers, or from encouraging or allowing the application of collective agreements which are more favourable to workers.

12. This Regulation does not apply to AI systems released under free and open-source licences, unless they are placed on the market or put into service as high-risk AI systems or as an AI system that falls under Article 5 or 50.

2.1. Recitals

504. **(2)** This Regulation should be applied in accordance with the values of the Union enshrined as in the Charter, facilitating the protection of natural persons, undertakings, democracy, the rule of law and environmental protection, while boosting innovation and employment and making the Union a leader in the uptake of trustworthy AI.

505. **(3)** AI systems can be easily deployed in a large variety of sectors of the economy and many parts of society, including across borders, and can easily circulate throughout the Union. Certain Member States have already explored the adoption of national rules to ensure that AI is trustworthy and safe and is developed and used in accordance with fundamental rights obligations. Diverging national rules may lead to the fragmentation of the internal market and may decrease legal certainty for operators that develop, import or use AI systems. A consistent and high level of protection throughout the Union should therefore be ensured in order to achieve trustworthy AI, while divergences hampering the free circulation, innovation, deployment and the uptake of AI systems and related products and services within the internal market should be prevented by laying down uniform obligations for operators and guaranteeing the uniform protection of overriding reasons of public interest and of rights of persons throughout the internal market on the basis of Article 114[18] of the Treaty on the Functioning of the European Union (TFEU). To the extent that this Regulation contains specific rules on the protection of individuals with regard to the processing of personal data concerning restrictions of the use of AI systems for remote biometric identification for the purpose of law enforcement, of the use of AI systems for risk assessments of natural persons for the purpose of law enforcement and of the use of AI systems of biometric categorisation for the purpose of law enforcement, it is appropriate to base this Regulation, in so far as those specific rules are concerned, on Article 16 TFEU. In light of those specific rules and the recourse to Article 16 TFEU, it is appropriate to consult the European Data Protection Board.

506. **(4)** AI is a fast evolving family of technologies that contributes to a wide array of economic, environmental and societal benefits across the entire spectrum of industries and social activities. By improving prediction, optimising

[18] Article on the approximation of laws.

operations and resource allocation, and personalising digital solutions available for individuals and organisations, the use of AI can provide key competitive advantages to undertakings and support socially and environmentally beneficial outcomes, for example in healthcare, agriculture, food safety, education and training, media, sports, culture, infrastructure management, energy, transport and logistics, public services, security, justice, resource and energy efficiency, environmental monitoring, the conservation and restoration of biodiversity and ecosystems and climate change mitigation and adaptation.

507. **(5)** At the same time, depending on the circumstances regarding its specific application, use, and level of technological development, AI may generate risks and cause harm to public interests and fundamental rights that are protected by Union law. Such harm might be material or immaterial, including physical, psychological, societal or economic harm.

508. **(6)** Given the major impact that AI can have on society and the need to build trust, it is vital for AI and its regulatory framework to be developed in accordance with Union values as enshrined in Article 2 of the Treaty on European Union (TEU), the fundamental rights and freedoms enshrined in the Treaties and, pursuant to Article 6 TEU, the Charter. As a prerequisite, AI should be a human-centric technology. It should serve as a tool for people, with the ultimate aim of increasing human well-being.

509. **(11)** This Regulation should be without prejudice to the provisions regarding the liability of providers of intermediary services as set out in Regulation (EU) 2022/2065 of the European Parliament and of the Council.[19]

510. **(21)** In order to ensure a level playing field and an effective protection of rights and freedoms of individuals across the Union, the rules established by this Regulation should apply to providers of AI systems in a non-discriminatory manner, irrespective of whether they are established within the Union or in a third country, and to deployers of AI systems established within the Union.

511. **(22)** In light of their digital nature, certain AI systems should fall within the scope of this Regulation even when they are not placed on the market, put into service, or used in the Union. This is the case, for example, where an operator established in the Union contracts certain services to an operator established in a third country in relation to an activity to be performed by an AI system that would qualify as high-risk. In those circumstances, the AI system used in a third country by the operator could process data lawfully collected in and transferred from the Union, and provide to the contracting operator in the Union the output of that AI system resulting from that processing, without that AI system

[19] Regulation (EU) 2022/2065 of the European Parliament and of the Council of 19 October 2022 on a Single Market For Digital Services and amending Directive 2000/31/EC (Digital Services Act), [2022] OJ L277/1.

being placed on the market, put into service or used in the Union. To prevent the circumvention of this Regulation and to ensure an effective protection of natural persons located in the Union, this Regulation should also apply to providers and deployers of AI systems that are established in a third country, to the extent the output produced by those systems is intended to be used in the Union. Nonetheless, to take into account existing arrangements and special needs for future cooperation with foreign partners with whom information and evidence is exchanged, this Regulation should not apply to public authorities of a third country and international organisations when acting in the framework of cooperation or international agreements concluded at Union or national level for law enforcement and judicial cooperation with the Union or the Member States, provided that the relevant third country or international organisation provides adequate safeguards with respect to the protection of fundamental rights and freedoms of individuals. Where relevant, this may cover activities of entities entrusted by the third countries to carry out specific tasks in support of such law enforcement and judicial cooperation. Such framework for cooperation or agreements have been established bilaterally between Member States and third countries or between the European Union, Europol and other Union agencies and third countries and international organisations. The authorities competent for supervision of the law enforcement and judicial authorities under this Regulation should assess whether those frameworks for cooperation or international agreements include adequate safeguards with respect to the protection of fundamental rights and freedoms of individuals. Recipient national authorities and Union institutions, bodies, offices and agencies making use of such outputs in the Union remain accountable to ensure their use complies with Union law. When those international agreements are revised or new ones are concluded in the future, the contracting parties should make utmost efforts to align those agreements with the requirements of this Regulation.

512. **(23)** This Regulation should also apply to Union institutions, bodies, offices and agencies when acting as a provider or deployer of an AI system.

513. **(24)** If, and insofar as, AI systems are placed on the market, put into service, or used with or without modification of such systems for military, defence or national security purposes, those should be excluded from the scope of this Regulation regardless of which type of entity is carrying out those activities, such as whether it is a public or private entity. As regards military and defence purposes, such exclusion is justified both by Article 4(2) TEU and by the specificities of the Member States' and the common Union defence policy covered by Chapter 2 of Title V TEU that are subject to public international law, which is therefore the more appropriate legal framework for the regulation of AI systems in the context of the use of lethal force and other AI systems in the context of military and defence activities. As regards national security purposes, the exclusion is justified both by the fact that national security remains the sole responsibility of

Member States in accordance with Article 4(2) TEU and by the specific nature and operational needs of national security activities and specific national rules applicable to those activities. Nonetheless, if an AI system developed, placed on the market, put into service or used for military, defence or national security purposes is used outside those temporarily or permanently for other purposes, for example, civilian or humanitarian purposes, law enforcement or public security purposes, such a system would fall within the scope of this Regulation. In that case, the entity using the AI system for other than military, defence or national security purposes should ensure the compliance of the AI system with this Regulation, unless the system is already compliant with this Regulation. AI systems placed on the market or put into service for an excluded purpose, namely military, defence or national security, and one or more non-excluded purposes, such as civilian purposes or law enforcement, fall within the scope of this Regulation and providers of those systems should ensure compliance with this Regulation. In those cases, the fact that an AI system may fall within the scope of this Regulation should not affect the possibility of entities carrying out national security, defence and military activities, regardless of the type of entity carrying out those activities, to use AI systems for national security, military and defence purposes, the use of which is excluded from the scope of this Regulation. An AI system placed on the market for civilian or law enforcement purposes which is used with or without modification for military, defence or national security purposes should not fall within the scope of this Regulation, regardless of the type of entity carrying out those activities

514. **(40)** In accordance with Article 6a of Protocol No 21 on the position of the United Kingdom and Ireland in respect of the area of freedom, security and justice, as annexed to the TEU and to the TFEU, Ireland is not bound by the rules laid down in Article 5(1), first subparagraph, point (g), to the extent it applies to the use of biometric categorisation systems for activities in the field of police cooperation and judicial cooperation in criminal matters, Article 5(1), first subparagraph, point (d), to the extent it applies to the use of AI systems covered by that provision, Article 5(1), first subparagraph, point (h), Article 5(2) to (6) and Article 26(10) of this Regulation adopted on the basis of Article 16 TFEU which relate to the processing of personal data by the Member States when carrying out activities falling within the scope of Chapter 4 or Chapter 5 of Title V of Part Three of the TFEU, where Ireland is not bound by the rules governing the forms of judicial cooperation in criminal matters or police cooperation which require compliance with the provisions laid down on the basis of Article 16 TFEU.

515. **(41)** In accordance with Articles 2 and 2a of Protocol No 22 on the position of Denmark, annexed to the TEU and to the TFEU, Denmark is not bound by rules laid down in Article 5(1), first subparagraph, point (g), to the extent it applies to the use of biometric categorisation systems for activities in the field of police cooperation and judicial cooperation in criminal matters, Article 5(1), first subparagraph, point (d), to the extent it applies to the use of AI systems covered by that provision, Article 5(1), first subparagraph, point (h), (2) to (6) and Article 26(10) of this Regulation adopted on the basis of Article 16 TFEU, or subject to their application, which relate to the processing of personal data by the Member States when carrying out activities falling within the scope of Chapter 4 or Chapter 5 of Title V of Part Three of the TFEU.

516. **(49)** As regards high-risk AI systems that are safety components of products or systems, or which are themselves products or systems falling within the scope of Regulation (EC) No 300/2008 of the European Parliament and of the Council,[20] Regulation (EU) No 167/2013 of the European Parliament and of the Council,[21] Regulation (EU) No 168/2013 of the European Parliament and of the Council,[22] Directive 2014/90/EU of the European Parliament and of the Council,[23] Directive (EU) 2016/797 of the European Parliament and of the Council,[24] Regulation (EU) 2018/858 of the European Parliament and of the Council,[25] Regulation (EU) 2018/1139 of the European Parliament and of the Council,[26] and Regulation (EU) 2019/2144 of the European Parliament and of the Council,[27] it is appropriate

---

20 Regulation (EC) No 300/2008 of the European Parliament and of the Council of 11 March 2008 on common rules in the field of civil aviation security and repealing Regulation (EC) No 2320/2002, [2008] OJ L97/72.

21 Regulation (EU) No 167/2013 of the European Parliament and of the Council of 5 February 2013 on the approval and market surveillance of agricultural and forestry vehicles, [2013] OJ L60/1.

22 Regulation (EU) No 168/2013 of the European Parliament and of the Council of 15 January 2013 on the approval and market surveillance of two- or three-wheel vehicles and quadricycles, [2013] OJ L60/52.

23 Directive 2014/90/EU of the European Parliament and of the Council of 23 July 2014 on marine equipment and repealing Council Directive 96/98/EC, [2014] OJ L257/146.

24 Directive (EU) 2016/797 of the European Parliament and of the Council of 11 May 2016 on the interoperability of the rail system within the European Union, [2016] OJ L138/44.

25 Regulation (EU) 2018/858 of the European Parliament and of the Council of 30 May 2018 on the approval and market surveillance of motor vehicles and their trailers, and of systems, components and separate technical units intended for such vehicles, amending Regulations (EC) No 715/2007 and (EC) No 595/2009 and repealing Directive 2007/46/EC, [2018] OJ L151/1.

26 Regulation (EU) 2018/1139 of the European Parliament and of the Council of 4 July 2018 on common rules in the field of civil aviation and establishing a European Union Aviation Safety Agency, and amending Regulations (EC) No 2111/2005, (EC) No 1008/2008, (EU) No 996/2010, (EU) No 376/2014 and Directives 2014/30/EU and 2014/53/EU of the European Parliament and of the Council, and repealing Regulations (EC) No 552/2004 and (EC) No 216/2008 of the European Parliament and of the Council and Council Regulation (EEC) No 3922/91, [2018] OJ L212/1.

27 Regulation (EU) 2019/2144 of the European Parliament and of the Council of 27 November 2019 on type-approval requirements for motor vehicles and their trailers, and systems, components and separate technical units intended for such vehicles, as regards their general safety and the protection of vehicle occupants and vulnerable road users, amending Regulation (EU) 2018/858 of the European Parliament and of the Council and repealing Regulations (EC) No 78/2009, (EC) No 79/2009 and (EC) No 661/2009 of the European Parliament and of the Council and Commission Regulations (EC) No 631/2009, (EU) No 406/2010,

to amend those acts to ensure that the Commission takes into account, on the basis of the technical and regulatory specificities of each sector, and without interfering with existing governance, conformity assessment and enforcement mechanisms and authorities established therein, the mandatory requirements for high-risk AI systems laid down in this Regulation when adopting any relevant delegated or implementing acts on the basis of those acts.

517. **(56)** The deployment of AI systems in education is important to promote high-quality digital education and training and to allow all learners and teachers to acquire and share the necessary digital skills and competences, including media literacy, and critical thinking, to take an active part in the economy, society, and in democratic processes. However, AI systems used in education or vocational training, in particular for determining access or admission, for assigning persons to educational and vocational training institutions or programmes at all levels, for evaluating learning outcomes of persons, for assessing the appropriate level of education for an individual and materially influencing the level of education and training that individuals will receive or will be able to access or for monitoring and detecting prohibited behaviour of students during tests should be classified as high-risk AI systems, since they may determine the educational and professional course of a person's life and therefore may affect that person's ability to secure a livelihood. When improperly designed and used, such systems may be particularly intrusive and may violate the right to education and training as well as the right not to be discriminated against and perpetuate historical patterns of discrimination, for example against women, certain age groups, persons with disabilities, or persons of certain racial or ethnic origins or sexual orientation.

518. **(57)** AI systems used in employment, workers management and access to self-employment, in particular for the recruitment and selection of persons, for making decisions affecting terms of the work-related relationship, promotion and termination of work-related contractual relationships, for allocating tasks on the basis of individual behaviour, personal traits or characteristics and for monitoring or evaluation of persons in work-related contractual relationships, should also be classified as high-risk, since those systems may have an appreciable impact on future career prospects, livelihoods of those persons and workers' rights. Relevant work-related contractual relationships should, in a meaningful manner, involve employees and persons providing services through platforms as referred to in the Commission Work Programme 2021. Throughout the recruitment process and in the evaluation, promotion, or retention of persons in work-related contractual relationships, such systems may perpetuate historical

(EU) No 672/2010, (EU) No 1003/2010, (EU) No 1005/2010, (EU) No 1008/2010, (EU) No 1009/2010, (EU) No 19/2011, (EU) No 109/2011, (EU) No 458/2011, (EU) No 65/2012, (EU) No 130/2012, (EU) No 347/2012, (EU) No 351/2012, (EU) No 1230/2012 and (EU) 2015/166, [2019] OJ L325/1.

patterns of discrimination, for example against women, certain age groups, persons with disabilities, or persons of certain racial or ethnic origins or sexual orientation. AI systems used to monitor the performance and behaviour of such persons may also undermine their fundamental rights to data protection and privacy.

519. **(58)** Another area in which the use of AI systems deserves special consideration is the access to and enjoyment of certain essential private and public services and benefits necessary for people to fully participate in society or to improve one's standard of living. In particular, natural persons applying for or receiving essential public assistance benefits and services from public authorities namely healthcare services, social security benefits, social services providing protection in cases such as maternity, illness, industrial accidents, dependency or old age and loss of employment and social and housing assistance, are typically dependent on those benefits and services and in a vulnerable position in relation to the responsible authorities. If AI systems are used for determining whether such benefits and services should be granted, denied, reduced, revoked or reclaimed by authorities, including whether beneficiaries are legitimately entitled to such benefits or services, those systems may have a significant impact on persons' livelihood and may infringe their fundamental rights, such as the right to social protection, non-discrimination, human dignity or an effective remedy and should therefore be classified as high-risk. Nonetheless, this Regulation should not hamper the development and use of innovative approaches in the public administration, which would stand to benefit from a wider use of compliant and safe AI systems, provided that those systems do not entail a high risk to legal and natural persons. In addition, AI systems used to evaluate the credit score or creditworthiness of natural persons should be classified as high-risk AI systems, since they determine those persons' access to financial resources or essential services such as housing, electricity, and telecommunication services. AI systems used for those purposes may lead to discrimination between persons or groups and may perpetuate historical patterns of discrimination, such as that based on racial or ethnic origins, gender, disabilities, age or sexual orientation, or may create new forms of discriminatory impacts. However, AI systems provided for by Union law for the purpose of detecting fraud in the offering of financial services and for prudential purposes to calculate credit institutions' and insurance undertakings' capital requirements should not be considered to be high-risk under this Regulation. Moreover, AI systems intended to be used for risk assessment and pricing in relation to natural persons for health and life insurance can also have a significant impact on persons' livelihood and if not duly designed, developed and used, can infringe their fundamental rights and can lead to serious consequences for people's life and health, including financial exclusion and discrimination. Finally, AI systems used to evaluate and classify emergency calls by natural persons or to dispatch or establish priority in the dispatching of emergency first response services, including by police, firefighters and medical aid, as well as of emergency healthcare patient triage systems, should also be classified as high-risk since they make decisions in very critical situations for the life and health of persons and their property.

520. (69) The right to privacy and to protection of personal data must be guaranteed throughout the entire lifecycle of the AI system. In this regard, the principles of data minimisation and data protection by design and by default, as set out in Union data protection law, are applicable when personal data are processed. Measures taken by providers to ensure compliance with those principles may include not only anonymisation and encryption, but also the use of technology that permits algorithms to be brought to the data and allows training of AI systems without the transmission between parties or copying of the raw or structured data themselves, without prejudice to the requirements on data governance provided for in this Regulation.

2.2. General Approach

521. The scope of the Regulation is divided into two categories:

- category 1: Application based on criteria;
- category 2: Exclusion based on a list of products and services.

2.3. Application Based on Criteria

522. The application criteria pertain to:

- five categories of main stakeholders;
- four types of activities:

NO.	ACTORS	PLACING ON THE MARKET	PUTTING INTO SERVICE	USE	OUTPUTS
1.	Provider	X	X	-	-
2.	Authorised representative	X	X	-	-
3.	Importer	X	X	-	-
4.	Distributor	-	X	-	-
5.	Deployer	-	X	X	X

523. Notes:

- (1) This scope applies to all AI systems.
- (2) The outputs are those of AI systems produced within the EU or originating from a third country outside the EU.

2.4. *Exclusions Based on a List*

2.4.1 Introduction

524. This list includes:

- areas that are excluded under the primary law of the EU;
- sectoral activities that have already undergone a harmonisation process according to specific standards.

2.4.2 Publicly Accessible Spaces

525. These refer to the following activities:

NO.	THEME	REFERENCE
1.	Defence activity[28]	AIA, Art. 2(3)
2.	Military activity[29]	AIA, Art. 2(3)
3.	Mixed civil activities with excluded activities as defined in the Regulation	AIA, Rec. 24
4.	National security[30]	AIA, Art. 2(3)

2.4.3 Sectoral Activities

526. These refer to the following activities:

NO.	THEME	SPECIFICATION
1.	Personal activity	Natural person for purely personal, non-professional activities. Note: • (1) This exclusion concerns AI systems but not AI models[31] or general-purpose AI systems[32]

28 Public or private actor.

29 Public or private actor.

30 Public or private actor.

31 AI Act, Art. 50.

32 Where an obligation is applied to a general-purpose AI system, it is explicitly stated in the Regulation, e.g., Article 50(2) on content creation.

NO.	THEME	SPECIFICATION
2.	Design (phase)	Research, testing or development activity regarding AI systems and before the placing on the market or putting into service Note: • (1) This derogation does not apply to testing in real-world conditions[33]
3.	International cooperation	Specific international agreements: • law enforcement cooperation • judicial cooperation
4.	Research	AI systems and AI models developed and put into service for such purposes but not placed on the market This exclusion includes: • research purposes • scientific development • associated outputs
5.	AI systems under free and open-source licence	Specific derogations applicable to these systems

2.4.4 Additions to the Regulation

527. Member States may supplement the Regulation in the following areas:

NO.	AREA	SPECIFICATION	STATUS
1.	Employees	User of AI systems	Higher protection
2.	Biometrics	Real-time identification in publicly accessible spaces	More restrictive derogations

2.4.5 Specific Areas

528. The following areas are excluded:

NO.	REGULATION	COMMENT
1.	Regulation (EC) No 300/2008	Regulation (EC) No 300/2008 of the European Parliament and of the Council of 11 March 2008 on common rules in the field of civil aviation security and repealing Regulation (EC) No 2320/2002

[33] AI Act, Art. 60.

NO.	REGULATION	COMMENT
2.	Regulation (EU) No 168/2013	Regulation (EU) No 168/2013 of the European Parliament and of the Council of 15 January 2013 on the approval and market surveillance of two- or three-wheel vehicles and quadricycles
3.	Regulation (EU) No 167/2013	Regulation (EU) No 167/2013 of the European Parliament and of the Council of 5 February 2013 on the approval and market surveillance of agricultural and forestry vehicles
4.	Directive 2014/90/EU	Directive 2014/90/EU of the European Parliament and of the Council of 23 July 2014 on marine equipment and repealing Council Directive 96/98/EC
5.	Directive (EU) 2016/797	Directive (EU) 2016/797 of the European Parliament and of the Council of 11 May 2016 on the interoperability of the rail system within the European Union
6.	Regulation (EU) 2018/858	Regulation (EU) 2018/858 of the European Parliament and of the Council of 30 May 2018 on the approval and market surveillance of motor vehicles and their trailers, and of systems, components and separate technical units intended for such vehicles, amending Regulations (EC) No 715/2007 and (EC) No 595/2009 and repealing Directive 2007/46/EC
7.	Regulation (EU) 2018/1139	Regulation (EU) 2018/1139 of the European Parliament and of the Council of 4 July 2018 on common rules in the field of civil aviation and establishing a European Union Aviation Safety Agency, and amending Regulations (EC) No 2111/2005, (EC) No 1008/2008, (EU) No 996/2010, (EU) No 376/2014 and Directives 2014/30/EU and 2014/53/EU of the European Parliament and of the Council, and repealing Regulations (EC) No 552/2004 and (EC) No 216/2008 of the European Parliament and of the Council and Council Regulation (EEC) No 3922/91
8.	Regulation (EU) 2019/2144	Regulation (EU) 2019/2144 of the European Parliament and of the Council of 27 November 2019 on type-approval requirements for motor vehicles and their trailers, and systems, components and separate technical units intended for such vehicles, as regards their general safety and the protection of vehicle occupants and vulnerable road users, amending Regulation (EU) 2018/858 of the European Parliament and of the Council and repealing Regulations (EC) No 78/2009, (EC) No 79/2009 and (EC) No 661/2009 of the European Parliament and of the Council and Commission Regulations (EC) No 631/2009, (EU) No 406/2010, (EU) No 672/2010, (EU) No 1003/2010, (EU) No 1005/2010, (EU) No 1008/2010, (EU) No 1009/2010, (EU) No 19/2011, (EU) No 109/2011, (EU) No 458/2011, (EU) No 65/2012, (EU) No 130/2012, (EU) No 347/2012, (EU) No 351/2012, (EU) No 1230/2012 and (EU) 2015/166

529. Notes:

- (1) This list only covers the high-risk systems referred to in Section B of Annex I;
- (2) These regulations must be updated to include AI systems.[34]

2.5. Relationship with the DSA

2.5.1 Introduction

530. A wide range of digital services implement AI technologies.

531. Sectoral regulations may present contradictions with a horizontal regulation such as the AI Act.

2.5.2 Guiding Principles

532. Explicitly, the AI Act does change the liability mechanism established by the Digital Services Regulation (DSA).[35]

533. Under the DSA, such liability mechanism is in particular set out as follows:

- '1. Where an information society service is provided that consists of the storage of information provided by a recipient of the service, the service provider shall not be liable for the information stored at the request of a recipient of the service, on condition that the provider:

(a) does not have actual knowledge of illegal activity or illegal content and, as regards claims for damages, is not aware of facts or circumstances from which the illegal activity or illegal content is apparent; or

(b) upon obtaining such knowledge or awareness, acts expeditiously to remove or to disable access to the illegal content.'

534. In any case, all obligations related to AI systems or models remain applicable notwithstanding the liability mechanism applicable to the aforementioned platforms.

---

[34] AI Act, Art. 84.

[35] Regulation (EU) 2022/2065 of 19 October 2022.

2.6. *Exclusion of Research*

2.6.1 Introduction

535. To strike a balance between innovation and regulation, the AI Act does not apply to scientific research and development activities.[36]

2.6.2 Definition

536. The field of scientific research and development encompasses:

- a scientific activity;
- fundamental or applied research;
- the public and private sectors;
- a field that is new in terms of knowledge;
- a purpose limited to research and development.

2.6.3 Guiding Principles

537. The exclusion concerns:

- AI systems;
- AI models;
- associated outputs.

538. Notes:

- (1) Over and above the concern not to hamper innovation in the field of AI, this exclusion echoes the principle according to which: 'The arts and scientific research shall be free of constraint.'[37]

2.6.4 Modalities

539. They are as follows:

NO.	MODALITIES	SPECIFICATION
1.	Design	Exclusion[38]
2.	Putting into service	For the sole purpose of research and development: exclusion[39]

36 AI Act, Art. 2(6).
37 Charter of Fundamental Rights of the European Union Art. 13.
38 AI Act, Art. 2(6).
39 Ibid.

NO.	MODALITIES	SPECIFICATION
3.	Internal testing	Exclusion
4.	Testing in real-world conditions	Application of the AIA[40]
5.	Placing on the market	Application of the AIA[41]

2.6.5 Research and Development Phase

540. Similarly, the AI Act does not apply to the research and development phase of AI systems or models prior to their being placed on the market or put into service.[42]

2.6.6 Personal Activities

541. The AI Act does not apply to personal activities as follows:[43]

NO.	FEATURE	SPECIFICATION
1.	Actor	Natural person
2.	Title	Deployer
3.	Use	Purely personal
4.	AI technology	AI system
5.	Purpose	Non-professional

542. Notes:

- (1) The derogation does not apply to general-purpose AI systems or general-purpose AI models.
- (2) Provider activities are subject to the AI Act.

40 Ibid.
41 Ibid., *a contrario*.
42 AI Act, Art. 2(8); however, testing in real-world conditions remains subject to the requirements of the AI Act.
43 AI Act, Art. 2(10).

2.7. *Open Source*

2.7.1 Introduction

543. In order to foster innovation and pool knowledge in relation to AI technologies, it is possible to derogate from the AI Act requirements by making AI systems available to all.

2.7.2 Guiding Principles

544. The derogation concerns free and open-source licences.

2.7.3 Modalities

545. They are as follows:

NO.	CONDITION	SPECIFICATION
1.	Technology	AI systems, and not general-purpose AI models
2.	Free and open-source licence	All types of licences (e.g. Apache licence, MIT licence, GNU GPL etc.)
3.	Exclusion	Prohibited systems (AIA, Art. 5) High-risk AI systems (AIA, Art. 6) AI systems subject to a transparency obligation (AIA, Art. 50)

546. Notes:

- (1) General-purpose AI models are not covered by this exclusion.
- (2) The use of free and open-source licences is taken into account for general-purpose AI models in the form of specific derogations.[44]

3 ARTICLE 3. DEFINITIONS

For the purposes of this Regulation, the following definitions apply:

(1) 'AI system' means a machine-based system that is designed to operate with varying levels of autonomy and that may exhibit adaptiveness after deployment, and that, for explicit or implicit objectives, infers, from the input it receives, how to generate outputs such as predictions, content, recommendations, or decisions that can influence physical or virtual environments;

---

44 AI Act, Art. 51 ff.

(2) 'risk' means the combination of the probability of an occurrence of harm and the severity of that harm;

(3) 'provider' means a natural or legal person, public authority, agency or other body that develops an AI system or a general-purpose AI model or that has an AI system or a general-purpose AI model developed and places it on the market or puts the AI system into service under its own name or trademark, whether for payment or free of charge;

(4) 'deployer' means a natural or legal person, public authority, agency or other body using an AI system under its authority except where the AI system is used in the course of a personal non-professional activity;

(5) 'authorised representative' means a natural or legal person located or established in the Union who has received and accepted a written mandate from a provider of an AI system or a general-purpose AI model to, respectively, perform and carry out on its behalf the obligations and procedures established by this Regulation;

(6) 'importer' means a natural or legal person located or established in the Union that places on the market an AI system that bears the name or trademark of a natural or legal person established in a third country;

(7) 'distributor' means a natural or legal person in the supply chain, other than the provider or the importer, that makes an AI system available on the Union market;

(8) 'operator' means a provider, product manufacturer, deployer, authorised representative, importer or distributor;

(9) 'placing on the market' means the first making available of an AI system or a general-purpose AI model on the Union market;

(10) 'making available on the market' means the supply of an AI system or a general-purpose AI model for distribution or use on the Union market in the course of a commercial activity, whether in return for payment or free of charge;

(11) 'putting into service' means the supply of an AI system for first use directly to the deployer or for own use in the Union for its intended purpose;

(12) 'intended purpose' means the use for which an AI system is intended by the provider, including the specific context and conditions of use, as specified in the information supplied by the provider in the instructions for use, promotional or sales materials and statements, as well as in the technical documentation;

(13) 'reasonably foreseeable misuse' means the use of an AI system in a way that is not in accordance with its intended purpose, but which may result from reasonably foreseeable human behaviour or interaction with other systems, including other AI systems;

(14) 'safety component' means a component of a product or of an AI system which fulfils a safety function for that product or AI system, or the failure or malfunctioning of which endangers the health and safety of persons or property;

(15) 'instructions for use' means the information provided by the provider to inform the deployer of, in particular, an AI system's intended purpose and proper use;

(16) 'recall of an AI system' means any measure aiming to achieve the return to the provider or taking out of service or disabling the use of an AI system made available to deployers;

(17) 'withdrawal of an AI system' means any measure aiming to prevent an AI system in the supply chain being made available on the market;

(18) 'performance of an AI system' means the ability of an AI system to achieve its intended purpose;

(19) 'notifying authority' means the national authority responsible for setting up and carrying out the necessary procedures for the assessment, designation and notification of conformity assessment bodies and for their monitoring;

(20) 'conformity assessment' means the process of demonstrating whether the requirements set out in Chapter III, Section 2 relating to a high-risk AI system have been fulfilled;

(21) 'conformity assessment body' means a body that performs third-party conformity assessment activities, including testing, certification and inspection;

(22) 'notified body' means a conformity assessment body notified in accordance with this Regulation and other relevant Union harmonisation legislation;

(23) 'substantial modification' means a change to an AI system after its placing on the market or putting into service which is not foreseen or planned in the initial conformity assessment carried out by the provider and as a result of which the compliance of the AI system with the requirements set out in Chapter III, Section 2 is affected or results in a modification to the intended purpose for which the AI system has been assessed;

(24) 'CE marking' means a marking by which a provider indicates that an AI system is in conformity with the requirements set out in Chapter III, Section 2 and other applicable Union harmonisation legislation providing for its affixing;

(25) 'post-market monitoring system' means all activities carried out by providers of AI systems to collect and review experience gained from the use of AI systems they place on the market or put into service for the purpose of identifying any need to immediately apply any necessary corrective or preventive actions;

(26) 'market surveillance authority' means the national authority carrying out the activities and taking the measures pursuant to Regulation (EU) 2019/1020;

(27) 'harmonised standard' means a harmonised standard as defined in Article 2(1), point (c), of Regulation (EU) No 1025/2012;

(28) **'common specification'** means a set of technical specifications as defined in Article 2, point (4) of Regulation (EU) No 1025/2012, providing means to comply with certain requirements established under this Regulation;

(29) **'training data'** means data used for training an AI system through fitting its learnable parameters;

(30) **'validation data'** means data used for providing an evaluation of the trained AI system and for tuning its non-learnable parameters and its learning process in order, inter alia, to prevent underfitting or overfitting;

(31) **'validation data set'** means a separate data set or part of the training data set, either as a fixed or variable split;

(32) **'testing data'** means data used for providing an independent evaluation of the AI system in order to confirm the expected performance of that system before its placing on the market or putting into service;

(33) **'input data'** means data provided to or directly acquired by an AI system on the basis of which the system produces an output;

(34) **'biometric data'** means personal data resulting from specific technical processing relating to the physical, physiological or behavioural characteristics of a natural person, such as facial images or dactyloscopic data;

(35) **'biometric identification'** means the automated recognition of physical, physiological, behavioural, or psychological human features for the purpose of establishing the identity of a natural person by comparing biometric data of that individual to biometric data of individuals stored in a database;

(36) **'biometric verification'** means the automated, one-to-one verification, including authentication, of the identity of natural persons by comparing their biometric data to previously provided biometric data;

(37) **'special categories of personal data'** means the categories of personal data referred to in Article 9(1) of Regulation (EU) 2016/679, Article 10 of Directive (EU) 2016/680 and Article 10(1) of Regulation (EU) 2018/1725;

(38) **'sensitive operational data'** means operational data related to activities of prevention, detection, investigation or prosecution of criminal offences, the disclosure of which could jeopardise the integrity of criminal proceedings;

(39) **'emotion recognition system'** means an AI system for the purpose of identifying or inferring emotions or intentions of natural persons on the basis of their biometric data;

(40) **'biometric categorisation system'** means an AI system for the purpose of assigning natural persons to specific categories on the basis of their biometric data, unless it is ancillary to another commercial service and strictly necessary for objective technical reasons;

(41) **'remote biometric identification system'** means an AI system for the purpose of identifying natural persons, without their active involvement, typically at a distance through the comparison of a person's biometric data with the biometric data contained in a reference database;

(42) 'real-time remote biometric identification system' means a remote biometric identification system, whereby the capturing of biometric data, the comparison and the identification all occur without a significant delay, comprising not only instant identification, but also limited short delays in order to avoid circumvention;

(43) 'post-remote biometric identification system' means a remote biometric identification system other than a real-time remote biometric identification system;

(44) 'publicly accessible space' means any publicly or privately owned physical place accessible to an undetermined number of natural persons, regardless of whether certain conditions for access may apply, and regardless of the potential capacity restrictions;

(45) 'law enforcement authority' means:

(a) any public authority competent for the prevention, investigation, detection or prosecution of criminal offences or the execution of criminal penalties, including the safeguarding against and the prevention of threats to public security; or

(b) any other body or entity entrusted by Member State law to exercise public authority and public powers for the purposes of the prevention, investigation, detection or prosecution of criminal offences or the execution of criminal penalties, including the safeguarding against and the prevention of threats to public security;

(46) 'law enforcement' means activities carried out by law enforcement authorities or on their behalf for the prevention, investigation, detection or prosecution of criminal offences or the execution of criminal penalties, including safeguarding against and preventing threats to public security;

(47) 'AI Office' means the Commission's function of contributing to the implementation, monitoring and supervision of AI systems and general-purpose AI models, and AI governance, provided for in Commission Decision of 24 January 2024; references in this Regulation to the AI Office shall be construed as references to the Commission;

(48) 'national competent authority' means a notifying authority or a market surveillance authority; as regards AI systems put into service or used by Union institutions, agencies, offices and bodies, references to national competent authorities or market surveillance authorities in this Regulation shall be construed as references to the European Data Protection Supervisor;

(49) 'serious incident' means an incident or malfunctioning of an AI system that directly or indirectly leads to any of the following:

(a) the death of a person, or serious harm to a person's health;

(b) a serious and irreversible disruption of the management or operation of critical infrastructure;

(c) the infringement of obligations under Union law intended to protect fundamental rights;

(d) serious harm to property or the environment;

(50) 'personal data' means personal data as defined in Article 4, point (1), of Regulation (EU) 2016/679;

(51) 'non-personal data' means data other than personal data as defined in Article 4, point (1), of Regulation (EU) 2016/679;

(52) 'profiling' means profiling as defined in Article 4, point (4), of Regulation (EU) 2016/679;

(53) 'real-world testing plan' means a document that describes the objectives, methodology, geographical, population and temporal scope, monitoring, organisation and conduct of testing in real-world conditions;

(54) 'sandbox plan' means a document agreed between the participating provider and the competent authority describing the objectives, conditions, timeframe, methodology and requirements for the activities carried out within the sandbox;

(55) 'AI regulatory sandbox' means a controlled framework set up by a competent authority which offers providers or prospective providers of AI systems the possibility to develop, train, validate and test, where appropriate in real-world conditions, an innovative AI system, pursuant to a sandbox plan for a limited time under regulatory supervision;

(56) 'AI literacy' means skills, knowledge and understanding that allow providers, deployers and affected persons, taking into account their respective rights and obligations in the context of this Regulation, to make an informed deployment of AI systems, as well as to gain awareness about the opportunities and risks of AI and possible harm it can cause;

(57) 'testing in real-world conditions' means the temporary testing of an AI system for its intended purpose in real-world conditions outside a laboratory or otherwise simulated environment, with a view to gathering reliable and robust data and to assessing and verifying the conformity of the AI system with the requirements of this Regulation and it does not qualify as placing the AI system on the market or putting it into service within the meaning of this Regulation, provided that all the conditions laid down in Article 57 or 60 are fulfilled;

(58) 'subject', for the purpose of real-world testing, means a natural person who participates in testing in real-world conditions;

(59) 'informed consent' means a subject's freely given, specific, unambiguous and voluntary expression of his or her willingness to participate in a particular testing in real-world conditions, after having been informed of all aspects of the testing that are relevant to the subject's decision to participate;

(60) 'deep fake' means AI-generated or manipulated image, audio or video content that resembles existing persons, objects, places, entities or events and would falsely appear to a person to be authentic or truthful;

(61) 'widespread infringement' means any act or omission contrary to Union law protecting the interest of individuals, which:

(a) has harmed or is likely to harm the collective interests of individuals residing in at least two Member States other than the Member State in which:

(i) the act or omission originated or took place;

(ii) the provider concerned, or, where applicable, its authorised representative is located or established; or

(iii) the deployer is established, when the infringement is committed by the deployer;

(b) has caused, causes or is likely to cause harm to the collective interests of individuals and has common features, including the same unlawful practice or the same interest being infringed, and is occurring concurrently, committed by the same operator, in at least three Member States;

(62) 'critical infrastructure' means critical infrastructure as defined in Article 2, point (4), of Directive (EU) 2022/2557;

(63) 'general-purpose AI model' means an AI model, including where such an AI model is trained with a large amount of data using self-supervision at scale, that displays significant generality and is capable of competently performing a wide range of distinct tasks regardless of the way the model is placed on the market and that can be integrated into a variety of downstream systems or applications, except AI models that are used for research, development or prototyping activities before they are placed on the market;

(64) 'high-impact capabilities' means capabilities that match or exceed the capabilities recorded in the most advanced general-purpose AI models;

(65) 'systemic risk' means a risk that is specific to the high-impact capabilities of general-purpose AI models, having a significant impact on the Union market due to their reach, or due to actual or reasonably foreseeable negative effects on public health, safety, public security, fundamental rights, or the society as a whole, that can be propagated at scale across the value chain;

(66) 'general-purpose AI system' means an AI system which is based on a general-purpose AI model and which has the capability to serve a variety of purposes, both for direct use as well as for integration in other AI systems;

(67) 'floating-point operation' means any mathematical operation or assignment involving floating-point numbers, which are a subset of the real numbers typically represented on computers by an integer of fixed precision scaled by an integer exponent of a fixed base;

(68) 'downstream provider' means a provider of an AI system, including a general-purpose AI system, which integrates an AI model, regardless of whether the AI model is provided by themselves and vertically integrated or provided by another entity based on contractual relations.

3.1. Recitals

547. **(12)** The notion of 'AI system' in this Regulation should be clearly defined and should be closely aligned with the work of international organisations working on AI to ensure legal certainty, facilitate international convergence and wide acceptance, while providing the flexibility to accommodate the rapid technological developments in this field. Moreover, the definition should be based on key characteristics of AI systems that distinguish it from simpler traditional software systems or programming approaches and should not cover systems that are based on the rules defined solely by natural persons to automatically execute operations. A key characteristic of AI systems is their capability to infer. This capability to infer refers to the process of obtaining the outputs, such as predictions, content, recommendations, or decisions, which can influence physical and virtual environments, and to a capability of AI systems to derive models or algorithms, or both, from inputs or data. The techniques that enable inference while building an AI system include machine learning approaches that learn from data how to achieve certain objectives, and logic- and knowledge-based approaches that infer from encoded knowledge or symbolic representation of the task to be solved. The capacity of an AI system to infer transcends basic data processing by enabling learning, reasoning or modelling. The term 'machine-based' refers to the fact that AI systems run on machines. The reference to explicit or implicit objectives underscores that AI systems can operate according to explicit defined objectives or to implicit objectives. The objectives of the AI system may be different from the intended purpose of the AI system in a specific context. For the purposes of this Regulation, environments should be understood to be the contexts in which the AI systems operate, whereas outputs generated by the AI system reflect different functions performed by AI systems and include predictions, content, recommendations or decisions. AI systems are designed to operate with varying levels of autonomy, meaning that they have some degree of independence of actions from human involvement and of capabilities to operate without human intervention. The adaptiveness that an AI system could exhibit after deployment, refers to self-learning capabilities, allowing the system to change while in use. AI systems can be used on a stand-alone basis or as a component of a product, irrespective of whether the system is physically integrated into the product (embedded) or serves the functionality of the product without being integrated therein (non-embedded).

548. **(13)** The notion of 'deployer' referred to in this Regulation should be interpreted as any natural or legal person, including a public authority, agency or other body, using an AI system under its authority, except where the AI system is used in the course of a personal non-professional activity. Depending on the type of AI system, the use of the system may affect persons other than the deployer.

549. **(14)** The notion of 'biometric data' used in this Regulation should be interpreted in light of the notion of biometric data as defined in Article 4, point (14) of Regulation (EU) 2016/679, Article 3, point (18) of Regulation (EU) 2018/1725 and Article 3, point (13) of Directive (EU) 2016/680. Biometric data can allow for the authentication, identification or categorisation of natural persons and for the recognition of emotions of natural persons.

550. **(15)** The notion of 'biometric identification' referred to in this Regulation should be defined as the automated recognition of physical, physiological and behavioural human features such as the face, eye movement, body shape, voice, prosody, gait, posture, heart rate, blood pressure, odour, keystrokes characteristics, for the purpose of establishing an individual's identity by comparing biometric data of that individual to stored biometric data of individuals in a reference database, irrespective of whether the individual has given its consent or not. This excludes AI systems intended to be used for biometric verification, which includes authentication, whose sole purpose is to confirm that a specific natural person is the person he or she claims to be and to confirm the identity of a natural person for the sole purpose of having access to a service, unlocking a device or having security access to premises.

551. **(16)** The notion of 'biometric categorisation' referred to in this Regulation should be defined as assigning natural persons to specific categories on the basis of their biometric data. Such specific categories can relate to aspects such as sex, age, hair colour, eye colour, tattoos, behavioural or personality traits, language, religion, membership of a national minority, sexual or political orientation. This does not include biometric categorisation systems that are a purely ancillary feature intrinsically linked to another commercial service, meaning that the feature cannot, for objective technical reasons, be used without the principal service, and the integration of that feature or functionality is not a means to circumvent the applicability of the rules of this Regulation. For example, filters categorising facial or body features used on online marketplaces could constitute such an ancillary feature as they can be used only in relation to the principal service which consists in selling a product by allowing the consumer to preview the display of the product on him or herself and help the consumer to make a purchase decision. Filters used on online social network services which categorise facial or body features to allow users to add or modify pictures or videos could also be considered to be ancillary feature as such filter cannot be used without the principal service of the social network services consisting in the sharing of content online.

552. **(17)** The notion of 'remote biometric identification system' referred to in this Regulation should be defined functionally, as an AI system intended for the identification of natural persons without their active involvement, typically at a distance, through the comparison of a person's biometric data with the biometric data contained in a reference database, irrespectively of the particular technology, processes or types of biometric data used. Such remote biometric identification systems are typically used to perceive multiple persons or their behaviour simultaneously in order to facilitate significantly the identification of natural persons without their active involvement. This excludes AI systems intended to be used for biometric verification, which includes authentication, the sole purpose of which is to confirm that a specific natural person is the person he or she claims to be and to confirm the identity of a natural person for the sole purpose of having access to a service, unlocking a device or having security access to premises. That exclusion is justified by the fact that such systems are likely to have a minor impact on fundamental rights of natural persons compared to the remote biometric identification systems which may be used for the processing of the biometric data of a large number of persons without their active involvement. In the case of 'real-time' systems, the capturing of the biometric data, the comparison and the identification occur all instantaneously, near-instantaneously or in any event without a significant delay. In this regard, there should be no scope for circumventing the rules of this Regulation on the 'real-time' use of the AI systems concerned by providing for minor delays. 'Real-time' systems involve the use of 'live' or 'near-live' material, such as video footage, generated by a camera or other device with similar functionality. In the case of 'post' systems, in contrast, the biometric data has already been captured and the comparison and identification occur only after a significant delay. This involves material, such as pictures or video footage generated by closed circuit television cameras or private devices, which has been generated before the use of the system in respect of the natural persons concerned.

553. (18) The notion of 'emotion recognition system' referred to in this Regulation should be defined as an AI system for the purpose of identifying or inferring emotions or intentions of natural persons on the basis of their biometric data. The notion refers to emotions or intentions such as happiness, sadness, anger, surprise, disgust, embarrassment, excitement, shame, contempt, satisfaction and amusement. It does not include physical states, such as pain or fatigue, including, for example, systems used in detecting the state of fatigue of professional pilots or drivers for the purpose of preventing accidents. This does also not include the mere detection of readily apparent expressions, gestures or movements, unless they are used for identifying or inferring emotions. Those expressions can be basic facial expressions, such as a frown or a smile, or gestures such as the movement of hands, arms or head, or characteristics of a person's voice, such as a raised voice or whispering.

554. (19) For the purposes of this Regulation the notion of 'publicly accessible space' should be understood as referring to any physical space that is accessible to an undetermined number of natural persons, and irrespective of whether the space in question is privately or publicly owned, irrespective of the activity for which the space may be used, such as for commerce, for example, shops, restaurants, cafés; for services, for example, banks, professional activities, hospitality; for sport, for example, swimming pools, gyms, stadiums; for transport, for example, bus, metro and railway stations, airports, means of transport; for entertainment, for example, cinemas, theatres, museums, concert and conference halls; or for leisure or otherwise, for example, public roads and squares, parks, forests, playgrounds. A space should also be classified as being publicly accessible if, regardless of potential capacity or security restrictions, access is subject to certain predetermined conditions which can be fulfilled by an undetermined number of persons, such as the purchase of a ticket or title of transport, prior registration or having a certain age. In contrast, a space should not be considered to be publicly accessible if access is limited to specific and defined natural persons through either Union or national law directly related to public safety or security or through the clear manifestation of will by the person having the relevant authority over the space. The factual possibility of access alone, such as an unlocked door or an open gate in a fence, does not imply that the space is publicly accessible in the presence of indications or circumstances suggesting the contrary, such as. signs prohibiting or restricting access. Company and factory premises, as well as offices and workplaces that are intended to be accessed only by relevant employees and service providers, are spaces that are not publicly accessible. Publicly accessible spaces should not include prisons or border control. Some other spaces may comprise both publicly accessible and non-publicly accessible spaces, such as the hallway of a private residential building necessary to access a doctor's office or an airport. Online spaces are not covered, as they are not physical spaces. Whether a given space is accessible to the public should however be determined on a case-by-case basis, having regard to the specificities of the individual situation at hand.

555. **(20)** In order to obtain the greatest benefits from AI systems while protecting fundamental rights, health and safety and to enable democratic control, AI literacy should equip providers, deployers and affected persons with the necessary notions to make informed decisions regarding AI systems. Those notions may vary with regard to the relevant context and can include understanding the correct application of technical elements during the AI system's development phase, the measures to be applied during its use, the suitable ways in which to interpret the AI system's output, and, in the case of affected persons, the knowledge necessary to understand how decisions taken with the assistance of AI will have an impact on them. In the context of the application this Regulation, AI literacy should provide all relevant actors in the AI value chain with the insights required to ensure the appropriate compliance and its correct enforcement. Furthermore, the wide implementation of AI literacy measures and the introduction of appropriate follow-up actions could contribute to improving working conditions and ultimately sustain the consolidation, and innovation path of trustworthy AI in the Union. The European Artificial Intelligence Board (the 'Board') should support the Commission, to promote AI literacy tools, public awareness and understanding of the benefits, risks, safeguards, rights and obligations in relation to the use of AI systems. In cooperation with the relevant stakeholders, the Commission and the Member States should facilitate the drawing up of voluntary codes of conduct to advance AI literacy among persons dealing with the development, operation and use of AI.

556. **(35)** Each use of a 'real-time' remote biometric identification system in publicly accessible spaces for the purpose of law enforcement should be subject to an express and specific authorisation by a judicial authority or by an independent administrative authority of a Member State whose decision is binding. Such authorisation should, in principle, be obtained prior to the use of the AI system with a view to identifying a person or persons. Exceptions to that rule should be allowed in duly justified situations on grounds of urgency, namely in situations where the need to use the systems concerned is such as to make it effectively and objectively impossible to obtain an authorisation before commencing the use of the AI system. In such situations of urgency, the use of the AI system should be restricted to the absolute minimum necessary and should be subject to appropriate safeguards and conditions, as determined in national law and specified in the context of each individual urgent use case by the law enforcement authority itself. In addition, the law enforcement authority should in such situations request such authorisation while providing the reasons for not having been able to request it earlier, without undue delay and at the latest within 24 hours. If such an authorisation is rejected, the use of real-time biometric identification systems linked to that authorisation should cease with immediate effect and all the data related to such use should be discarded and deleted. Such data includes input data directly acquired by an AI system in the course of the use of such system as well as the results and outputs of the use linked to that authorisation. It should not include input that is legally acquired in accordance with another Union or national law. In any case, no decision producing an adverse legal effect on a person should be taken based solely on the output of the remote biometric identification system.

557. **(36)** In order to carry out their tasks in accordance with the requirements set out in this Regulation as well as in national rules, the relevant market surveillance authority and the national data protection authority should be notified of each use of the real-time biometric identification system. Market surveillance authorities and the national data protection authorities that have been notified should submit to the Commission an annual report on the use of real-time biometric identification systems.

558. **(37)** Furthermore, it is appropriate to provide, within the exhaustive framework set by this Regulation that such use in the territory of a Member State in accordance with this Regulation should only be possible where and in as far as the Member State concerned has decided to expressly provide for the possibility to authorise such use in its detailed rules of national law. Consequently, Member

States remain free under this Regulation not to provide for such a possibility at all or to only provide for such a possibility in respect of some of the objectives capable of justifying authorised use identified in this Regulation. Such national rules should be notified to the Commission within 30 days of their adoption.

559. **(38)** The use of AI systems for real-time remote biometric identification of natural persons in publicly accessible spaces for the purpose of law enforcement necessarily involves the processing of biometric data. The rules of this Regulation that prohibit, subject to certain exceptions, such use, which are based on Article 16 TFEU, should apply as *lex specialis* in respect of the rules on the processing of biometric data contained in Article 10 of Directive (EU) 2016/680, thus regulating such use and the processing of biometric data involved in an exhaustive manner. Therefore, such use and processing should be possible only in as far as it is compatible with the framework set by this Regulation, without there being scope, outside that framework, for the competent authorities, where they act for purpose of law enforcement, to use such systems and process such data in connection thereto on the grounds listed in Article 10 of Directive (EU) 2016/680. In that context, this Regulation is not intended to provide the legal basis for the processing of personal data under Article 8 of Directive (EU) 2016/680. However, the use of real-time remote biometric identification systems in publicly accessible spaces for purposes other than law enforcement, including by competent authorities, should not be covered by the specific framework regarding such use for the purpose of law enforcement set by this Regulation. Such use for purposes other than law enforcement should therefore not be subject to the requirement of an authorisation under this Regulation and the applicable detailed rules of national law that may give effect to that authorisation.

560. **(39)** Any processing of biometric data and other personal data involved in the use of AI systems for biometric identification, other than in connection to the use of real-time remote biometric identification systems in publicly accessible spaces for the purpose of law enforcement as regulated by this Regulation, should continue to comply with all requirements resulting from Article 10 of Directive (EU) 2016/680. For purposes other than law enforcement, Article 9(1) of Regulation (EU) 2016/679 and Article 10(1) of Regulation (EU) 2018/1725 prohibit the processing of biometric data subject to limited exceptions as provided in those Articles. In the application of Article 9(1) of Regulation (EU) 2016/679, the use of remote biometric identification for purposes other than law enforcement has already been subject to prohibition decisions by national data protection authorities.

561. **(40)** In accordance with Article 6a of Protocol No 21 on the position of the United Kingdom and Ireland in respect of the area of freedom, security and justice, as annexed to the TEU and to the TFEU, Ireland is not bound by the rules laid down in Article 5(1), first subparagraph, point (g), to the extent it applies to the use of biometric categorisation systems for activities in the field of police cooperation and judicial cooperation in criminal matters, Article 5(1), first subparagraph, point (d), to the extent it applies to the use of AI systems covered by that provision, Article 5(1), first subparagraph, point (h), Article 5(2) to (6) and Article 26(10) of this Regulation adopted on the basis of Article 16 TFEU which relate to the processing of personal data by the Member States when carrying out activities falling within the scope of Chapter 4 or Chapter 5 of Title V of Part Three of the TFEU, where Ireland is not bound by the rules governing the forms of judicial cooperation in criminal matters or police cooperation which require compliance with the provisions laid down on the basis of Article 16 TFEU.

562. **(41)** In accordance with Articles 2 and 2a of Protocol No 22 on the position of Denmark, annexed to the TEU and to the TFEU, Denmark is not bound by rules laid down in Article 5(1), first subparagraph, point (g), to the extent it applies to the use of biometric categorisation systems for activities in the field of police cooperation and judicial cooperation in criminal matters, Article 5(1), first subparagraph, point (d), to the extent it applies to the use of AI systems covered by that provision, Article 5(1), first subparagraph, point (h), (2) to (6) and Article 26(10) of this Regulation adopted on the basis of Article 16 TFEU, or subject to their application, which relate to the processing of personal data by the Member States when carrying out activities falling within the scope of Chapter 4 or Chapter 5 of Title V of Part Three of the TFEU.

563. **(52)** As regards stand-alone AI systems, namely high-risk AI systems other than those that are safety components of products, or that are themselves products, it is appropriate to classify them as high-risk if, in light of their intended purpose, they pose a high risk of harm to the health and safety or the fundamental rights of persons, taking into account both the severity of the possible harm and its probability of occurrence and they are used in a number of specifically pre-defined areas specified in this Regulation. The identification of those systems is based on the same methodology and criteria envisaged also for any future amendments of the list of high-risk AI systems that the Commission should be empowered to adopt, via delegated acts, to take into account the rapid pace of technological development, as well as the potential changes in the use of AI systems.

564. **(55)** As regards the management and operation of critical infrastructure, it is appropriate to classify as high-risk the AI systems intended to be used as safety components in the management and operation of critical digital infrastructure as listed in point (8) of the Annex to Directive (EU) 2022/2557, road traffic and the supply of water, gas, heating and electricity, since their failure or malfunctioning may put at risk the life and health of persons at large scale and lead to appreciable disruptions in the ordinary conduct of social and economic activities. Safety components of critical infrastructure, including critical digital infrastructure, are systems used to directly protect the physical integrity of critical infrastructure or the health and safety of persons and property but which are not necessary in order for the system to function. The failure or malfunctioning of such components might directly lead to risks to the physical integrity of critical infrastructure and thus to risks to health and safety of persons and property. Components intended to be used solely for cybersecurity purposes should not qualify as safety components. Examples of safety components of such critical infrastructure may include systems for monitoring water pressure or fire alarm controlling systems in cloud computing centres.

565. **(97)** The notion of general-purpose AI models should be clearly defined and set apart from the notion of AI systems to enable legal certainty. The definition should be based on the key functional characteristics of a general-purpose AI model, in particular the generality and the capability to competently perform a wide range of distinct tasks. These models are typically trained on large amounts of data, through various methods, such as self-supervised, unsupervised or reinforcement learning. General-purpose AI models may be placed on the market in various ways, including through libraries, application programming interfaces (APIs), as direct download, or as physical copy. These models may be further modified or fine-tuned into new models. Although AI models are essential components of AI systems, they do not constitute AI systems on their own. AI models require the addition of further components, such as for example a user interface, to become AI systems. AI models are typically integrated into and form part of AI systems. This Regulation provides specific rules for general-purpose AI models and for general-purpose AI models that pose systemic risks, which should apply also when these models are integrated or form part of an AI system. It should be understood that the obligations for the providers of general-purpose AI models should apply once the general-purpose AI models are placed on the market. When the provider of a general-purpose AI model integrates an own model into its own AI system that is made available on the market or put into service, that model should be considered to be placed on the market and, therefore, the obligations in this Regulation for models should continue to apply in addition to those for AI systems. The obligations laid down for models should in any case not apply when an own model is used for purely internal processes that are not essential for providing a product or a service to third parties and the rights of natural persons are not affected. Considering their potential significantly negative effects, the general-purpose AI models with systemic risk should always be subject to the relevant obligations under this Regulation. The definition should not cover AI models used before their placing on the market for the sole purpose of research, development and prototyping activities. This is without prejudice to the obligation to comply with this Regulation when, following such activities, a model is placed on the market.

566. **(133)** A variety of AI systems can generate large quantities of synthetic content that becomes increasingly hard for humans to distinguish from human-generated and authentic content. The wide availability and increasing capabilities of those systems have a significant impact on the integrity and trust in the information ecosystem, raising new risks of misinformation and manipulation at scale, fraud, impersonation and consumer deception. In light of those impacts, the fast technological pace and the need for new methods and techniques to trace origin of information, it is appropriate to require providers of those systems to embed technical solutions that enable marking in a machine readable format and detection that the output has been generated or manipulated by an AI system and not a human. Such techniques and methods should be sufficiently reliable, interoperable, effective and robust as far as this is technically feasible, taking into account available techniques or a combination of such techniques, such as watermarks, metadata identifications, cryptographic methods for proving provenance and authenticity of content, logging methods, fingerprints or other techniques, as may be appropriate. When implementing this obligation, providers should also take into account the specificities and the limitations of the different types of content and the relevant technological and market developments in the field, as reflected in the generally acknowledged state of the Art. Such techniques and methods can be implemented at the level of the AI system or at the level of the AI model, including general-purpose AI models generating content, thereby facilitating fulfilment of this obligation by the downstream provider of the AI system. To remain proportionate, it is appropriate to envisage that this marking obligation should not cover AI systems performing primarily an assistive function for standard editing or AI systems not substantially altering the input data provided by the deployer or the semantics thereof.

3.2. General Approach

567. The analysis of the definitions can be found in the Articles implementing such definitions.

4 ARTICLE 4. AI LITERACY

> Providers and deployers of AI systems shall take measures to ensure, to their best extent, a sufficient level of AI literacy of their staff and other persons dealing with the operation and use of AI systems on their behalf, taking into account their technical knowledge, experience, education and training and the context the AI systems are to be used in, and considering the persons or groups of persons on whom the AI systems are to be used.

4.1. Recitals

568. **(20)** In order to obtain the greatest benefits from AI systems while protecting fundamental rights, health and safety and to enable democratic control, AI literacy should equip providers, deployers and affected persons with the necessary notions to make informed decisions regarding AI systems. Those notions may vary with regard to the relevant context and can include understanding the correct application of technical elements during the AI system's development phase, the measures to be applied during its use, the suitable ways in which to interpret the AI system's output, and, in the case of affected persons, the knowledge necessary to understand how decisions taken with the assistance of AI will have an impact on them. In the context of the application this Regulation, AI literacy should provide all relevant actors in the AI value chain with the insights required to ensure the appropriate compliance and its correct enforcement. Furthermore, the wide implementation of AI literacy measures and the introduction of appropriate follow-up actions could contribute to improving working conditions and ultimately sustain the consolidation, and innovation path of trustworthy AI in the Union. The European Artificial Intelligence Board (the 'Board') should support the Commission, to promote AI literacy tools, public awareness and understanding of the benefits, risks, safeguards, rights and obligations in relation to the use of AI systems. In cooperation with the relevant stakeholders, the Commission and the Member States should facilitate the drawing up of voluntary codes of conduct to advance AI literacy among persons dealing with the development, operation and use of AI.

4.2. General Approach

4.2.1 Preamble

569. The notion of AI technology literacy is very difficult to grasp. It imposes specific obligations on employers, in addition to the general training obligations already imposed by labour laws.

570. It covers all AI systems.

571. Notes:

- (1) This does not apply to general-purpose AI models.[45]
- (2) This does not apply to general-purpose AI systems; where general-purpose AI systems are concerned, it is then explicitly stated in the Regulation. This is the case for example for AI systems used for content generation, as set out below:

[45] AI Act, Art. 51.

  - o 'Providers of AI systems, including general-purpose AI systems, generating synthetic audio, image, video or text content, shall ensure that the outputs of the AI system are marked in a machine-readable format and detectable as artificially generated or manipulated. Providers shall ensure their technical solutions are effective, interoperable, robust and reliable as far as this is technically feasible, taking into account the specificities and limitations of various types of content, the costs of implementation and the generally acknowledged state of the art, as may be reflected in relevant technical standards. This obligation shall not apply to the extent the AI systems perform an assistive function for standard editing or do not substantially alter the input data provided by the deployer or the semantics thereof, or where authorised by law to detect, prevent, investigate or prosecute criminal offences.'[46]
- The above two implicit exclusions stem from the late-stage introduction of general-purpose AI models, following the exponential development of generative artificial intelligence such as ChatGPT, Gemini, or Claude. However, common sense, the objective of the Regulation in this area, and the protection of employees would require an application to general-purpose AI models[47] and general-purpose AI systems.[48]

4.2.2 Actors

572. The affected persons are:
- employees of providers;
- employees of deployers.

573. Other actors, such as authorised representatives, importers, and distributors, are not targeted as such.

4.2.3 Activities

574. AI literacy involves:
- how AI works;
- how AI is used.

4.2.4 Purpose

575. The definition of skills depends on the purpose or intended use of the AI system.

46 AI Act, Art. 50(2).
47 AI Act, Arts. 3(63) and 51.
48 AI Act, Art. 3(66).

576. The objective is to equip the affected persons with 'the necessary notions to make informed decisions'.[49]

577. AI literacy should allow users of high-risk AI systems to exercise effective oversight.[50]

4.2.5 Essential Requirements

578. The notion of literacy assumes that the employer is capable of ensuring the safety of employees by implementing the following constraints, regardless of the type of AI system and throughout its lifecycle (from design to archiving):

- risk mapping;
- risk management;
- risk minimisation;
- information, awareness, and training;
- maintaining the operational condition of all reasonable protection measures;
- incident monitoring and adjustment of protections.

4.2.6 Nature of Requirement

579. This constitutes a best efforts obligation based on the state of the art, notwithstanding the legal obligations for employee protection in terms of health or work-related illness.

4.2.7 Proof

580. The burden of proof lies with the actors involved, i.e. providers or deployers.

581. Proof should be provided for the obligations in relation to:

- awareness;
- training;
- evaluation;
- maintaining operational conditions.

582. Note:

- (1) One of the tasks assigned to the AI Board is specifically to promote AI literacy.[51]

[49] AI Act, Rec. 25.
[50] AI Act, Art. 16.
[51] AI Act, Art. 66(f).

4.3. *Legal Algorithm*

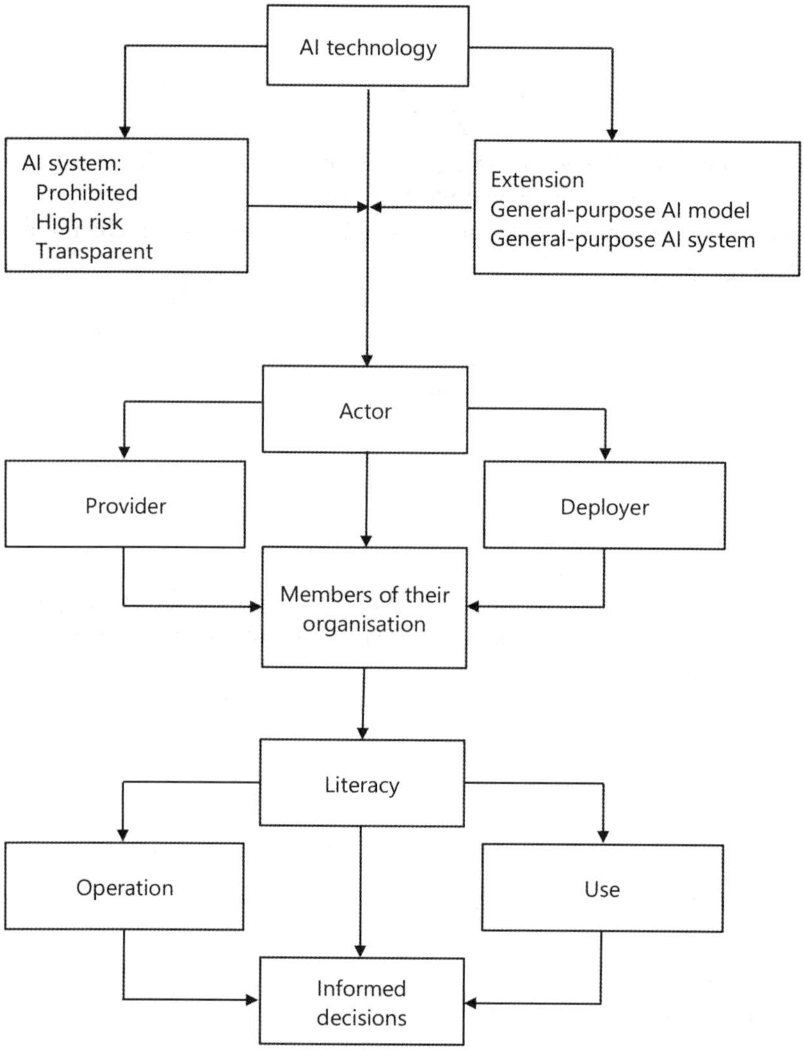

4.4. *Find Out More*

4.4.1 Toolbox

583. 'Ethical guidelines on the use of artificial intelligence (AI) and data in teaching and learning for educators', European Commission and Directorate-General for Education, Youth, Sport and Culture, September 2022.

4.5. *Closing Remarks*

4.5.1 Timetable

584. This Article came into effect on 2 February 2025.[52]

[52] AI Act, Art. 113(a).

CHAPTER II
PROHIBITED AI PRACTICES

585. Key takeaways: This Chapter focuses on the eight categories of prohibited practices in the field of AI.

5 ARTICLE 5. PROHIBITED AI PRACTICES

1. The following AI practices:

(a) the placing on the market, the putting into service or the use of an AI system that deploys subliminal techniques beyond a person's consciousness or purposefully manipulative or deceptive techniques, with the objective, or the effect of materially distorting the behaviour of a person or a group of persons by appreciably impairing their ability to make an informed decision, thereby causing them to take a decision that they would not have otherwise taken in a manner that causes or is reasonably likely to cause that person, another person or group of persons significant harm;

(b) the placing on the market, the putting into service or the use of an AI system that exploits any of the vulnerabilities of a natural person or a specific group of persons due to their age, disability or a specific social or economic situation, with the objective, or the effect, of materially distorting the behaviour of that person or a person belonging to that group in a manner that causes or is reasonably likely to cause that person or another person significant harm;

(c) the placing on the market, the putting into service or the use of AI systems for the evaluation or classification of natural persons or groups of persons over a certain period of time based on their social behaviour or known, inferred or predicted personal or personality characteristics, with the social score leading to either or both of the following:

(i) detrimental or unfavourable treatment of certain natural persons or groups of persons in social contexts that are unrelated to the contexts in which the data was originally generated or collected;

(ii) detrimental or unfavourable treatment of certain natural persons or groups of persons that is unjustified or disproportionate to their social behaviour or its gravity;

(d) the placing on the market, the putting into service for this specific purpose, or the use of an AI system for making risk assessments of natural persons in order to assess or predict the risk of a natural person committing a criminal offence, based solely on the profiling of a natural person or on assessing their personality traits and characteristics; this prohibition shall not apply to AI systems used to support the human assessment of the involvement of a person in a criminal activity, which is already based on objective and verifiable facts directly linked to a criminal activity;

(e) the placing on the market, the putting into service for this specific purpose, or the use of AI systems that create or expand facial recognition databases through the untargeted scraping of facial images from the internet or CCTV footage;

(f) the placing on the market, the putting into service for this specific purpose, or the use of AI systems to infer emotions of a natural person in the areas of workplace and education institutions, except where the use of the AI system is intended to be put in place or into the market for medical or safety reasons;

(g) the placing on the market, the putting into service for this specific purpose, or the use of biometric categorisation systems that categorise individually natural persons based on their biometric data to deduce or infer their race, political opinions, trade union membership, religious or philosophical beliefs, sex life or sexual orientation; this prohibition does not cover any labelling or filtering of lawfully acquired biometric datasets, such as images, based on biometric data or categorizing of biometric data in the area of law enforcement;

(h) the use of 'real-time' remote biometric identification systems in publicly accessible spaces for the purposes of law enforcement, unless and in so far as such use is strictly necessary for one of the following objectives:

(i) the targeted search for specific victims of abduction, trafficking in human beings or sexual exploitation of human beings, as well as the search for missing persons;

(ii) the prevention of a specific, substantial and imminent threat to the life or physical safety of natural persons or a genuine and present or genuine and foreseeable threat of a terrorist attack;

(iii) the localisation or identification of a person suspected of having committed a criminal offence, for the purpose of conducting a criminal investigation or prosecution or executing a criminal penalty for offences referred to in Annex II and punishable in the Member State concerned by a custodial sentence or a detention order for a maximum period of at least four years.

Point (h) of the first subparagraph is without prejudice to Article 9 of Regulation (EU) 2016/679 for the processing of biometric data for purposes other than law enforcement.

2. The use of 'real-time' remote biometric identification systems in publicly accessible spaces for the purposes of law enforcement for any of the objectives referred to in paragraph 1, first subparagraph, point (h), shall be deployed for the purposes set out in that point only to confirm the identity of the specifically targeted individual, and it shall take into account the following elements:

(a) the nature of the situation giving rise to the possible use, in particular the seriousness, probability and scale of the harm that would be caused if the system were not used;

(b) the consequences of the use of the system for the rights and freedoms of all persons concerned, in particular the seriousness, probability and scale of those consequences.

In addition, the use of 'real-time' remote biometric identification systems in publicly accessible spaces for the purposes of law enforcement for any of the objectives referred to in paragraph 1, first subparagraph, point (h), of this Article shall comply with necessary and proportionate safeguards and conditions in relation to the use in accordance with the national law authorising the use thereof, in particular as regards the temporal, geographic and personal limitations. The use of the 'real-time' remote biometric identification system in publicly accessible spaces shall be authorised only if the law enforcement authority has completed a fundamental rights impact assessment as provided for in Article 27 and has registered the system in the EU database according to Article 49. However, in duly justified cases of urgency, the use of such systems may be commenced without the registration in the EU database, provided that such registration is completed without undue delay.

3. For the purposes of paragraph 1, first subparagraph, point (h) and paragraph 2, each use for the purposes of law enforcement of a 'real-time' remote biometric identification system in publicly accessible spaces shall be subject to a prior authorisation granted by a judicial authority or an independent administrative authority whose decision is binding of the Member State in which the use is to take place, issued upon a reasoned request and in accordance with the detailed rules of national law referred to in paragraph 5. However, in a duly justified situation of urgency, the use of such system may be commenced without an authorisation provided that such authorisation is requested without undue delay, at the latest within 24 hours. If such authorisation is rejected, the use shall be stopped with immediate effect and all the data, as well as the results and outputs of that use shall be immediately discarded and deleted.

The competent judicial authority or an independent administrative authority whose decision is binding shall grant the authorisation only where it is satisfied, on the basis of objective evidence or clear indications presented to it, that the use of the 'real-time' remote biometric identification system concerned is necessary for, and proportionate to, achieving one of the objectives specified in paragraph 1, first subparagraph, point (h), as identified in the request and, in particular, remains limited to what is strictly necessary concerning the period of time as well as the geographic and personal scope. In deciding on the request, that authority shall take into account the elements referred to in paragraph 2. No decision that produces an adverse legal effect on a person may be taken based solely on the output of the 'real-time' remote biometric identification system.

4. Without prejudice to paragraph 3, each use of a 'real-time' remote biometric identification system in publicly accessible spaces for law enforcement purposes shall be notified to the relevant market surveillance authority and the national data protection authority in accordance with the national rules referred to in paragraph 5. The notification shall, as a minimum, contain the information specified under paragraph 6 and shall not include sensitive operational data.

5. A Member State may decide to provide for the possibility to fully or partially authorise the use of 'real-time' remote biometric identification systems in publicly accessible spaces for the purposes of law enforcement within the limits and under the conditions listed in paragraph 1, first subparagraph, point (h), and paragraphs 2 and 3. Member States concerned shall lay down in their national law the necessary detailed rules for the request, issuance and exercise of, as well as supervision and reporting relating to, the authorisations referred to in paragraph 3. Those rules shall also specify in respect of which of the objectives listed in paragraph 1, first subparagraph, point (h), including which of the criminal offences referred to in point (h)(iii) thereof, the competent authorities may be authorised to use those systems for the purposes of law enforcement. Member States shall notify those rules to the Commission at the latest 30 days following the adoption thereof. Member States may introduce, in accordance with Union law, more restrictive laws on the use of remote biometric identification systems.

6. National market surveillance authorities and the national data protection authorities of Member States that have been notified of the use of 'real-time' remote biometric identification systems in publicly accessible spaces for law enforcement purposes pursuant to paragraph 4 shall submit to the Commission annual reports on such use. For that purpose, the Commission shall provide Member States and national market surveillance and data protection authorities with a template, including information on the number of the decisions taken by competent judicial authorities or an independent administrative authority whose decision is binding upon requests for authorisations in accordance with paragraph 3 and their result.

7. The Commission shall publish annual reports on the use of real-time remote biometric identification systems in publicly accessible spaces for law enforcement purposes, based on aggregated data in Member States on the basis of the annual reports referred to in paragraph 6. Those annual reports shall not include sensitive operational data of the related law enforcement activities.

8. This Article shall not affect the prohibitions that apply where an AI practice infringes other Union law.

5.1. Recitals

586. (26) In order to introduce a proportionate and effective set of binding rules for AI systems, a clearly defined risk-based approach should be followed. That approach should tailor the type and content of such rules to the intensity and scope of the risks that AI systems can generate. It is therefore necessary to prohibit certain unacceptable AI practices, to lay down requirements for high-risk AI systems and obligations for the relevant operators, and to lay down transparency obligations for certain AI systems.

587. (28) Aside from the many beneficial uses of AI, it can also be misused and provide novel and powerful tools for manipulative, exploitative and social control practices. Such practices are particularly harmful and abusive and should be prohibited because they contradict Union values of respect for human dignity, freedom, equality, democracy and the rule of law and fundamental rights enshrined in the Charter, including the right to non-discrimination, to data protection and to privacy and the rights of the child.

588. (29) AI-enabled manipulative techniques can be used to persuade persons to engage in unwanted behaviours, or to deceive them by nudging them into decisions in a way that subverts and impairs their autonomy, decision-making and free choices. The placing on the market, the putting into service or the use of certain AI systems with the objective to or the effect of materially distorting human behaviour, whereby significant harms, in particular having sufficiently important adverse impacts on physical, psychological health or financial interests are likely to occur, are particularly dangerous and should therefore be prohibited. Such AI systems deploy subliminal components such as audio, image, video stimuli that persons cannot perceive, as those stimuli are beyond human perception, or other manipulative or deceptive techniques that subvert or impair person's autonomy, decision-making or free choice in ways that people are not consciously aware of those techniques or, where they are aware of them, can still be deceived or are not able to control or resist them. This could be facilitated, for example, by machine-brain interfaces or virtual reality as they allow for a higher degree of control of what stimuli are presented to persons, insofar as they may materially distort their behaviour in a significantly harmful manner. In addition, AI systems may also otherwise exploit the vulnerabilities of a person or a specific group of persons due to their age, disability within the meaning of Directive (EU) 2019/882 of the European Parliament and of the Council,[1] or a specific social or economic situation that is likely to make those persons more vulnerable to exploitation such as persons living in extreme poverty, ethnic or religious minorities. Such AI systems can be placed on the market, put into service or used with the objective to or the effect of materially distorting the behaviour of a person and in a manner that causes or is reasonably likely to cause significant harm to that or another person or groups of persons, including harms that may be accumulated over time and should therefore be prohibited. It may not be possible to assume that there is an intention to distort behaviour where the distortion results from factors external to the AI system which are outside the control of the provider or the deployer, namely factors that may not be reasonably foreseeable and therefore not possible for the provider or the deployer of the AI system to mitigate. In any case, it is not necessary for the provider or the deployer to have the intention to cause significant harm, provided that such harm results from the manipulative or exploitative AI-enabled practices. The prohibitions for such AI practices are complementary to the provisions contained in Directive 2005/29/EC of the European Parliament and of the Council,[2] in particular unfair commercial practices leading to economic or financial harms to consumers are prohibited under all circumstances, irrespective of whether they are put in place through AI systems or otherwise. The prohibitions of manipulative and exploitative practices in this Regulation should not affect lawful practices in the context of medical treatment such as psychological treatment of a mental disease or physical rehabilitation, when those practices are carried out in accordance with the applicable law and medical standards, for example explicit consent of the individuals or their legal representatives. In addition, common and legitimate commercial practices, for example in the field of advertising, that comply with the applicable law should not, in themselves, be regarded as constituting harmful manipulative AI-enabled practices.

589. (30) Biometric categorisation systems that are based on natural persons' biometric data, such as an individual person's face or fingerprint, to deduce or infer an individuals' political opinions, trade union membership, religious or philosophical beliefs, race, sex life or sexual orientation should be prohibited. That prohibition should not cover the lawful labelling, filtering or categorisation of biometric data sets acquired in line with Union or national law according to

---

1 Directive (EU) 2019/882 of the European Parliament and of the Council of 17 April 2019 on the accessibility requirements for products and services, [2019] OJ L151/70.

2 Directive 2005/29/EC of the European Parliament and of the Council of 11 May 2005 concerning unfair business-to-consumer commercial practices in the internal market and amending Council Directive 84/450/EEC, Directives 97/7/EC, 98/27/EC and 2002/65/EC of the European Parliament and of the Council and Regulation (EC) No 2006/2004 of the European Parliament and of the Council ('Unfair Commercial Practices Directive'), [2005] OJ L149/22.

biometric data, such as the sorting of images according to hair colour or eye colour, which can for example be used in the area of law enforcement.

590. **(31)** AI systems providing social scoring of natural persons by public or private actors may lead to discriminatory outcomes and the exclusion of certain groups. They may violate the right to dignity and non-discrimination and the values of equality and justice. Such AI systems evaluate or classify natural persons or groups thereof on the basis of multiple data points related to their social behaviour in multiple contexts or known, inferred or predicted personal or personality characteristics over certain periods of time. The social score obtained from such AI systems may lead to the detrimental or unfavourable treatment of natural persons or whole groups thereof in social contexts, which are unrelated to the context in which the data was originally generated or collected or to a detrimental treatment that is disproportionate or unjustified to the gravity of their social behaviour. AI systems entailing such unacceptable scoring practices and leading to such detrimental or unfavourable outcomes should therefore be prohibited. That prohibition should not affect lawful evaluation practices of natural persons that are carried out for a specific purpose in accordance with Union and national law.

591. **(33)** The use of those systems for the purpose of law enforcement should therefore be prohibited, except in exhaustively listed and narrowly defined situations, where the use is strictly necessary to achieve a substantial public interest, the importance of which outweighs the risks. Those situations involve the search for certain victims of crime including missing persons; certain threats to the life or to the physical safety of natural persons or of a terrorist attack; and the localisation or identification of perpetrators or suspects of the criminal offences listed in an annex to this Regulation, where those criminal offences are punishable in the Member State concerned by a custodial sentence or a detention order for a maximum period of at least four years and as they are defined in the law of that Member State. Such a threshold for the custodial sentence or detention order in accordance with national law contributes to ensuring that the offence should be serious enough to potentially justify the use of 'real-time' remote biometric identification systems. Moreover, the list of criminal offences provided in an annex to this Regulation is based on the 32 criminal offences listed in the Council Framework Decision 2002/584/JHA,[3] taking into account that some of those offences are, in practice, likely to be more relevant than others, in that the recourse to 'real-time' remote biometric identification could, foreseeably, be necessary and proportionate to highly varying degrees for the practical pursuit of the localisation or identification of a perpetrator or suspect of the different criminal offences listed and having regard to the likely differences

3 Council Framework Decision 2002/584/JHA of 13 June 2002 on the European arrest warrant and the surrender procedures between Member States, [2002] OJ L190/1.

in the seriousness, probability and scale of the harm or possible negative consequences. An imminent threat to life or the physical safety of natural persons could also result from a serious disruption of critical infrastructure, as defined in Article 2, point (4) of Directive (EU) 2022/2557 of the European Parliament and of the Council,[4] where the disruption or destruction of such critical infrastructure would result in an imminent threat to life or the physical safety of a person, including through serious harm to the provision of basic supplies to the population or to the exercise of the core function of the State. In addition, this Regulation should preserve the ability for law enforcement, border control, immigration or asylum authorities to carry out identity checks in the presence of the person concerned in accordance with the conditions set out in Union and national law for such checks. In particular, law enforcement, border control, immigration or asylum authorities should be able to use information systems, in accordance with Union or national law, to identify persons who, during an identity check, either refuse to be identified or are unable to state or prove their identity, without being required by this Regulation to obtain prior authorisation. This could be, for example, a person involved in a crime, being unwilling, or unable due to an accident or a medical condition, to disclose their identity to law enforcement authorities.

592. (35) Each use of a 'real-time' remote biometric identification system in publicly accessible spaces for the purpose of law enforcement should be subject to an express and specific authorisation by a judicial authority or by an independent administrative authority of a Member State whose decision is binding. Such authorisation should, in principle, be obtained prior to the use of the AI system with a view to identifying a person or persons. Exceptions to that rule should be allowed in duly justified situations on grounds of urgency, namely in situations where the need to use the systems concerned is such as to make it effectively and objectively impossible to obtain an authorisation before commencing the use of the AI system. In such situations of urgency, the use of the AI system should be restricted to the absolute minimum necessary and should be subject to appropriate safeguards and conditions, as determined in national law and specified in the context of each individual urgent use case by the law enforcement authority itself. In addition, the law enforcement authority should in such situations request such authorisation while providing the reasons for not having been able to request it earlier, without undue delay and at the latest within 24 hours. If such an authorisation is rejected, the use of real-time biometric identification systems linked to that authorisation should cease with immediate effect and all the data related to such use should be discarded and deleted. Such data includes input data directly acquired by an AI system in the

[4] Directive (EU) 2022/2557 of the European Parliament and of the Council of 14 December 2022 on the resilience of critical entities and repealing Council Directive 2008/114/EC, [2022] OJ L333/164.

course of the use of such system as well as the results and outputs of the use linked to that authorisation. It should not include input that is legally acquired in accordance with another Union or national law. In any case, no decision producing an adverse legal effect on a person should be taken based solely on the output of the remote biometric identification system.

593. **(36)** In order to carry out their tasks in accordance with the requirements set out in this Regulation as well as in national rules, the relevant market surveillance authority and the national data protection authority should be notified of each use of the real-time biometric identification system. Market surveillance authorities and the national data protection authorities that have been notified should submit to the Commission an annual report on the use of real-time biometric identification systems.

594. **(37)** Furthermore, it is appropriate to provide, within the exhaustive framework set by this Regulation that such use in the territory of a Member State in accordance with this Regulation should only be possible where and in as far as the Member State concerned has decided to expressly provide for the possibility to authorise such use in its detailed rules of national law. Consequently, Member States remain free under this Regulation not to provide for such a possibility at all or to only provide for such a possibility in respect of some of the objectives capable of justifying authorised use identified in this Regulation. Such national rules should be notified to the Commission within 30 days of their adoption.

595. **(38)** The use of AI systems for real-time remote biometric identification of natural persons in publicly accessible spaces for the purpose of law enforcement necessarily involves the processing of biometric data. The rules of this Regulation that prohibit, subject to certain exceptions, such use, which are based on Article 16 TFEU, should apply as *lex specialis* in respect of the rules on the processing of biometric data contained in Article 10 of Directive (EU) 2016/680, thus regulating such use and the processing of biometric data involved in an exhaustive manner. Therefore, such use and processing should be possible only in as far as it is compatible with the framework set by this Regulation, without there being scope, outside that framework, for the competent authorities, where they act for purpose of law enforcement, to use such systems and process such data in connection thereto on the grounds listed in Article 10 of Directive (EU) 2016/680. In that context, this Regulation is not intended to provide the legal basis for the processing of personal data under Article 8 of Directive (EU) 2016/680. However, the use of real-time remote biometric identification systems in publicly accessible spaces for purposes other than law enforcement, including by competent authorities, should not be covered by the specific framework regarding such use for the purpose of law enforcement set by this Regulation. Such use for purposes other than law enforcement should therefore not be subject to the requirement of an authorisation under this Regulation and the applicable detailed rules of national law that may give effect to that authorisation.

596. **(39)** Any processing of biometric data and other personal data involved in the use of AI systems for biometric identification, other than in connection to the use of real-time remote biometric identification systems in publicly accessible spaces for the purpose of law enforcement as regulated by this Regulation, should continue to comply with all requirements resulting from Article 10 of Directive (EU) 2016/680. For purposes other than law enforcement, Article 9(1) of Regulation (EU) 2016/679 and Article 10(1) of Regulation (EU) 2018/1725 prohibit the processing of biometric data subject to limited exceptions as provided in those Articles. In the application of Article 9(1) of Regulation (EU) 2016/679, the use of remote biometric identification for purposes other than law enforcement has already been subject to prohibition decisions by national data protection authorities.

597. **(40)** In accordance with Article 6a of Protocol No 21 on the position of the United Kingdom and Ireland in respect of the area of freedom, security and justice, as annexed to the TEU and to the TFEU, Ireland is not bound by the rules laid down in Article 5(1), first subparagraph, point (g), to the extent it applies to the use of biometric categorisation systems for activities in the field of police cooperation and judicial cooperation in criminal matters, Article 5(1), first subparagraph, point (d), to the extent it applies to the use of AI systems covered by that provision, Article 5(1), first subparagraph, point (h), Article 5(2) to (6) and Article 26(10) of this Regulation adopted on the basis of Article 16 TFEU which relate to the processing of personal data by the Member States when carrying out activities falling within the scope of Chapter 4 or Chapter 5 of Title V of Part Three of the TFEU, where Ireland is not bound by the rules governing the forms of judicial cooperation in criminal matters or police cooperation which require compliance with the provisions laid down on the basis of Article 16 TFEU.

598. **(41)** In accordance with Articles 2 and 2a of Protocol No 22 on the position of Denmark, annexed to the TEU and to the TFEU, Denmark is not bound by rules laid down in Article 5(1), first subparagraph, point (g), to the extent it applies to the use of biometric categorisation systems for activities in the field of police cooperation and judicial cooperation in criminal matters, Article 5(1), first subparagraph, point (d), to the extent it applies to the use of AI systems covered by that provision, Article 5(1), first subparagraph, point (h), (2) to (6) and Article 26(10) of this Regulation adopted on the basis of Article 16 TFEU, or subject to their application, which relate to the processing of personal data by the Member States when carrying out activities falling within the scope of Chapter 4 or Chapter 5 of Title V of Part Three of the TFEU.

599. **(42)** In line with the presumption of innocence, natural persons in the Union should always be judged on their actual behaviour. Natural persons should never be judged on AI-predicted behaviour based solely on their profiling, personality traits or characteristics, such as nationality, place of birth, place of residence, number of children, level of debt or type of car, without a reasonable suspicion of that person being involved in a criminal activity based on objective verifiable facts and without human assessment thereof. Therefore, risk assessments carried out with regard to natural persons in order to assess the likelihood of their offending or to predict the occurrence of an actual or potential criminal offence based solely on profiling them or on assessing their personality traits and characteristics should be prohibited. In any case, that prohibition does not refer to or touch upon risk analytics that are not based on the profiling of individuals or on the personality traits and characteristics of individuals, such as AI systems using risk analytics to assess the likelihood of financial fraud by undertakings on the basis of suspicious transactions or risk analytic tools to predict the likelihood of the localisation of narcotics or illicit goods by customs authorities, for example on the basis of known trafficking routes.

600. **(43)** The placing on the market, the putting into service for that specific purpose, or the use of AI systems that create or expand facial recognition databases through the untargeted scraping of facial images from the internet or CCTV footage, should be prohibited because that practice adds to the feeling of mass surveillance and can lead to gross violations of fundamental rights, including the right to privacy.

601. **(44)** There are serious concerns about the scientific basis of AI systems aiming to identify or infer emotions, particularly as expression of emotions vary considerably across cultures and situations, and even within a single individual. Among the key shortcomings of such systems are the limited reliability, the lack of specificity and the limited generalisability. Therefore, AI systems identifying or inferring emotions or intentions of natural persons on the basis of their biometric data may lead to discriminatory outcomes and can be intrusive to the rights and freedoms of the concerned persons. Considering the imbalance of power in the context of work or education, combined with the intrusive nature of these systems, such systems could lead to detrimental or unfavourable treatment of certain natural persons or whole groups thereof. Therefore, the placing on the market, the putting into service, or the use of AI systems intended to be used to detect the emotional state of individuals in situations related to the workplace and education should be prohibited. That prohibition should not cover AI systems placed on the market strictly for medical or safety reasons, such as systems intended for therapeutical use.

602. **(45)** Practices that are prohibited by Union law, including data protection law, non-discrimination law, consumer protection law, and competition law, should not be affected by this Regulation.

603. **(72)** To address concerns related to opacity and complexity of certain AI systems and help deployers to fulfil their obligations under this Regulation, transparency should be required for high-risk AI systems before they are placed on the market or put it into service. High-risk AI systems should be designed in a manner to enable deployers to understand how the AI system works, evaluate its functionality, and comprehend its strengths and limitations. High-risk AI systems should be accompanied by appropriate information in the form of instructions of use. Such information should include the characteristics, capabilities and limitations of performance of the AI system. Those would cover information on possible known and foreseeable circumstances related to the use of the high-risk AI system, including deployer action that may influence system behaviour and performance, under which the AI system can lead to risks to health, safety, and fundamental rights, on the changes that have been pre-determined and assessed for conformity by the provider and on the relevant human oversight measures, including the measures to facilitate the interpretation of the outputs of the AI system by the deployers. Transparency, including the accompanying instructions for use, should assist deployers in the use of the system and support informed decision making by them. Deployers should, inter alia, be in a better position to make the correct choice of the system that they intend to use in light of the obligations applicable to them, be educated about the intended and precluded uses, and use the AI system correctly and as appropriate. In order to enhance legibility and accessibility of the information included in the instructions of use, where appropriate, illustrative examples, for instance on the limitations and on the intended and precluded uses of the AI system, should be included. Providers should ensure that all documentation, including the instructions for use, contains meaningful, comprehensive, accessible and understandable information, taking into account the needs and foreseeable knowledge of the target deployers. Instructions for use should be made available in a language which can be easily understood by target deployers, as determined by the Member State concerned.

604. **(79)** It is appropriate that a specific natural or legal person, defined as the provider, takes responsibility for the placing on the market or the putting into service of a high-risk AI system, regardless of whether that natural or legal person is the person who designed or developed the system.

605. **(133)** A variety of AI systems can generate large quantities of synthetic content that becomes increasingly hard for humans to distinguish from human-generated and authentic content. The wide availability and increasing capabilities of those systems have a significant impact on the integrity and trust in the information ecosystem, raising new risks of misinformation and manipulation at scale, fraud, impersonation and consumer deception. In light of those impacts, the fast technological pace and the need for new methods and techniques to trace origin of information, it is appropriate to require providers of those systems to embed technical solutions that enable marking in a machine readable format and detection that the output has been generated or manipulated by an AI system and not a human. Such techniques and methods should be sufficiently reliable, interoperable, effective and robust as far as this is technically feasible, taking into account available techniques or a combination of such techniques, such as watermarks, metadata identifications, cryptographic methods for proving provenance and authenticity of content, logging methods, fingerprints or other techniques, as may be appropriate. When implementing this obligation, providers should also take into account the specificities and the limitations of the different types of content and the relevant technological and market developments in the field, as reflected in the generally acknowledged state of the Art. Such techniques and methods can be implemented at the level of the AI system or at the level of the AI model, including general-purpose AI models generating content, thereby facilitating fulfilment of this obligation by the downstream provider of the AI system. To remain proportionate, it is appropriate to envisage that this marking obligation should not cover AI systems performing primarily an assistive function for standard editing or AI systems not substantially altering the input data provided by the deployer or the semantics thereof.

606. **(134)** Further to the technical solutions employed by the providers of the AI system, deployers who use an AI system to generate or manipulate image, audio or video content that appreciably resembles existing persons, objects, places, entities or events and would falsely appear to a person to be authentic or truthful (deep fakes), should also clearly and distinguishably disclose that the content has been artificially created or manipulated by labelling the AI output accordingly and disclosing its artificial origin. Compliance with this transparency obligation should not be interpreted as indicating that the use of the AI system or its output impedes the right to freedom of expression and the right to freedom of the arts and sciences guaranteed in the Charter, in particular where the content is part of an evidently creative, satirical, artistic, fictional or analogous work or programme, subject to appropriate safeguards for the rights and freedoms of third parties. In those cases, the transparency obligation for deep fakes set out in this Regulation is limited to disclosure of the existence of such generated or manipulated content in an appropriate manner that does not hamper the display or enjoyment of the work, including its normal exploitation and use, while maintaining the utility and quality of the work. In addition, it is also appropriate to envisage a similar disclosure obligation in relation to AI-generated or manipulated text to the extent it is published with the purpose of informing the public on matters of public interest unless the AI-generated content has undergone a process of human review or editorial control and a natural or legal person holds editorial responsibility for the publication of the content.

607. **(174)** Given the rapid technological developments and the technical expertise required to effectively apply this Regulation, the Commission should evaluate and review this Regulation by 2 August 2029 and every four years thereafter and report to the European Parliament and the Council. In addition, taking into account the implications for the scope of this Regulation, the Commission should carry out an assessment of the need to amend the list of high-risk AI systems and the list of prohibited practices once a year. Moreover, by 2 August 2028 and every four years thereafter, the Commission should evaluate and report to the European Parliament and to the Council on the need to amend the list of high-risk areas headings in the annex to this Regulation, the AI systems within the scope of the transparency obligations, the effectiveness of the supervision and governance system and the progress on the development of standardisation deliverables on energy efficient development of general-purpose AI models, including the need for further measures or actions. Finally, by 2 August 2028 and every three years thereafter, the Commission should evaluate the impact and effectiveness of voluntary codes of conduct to foster the application of the requirements provided for high-risk AI systems in the case of AI systems other than high-risk AI systems and possibly other additional requirements for such AI systems.

5.2. Prohibited AI Systems

5.2.1 Introduction

608. Prohibited AI systems pertain to the following eight categories of AI systems:

- AI systems and consciousness;
- AI systems and the protection of vulnerable persons;
- AI systems and social scoring;
- profiling for criminal purposes;
- scraping of facial images;
- emotion inference;
- biometric categorisation;
- real-time biometric identification in publicly accessible spaces.

5.2.2 Guiding Principles

609. Prohibited AI systems include AI systems that pose unacceptable risks to democracy.

610. The principle of prohibition applies because this type of AI system is contrary to the values established in the Charter of Fundamental Rights.

611. The prohibition extends from design to use of that kid of AI systems, as well as to the outputs they can generate, even when those outputs originated from AI systems operated outside the European Union.

612. Similarly, the prohibition extends to export operations to countries without regulations banning this category of AI systems.

613. Notes:

- (1) The prohibition targets AI systems, and not general-purpose AI systems and general-purpose AI models.
- (2) However, these two other categories are affected insofar as the prohibition applies to AI technologies with the following terms:
    - o 'The following AI practices shall be prohibited: […].'[5]

5.2.3 Consensus

614. There is no global consensus on this prohibition. The main reasons include:

- difficulties in definition and implementation (e.g. consciousness).
- existing practices where AI systems serve as methods.
- AI systems developed in other countries with continuous interaction with the European Union (e.g. USA, UK, or China).
- regulations hindering innovation in these fields, providing significant advantages to foreign AI industries.

5.3. *AI Systems and Consciousness*

5.3.1 Introduction

615. The prohibition of AI systems that violate individuals' freedom of conscience by subjecting humanity to subjugation is the greatest challenge posed by the advent of artificial intelligence.

616. The risk of technological dependence is not science fiction.

617. This prohibition establishes an initial regulation of neurorights or the right of consciousness, a component of the right to dignity.

5.3.2 Guiding Principles

618. AI systems must not enable the implementation of techniques that are:

- subliminal;
- deceptive;
- distorting the behaviour.

619. This prohibition applies to all AI systems that make an individual dependent by impairing that individual's decision-making.

---

5 AI Act, Art. 5(1).

5.3.3 Actors

620. All AI system operators[6] are concerned, from the design phase to the use phase.

5.3.4 Activities

621. These involve the three regulated activities:
- placing on the market;
- putting into service;
- use.

5.3.5 Criteria

622. They are as follows:

NO.	THEME	SPECIFICATION	REFERENCE
1.	Subliminal technique	Beyond a person's consciousness	Art. 5(1)(a)
2.	Manipulative technique	Purposefully	Art. 5(1)(a)
3.	Deceptive technique	Purposefully	Art. 5(1)(a)

5.3.5.1 *Subliminal Techniques*

623. According to the *Académie Française*,[7] in philosophy or psychology, the adjective subliminal means 'that which remains beyond consciousness'. Consequently, the addition of 'beyond a person's consciousness' is tautological, in France at least.

624. Note:
- (1) This prohibition is already established in the advertising sector with the following provision:
  - o 'Advertising shall not use subliminal techniques.'[8]

625. The prohibition is general.

[6] 'Operator' means a provider, product manufacturer, deployer, authorised representative, importer or distributor (AI Act, Art. 3(8)).

[7] *Académie Française* (French Academy) is the principal French council for matters pertaining to the French language.

[8] French Decree No 92-280 of 27 March 1992, Art. 10.

5.3.5.2 *Manipulative or Deceptive Techniques*

626. This applies to all implementations of AI systems, including text, image, video, or podcast generation.

627. The prohibition applies when those techniques are deployed 'purposefully', from design to use.

5.3.6 Purposes

628. The prohibition focuses on intended purposes of those techniques, which are either:
- to distort behaviour, or
- to impair the ability to make an informed decision.

5.3.7 Protected Persons

629. The protection applies to:
- an individual;
- a group of natural persons;
- affected third parties.

5.3.8 Harm

630. The prohibition applies only if individuals are at risk of, or suffer, 'significant' harm.

631. Harm includes:
- psychological harm;
- the consequences suffered;
- losses incurred, loss of profit, or loss of opportunity.

5.3.9 Legal Algorithm

632. It can be represented as follows:

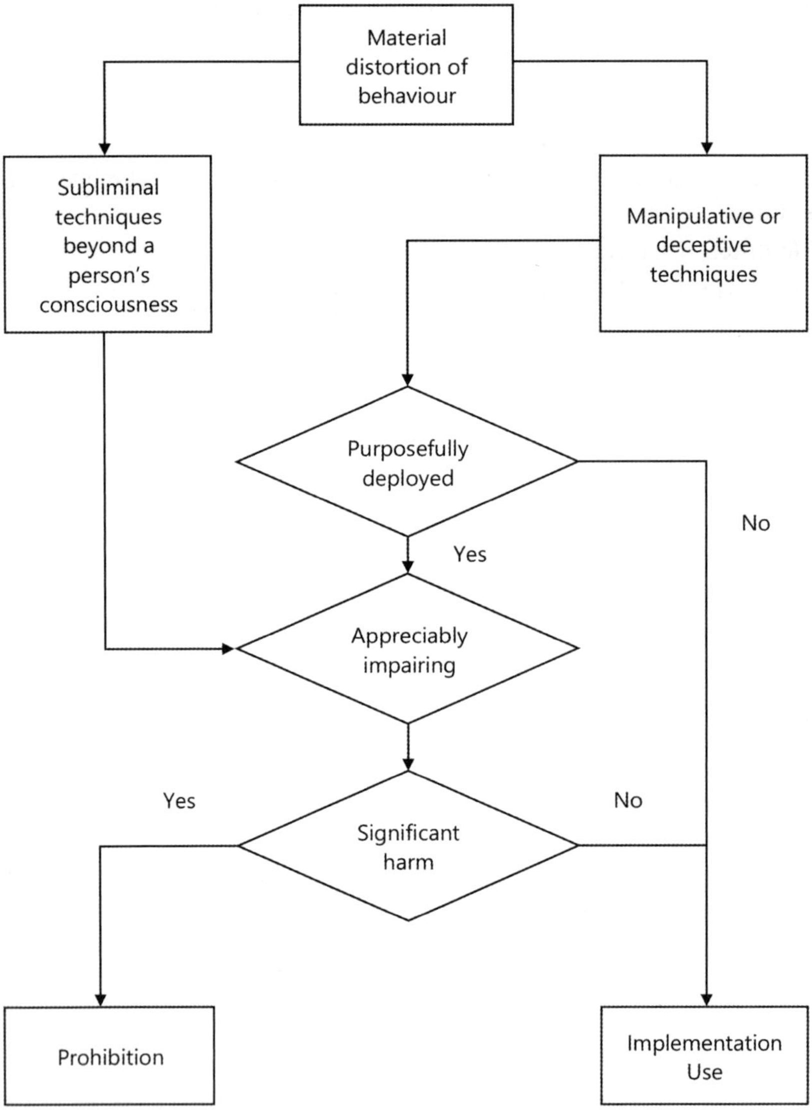

633. Notes:

- (1) The concept of significant harm is not defined.
- (2) No clarification is provided in the Recitals, including in Recital 29.

5.4. *AI Systems and Vulnerable Persons*

5.4.1 Introduction

634. The exploitation of vulnerable individuals in all areas is prohibited. This applies to AI systems, from design to implementation. Numerous regulations concerning products and services already address this. It is not clear that this prohibition was not already regulated.

5.4.2 Guiding Principles

635. The objective is to prevent the exploitation of vulnerabilities specific to an individual or a group of individuals.

5.4.3 Actors

636. All AI system operators[9] are concerned, from the design phase to the use phase.

5.4.4 Activities

637. These involve the three regulated activities:
- placing on the market;
- putting into service;
- use.

5.4.5 Vulnerabilities

638. They are related to:
- age;
- disability;
- social or economic situation.

5.4.6 Recipients

639. The AI system must materially distort the behaviour.

---

9 'Operator' means a provider, product manufacturer, deployer, authorised representative, importer or distributor (AI Act, Art. 3(8)).

5.4.7 Protected Persons

640. The protection applies to:

- an individual; or
- a group of natural persons.

5.4.8 Harm

641. The prohibition applies only if individuals are at risk of, or suffer, 'significant' harm.

642. Harm includes:

- psychological harm.
- the consequences suffered.
- losses incurred, loss of profit, or loss of opportunity.

643. Notes:

- (1) The concept of significant harm is not defined.
- (2) No clarification is provided in the Recitals, including in Recital 29.

5.4.9 Legal Algorithm

644. It can be represented as follows:

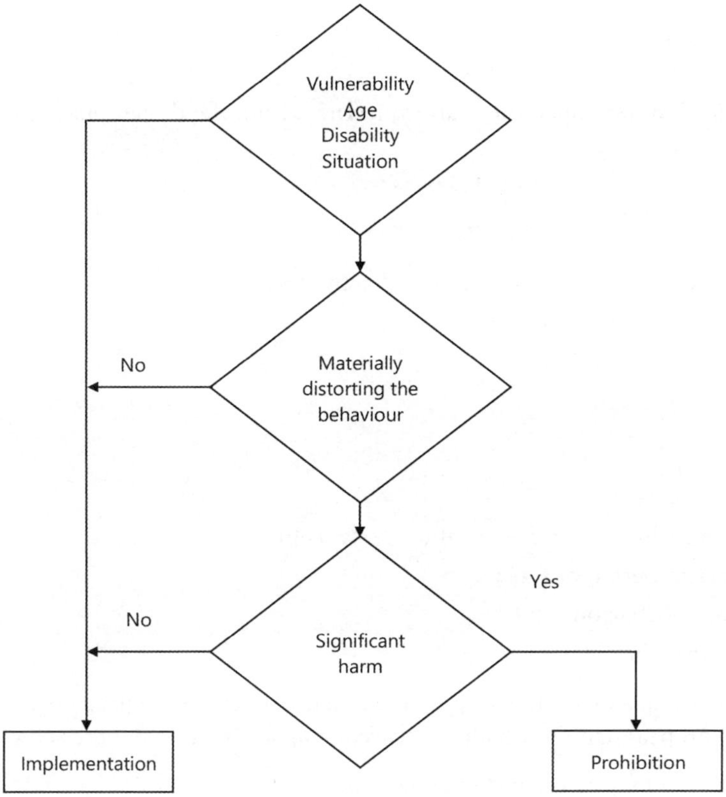

5.5. Social Scoring

5.5.1 Introduction

645. In the initial version proposed by the European Commission, the prohibition was limited to AI systems 'by public authorities or on their behalf'.[10]

646. Now, the prohibition applies to both the public and private sectors.[11]

---

10 Proposal for a Regulation on AI COM(2021) 206 of 21 April 2021, Art. 5(1)(c).

11 AI Act, Art. 5(1)(c).

5.5.2 Guiding Principles

647. The objective is to prevent the categorisation of individuals through social scoring for regulatory purposes.

5.5.3 Actors

648. All AI system operators[12] are concerned, from the design phase to the use phase.

5.5.4 Activities

649. These involve the three regulated activities:
- placing on the market;
- putting into service;
- use.

5.5.5 Criteria

650. The evaluation or classification pertains to:
- a certain period of time;
- a social behaviour; or
- personal characteristics.

651. Adopting a quantitative approach to natural persons contradicts the values of the European Union, which rejects reducing a person to a mere score.

652. Scoring may be calculated based on:
- direct assessments;
- inferences;
- predictions.

5.5.6 Purpose

653. It leads to either or both of the following:
- detrimental treatment in social contexts that are unrelated to the contexts in which the data was collected;
- detrimental treatment that is unjustified or disproportionate.

---

[12] 'Operator' means a provider, product manufacturer, deployer, authorised representative, importer or distributor (AI Act, Art. 3(8)).

5.5.7 Protected Persons

654. The protection applies to:
- natural persons;
- groups of natural persons.

655. Although this prohibited practice does not specify the nature of the groups of persons concerned, it should be understood that legal entities are excluded.[13]

5.5.8 Legal Algorithm

656. It can be represented as follows:

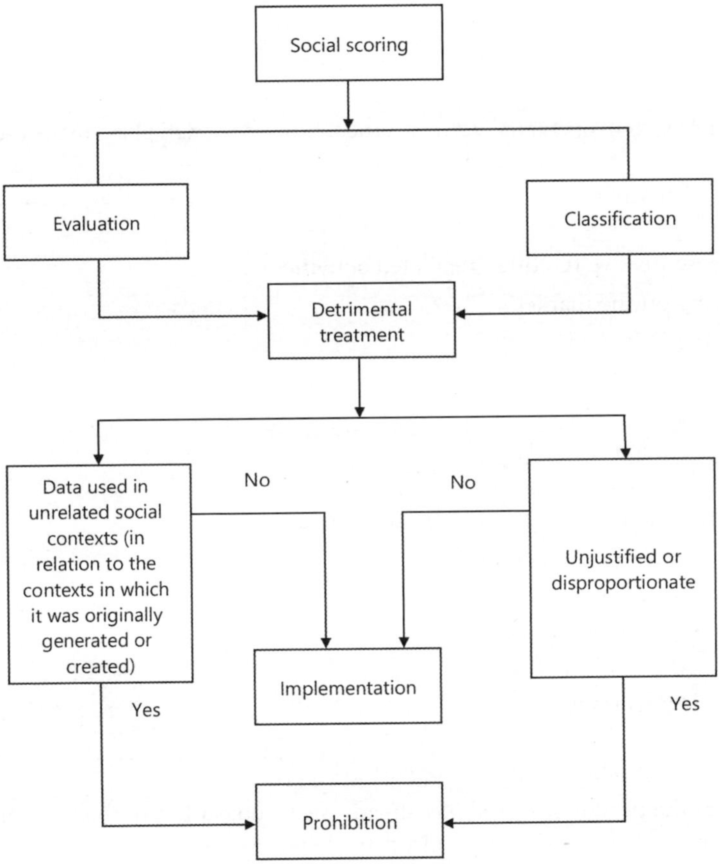

[13] AI Act, Art. 5(1)(c).

5.6. *Profiling for Criminal Purposes*

5.6.1 Introduction

657. This new addition compared to the European Commission's[14] initial proposal aims to limit the development of a generalised surveillance society based on behaviours that are dangerous or outside of prevailing social norms in European democracies.

5.6.2 Guiding Principles

658. The prohibition applies to the inference of criminal behaviours through probability calculations based on various objective or subjective factors.

5.6.3 Actors

659. All AI system operators[15] are concerned, from the design phase to the use phase.

5.6.4 Activities

660. These involve the three regulated activities:

- placing on the market;
- putting into service;
- use.

5.6.5 Criteria

661. The AI systems concerned are those relating to:

- assessments or predictions;
- personality traits and;
- personal characteristics.

5.6.6 Derogations

662. This prohibition does not apply:

- where the person observed has already been subject to prior assessment procedures based on objective and verifiable facts;
- as part of an investigation of criminal activities.

---

[14] Proposal for a Regulation on AI COM(2021) 206 of 21 April 2021.

[15] 'Operator' means a provider, product manufacturer, deployer, authorised representative, importer or distributor (AI Act, Art. 3(8)).

5.6.7 Affected Persons

663. All natural persons are protected against such profiling.

664. Note:

- (1) AI systems allowing such personal qualifications are applicable to legal persons for minor offences, serious offences, and crimes.

5.6.8 Legal Algorithm

665. It can be represented as follows:

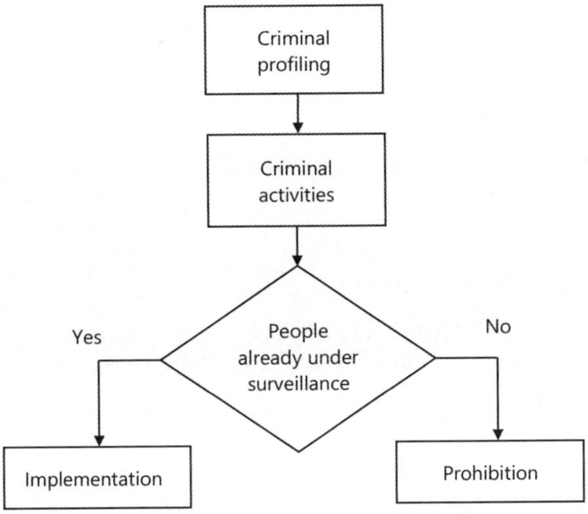

5.7. *Scraping of Facial Images*

5.7.1 Introduction

666. In line with the right to privacy and the protection of individuals' images, this prohibition helps prevent the creation of global facial recognition databases.

5.7.2 Guiding Principles

667. Scraping of facial images is not prohibited, particularly for AI system training purposes. Only the 'untargeted' scraping is prohibited.

5.7.3 Actors

668. All AI system operators[16] are concerned, from the design phase to the use phase.

5.7.4 Activities

669. These involve the three regulated activities:
- placing on the market;
- putting into service;
- use.

5.7.5 Database

670. The prohibition applies to:
- creation;
- development;
- updating.

671. Facial images may come from:
- photographs;
- images of a physical person generated from templates;
- videos from any source.

5.7.6 Criteria

672. The first criterion concerns scraping from the internet.

673. The second criterion targets facial images from CCTV footage.

674. Notes:
- (1) This should also include facial images resulting from recordings made by video protection systems.

675. The third criterion corresponds to untargeted or indiscriminate scraping.

5.7.7 Affected Persons

676. This applies to all individuals located within the European Union.

---

[16] 'Operator' means a provider, product manufacturer, deployer, authorised representative, importer or distributor (AI Act, Art. 3(8)).

677. Notes:

- (1) It can be considered that this prohibition also applies to individuals outside the EU.
- (2) This approach also concerns nationals of countries where the creation of facial recognition databases is permitted for both the public and private sectors.
- (3) A database created on the basis of consent cannot be classified as untargeted.

5.7.8 Consequences

678. The prohibition is relevant even in the absence of direct harm to the affected persons.

5.7.9 Legal Algorithm

679. It can be represented as follows:

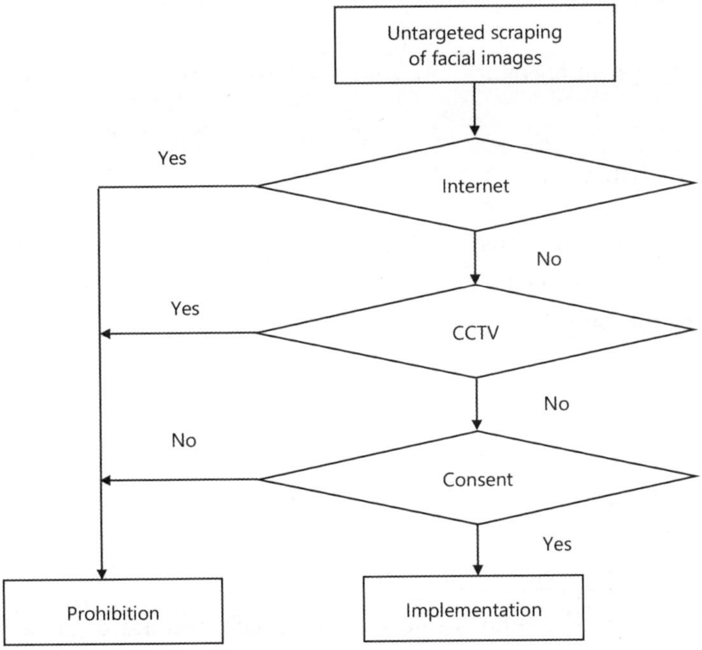

680. Note:

- The requirement for consent falls under the application of the GDPR, Regulation (EU) 2016/679.

5.8. *Emotion Inference*

5.8.1 Introduction

681. The manipulation of crowds, groups, or an individual can result from various ways, including emotion inference.

5.8.2 Guiding Principles

682. To protect human dignity and the ability to make free decisions, this prohibition prevents the implementation of AI systems designed to alter the initial emotional state of an individual.

5.8.3 Actors

683. All AI system operators[17] are concerned, from the design phase to the use phase.

5.8.4 Activities

684. These involve the three regulated activities:

- placing on the market;
- putting into service;
- use.

5.8.5 Criteria

685. There are two criteria:

- emotions;
- the places where such emotions are collected.

686. The notion of emotions refers to all specific feelings of an individual, whether positive or negative, objective or subjective.

---

[17] 'Operator' means a provider, product manufacturer, deployer, authorised representative, importer or distributor (AI Act, Art. 3(8)).

687. The places concerned are:
- workplaces;
- education institutions.

5.8.6 Derogations

688. There are derogations for:
- safety reasons;
- medical reasons.

5.8.7 Affected Persons

689. This applies to all individuals located within the European Union.

5.8.8 Legal Algorithm

690. It can be represented as follows:

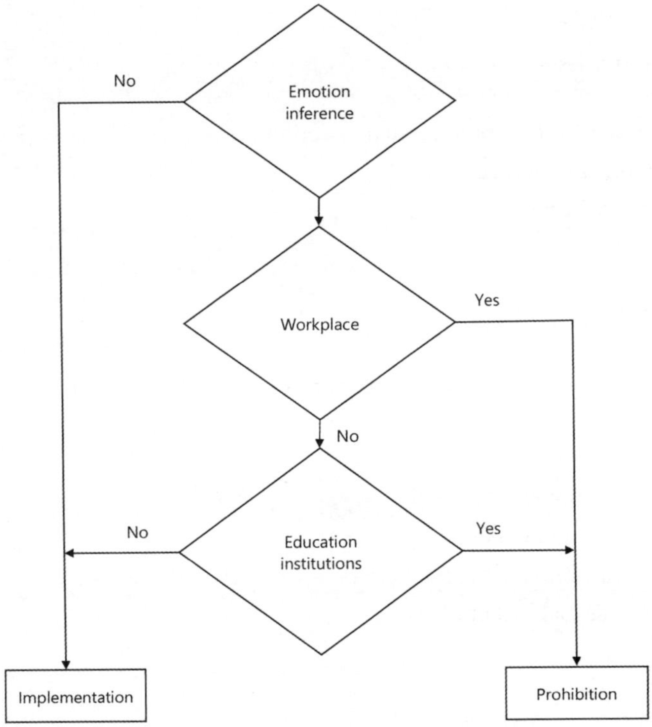

691. Note:
- Exceptions for medical or safety reasons.

5.9. *Biometric Categorisation*

5.9.1 Introduction

692. This prohibition is a new addition compared to the European Commission's initial draft.[18] It reflects concerns about the power of AI systems geared towards the surveillance and control of individuals.

5.9.2 Guiding Principles

693. The prohibition pertains to the use of an individual's biometric characteristics in a democratic society, except in cases of explicit exemptions, which are by nature limited to very high-level objectives in terms of public policy and regulation.

5.9.3 Actors

694. All AI system operators[19] are concerned, from the design phase to the use phase.

5.9.4 Activities

695. These involve the three regulated activities:
- placing on the market;
- putting into service;
- use.

5.9.5 Criteria

696. Biometric categorisation is prohibited for deducing or inferring the following:
- race;
- political opinions;
- trade union membership;
- religious or philosophical beliefs;
- sex life or sexual orientation.

---

18 Proposal for a regulation on AI, COM(2021) 206 of 21 April 2021.

19 'Operator' means a provider, product manufacturer, deployer, authorised representative, importer or distributor (AI Act, Art. 3(8)).

5.9.6 Derogations

697. They pertain to:

- the labelling or filtering of lawfully acquired biometric datasets;
- the categorisation of biometric data in the area of law enforcement.

5.9.7 Affected Persons

698. This applies to all individuals located within the European Union.

699. Notes:

- (1) It can be considered that this prohibition also applies to individuals outside the European Union.
- (2) This approach also concerns nationals of countries where the creation of facial recognition databases is permitted for both the public and private sectors.

5.9.8 Consequences

700. The prohibition is relevant even in the absence of direct harm to the affected persons.

5.9.9 Legal Algorithm

701. It can be represented as follows:

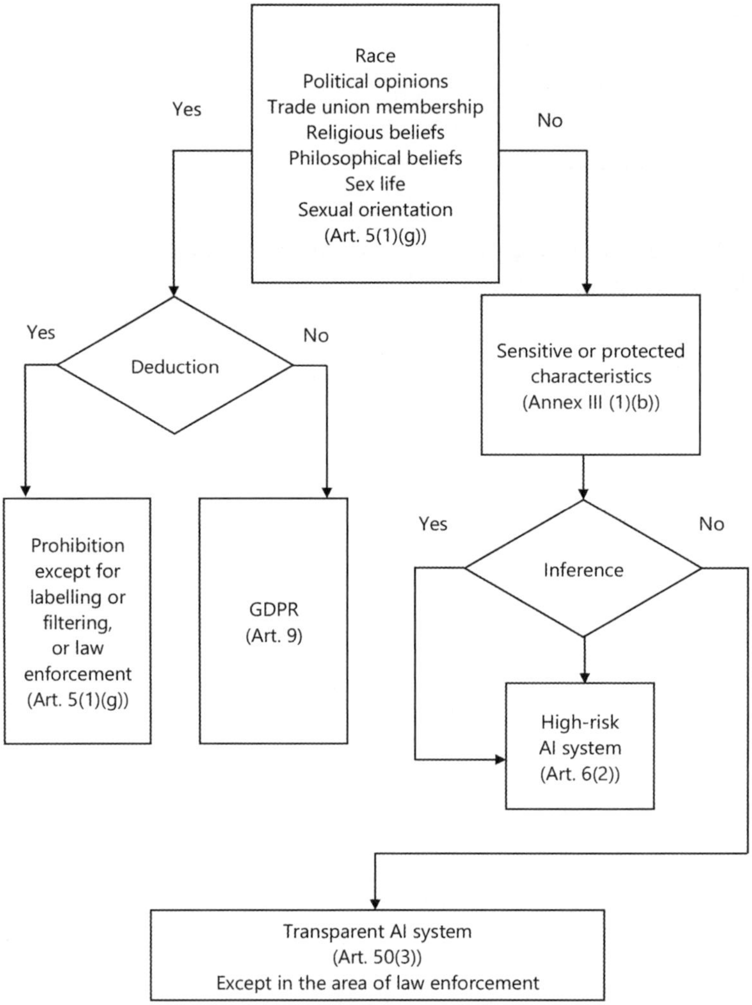

5.10. Biometrics in Publicly Accessible Spaces

5.10.1 Introduction

702. Biometrics is regulated by the GDPR (2016/679). In general, biometric techniques fall under the legal framework governing special categories of data.[20]

[20] GDPR (2016/679), Art. 9.

703. The general rule is that individuals must give their consent, except in specific cases. In this context, 'biometric data' means:[21]

- 'personal data resulting from specific technical processing relating to the physical, physiological or behavioural characteristics of a natural person, which allow or confirm the unique identification of that natural person, such as facial images or dactyloscopic data'.

704. The AI Act allows Member States to impose further conditions.[22] This is, for example, the case in France.

705. Under French law, there is a prohibition principle that applies to the processing of biometric data 'for the purpose of uniquely identifying a natural person'.[23]

706. Notes:

- (1) This prohibition does not apply to processing whose legal basis is 'the public interest and authorised in accordance with the provisions of Article 31-II and Article 32' of the French Data Protection Act.[24]
- (2) Authorisation pertains to processing 'carried out on behalf of the State, acting in the exercise of its public powers'. In France, this authorisation requires a decree issued by the Council of State, following a reasoned and published opinion from the French data protection authority (CNIL).[25]

5.10.2 Definition

707. A 'remote biometric identification system' means "an AI system for the purpose of identifying natural persons, without their active involvement, typically at a distance through the comparison of a person's biometric data with the biometric data contained in a reference database[26]".

708. The notion of 'real-time' means "without a significant delay".[27]

5.10.3 Guiding Principles

709. In general, the practice of widespread real-time surveillance of publicly accessible spaces is prohibited.[28] By way of exception, the Regulation provides

---

[21] GDPR (2016/679), Art. 4(14).
[22] GDPR (2016/679), Art. 9(4).
[23] French Data Protection Act (Loi 78-17 Informatique et libertés), Art. 6, I.
[24] French Data Protection Act (Loi 78-17 Informatique et libertés), Art. 6, III.
[25] French Data Protection Act (Loi 78-17 Informatique et libertés), Art. 32.
[26] AI Act, Art. 3(41).
[27] AI Act, Art. 3(42).
[28] AI Act, Art. 5(1)(h).

a very strict framework for biometric surveillance in the very limited context of combating serious crime and protecting victims.

5.10.4 Actors

710. All AI system operators[29] are concerned, from the design phase to the use phase.

5.10.5 Activities

711. The prohibition applies only to the use.[30]

5.10.6 Criteria

712. They are as follows:

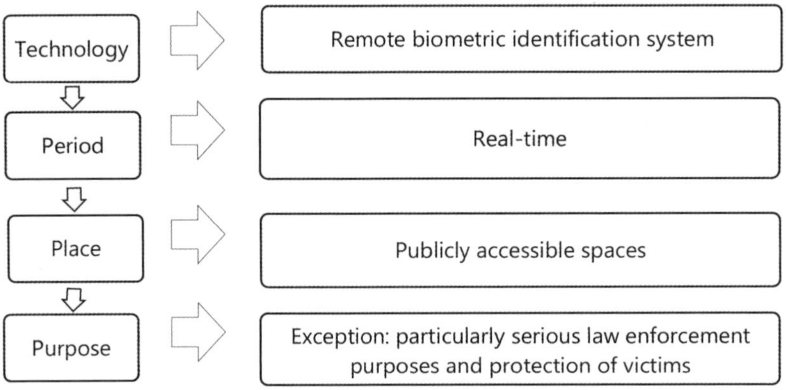

713. These criteria are cumulative.

5.10.7 Publicly Accessible Spaces

714. A publicly accessible space refers to the following places:

- a 'publicly or privately owned physical place accessible to an undetermined number of natural persons, regardless of whether certain conditions for access may apply, and regardless of the potential capacity restrictions';[31]
- places accessible to an undetermined number of natural persons;
- places that are privately or publicly owned.

---

[29] 'Operator' means a provider, product manufacturer, deployer, authorised representative, importer or distributor (AI Act, Art. 3(8)).

[30] AI Act, Art. 5(1)(h).

[31] AI Act, Art. 3(44).

715. Note:

- (1) Online spaces are not concerned.

716. There are numerous regulations that govern large-scale surveillance, on the one hand, and biometrics, on the other hand. The Regulation introduces just another principle of prohibition.[32]

5.10.8 Derogations

717. Real-time remote biometric identification in publicly accessible spaces is prohibited, except for law enforcement purposes.[33]

718. A derogation is introduced in particular for the following purposes:

- the targeted search for potential victims,[34] including minors;[35]
- the prevention of a terrorist attack;[36]
- the prosecution of specific offences.[37]

5.10.9 Modalities

719. The use of identification systems to confirm the identity of specifically targeted individuals is subject to:

- characterising the consequences of not using such a system;
- assessing the consequences of the use of such a system for the persons concerned.

5.10.10 Safeguards

720. The implementation requires specific safeguards such as:

- a legal authorisation scheme, which provides for temporal and geographic limitations;
- a fundamental rights impact assessment;
- a registration with the European Commission;[38]
- an authorisation by a national competent authority;

---

32 All of these regulations are not homogeneous and leave room for many uncertainties.

33 European Parliament study, Biometric Recognition and Behavioural Detection: Assessing the ethical aspects of biometric recognition and behavioural detection techniques with a focus on their current and future use in public spaces, August 2021.

34 AI Act, Art. 5(1)(h), (i).

35 AI Act, Rec. 9.

36 AI Act, 5(1)(h)(ii).

37 AI Act, Art. 5(1)(h)(iii) and Annex II; Council Framework Decision 2002/584/JHA, Art. 2(2).

38 Possibility of derogations in case of urgency.

- a notification to the market surveillance authority.

5.10.11 Protection of Persons

721. The identification system cannot be used to make a decision based solely on real-time remote biometric identification.

5.10.12 Special Legislation

722. The use of a biometric system in a publicly accessible space where real-time identification must be regulated by national legislation that should specify:

- the conditions of implementation;
- the terms of authorisation;
- the remedies.

723. These provisions must be notified to the European Commission at the latest 30 days following the adoption thereof.

724. Notes:

- (1) These complementary rules are not limited to real-time systems.
- (2) They apply to remote biometric systems for purposes not limited to law enforcement.
- (3) They may apply to the public or private sector with different rules depending on the objectives pursued.

725. Member states may define more restrictive rules regarding remote biometric identification systems.

5.10.13 Legal Algorithm

726. It can be represented as follows:

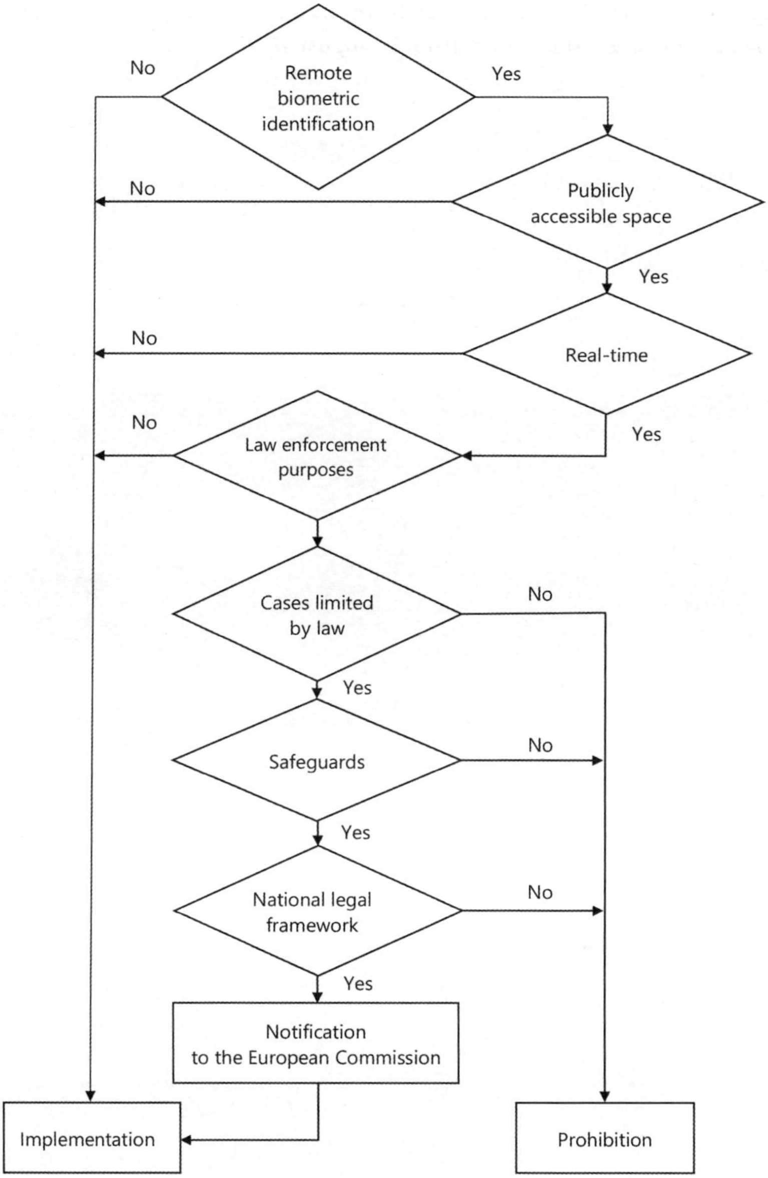

5.11. *Find Out More*

5.11.1 Timetable

727. The prohibited AI practices shall be prohibited from 2 February 2025.[39] The associated penalties[40] shall apply from 2 August 2025.[41]

[39] AI Act, Art. 113(a).
[40] AI Act, Art. 99(3).
[41] AI Act, Art. 113(b).

CHAPTER III
HIGH-RISK AI SYSTEMS

728. Key takeaways: Regulating high-risk systems is crucial for trustworthy AI technologies. It concerns the following:

- classification of high-risk systems (Annex I and Annex III);
- risk management (requirements);
- obligations of providers and deployers;
- organisation and implementation of certification mechanisms (notifying authorities and notified bodies);
- conformity standards (certificates, CE marking, EU declaration).

SECTION 1. CLASSIFICATION OF AI SYSTEMS AS HIGH-RISK

6 ARTICLE 6. CLASSIFICATION RULES FOR HIGH-RISK AI SYSTEMS

1. Irrespective of whether an AI system is placed on the market or put into service independently of the products referred to in points (a) and (b), that AI system shall be considered to be high-risk where both of the following conditions are fulfilled:

(a) the AI system is intended to be used as a safety component of a product, or the AI system is itself a product, covered by the Union harmonisation legislation listed in Annex I;

(b) the product whose safety component pursuant to point (a) is the AI system, or the AI system itself as a product, is required to undergo a third-party conformity assessment, with a view to the placing on the market or the putting into service of that product pursuant to the Union harmonisation legislation listed in Annex I.

2. In addition to the high-risk AI systems referred to in paragraph 1, AI systems referred to in Annex III shall be considered to be high-risk.

3. By derogation from paragraph 2, an AI system referred to in Annex III shall not be considered to be high-risk where it does not pose a significant risk of harm to the health, safety or fundamental rights of natural persons, including by not materially influencing the outcome of decision making.

The first subparagraph shall apply where any of the following conditions is fulfilled:

(a) the AI system is intended to perform a narrow procedural task;

(b) the AI system is intended to improve the result of a previously completed human activity;

(c) the AI system is intended to detect decision-making patterns or deviations from prior decision-making patterns and is not meant to replace or influence the previously completed human assessment, without proper human review; or

(d) the AI system is intended to perform a preparatory task to an assessment relevant for the purposes of the use cases listed in Annex III.

Notwithstanding the first subparagraph, an AI system referred to in Annex III shall always be considered to be high-risk where the AI system performs profiling of natural persons.

4. A provider who considers that an AI system referred to in Annex III is not high-risk shall document its assessment before that system is placed on the market or put into service. Such provider shall be subject to the registration obligation set out in Article 49(2). Upon request of national competent authorities, the provider shall provide the documentation of the assessment.

5. The Commission shall, after consulting the European Artificial Intelligence Board (the 'Board'), and no later than 2 February 2026, provide guidelines specifying the practical implementation of this Article in line with Article 96 together with a comprehensive list of practical examples of use cases of AI systems that are high-risk and not high-risk.

6. The Commission is empowered to adopt delegated acts in accordance with Article 97 in order to amend paragraph 3, second subparagraph, of this Article by adding new conditions to those laid down therein, or by modifying them, where there is concrete and reliable evidence of the existence of AI systems that fall under the scope of Annex III, but do not pose a significant risk of harm to the health, safety or fundamental rights of natural persons.

7. The Commission shall adopt delegated acts in accordance with Article 97 in order to amend paragraph 3, second subparagraph, of this Article by deleting any of the conditions laid down therein, where there is concrete and reliable evidence that this is necessary to maintain the level of protection of health, safety and fundamental rights provided for by this Regulation.

8. Any amendment to the conditions laid down in paragraph 3, second subparagraph, adopted in accordance with paragraphs 6 and 7 of this Article shall not decrease the overall level of protection of health, safety and fundamental rights provided for by this Regulation and shall ensure consistency with the delegated acts adopted pursuant to Article 7(1), and take account of market and technological developments.

6.1. Recitals

729. (46) High-risk AI systems should only be placed on the Union market, put into service or used if they comply with certain mandatory requirements. Those requirements should ensure that high-risk AI systems available in the Union or whose output is otherwise used in the Union do not pose unacceptable risks to important Union public interests as recognised and protected by Union law. On the basis of the New Legislative Framework, as clarified in the Commission notice 'The "Blue Guide" on the implementation of EU product rules 2022',[1] the general rule is that more than one legal act of Union harmonisation legislation, such as Regulations (EU) 2017/745[2] and (EU) 2017/746[3] of the European Parliament and of the Council or Directive 2006/42/EC of the European Parliament and of the Council,[4] may be applicable to one product, since the making available or putting into service can take place only when the product complies with all applicable Union harmonisation legislation. To ensure consistency and avoid unnecessary administrative burdens or costs, providers of a product that contains one or more high-risk AI systems, to which the requirements of this Regulation and of the Union harmonisation legislation listed in an annex to this Regulation apply, should have flexibility with regard to operational decisions on how to ensure compliance of a product that contains one or more AI systems with all applicable requirements of the Union harmonisation legislation in an optimal manner. AI systems identified as high-risk should be limited to those that have a significant harmful impact on the health, safety and fundamental rights of persons in the Union and such limitation should minimise any potential restriction to international trade.

730. (47) AI systems could have an adverse impact on the health and safety of persons, in particular when such systems operate as safety components of products. Consistent with the objectives of Union harmonisation legislation to facilitate the free movement of products in the internal market and to ensure that only safe and otherwise compliant products find their way into the market, it is important that the safety risks that may be generated by a product as a whole due to its digital components, including AI systems, are duly prevented and mitigated. For instance, increasingly autonomous robots, whether in the context

---

1 OJ C247/ 1.

2 Regulation (EU) 2017/745 of the European Parliament and of the Council of 5 April 2017 on medical devices, amending Directive 2001/83/EC, Regulation (EC) No 178/2002 and Regulation (EC) No 1223/2009 and repealing Council Directives 90/385/EEC and 93/42/EEC, [2017] OJ L117/1.

3 Regulation (EU) 2017/746 of the European Parliament and of the Council of 5 April 2017 on in vitro diagnostic medical devices and repealing Directive 98/79/EC and Commission Decision 2010/227/EU, [2017] OJ L117/176.

4 Directive 2006/42/EC of the European Parliament and of the Council of 17 May 2006 on machinery, and amending Directive 95/16/EC, [2006] OJ L157/24.

of manufacturing or personal assistance and care should be able to safely operate and performs their functions in complex environments. Similarly, in the health sector where the stakes for life and health are particularly high, increasingly sophisticated diagnostics systems and systems supporting human decisions should be reliable and accurate.

731. (51) The classification of an AI system as high-risk pursuant to this Regulation should not necessarily mean that the product whose safety component is the AI system, or the AI system itself as a product, is considered to be high-risk under the criteria established in the relevant Union harmonisation legislation that applies to the product. This is, in particular, the case for Regulations (EU) 2017/745 and (EU) 2017/746, where a third-party conformity assessment is provided for medium-risk and high-risk products.

732. (52) As regards stand-alone AI systems, namely high-risk AI systems other than those that are safety components of products, or that are themselves products, it is appropriate to classify them as high-risk if, in light of their intended purpose, they pose a high risk of harm to the health and safety or the fundamental rights of persons, taking into account both the severity of the possible harm and its probability of occurrence and they are used in a number of specifically pre-defined areas specified in this Regulation. The identification of those systems is based on the same methodology and criteria envisaged also for any future amendments of the list of high-risk AI systems that the Commission should be empowered to adopt, via delegated acts, to take into account the rapid pace of technological development, as well as the potential changes in the use of AI systems.

733. (53) It is also important to clarify that there may be specific cases in which AI systems referred to in pre-defined areas specified in this Regulation do not lead to a significant risk of harm to the legal interests protected under those areas because they do not materially influence the decision-making or do not harm those interests substantially. For the purposes of this Regulation, an AI system that does not materially influence the outcome of decision-making should be understood to be an AI system that does not have an impact on the substance, and thereby the outcome, of decision-making, whether human or automated. An AI system that does not materially influence the outcome of decision-making could include situations in which one or more of the following conditions are fulfilled. The first such condition should be that the AI system is intended to perform a narrow procedural task, such as an AI system that transforms unstructured data into structured data, an AI system that classifies incoming documents into categories or an AI system that is used to detect duplicates among a large number of applications. Those tasks are of such narrow and limited nature that they pose only limited risks which are not increased through the use of an AI system in a context that is listed as a high-risk use in an annex to this Regulation. The second condition should be that the task performed by the AI system is intended to improve the result of a previously completed human activity that may be relevant for the purposes of the high-risk uses listed in an annex to this Regulation. Considering those characteristics, the AI system provides only an additional layer to a human activity with consequently lowered risk. That condition would, for example, apply to AI systems that are intended to improve the language used in previously drafted documents, for example in relation to professional tone, academic style of language or by aligning text to a certain brand messaging. The third condition should be that the AI system is intended to detect decision-making patterns or deviations from prior decision-making patterns. The risk would be lowered because the use of the AI system follows a previously completed human assessment which it is not meant to replace or influence, without proper human review. Such AI systems include for instance those that, given a certain grading pattern of a teacher, can be used to check ex post whether the teacher may have deviated from the grading pattern so as to flag potential inconsistencies or anomalies. The fourth condition should be that the AI system is intended to perform a task that is only preparatory to an assessment relevant for the purposes of the AI systems listed in an annex to this Regulation, thus making the possible impact of the output of the system very low in terms of representing a risk for the assessment to follow. That condition covers, inter alia, smart solutions for file handling, which include various functions from indexing, searching, text and speech processing or linking data to other data sources, or AI systems used for translation of initial documents. In any case, AI systems used in high-risk use-cases listed in an annex to this Regulation should be considered to pose significant risks of harm to the health, safety or fundamental rights if the AI system implies profiling within the meaning of Article 4, point (4) of Regulation (EU) 2016/679 or Article 3, point (4) of Directive (EU) 2016/680 or Article 3, point (5) of Regulation (EU) 2018/1725. To ensure traceability and transparency, a provider who considers that an AI system is not high-risk on the basis of the conditions referred to above should draw up documentation of the assessment before that system is placed on the market or put into service and should provide that documentation to national competent authorities upon request. Such a provider should be obliged to register the AI system in the EU database established under this Regulation. With a view to providing further guidance for the practical implementation of the conditions under which the AI systems listed in an annex to this Regulation are, on an exceptional basis, non-high-risk, the Commission should, after consulting the Board, provide guidelines specifying that practical implementation, completed by a comprehensive list of practical examples of use cases of AI systems that are high-risk and use cases that are not.

734. **(54)** As biometric data constitutes a special category of personal data, it is appropriate to classify as high-risk several critical-use cases of biometric systems, insofar as their use is permitted under relevant Union and national law. Technical inaccuracies of AI systems intended for the remote biometric identification of natural persons can lead to biased results and entail discriminatory effects. The risk of such biased results and discriminatory effects is particularly relevant with regard to age, ethnicity, race, sex or disabilities. Remote biometric identification systems should therefore be classified as high-risk in view of the risks that they pose. Such a classification excludes AI systems intended to be used for biometric verification, including authentication, the sole purpose of which is to confirm that a specific natural person is who that person claims to be and to confirm the identity of a natural person for the sole purpose of having access to a service, unlocking a device or having secure access to premises. In addition, AI systems intended to be used for biometric categorisation according to sensitive attributes or characteristics protected under Article 9(1) of Regulation (EU) 2016/679 on the basis of biometric data, in so far as these are not prohibited under this Regulation, and emotion recognition systems that are not prohibited under this Regulation, should be classified as high-risk. Biometric systems which are intended to be used solely for the purpose of enabling cybersecurity and personal data protection measures should not be considered to be high-risk AI systems.

735. (61) Certain AI systems intended for the administration of justice and democratic processes should be classified as high-risk, considering their potentially significant impact on democracy, the rule of law, individual freedoms as well as the right to an effective remedy and to a fair trial. In particular, to address the risks of potential biases, errors and opacity, it is appropriate to qualify as high-risk AI systems intended to be used by a judicial authority or on its behalf to assist judicial authorities in researching and interpreting facts and the law and in applying the law to a concrete set of facts. AI systems intended to be used by alternative dispute resolution bodies for those purposes should also be considered to be high-risk when the outcomes of the alternative dispute resolution proceedings produce legal effects for the parties. The use of AI tools can support the decision-making power of judges or judicial independence, but should not replace it: the final decision-making must remain a human-driven activity. The classification of AI systems as high-risk should not, however, extend to AI systems intended for purely ancillary administrative activities that do not affect the actual administration of justice in individual cases, such as anonymisation or pseudonymisation of judicial decisions, documents or data, communication between personnel, administrative tasks.

736. (110) General-purpose AI models could pose systemic risks which include, but are not limited to, any actual or reasonably foreseeable negative effects in relation to major accidents, disruptions of critical sectors and serious consequences to public health and safety; any actual or reasonably foreseeable negative effects on democratic processes, public and economic security; the dissemination of illegal, false, or discriminatory content. Systemic risks should be understood to increase with model capabilities and model reach, can arise along the entire lifecycle of the model, and are influenced by conditions of misuse, model reliability, model fairness and model security, the level of autonomy of the model, its access to tools, novel or combined modalities, release and distribution strategies, the potential to remove guardrails and other factors. In particular, international approaches have so far identified the need to pay attention to risks from potential intentional misuse or unintended issues of control relating to alignment with human intent; chemical, biological, radiological, and nuclear risks, such as the ways in which barriers to entry can be lowered, including for weapons development, design acquisition, or use; offensive cyber capabilities, such as the ways in vulnerability discovery, exploitation, or operational use can be enabled; the effects of interaction and tool use, including for example the capacity to control physical systems and interfere with critical infrastructure; risks from models of making copies of themselves or 'self-replicating' or training other models; the ways in which models can give rise to harmful bias and discrimination with risks to individuals, communities or societies; the facilitation of disinformation or harming privacy with threats to democratic values and human rights; risk that a particular event could lead to a chain reaction with considerable negative effects that could affect up to an entire city, an entire domain activity or an entire community.

737. (111) It is appropriate to establish a methodology for the classification of general-purpose AI models as general-purpose AI model with systemic risks. Since systemic risks result from particularly high capabilities, a general-purpose AI model should be considered to present systemic risks if it has high-impact capabilities, evaluated on the basis of appropriate technical tools and methodologies, or significant impact on the internal market due to its reach. High-impact capabilities in general-purpose AI models means capabilities that match or exceed the capabilities recorded in the most advanced general-purpose AI models. The full range of capabilities in a model could be better understood after its placing on the market or when deployers interact with the model. According to the state of the art at the time of entry into force of this Regulation, the cumulative amount of computation used for the training of the general-purpose AI model measured in floating point operations is one of the relevant approximations for model capabilities. The cumulative amount of computation used for training includes the computation used across the activities and methods that are intended to enhance the capabilities of the model prior to deployment, such as pre-training, synthetic data generation and fine-tuning. Therefore, an initial threshold of floating point operations should be set, which, if met by a general-purpose AI model, leads to a presumption that the model is a general-purpose AI model with systemic risks. This threshold should be adjusted over time to reflect technological and industrial changes, such as algorithmic improvements or increased hardware efficiency, and should be supplemented with benchmarks and indicators for model capability. To inform this, the AI Office should engage with the scientific community, industry, civil society and other experts. Thresholds, as well as tools and benchmarks for the assessment of high-impact capabilities, should be strong predictors of generality, its capabilities and associated systemic risk of general-purpose AI models, and could take into account the way the model will be placed on the market or the number of users it may affect. To complement this system, there should be a possibility for the Commission to take individual decisions designating a general-purpose AI model as a general-purpose AI model with systemic risk if it is found that such model has capabilities or an impact equivalent to those captured by the set threshold. That decision should be taken on the basis of an overall assessment of the criteria for the designation of a general-purpose AI model with systemic risk set out in an annex to this Regulation, such as quality or size of the training data set, number of business and end users, its input and output modalities, its level of autonomy and scalability, or the tools it has access to. Upon a reasoned request of a provider whose model has been designated as a general-purpose AI model with systemic risk, the Commission should take the request into account and may decide to reassess whether the general-purpose AI model can still be considered to present systemic risks.

738. **(112)** It is also necessary to clarify a procedure for the classification of a general-purpose AI model with systemic risks. A general-purpose AI model that meets the applicable threshold for high-impact capabilities should be presumed to be a general-purpose AI models with systemic risk. The provider should notify the AI Office at the latest two weeks after the requirements are met or it becomes known that a general-purpose AI model will meet the requirements that lead to the presumption. This is especially relevant in relation to the threshold of floating point operations because training of general-purpose AI models takes considerable planning which includes the upfront allocation of compute resources and, therefore, providers of general-purpose AI models are able to know if their model would meet the threshold before the training is completed. In the context of that notification, the provider should be able to demonstrate that, because of its specific characteristics, a general-purpose AI model exceptionally does not present systemic risks, and that it thus should not be classified as a general-purpose AI model with systemic risks. That information is valuable for the AI Office to anticipate the placing on the market of general-purpose AI models with systemic risks and the providers can start to engage with the AI Office early on. That information is especially important with regard to general-purpose AI models that are planned to be released as open-source, given that, after the open-source model release, necessary measures to ensure compliance with the obligations under this Regulation may be more difficult to implement.

739. **(113)** If the Commission becomes aware of the fact that a general-purpose AI model meets the requirements to classify as a general-purpose AI model with systemic risk, which previously had either not been known or of which the relevant provider has failed to notify the Commission, the Commission should be empowered to designate it so. A system of qualified alerts should ensure that the AI Office is made aware by the scientific panel of general-purpose AI models that should possibly be classified as general-purpose AI models with systemic risk, in addition to the monitoring activities of the AI Office.

740. (163) With a view to complementing the governance systems for general-purpose AI models, the scientific panel should support the monitoring activities of the AI Office and may, in certain cases, provide qualified alerts to the AI Office which trigger follow-ups, such as investigations. This should be the case where the scientific panel has reason to suspect that a general-purpose AI model poses a concrete and identifiable risk at Union level. Furthermore, this should be the case where the scientific panel has reason to suspect that a general-purpose AI model meets the criteria that would lead to a classification as general-purpose AI model with systemic risk. To equip the scientific panel with the information necessary for the performance of those tasks, there should be a mechanism whereby the scientific panel can request the Commission to require documentation or information from a provider.

741. (173) In order to ensure that the regulatory framework can be adapted where necessary, the power to adopt acts in accordance with Article 290 TFEU should be delegated to the Commission to amend the conditions under which an AI system is not to be considered to be high-risk, the list of high-risk AI systems, the provisions regarding technical documentation, the content of the EU declaration of conformity the provisions regarding the conformity assessment procedures, the provisions establishing the high-risk AI systems to which the conformity assessment procedure based on assessment of the quality management system and assessment of the technical documentation should apply, the threshold, benchmarks and indicators, including by supplementing those benchmarks and indicators, in the rules for the classification of general-purpose AI models with systemic risk, the criteria for the designation of general-purpose AI models with systemic risk, the technical documentation for providers of general-purpose AI models and the transparency information for providers of general-purpose AI models. It is of particular importance that the Commission carry out appropriate consultations during its preparatory work, including at expert level, and that those consultations be conducted in accordance with the principles laid down in the Interinstitutional Agreement of 13 April 2016 on Better Law-Making.[5] In particular, to ensure equal participation in the preparation of delegated acts, the European Parliament and the Council receive all documents at the same time as Member States' experts, and their experts systematically have access to meetings of Commission expert groups dealing with the preparation of delegated acts.

5 [2016] OJ L123/1.

742. **(179)** This Regulation should apply from 2 August 2026. However, taking into account the unacceptable risk associated with the use of AI in certain ways, the prohibitions as well as the general provisions of this Regulation should already apply from 2 February 2025. While the full effect of those prohibitions follows with the establishment of the governance and enforcement of this Regulation, anticipating the application of the prohibitions is important to take account of unacceptable risks and to have an effect on other procedures, such as in civil law. Moreover, the infrastructure related to the governance and the conformity assessment system should be operational before 2 August 2026, therefore the provisions on notified bodies and governance structure should apply from 2 August 2025. Given the rapid pace of technological advancements and adoption of general-purpose AI models, obligations for providers of general-purpose AI models should apply from 2 August 2025. Codes of practice should be ready by 2 May 2025 in view of enabling providers to demonstrate compliance on time. The AI Office should ensure that classification rules and procedures are up to date in light of technological developments. In addition, Member States should lay down and notify to the Commission the rules on penalties, including administrative fines, and ensure that they are properly and effectively implemented by the date of application of this Regulation. Therefore the provisions on penalties should apply from 2 August 2025.

6.2. *General Approach*

6.2.1 Preamble

743. The regulation of high-risk AI systems is at the core of the AI Act. The goal is to find a balance between the protection of individuals and the development of innovation within the European Union.

6.2.2 Guiding Principles

744. The regulation of high-risk AI systems consists of:

- accepting risk based on a cost-benefit analysis;
- implementing a risk minimisation policy to an acceptable level;
- monitoring risks and associated outcomes to implement corrective actions;
- managing everything under the supervision of a local market surveillance authority.

6.2.3 Actors

745. All AI system operators[6] are concerned, from the design phase to the use phase.

6.2.4 Activities

746. These involve the three regulated activities:

- placing on the market;
- putting into service;
- use.

6.2.5 Definition

747. Risk means 'the combination of the probability of an occurrence of harm and the severity of that harm'.[7] However, the qualification of 'high' associated with the concept of 'risk' is not specified.

748. It is common practice in the field of risk management to use the following matrix:

Severity[8] \ **Likelihood**	Very Unlikely	Unlikely	Likely	Very Likely
Critical	O	O	R	R
Major	Y	O	R	R
Medium	G	Y	O	O
Minor	G	G	Y	Y

6.2.6 Qualification

749. On the one hand, the concept of 'high risk' is assessed in the AI Act in a formal manner. The mere fact that an AI system falls under the scope of the legislation listed in Annex I or the areas listed in Annex III results in that said

6 'Operator' means a provider, product manufacturer, deployer, authorised representative, importer or distributor (AI Act, Art. 3(8)).

7 AI Act, Art. 3(2).

8 Y = (Yellow); R = (Red); G = (Green); O = (Orange).

AI system to be classified as high risk; operators do not have to carry out any assessment.[9]

750. On the other hand, to obtain a de-classification, i.e., to be downgraded from the 'high-risk' classification for AI systems listed in Annex III, a subjective assessment of risks is to be taken into account.

6.2.7 Classification

751. High-risk AI systems are divided into two categories:

- AI systems considered as safety products or safety components of products listed in Annex I;
- AI systems related to the areas listed in Annex III.[10]

6.3. *High-Risk AI Systems That Are Safety Products or Safety Components of Products (Annex I)*

6.3.1 Introduction

752. This first category of high-risk AI systems includes all high-risk AI systems that are not specifically otherwise qualified because of their sector or intended purpose.[11] In general terms, this category is defined by two cumulative criteria related to the European Union harmonisation legislation listed in Annex I.

6.3.2 Classification

753. It includes AI systems that are:

- safety components of products;
- safety products as such.

6.4. *Criteria*

754. There are two criteria that should be both fulfilled:

- the component or product concerns one of the legislative acts listed in Annex I;
- the component or product is required to undergo a third-party conformity assessment in accordance with the legislative acts listed in Annex I.

---

9 This approach is very different from the rules concerning the protection of personal data: GDPR (EU) 2016/679 Art. 35.

10 Annex III: High-risk AI systems referred to in Article 6(2).

11 As referred to in Annex I.

755. Notes:

- (1) Annex I includes the list of European Union harmonisation legislation.
- (2) Annex I is divided into two sections:
  - o Section A: List of Union harmonisation legislation based on the New Legislative Framework;
  - o Section B: List of other Union harmonisation legislation.

6.4.1 List of European Union Harmonisation Legislation Based on the New Legislative Framework

756. This first list, corresponding to Section A of Annex I, includes the following legislation:

NO.	THEME	DATE	SPECIFICATION
1.	Directive 2006/42/EC[12]	17 May 2006	Machinery and amending Directive 95/16/EC
2.	Directive 2009/48/EC	18 June 2009	Safety of toys
3.	Directive 2013/53/EU	20 November 2013	Recreational craft and personal watercraft
4.	Directive 2014/33/EU	26 February 2014	Lifts and safety components for lifts
5.	Directive 2014/34/EU	26 February 2014	Equipment and protective systems intended for use in potentially explosive atmospheres
6.	Directive 2014/53/EU	16 April 2014	Making available on the market of radio equipment
7.	Directive 2014/68/EU	15 May 2014	Making available on the market of pressure equipment
8.	Regulation (EU) 2016/424	9 March 2016	Cableway installations
9.	Regulation (EU) 2016/425	9 March 2016	Personal protective equipment
10.	Regulation (EU) 2016/426	9 March 2016	Appliances burning gaseous fuels
11.	Regulation (EU) 2017/745	5 April 2017	Medical devices

12 This directive, which is still in force, will gradually be replaced by Regulation (EU) 2023/1230 of the European Parliament and of the Council of 14 June 2023 on machinery and repealing Directive 2006/42/EC of the European Parliament and of the Council and Council Directive 73/361/EEC ([2023] OJ L165/1), which will apply from 14 January 2027.

NO.	THEME	DATE	SPECIFICATION
12.	Regulation (EU) 2017/746	5 April 2017	*In vitro* diagnostic medical devices

6.4.2 List of Other European Union Harmonisation Legislation

757. This second list, corresponding to Section B of Annex I, includes the following legislation:

NO.	THEME	DATE	SPECIFICATION
1.	Regulation (EC) No 300/2008	11 March 2008	Common rules in the field of civil aviation security
2.	Regulation (EU) No 168/2013	15 January 2013	Approval and market surveillance of two- or three-wheel vehicles and quadricycles
3.	Regulation (EU) No 167/2013	5 February 2013	Approval and market surveillance of agricultural and forestry vehicles
4.	Directive No 2014/90/ EU	23 July 2014	Marine equipment
5.	Directive (EU) No 2016/797	11 May 2016	Interoperability of the rail system within the European Union
6.	Regulation (EU) No 2018/858	30 May 2018	Approval and market surveillance of motor vehicles and their trailers, and of systems, components and separate technical units intended for such vehicles, amending Regulations (EC) No 715/2007 and (EC) No 595/2009
7.	Regulation (EU) No 2018/1139	4 July 2018	Common rules in the field of civil aviation and establishing a European Union Aviation Safety Agency, and amending Regulations (EC) No 2111/2005, (EC) No 1008/2008, (EU) No 996/2010, (EU) No 376/2014 and Directives 2014/30/EU and 2014/53/EU
8.	Regulation (EU) No 2019/2144	27 November 2019	Type-approval requirements for motor vehicles and their trailers, and systems, components and separate technical units intended for such vehicles, as regards their general safety and the protection of vehicle occupants and vulnerable road users, amending Regulation (EU) 2018/858

6.4.3 Exclusions

758. The harmonisation legislation listed in Section B of Annex I is excluded from the legal framework related to AI. Those laws have been modified to account for the use of high-risk AI as a security component of a product or as security products as such. Only the following elements are to be considered:

NO.	THEME	SPECIFICATION
1.	Legal rules for high-risk AI systems listed in Section B	Exclusion of all obligations except
2.	Qualification	Application of Article 6(1) relating to one of the two definitions of high-risk AI systems associated with Section B of Annex I[13]
3.	Civil aviation	Application of Article 102 of the AIA amending Regulation (EC) No 300/2008
4.	Agricultural and forestry vehicles	Application of Article 103 of the AIA amending Regulation (EU) No 167/2013
5.	Two- or three-wheel vehicles and quadricycles	Application of Article 104 of the AIA amending Regulation (EU) No 168/2013
6.	Marine equipment	Application of Article 105 of the AIA amending Directive 2014/90/EU
7.	Rail system	Application of Article 106 of the AIA amending Directive (EU) 2016/797
8.	Motor vehicles and their trailers	Application of Article 107 of the AIA amending Regulation (EU) No 2018/858
9.	European Union Aviation Safety Agency	Application of Article 108 of the AIA amending Regulation (EU) No 2018/1139
10.	Motor vehicles and their trailers (approval)	Application of Article 109 of the AIA amending Regulation (EU) No 2019/2144
11.	Evaluation and review procedure	Trajectory for updating legislation to take into account developments in AI technologies. Application of Article 102
12.	Regulatory sandboxes (Art. 57)	Application of Article 50 of the AIA if EU harmonisation legislation has taken into account the AI Act requirements for high-risk AI systems

[13] See the above list.

759. Notes:

- (1) The inclusion of a safety component based on a high-risk AI system is not intended to alter the risk level of the product concerned by the aforementioned harmonisation legislation.[14]
- (2) The same applies if the high-risk AI system is a product as such.
- (3) Examples: medical devices[15] or *in vitro* diagnostic medical devices.[16]

6.5. *High-Risk Sectoral AI Systems (Annex III)*

6.5.1 Introduction

760. This second category of high-risk AI systems is defined according to sector-specific criteria and functional specifications, which are outlined in Annex III.

6.5.2 Classification

761. It is classified alphabetically as follows:

NO.	THEME	SPECIFICATION	REFERENCE
1.	Access to self-employment		Annex III(4)
2.	Asylum	In so far as use is permitted under relevant Union or national law	Annex III(7)
3.	Biometrics	In so far as use is permitted under relevant Union or national law	Annex III(1)
4.	Border control management	In so far as use is permitted under relevant Union or national law	Annex III(7)
5.	Critical infrastructure	E.g. road traffic, supply of water, gas, heating or electricity	Annex III(2)
6.	Democracy	Democratic processes	Annex III(8)
7.	Education		Annex III(3)
8.	Employment		Annex III(4)
9.	Essential private services	Access and enjoyment	Annex III(5)
10.	Essential public benefits	Access and enjoyment	Annex III(5)

14 AI Act, Rec. 51.
15 Regulation (EU) 2017/745 of 5 April 2017.
16 Regulation (EU) 2017/746 of 5 April 2017.

NO.	THEME	SPECIFICATION	REFERENCE
11.	Essential public services	Access and enjoyment	Annex III(5)
12.	Justice	Administration of justice	Annex III(8)
13.	Law enforcement	In so far as use is permitted under relevant Union or national law	Annex III(6)
14.	Migration	In so far as use is permitted under relevant Union or national law	Annex III(7)
15.	Training		Annex III(3)
16.	Workers' management		Annex III(4)

6.5.3 Qualification

762. The concept of 'high risk' applies based on all of the following three criteria:

- the type of activity specified in the aforementioned classification;
- the assessment of the risk level;
- the nature and severity of the harm.

6.5.3.1 *Values*

763. The AI Act specifies only the following protected values:

- health;
- safety;
- fundamental rights.

764. Notes:

- (1) These three values were included in the scope of the AI Act in its first version.[17]
- (2) New values, added subsequently, are not mentioned in the derogation, namely:
  - o environmental protection;
  - o the rule of law;
  - o democracy.[18]
- (3) However, given the objectives of the Regulation, one can consider that they apply to high-risk AI systems.

---

17 Proposal for a Regulation on IA COM(2021) 206 final of 21 April 2021.

18 No immediate reason justifies this particularity other than a defect.

6.5.3.2 *Risk Assessment*

765. A risk is considered not significant in terms of harmful consequences in the following contexts:

NO.	THEME	SPECIFICATION
1.	Decision support	The AI system performs a preparatory task to an assessment
2.	Improvement	The AI system improves the result of a previously completed human activity
3.	Decision-making	The AI system detects patterns or deviations and is not meant to replace human assessment
4.	Process	The AI system performs a narrow procedural task

6.5.3.3 *Harm*

766. The derogation applies where:

- the AI system does not pose a significant risk of harm;
- the AI system does not materially influence the outcome of decision making.

6.5.3.4 *Presumption*

767. An AI system referred to in Annex III will always be considered to be high-risk where the AI system performs profiling of natural persons.

6.5.3.5 *Specific Derogations*

768. The classification as a high-risk AI system for AI systems listed in Annex III is a rebuttable presumption.[19]

769. The provider can avoid this classification by implementing the following measures:

NO.	OBLIGATION	SPECIFICATION
1.	Documentation	Evidence file demonstrating the absence of significant risk as per the aforementioned criteria[20]
2.	EU database[21]	Registration, like all other high-risk AI systems
3.	Control	Provision of documentation upon request of national competent authorities

19 AI Act, Art. 6(4).
20 See 6.5.3 Qualification.
21 AI Act, Art. 49.

6.6. *Information and Examples*

770. The European Commission must, after consulting the AI Board:

- provide operators with guidelines and examples;
- supply use cases of AI systems that are not subject to the requirements for high-risk systems listed in Annex III.

6.7. *Legal Algorithm*

771. It can be represented as follows:

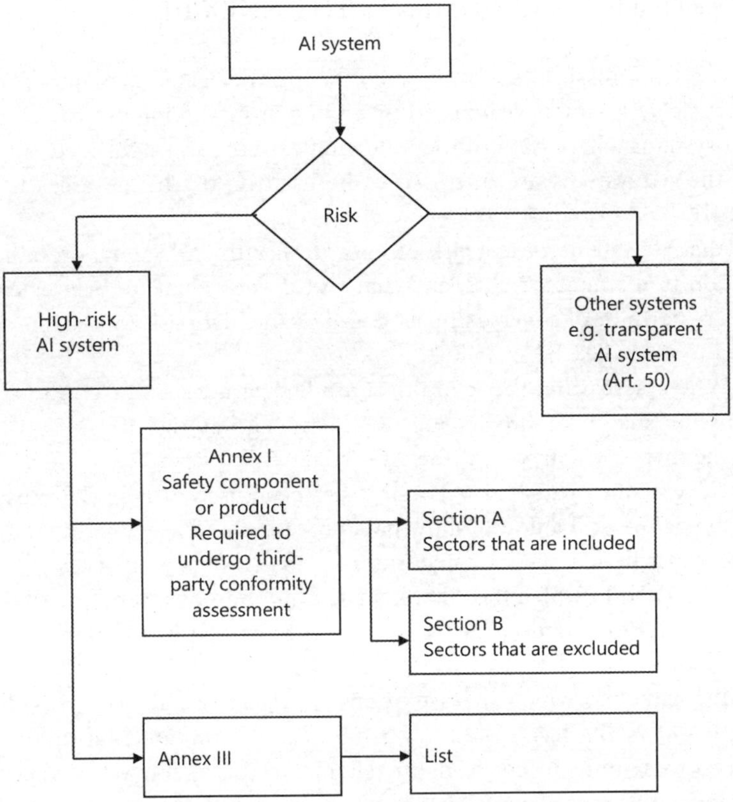

6.8. *Find Out More*

6.8.1 Coordinated Texts

772. When an AI system is removed from the "high-risk" classification under the AI Act, Regulation (EU) 2023/988 on general product safety must be applied.

6.8.2 Timetable

773. The application dates are as follows:

NO.	HIGH-RISK AI SYSTEM	DATE
1.	Annex I	2 August 2027[22]
2.	Annex III	2 August 2026[23]

7 ARTICLE 7. AMENDMENTS TO ANNEX III

1. The Commission is empowered to adopt delegated acts in accordance with Article 97 to amend Annex III by adding or modifying use-cases of high-risk AI systems where both of the following conditions are fulfilled:

(a) the AI systems are intended to be used in any of the areas listed in Annex III;

(b) the AI systems pose a risk of harm to health and safety, or an adverse impact on fundamental rights, and that risk is equivalent to, or greater than, the risk of harm or of adverse impact posed by the high-risk AI systems already referred to in Annex III.

2. When assessing the condition under paragraph 1, point (b), the Commission shall take into account the following criteria:

(a) the intended purpose of the AI system;

(b) the extent to which an AI system has been used or is likely to be used;

(c) the nature and amount of the data processed and used by the AI system, in particular whether special categories of personal data are processed;

(d) the extent to which the AI system acts autonomously and the possibility for a human to override a decision or recommendations that may lead to potential harm;

(e) the extent to which the use of an AI system has already caused harm to health and safety, has had an adverse impact on fundamental rights or has given rise to significant concerns in relation to the likelihood of such harm or adverse impact, as demonstrated, for example, by reports or documented allegations submitted to national competent authorities or by other reports, as appropriate;

[22] AI Act, Art. 113(c).

[23] AI Act, Art. 113.

(f) the potential extent of such harm or such adverse impact, in particular in terms of its intensity and its ability to affect multiple persons or to disproportionately affect a particular group of persons;

(g) the extent to which persons who are potentially harmed or suffer an adverse impact are dependent on the outcome produced with an AI system, in particular because for practical or legal reasons it is not reasonably possible to opt-out from that outcome;

(h) the extent to which there is an imbalance of power, or the persons who are potentially harmed or suffer an adverse impact are in a vulnerable position in relation to the deployer of an AI system, in particular due to status, authority, knowledge, economic or social circumstances, or age;

(i) the extent to which the outcome produced involving an AI system is easily corrigible or reversible, taking into account the technical solutions available to correct or reverse it, whereby outcomes having an adverse impact on health, safety or fundamental rights, shall not be considered to be easily corrigible or reversible;

(j) the magnitude and likelihood of benefit of the deployment of the AI system for individuals, groups, or society at large, including possible improvements in product safety;

(k) the extent to which existing Union law provides for:

(i) effective measures of redress in relation to the risks posed by an AI system, with the exclusion of claims for damages;

(ii) effective measures to prevent or substantially minimise those risks.

3. The Commission is empowered to adopt delegated acts in accordance with Article 97 to amend the list in Annex III by removing high-risk AI systems where both of the following conditions are fulfilled:

(a) the high-risk AI system concerned no longer poses any significant risks to fundamental rights, health or safety, taking into account the criteria listed in paragraph 2;

(b) the deletion does not decrease the overall level of protection of health, safety and fundamental rights under Union law.

7.1. Recitals

774. (48) The extent of the adverse impact caused by the AI system on the fundamental rights protected by the Charter is of particular relevance when classifying an AI system as high risk. Those rights include the right to human dignity, respect for private and family life, protection of personal data, freedom of expression and information, freedom of assembly and of association, the right to non-discrimination, the right to education, consumer protection, workers' rights, the rights of persons with disabilities, gender equality, intellectual property rights, the right to an effective remedy and to a fair trial, the right of defence and the presumption of innocence, and the right to good administration. In addition to those rights, it is important to highlight the fact that children have specific rights as enshrined in Article 24 of the Charter and in the United Nations Convention on the Rights of the Child, further developed in the UNCRC General Comment No 25 as regards the digital environment, both of which require consideration of the children's vulnerabilities and provision of such protection and care as necessary for their well-being. The fundamental right to a high level of environmental protection enshrined in the Charter and implemented in Union policies should also be considered when assessing the severity of the harm that an AI system can cause, including in relation to the health and safety of persons.

775. **(53)** It is also important to clarify that there may be specific cases in which AI systems referred to in pre-defined areas specified in this Regulation do not lead to a significant risk of harm to the legal interests protected under those areas because they do not materially influence the decision-making or do not harm those interests substantially. For the purposes of this Regulation, an AI system that does not materially influence the outcome of decision-making should be understood to be an AI system that does not have an impact on the substance, and thereby the outcome, of decision-making, whether human or automated. An AI system that does not materially influence the outcome of decision-making could include situations in which one or more of the following conditions are fulfilled. The first such condition should be that the AI system is intended to perform a narrow procedural task, such as an AI system that transforms unstructured data into structured data, an AI system that classifies incoming documents into categories or an AI system that is used to detect duplicates among a large number of applications. Those tasks are of such narrow and limited nature that they pose only limited risks which are not increased through the use of an AI system in a context that is listed as a high-risk use in an annex to this Regulation. The second condition should be that the task performed by the AI system is intended to improve the result of a previously completed human activity that may be relevant for the purposes of the high-risk uses listed in an annex to this Regulation. Considering those characteristics, the AI system provides only an additional layer to a human activity with consequently lowered risk. That condition would, for example, apply to AI systems that are intended to improve the language used in previously drafted documents, for example in relation to professional tone, academic style of language or by aligning text to a certain brand messaging. The third condition should be that the AI system is intended to detect decision-making patterns or deviations from prior decision-making patterns. The risk would be lowered because the use of the AI system follows a previously completed human assessment which it is not meant to replace or influence, without proper human review. Such AI systems include for instance those that, given a certain grading pattern of a teacher, can be used to check ex post whether the teacher may have deviated from the grading pattern so as to flag potential inconsistencies or anomalies. The fourth condition should be that the AI system is intended to perform a task that is only preparatory to an assessment relevant for the purposes of the AI systems listed in an annex to this Regulation, thus making the possible impact of the output of the system very low in terms of representing a risk for the assessment to follow. That condition covers, inter alia, smart solutions for file handling, which include various functions from indexing, searching, text and speech processing or linking data to other data sources, or AI systems used for translation of initial documents. In any case, AI systems used in high-risk use-cases listed in an annex to this Regulation should be considered to pose significant risks of harm to the health, safety or fundamental rights if the AI system implies profiling within the meaning of Article 4, point (4) of Regulation (EU) 2016/679 or Article 3, point (4) of Directive (EU) 2016/680 or Article 3, point (5) of Regulation (EU) 2018/1725. To ensure traceability and transparency, a provider who considers that an AI system is not high-risk on the basis of the conditions referred to above should draw up documentation of the assessment before that system is placed on the market or put into service and should provide that documentation to national competent authorities upon request. Such a provider should be obliged to register the AI system in the EU database established under this Regulation. With a view to providing further guidance for the practical implementation of the conditions under which the AI systems listed in an annex to this Regulation are, on an exceptional basis, non-high-risk, the Commission should, after consulting the Board, provide guidelines specifying that practical implementation, completed by a comprehensive list of practical examples of use cases of AI systems that are high-risk and use cases that are not.

776. (67) High-quality data and access to high-quality data plays a vital role in providing structure and in ensuring the performance of many AI systems, especially when techniques involving the training of models are used, with a view to ensure that the high-risk AI system performs as intended and safely and it does not become a source of discrimination prohibited by Union law. High-quality data sets for training, validation and testing require the implementation of appropriate data governance and management practices. Data sets for training, validation and testing, including the labels, should be relevant, sufficiently representative, and to the best extent possible free of errors and complete in view of the intended purpose of the system. In order to facilitate compliance with Union data protection law, such as Regulation (EU) 2016/679, data governance and management practices should include, in the case of personal data, transparency about the original purpose of the data collection. The data sets should also have the appropriate statistical properties, including as regards the persons or groups of persons in relation to whom the high-risk AI system is intended to be used, with specific attention to the mitigation of possible biases in the data sets, that are likely to affect the health and safety of persons, have a negative impact on fundamental rights or lead to discrimination prohibited under Union law, especially where data outputs influence inputs for future operations (feedback loops). Biases can for example be inherent in underlying data sets, especially when historical data is being used, or generated when the systems are implemented in real world settings. Results provided by AI systems could be influenced by such inherent biases that are inclined to gradually increase and thereby perpetuate and amplify existing discrimination, in particular for persons belonging to certain vulnerable groups, including racial or ethnic groups. The requirement for the data sets to be to the best extent possible complete and free of errors should not affect the use of privacy-preserving techniques in the context of the development and testing of AI systems. In particular, data sets should take into account, to the extent required by their intended purpose, the features, characteristics or elements that are particular to the specific geographical, contextual, behavioural or functional setting which the AI system is intended to be used. The requirements related to data governance can be complied with by having recourse to third parties that offer certified compliance services including verification of data governance, data set integrity, and data training, validation and testing practices, as far as compliance with the data requirements of this Regulation are ensured.

777. **(171)** Affected persons should have the right to obtain an explanation where a deployer's decision is based mainly upon the output from certain high-risk AI systems that fall within the scope of this Regulation and where that decision produces legal effects or similarly significantly affects those persons in a way that they consider to have an adverse impact on their health, safety or fundamental rights. That explanation should be clear and meaningful and should provide a basis on which the affected persons are able to exercise their rights. The right to obtain an explanation should not apply to the use of AI systems for which exceptions or restrictions follow from Union or national law and should apply only to the extent this right is not already provided for under Union law.

7.2. General Approach

7.2.1 Preamble

778. The pace of innovation in the field of artificial intelligence systems is exponential. This is exemplified by ChatGPT.[24]

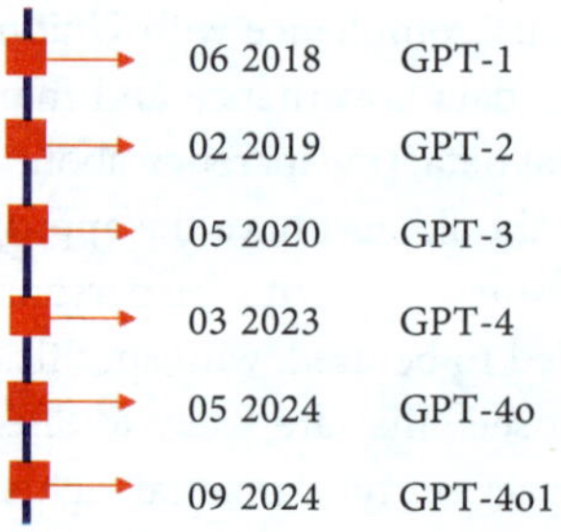

24 OpenAI.

7.2.2 Classification

779. The list of high-risk AI systems set out in Annex III can be amended to adapt to changes according to sectoral and functional criteria.

7.3. Empowerment

780. The European Commission is empowered to update the list of systems subject to high-risk requirements where both of the following conditions are fulfilled:

- the AI systems are intended to be used in any of the areas listed in Annex III;
- the AI systems pose a risk that is equivalent to, or greater than, the risk specified in Annex III.

7.4. Risk Criteria

7.4.1 Areas

781. These risks pertain to:

- health;
- safety;
- fundamental rights.

782. Note:

- (1) The following three other types of risk are not mentioned:
    - o environmental protection;
    - o the rule of law;
    - o democracy.

7.4.2 Assessment

783. These risks are assessed based on:

- severity;
- probability of occurrence.

7.4.3 Assessment Protocol

784. The assessment protocol must take into account all the following elements:[25]

NO.	THEME
1.	(a) the intended purpose of the AI system
2.	(b) the extent to which an AI system has been used or is likely to be used
3.	(c) the nature and amount of the data processed and used by the AI system, in particular whether special categories of personal data are processed
4.	(d) the extent to which the AI system acts autonomously and the possibility for a human to override a decision or recommendations that may lead to potential harm
5.	(e) the extent to which the use of an AI system has already caused harm to health and safety, has had an adverse impact on fundamental rights or has given rise to significant concerns in relation to the likelihood of such harm or adverse impact, as demonstrated, for example, by reports or documented allegations submitted to national competent authorities or by other reports, as appropriate
6.	(f) the potential extent of such harm or such adverse impact, in particular in terms of its intensity and its ability to affect multiple persons or to disproportionately affect a particular group of persons
7.	(g) the extent to which persons who are potentially harmed or suffer an adverse impact are dependent on the outcome produced with an AI system, in particular because for practical or legal reasons it is not reasonably possible to opt-out from that outcome
8.	(h) the extent to which there is an imbalance of power, or the persons who are potentially harmed or suffer an adverse impact are in a vulnerable position in relation to the deployer of an AI system, in particular due to status, authority, knowledge, economic or social circumstances, or age
9.	(i) the extent to which the outcome produced involving an AI system is easily corrigible or reversible, taking into account the technical solutions available to correct or reverse it, whereby outcomes having an adverse impact on health, safety or fundamental rights, shall not be considered to be easily corrigible or reversible
10.	(j) the magnitude and likelihood of benefit of the deployment of the AI system for individuals, groups, or society at large, including possible improvements in product safety
11.	(k) the extent to which existing Union law provides for: (i) effective measures of redress in relation to the risks posed by an AI system, with the exclusion of claims for damages (ii) effective measures to prevent or substantially minimise those risks

25 AI Act, Art. 7.

7.5. Empowerment

785. The European Commission is empowered to adopt delegated acts to amend the list in Annex III.[26]

786. A review must be conducted once a year following the entry into force of the AI Act to account for the development of AI technologies.[27]

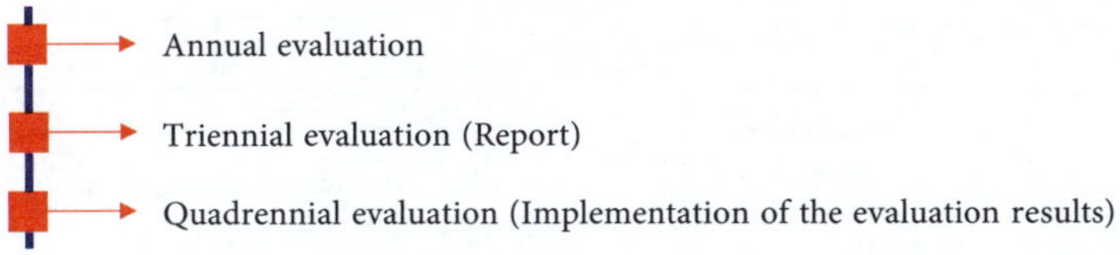

7.6. De-Classification

787. Still through delegated acts,[28] the European Commission is empowered to remove an AI system from the high-risk list where both of the following conditions are fulfilled:

- absence of significant risks to health, safety, and fundamental rights; and
- absence of decrease of the overall level of protection of these values under EU law.

26 AI Act, Art. 97.
27 AI Act, Art. 112.
28 AI Act, Art. 97.

788. This change in status can be illustrated as follows:[29]

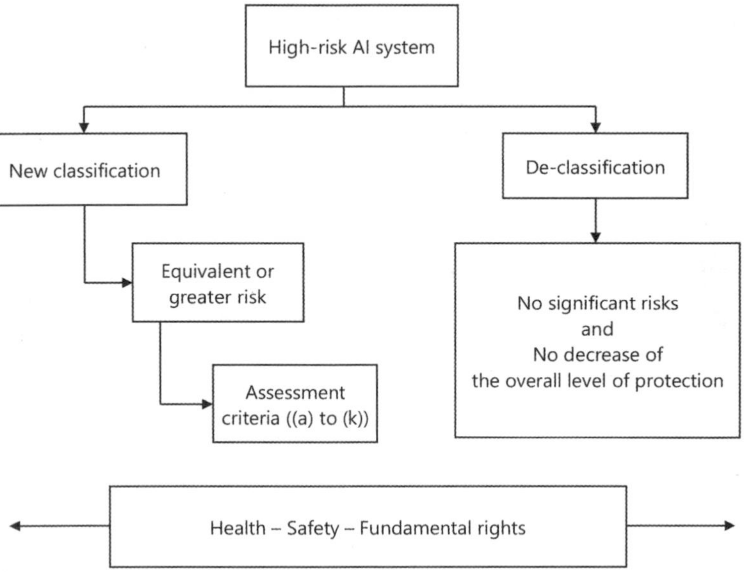

SECTION 2. REQUIREMENTS FOR HIGH-RISK AI SYSTEMS

8 ARTICLE 8. COMPLIANCE WITH THE REQUIREMENTS

1. High-risk AI systems shall comply with the requirements laid down in this Section, taking into account their intended purpose as well as the generally acknowledged state of the art on AI and AI-related technologies. The risk management system referred to in Article 9 shall be taken into account when ensuring compliance with those requirements.

2. Where a product contains an AI system, to which the requirements of this Regulation as well as requirements of the Union harmonisation legislation listed in Section A of Annex I apply, providers shall be responsible for ensuring that their product is fully compliant with all applicable requirements under applicable Union harmonisation legislation. In ensuring the compliance of high-risk AI systems referred to in paragraph 1 with the requirements set out in this Section, and in order to ensure consistency, avoid duplication and minimise additional burdens, providers shall have a choice of integrating, as appropriate, the necessary testing and reporting processes, information and documentation

[29] The other values (environmental protection, rule of law, democracy) are not cited.

they provide with regard to their product into documentation and procedures that already exist and are required under the Union harmonisation legislation listed in Section A of Annex I.

8.1. Recitals

789. (166) It is important that AI systems related to products that are not high-risk in accordance with this Regulation and thus are not required to comply with the requirements set out for high-risk AI systems are nevertheless safe when placed on the market or put into service. To contribute to this objective, Regulation (EU) 2023/988 of the European Parliament and of the Council[30] would apply as a safety net.

790. (174) Given the rapid technological developments and the technical expertise required to effectively apply this Regulation, the Commission should evaluate and review this Regulation by 2 August 2029 and every four years thereafter and report to the European Parliament and the Council. In addition, taking into account the implications for the scope of this Regulation, the Commission should carry out an assessment of the need to amend the list of high-risk AI systems and the list of prohibited practices once a year. Moreover, by 2 August 2028 and every four years thereafter, the Commission should evaluate and report to the European Parliament and to the Council on the need to amend the list of high-risk areas headings in the annex to this Regulation, the AI systems within the scope of the transparency obligations, the effectiveness of the supervision and governance system and the progress on the development of standardisation deliverables on energy efficient development of general-purpose AI models, including the need for further measures or actions. Finally, by 2 August 2028 and every three years thereafter, the Commission should evaluate the impact and effectiveness of voluntary codes of conduct to foster the application of the requirements provided for high-risk AI systems in the case of AI systems other than high-risk AI systems and possibly other additional requirements for such AI systems.

---

[30] Regulation (EU) No 1025/2012 of the European Parliament and of the Council of 25 October 2012 on European standardisation, amending Council Directives 89/686/EEC and 93/15/EEC and Directives 94/9/EC, 94/25/EC, 95/16/EC, 97/23/EC, 98/34/EC, 2004/22/EC, 2007/23/EC, 2009/23/EC and 2009/105/EC of the European Parliament and of the Council and repealing Council Decision 87/95/EEC and Decision No 1673/2006/EC of the European Parliament and of the Council, [2012] OJ L316/1.

8.2. *General Approach*

8.2.1 Preamble

791. Risk-based management requires operators[31] to comply with a series of essential requirements structured as follows:

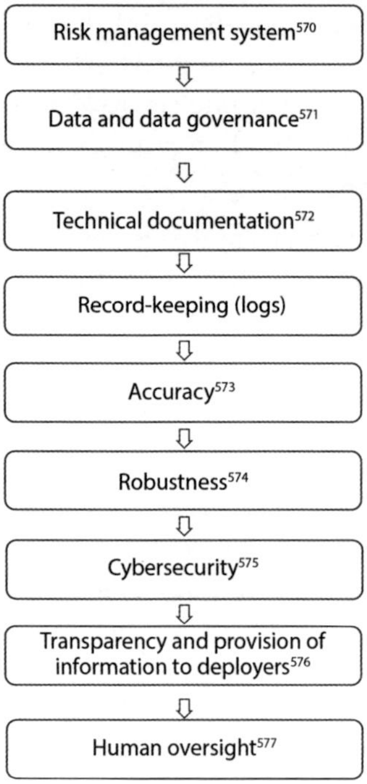

8.2.2 Classification

792. These requirements are grouped into two categories:[32]

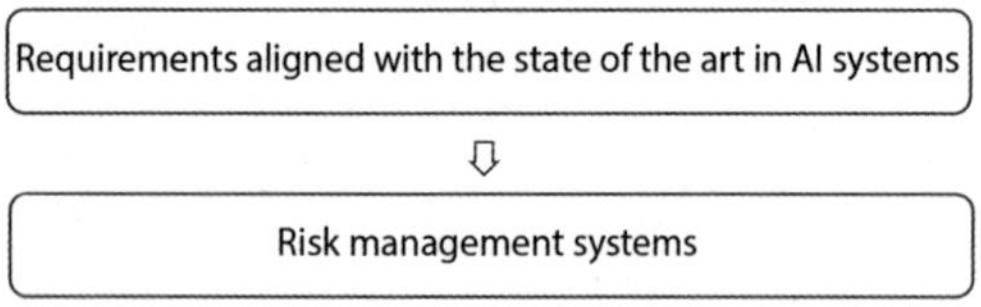

793. Notes:

- (1) Each requirement must be met, and its operational maintenance must be ensured over time.

---

[31] Providers, authorised representatives, deployers, importers and distributors. AI Act, Art. 3.
[32] AI Act, Art. 9.

9 ARTICLE 9. RISK MANAGEMENT SYSTEM

1. A risk management system shall be established, implemented, documented and maintained in relation to high-risk AI systems.

2. The risk management system shall be understood as a continuous iterative process planned and run throughout the entire lifecycle of a high-risk AI system, requiring regular systematic review and updating. It shall comprise the following steps:

(a) the identification and analysis of the known and the reasonably foreseeable risks that the high-risk AI system can pose to health, safety or fundamental rights when the high-risk AI system is used in accordance with its intended purpose;

(b) the estimation and evaluation of the risks that may emerge when the high-risk AI system is used in accordance with its intended purpose, and under conditions of reasonably foreseeable misuse;

(c) the evaluation of other risks possibly arising, based on the analysis of data gathered from the post-market monitoring system referred to in Article 72;

(d) the adoption of appropriate and targeted risk management measures designed to address the risks identified pursuant to point (a).

3. The risks referred to in this Article shall concern only those which may be reasonably mitigated or eliminated through the development or design of the high-risk AI system, or the provision of adequate technical information.

4. The risk management measures referred to in paragraph 2, point (d), shall give due consideration to the effects and possible interaction resulting from the combined application of the requirements set out in this Section, with a view to minimising risks more effectively while achieving an appropriate balance in implementing the measures to fulfil those requirements.

5. The risk management measures referred to in paragraph 2, point (d), shall be such that the relevant residual risk associated with each hazard, as well as the overall residual risk of the high-risk AI systems is judged to be acceptable.

In identifying the most appropriate risk management measures, the following shall be ensured:

(a) elimination or reduction of risks identified and evaluated pursuant to paragraph 2 in as far as technically feasible through adequate design and development of the high-risk AI system;

(b) where appropriate, implementation of adequate mitigation and control measures addressing risks that cannot be eliminate;

(c) provision of information required pursuant to Article 13 and, where appropriate, training to deployers.

With a view to eliminating or reducing risks related to the use of the high-risk AI system, due consideration shall be given to the technical knowledge, experience, education, the training to be expected by the deployer, and the presumable context in which the system is intended to be used.

6. High-risk AI systems shall be tested for the purpose of identifying the most appropriate and targeted risk management measures. Testing shall ensure that high-risk AI systems perform consistently for their intended purpose and that they are in compliance with the requirements set out in this Section.

7. Testing procedures may include testing in real-world conditions in accordance with Article 60.

8. The testing of high-risk AI systems shall be performed, as appropriate, at any time throughout the development process, and, in any event, prior to their being placed on the market or put into service. Testing shall be carried out against prior defined metrics and probabilistic thresholds that are appropriate to the intended purpose of the high-risk AI system.

9. When implementing the risk management system as provided for in paragraphs 1 to 7, providers shall give consideration to whether in view of its intended purpose the high-risk AI system is likely to have an adverse impact on persons under the age of 18 and, as appropriate, other vulnerable groups.

10. For providers of high-risk AI systems that are subject to requirements regarding internal risk management processes under other relevant provisions of Union law, the aspects provided in paragraphs 1 to 9 may be part of, or combined with, the risk management procedures established pursuant to that law.

9.1. Recitals

794. (64) To mitigate the risks from high-risk AI systems placed on the market or put into service and to ensure a high level of trustworthiness, certain mandatory requirements should apply to high-risk AI systems, taking into account the intended purpose and the context of use of the AI system and according to the risk-management system to be established by the provider. The measures adopted by the providers to comply with the mandatory requirements of this Regulation should take into account the generally acknowledged state of the art on AI, be proportionate and effective to meet the objectives of this Regulation. Based on the New Legislative Framework, as clarified in Commission notice 'The "Blue Guide" on the implementation of EU product rules 2022', the general rule is that more than one legal act of Union harmonisation legislation may be applicable to one product, since the making available or putting into service can take place only when the product complies with all applicable Union harmonisation legislation. The hazards of AI systems covered by the requirements of this Regulation concern different aspects than the existing Union harmonisation legislation and therefore the requirements of this Regulation would complement the existing body of the Union harmonisation legislation. For example, machinery or medical devices products incorporating an AI system might present risks not addressed by the essential health and safety requirements set out in the relevant Union harmonised legislation, as that sectoral law does not deal with risks specific to AI systems. This calls for a simultaneous and complementary application of the various legislative acts. To ensure consistency and to avoid an unnecessary administrative burden and unnecessary costs, providers of a product that contains one or more high-risk AI system, to which the requirements of this Regulation and of the Union harmonisation legislation based on the New Legislative Framework and listed in an annex to this Regulation apply, should have flexibility with regard to operational decisions on how to ensure compliance of a product that contains one or more AI systems with all the applicable requirements of that Union harmonised legislation in an optimal manner. That flexibility could mean, for example a decision by the provider to integrate a part of the necessary testing and reporting processes, information and documentation required under this Regulation into already existing documentation and procedures required under existing Union harmonisation legislation based on the New Legislative Framework and listed in an annex to this Regulation. This should not, in any way, undermine the obligation of the provider to comply with all the applicable requirements.

795. **(65)** The risk-management system should consist of a continuous, iterative process that is planned and run throughout the entire lifecycle of a high-risk AI system. That process should be aimed at identifying and mitigating the relevant risks of AI systems on health, safety and fundamental rights. The risk-management system should be regularly reviewed and updated to ensure its continuing effectiveness, as well as justification and documentation of any significant decisions and actions taken subject to this Regulation. This process should ensure that the provider identifies risks or adverse impacts and implements mitigation measures for the known and reasonably foreseeable risks of AI systems to the health, safety and fundamental rights in light of their intended purpose and reasonably foreseeable misuse, including the possible risks arising from the interaction between the AI system and the environment within which it operates. The risk-management system should adopt the most appropriate risk-management measures in light of the state of the art in AI. When identifying the most appropriate risk-management measures, the provider should document and explain the choices made and, when relevant, involve experts and external stakeholders. In identifying the reasonably foreseeable misuse of high-risk AI systems, the provider should cover uses of AI systems which, while not directly covered by the intended purpose and provided for in the instruction for use may nevertheless be reasonably expected to result from readily predictable human behaviour in the context of the specific characteristics and use of a particular AI system. Any known or foreseeable circumstances related to the use of the high-risk AI system in accordance with its intended purpose or under conditions of reasonably foreseeable misuse, which may lead to risks to the health and safety or fundamental rights should be included in the instructions for use that are provided by the provider. This is to ensure that the deployer is aware and takes them into account when using the high-risk AI system. Identifying and implementing risk mitigation measures for foreseeable misuse under this Regulation should not require specific additional training for the high-risk AI system by the provider to address foreseeable misuse. The providers however are encouraged to consider such additional training measures to mitigate reasonable foreseeable misuses as necessary and appropriate.

796. **(71)** Having comprehensible information on how high-risk AI systems have been developed and how they perform throughout their lifetime is essential to enable traceability of those systems, verify compliance with the requirements under this Regulation, as well as monitoring of their operations and post market monitoring. This requires keeping records and the availability of technical documentation, containing information which is necessary to assess the compliance of the AI system with the relevant requirements and facilitate post market monitoring. Such information should include the general characteristics, capabilities and limitations of the system, algorithms, data, training, testing and validation processes used as well as documentation on the relevant risk-management system and drawn in a clear and comprehensive form. The technical documentation should be kept up to date, appropriately throughout the lifetime of the AI system. Furthermore, high-risk AI systems should technically allow for the automatic recording of events, by means of logs, over the duration of the lifetime of the system.

9.2. *General Approach*

9.2.1 Preamble

797. The core of AI systems regulation is embodied in risk management entrusted to operators. This risk management serves as the counterpart to the freedom of design and development.

798. The balance between innovation and regulation is founded on this obligation to manage risks, which is an essential component of the new legal requirements.

9.2.2 Guiding Principles

799. Each operator must take responsibility for the risks arising from AI systems. The Regulation provides guidance in the form of requirements aimed at promoting the deployment of trustworthy AI systems under dual oversight by:

- operators, for all operations throughout the entire lifecycle of high-risk AI systems;
- national competent authorities.

800. Every link in the chain, from design to development, from distribution to placing on the market, and from putting into service to use, must implement a risk management system.

9.3. *Composition*

801. The system includes the following:

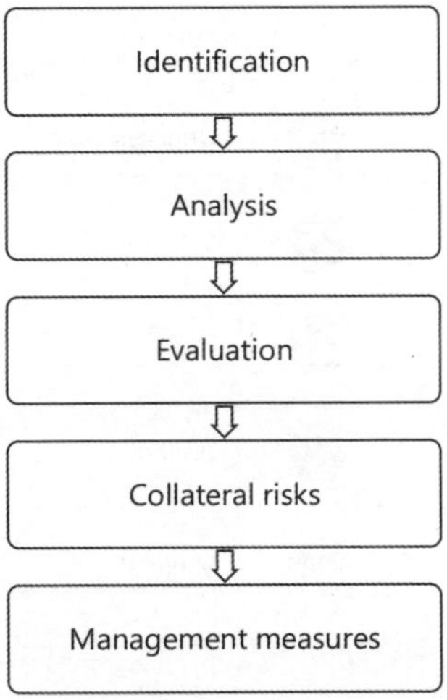

9.4. *Approach*

802. The steps are as follows:

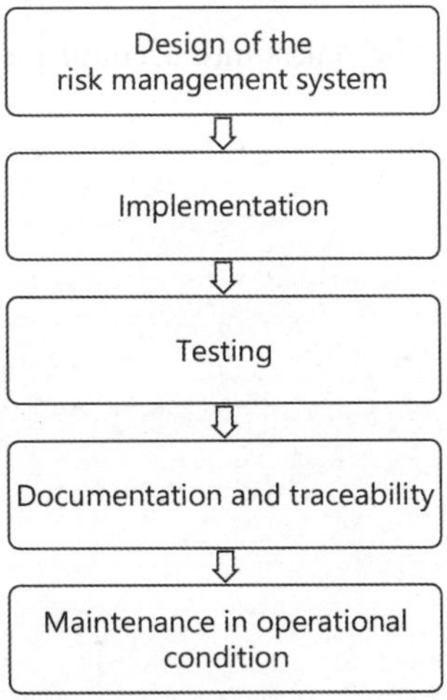

9.5. *Definition*

803. The concept of risk is defined as 'the combination of the probability of an occurrence of harm and the severity of that harm'.[33]

9.5.1 Risk Scale

804. It is as follows:

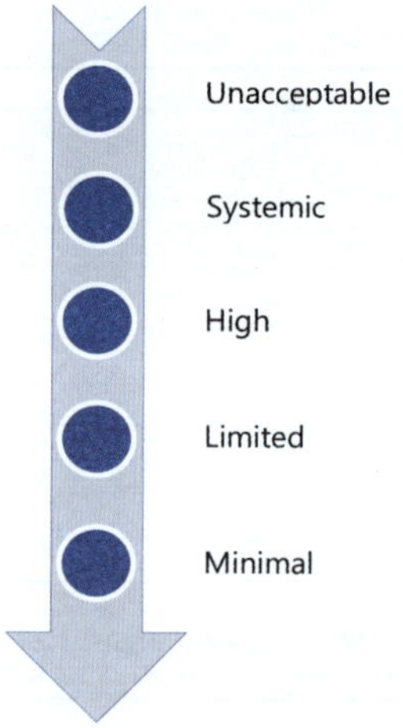

9.5.2 Evaluation

805. Risk assessment is conducted in two stages:

- an objective evaluation;
- a risk detection process that takes into account the contexts of use.

[33] AI Act, Art. 3(2).

806. The assessment must be carried out according to the following areas:

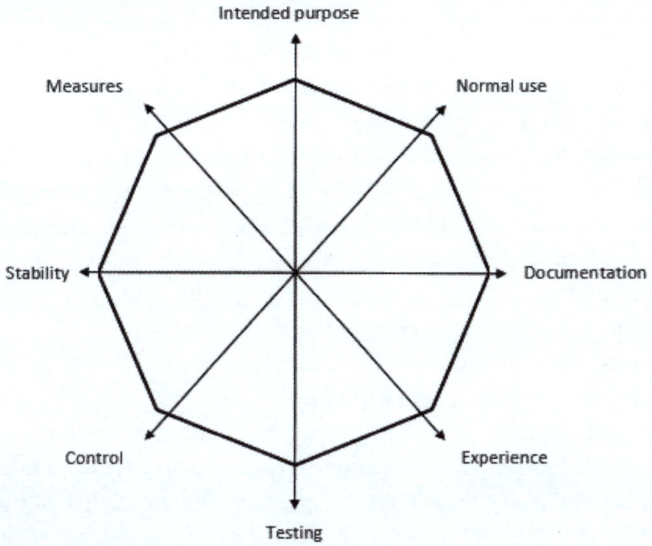

807. Based on this assessment, operators must implement a series of technical, organisational, and legal measures aimed at simultaneously:

- mitigating risks;
- monitoring their developments.

808. This approach is assessed according to the following implementation context:

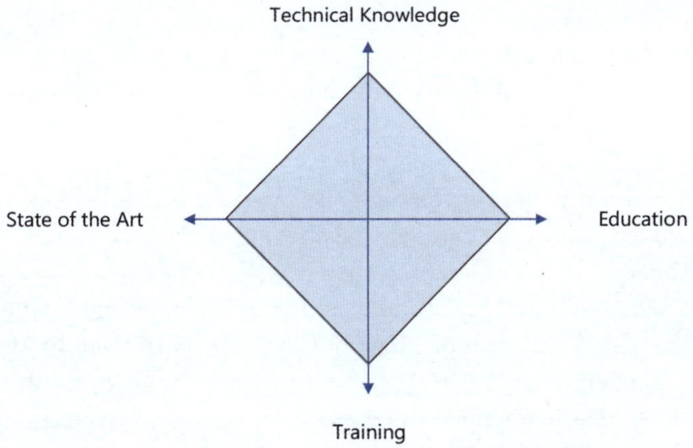

10 ARTICLE 10. DATA AND DATA GOVERNANCE

1. High-risk AI systems which make use of techniques involving the training of AI models with data shall be developed on the basis of training, validation and testing data sets that meet the quality criteria referred to in paragraphs 2 to 5 whenever such data sets are used.

2. Training, validation and testing data sets shall be subject to data governance and management practices appropriate for the intended purpose of the high-risk AI system. Those practices shall concern in particular:

(a) the relevant design choices;

(b) data collection processes and the origin of data, and in the case of personal data, the original purpose of the data collection;

(c) relevant data-preparation processing operations, such as annotation, labelling, cleaning, updating, enrichment and aggregation;

(d) the formulation of assumptions, in particular with respect to the information that the data are supposed to measure and represent;

(e) an assessment of the availability, quantity and suitability of the data sets that are needed;

(f) examination in view of possible biases that are likely to affect the health and safety of persons, have a negative impact on fundamental rights or lead to discrimination prohibited under Union law, especially where data outputs influence inputs for future operations;

(g) appropriate measures to detect, prevent and mitigate possible biases identified according to point (f);

(h) the identification of relevant data gaps or shortcomings that prevent compliance with this Regulation, and how those gaps and shortcomings can be addressed.

3. Training, validation and testing data sets shall be relevant, sufficiently representative, and to the best extent possible, free of errors and complete in view of the intended purpose. They shall have the appropriate statistical properties, including, where applicable, as regards the persons or groups of persons in relation to whom the high-risk AI system is intended to be used. Those characteristics of the data sets may be met at the level of individual data sets or at the level of a combination thereof.

4. Data sets shall take into account, to the extent required by the intended purpose, the characteristics or elements that are particular to the specific geographical, contextual, behavioural or functional setting within which the high-risk AI system is intended to be used.

5. To the extent that it is strictly necessary for the purpose of ensuring bias detection and correction in relation to the high-risk AI systems in accordance with paragraph (2), points (f) and (g) of this Article, the providers of such systems may exceptionally process special categories of personal data, subject to appropriate safeguards for the fundamental rights and freedoms of natural persons. In addition to the provisions set out in Regulations (EU) 2016/679 and (EU) 2018/1725 and Directive (EU) 2016/680, all the following conditions must be met in order for such processing to occur:

(a) the bias detection and correction cannot be effectively fulfilled by processing other data, including synthetic or anonymised data;

(b) the special categories of personal data are subject to technical limitations on the re-use of the personal data, and state-of-the-art security and privacy-preserving measures, including pseudonymisation;

(c) the special categories of personal data are subject to measures to ensure that the personal data processed are secured, protected, subject to suitable safeguards, including strict controls and documentation of the access, to avoid misuse and ensure that only authorised persons have access to those personal data with appropriate confidentiality obligations;

(d) the special categories of personal data are not to be transmitted, transferred or otherwise accessed by other parties;

(e) the special categories of personal data are deleted once the bias has been corrected or the personal data has reached the end of its retention period, whichever comes first;

(f) the records of processing activities pursuant to Regulations (EU) 2016/679 and (EU) 2018/1725 and Directive (EU) 2016/680 include the reasons why the processing of special categories of personal data was strictly necessary to detect and correct biases, and why that objective could not be achieved by processing other data.

6. For the development of high-risk AI systems not using techniques involving the training of AI models, paragraphs 2 to 5 apply only to the testing data sets.

10.1. Recitals

809. (66) Requirements should apply to high-risk AI systems as regards risk management, the quality and relevance of data sets used, technical documentation and record-keeping, transparency and the provision of information to deployers, human oversight, and robustness, accuracy and cybersecurity. Those requirements are necessary to effectively mitigate the risks for health, safety and fundamental rights. As No other less trade restrictive measures are reasonably available those requirements are not unjustified restrictions to trade.

810. (67) High-quality data and access to high-quality data plays a vital role in providing structure and in ensuring the performance of many AI systems, especially when techniques involving the training of models are used, with a view to ensure that the high-risk AI system performs as intended and safely and it does not become a source of discrimination prohibited by Union law. High-quality data sets for training, validation and testing require the implementation of appropriate data governance and management practices. Data sets for training, validation and testing, including the labels, should be relevant, sufficiently representative, and to the best extent possible free of errors and complete in view of the intended purpose of the system. In order to facilitate compliance with Union data protection law, such as Regulation (EU) 2016/679, data governance and management practices should include, in the case of personal data, transparency about the original purpose of the data collection. The data sets should also have the appropriate statistical properties, including as regards the persons or groups of persons in relation to whom the high-risk AI system is intended to be used, with specific attention to the mitigation of possible biases in the data sets, that are likely to affect the health and safety of persons, have a negative impact on fundamental rights or lead to discrimination prohibited under Union law, especially where data outputs influence inputs for future operations (feedback loops). Biases can for example be inherent in underlying data sets, especially when historical data is being used, or generated when the systems are implemented in real world settings. Results provided by AI systems could be influenced by such inherent biases that are inclined to gradually increase and thereby perpetuate and amplify existing discrimination, in particular for persons belonging to certain vulnerable groups, including racial or ethnic groups. The requirement for the data sets to be to the best extent possible complete and free of errors should not affect the use of privacy-preserving techniques in the context of the development and testing of AI systems. In particular, data sets should take into account, to the extent required by their intended purpose, the features, characteristics or elements that are particular to the specific geographical, contextual, behavioural or functional setting which the AI system is intended to be used. The requirements related to data governance can be complied with by having recourse to third parties that offer certified compliance services including verification of data governance, data set integrity, and data training, validation and testing practices, as far as compliance with the data requirements of this Regulation are ensured.

811. **(68)** For the development and assessment of high-risk AI systems, certain actors, such as providers, notified bodies and other relevant entities, such as European Digital Innovation Hubs, testing experimentation facilities and researchers, should be able to access and use high-quality data sets within the fields of activities of those actors which are related to this Regulation. European common data spaces established by the Commission and the facilitation of data sharing between businesses and with government in the public interest will be instrumental to provide trustful, accountable and non-discriminatory access to high-quality data for the training, validation and testing of AI systems. For example, in health, the European health data space will facilitate non-discriminatory access to health data and the training of AI algorithms on those data sets, in a privacy-preserving, secure, timely, transparent and trustworthy manner, and with an appropriate institutional governance. Relevant competent authorities, including sectoral ones, providing or supporting the access to data may also support the provision of high-quality data for the training, validation and testing of AI systems.

812. **(70)** In order to protect the right of others from the discrimination that might result from the bias in AI systems, the providers should, exceptionally, to the extent that it is strictly necessary for the purpose of ensuring bias detection and correction in relation to the high-risk AI systems, subject to appropriate safeguards for the fundamental rights and freedoms of natural persons and following the application of all applicable conditions laid down under this Regulation in addition to the conditions laid down in Regulations (EU) 2016/679 and (EU) 2018/1725 and Directive (EU) 2016/680, be able to process also special categories of personal data, as a matter of substantial public interest within the meaning of Article 9(2), point (g) of Regulation (EU) 2016/679 and Article 10(2), point (g) of Regulation (EU) 2018/1725.

813. **(76)** Cybersecurity plays a crucial role in ensuring that AI systems are resilient against attempts to alter their use, behaviour, performance or compromise their security properties by malicious third parties exploiting the system's vulnerabilities. Cyberattacks against AI systems can leverage AI specific assets, such as training data sets (e.g. data poisoning) or trained models (e.g. adversarial attacks or membership inference)), or exploit vulnerabilities in the AI system's digital assets or the underlying ICT infrastructure. To ensure a level of cybersecurity appropriate to the risks, suitable measures, such as security controls, should therefore be taken by the providers of high-risk AI systems, also taking into account as appropriate the underlying ICT infrastructure.

814. **(115)** Providers of general-purpose AI models with systemic risks should assess and mitigate possible systemic risks. If, despite efforts to identify and prevent risks related to a general-purpose AI model that may present systemic risks, the development or use of the model causes a serious incident, the general-purpose AI model provider should without undue delay keep track of the incident and report any relevant information and possible corrective measures to the Commission and national competent authorities. Furthermore, providers should ensure an adequate level of cybersecurity protection for the model and its physical infrastructure, if appropriate, along the entire model lifecycle. Cybersecurity protection related to systemic risks associated with malicious use or attacks should duly consider accidental model leakage, unauthorised releases, circumvention of safety measures, and defence against cyberattacks, unauthorised access or model theft. That protection could be facilitated by securing model weights, algorithms, servers, and data sets, such as through operational security measures for information security, specific cybersecurity policies, adequate technical and established solutions, and cyber and physical access controls, appropriate to the relevant circumstances and the risks involved.

10.2. General Approach

815. Training data play a critical role in the quality of outputs.

816. Numerous studies have highlighted the risks posed by data sets that are not representative of general usage conditions.

817. Training data means 'data used for training an AI system through fitting its learnable parameters'.[34]

10.3. Approach

818. Managing risks associated with the use of data sets involves:

- requirements related to data quality requirements;
- governance obligations.

10.4. Governance

819. It is implemented as follows:

- a general policy outlining the rules for data set implementation;
- a steering and validation committee;
- rules of procedure for the organisation and administration of the committee;
- regular reports on risk monitoring related to data sets;
- a feedback policy.

10.5. Purpose

820. Insights derived from this governance should be documented in a risk management system.[35]

10.6. Period

821. All these analyses must be completed before the placing on the market. They are monitored during the putting into service and use phases.

34 AI Act, Art. 3(29).

35 AI Act, Art. 9(8).

10.7. Combating Bias

822. Addressing bias is essential to counter discrimination, given the characteristics of the learning phase.[36]

823. In this context, the quality of validation data is crucial to reducing or eliminating bias. 'Validation data' are 'data used for providing an evaluation of the trained AI system and for tuning its non-learnable parameters and its learning process in order, inter alia, to prevent underfitting or overfitting'.[37]

10.8. Find Out More

10.8.1 Toolbox

824. CNIL, 'IA et libre-arbitre: sommes-nous des moutons numériques?' ['AI and Free Will: Are We Digital Sheep?'], Cahier air2023, 22 April 2024.

825. LINC, 'Sécurité des systèmes d'IA' ['AI system security'], Report from the CNIL's Digital Innovation Lab, *LINC-Cnil*, April 2022.

826. Prud'homme, B., Régis, C., Farnadi, G., Dreier, V. and Rubel, S., 'Missing links in AI governance', *UNESCO-Mila*, 17 March 2023.

11 ARTICLE 11. TECHNICAL DOCUMENTATION

> **1.** The technical documentation of a high-risk AI system shall be drawn up before that system is placed on the market or put into service and shall be kept up-to date.
>
> The technical documentation shall be drawn up in such a way as to demonstrate that the high-risk AI system complies with the requirements set out in this Section and to provide national competent authorities and notified bodies with the necessary information in a clear and comprehensive form to assess the compliance of the AI system with those requirements. It shall contain, at a minimum, the elements set out in Annex IV. SMEs, including start-ups, may provide the elements of the technical documentation specified in Annex IV in a simplified manner. To that end, the Commission shall establish a simplified technical documentation form targeted at the needs of small and microenterprises. Where an SME, including a start-up, opts to provide the

---

36 'Yet 80% of coders are men and 80% of chatbots (Sofia, Alexa) are feminised (voice, face, body)' [Translated by the author]: L. Deviller,' Les systèmes d'intelligence artificielle font amplifier les biais de genre dans tous les domaines' ['Artificial intelligence systems amplify gender bias in all fields'], *Le Monde*, 6 June 2023.

37 AI Act, Art. 3(30).

information required in Annex IV in a simplified manner, it shall use the form referred to in this paragraph. Notified bodies shall accept the form for the purposes of the conformity assessment.

2. Where a high-risk AI system related to a product covered by the Union harmonisation legislation listed in Section A of Annex I is placed on the market or put into service, a single set of technical documentation shall be drawn up containing all the information set out in paragraph 1, as well as the information required under those legal acts.

3. The Commission is empowered to adopt delegated acts in accordance with Article 97 in order to amend Annex IV, where necessary, to ensure that, in light of technical progress, the technical documentation provides all the information necessary to assess the compliance of the system with the requirements set out in this Section.

11.1. Recitals

827. **(9)** Harmonised rules applicable to the placing on the market, the putting into service and the use of high-risk AI systems should be laid down consistently with Regulation (EC) No 765/2008 of the European Parliament and of the Council,[38] Decision No 768/2008/EC of the European Parliament and of the Council[39] and Regulation (EU) 2019/1020 of the European Parliament and of the Council[40] (New Legislative Framework). The harmonised rules laid down in this Regulation should apply across sectors and, in line with the New Legislative Framework, should be without prejudice to existing Union law, in particular on data protection, consumer protection, fundamental rights, employment, and protection of workers, and product safety, to which this Regulation is complementary. As a consequence, all rights and remedies provided for by such Union law to consumers, and other persons on whom AI systems may have a negative impact, including as regards the compensation of possible damages pursuant to Council Directive 85/374/EEC[41] remain unaffected and fully applicable. Furthermore, in the context of employment and protection of workers, this Regulation should therefore not affect Union law on social policy

---

38 Regulation (EC) No 765/2008 of the European Parliament and of the Council of 9 July 2008 setting out the requirements for accreditation and repealing Regulation (EEC) No 339/93, [2008] OJ L218/30.

39 Decision No 768/2008/EC of the European Parliament and of the Council of 9 July 2008 on a common framework for the marketing of products, and repealing Council Decision 93/465/EEC, [2008] OJ L218/82.

40 Regulation (EU) 2019/1020 of the European Parliament and of the Council of 20 June 2019 on market surveillance and compliance of products and amending Directive 2004/42/EC and Regulations (EC) No 765/2008 and (EU) No 305/2011, [2019] OJ L169/1.

41 Council Directive 85/374/EEC of 25 July 1985 on the approximation of the laws, regulations and administrative provisions of the Member States concerning liability for defective products, [1985] OJ L210/29.

and national labour law, in compliance with Union law, concerning employment and working conditions, including health and safety at work and the relationship between employers and workers. This Regulation should also not affect the exercise of fundamental rights as recognised in the Member States and at Union level, including the right or freedom to strike or to take other action covered by the specific industrial relations systems in Member States as well as the right to negotiate, to conclude and enforce collective agreements or to take collective action in accordance with national law. This Regulation should not affect the provisions aiming to improve working conditions in platform work laid down in a Directive of the European Parliament and of the Council on improving working conditions in platform work. Moreover, this Regulation aims to strengthen the effectiveness of such existing rights and remedies by establishing specific requirements and obligations, including in respect of the transparency, technical documentation and record-keeping of AI systems. Furthermore, the obligations placed on various operators involved in the AI value chain under this Regulation should apply without prejudice to national law, in compliance with Union law, having the effect of limiting the use of certain AI systems where such law falls outside the scope of this Regulation or pursues legitimate public interest objectives other than those pursued by this Regulation. For example, national labour law and law on the protection of minors, namely persons below the age of 18, taking into account the UNCRC General Comment No 25 (2021) on children's rights in relation to the digital environment, insofar as they are not specific to AI systems and pursue other legitimate public interest objectives, should not be affected by this Regulation.

828. **(66)** Requirements should apply to high-risk AI systems as regards risk management, the quality and relevance of data sets used, technical documentation and record-keeping, transparency and the provision of information to deployers, human oversight, and robustness, accuracy and cybersecurity. Those requirements are necessary to effectively mitigate the risks for health, safety and fundamental rights. As no other less trade restrictive measures are reasonably available those requirements are not unjustified restrictions to trade.

829. **(71)** Having comprehensible information on how high-risk AI systems have been developed and how they perform throughout their lifetime is essential to enable traceability of those systems, verify compliance with the requirements under this Regulation, as well as monitoring of their operations and post market monitoring. This requires keeping records and the availability of technical documentation, containing information which is necessary to assess the compliance of the AI system with the relevant requirements and facilitate post market monitoring. Such information should include the general characteristics, capabilities and limitations of the system, algorithms, data, training, testing and validation processes used as well as documentation on the relevant risk-management system and drawn in a clear and comprehensive form. The technical documentation should be kept up to date, appropriately throughout the lifetime of the AI system. Furthermore, high-risk AI systems should technically allow for the automatic recording of events, by means of logs, over the duration of the lifetime of the system.

830. **(101)** Providers of general-purpose AI models have a particular role and responsibility along the AI value chain, as the models they provide may form the basis for a range of downstream systems, often provided by downstream providers that necessitate a good understanding of the models and their capabilities, both to enable the integration of such models into their products, and to fulfil their obligations under this or other regulations. Therefore, proportionate transparency measures should be laid down, including the drawing up and keeping up to date of documentation, and the provision of information on the general-purpose AI model for its usage by the downstream providers. Technical documentation should be prepared and kept up to date by the general-purpose AI model provider for the purpose of making it available, upon request, to the AI Office and the national competent authorities. The minimal set of elements to be included in such documentation should be set out in specific annexes to this Regulation. The Commission should be empowered to amend those annexes by means of delegated acts in light of evolving technological developments.

831. **(109)** Compliance with the obligations applicable to the providers of general-purpose AI models should be commensurate and proportionate to the type of model provider, excluding the need for compliance for persons who develop or use models for non-professional or scientific research purposes, who should nevertheless be encouraged to voluntarily comply with these requirements. Without prejudice to Union copyright law, compliance with those obligations should take due account of the size of the provider and allow simplified ways of compliance for SMEs, including start-ups, that should not represent an excessive cost and not discourage the use of such models. In the case of a modification or fine-tuning of a model, the obligations for providers of general-purpose AI models should be limited to that modification or fine-tuning, for example by complementing the already existing technical documentation with information on the modifications, including new training data sources, as a means to comply with the value chain obligations provided in this Regulation.

832. **(173)** In order to ensure that the regulatory framework can be adapted where necessary, the power to adopt acts in accordance with Article 290 TFEU should be delegated to the Commission to amend the conditions under which an AI system is not to be considered to be high-risk, the list of high-risk AI systems, the provisions regarding technical documentation, the content of the EU declaration of conformity the provisions regarding the conformity assessment procedures, the provisions establishing the high-risk AI systems to which the conformity assessment procedure based on assessment of the quality management system and assessment of the technical documentation should apply, the threshold, benchmarks and indicators, including by supplementing those benchmarks and indicators, in the rules for the classification of general-purpose AI models with systemic risk, the criteria for the designation of general-purpose AI models with systemic risk, the technical documentation for providers of general-purpose AI models and the transparency information for providers of general-purpose AI models. It is of particular importance that the Commission carry out appropriate consultations during its preparatory work, including at expert level, and that those consultations be conducted in accordance with the principles laid down in the Interinstitutional Agreement of 13 April 2016 on Better Law-Making.[42] In particular, to ensure equal participation in the preparation of delegated acts, the European Parliament and the Council receive all documents at the same time as Member States' experts, and their experts systematically have access to meetings of Commission expert groups dealing with the preparation of delegated acts.

11.2. General Approach

11.2.1 Preamble

833. The risk management system requires traceability. This is why the requirement to produce technical documentation is essential.

11.2.2 Guiding Principles

834. The technical documentation serves the following four main purposes:[43]

- to monitor the evolution of residual risks;
- to enable urgent response in case of incidents;
- to demonstrate to the supervisory authority that risks are under control;
- to defend reasonable deployment practices on the market in the event of problematic or even severe accidents.

[42] [2016] OJ L123/1.
[43] AI Act, Annex IV.

11.3. *Classification*

835. The technical documentation includes the following:

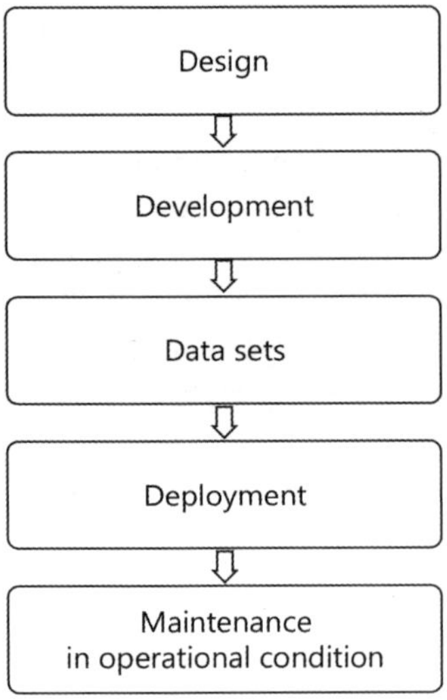

11.4. *Approach*

836. It is divided into two steps:

Step 1: Drawn up before the placing on the market

Step 2: Kept up-to-date as needed

11.5. *Definition*

837. The technical documentation is not defined as such but is characterised by its features.[44] It must be distinguished from the instructions for use, which are intended for the end user.[45]

44 See below.
45 AI Act, Art. 3(15).

11.6. *Characteristics*

838. The technical documentation must contain at least the following information:

- the methods and steps performed for the development of the AI system, including, where relevant, recourse to pre-trained systems or tools provided by third parties and how those were used, integrated or modified by the provider;
- the design specifications of the system, namely the general logic of the AI system and of the algorithms; the key design choices including the rationale and assumptions made, including with regard to persons or groups of persons in respect of who, the system is intended to be used; the main classification choices; what the system is designed to optimise for, and the relevance of the different parameters; the description of the expected output and output quality of the system; the decisions about any possible trade-off made regarding the technical solutions adopted to comply with the requirements set out in Chapter III, Section 2;
- the description of the system architecture explaining how software components build on or feed into each other and integrate into the overall processing; the computational resources used to develop, train, test and validate the AI system;
- where relevant, the data requirements in terms of datasheets describing the training methodologies and techniques and the training data sets used, including a general description of these data sets, information about their provenance, scope and main characteristics; how the data was obtained and selected; labelling procedures (e.g. for supervised learning), data cleaning methodologies (e.g. outliers detection);
- assessment of the human oversight measures needed in accordance with Article 14, including an assessment of the technical measures needed to facilitate the interpretation of the outputs of AI systems by the deployers, in accordance with Article 13(3), point (d).

11.7. *Limitations*

839. The technical documentation does not include know-how or trade secrets unless they are a component of risk management.

11.8. *Formalities*

840. Providers must be able to make the technical documentation available at: any time.

11.9. *Period*

841. The documentation must be continuously updated according to the severity of the risks.

11.10. *Change*

842. Under the Regulation, the European Commission is empowered to adopt delegated acts in order to adjust these requirements in light of technical progress.[46]

11.11. *Summary*

843. It is as follows:

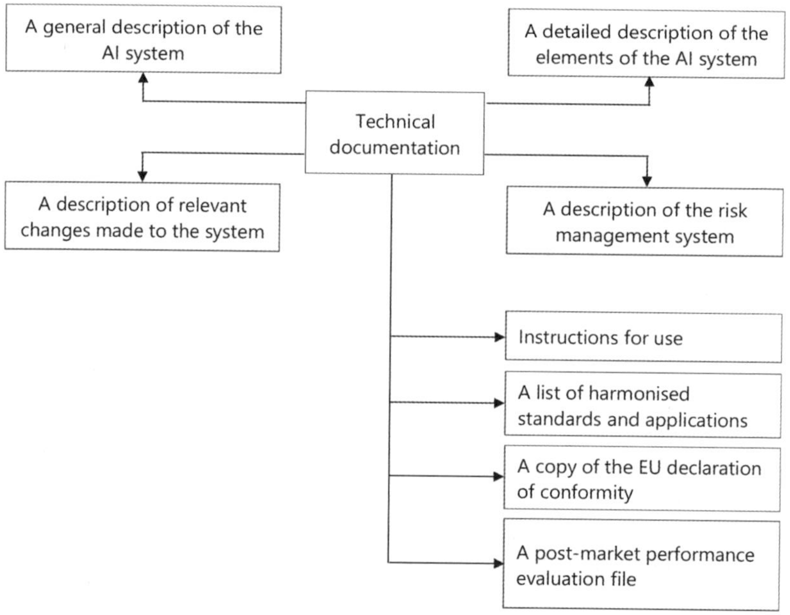

12 ARTICLE 12. RECORD-KEEPING

1. High-risk AI systems shall technically allow for the automatic recording of events (logs) over the lifetime of the system.

46 AI Act, Art. 112 (Evaluation and review).

2. In order to ensure a level of traceability of the functioning of a high-risk AI system that is appropriate to the intended purpose of the system, logging capabilities shall enable the recording of events relevant for:

(a) Identifying situations that may result in the high-risk AI system presenting a risk within the meaning of Article 79(1) or in a substantial modification;

(b) facilitating the post-market monitoring referred to in Article 72; and

(c) monitoring the operation of high-risk AI systems referred to in Article 26(5).

3. For high-risk AI systems referred to in point 1 (a), of Annex III, the logging capabilities shall provide, at a minimum:

(a) recording of the period of each use of the system (start date and time and end date and time of each use);

(b) the reference database against which input data has been checked by the system;

(c) the input data for which the search has led to a match;

(d) the identification of the natural persons involved in the verification of the results, as referred to in Article 14(5).

12.1. Recitals

844. **(71)** Having comprehensible information on how high-risk AI systems have been developed and how they perform throughout their lifetime is essential to enable traceability of those systems, verify compliance with the requirements under this Regulation, as well as monitoring of their operations and post market monitoring. This requires keeping records and the availability of technical documentation, containing information which is necessary to assess the compliance of the AI system with the relevant requirements and facilitate post market monitoring. Such information should include the general characteristics, capabilities and limitations of the system, algorithms, data, training, testing and validation processes used as well as documentation on the relevant risk-management system and drawn in a clear and comprehensive form. The technical documentation should be kept up to date, appropriately throughout the lifetime of the AI system. Furthermore, high-risk AI systems should technically allow for the automatic recording of events, by means of logs, over the duration of the lifetime of the system.

845. **(131)** In order to facilitate the work of the Commission and the Member States in the AI field as well as to increase the transparency towards the public, providers of high-risk AI systems other than those related to products falling within the scope of relevant existing Union harmonisation legislation, as well as providers who consider that an AI system listed in the high-risk use cases in an annex to this Regulation is not high-risk on the basis of a derogation, should be required to register themselves and information about their AI system in an EU database, to be established and managed by the Commission. Before using an AI system listed in the high-risk use cases in an annex to this Regulation, deployers of high-risk AI systems that are public authorities, agencies or bodies, should register themselves in such database and select the system that they envisage to use. Other deployers should be entitled to do so voluntarily. This section of the EU database should be publicly accessible, free of charge, the information should be easily navigable, understandable and machine-readable. The EU database should also be user-friendly, for example by providing search functionalities, including through keywords, allowing the general public to find relevant information to be submitted upon the registration of high-risk AI systems and on the use case of high-risk AI systems, set out in an annex to this Regulation, to which the high-risk AI systems correspond. Any substantial modification of high-risk AI systems should also be registered in the EU database. For high-risk AI systems in the area of law enforcement, migration, asylum and border control management, the registration obligations should be fulfilled in a secure non-public section of the EU database. Access to the secure non-public section should be strictly limited to the Commission as well as to market surveillance authorities with regard to their national section of that database. High-risk AI systems in the area of critical infrastructure should only be registered at national level. The Commission should be the controller of the EU database, in accordance with Regulation (EU) 2018/1725. In order to ensure the full functionality of the EU database, when deployed, the procedure for setting the database should include the development of functional specifications by the Commission and an independent audit report. The Commission should take into account cybersecurity risks when carrying out its tasks as data controller on the EU database. In order to maximise the availability and use of the EU database by the public, the EU database, including the information made available through it, should comply with requirements under the Directive (EU) 2019/882.

12.2. General Approach

12.2.1 Preamble

846. Traceability is an essential component of risk-based management.

12.2.2 Guiding Principles

847. Events that are representative of risk management must be recorded in logs.

848. The scope of traceability includes the following generic elements:

NO.	THEME
1.	Events and event history
2.	Protection measures and protection evaluation
3.	Evolution of risk indicators based on potential or actual breach of the six values of the European Union

12.3. Implementation

849. Traceability must be considered during the design phase. Throughout development, traceable elements must be integrated into the relevant processes.

850. Logging must be determined according to the intended use of AI systems to:

- monitor elements that present a risk;
- track substantial modifications to the AI system;
- manage post-market risks.

12.4. Special Cases

851. Specific logging is required for biometric systems such as AI systems:

- for remote biometric identification;[47]
- for biometric categorisation;
- for emotion recognition.

852. Such logging must include at a minimum the following:

NO.	THEME	MEANING
1.	Start of the system's period of use	Date and time
2.	Reference database	Monitoring access to identification data
3.	Input data	For which the search has led to a match
4.	Identification	List of natural persons directly involved in the verification of the results[48]
5.	End of the system's period of use	Date and time

[47] In real time or post-remote.

[48] At least two natural persons. AI Act, Art. 14(5)(2).

13 ARTICLE 13. TRANSPARENCY AND PROVISION OF INFORMATION TO DEPLOYERS

1. High-risk AI systems shall be designed and developed in such a way as to ensure that their operation is sufficiently transparent to enable deployers to interpret a system's output and use it appropriately. An appropriate type and degree of transparency shall be ensured with a view to achieving compliance with the relevant obligations of the provider and deployer set out in Section 3.

2. High-risk AI systems shall be accompanied by instructions for use in an appropriate digital format or otherwise that include concise, complete, correct and clear information that is relevant, accessible and comprehensible to deployers.

3. The instructions for use shall contain at least the following information:

(a) the identity and the contact details of the provider and, where applicable, of its authorised representative;

(b) the characteristics, capabilities and limitations of performance of the high-risk AI system, including:

(i) its intended purpose;

(ii) the level of accuracy, including its metrics, robustness and cybersecurity referred to in Article 15 against which the high-risk AI system has been tested and validated and which can be expected, and any known and foreseeable circumstances that may have an impact on that expected level of accuracy, robustness and cybersecurity;

(iii) any known or foreseeable circumstance, related to the use of the high-risk AI system in accordance with its intended purpose or under conditions of reasonably foreseeable misuse, which may lead to risks to the health and safety or fundamental rights referred to in Article 9(2);

(iv) where applicable, the technical capabilities and characteristics of the high-risk AI system to provide information that is relevant to explain its output;

(v) when appropriate, its performance regarding specific persons or groups of persons on which the system is intended to be used;

(vi) when appropriate, specifications for the input data, or any other relevant information in terms of the training, validation and testing data sets used, taking into account the intended purpose of the high-risk AI system;

(vii) where applicable, information to enable deployers to interpret the output of the high-risk AI system and use it appropriately;

(c) the changes to the high-risk AI system and its performance which have been pre-determined by the provider at the moment of the initial conformity assessment, if any;

(d) the human oversight measures referred to in Article 14, including the technical measures put in place to facilitate the interpretation of the outputs of the high-risk AI systems by the deployers;

(e) the computational and hardware resources needed, the expected lifetime of the high-risk AI system and any necessary maintenance and care measures, including their frequency, to ensure the proper functioning of that AI system, including as regards software updates;

(f) where relevant, a description of the mechanisms included within the high-risk AI system that allows deployers to properly collect, store and interpret the logs in accordance with Article 12.

13.1. Recitals

853. (26) In order to introduce a proportionate and effective set of binding rules for AI systems, a clearly defined risk-based approach should be followed. That approach should tailor the type and content of such rules to the intensity and scope of the risks that AI systems can generate. It is therefore necessary to prohibit certain unacceptable AI practices, to lay down requirements for high-risk AI systems and obligations for the relevant operators, and to lay down transparency obligations for certain AI systems.

854. (27) While the risk-based approach is the basis for a proportionate and effective set of binding rules, it is important to recall the 2019 Ethics guidelines for trustworthy AI developed by the independent AI HLEG appointed by the Commission. In those guidelines, the AI HLEG developed seven non-binding ethical principles for AI which are intended to help ensure that AI is trustworthy and ethically sound. The seven principles include human agency and oversight; technical robustness and safety; privacy and data governance; transparency; diversity, non-discrimination and fairness; societal and environmental well-being and accountability. Without prejudice to the legally binding requirements of this Regulation and any other applicable Union law, those guidelines contribute to the design of coherent, trustworthy and human-centric AI, in line with the Charter and with the values on which the Union is founded. According to the guidelines of the AI HLEG, human agency and oversight means that AI systems are developed and used as a tool that serves people, respects human dignity and personal autonomy, and that is functioning in a way that can be appropriately controlled and overseen by humans. Technical robustness and safety means that AI systems are developed and used in a way that allows robustness in the case of problems and resilience against attempts to alter the use or performance of the AI system so as to allow unlawful use by third parties, and minimise unintended harm. Privacy and data governance means that AI systems are developed and used in accordance with privacy and data protection rules, while processing data that meets high standards in terms of quality and integrity. Transparency means that AI systems are developed and used in a way that allows appropriate traceability and explainability, while making humans aware that they communicate or interact with an AI system, as well as duly informing deployers of the capabilities and limitations of that AI system and affected persons about their rights. Diversity, non-discrimination and fairness means that AI systems are developed and used in a way that includes diverse actors and promotes equal access, gender equality and cultural diversity, while avoiding discriminatory impacts and unfair biases that are prohibited by Union or national law. Social and environmental well-being means that AI systems are developed and used in a sustainable and environmentally friendly manner as well as in a way to benefit all human beings, while monitoring and assessing the long-term impacts on the individual, society and democracy. The application of those principles should be translated, when possible, in the design and use of AI models. They should in any case serve as a basis for the drafting of codes of conduct under this Regulation. All stakeholders, including industry, academia, civil society and standardisation organisations, are encouraged to take into account, as appropriate, the ethical principles for the development of voluntary best practices and standards.

855. (53) It is also important to clarify that there may be specific cases in which AI systems referred to in pre-defined areas specified in this Regulation do not lead to a significant risk of harm to the legal interests protected under those areas because they do not materially influence the decision-making or do not harm those interests substantially. For the purposes of this Regulation, an AI system that does not materially influence the outcome of decision-making should be understood to be an AI system that does not have an impact on the substance, and thereby the outcome, of decision-making, whether human or automated. An AI system that does not materially influence the outcome of decision-making could include situations in which one or more of the following conditions are fulfilled. The first such condition should be that the AI system is intended to perform a narrow procedural task, such as an AI system that transforms unstructured data into structured data, an AI system that classifies incoming documents into categories or an AI system that is used to detect duplicates among a large number of applications. Those tasks are of such narrow and limited nature that they pose only limited risks which are not increased through the use of an AI system in a context that is listed as a high-risk use in an annex to this Regulation. The second condition should be that the task performed by the AI system is intended to improve the result of a previously completed human activity that may be relevant for the purposes of the high-risk uses listed in an annex to this Regulation. Considering those characteristics, the AI system provides only an additional layer to a human activity with consequently lowered risk. That condition would, for example, apply to AI systems that are intended to improve the language used in previously drafted documents, for example in relation to professional tone, academic style of language or by aligning text to a certain brand messaging. The third condition should be that the AI system is intended to detect decision-making patterns or deviations from prior decision-making patterns. The risk would be lowered because the use of the AI system follows a previously completed human assessment which it is not meant to replace or influence, without proper human review. Such AI systems include for instance those that, given a certain grading pattern of a teacher, can be used to check ex post whether the teacher may have deviated from the grading pattern so as to flag potential inconsistencies or anomalies. The fourth condition should be that the AI system is intended to perform a task that is only preparatory to an assessment relevant for the purposes of the AI systems listed in an annex to this Regulation, thus making the possible impact of the output of the system very low in terms of representing a risk for the assessment to follow. That condition covers, inter alia, smart solutions for file handling, which include various functions from indexing, searching, text and speech processing or linking data to other data sources, or AI systems used for translation of initial documents. In any case, AI systems used in high-risk use-cases listed in an annex to this Regulation should be considered to pose significant risks of harm to the health, safety or fundamental rights if the AI system implies profiling within the meaning of Article 4, point (4) of Regulation (EU) 2016/679 or Article 3, point (4) of Directive (EU) 2016/680 or Article 3, point (5) of Regulation (EU) 2018/1725. To ensure traceability and transparency, a provider who considers that an AI system is not high-risk on the basis of the conditions referred to above should draw up documentation of the assessment before that system is placed on the market or put into service and should provide that documentation to national competent authorities upon request. Such a provider should be obliged to register the AI system in the EU database established under this Regulation. With a view to providing further guidance for the practical implementation of the conditions under which the AI systems listed in an annex to this Regulation are, on an exceptional basis, non-high-risk, the Commission should, after consulting the Board, provide guidelines specifying that practical implementation, completed by a comprehensive list of practical examples of use cases of AI systems that are high-risk and use cases that are not.

856. (59) Given their role and responsibility, actions by law enforcement authorities involving certain uses of AI systems are characterised by a significant degree of power imbalance and may lead to surveillance, arrest or deprivation of a natural person's liberty as well as other adverse impacts on fundamental rights guaranteed in the Charter. In particular, if the AI system is not trained with high-quality data, does not meet adequate requirements in terms of its performance, its accuracy or robustness, or is not properly designed and tested before being put on the market or otherwise put into service, it may single out people in a discriminatory or otherwise incorrect or unjust manner. Furthermore, the exercise of important procedural fundamental rights, such as the right to an effective remedy and to a fair trial as well as the right of defence and the presumption of innocence, could be hampered, in particular, where such AI systems are not sufficiently transparent, explainable and documented. It is therefore appropriate to classify as high-risk, insofar as their use is permitted under relevant Union and national law, a number of AI systems intended to be used in the law enforcement context where accuracy, reliability and transparency is particularly important to avoid adverse impacts, retain public trust and ensure accountability and effective redress. In view of the nature of the activities and the risks relating thereto, those high-risk AI systems should include in particular AI systems intended to be used by or on behalf of law enforcement authorities or by Union institutions, bodies, offices, or agencies in support of law enforcement authorities for assessing the risk of a natural person to become a victim of criminal offences, as polygraphs and similar tools, for the evaluation of the reliability of evidence in in the course of investigation or prosecution of criminal offences, and, insofar as not prohibited under this Regulation, for assessing the risk of a natural person offending or reoffending not solely on the basis of the profiling of natural persons or the assessment of personality traits and characteristics or the past criminal behaviour of natural persons or groups, for profiling in the course of detection, investigation or prosecution of criminal offences. AI systems specifically intended to be used for administrative proceedings by tax and customs authorities as well as by financial intelligence units carrying out administrative tasks analysing information pursuant to Union anti-money laundering law should not be classified as high-risk AI systems used by law enforcement authorities for the purpose of prevention, detection, investigation and prosecution of criminal offences. The use of AI tools by law enforcement and other relevant authorities should not become a factor of inequality, or exclusion. The impact of the use of AI tools on the defence rights of suspects should not be ignored, in particular the difficulty in obtaining meaningful information on the functioning of those systems and the resulting difficulty in challenging their results in court, in particular by natural persons under investigation.

857. **(60)** AI systems used in migration, asylum and border control management affect persons who are often in particularly vulnerable position and who are dependent on the outcome of the actions of the competent public authorities. The accuracy, non-discriminatory nature and transparency of the AI systems used in those contexts are therefore particularly important to guarantee respect for the fundamental rights of the affected persons, in particular their rights to free movement, non-discrimination, protection of private life and personal data, international protection and good administration. It is therefore appropriate to classify as high-risk, insofar as their use is permitted under relevant Union and national law, AI systems intended to be used by or on behalf of competent public authorities or by Union institutions, bodies, offices or agencies charged with tasks in the fields of migration, asylum and border control management as polygraphs and similar tools, for assessing certain risks posed by natural persons entering the territory of a Member State or applying for visa or asylum, for assisting competent public authorities for the examination, including related assessment of the reliability of evidence, of applications for asylum, visa and residence permits and associated complaints with regard to the objective to establish the eligibility of the natural persons applying for a status, for the purpose of detecting, recognising or identifying natural persons in the context of migration, asylum and border control management, with the exception of verification of travel documents. AI systems in the area of migration, asylum and border control management covered by this Regulation should comply with the relevant procedural requirements set by the Regulation (EC) No 810/2009 of the European Parliament and of the Council,[49] the Directive 2013/32/EU of the European Parliament and of the Council,[50] and other relevant Union law. The use of AI systems in migration, asylum and border control management should, in no circumstances, be used by Member States or Union institutions, bodies, offices or agencies as a means to circumvent their international obligations under the UN Convention relating to the Status of Refugees done at Geneva on 28 July 1951 as amended by the Protocol of 31 January 1967. Nor should they be used to in any way infringe on the principle of non-refoulement, or to deny safe and effective legal avenues into the territory of the Union, including the right to international protection.

858. (62) Without prejudice to the rules provided for in Regulation (EU) 2024/900 of the European Parliament and of the Council,[51] and in order to address the risks of undue external interference with the right to vote enshrined in Article 39 of the Charter, and of adverse effects on democracy and the rule of law, AI systems intended to be used to influence the outcome of an election or referendum or the voting behaviour of natural persons in the exercise of their vote in elections or referenda should be classified as high-risk AI systems with the exception of AI systems whose output natural persons are not directly exposed to, such as tools used to organise, optimise and structure political campaigns from an administrative and logistical point of view.

859. (66) Requirements should apply to high-risk AI systems as regards risk management, the quality and relevance of data sets used, technical documentation and record-keeping, transparency and the provision of information to deployers, human oversight, and robustness, accuracy and cybersecurity. Those requirements are necessary to effectively mitigate the risks for health, safety and fundamental rights. As no other less trade restrictive measures are reasonably available those requirements are not unjustified restrictions to trade.

860. (67) High-quality data and access to high-quality data plays a vital role in providing structure and in ensuring the performance of many AI systems, especially when techniques involving the training of models are used, with a view to ensure that the high-risk AI system performs as intended and safely and it

---

[49] Regulation (EC) No 810/2009 of the European Parliament and of the Council of 13 July 2009 establishing a Community Code on Visas (Visa Code), [2009] OJ L243/1.

[50] Directive 2013/32/EU of the European Parliament and of the Council of 26 June 2013 on common procedures for granting and withdrawing international protection, [2013] OJ L180/60.

[51] Regulation (EU) 2024/900 of the European parliament and of the Council of 13 March 2024 on the transparency and targeting of political advertising, [2024] OJ L, 2024/900.

does not become a source of discrimination prohibited by Union law. High-quality data sets for training, validation and testing require the implementation of appropriate data governance and management practices. Data sets for training, validation and testing, including the labels, should be relevant, sufficiently representative, and to the best extent possible free of errors and complete in view of the intended purpose of the system. In order to facilitate compliance with Union data protection law, such as Regulation (EU) 2016/679, data governance and management practices should include, in the case of personal data, transparency about the original purpose of the data collection. The data sets should also have the appropriate statistical properties, including as regards the persons or groups of persons in relation to whom the high-risk AI system is intended to be used, with specific attention to the mitigation of possible biases in the data sets, that are likely to affect the health and safety of persons, have a negative impact on fundamental rights or lead to discrimination prohibited under Union law, especially where data outputs influence inputs for future operations (feedback loops). Biases can for example be inherent in underlying data sets, especially when historical data is being used, or generated when the systems are implemented in real world settings. Results provided by AI systems could be influenced by such inherent biases that are inclined to gradually increase and thereby perpetuate and amplify existing discrimination, in particular for persons belonging to certain vulnerable groups, including racial or ethnic groups. The requirement for the data sets to be to the best extent possible complete and free of errors should not affect the use of privacy-preserving techniques in the context of the development and testing of AI systems. In particular, data sets should take into account, to the extent required by their intended purpose, the features, characteristics or elements that are particular to the specific geographical, contextual, behavioural or functional setting which the AI system is intended to be used. The requirements related to data governance can be complied with by having recourse to third parties that offer certified compliance services including verification of data governance, data set integrity, and data training, validation and testing practices, as far as compliance with the data requirements of this Regulation are ensured.

861. (72) To address concerns related to opacity and complexity of certain AI systems and help deployers to fulfil their obligations under this Regulation, transparency should be required for high-risk AI systems before they are placed on the market or put it into service. High-risk AI systems should be designed in a manner to enable deployers to understand how the AI system works, evaluate its functionality, and comprehend its strengths and limitations. High-risk AI systems should be accompanied by appropriate information in the form of instructions of use. Such information should include the characteristics, capabilities and limitations of performance of the AI system. Those would cover information on possible known and foreseeable circumstances related to the use of the high-risk AI system, including deployer action that may influence system behaviour and performance, under which the AI system can lead to risks to health, safety, and fundamental rights, on the changes that have been pre-determined and assessed for conformity by the provider and on the relevant human oversight measures, including the measures to facilitate the interpretation of the outputs of the AI system by the deployers. Transparency, including the accompanying instructions for use, should assist deployers in the use of the system and support informed decision making by them. Deployers should, inter alia, be in a better position to make the correct choice of the system that they intend to use in light of the obligations applicable to them, be educated about the intended and precluded uses, and use the AI system correctly and as appropriate. In order to enhance legibility and accessibility of the information included in the instructions of use, where appropriate, illustrative examples, for instance on the limitations and on the intended and precluded uses of the AI system, should be included. Providers should ensure that all documentation, including the instructions for use, contains meaningful, comprehensive, accessible and understandable information, taking into account the needs and foreseeable knowledge of the target deployers. Instructions for use should be made available in a language which can be easily understood by target deployers, as determined by the Member State concerned.

862. **(74)** High-risk AI systems should perform consistently throughout their lifecycle and meet an appropriate level of accuracy, robustness and cybersecurity, in light of their intended purpose and in accordance with the generally acknowledged state of the Art. The Commission and relevant organisations and stakeholders are encouraged to take due consideration of the mitigation of risks and the negative impacts of the AI system. The expected level of performance metrics should be declared in the accompanying instructions of use. Providers are urged to communicate that information to deployers in a clear and easily understandable way, free of misunderstandings or misleading statements. Union law on legal metrology, including Directives 2014/31/EU[52] and 2014/32/EU[53] of the European Parliament and of the Council, aims to ensure the accuracy of measurements and to help the transparency and fairness of commercial transactions. In that context, in cooperation with relevant stakeholders and organisation, such as metrology and benchmarking authorities, the Commission should encourage, as appropriate, the development of benchmarks and measurement methodologies for AI systems. In doing so, the Commission should

---

[52] Directive 2014/31/EU of the European Parliament and of the Council of 26 February 2014 on the harmonisation of the laws of the Member States relating to the making available on the market of non-automatic weighing instruments, [2024] OJ L96/107.

[53] Directive 2014/32/EU of the European Parliament and of the Council of 26 February 2014 on the harmonisation of the laws of the Member States relating to the making available on the market of measuring instruments, [2014] OJ L96/149.

take note and collaborate with international partners working on metrology and relevant measurement indicators relating to AI.

863. **(94)** Any processing of biometric data involved in the use of AI systems for biometric identification for the purpose of law enforcement needs to comply with Article 10 of Directive (EU) 2016/680, that allows such processing only where strictly necessary, subject to appropriate safeguards for the rights and freedoms of the data subject, and where authorised by Union or Member State law. Such use, when authorised, also needs to respect the principles laid down in Article 4 (1) of Directive (EU) 2016/680 including lawfulness, fairness and transparency, purpose limitation, accuracy and storage limitation.

864. **(101)** Providers of general-purpose AI models have a particular role and responsibility along the AI value chain, as the models they provide may form the basis for a range of downstream systems, often provided by downstream providers that necessitate a good understanding of the models and their capabilities, both to enable the integration of such models into their products, and to fulfil their obligations under this or other regulations. Therefore, proportionate transparency measures should be laid down, including the drawing up and keeping up to date of documentation, and the provision of information on the general-purpose AI model for its usage by the downstream providers. Technical documentation should be prepared and kept up to date by the general-purpose AI model provider for the purpose of making it available, upon request, to the AI Office and the national competent authorities. The minimal set of elements to be included in such documentation should be set out in specific annexes to this Regulation. The Commission should be empowered to amend those annexes by means of delegated acts in light of evolving technological developments.

865. **(102)** Software and data, including models, released under a free and open-source licence that allows them to be openly shared and where users can freely access, use, modify and redistribute them or modified versions thereof, can contribute to research and innovation in the market and can provide significant growth opportunities for the Union economy. General-purpose AI models released under free and open-source licences should be considered to ensure high levels of transparency and openness if their parameters, including the weights, the information on the model architecture, and the information on model usage are made publicly available. The licence should be considered to be free and open-source also when it allows users to run, copy, distribute, study, change and improve software and data, including models under the condition that the original provider of the model is credited, the identical or comparable terms of distribution are respected.

866. **(104)** The providers of general-purpose AI models that are released under a free and open-source licence, and whose parameters, including the weights, the information on the model architecture, and the information on model usage, are made publicly available should be subject to exceptions as regards the transparency-related requirements imposed on general-purpose AI models, unless they can be considered to present a systemic risk, in which case the circumstance that the model is transparent and accompanied by an open-source license should not be considered to be a sufficient reason to exclude compliance with the obligations under this Regulation. In any case, given that the release of general-purpose AI models under free and open-source licence does not necessarily reveal substantial information on the data set used for the training or fine-tuning of the model and on how compliance of copyright law was thereby ensured, the exception provided for general-purpose AI models from compliance with the transparency-related requirements should not concern the obligation to produce a summary about the content used for model training and the obligation to put in place a policy to comply with Union copyright law, in particular to identify and comply with the reservation of rights pursuant to Article 4(3) of Directive (EU) 2019/790 of the European Parliament and of the Council.[54]

867. (107) In order to increase transparency on the data that is used in the pre-training and training of general-purpose AI models, including text and data protected by copyright law, it is adequate that providers of such models draw up and make publicly available a sufficiently detailed summary of the content used for training the general-purpose AI model. While taking into due account the need to protect trade secrets and confidential business information, this summary should be generally comprehensive in its scope instead of technically detailed to facilitate parties with legitimate interests, including copyright holders, to exercise and enforce their rights under Union law, for example by listing the main data collections or sets that went into training the model, such as large private or public databases or data archives, and by providing a narrative explanation about other data sources used. It is appropriate for the AI Office to provide a template for the summary, which should be simple, effective, and allow the provider to provide the required summary in narrative form.

868. (131) In order to facilitate the work of the Commission and the Member States in the AI field as well as to increase the transparency towards the public, providers of high-risk AI systems other than those related to products falling within the scope of relevant existing Union harmonisation legislation, as well as providers who consider that an AI system listed in the high-risk use cases in an annex to this Regulation is not high-risk on the basis of a derogation, should be required to register themselves and information about their AI system in an EU database, to be established and managed by the Commission. Before using an AI system listed in the high-risk use cases in an annex to this Regulation, deployers

[54] Directive (EU) 2019/790 of the European Parliament and of the Council of 17 April 2019 on copyright and related rights in the Digital Single Market and amending Directives 96/9/EC and 2001/29/EC, [2019] OJ L130/92.

of high-risk AI systems that are public authorities, agencies or bodies, should register themselves in such database and select the system that they envisage to use. Other deployers should be entitled to do so voluntarily. This section of the EU database should be publicly accessible, free of charge, the information should be easily navigable, understandable and machine-readable. The EU database should also be user-friendly, for example by providing search functionalities, including through keywords, allowing the general public to find relevant information to be submitted upon the registration of high-risk AI systems and on the use case of high-risk AI systems, set out in an annex to this Regulation, to which the high-risk AI systems correspond. Any substantial modification of high-risk AI systems should also be registered in the EU database. For high-risk AI systems in the area of law enforcement, migration, asylum and border control management, the registration obligations should be fulfilled in a secure non-public section of the EU database. Access to the secure non-public section should be strictly limited to the Commission as well as to market surveillance authorities with regard to their national section of that database. High-risk AI systems in the area of critical infrastructure should only be registered at national level. The Commission should be the controller of the EU database, in accordance with Regulation (EU) 2018/1725. In order to ensure the full functionality of the EU database, when deployed, the procedure for setting the database should include the development of functional specifications by the Commission and an independent audit report. The Commission should take into account cybersecurity risks when carrying out its tasks as data controller on the EU database. In order to maximise the availability and use of the EU database by the public, the EU database, including the information made available through it, should comply with requirements under the Directive (EU) 2019/882.

869. (132) Certain AI systems intended to interact with natural persons or to generate content may pose specific risks of impersonation or deception irrespective of whether they qualify as high-risk or not. In certain circumstances, the use of these systems should therefore be subject to specific transparency obligations without prejudice to the requirements and obligations for high-risk AI systems and subject to targeted exceptions to take into account the special need of law enforcement. In particular, natural persons should be notified that they are interacting with an AI system, unless this is obvious from the point of view of a natural person who is reasonably well-informed, observant and circumspect taking into account the circumstances and the context of use. When implementing that obligation, the characteristics of natural persons belonging to vulnerable groups due to their age or disability should be taken into account to the extent the AI system is intended to interact with those groups as well. Moreover, natural persons should be notified when they are exposed to AI systems that, by processing their biometric data, can identify or infer the emotions or intentions of those persons or assign them to specific categories. Such specific categories can relate to aspects such as sex, age, hair colour, eye colour, tattoos, personal traits, ethnic origin, personal preferences and interests. Such information and notifications should be provided in accessible formats for persons with disabilities.

870. **(134)** Further to the technical solutions employed by the providers of the AI system, deployers who use an AI system to generate or manipulate image, audio or video content that appreciably resembles existing persons, objects, places, entities or events and would falsely appear to a person to be authentic or truthful (deep fakes), should also clearly and distinguishably disclose that the content has been artificially created or manipulated by labelling the AI output accordingly and disclosing its artificial origin. Compliance with this transparency obligation should not be interpreted as indicating that the use of the AI system or its output impedes the right to freedom of expression and the right to freedom of the arts and sciences guaranteed in the Charter, in particular where the content is part of an evidently creative, satirical, artistic, fictional or analogous work or programme, subject to appropriate safeguards for the rights and freedoms of third parties. In those cases, the transparency obligation for deep fakes set out in this Regulation is limited to disclosure of the existence of such generated or manipulated content in an appropriate manner that does not hamper the display or enjoyment of the work, including its normal exploitation and use, while maintaining the utility and quality of the work. In addition, it is also appropriate to envisage a similar disclosure obligation in relation to AI-generated or manipulated text to the extent it is published with the purpose of informing the public on matters of public interest unless the AI-generated content has undergone a process of human review or editorial control and a natural or legal person holds editorial responsibility for the publication of the content.

871. **(135)** Without prejudice to the mandatory nature and full applicability of the transparency obligations, the Commission may also encourage and facilitate the drawing up of codes of practice at Union level to facilitate the effective implementation of the obligations regarding the detection and labelling of artificially generated or manipulated content, including to support practical arrangements for making, as appropriate, the detection mechanisms accessible and facilitating cooperation with other actors along the value chain, disseminating content or checking its authenticity and provenance to enable the public to effectively distinguish AI-generated content.

872. **(137)** Compliance with the transparency obligations for the AI systems covered by this Regulation should not be interpreted as indicating that the use of the AI system or its output is lawful under this Regulation or other Union and Member State law and should be without prejudice to other transparency obligations for deployers of AI systems laid down in Union or national law.

873. (157) This Regulation is without prejudice to the competences, tasks, powers and independence of relevant national public authorities or bodies which supervise the application of Union law protecting fundamental rights, including equality bodies and data protection authorities. Where necessary for their mandate, those national public authorities or bodies should also have access to any documentation created under this Regulation. A specific safeguard procedure should be set for ensuring adequate and timely enforcement against AI systems presenting a risk to health, safety and fundamental rights. The procedure for such AI systems presenting a risk should be applied to high-risk AI systems presenting a risk, prohibited systems which have been placed on the market, put into service or used in violation of the prohibited practices laid down in this Regulation and AI systems which have been made available in violation of the transparency requirements laid down in this Regulation and present a risk.

874. (173) In order to ensure that the regulatory framework can be adapted where necessary, the power to adopt acts in accordance with Article 290 TFEU should be delegated to the Commission to amend the conditions under which an AI system is not to be considered to be high-risk, the list of high-risk AI systems, the provisions regarding technical documentation, the content of the EU declaration of conformity the provisions regarding the conformity assessment procedures, the provisions establishing the high-risk AI systems to which the conformity assessment procedure based on assessment of the quality management system and assessment of the technical documentation should apply, the threshold, benchmarks and indicators, including by supplementing those benchmarks and indicators, in the rules for the classification of general-purpose AI models with systemic risk, the criteria for the designation of general-purpose AI models with systemic risk, the technical documentation for providers of general-purpose AI models and the transparency information for providers of general-purpose AI models. It is of particular importance that the Commission carry out appropriate consultations during its preparatory work, including at expert level, and that those consultations be conducted in accordance with the principles laid down in the Interinstitutional Agreement of 13 April 2016 on Better Law-Making.[55] In particular, to ensure equal participation in the preparation of delegated acts, the European Parliament and the Council receive all documents at the same time as Member States' experts, and their experts systematically have access to meetings of Commission expert groups dealing with the preparation of delegated acts.

[55] [2016] OJ L123/1.

13.2. General Approach

13.2.1 Preamble

875. The principle of transparency[56] is a cardinal principle in risk management by deployers. It is critical for the implementation of trustworthy AI systems.

13.2.2 Guiding Principles

876. Where applied to high-risk AI systems, this transparency serves two complementary purposes:

- understanding the system;
- interpreting the outputs.

877. Compliance with the transparency obligation primarily requires complying with the requirement of providing instructions for use.

13.3. Content of the Instructions for Use

878. They must contain at least the following sections:

NO.	THEME	SPECIFICATION	COMMENT
1.	Identity	Provider or authorised representative	
2.	Intended purpose	Main purposes of the AI system	
3.	Accuracy	Level against which the system has been tested	
4.	Robustness	Level against which the system has been tested	
5.	Cybersecurity	Level against which the system has been tested	
6.	Events with an impact on risk levels	Accuracy, robustness and cybersecurity	Known or foreseeable circumstances
7.	Events with an impact on risk levels	Health, safety and fundamental rights	Known or foreseeable circumstances

56 AI Act, Art. 13.

NO.	THEME	SPECIFICATION	COMMENT
8.	Performance	Use	Persons or groups of persons on which the system is intended to be used
9.	Information on data sets		
10.	Changes to the system	Pre-determined by the provider	At the moment of the initial conformity
11.	Changes to the system performance	Pre-determined by the provider	At the moment of the initial conformity
12.	Information on human oversight	Technical measures and interpretation of outputs	
13.	Maintenance	Service information (threats and monitoring)	
14.	Software updates	Periodicity, version and content	
15.	Incident logs	Interpretation of events in recording logs	

14 ARTICLE 14. HUMAN OVERSIGHT

1. High-risk AI systems shall be designed and developed in such a way, including with appropriate human-machine interface tools, that they can be effectively overseen by natural persons during the period in which they are in use.

2. Human oversight shall aim to prevent or minimise the risks to health, safety or fundamental rights that may emerge when a high-risk AI system is used in accordance with its intended purpose or under conditions of reasonably foreseeable misuse, in particular where such risks persist despite the application of other requirements set out in this Section.

3. The oversight measures shall be commensurate with the risks, level of autonomy and context of use of the high-risk AI system, and shall be ensured through either one or both of the following types of measures:

(a) measures identified and built, when technically feasible, into the high-risk AI system by the provider before it is placed on the market or put into service;

(b) measures identified by the provider before placing the high-risk AI system on the market or putting it into service and that are appropriate to be implemented by the deployer.

4. For the purpose of implementing paragraphs 1, 2 and 3, the high-risk AI system shall be provided to the deployer in such a way that natural persons to whom human oversight is assigned are enabled, as appropriate and proportionate:

(a) to properly understand the relevant capacities and limitations of the high-risk AI system and be able to duly monitor its operation, including in view of detecting and addressing anomalies, dysfunctions and unexpected performance;

(b) to remain aware of the possible tendency of automatically relying or over-relying on the output produced by a high-risk AI system (automation bias), in particular for high-risk AI systems used to provide information or recommendations for decisions to be taken by natural persons;

(c) to correctly interpret the high-risk AI system's output, taking into account, for example, the interpretation tools and methods available;

(d) to decide, in any particular situation, not to use the high-risk AI system or to otherwise disregard, override or reverse the output of the high-risk AI system;

(e) to intervene in the operation of the high-risk AI system or interrupt the system through a 'stop' button or a similar procedure that allows the system to come to a halt in a safe state.

5. For high-risk AI systems referred to in point 1(a) of Annex III, the measures referred to in paragraph 3 of this Article shall be such as to ensure that, in addition, no action or decision is taken by the deployer on the basis of the identification resulting from the system unless that identification has been separately verified and confirmed by at least two natural persons with the necessary competence, training and authority.

The requirement for a separate verification by at least two natural persons shall not apply to high-risk AI systems used for the purposes of law enforcement, migration, border control or asylum, where Union or national law considers the application of this requirement to be disproportionate.

14.1. Recitals

879. (27) While the risk-based approach is the basis for a proportionate and effective set of binding rules, it is important to recall the 2019 Ethics guidelines for trustworthy AI developed by the independent AI HLEG appointed by the Commission. In those guidelines, the AI HLEG developed seven non-binding ethical principles for AI which are intended to help ensure that AI is trustworthy and ethically sound. The seven principles include human agency and oversight; technical robustness and safety; privacy and data governance; transparency; diversity, non-discrimination and fairness; societal and environmental well-being and accountability. Without prejudice to the legally binding requirements of this Regulation and any other applicable Union law, those guidelines contribute to the design of coherent, trustworthy and human-centric AI, in line with the Charter and with the values on which the Union is founded. According to the guidelines of the AI HLEG, human agency and oversight means that AI systems are developed and used as a tool that serves people, respects human dignity and personal autonomy, and that is functioning in a way that can be appropriately controlled and overseen by humans. Technical robustness and safety means that AI systems are developed and used in a way that allows robustness in the case of problems and resilience against attempts to alter the use or performance of the AI system so as to allow unlawful use by third parties, and minimise unintended harm. Privacy and data governance means that AI systems are developed and used in accordance with privacy and data protection rules, while processing data that meets high standards in terms of quality and integrity. Transparency means that AI systems are developed and used in a way that allows appropriate traceability and explainability, while making humans aware that they communicate or interact with an AI system, as well as duly informing deployers of the capabilities and limitations of that AI system and affected persons about their rights. Diversity, non-discrimination and fairness means that AI systems are developed and used in a way that includes diverse actors and promotes equal access, gender equality and cultural diversity, while avoiding discriminatory impacts and unfair biases that are prohibited by Union or national law. Social and environmental well-being means that AI systems are developed and used in a sustainable and environmentally friendly manner as well as in a way to benefit all human beings, while monitoring and assessing the long-term impacts on the individual, society and democracy. The application of those principles should be translated, when possible, in the design and use of AI models. They should in any case serve as a basis for the drafting of codes of conduct under this Regulation. All stakeholders, including industry, academia, civil society and standardisation organisations, are encouraged to take into account, as appropriate, the ethical principles for the development of voluntary best practices and standards.

880. **(33)** The use of those systems for the purpose of law enforcement should therefore be prohibited, except in exhaustively listed and narrowly defined situations, where the use is strictly necessary to achieve a substantial public interest, the importance of which outweighs the risks. Those situations involve the search for certain victims of crime including missing persons; certain threats to the life or to the physical safety of natural persons or of a terrorist attack; and the localisation or identification of perpetrators or suspects of the criminal offences listed in an annex to this Regulation, where those criminal offences are punishable in the Member State concerned by a custodial sentence or a detention order for a maximum period of at least four years and as they are defined in the law of that Member State. Such a threshold for the custodial sentence or detention order in accordance with national law contributes to ensuring that the offence should be serious enough to potentially justify the use of 'real-time' remote biometric identification systems. Moreover, the list of criminal offences provided in an annex to this Regulation is based on the 32 criminal offences listed in the Council Framework Decision 2002/584/JHA,[57] taking into account that some of those offences are, in practice, likely to be more relevant than others, in that the recourse to 'real-time' remote biometric identification could, foreseeably, be necessary and proportionate to highly varying degrees for the practical pursuit of the localisation or identification of a perpetrator or suspect of the different criminal offences listed and having regard to the likely differences in the seriousness, probability and scale of the harm or possible negative consequences. An imminent threat to life or the physical safety of natural persons could also result from a serious disruption of critical infrastructure, as defined in Article 2, point (4) of Directive (EU) 2022/2557 of the European Parliament and of the Council,[58] where the disruption or destruction of such critical infrastructure would result in an imminent threat to life or the physical safety of a person, including through serious harm to the provision of basic supplies to the population or to the exercise of the core function of the State. In addition, this Regulation should preserve the ability for law enforcement, border control, immigration or asylum authorities to carry out identity checks in the presence of the person concerned in accordance with the conditions set out in Union and national law for such checks. In particular, law enforcement, border control, immigration or asylum authorities should be able to use information systems, in accordance with Union or national law, to identify persons who, during an identity check, either refuse to be identified or are unable to state or prove their identity, without being required by this Regulation to obtain prior authorisation. This could be, for example, a person involved in a crime, being unwilling, or unable due to an accident or a medical condition, to disclose their identity to law enforcement authorities.

881. (66) Requirements should apply to high-risk AI systems as regards risk management, the quality and relevance of data sets used, technical documentation and record-keeping, transparency and the provision of information to deployers, human oversight, and robustness, accuracy and cybersecurity. Those requirements are necessary to effectively mitigate the risks for health, safety and fundamental rights. As no other less trade restrictive measures are reasonably available those requirements are not unjustified restrictions to trade.

882. (72) To address concerns related to opacity and complexity of certain AI systems and help deployers to fulfil their obligations under this Regulation, transparency should be required for high-risk AI systems before they are placed on the market or put it into service. High-risk AI systems should be

[57] Council Framework Decision 2002/584/JHA of 13 June 2002 on the European arrest warrant and the surrender procedures between Member States, [2002] OJ L190/1.

[58] Directive (EU) 2022/2557 of the European Parliament and of the Council of 14 December 2022 on the resilience of critical entities and repealing Council Directive 2008/114/EC, [2022] OJ L333/164.

designed in a manner to enable deployers to understand how the AI system works, evaluate its functionality, and comprehend its strengths and limitations. High-risk AI systems should be accompanied by appropriate information in the form of instructions of use. Such information should include the characteristics, capabilities and limitations of performance of the AI system. Those would cover information on possible known and foreseeable circumstances related to the use of the high-risk AI system, including deployer action that may influence system behaviour and performance, under which the AI system can lead to risks to health, safety, and fundamental rights, on the changes that have been pre-determined and assessed for conformity by the provider and on the relevant human oversight measures, including the measures to facilitate the interpretation of the outputs of the AI system by the deployers. Transparency, including the accompanying instructions for use, should assist deployers in the use of the system and support informed decision making by them. Deployers should, inter alia, be in a better position to make the correct choice of the system that they intend to use in light of the obligations applicable to them, be educated about the intended and precluded uses, and use the AI system correctly and as appropriate. In order to enhance legibility and accessibility of the information included in the instructions of use, where appropriate, illustrative examples, for instance on the limitations and on the intended and precluded uses of the AI system, should be included. Providers should ensure that all documentation, including the instructions for use, contains meaningful, comprehensive, accessible and understandable information, taking into account the needs and foreseeable knowledge of the target deployers. Instructions for use should be made available in a language which can be easily understood by target deployers, as determined by the Member State concerned.

883. (73) High-risk AI systems should be designed and developed in such a way that natural persons can oversee their functioning, ensure that they are used as intended and that their impacts are addressed over the system's lifecycle. To that end, appropriate human oversight measures should be identified by the provider of the system before its placing on the market or putting into service. In particular, where appropriate, such measures should guarantee that the system is subject to in-built operational constraints that cannot be overridden by the system itself and is responsive to the human operator, and that the natural persons to whom human oversight has been assigned have the necessary competence, training and authority to carry out that role. It is also essential, as appropriate, to ensure that high-risk AI systems include mechanisms to guide and inform a natural person to whom human oversight has been assigned to make informed decisions if, when and how to intervene in order to avoid negative consequences or risks, or stop the system if it does not perform as intended. Considering the significant consequences for persons in the case of an incorrect match by certain biometric identification systems, it is appropriate to provide for an enhanced human oversight requirement for those systems so that no action or decision may be taken by the deployer on the basis of the identification resulting from the system unless this has been separately verified and confirmed by at least two natural persons. Those persons could be from one or more entities and include the person operating or using the system. This requirement should not pose unnecessary burden or delays and it could be sufficient that the separate verifications by the different persons are automatically recorded in the logs generated by the system. Given the specificities of the areas of law enforcement, migration, border control and asylum, this requirement should not apply where Union or national law considers the application of that requirement to be disproportionate.

884. **(91)** Given the nature of AI systems and the risks to safety and fundamental rights possibly associated with their use, including as regards the need to ensure proper monitoring of the performance of an AI system in a real-life setting, it is appropriate to set specific responsibilities for deployers. Deployers should in particular take appropriate technical and organisational measures to ensure they use high-risk AI systems in accordance with the instructions of use and certain other obligations should be provided for with regard to monitoring of the functioning of the AI systems and with regard to record-keeping, as appropriate. Furthermore, deployers should ensure that the persons assigned to implement the instructions for use and human oversight as set out in this Regulation have the necessary competence, in particular an adequate level of AI literacy, training and authority to properly fulfil those tasks. Those obligations should be without prejudice to other deployer obligations in relation to high-risk AI systems under Union or national law.

885. **(96)** In order to efficiently ensure that fundamental rights are protected, deployers of high-risk AI systems that are bodies governed by public law, or private entities providing public services and deployers of certain high-risk AI systems listed in an annex to this Regulation, such as banking or insurance entities, should carry out a fundamental rights impact assessment prior to putting it into use. Services important for individuals that are of public nature may also be provided by private entities. Private entities providing such public services are linked to tasks in the public interest such as in the areas of education, healthcare, social services, housing, administration of justice. The aim of the fundamental rights impact assessment is for the deployer to identify the specific risks to the rights of individuals or groups of individuals likely to be affected, identify measures to be taken in the case of a materialisation of those risks. The impact assessment should be performed prior to deploying the high-risk AI system, and should be updated when the deployer considers that any of the relevant factors have changed. The impact assessment should identify the deployer's relevant processes in which the high-risk AI system will be used in line with its intended purpose, and should include a description of the period of time and frequency in which the system is intended to be used as well as of specific categories of natural persons and groups who are likely to be affected in the specific context of use. The assessment should also include the identification of specific risks of harm likely to have an impact on the fundamental rights of those persons or groups. While performing this assessment, the deployer should take into account information relevant to a proper assessment of the impact, including but not limited to the information given by the provider of the high-risk AI system in the instructions for use. In light of the risks identified, deployers should determine measures to be taken in the case of a materialisation of those risks, including for example governance arrangements in that specific context of use, such as arrangements for human oversight according to the instructions of use or, complaint handling and redress procedures, as they could be instrumental in mitigating risks to fundamental rights in concrete use-cases. After performing that impact assessment, the deployer should notify the relevant market surveillance authority. Where appropriate, to collect relevant information necessary to perform the impact assessment, deployers of high-risk AI system, in particular when AI systems are used in the public sector, could involve relevant stakeholders, including the representatives of groups of persons likely to be affected by the AI system, independent experts, and civil society organisations in conducting such impact assessments and designing measures to be taken in the case of materialisation of the risks. The European Artificial Intelligence Office (AI Office) should develop a template for a questionnaire in order to facilitate compliance and reduce the administrative burden for deployers.

14.2. General Approach

14.2.1 Preamble

886. This Article, which provides for the possibility of interrupting the AI system, concerns one of the most fundamental issues in AI systems regulation. Should there be a 'red button', a 'kill switch' or 'stop button' so that a human can retain control over situations under all circumstances?

887. The key is not merely to integrate AI but to define its role in balancing human and automated tasks. We must build an evolving partnership (a new human-machine social contract) that respects and leverages the strengths of both human and artificial intelligence. This partnership is one of hybrid intelligence, a managerial imperative.[59]

[59] V. Vinzi, 'Réinventer le management: l'ère de l'intelligence hybride' ['Reinventing management: the era of hybrid intelligence"], *Les Échos*, 22 January 2024.

14.2.2 Guiding Principles

888. Between artificial intelligence and human intelligence, the final decision must always remain the privilege of humans.

889. This principle requires an approach that is human-centric by design to ensure that AI systems never operate entirely autonomously.

890. To that end, the architecture of AI systems must incorporate two complementary requirements:

- the creation of a containment area for AI systems to limit their autonomy;
- the existence of a stop button to neutralize such systems at any time.

14.3. Classification

891. This control can be classified into the following three categories:

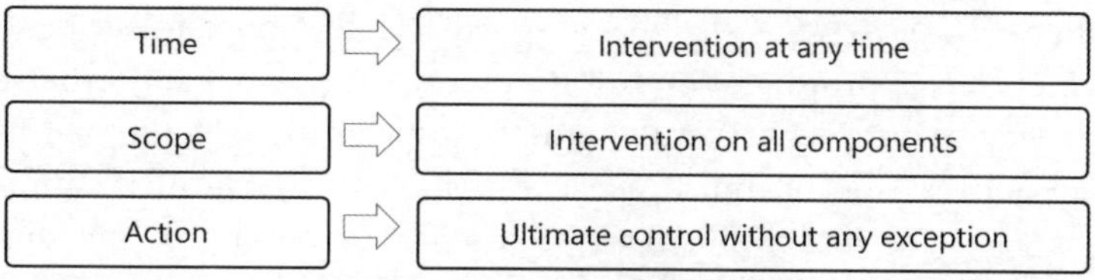

14.4. Purposes

892. They are organised into the following two themes:

- prevention;
- risk reduction.

14.5. Characteristics

893. The methods for exercising oversight are carried out through the following processes.

NO.	THEME	SPECIFICATION
1.	Measures before the system is placed on the market	Implementation of an effective oversight system
2.	Intervention	Actions that can be implemented in terms of: • monitoring; • control; • returning to the initial phase; • emergency stop.
3.	Control	Normal use or foreseeable misuse

14.6. *Find Out More*

14.6.1 Toolbox

894. AIA, 'Algorithmic Impact Assessment', v0.10.0, canada.ca.

895. AIA, 'Algorithmic Impact Assessment tool', canada.ca.

896. Conseil d'État, 'Intelligence artificielle et action publique: construire la confiance, servir la performance' ['Artificial intelligence and public action: building trust, serving performance'], Study by the Conseil d'État at the request of the Prime Minister, 31 March 2022.

15 ARTICLE 15. ACCURACY, ROBUSTNESS AND CYBERSECURITY

1. High-risk AI systems shall be designed and developed in such a way that they achieve an appropriate level of accuracy, robustness, and cybersecurity, and that they perform consistently in those respects throughout their lifecycle.

2. To address the technical aspects of how to measure the appropriate levels of accuracy and robustness set out in paragraph 1 and any other relevant performance metrics, the Commission shall, in cooperation with relevant stakeholders and organisations such as metrology and benchmarking authorities, encourage, as appropriate, the development of benchmarks and measurement methodologies.

3. The levels of accuracy and the relevant accuracy metrics of high-risk AI systems shall be declared in the accompanying instructions of use.

4. High-risk AI systems shall be as resilient as possible regarding errors, faults or inconsistencies that may occur within the system or the environment in which the system operates, in particular due to their interaction with natural persons or other systems. Technical and organisational measures shall be taken in this regard.

The robustness of high-risk AI systems may be achieved through technical redundancy solutions, which may include backup or fail-safe plans.

High-risk AI systems that continue to learn after being placed on the market or put into service shall be developed in such a way as to eliminate or reduce as far as possible the risk of possibly biased outputs influencing input for future operations (feedback loops), and as to ensure that any such feedback loops are duly addressed with appropriate mitigation measures.

5. High-risk AI systems shall be resilient against attempts by unauthorised third parties to alter their use, outputs or performance by exploiting system vulnerabilities.

The technical solutions aiming to ensure the cybersecurity of high-risk AI systems shall be appropriate to the relevant circumstances and the risks.

The technical solutions to address AI specific vulnerabilities shall include, where appropriate, measures to prevent, detect, respond to, resolve and control for attacks trying to manipulate the training data set (data poisoning), or pre-trained components used in training (model poisoning), inputs designed to cause the AI model to make a mistake (adversarial examples or model evasion), confidentiality attacks or model flaws.

15.1. Recitals

897. **(27)** While the risk-based approach is the basis for a proportionate and effective set of binding rules, it is important to recall the 2019 Ethics guidelines for trustworthy AI developed by the independent AI HLEG appointed by the Commission. In those guidelines, the AI HLEG developed seven non-binding ethical principles for AI which are intended to help ensure that AI is trustworthy and ethically sound. The seven principles include human agency and oversight; technical robustness and safety; privacy and data governance; transparency; diversity, non-discrimination and fairness; societal and environmental well-being and accountability. Without prejudice to the legally binding requirements of this Regulation and any other applicable Union law, those guidelines contribute to the design of coherent, trustworthy and human-centric AI, in line with the Charter and with the values on which the Union is founded. According to the guidelines of the AI HLEG, human agency and oversight means that AI systems are developed and used as a tool that serves people, respects human dignity and personal autonomy, and that is functioning in a way that can be appropriately controlled and overseen by humans. Technical robustness and safety means that AI systems are developed and used in a way that allows robustness in the case of problems and resilience against attempts to alter the use or performance of the AI system so as to allow unlawful use by third parties, and minimise unintended harm. Privacy and data governance means that AI systems are developed and used in accordance with privacy and data protection rules, while processing data that meets high standards in terms of quality and integrity. Transparency means that AI systems are developed and used in a way that allows appropriate traceability and explainability, while making humans aware that they communicate or interact with an AI system, as well as duly informing deployers of the capabilities and limitations of that AI system and affected persons about their rights. Diversity, non-discrimination and fairness means that AI systems are developed and used in a way that includes diverse actors and promotes equal access, gender equality and cultural diversity, while avoiding discriminatory impacts and unfair biases that are prohibited by Union or national law. Social and environmental well-being means that AI systems are developed and used in a sustainable and environmentally friendly manner as well as in a way to benefit all human beings, while monitoring and assessing the long-term impacts on the individual, society and democracy. The application of those principles should be translated, when possible, in the design and use of AI models. They should in any case serve as a basis for the drafting of codes of conduct under this Regulation. All stakeholders, including industry, academia, civil society and standardisation organisations, are encouraged to take into account, as appropriate, the ethical principles for the development of voluntary best practices and standards.

898. **(32)** The use of AI systems for 'real-time' remote biometric identification of natural persons in publicly accessible spaces for the purpose of law enforcement is particularly intrusive to the rights and freedoms of the concerned persons, to the extent that it may affect the private life of a large part of the population, evoke a feeling of constant surveillance and indirectly dissuade the exercise of the freedom of assembly and other fundamental rights. Technical inaccuracies of AI systems intended for the remote biometric identification of natural persons can lead to biased results and entail discriminatory effects. Such possible biased results and discriminatory effects are particularly relevant with regard to age, ethnicity, race, sex or disabilities. In addition, the immediacy of the impact and the limited opportunities for further checks or corrections in relation to the use of such systems operating in real-time carry heightened risks for the rights and freedoms of the persons concerned in the context of, or impacted by, law enforcement activities.

899. **(59)** Given their role and responsibility, actions by law enforcement authorities involving certain uses of AI systems are characterised by a significant degree of power imbalance and may lead to surveillance, arrest or deprivation of a natural person's liberty as well as other adverse impacts on fundamental rights guaranteed in the Charter. In particular, if the AI system is not trained with high-quality data, does not meet adequate requirements in terms of its performance, its accuracy or robustness, or is not properly designed and tested before being put on the market or otherwise put into service, it may single out people in a discriminatory or otherwise incorrect or unjust manner. Furthermore, the exercise of important procedural fundamental rights, such as the right to an effective remedy and to a fair trial as well as the right of defence and the presumption of innocence, could be hampered, in particular, where such AI systems are not sufficiently transparent, explainable and documented. It is therefore appropriate to classify as high-risk, insofar as their use is permitted under relevant Union and national law, a number of AI systems intended to be used in the law enforcement context where accuracy, reliability and transparency is particularly important to avoid adverse impacts, retain public trust and ensure accountability and effective redress.

900. In view of the nature of the activities and the risks relating thereto, those high-risk AI systems should include in particular AI systems intended to be used by or on behalf of law enforcement authorities or by Union institutions, bodies, offices, or agencies in support of law enforcement authorities for assessing the risk of a natural person to become a victim of criminal offences, as polygraphs and similar tools, for the evaluation of the reliability of evidence in in the course of investigation or prosecution of criminal offences, and, insofar as not prohibited under this Regulation, for assessing the risk of a natural person offending or reoffending not solely on the basis of the profiling of natural persons or the assessment of personality traits and characteristics or the past criminal behaviour of natural persons or groups, for profiling in the course of detection, investigation or prosecution of criminal offences. AI systems specifically intended to be used for administrative proceedings by tax and customs authorities as well as by financial intelligence units carrying out administrative tasks analysing information pursuant to Union anti-money laundering law should not be classified as high-risk AI systems used by law enforcement authorities for the purpose of prevention, detection, investigation and prosecution of criminal offences. The use of AI tools by law enforcement and other relevant authorities should not become a factor of inequality, or exclusion. The impact of the use of AI tools on the defence rights of suspects should not be ignored, in particular the difficulty in obtaining meaningful information on the functioning of those systems and the resulting difficulty in challenging their results in court, in particular by natural persons under investigation.

901. **(60)** AI systems used in migration, asylum and border control management affect persons who are often in particularly vulnerable position and who are dependent on the outcome of the actions of the competent public authorities. The accuracy, non-discriminatory nature and transparency of the AI systems used in those contexts are therefore particularly important to guarantee respect for the fundamental rights of the affected persons, in particular their rights to free movement, non-discrimination, protection of private life and personal data, international protection and good administration. It is therefore appropriate to classify as high-risk, insofar as their use is permitted under relevant Union and national law, AI systems intended to be used by or on behalf of competent public authorities or by Union institutions, bodies, offices or agencies charged with tasks in the fields of migration, asylum and border control management as polygraphs and similar tools, for assessing certain risks posed by natural persons entering the territory of a Member State or applying for visa or asylum, for assisting competent public authorities for the examination, including related assessment of the reliability of evidence, of applications for asylum, visa and residence permits and associated complaints with regard to the objective to establish the eligibility of the natural persons applying for a status, for the purpose of detecting, recognising or identifying natural persons in the context of migration, asylum and border control management, with the exception of verification of travel documents.

902. AI systems in the area of migration, asylum and border control management covered by this Regulation should comply with the relevant procedural requirements set by the Regulation (EC) No 810/2009 of the European Parliament and of the Council,[60] the Directive 2013/32/EU of the European Parliament and of the Council,[61] and other relevant Union law. The use of AI systems in migration, asylum and border control management should, in no circumstances, be used by Member States or Union institutions, bodies, offices or agencies as a means to circumvent their international obligations under the UN Convention relating to the Status of Refugees done at Geneva on 28 July 1951 as amended by the Protocol of 31 January 1967. Nor should they be used to in any way infringe on the principle of non-refoulement, or to deny safe and effective legal avenues into the territory of the Union, including the right to international protection.

903. (66) Requirements should apply to high-risk AI systems as regards risk management, the quality and relevance of data sets used, technical documentation and record-keeping, transparency and the provision of information to deployers, human oversight, and robustness, accuracy and cybersecurity. Those requirements are necessary to effectively mitigate the risks for health, safety and fundamental rights. As no other less trade restrictive measures are reasonably available those requirements are not unjustified restrictions to trade.

904. (74) High-risk AI systems should perform consistently throughout their lifecycle and meet an appropriate level of accuracy, robustness and cybersecurity, in light of their intended purpose and in accordance with the generally acknowledged state of the Art. The Commission and relevant organisations and stakeholders are encouraged to take due consideration of the mitigation of risks and the negative impacts of the AI system. The expected level of performance metrics should be declared in the accompanying instructions of use. Providers are urged to communicate that information to deployers in a clear and easily understandable way, free of misunderstandings or misleading statements. Union law on legal metrology, including Directives 2014/31/EU[62] and 2014/32/EU[63] of the European Parliament and of the Council, aims to ensure the accuracy of measurements and to help the transparency and fairness of commercial transactions. In that context, in cooperation with relevant stakeholders and

---

[60] Regulation (EC) No 810/2009 of the European Parliament and of the Council of 13 July 2009 establishing a Community Code on Visas (Visa Code), [2009] OJ L243/1.

[61] Directive 2013/32/EU of the European Parliament and of the Council of 26 June 2013 on common procedures for granting and withdrawing international protection, [2013] OJ L180/60.

[62] Directive 2014/31/EU of the European Parliament and of the Council of 26 February 2014 on the harmonisation of the laws of the Member States relating to the making available on the market of non-automatic weighing instruments, [2014] OJ L96/107.

[63] Directive 2014/32/EU of the European Parliament and of the Council of 26 February 2014 on the harmonisation of the laws of the Member States relating to the making available on the market of measuring instruments, [2014] OJ L96/149.

organisation, such as metrology and benchmarking authorities, the Commission should encourage, as appropriate, the development of benchmarks and measurement methodologies for AI systems. In doing so, the Commission should take note and collaborate with international partners working on metrology and relevant measurement indicators relating to AI.

905. (75) Technical robustness is a key requirement for high-risk AI systems. They should be resilient in relation to harmful or otherwise undesirable behaviour that may result from limitations within the systems or the environment in which the systems operate (e.g. errors, faults, inconsistencies, unexpected situations). Therefore, technical and organisational measures should be taken to ensure robustness of high-risk AI systems, for example by designing and developing appropriate technical solutions to prevent or minimise harmful or otherwise undesirable behaviour. Those technical solution may include for instance mechanisms enabling the system to safely interrupt its operation (fail-safe plans) in the presence of certain anomalies or when operation takes place outside certain predetermined boundaries. Failure to protect against these risks could lead to safety impacts or negatively affect the fundamental rights, for example due to erroneous decisions or wrong or biased outputs generated by the AI system.

906. (76) Cybersecurity plays a crucial role in ensuring that AI systems are resilient against attempts to alter their use, behaviour, performance or compromise their security properties by malicious third parties exploiting the system's vulnerabilities. Cyberattacks against AI systems can leverage AI specific assets, such as training data sets (e.g. data poisoning) or trained models (e.g. adversarial attacks or membership inference)), or exploit vulnerabilities in the AI system's digital assets or the underlying ICT infrastructure. To ensure a level of cybersecurity appropriate to the risks, suitable measures, such as security controls, should therefore be taken by the providers of high-risk AI systems, also taking into account as appropriate the underlying ICT infrastructure.

907. (77) Without prejudice to the requirements related to robustness and accuracy set out in this Regulation, high-risk AI systems which fall within the scope of a regulation of the European Parliament and of the Council on horizontal cybersecurity requirements for products with digital elements, in accordance with that regulation may demonstrate compliance with the cybersecurity requirements of this Regulation by fulfilling the essential cybersecurity requirements set out in that regulation. When high-risk AI systems fulfil the essential requirements of a regulation of the European Parliament and of the Council on horizontal cybersecurity requirements for products with digital elements, they should be deemed compliant with the cybersecurity requirements set out in this Regulation in so far as the achievement of those requirements is demonstrated in the EU declaration of conformity or parts thereof issued under that regulation. To that end, the assessment of the cybersecurity risks, associated to a product with digital elements classified as high-risk AI system according to this Regulation, carried out under a regulation of the European Parliament and of the Council on horizontal cybersecurity requirements for products with digital elements, should consider risks to the cyber resilience of an AI system as regards attempts by unauthorised third parties to alter its use, behaviour or performance, including AI specific vulnerabilities such as data poisoning or adversarial attacks, as well as, as relevant, risks to fundamental rights as required by this Regulation.

908. **(78)** The conformity assessment procedure provided by this Regulation should apply in relation to the essential cybersecurity requirements of a product with digital elements covered by a regulation of the European Parliament and of the Council on horizontal cybersecurity requirements for products with digital elements and classified as a high-risk AI system under this Regulation. However, this rule should not result in reducing the necessary level of assurance for critical products with digital elements covered by a regulation of the European Parliament and of the Council on horizontal cybersecurity requirements for products with digital elements. Therefore, by way of derogation from this rule, high-risk AI systems that fall within the scope of this Regulation and are also qualified as important and critical products with digital elements pursuant to a regulation of the European Parliament and of the Council on horizontal cybersecurity requirements for products with digital elements and to which the conformity assessment procedure based on internal control set out in an annex to this Regulation applies, are subject to the conformity assessment provisions of a regulation of the European Parliament and of the Council on horizontal cybersecurity requirements for products with digital elements insofar as the essential cybersecurity requirements of that regulation are concerned. In this case, for all the other aspects covered by this Regulation the respective provisions on conformity assessment based on internal control set out in an annex to this Regulation should apply. Building on the knowledge and expertise of ENISA on the cybersecurity policy and tasks assigned to ENISA under the Regulation (EU) 2019/881 of the European Parliament and of the Council,[64] the Commission should cooperate with ENISA on issues related to cybersecurity of AI systems.

909. **(94)** Any processing of biometric data involved in the use of AI systems for biometric identification for the purpose of law enforcement needs to comply with Article 10 of Directive (EU) 2016/680, that allows such processing only where strictly necessary, subject to appropriate safeguards for the rights and freedoms of the data subject, and where authorised by Union or Member State law. Such use, when authorised, also needs to respect the principles laid down

---

[64] Regulation (EU) 2019/881 of the European Parliament and of the Council of 17 April 2019 on ENISA (the European Union Agency for Cybersecurity) and on information and communications technology cybersecurity certification and repealing Regulation (EU) No 526/2013 (Cybersecurity Act), [2019] OJ L151/15.

in Article 4 (1) of Directive (EU) 2016/680 including lawfulness, fairness and transparency, purpose limitation, accuracy and storage limitation.

910. **(114)** The providers of general-purpose AI models presenting systemic risks should be subject, in addition to the obligations provided for providers of general-purpose AI models, to obligations aimed at identifying and mitigating those risks and ensuring an adequate level of cybersecurity protection, regardless of whether it is provided as a standalone model or embedded in an AI system or a product. To achieve those objectives, this Regulation should require providers to perform the necessary model evaluations, in particular prior to its first placing on the market, including conducting and documenting adversarial testing of models, also, as appropriate, through internal or independent external testing. In addition, providers of general-purpose AI models with systemic risks should continuously assess and mitigate systemic risks, including for example by putting in place risk-management policies, such as accountability and governance processes, implementing post-market monitoring, taking appropriate measures along the entire model's lifecycle and cooperating with relevant actors along the AI value chain.

911. **(115)** Providers of general-purpose AI models with systemic risks should assess and mitigate possible systemic risks. If, despite efforts to identify and prevent risks related to a general-purpose AI model that may present systemic risks, the development or use of the model causes a serious incident, the general-purpose AI model provider should without undue delay keep track of the incident and report any relevant information and possible corrective measures to the Commission and national competent authorities. Furthermore, providers should ensure an adequate level of cybersecurity protection for the model and its physical infrastructure, if appropriate, along the entire model lifecycle. Cybersecurity protection related to systemic risks associated with malicious use or attacks should duly consider accidental model leakage, unauthorised releases, circumvention of safety measures, and defence against cyberattacks, unauthorised access or model theft. That protection could be facilitated by securing model weights, algorithms, servers, and data sets, such as through operational security measures for information security, specific cybersecurity policies, adequate technical and established solutions, and cyber and physical access controls, appropriate to the relevant circumstances and the risks involved.

912. **(122)** It is appropriate that, without prejudice to the use of harmonised standards and common specifications, providers of a high-risk AI system that has been trained and tested on data reflecting the specific geographical, behavioural, contextual or functional setting within which the AI system is intended to be used, should be presumed to comply with the relevant measure provided for under the requirement on data governance set out in this Regulation. Without prejudice to the requirements related to robustness and accuracy set out in this Regulation, in accordance with Article 54(3) of Regulation (EU) 2019/881, high-risk AI systems that have been certified or for which a statement of conformity has been issued under a cybersecurity scheme pursuant to that Regulation and the references of which have been published in the Official Journal of the European Union should be presumed to comply with the cybersecurity requirement of this Regulation in so far as the cybersecurity certificate or statement of conformity or parts thereof cover the cybersecurity requirement of this Regulation. This remains without prejudice to the voluntary nature of that cybersecurity scheme.

913. (126) In order to carry out third-party conformity assessments when so required, notified bodies should be notified under this Regulation by the national competent authorities, provided that they comply with a set of requirements, in particular on independence, competence, absence of conflicts of interests and suitable cybersecurity requirements. Notification of those bodies should be sent by national competent authorities to the Commission and the other Member States by means of the electronic notification tool developed and managed by the Commission pursuant to Article R23 of Annex I to Decision No 768/2008/EC.

914. (131) In order to facilitate the work of the Commission and the Member States in the AI field as well as to increase the transparency towards the public, providers of high-risk AI systems other than those related to products falling within the scope of relevant existing Union harmonisation legislation, as well as providers who consider that an AI system listed in the high-risk use cases in an annex to this Regulation is not high-risk on the basis of a derogation, should be required to register themselves and information about their AI system in an EU database, to be established and managed by the Commission. Before using an AI system listed in the high-risk use cases in an annex to this Regulation, deployers of high-risk AI systems that are public authorities, agencies or bodies, should register themselves in such database and select the system that they envisage to use. Other deployers should be entitled to do so voluntarily. This section of the EU database should be publicly accessible, free of charge, the information should be easily navigable, understandable and machine-readable. The EU database should also be user-friendly, for example by providing search functionalities, including through keywords, allowing the general public to find relevant information to be submitted upon the registration of high-risk AI systems and on the use case of high-risk AI systems, set out in an annex to this Regulation, to which the high-risk AI systems correspond. Any substantial modification of high-risk AI systems should also be registered in the EU database. For high-risk AI systems in the area of law enforcement, migration, asylum and border control management, the registration obligations should be fulfilled in a secure non-public section of the EU database. Access to the secure non-public section should be strictly limited to the Commission as well as to market surveillance authorities with regard to their national section of that database. High-risk AI systems in the area of critical infrastructure should only be registered at national level. The Commission should be the controller of the EU database, in accordance with Regulation (EU)

2018/1725. In order to ensure the full functionality of the EU database, when deployed, the procedure for setting the database should include the development of functional specifications by the Commission and an independent audit report. The Commission should take into account cybersecurity risks when carrying out its tasks as data controller on the EU database. In order to maximise the availability and use of the EU database by the public, the EU database, including the information made available through it, should comply with requirements under the Directive (EU) 2019/882.

15.2. General Approach

15.2.1 Preamble

915. The last three requirements that high-risk AI systems must meet are aimed at ensuring the reliability of the systems. They are structured according to the following classification:

Accuracy	Ability to deliver high-quality results
Robustness	Maintaining operational characteristics with regard to purposes
Cybersecurity	Ability to combat fraud

15.2.2 Guiding Principles

916. These requirements are not defined as such.

917. They pertain to the following phases:

- design;
- development;
- testing;
- use.

15.3. Accuracy

15.3.1 Introduction

918. The notion of accuracy is determined by metrics.

15.3.2 Metrics

919. These metrics are described in the instructions for use according to the purpose and nature of the risks.[65]

920. They are one of the characteristics of compliance with the transparency obligation, enabling users to assess the nature and level of risk.

15.4. Robustness

15.4.1 Introduction

921. Robustness is defined during the design phase and implemented during the deployment phase. It is characterised by the system's resilience to limit predefined risks through implemented technical and organisational measures.

15.4.2 Guiding Principles

922. AI systems must be resilient against:

- errors;
- faults;
- inconsistencies.

15.5. Resilience

923. Resilience concerns:

- technical state;
- redundancy solutions;
- interactions with natural persons.

924. Robustness must be managed during subsequent learning phases to prevent serial biases or degradation of robustness.

15.6. Cybersecurity

15.6.1 Introduction

925. Cybersecurity concerns:

- data sets (data poisoning);
- the systems themselves.

---

[65] AI Act, Art. 13.

15.6.2 Guiding Principles

926. The specific requirements are outlined as follows:

NO.	THEME	SPECIFICATION
1.	Access control	Monitoring attempts of unauthorised third-party access
2.	Impact	Integrity Performance Use Misuse
3.	Measures	Appropriate to the relevant circumstances and the risks
4.	Data	Control and monitoring of data (training data sets and input data).

15.6.3 Special Cases

927. For high-risk AI systems that continue to learn after being placed on the market, the following protocol must be followed:

- Step 1: Barriers against bias;
- Step 2: Monitoring for drifts;
- Step 3: Mitigation measure plan;
- Step 4: Verification that learning does not result in changes to the risk levels specified in the instructions for use.

15.7. Find Out More

15.7.1 Toolbox

928. ANSSI, 'Security recommendations for a generative AI system', Guide No ANSSI-PA-102, 29 April 2024.

929. Vallet, F., 'Sécurité des systèmes d'IA, les gestes qui sauvent' ['AI system security, a first aid guide'], *LINC* (Laboratoire d'innovation numérique de la CNIL), 21 January 2022.

SECTION 3. OBLIGATIONS OF PROVIDERS AND DEPLOYERS OF HIGH-RISK AI SYSTEMS AND OTHER PARTIES

16 ARTICLE 16. OBLIGATIONS OF PROVIDERS OF HIGH-RISK AI SYSTEMS

Providers of high-risk AI systems shall:

(a) ensure that their high-risk AI systems are compliant with the requirements set out in Section 2;

(b) indicate on the high-risk AI system or, where that is not possible, on its packaging or its accompanying documentation, as applicable, their name, registered trade name or registered trade mark, the address at which they can be contacted;

(c) have a quality management system in place which complies with Article 17;

(d) keep the documentation referred to in Article 18;

(e) when under their control, keep the logs automatically generated by their high-risk AI systems as referred to in Article 19;

(f) ensure that the high-risk AI system undergoes the relevant conformity assessment procedure as referred to in Article 43, prior to its being placed on the market or put into service;

(g) draw up an EU declaration of conformity in accordance with Article 47;

(h) affix the CE marking to the high-risk AI system or, where that is not possible, on its packaging or its accompanying documentation, to indicate conformity with this Regulation, in accordance with Article 48;

(i) comply with the registration obligations referred to in Article 49(1);

(j) take the necessary corrective actions and provide information as required in Article 20;

(k) upon a reasoned request of a national competent authority, demonstrate the conformity of the high-risk AI system with the requirements set out in Section 2;

l) ensure that the high-risk AI system complies with accessibility requirements in accordance (with Directives (EU) 2016/2102 and (EU) 2019/882.

16.1. Recitals

930. **(10)** The fundamental right to the protection of personal data is safeguarded in particular by Regulations (EU) 2016/679[66] and (EU) 2018/1725[67] of the European Parliament and of the Council and Directive (EU) 2016/680 of the European Parliament and of the Council.[68] Directive 2002/58/EC of the European Parliament and of the Council[69] additionally protects private life and the confidentiality of communications, including by way of providing conditions for any storing of personal and non-personal data in, and access from, terminal equipment. Those Union legal acts provide the basis for sustainable and responsible data processing, including where data sets include a mix of personal and non-personal data. This Regulation does not seek to affect the application of existing Union law governing the processing of personal data, including the tasks and powers of the independent supervisory authorities competent to monitor compliance with those instruments. It also does not affect the obligations of providers and deployers of AI systems in their role as data controllers or processors stemming from Union or national law on the protection of personal data in so far as the design, the development or the use of AI systems involves the processing of personal data. It is also appropriate to clarify that data subjects continue to enjoy all the rights and guarantees awarded to them by such Union law, including the rights related to solely automated individual decision-making, including profiling. Harmonised rules for the placing on the market, the putting into service and the use of AI systems established under this Regulation should facilitate the effective implementation and enable the exercise of the data subjects' rights and other remedies guaranteed under Union law on the protection of personal data and of other fundamental rights.

---

[66] Regulation (EU) 2016/679 of the European Parliament and of the Council of 27 April 2016 on the protection of natural persons with regard to the processing of personal data and on the free movement of such data, and repealing Directive 95/46/EC (General Data Protection Regulation), [2016] OJ L119/1.

[67] Regulation (EU) 2018/1725 of the European Parliament and of the Council of 23 October 2018 on the protection of natural persons with regard to the processing of personal data by the Union institutions, bodies, offices and agencies and on the free movement of such data, and repealing Regulation (EC) No 45/2001 and Decision No 1247/2002/EC, [2018] OJ L295/39.

[68] Directive (EU) 2016/680 of the European Parliament and of the Council of 27 April 2016 on the protection of natural persons with regard to the processing of personal data by competent authorities for the purposes of the prevention, investigation, detection or prosecution of criminal offences or the execution of criminal penalties, and on the free movement of such data, and repealing Council Framework Decision 2008/977/JHA, [2016] OJ L119/89.

[69] Directive 2002/58/EC of the European Parliament and of the Council of 12 July 2002 concerning the processing of personal data and the protection of privacy in the electronic communications sector (Directive on privacy and electronic communications), [2002] OJ L201/37.

931. (26) In order to introduce a proportionate and effective set of binding rules for AI systems, a clearly defined risk-based approach should be followed. That approach should tailor the type and content of such rules to the intensity and scope of the risks that AI systems can generate. It is therefore necessary to prohibit certain unacceptable AI practices, to lay down requirements for high-risk AI systems and obligations for the relevant operators, and to lay down transparency obligations for certain AI systems.

932. (79) It is appropriate that a specific natural or legal person, defined as the provider, takes responsibility for the placing on the market or the putting into service of a high-risk AI system, regardless of whether that natural or legal person is the person who designed or developed the system.

933. (81) The provider should establish a sound quality management system, ensure the accomplishment of the required conformity assessment procedure, draw up the relevant documentation and establish a robust post-market monitoring system. Providers of high-risk AI systems that are subject to obligations regarding quality management systems under relevant sectoral Union law should have the possibility to include the elements of the quality management system provided for in this Regulation as part of the existing quality management system provided for in that other sectoral Union law. The complementarity between this Regulation and existing sectoral Union law should also be taken into account in future standardisation activities or guidance adopted by the Commission. Public authorities which put into service high-risk AI systems for their own use may adopt and implement the rules for the quality management system as part of the quality management system adopted at a national or regional level, as appropriate, taking into account the specificities of the sector and the competences and organisation of the public authority concerned.

934. (82) To enable enforcement of this Regulation and create a level playing field for operators, and, taking into account the different forms of making available of digital products, it is important to ensure that, under all circumstances, a person established in the Union can provide authorities with all the necessary information on the compliance of an AI system. Therefore, prior to making their AI systems available in the Union, providers established in third countries should, by written mandate, appoint an authorised representative established in the Union. This authorised representative plays a pivotal role in ensuring the compliance of the high-risk AI systems placed on the market or put into service in the Union by those providers who are not established in the Union and in serving as their contact person established in the Union.

935. (83) In light of the nature and complexity of the value chain for AI systems and in line with the New Legislative Framework, it is essential to ensure legal certainty and facilitate the compliance with this Regulation. Therefore, it is necessary to clarify the role and the specific obligations of relevant operators along that value chain, such as importers and distributors who may contribute to the development of AI systems. In certain situations those operators could act in more than one role at the same time and should therefore fulfil cumulatively all relevant obligations associated with those roles. For example, an operator could act as a distributor and an importer at the same time.

936. **(84)** To ensure legal certainty, it is necessary to clarify that, under certain specific conditions, any distributor, importer, deployer or other third-party should be considered to be a provider of a high-risk AI system and therefore assume all the relevant obligations. This would be the case if that party puts its name or trademark on a high-risk AI system already placed on the market or put into service, without prejudice to contractual arrangements stipulating that the obligations are allocated otherwise. This would also be the case if that party makes a substantial modification to a high-risk AI system that has already been placed on the market or has already been put into service in a way that it remains a high-risk AI system in accordance with this Regulation, or if it modifies the intended purpose of an AI system, including a general-purpose AI system, which has not been classified as high-risk and has already been placed on the market or put into service, in a way that the AI system becomes a high-risk AI system in accordance with this Regulation. Those provisions should apply without prejudice to more specific provisions established in certain Union harmonisation legislation based on the New Legislative Framework, together with which this Regulation should apply. For example, Article 16(2) of Regulation (EU) 2017/745, establishing that certain changes should not be considered to be modifications of a device that could affect its compliance with the applicable requirements, should continue to apply to high-risk AI systems that are medical devices within the meaning of that Regulation.

937. **(85)** General-purpose AI systems may be used as high-risk AI systems by themselves or be components of other high-risk AI systems. Therefore, due to their particular nature and in order to ensure a fair sharing of responsibilities along the AI value chain, the providers of such systems should, irrespective of whether they may be used as high-risk AI systems as such by other providers or as components of high-risk AI systems and unless provided otherwise under this Regulation, closely cooperate with the providers of the relevant high-risk AI systems to enable their compliance with the relevant obligations under this Regulation and with the competent authorities established under this Regulation.

938. **(86)** Where, under the conditions laid down in this Regulation, the provider that initially placed the AI system on the market or put it into service should no longer be considered to be the provider for the purposes of this Regulation, and when that provider has not expressly excluded the change of the AI system into a high-risk AI system, the former provider should nonetheless closely cooperate and make available the necessary information and provide the reasonably expected technical access and other assistance that are required for the fulfilment of the obligations set out in this Regulation, in particular regarding the compliance with the conformity assessment of high-risk AI systems.

939. **(87)** In addition, where a high-risk AI system that is a safety component of a product which falls within the scope of Union harmonisation legislation based on the New Legislative Framework is not placed on the market or put into service independently from the product, the product manufacturer defined in that legislation should comply with the obligations of the provider established in this Regulation and should, in particular, ensure that the AI system embedded in the final product complies with the requirements of this Regulation.

940. **(88)** Along the AI value chain multiple parties often supply AI systems, tools and services but also components or processes that are incorporated by the provider into the AI system with various objectives, including the model training, model retraining, model testing and evaluation, integration into software, or other aspects of model development. Those parties have an important role to play in the value chain towards the provider of the high-risk AI system into which their AI systems, tools, services, components or processes are integrated, and should provide by written agreement this provider with the necessary information, capabilities, technical access and other assistance based on the generally acknowledged state of the art, in order to enable the provider to fully comply with the obligations set out in this Regulation, without compromising their own intellectual property rights or trade secrets.

941. **(93)** Whilst risks related to AI systems can result from the way such systems are designed, risks can as well stem from how such AI systems are used. Deployers of high-risk AI system therefore play a critical role in ensuring that fundamental rights are protected, complementing the obligations of the provider when developing the AI system. Deployers are best placed to understand how the high-risk AI system will be used concretely and can therefore identify potential significant risks that were not foreseen in the development phase, due to a more precise knowledge of the context of use, the persons or groups of persons likely to be affected, including vulnerable groups. Deployers of high-risk AI systems listed in an annex to this Regulation also play a critical role in informing natural persons and should, when they make decisions or assist in making decisions related to natural persons, where applicable, inform the natural persons that they are subject to the use of the high-risk AI system. This information should include the intended purpose and the type of decisions it makes. The deployer should also inform the natural persons about their right to an explanation provided under this Regulation. With regard to high-risk AI systems used for law enforcement purposes, that obligation should be implemented in accordance with Article 13 of Directive (EU) 2016/680.

942. **(97)** The notion of general-purpose AI models should be clearly defined and set apart from the notion of AI systems to enable legal certainty. The definition should be based on the key functional characteristics of a general-purpose AI model, in particular the generality and the capability to competently perform a wide range of distinct tasks. These models are typically trained on large amounts of data, through various methods, such as self-supervised, unsupervised or reinforcement learning. General-purpose AI models may be placed on the market in various ways, including through libraries, application programming interfaces (APIs), as direct download, or as physical copy. These models may be further modified or fine-tuned into new models. Although AI models are essential components of AI systems, they do not constitute AI systems on their own. AI models require the addition of further components, such as for example a user interface, to become AI systems. AI models are typically integrated into and form part of AI systems. This Regulation provides specific rules for general-purpose AI models and for general-purpose AI models that pose systemic risks, which should apply also when these models are integrated or form part of an AI system. It should be understood that the obligations for the providers of general-purpose AI models should apply once the general-purpose AI models are placed on the market.

943. When the provider of a general-purpose AI model integrates an own model into its own AI system that is made available on the market or put into service, that model should be considered to be placed on the market and, therefore, the obligations in this Regulation for models should continue to apply in addition to those for AI systems. The obligations laid down for models should in any case not apply when an own model is used for purely internal processes that are not essential for providing a product or a service to third parties and the rights of natural persons are not affected. Considering their potential significantly negative effects, the general-purpose AI models with systemic risk should always be subject to the relevant obligations under this Regulation. The definition should not cover AI models used before their placing on the market for the sole purpose of research, development and prototyping activities. This is without prejudice to the obligation to comply with this Regulation when, following such activities, a model is placed on the market.

944. (101) Providers of general-purpose AI models have a particular role and responsibility along the AI value chain, as the models they provide may form the basis for a range of downstream systems, often provided by downstream providers that necessitate a good understanding of the models and their capabilities, both to enable the integration of such models into their products, and to fulfil their obligations under this or other regulations. Therefore, proportionate transparency measures should be laid down, including the drawing up and keeping up to date of documentation, and the provision of information on the general-purpose AI model for its usage by the downstream providers. Technical documentation should be prepared and kept up to date by the general-purpose AI model provider for the purpose of making it available, upon request, to the

AI Office and the national competent authorities. The minimal set of elements to be included in such documentation should be set out in specific annexes to this Regulation. The Commission should be empowered to amend those annexes by means of delegated acts in light of evolving technological developments.

945. **(104)** The providers of general-purpose AI models that are released under a free and open-source licence, and whose parameters, including the weights, the information on the model architecture, and the information on model usage, are made publicly available should be subject to exceptions as regards the transparency-related requirements imposed on general-purpose AI models, unless they can be considered to present a systemic risk, in which case the circumstance that the model is transparent and accompanied by an open-source license should not be considered to be a sufficient reason to exclude compliance with the obligations under this Regulation. In any case, given that the release of general-purpose AI models under free and open-source licence does not necessarily reveal substantial information on the data set used for the training or fine-tuning of the model and on how compliance of copyright law was thereby ensured, the exception provided for general-purpose AI models from compliance with the transparency-related requirements should not concern the obligation to produce a summary about the content used for model training and the obligation to put in place a policy to comply with Union copyright law, in particular to identify and comply with the reservation of rights pursuant to Article 4(3) of Directive (EU) 2019/790 of the European Parliament and of the Council.[70]

946. **(106)**, Providers that place general-purpose AI models on the Union market should ensure compliance with the relevant obligations in this Regulation. To that end, providers of general-purpose AI models should put in place a policy to comply with Union law on copyright and related rights, in particular to identify and comply with the reservation of rights expressed by rightsholders pursuant to Article 4(3) of Directive (EU) 2019/790. Any provider placing a general-purpose AI model on the Union market should comply with this obligation, regardless of the jurisdiction in which the copyright-relevant acts underpinning the training of those general-purpose AI models take place. This is necessary to ensure a level playing field among providers of general-purpose AI models where no provider should be able to gain a competitive advantage in the Union market by applying lower copyright standards than those provided in the Union.

947. **(109)** Compliance with the obligations applicable to the providers of general-purpose AI models should be commensurate and proportionate to the type of model provider, excluding the need for compliance for persons who develop

[70] Directive (EU) 2019/790 of the European Parliament and of the Council of 17 April 2019 on copyright and related rights in the Digital Single Market and amending Directives 96/9/EC and 2001/29/EC, [2019] OJ L130/92.

or use models for non-professional or scientific research purposes, who should nevertheless be encouraged to voluntarily comply with these requirements. Without prejudice to Union copyright law, compliance with those obligations should take due account of the size of the provider and allow simplified ways of compliance for SMEs, including start-ups, that should not represent an excessive cost and not discourage the use of such models. In the case of a modification or fine-tuning of a model, the obligations for providers of general-purpose AI models should be limited to that modification or fine-tuning, for example by complementing the already existing technical documentation with information on the modifications, including new training data sources, as a means to comply with the value chain obligations provided in this Regulation.

948. **(112)** It is also necessary to clarify a procedure for the classification of a general-purpose AI model with systemic risks. A general-purpose AI model that meets the applicable threshold for high-impact capabilities should be presumed to be a general-purpose AI models with systemic risk. The provider should notify the AI Office at the latest two weeks after the requirements are met or it becomes known that a general-purpose AI model will meet the requirements that lead to the presumption. This is especially relevant in relation to the threshold of floating point operations because training of general-purpose AI models takes considerable planning which includes the upfront allocation of compute resources and, therefore, providers of general-purpose AI models are able to know if their model would meet the threshold before the training is completed. In the context of that notification, the provider should be able to demonstrate that, because of its specific characteristics, a general-purpose AI model exceptionally does not present systemic risks, and that it thus should not be classified as a general-purpose AI model with systemic risks. That information is valuable for the AI Office to anticipate the placing on the market of general-purpose AI models with systemic risks and the providers can start to engage with the AI Office early on. That information is especially important with regard to general-purpose AI models that are planned to be released as open-source, given that, after the open-source model release, necessary measures to ensure compliance with the obligations under this Regulation may be more difficult to implement.

949. **(114)** The providers of general-purpose AI models presenting systemic risks should be subject, in addition to the obligations provided for providers of general-purpose AI models, to obligations aimed at identifying and mitigating those risks and ensuring an adequate level of cybersecurity protection, regardless of whether it is provided as a standalone model or embedded in an AI system or a product. To achieve those objectives, this Regulation should require providers to perform the necessary model evaluations, in particular prior to its first placing on the market, including conducting and documenting adversarial testing of models, also, as appropriate, through internal or independent external testing.

In addition, providers of general-purpose AI models with systemic risks should continuously assess and mitigate systemic risks, including for example by putting in place risk-management policies, such as accountability and governance processes, implementing post-market monitoring, taking appropriate measures along the entire model's lifecycle and cooperating with relevant actors along the AI value chain.

950. **(116)** The AI Office should encourage and facilitate the drawing up, review and adaptation of codes of practice, taking into account international approaches. All providers of general-purpose AI models could be invited to participate. To ensure that the codes of practice reflect the state of the art and duly take into account a diverse set of perspectives, the AI Office should collaborate with relevant national competent authorities, and could, where appropriate, consult with civil society organisations and other relevant stakeholders and experts, including the Scientific Panel, for the drawing up of such codes. Codes of practice should cover obligations for providers of general-purpose AI models and of general-purpose AI models presenting systemic risks. In addition, as regards systemic risks, codes of practice should help to establish a risk taxonomy of the type and nature of the systemic risks at Union level, including their sources. Codes of practice should also be focused on specific risk assessment and mitigation measures.

951. **(117)** The codes of practice should represent a central tool for the proper compliance with the obligations provided for under this Regulation for providers of general-purpose AI models. Providers should be able to rely on codes of practice to demonstrate compliance with the obligations. By means of implementing acts, the Commission may decide to approve a code of practice and give it a general validity within the Union, or, alternatively, to provide common rules for the implementation of the relevant obligations, if, by the time this Regulation becomes applicable, a code of practice cannot be finalised or is not deemed adequate by the AI Office. Once a harmonised standard is published and assessed as suitable to cover the relevant obligations by the AI Office, compliance with a European harmonised standard should grant providers the presumption of conformity. Providers of general-purpose AI models should furthermore be able to demonstrate compliance using alternative adequate means, if codes of practice or harmonised standards are not available, or they choose not to rely on those.

952. **(118)** This Regulation regulates AI systems and AI models by imposing certain requirements and obligations for relevant market actors that are placing them on the market, putting into service or use in the Union, thereby complementing obligations for providers of intermediary services that embed such systems or models into their services regulated by Regulation (EU) 2022/2065. To the extent that such systems or models are embedded into designated very large online platforms or very large online search engines, they are subject to the risk-management framework provided for in Regulation (EU)

2022/2065. Consequently, the corresponding obligations of this Regulation should be presumed to be fulfilled, unless significant systemic risks not covered by Regulation (EU) 2022/2065 emerge and are identified in such models. Within this framework, providers of very large online platforms and very large online search engines are obliged to assess potential systemic risks stemming from the design, functioning and use of their services, including how the design of algorithmic systems used in the service may contribute to such risks, as well as systemic risks stemming from potential misuses. Those providers are also obliged to take appropriate mitigating measures in observance of fundamental rights.

953. (119) Considering the quick pace of innovation and the technological evolution of digital services in scope of different instruments of Union law in particular having in mind the usage and the perception of their recipients, the AI systems subject to this Regulation may be provided as intermediary services or parts thereof within the meaning of Regulation (EU) 2022/2065, which should be interpreted in a technology-neutral manner. For example, AI systems may be used to provide online search engines, in particular, to the extent that an AI system such as an online chatbot performs searches of, in principle, all websites, then incorporates the results into its existing knowledge and uses the updated knowledge to generate a single output that combines different sources of information.

954. (120) Furthermore, obligations placed on providers and deployers of certain AI systems in this Regulation to enable the detection and disclosure that the outputs of those systems are artificially generated or manipulated are particularly relevant to facilitate the effective implementation of Regulation (EU) 2022/2065. This applies in particular as regards the obligations of providers of very large online platforms or very large online search engines to identify and mitigate systemic risks that may arise from the dissemination of content that has been artificially generated or manipulated, in particular risk of the actual or foreseeable negative effects on democratic processes, civic discourse and electoral processes, including through disinformation.

955. (136) The obligations placed on providers and deployers of certain AI systems in this Regulation to enable the detection and disclosure that the outputs of those systems are artificially generated or manipulated are particularly relevant to facilitate the effective implementation of Regulation (EU) 2022/2065. This applies in particular as regards the obligations of providers of very large online platforms or very large online search engines to identify and mitigate systemic risks that may arise from the dissemination of content that has been artificially generated or manipulated, in particular the risk of the actual or foreseeable negative effects on democratic processes, civic discourse and electoral processes, including through disinformation. The requirement to label content generated by AI systems under this Regulation is without prejudice to the obligation in

Article 16(6) of Regulation (EU) 2022/2065 for providers of hosting services to process notices on illegal content received pursuant to Article 16(1) of that Regulation and should not influence the assessment and the decision on the illegality of the specific content. That assessment should be performed solely with reference to the rules governing the legality of the content.

956. (145) In order to minimise the risks to implementation resulting from lack of knowledge and expertise in the market as well as to facilitate compliance of providers, in particular SMEs, including start-ups, and notified bodies with their obligations under this Regulation, the AI-on-demand platform, the European Digital Innovation Hubs and the testing and experimentation facilities established by the Commission and the Member States at Union or national level should contribute to the implementation of this Regulation. Within their respective mission and fields of competence, the AI-on-demand platform, the European Digital Innovation Hubs and the testing and experimentation Facilities are able to provide in particular technical and scientific support to providers and notified bodies.

957. (158) Union financial services law includes internal governance and risk-management rules and requirements which are applicable to regulated financial institutions in the course of provision of those services, including when they make use of AI systems. In order to ensure coherent application and enforcement of the obligations under this Regulation and relevant rules and requirements of the Union financial services legal acts, the competent authorities for the supervision and enforcement of those legal acts, in particular competent authorities as defined in Regulation (EU) No 575/2013 of the European Parliament and of the Council[71] and Directives 2008/48/EC,[72] 2009/138/EC,[73] 2013/36/EU,[74] 2014/17/EU[75] and (EU) 2016/97[76] of the European Parliament and of the Council, should

[71] Regulation (EU) No 575/2013 of the European Parliament and of the Council of 26 June 2013 on prudential requirements for credit institutions and investment firms and amending Regulation (EU) No 648/2012, [2013] OJ L176/1.

[72] Directive 2008/48/EC of the European Parliament and of the Council of 23 April 2008 on credit agreements for consumers and repealing Council Directive 87/102/EEC, [2008] OJ L133/66.

[73] Directive 2009/138/EC of the European Parliament and of the Council of 25November 2009 on the taking-up and pursuit of the business of Insurance and Reinsurance (Solvency II), [2009] OJ L335/1.

[74] Directive 2013/36/EU of the European Parliament and of the Council of 26 June 2013 on access to the activity of credit institutions and the prudential supervision of credit institutions and investment firms, amending Directive 2002/87/EC and repealing Directives 2006/48/EC and 2006/49/EC, [2013] OJ L176/338.

[75] Directive 2014/17/EU of the European Parliament and of the Council of 4 February 2014 on credit agreements for consumers relating to residential immovable property and amending Directives 2008/48/EC and 2013/36/EU and Regulation (EU) No 1093/2010, [214] OJ L60/34.

[76] Directive (EU) 2016/97 of the European Parliament and of the Council of 20 January 2016 on insurance distribution, [2016] OJ L26/19.

be designated, within their respective competences, as competent authorities for the purpose of supervising the implementation of this Regulation, including for market surveillance activities, as regards AI systems provided or used by regulated and supervised financial institutions unless Member States decide to designate another authority to fulfil these market surveillance tasks.

958. Those competent authorities should have all powers under this Regulation and Regulation (EU) 2019/1020 to enforce the requirements and obligations of this Regulation, including powers to carry our *ex post* market surveillance activities that can be integrated, as appropriate, into their existing supervisory mechanisms and procedures under the relevant Union financial services law. It is appropriate to envisage that, when acting as market surveillance authorities under this Regulation, the national authorities responsible for the supervision of credit institutions regulated under Directive 2013/36/EU, which are participating in the Single Supervisory Mechanism established by Council Regulation (EU) No 1024/2013,[77] should report, without delay, to the European Central Bank any information identified in the course of their market surveillance activities that may be of potential interest for the European Central Bank's prudential supervisory tasks as specified in that Regulation. To further enhance the consistency between this Regulation and the rules applicable to credit institutions regulated under Directive 2013/36/EU, it is also appropriate to integrate some of the providers' procedural obligations in relation to risk management, post marketing monitoring and documentation into the existing obligations and procedures under Directive 2013/36/EU. In order to avoid overlaps, limited derogations should also be envisaged in relation to the quality management system of providers and the monitoring obligation placed on deployers of high-risk AI systems to the extent that these apply to credit institutions regulated by Directive 2013/36/EU. The same regime should apply to insurance and re-insurance undertakings and insurance holding companies under Directive 2009/138/EC and the insurance intermediaries under Directive (EU) 2016/97 and other types of financial institutions subject to requirements regarding internal governance, arrangements or processes established pursuant to the relevant Union financial services law to ensure consistency and equal treatment in the financial sector.

959. (162) To make best use of the centralised Union expertise and synergies at Union level, the powers of supervision and enforcement of the obligations on providers of general-purpose AI models should be a competence of the Commission. The AI Office should be able to carry out all necessary actions to monitor the effective implementation of this Regulation as regards

---

[77] Council Regulation (EU) No 1024/2013 of 15 October 2013 conferring specific tasks on the European Central Bank concerning policies relating to the prudential supervision of credit institutions, [2013] OJ L287/63.

general-purpose AI models. It should be able to investigate possible infringements of the rules on providers of general-purpose AI models both on its own initiative, following the results of its monitoring activities, or upon request from market surveillance authorities in line with the conditions set out in this Regulation. To support effective monitoring of the AI Office, it should provide for the possibility that downstream providers lodge complaints about possible infringements of the rules on providers of general-purpose AI models and systems.

960. **(164)** The AI Office should be able to take the necessary actions to monitor the effective implementation of and compliance with the obligations for providers of general-purpose AI models laid down in this Regulation. The AI Office should be able to investigate possible infringements in accordance with the powers provided for in this Regulation, including by requesting documentation and information, by conducting evaluations, as well as by requesting measures from providers of general-purpose AI models. When conducting evaluations, in order to make use of independent expertise, the AI Office should be able to involve independent experts to carry out the evaluations on its behalf. Compliance with the obligations should be enforceable, inter alia, through requests to take appropriate measures, including risk mitigation measures in the case of identified systemic risks as well as restricting the making available on the market, withdrawing or recalling the model. As a safeguard, where needed beyond the procedural rights provided for in this Regulation, providers of general-purpose AI models should have the procedural rights provided for in Article 18 of Regulation (EU) 2019/1020, which should apply *mutatis mutandis*, without prejudice to more specific procedural rights provided for by this Regulation.

961. **(169)** Compliance with the obligations on providers of general-purpose AI models imposed under this Regulation should be enforceable, inter alia, by means of fines. To that end, appropriate levels of fines should also be laid down for infringement of those obligations, including the failure to comply with measures requested by the Commission in accordance with this Regulation, subject to appropriate limitation periods in accordance with the principle of proportionality. All decisions taken by the Commission under this Regulation are subject to review by the Court of Justice of the European Union in accordance with the TFEU, including the unlimited jurisdiction of the Court of Justice with regard to penalties pursuant to Article 261 TFEU.

962. **(177)** In order to ensure legal certainty, ensure an appropriate adaptation period for operators and avoid disruption to the market, including by ensuring continuity of the use of AI systems, it is appropriate that this Regulation applies to the high-risk AI systems that have been placed on the market or put into service before the general date of application thereof, only if, from that date, those systems are subject to significant changes in their design or intended purpose. It is appropriate to clarify that, in this respect, the concept of significant change should be understood as equivalent in substance to the notion of substantial modification, which is used with regard only to high-risk AI systems pursuant to this Regulation. On an exceptional basis and in light of public accountability, operators of AI systems which are components of the large-scale IT systems established by the legal acts listed in an annex to this Regulation and operators of high-risk AI systems that are intended to be used by public authorities should, respectively, take the necessary steps to comply with the requirements of this Regulation by end of 2030 and by 2 August 2030.

963. **(178)** Providers of high-risk AI systems are encouraged to start to comply, on a voluntary basis, with the relevant obligations of this Regulation already during the transitional period.

16.2. General Approach

16.2.1 Preamble

964. After the requirements outlined for managing high-risk AI systems, the Regulation imposes obligations on the various stakeholders.

965. These obligations, grouped in Section 3, apply to all actors operating in the economic sphere of high-risk AI systems, albeit to varying degrees.

16.2.2 Guiding Principles

966. The structure of the obligations imposed on providers is as follows:

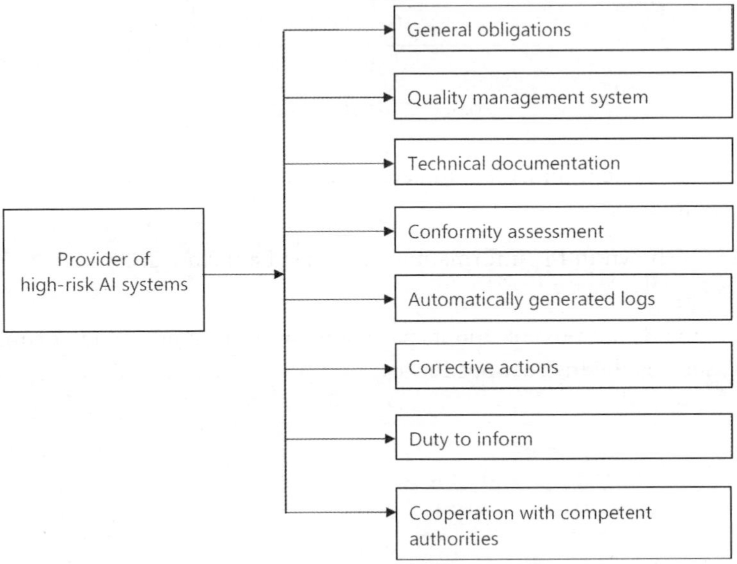

16.3. *General Obligations*

967. These obligations address the essential requirements applicable to the design, development, placing on the market, putting into service, and use of high-risk AI systems, such as:

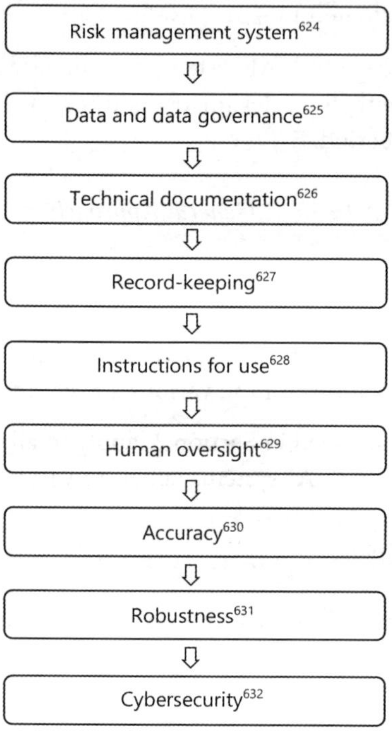

16.4. *Identification*

968. The AI system must be linked to a provider who assumes primary responsibility for it.

969. This is shown in the information that must be included:

- on the system;
- where that is not possible, on its packaging or its accompanying documentation, such as the instructions for use.[78]

[78] AI Act, Art. 13.

970. The information includes the following:

NO.	THEME	SPECIFICATION
1.	Name	As indicated in the certificate of good standing[79]
2.	Registered trade name	In connection with the name
3.	Registered trademark	In connection with the name
4.	Contact address	Electronic or physical

16.5. Quality System

971. Risk management necessarily relies on a quality system as defined in Article 17.

16.6. Technical Documentation

972. Effective risk management over time requires that documentation be kept.[80]

973. The same applies to logs of recorded events.[81]

16.7. Evaluation Procedure

974. This procedure falls under the responsibility of the provider of the high-risk AI system and must be conducted before such system is placed on the market or put into service.

16.8. EU Declaration and CE Marking

975. These obligations fall under the provider's responsibility.[82]

16.9. Conformity

976. The provider bears the burden of proof for conformity.

---

79 In France, '*extrait K-bis*'.

80 AI Act, Art. 18.

81 AI Act, Art. 12.

82 AI Act, Art. 47.

16.10. Additional Requirements

977. These include:

- complying with registration obligations;
- taking corrective actions and providing associated information;
- complying with accessibility requirements.[83]

17 ARTICLE 17. QUALITY MANAGEMENT SYSTEM

1. Providers of high-risk AI systems shall put a quality management system in place that ensures compliance with this Regulation. That system shall be documented in a systematic and orderly manner in the form of written policies, procedures and instructions, and shall include at least the following aspects:

(a) a strategy for regulatory compliance, including compliance with conformity assessment procedures and procedures for the management of modifications to the high-risk AI system;

(b) techniques, procedures and systematic actions to be used for the design, design control and design verification of the high-risk AI system;

(c) techniques, procedures and systematic actions to be used for the development, quality control and quality assurance of the high-risk AI system;

(d) examination, test and validation procedures to be carried out before, during and after the development of the high-risk AI system, and the frequency with which they have to be carried out;

(e) technical specifications, including standards, to be applied and, where the relevant harmonised standards are not applied in full or do not cover all of the relevant requirements set out in Section 2, the means to be used to ensure that the high-risk AI system complies with those requirements;

(f) systems and procedures for data management, including data acquisition, data collection, data analysis, data labelling, data storage, data filtration, data mining, data aggregation, data retention and any other operation regarding the data that is performed before and for the purpose of the placing on the market or the putting into service of high-risk AI systems;

(g) the risk management system referred to in Article 9;

(h) the setting-up, implementation and maintenance of a post-market monitoring system, in accordance with Article 72;

(i) procedures related to the reporting of a serious incident in accordance with Article 73;

[83] Directive 2016/2102 and Directive 2019/882.

(j) the handling of communication with national competent authorities, other relevant authorities, including those providing or supporting the access to data, notified bodies, other operators, customers or other interested parties;

(k) systems and procedures for record-keeping of all relevant documentation and information;

(l) resource management, including security-of-supply related measures;

(m) an accountability framework setting out the responsibilities of the management and other staff with regard to all the aspects listed in this paragraph.

2. The implementation of the aspects referred to in paragraph 1 shall be proportionate to the size of the provider's organisation. Providers shall, in any event, respect the degree of rigour and the level of protection required to ensure the compliance of their high-risk AI systems with this Regulation.

3. Providers of high-risk AI systems that are subject to obligations regarding quality management systems or an equivalent function under relevant sectoral Union law may include the aspects listed in paragraph 1 as part of the quality management systems pursuant to that law.

4. For providers that are financial institutions subject to requirements regarding their internal governance, arrangements or processes under Union financial services law, the obligation to put in place a quality management system, with the exception of paragraph 1, points (g), (h) and (i) of this Article, shall be deemed to be fulfilled by complying with the rules on internal governance arrangements or processes pursuant to the relevant Union financial services law. To that end, any harmonised standards referred to in Article 40 shall be taken into account.

17.1. Recitals

978. (81) The provider should establish a sound quality management system, ensure the accomplishment of the required conformity assessment procedure, draw up the relevant documentation and establish a robust post-market monitoring system. Providers of high-risk AI systems that are subject to obligations regarding quality management systems under relevant sectoral Union law should have the possibility to include the elements of the quality management system provided for in this Regulation as part of the existing quality management system provided for in that other sectoral Union law. The complementarity between this Regulation and existing sectoral Union law should also be taken into account in future standardisation activities or guidance adopted by the Commission. Public authorities which put into service high-risk AI systems for their own use may adopt and implement the rules for the quality management system as part of the quality management system adopted at a national or regional level, as appropriate, taking into account the specificities of the sector and the competences and organisation of the public authority concerned.

979. **(146)** Moreover, in light of the very small size of some operators and in order to ensure proportionality regarding costs of innovation, it is appropriate to allow microenterprises to fulfil one of the most costly obligations, namely to establish a quality management system, in a simplified manner which would reduce the administrative burden and the costs for those enterprises without affecting the level of protection and the need for compliance with the requirements for high-risk AI systems. The Commission should develop guidelines to specify the elements of the quality management system to be fulfilled in this simplified manner by microenterprises.

980. **(158)** Union financial services law includes internal governance and risk-management rules and requirements which are applicable to regulated financial institutions in the course of provision of those services, including when they make use of AI systems. In order to ensure coherent application and enforcement of the obligations under this Regulation and relevant rules and requirements of the Union financial services legal acts, the competent authorities for the supervision and enforcement of those legal acts, in particular competent authorities as defined in Regulation (EU) No 575/2013 of the European Parliament and of the Council[84] and Directives 2008/48/EC,[85] 2009/138/EC,[86] 2013/36/EU,[87] 2014/17/EU[88] and (EU) 2016/97[89] of the European Parliament and of the Council, should be designated, within their respective competences, as competent authorities for the purpose of supervising the implementation of this Regulation, including for market surveillance activities, as regards AI systems provided or used by regulated and supervised financial institutions unless Member States decide to designate another authority to fulfil these market surveillance tasks.

981. Those competent authorities should have all powers under this Regulation and Regulation (EU) 2019/1020 to enforce the requirements and obligations

---

84 Regulation (EU) No 575/2013 of the European Parliament and of the Council of 26 June 2013 on prudential requirements for credit institutions and investment firms and amending Regulation (EU) No 648/2012, [2013] OJ L176/1.

85 Directive 2008/48/EC of the European Parliament and of the Council of 23 April 2008 on credit agreements for consumers and repealing Council Directive 87/102/EEC, [2008] OJ L133/66.

86 Directive 2009/138/EC of the European Parliament and of the Council of 25 November 2009 on the taking-up and pursuit of the business of Insurance and Reinsurance (Solvency II), [2009] OJE L335/1.

87 Directive 2013/36/EU of the European Parliament and of the Council of 26 June 2013 on access to the activity of credit institutions and the prudential supervision of credit institutions and investment firms, amending Directive 2002/87/EC and repealing Directives 2006/48/EC and 2006/49/EC, [2013] OJ L176/338.

88 Directive 2014/17/EU of the European Parliament and of the Council of 4 February 2014 on credit agreements for consumers relating to residential immovable property and amending Directives 2008/48/EC and 2013/36/EU and Regulation (EU) No 1093/2010, [2014] OJ L60/34.

89 Directive (EU) 2016/97 of the European Parliament and of the Council of 20 January 2016 on insurance distribution, [2016] OJEU, L26/19.

of this Regulation, including powers to carry our *ex post* market surveillance activities that can be integrated, as appropriate, into their existing supervisory mechanisms and procedures under the relevant Union financial services law. It is appropriate to envisage that, when acting as market surveillance authorities under this Regulation, the national authorities responsible for the supervision of credit institutions regulated under Directive 2013/36/EU, which are participating in the Single Supervisory Mechanism established by Council Regulation (EU) No 1024/2013,[90] should report, without delay, to the European Central Bank any information identified in the course of their market surveillance activities that may be of potential interest for the European Central Bank's prudential supervisory tasks as specified in that Regulation. To further enhance the consistency between this Regulation and the rules applicable to credit institutions regulated under Directive 2013/36/EU, it is also appropriate to integrate some of the providers' procedural obligations in relation to risk management, post marketing monitoring and documentation into the existing obligations and procedures under Directive 2013/36/EU. In order to avoid overlaps, limited derogations should also be envisaged in relation to the quality management system of providers and the monitoring obligation placed on deployers of high-risk AI systems to the extent that these apply to credit institutions regulated by Directive 2013/36/EU. The same regime should apply to insurance and re-insurance undertakings and insurance holding companies under Directive 2009/138/EC and the insurance intermediaries under Directive (EU) 2016/97 and other types of financial institutions subject to requirements regarding internal governance, arrangements or processes established pursuant to the relevant Union financial services law to ensure consistency and equal treatment in the financial sector.

982. **(173)** In order to ensure that the regulatory framework can be adapted where necessary, the power to adopt acts in accordance with Article 290 TFEU should be delegated to the Commission to amend the conditions under which an AI system is not to be considered to be high-risk, the list of high-risk AI systems, the provisions regarding technical documentation, the content of the EU declaration of conformity the provisions regarding the conformity assessment procedures, the provisions establishing the high-risk AI systems to which the conformity assessment procedure based on assessment of the quality management system and assessment of the technical documentation should apply, the threshold, benchmarks and indicators, including by supplementing those benchmarks and indicators, in the rules for the classification of general-purpose AI models with systemic risk, the criteria for the designation of general-purpose AI models with systemic risk, the technical documentation for providers of general-purpose AI

[90] Council Regulation (EU) No 1024/2013 of 15 October 2013 conferring specific tasks on the European Central Bank concerning policies relating to the prudential supervision of credit institutions, [2013] OJ L287/63.

models and the transparency information for providers of general-purpose AI models. It is of particular importance that the Commission carry out appropriate consultations during its preparatory work, including at expert level, and that those consultations be conducted in accordance with the principles laid down in the Interinstitutional Agreement of 13 April 2016 on Better Law-Making.[91] In particular, to ensure equal participation in the preparation of delegated acts, the European Parliament and the Council receive all documents at the same time as Member States' experts, and their experts systematically have access to meetings of Commission expert groups dealing with the preparation of delegated acts.

17.2. General Approach

17.2.1 Preamble

983. The requirement for a quality management system is part of:

- a risk-based trust process;[92]
- an approach rooted in quality management;[93]
- a deployment despite the inherent risks of this technology.

17.3. Guiding Principles

984. The system is based on a set of documentation aimed at ensuring the traceability of key management elements to guarantee a trustworthy high-risk AI system. Such a system includes the following elements:

91 [2016] OJ L123/1.
92 Obligation to establish a risk management system. AI Act, Art. 9.
93 Similar to ISO 9000:2015.

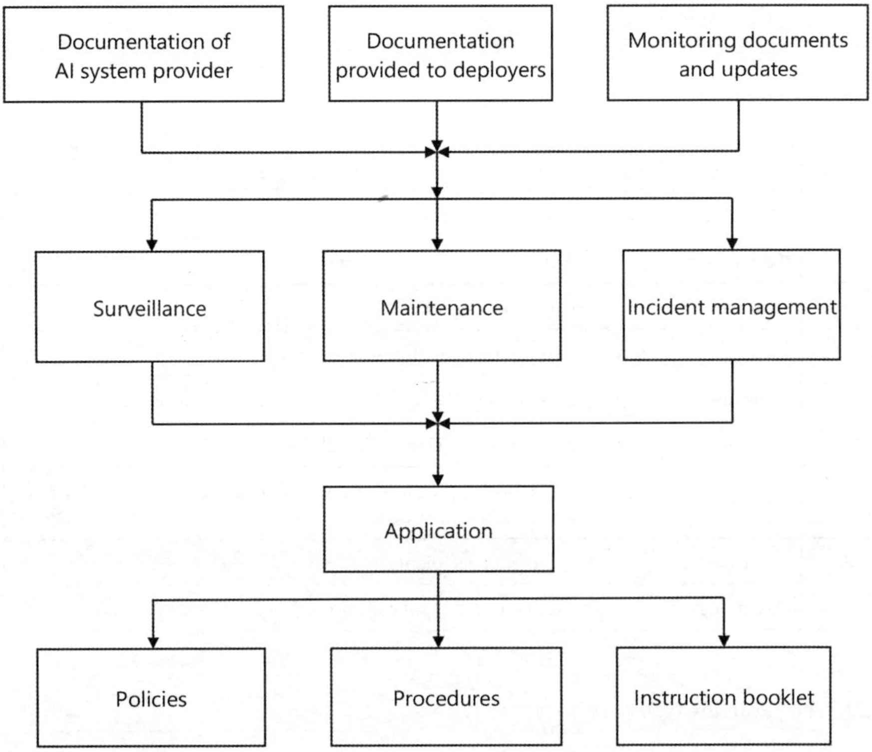

17.3.1 Typology

985. More specifically, the quality management system includes three types of documentation corresponding to three levels of quality management and incident resolution:

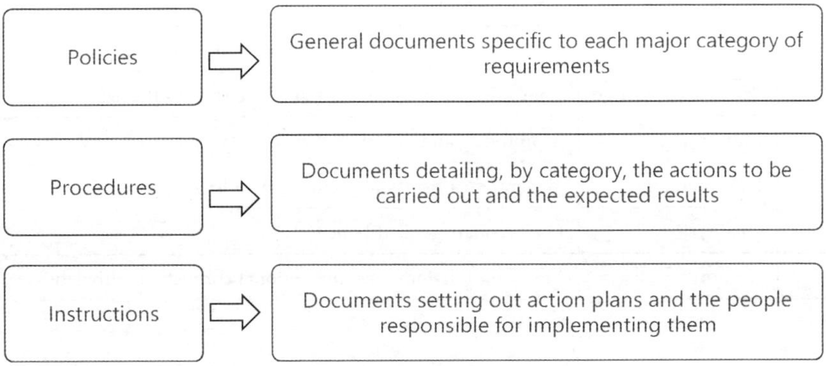

17.3.2 Characteristics

986. They are as follows:

NO.	THEME	SPECIFICATION
1.	Organisation	Systematic numbering
2.	Periodicity	Continuous for each event
3.	Traceability	Consistent system
4.	Link	Requirements with associated documentation
5.	Duration	Retention based on monitoring of each requirement
6.	Version	Monitoring of changes to all documentation
7.	Person responsible	Department in charge of documentation or its consolidation into a coherent system
8.	Distribution	Control of recipients
9.	Archiving	All documents (policies, procedures and instructions)

17.3.3 Policies

987. They include the following sections:

NO.	THEME	SPECIFICATION
1.	Strategy	General risk management policy
2.	Risks	Detailed policy for each risk
3.	Regulations	Policy on knowledge of applicable regulations
4.	Standard	Policy for controlling the application of standards
5.	State of knowledge	Policy for the implementation of the state of the art
6.	Monitoring	Monitoring and control policy
7.	Documentation	General documentation policy (including logs)
8.	Quality	Quality management policy
9.	Authority	Policy on relations with the national competent authorities

17.3.4 Procedures

988. They include the following sections:

NO.	THEME	SPECIFICATION
1.	Design	Procedure by homogeneous functional element
2.	Study	Risk management and human control procedures
3.	Software code	Quality
4.	Test cases	Quality
5.	Learning data	Absence of bias and poisoning
6.	Compliance	Procedures, CE certificates and EU declarations
7.	Monitoring	Terms and conditions
8.	Feedback	Taking incidents into account
9.	Documentation	Documentation management

17.3.5 Instructions

989. They include the following sections:

NO.	THEME	SPECIFICATION
1.	Requirement	Typology of requirements
2.	Link	Associated procedures and policies
3.	Action	List of actions: • implementation • control • monitoring
4.	Programming	Action plan indicating: • priorities • responsibilities
5.	Documentation	Archiving of instructions

17.4. Differentiating Elements

990. The quality management system is defined according to complementary axes:
- the size of the provider's organisation;
- the level of protection to be established in relation to the degree of high risk.

991. Note:

- (1) Such a quality management system can be integrated as a component of another legally mandated quality management system.

18 ARTICLE 18. DOCUMENTATION KEEPING

1. The provider shall, for a period ending 10 years after the high-risk AI system has been placed on the market or put into service, keep at the disposal of the national competent authorities:

(a) the technical documentation referred to in Article 11;

(b) the documentation concerning the quality management system referred to in Article 17;

(c) the documentation concerning the changes approved by notified bodies, where applicable;

(d) the decisions and other documents issued by the notified bodies, where applicable;

(e) the EU declaration of conformity referred to in Article 47.

2. Each Member State shall determine conditions under which the documentation referred to in paragraph 1 remains at the disposal of the national competent authorities for the period indicated in that paragraph for the cases when a provider or its authorised representative established on its territory goes bankrupt or ceases its activity prior to the end of that period.

3. Providers that are financial institutions subject to requirements regarding their internal governance, arrangements or processes under Union financial services law shall maintain the technical documentation as part of the documentation kept under the relevant Union financial services law.

18.1. Recitals

992. (66) Requirements should apply to high-risk AI systems as regards risk management, the quality and relevance of data sets used, technical documentation and record-keeping, transparency and the provision of information to deployers, human oversight, and robustness, accuracy and cybersecurity. Those requirements are necessary to effectively mitigate the risks for health, safety and fundamental rights. As no other less trade restrictive measures are reasonably available those requirements are not unjustified restrictions to trade.

993. (158) Union financial services law includes internal governance and risk-management rules and requirements which are applicable to regulated financial institutions in the course of provision of those services, including when they make use of AI systems. In order to ensure coherent application and enforcement of the obligations under this Regulation and relevant rules and requirements of the

Union financial services legal acts, the competent authorities for the supervision and enforcement of those legal acts, in particular competent authorities as defined in Regulation (EU) No 575/2013 of the European Parliament and of the Council[94] and Directives 2008/48/EC,[95] 2009/138/EC,[96] 2013/36/EU,[97] 2014/17/EU[98] and (EU) 2016/97[99] of the European Parliament and of the Council, should be designated, within their respective competences, as competent authorities for the purpose of supervising the implementation of this Regulation, including for market surveillance activities, as regards AI systems provided or used by regulated and supervised financial institutions unless Member States decide to designate another authority to fulfil these market surveillance tasks.

994. Those competent authorities should have all powers under this Regulation and Regulation (EU) 2019/1020 to enforce the requirements and obligations of this Regulation, including powers to carry our *ex post* market surveillance activities that can be integrated, as appropriate, into their existing supervisory mechanisms and procedures under the relevant Union financial services law. It is appropriate to envisage that, when acting as market surveillance authorities under this Regulation, the national authorities responsible for the supervision of credit institutions regulated under Directive 2013/36/EU, which are participating in the Single Supervisory Mechanism established by Council Regulation (EU) No 1024/2013,[100] should report, without delay, to the European Central Bank any information identified in the course of their market surveillance activities that may be of potential interest for the European Central Bank's prudential supervisory tasks as specified in that Regulation. To further enhance the consistency between this Regulation and the rules applicable to credit institutions

94 Regulation (EU) No 575/2013 of the European Parliament and of the Council of 26 June 2013 on prudential requirements for credit institutions and investment firms and amending Regulation (EU) No 648/2012, [2013] OJ L176/1.

95 Directive 2008/48/EC of the European Parliament and of the Council of 23 April 2008 on credit agreements for consumers and repealing Council Directive 87/102/EEC, [2008] OJ L133/66.

96 Directive 2009/138/EC of the European Parliament and of the Council of 25 November 2009 on the taking-up and pursuit of the business of Insurance and Reinsurance (Solvency II), [2009] OJ L335/1.

97 Directive 2013/36/EU of the European Parliament and of the Council of 26 June 2013 on access to the activity of credit institutions and the prudential supervision of credit institutions and investment firms, amending Directive 2002/87/EC and repealing Directives 2006/48/EC and 2006/49/EC, [2013] OJ L176/338.

98 Directive 2014/17/EU of the European Parliament and of the Council of 4 February 2014 on credit agreements for consumers relating to residential immovable property and amending Directives 2008/48/EC and 2013/36/EU and Regulation (EU) No 1093/2010, [2014] OJ L60/34.

99 Directive (EU) 2016/97 of the European Parliament and of the Council of 20 January 2016 on insurance distribution, [2016] OJ L26/19.

100 Council Regulation (EU) No 1024/2013 of 15 October 2013 conferring specific tasks on the European Central Bank concerning policies relating to the prudential supervision of credit institutions, [2013] OJ L287/63.

regulated under Directive 2013/36/EU, it is also appropriate to integrate some of the providers' procedural obligations in relation to risk management, post marketing monitoring and documentation into the existing obligations and procedures under Directive 2013/36/EU. In order to avoid overlaps, limited derogations should also be envisaged in relation to the quality management system of providers and the monitoring obligation placed on deployers of high-risk AI systems to the extent that these apply to credit institutions regulated by Directive 2013/36/EU. The same regime should apply to insurance and re-insurance undertakings and insurance holding companies under Directive 2009/138/EC and the insurance intermediaries under Directive (EU) 2016/97 and other types of financial institutions subject to requirements regarding internal governance, arrangements or processes established pursuant to the relevant Union financial services law to ensure consistency and equal treatment in the financial sector.

18.2. General Approach

18.2.1 Preamble

995. High-risk AI systems must be accompanied by technical documentation. This documentation is part of a set of documents, which includes the following four main categories of documentation.

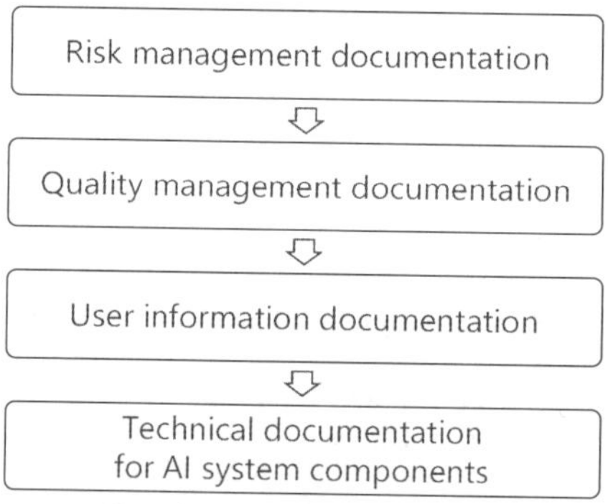

18.2.2 Guiding Principles

996. The technical documentation is:

- specified within the framework of requirements applicable to high-risk AI systems;[101]
- detailed in Annex IV.

[101] AI Act, Art. 11.

997. It must be kept at the disposal of the national competent authorities for a period of ten years after the placing on the market or the putting into service of each high-risk AI system.

998. This documentation keeping requirement aims to monitor risk containment and ensure the operational reliability of a trustworthy AI.

18.3. Classification

999. Documentation keeping requirements can be organised as follows:

NO.	THEME	SPECIFICATION	REFERENCE
1.	Provider (identification)	Name	AIA, Annex IV(1)(a)
	Harmonised standards	List of the harmonised standards. Failing that, a description of the solutions adopted to meet the requirements applicable to the high-risk AI system	AIA, Arts. 6–15 AIA, Annex IV(7)
2.	Description of the high-risk AI system	Intended purpose	AIA, Annex IV(1)(a)
		Version and version history	AIA, Annex IV(1)(a)
		Component of products: • photograph • illustrations showing external features	AIA, Annex IV(1)(f)
		CE marking	AIA, Annex IV(1)(f)
		Internal layout of the component in the product	AIA, Annex IV(1)(f)
		User interface provided to the deployer with a basic description	AIA, Annex IV(1)(g)
		Instructions for use provided to the deployer	AIA, Annex IV(1)(h)
3.	Development process	Methods and steps	AIA, Annex IV(2)(a)
		Pre-trained tools provided by third parties	AIA, Annex IV(2)(a)

NO.	THEME	SPECIFICATION	REFERENCE
4.	Design	Design specifications including: • general logic; • algorithms; • assumptions; • rationale.	AIA, Annex IV(2)(b)
		Persons concerned	AIA, Annex IV(2)(b)
		Parameters	AIA, Annex IV(2)(b)
		Optimisation	AIA, Annex IV(2)(b)
		Technical solutions (Chap. III, sec. 2)	AIA, Annex IV(2)(b)
		Validation procedure	AIA, Annex IV(2)(g)
5.	Computer specifications	Hardware (running and interaction)	AIA, Annex IV(1)(b) and (e)
		Software	AIA, Annex IV(1)(b)
		Linking of high-risk and non-high-risk AI systems	AIA, Annex IV(1)(c)
		Relevant software or firmware with associated version history	AIA, Annex IV(1)(c)
		Software component architecture	AIA, Annex IV(2)(c)
		Computational resources used (development, training, testing)	AIA, Annex IV(2)(c)
		Files	AIA, Annex IV(2)(d)
6.	Documentation	Technical documentation (proof of compliance with all requirements)	AIA, Art. 11
		Documentation (proof of the quality management system)	AIA, Art. 17
		Risk management documentation	AIA, Annex IV(5)
		Documentation of the appropriateness and development of metrics	AIA, Annex IV(4)
		Documentation of relevant changes to the system through its lifecycle	AIA, Annex IV(6)
		AI system functioning monitoring file	AIA, Annex IV(3)

NO.	THEME	SPECIFICATION	REFERENCE
7.	Technical deployment during placing on the market or putting into service	Software package	AIA, Annex IV(1)(d)
		Download	
		API	
8.	Human oversight	Threat assessment and controls	AIA, Annex IV(2)(e)
9.	Cybersecurity	Identification of threats	AIA, Annex IV(2)(h)
10.	Compliance	Assessment of the measures implemented	AIA, Annex IV(2)(f)
11.	Monitoring	Post-market	AIA, Annex IV(9)
12.	Certification	EU declaration of conformity	AIA, Art. 47
		CE marking	AIA, Art. 48
		Documentation concerning the changes approved by notified bodies	AIA, Art. 18(1)(c)
		Decisions and other documents issued by the notified bodies	AIA, Art. 18(1)(d)

1000. Notes:

- (1) National legislations must address the status of this documentation in the event of bankruptcy or cessation of activity.
- (2) For financial services, the documentation keeping requirement must be incorporated into the specific requirements applicable to this type of service.

19 ARTICLE 19. AUTOMATICALLY GENERATED LOGS

1. Providers of high-risk AI systems shall keep the logs referred to in Article 12(1), automatically generated by their high-risk AI systems, to the extent such logs are under their control. Without prejudice to applicable Union or national law, the logs shall be kept for a period appropriate to the intended purpose of the high-risk AI system, of at least six months, unless provided otherwise in the applicable Union or national law, in particular in Union law on the protection of personal data.

2. Providers that are financial institutions subject to requirements regarding their internal governance, arrangements or processes under Union financial services law shall maintain the logs automatically generated by their high-risk AI systems as part of the documentation kept under the relevant financial services law.

19.1. Recitals

1001. (71) Having comprehensible information on how high-risk AI systems have been developed and how they perform throughout their lifetime is essential to enable traceability of those systems, verify compliance with the requirements under this Regulation, as well as monitoring of their operations and post market monitoring. This requires keeping records and the availability of technical documentation, containing information which is necessary to assess the compliance of the AI system with the relevant requirements and facilitate post market monitoring. Such information should include the general characteristics, capabilities and limitations of the system, algorithms, data, training, testing and validation processes used as well as documentation on the relevant risk-management system and drawn in a clear and comprehensive form. The technical documentation should be kept up to date, appropriately throughout the lifetime of the AI system. Furthermore, high-risk AI systems should technically allow for the automatic recording of events, by means of logs, over the duration of the lifetime of the system.

1002. (73) High-risk AI systems should be designed and developed in such a way that natural persons can oversee their functioning, ensure that they are used as intended and that their impacts are addressed over the system's lifecycle. To that end, appropriate human oversight measures should be identified by the provider of the system before its placing on the market or putting into service. In particular, where appropriate, such measures should guarantee that the system is subject to in-built operational constraints that cannot be overridden by the system itself and is responsive to the human operator, and that the natural persons to whom human oversight has been assigned have the necessary competence, training and authority to carry out that role. It is also essential, as appropriate, to ensure that high-risk AI systems include mechanisms to guide and inform a natural person to whom human oversight has been assigned to make informed decisions if, when and how to intervene in order to avoid negative consequences or risks, or stop the system if it does not perform as intended. Considering the significant consequences for persons in the case of an incorrect match by certain biometric identification systems, it is appropriate to provide for an enhanced human oversight requirement for those systems so that no action or decision may be taken by the deployer on the basis of the identification resulting from the system unless this has been separately verified and confirmed by at least two natural persons. Those persons could be from one or more entities and include the person operating or using the system. This requirement should not pose unnecessary burden or delays and it could be sufficient that the separate verifications by the different persons are automatically recorded in the logs generated by the system. Given the specificities of the areas of law enforcement, migration, border control and asylum, this requirement should not apply where Union or national law considers the application of that requirement to be disproportionate.

19.2. General Approach

19.2.1 Preamble

1003. Logs automatically generated by high-risk AI systems are one of the components of the documentation.

19.2.2 Guiding Principles

1004. Maintaining these logs is a requirement that applies only to the automatic logs integrated into the various digital elements that make up high-risk AI systems.

1005. The high-risk AI system must be designed by the provider to enable the recording of a set of events intended for risk management and incident monitoring in an automated manner.[102]

1006. Automatically generated logs must be kept by the operators responsible for the concerned AI systems.

19.3. Characteristics

1007. They are as follows:

NO.	THEME	SPECIFICATION
1.	Management	By the provider directly or by contract with other operators
2.	Archiving	Minimum duration of 6 months and until the end of the applicable legal requirements
3.	Personal data	This requirement must be combined with the GDPR, with Regulation 2019/679, and with Directive 2016/680

20 ARTICLE 20. CORRECTIVE ACTIONS AND DUTY OF INFORMATION

1. Providers of high-risk AI systems which consider or have reason to consider that a high-risk AI system that they have placed on the market or

[102] AI Act, Art. 12.

put into service is not in conformity with this Regulation shall immediately take the necessary corrective actions to bring that system into conformity, to withdraw it, to disable it, or to recall it, as appropriate. They shall inform the distributors of the high-risk AI system concerned and, where applicable, the deployers, the authorised representative and importers accordingly.

2. Where the high-risk AI system presents a risk within the meaning of Article 79(1) and the provider becomes aware of that risk, it shall immediately investigate the causes, in collaboration with the reporting deployer, where applicable, and inform the market surveillance authorities competent for the high-risk AI system concerned and, where applicable, the notified body that issued a certificate for that high-risk AI system in accordance with Article 44, in particular, of the nature of the non-compliance and of any relevant corrective action taken.

20.1. Recitals

1008. **(155)** In order to ensure that providers of high-risk AI systems can take into account the experience on the use of high-risk AI systems for improving their systems and the design and development process or can take any possible corrective action in a timely manner, all providers should have a post-market monitoring system in place. Where relevant, post-market monitoring should include an analysis of the interaction with other AI systems including other devices and software. Post-market monitoring should not cover sensitive operational data of deployers which are law enforcement authorities. This system is also key to ensure that the possible risks emerging from AI systems which continue to 'learn' after being placed on the market or put into service can be more efficiently and timely addressed. In this context, providers should also be required to have a system in place to report to the relevant authorities any serious incidents resulting from the use of their AI systems, meaning incident or malfunctioning leading to death or serious damage to health, serious and irreversible disruption of the management and operation of critical infrastructure, infringements of obligations under Union law intended to protect fundamental rights or serious damage to property or the environment.

1009. **(159)** Each market surveillance authority for high-risk AI systems in the area of biometrics, as listed in an annex to this Regulation insofar as those systems are used for the purposes of law enforcement, migration, asylum and border control management, or the administration of justice and democratic processes, should have effective investigative and corrective powers, including at least the power to obtain access to all personal data that are being processed and to all information necessary for the performance of its tasks. The market surveillance authorities should be able to exercise their powers by acting with complete independence. Any limitations of their access to sensitive operational data under this Regulation should be without prejudice to the powers conferred to them by Directive (EU) 2016/680. No exclusion on disclosing data to national data protection authorities under this Regulation should affect the current or future powers of those authorities beyond the scope of this Regulation.

20.2. General Approach

20.2.1 Preamble

1010. The requirement for corrective actions applies to all providers who are informed of faults in their high-risk AI systems.

20.2.2 Guiding Principles

1011. The requirement implies taking the following corrective actions:
- bringing the system into conformity;
- disabling the system;
- recalling the system;
- withdrawing the system.

1012. To ensure trustworthy AI, the provider has a duty to promptly inform the entire chain of stakeholders.

1013. Two categories of risks are involved:
- a risk of non-compliance;
- a risk of actual harm.

20.3. Risks of Non-Compliance

20.3.1 Characteristics

1014. The obligations are as follows:

NO.	THEME	SPECIFICATION
1.	Deadline	As soon as it is known
2.	Intervention	Directly or through the distribution network
3.	Coverage	Hardware or software
4.	Making safe	Stop any use
5.	Authorisation	Correction in complete safety
6.	Traceability	Entry into the system only with prior authorisation from the user
7.	Testing	Log of all operations carried out
8.	Impact	Return to compliance with success report

20.3.2 Mandatory Information

1015. The situation and corrective actions are notified under the following conditions:

NO.	THEME	SPECIFICATION
1.	Recipients	Authorised representative, importers, distributors and deployers
		National competent authorities
		Notified body
2.	Information	Causes and actions concerned
3.	Period	As soon as it becomes aware of the risk, depending on the occurrence of risks

20.4. Actual Risk

20.4.1 Characteristics

1016. The obligations are as follows:

NO.	THEME	SPECIFICATION
1.	Notion	Actual risk or risk in the process of materialising
2.	Time limit	As soon as it is known
3.	Notification	Deployer
4.	Procedure	Investigation of causes with deployer
5.	Information and cooperation	Market surveillance authority Notified body
6.	Non-compliance	List of non-conformities involved
7.	Measures	Detailed list of corrective operations

21 ARTICLE 21. COOPERATION WITH COMPETENT AUTHORITIES

1. Providers of high-risk AI systems shall, upon a reasoned request by a competent authority, provide that authority all the information and documentation necessary to demonstrate the conformity of the high-risk AI system with the requirements set out in Section 2, in a language which can be easily understood by the authority in one of the official languages of the institutions of the Union as indicated by the Member State concerned.

2. Upon a reasoned request by a competent authority, providers shall also give the requesting competent authority, as applicable, access to the automatically generated logs of the high-risk AI system referred to in Article 12(1), to the extent such logs are under their control.

3. Any information obtained by a competent authority pursuant to this Article shall be treated in accordance with the confidentiality obligations set out in Article 78.

21.1. Recitals

1017. **(74)** High-risk AI systems should perform consistently throughout their lifecycle and meet an appropriate level of accuracy, robustness and cybersecurity, in light of their intended purpose and in accordance with the generally acknowledged state of the Art. The Commission and relevant organisations and stakeholders are encouraged to take due consideration of the mitigation of risks and the negative impacts of the AI system. The expected level of performance metrics should be declared in the accompanying instructions of use. Providers are urged to communicate that information to deployers in a clear and easily understandable way, free of misunderstandings or misleading statements. Union law on legal metrology, including Directives 2014/31/EU[103] and 2014/32/EU[104] of the European Parliament and of the Council, aims to ensure the accuracy of measurements and to help the transparency and fairness of commercial transactions. In that context, in cooperation with relevant stakeholders and organisation, such as metrology and benchmarking authorities, the Commission should encourage, as appropriate, the development of benchmarks and measurement methodologies for AI systems. In doing so, the Commission should take note and collaborate with international partners working on metrology and relevant measurement indicators relating to AI.

---

[103] Directive 2014/31/EU of the European Parliament and of the Council of 26 February 2014 on the harmonisation of the laws of the Member States relating to the making available on the market of non-automatic weighing instruments, *OJEU*, L 96, 29 March 2014, p. 107.

[104] Directive 2014/32/EU of the European Parliament and of the Council of 26 February 2014 on the harmonisation of the laws of the Member States relating to the making available on the market of measuring instruments, *OJEU*, L 96, 29 March 2014, p. 149.

21.2. General Approach

21.2.1 Preamble

1018. The entire regulatory system is based on three main pillars:
- a compliance mechanism;
- national regulatory authorities;
- continuous information exchange to confirm risks and mitigate their consequences.

21.2.2 Guiding Principles

1019. Cooperation requires providers to provide all information to the national competent authority regarding:
- the documentation and associated quality system;
- events that are relevant to risk assessment.

21.2.3 Characteristics

1020. They are as follows:

NO.	THEME	SPECIFICATION
1.	Request	Reasoned
2.	Documentation	Conformity
3.	Language	Official EU language
4.	Logs	Logs under the control of the providers
5.	Deadline	As soon as possible
6.	Service	Confidentiality[105]

22 ARTICLE 22. AUTHORISED REPRESENTATIVES OF PROVIDERS OF HIGH-RISK AI SYSTEMS

1. Prior to making their high-risk AI systems available on the Union market, providers established in third countries shall, by written mandate, appoint an authorised representative which is established in the Union.

[105] AI Act, Art. 78.

2. The provider shall enable its authorised representative to perform the tasks specified in the mandate received from the provider.

3. The authorised representative shall perform the tasks specified in the mandate received from the provider. It shall provide a copy of the mandate to the market surveillance authorities upon request, in one of the official languages of the institutions of the Union, as indicated by the competent authority. For the purposes of this Regulation, the mandate shall empower the authorised representative to carry out the following tasks:

(a) verify that the EU declaration of conformity referred to in Article 47 and the technical documentation referred to in Article 11 have been drawn up and that an appropriate conformity assessment procedure has been carried out by the provider;

(b) keep at the disposal of the competent authorities and national authorities or bodies referred to in Article 74(10), for a period of 10 years after the high-risk AI system has been placed on the market or put into service, the contact details of the provider that appointed the authorised representative, a copy of the EU declaration of conformity referred to in Article 47, the technical documentation and, if applicable, the certificate issued by the notified body;

(c) provide a competent authority, upon a reasoned request, with all the information and documentation, including that referred to in point (b) of this subparagraph, necessary to demonstrate the conformity of a high-risk AI system with the requirements set out in Section 2, including access to the logs, as referred to in Article 12(1), automatically generated by the high-risk AI system, to the extent such logs are under the control of the provider;

(d) cooperate with competent authorities, upon a reasoned request, in any action the latter take in relation to the high-risk AI system, in particular to reduce and mitigate the risks posed by the high-risk AI system;

(e) where applicable, comply with the registration obligations referred to in Article 49(1), or, if the registration is carried out by the provider itself, ensure that the information referred to in point 3 of Section A of Annex VIII is correct.

The mandate shall empower the authorised representative to be addressed, in addition to or instead of the provider, by the competent authorities, on all issues related to ensuring compliance with this Regulation.

4. The authorised representative shall terminate the mandate if it considers or has reason to consider the provider to be acting contrary to its obligations pursuant to this Regulation. In such a case, it shall immediately inform the relevant market surveillance authority, as well as, where applicable, the relevant notified body, about the termination of the mandate and the reasons therefor.

22.1. Recitals

1021. (82) To enable enforcement of this Regulation and create a level playing field for operators, and, taking into account the different forms of making available of digital products, it is important to ensure that, under all circumstances, a person established in the Union can provide authorities with all the necessary information on the compliance of an AI system. Therefore, prior to making their AI systems available in the Union, providers established in third countries should, by written mandate, appoint an authorised representative established in the Union. This authorised representative plays a pivotal role in ensuring the compliance of the high-risk AI systems placed on the market or put into service in the Union by those providers who are not established in the Union and in serving as their contact person established in the Union.

22.2. General Approach

22.2.1 Preamble

1022. The placing on the market, putting into service, and deployment of high-risk AI systems by providers established in third countries cannot occur without the prior appointment of an authorised representative established within the European Union.

22.2.2 Guiding Principles

1023. The objective is to have a representative within the European Union responsible for ensuring compliance with the requirements established by the Regulation, identical to the obligations imposed on providers established within the European Union.

22.2.3 Characteristics

1024. The role of the authorised representative requires fulfilling the following conditions:

NO.	THEME	SPECIFICATION
1.	Form	Mandate that is written, dated and signed by the provider
2.	Location	Authorised representative established in the EU with a permanent establishment
3.	Operation	List of delegated tasks
4.	Duration	Period of use of the high-risk AI system

NO.	THEME	SPECIFICATION
5.	Communication	Copy of the mandate to the competent national authorities corresponding to the various Member States in which the high-risk AI system is distributed

22.2.4 Modalities

1025. They are as follows:

NO.	THEME	SPECIFICATION
1.	EU declaration	Verification of conformity (referred to in Art. 47)
2.	Technical documentation	Verification of conformity (referred to in Art. 11)
3.	Keeping of documentation	10 years after the placing on the market or putting in to service
4.	Monitoring documents	Contact details of the provider Copy of the technical documentation Certificate issued by the notified body, if applicable Automatically generated logs
5.	National competent authority	Provision of all mandatory information corresponding to the high-risk AI system in question
6.	Cooperation	Obligation of the authorised representative to cooperate with the supervisory authorities to reduce and mitigate risks
7.	Registration	Completion or verification of the mandatory registration of the high-risk AI system in the EU database[106]

23 ARTICLE 23. OBLIGATIONS OF IMPORTERS

1. Before placing a high-risk AI system on the market, importers shall ensure that the system is in conformity with this Regulation by verifying that:

(a) the relevant conformity assessment procedure referred to in Article 43 has been carried out by the provider of the high-risk AI system;

(b) the provider has drawn up the technical documentation in accordance with Article 11 and Annex IV;

[106] AI Act, Art. 71.

(c) the system bears the required CE marking and is accompanied by the EU declaration of conformity referred to in Article 47 and instructions for use;

(d) the provider has appointed an authorised representative in accordance with Article 22(1).

2. Where an importer has sufficient reason to consider that a high-risk AI system is not in conformity with this Regulation, or is falsified, or accompanied by falsified documentation, it shall not place the system on the market until it has been brought into conformity. Where the high-risk AI system presents a risk within the meaning of Article 79(1), the importer shall inform the provider of the system, the authorised representative and the market surveillance authorities to that effect.

3. Importers shall indicate their name, registered trade name or registered trade mark, and the address at which they can be contacted on the high-risk AI system and on its packaging or its accompanying documentation, where applicable.

4. Importers shall ensure that, while a high-risk AI system is under their responsibility, storage or transport conditions, where applicable, do not jeopardise its compliance with the requirements set out in Section 2.

5. Importers shall keep, for a period of 10 years after the high-risk AI system has been placed on the market or put into service, a copy of the certificate issued by the notified body, where applicable, of the instructions for use, and of the EU declaration of conformity referred to in Article 47.

6. Importers shall provide the relevant competent authorities, upon a reasoned request, with all the necessary information and documentation, including that referred to in paragraph 5, to demonstrate the conformity of a high-risk AI system with the requirements set out in Section 2 in a language which can be easily understood by them. For this purpose, they shall also ensure that the technical documentation can be made available to those authorities.

7. Importers shall cooperate with the relevant competent authorities in any action those authorities take in relation to a high-risk AI system placed on the market by the importers, in particular to reduce and mitigate the risks posed by it.

23.1. Recitals

1026. (83) In light of the nature and complexity of the value chain for AI systems and in line with the New Legislative Framework, it is essential to ensure legal certainty and facilitate the compliance with this Regulation. Therefore, it is necessary to clarify the role and the specific obligations of relevant operators along that value chain, such as importers and distributors who may contribute to the development of AI systems. In certain situations those operators could act in more than one role at the same time and should therefore fulfil cumulatively all relevant obligations associated with those roles. For example, an operator could act as a distributor and an importer at the same time.

1027. **(84)** To ensure legal certainty, it is necessary to clarify that, under certain specific conditions, any distributor, importer, deployer or other third-party should be considered to be a provider of a high-risk AI system and therefore assume all the relevant obligations. This would be the case if that party puts its name or trademark on a high-risk AI system already placed on the market or put into service, without prejudice to contractual arrangements stipulating that the obligations are allocated otherwise. This would also be the case if that party makes a substantial modification to a high-risk AI system that has already been placed on the market or has already been put into service in a way that it remains a high-risk AI system in accordance with this Regulation, or if it modifies the intended purpose of an AI system, including a general-purpose AI system, which has not been classified as high-risk and has already been placed on the market or put into service, in a way that the AI system becomes a high-risk AI system in accordance with this Regulation. Those provisions should apply without prejudice to more specific provisions established in certain Union harmonisation legislation based on the New Legislative Framework, together with which this Regulation should apply. For example, Article 16(2) of Regulation (EU) 2017/745, establishing that certain changes should not be considered to be modifications of a device that could affect its compliance with the applicable requirements, should continue to apply to high-risk AI systems that are medical devices within the meaning of that Regulation.

23.2. General Approach

23.2.1 Preamble

1028. The importer acts as the intermediary for providers of high-risk AI systems that are established in third countries, regardless of the presence of an authorised representative.[107]

23.2.2 Guiding Principles

1029. The importer:

- verifies that the non-EU provider has fulfilled its obligations;
- verifies that the conformity requirements are met before placing the system on the market or putting it into service;
- collaborates with the authorised representative.

[107] AI Act, Art. 24.

23.2.3 Characteristics

1030. They are as follows:

NO.	THEME	SPECIFICATION
1.	Effectiveness	Before the placing on the market
2.	Conformity	Verification of conformity made for the provider
3.	Technical documentation	Verification of availability
4.	CE marking	
5.	Documentation	Risk management and quality management
6.	Instructions for use	Availability of a copy
7.	Risks	Information of the provider
8.	Information of the national competent authority	Information and collaboration

24 ARTICLE 24. OBLIGATIONS OF DISTRIBUTORS

1. Before making a high-risk AI system available on the market, distributors shall verify that it bears the required CE marking, that it is accompanied by a copy of the EU declaration of conformity referred to in Article 47 and instructions for use, and that the provider and the importer of that system, as applicable, have complied with their respective obligations as laid down in Article 16, points (b) and (c) and Article 23(3).

2. Where a distributor considers or has reason to consider, on the basis of the information in its possession, that a high-risk AI system is not in conformity with the requirements set out in Section 2, it shall not make the high-risk AI system available on the market until the system has been brought into conformity with those requirements. Furthermore, where the high-risk AI system presents a risk within the meaning of Article 79(1), the distributor shall inform the provider or the importer of the system, as applicable, to that effect.

3. Distributors shall ensure that, while a high-risk AI system is under their responsibility, storage or transport conditions, where applicable, do not jeopardise the compliance of the system with the requirements set out in Section 2.

4. A distributor that considers or has reason to consider, on the basis of the information in its possession, a high-risk AI system which it has made available on the market not to be in conformity with the requirements set out in Section 2, shall take the corrective actions necessary to bring that system into conformity with those requirements, to withdraw it or recall it, or shall ensure that the provider, the importer or any relevant operator, as appropriate, takes those corrective actions. Where the high-risk AI system presents a risk within the meaning of Article 79(1), the distributor shall immediately inform the provider or importer of the system and the authorities competent for the high-risk AI system concerned, giving details, in particular, of the non-compliance and of any corrective actions taken.

5. Upon a reasoned request from a relevant competent authority, distributors of a high-risk AI system shall provide that authority with all the information and documentation regarding their actions pursuant to paragraphs 1 to 4 necessary to demonstrate the conformity of that system with the requirements set out in Section 2.

6. Distributors shall cooperate with the relevant competent authorities in any action those authorities take in relation to a high-risk AI system made available on the market by the distributors, in particular to reduce or mitigate the risk posed by it.

24.1. Recitals

1031. (83) In light of the nature and complexity of the value chain for AI systems and in line with the New Legislative Framework, it is essential to ensure legal certainty and facilitate the compliance with this Regulation. Therefore, it is necessary to clarify the role and the specific obligations of relevant operators along that value chain, such as importers and distributors who may contribute to the development of AI systems. In certain situations those operators could act in more than one role at the same time and should therefore fulfil cumulatively all relevant obligations associated with those roles. For example, an operator could act as a distributor and an importer at the same time.

1032. (84) To ensure legal certainty, it is necessary to clarify that, under certain specific conditions, any distributor, importer, deployer or other third-party should be considered to be a provider of a high-risk AI system and therefore assume all the relevant obligations. This would be the case if that party puts its name or trademark on a high-risk AI system already placed on the market or put into service, without prejudice to contractual arrangements stipulating that the obligations are allocated otherwise. This would also be the case if that party makes a substantial modification to a high-risk AI system that has already been placed on the market or has already been put into service in a way that it remains a high-risk AI system in accordance with this Regulation, or if it modifies the intended purpose of an AI system, including a general-purpose AI system, which has not been classified as high-risk and has already been placed on the market or put into service, in a way that the AI system becomes a high-risk AI system in accordance with this Regulation. Those provisions should apply without prejudice to more specific provisions established in certain Union harmonisation legislation based on the New Legislative Framework, together with which this Regulation should apply. For example, Article 16(2) of Regulation (EU) 2017/745, establishing that certain changes should not be considered to be modifications of a device that could affect its compliance with the applicable requirements, should continue to apply to high-risk AI systems that are medical devices within the meaning of that Regulation.

24.2. General Approach

24.2.1 Preamble

1033. Maintaining trust requires that all parties involved in the supply chain ensure the 'continuity' of compliance.

24.2.2 Guiding Principles

1034. Distributors act as a key link in the market, and their obligations include verifying that the high-risk AI systems they distribute comply with the requirements before being made available on the market.

24.2.3 Characteristics

1035. They are as follows:

NO.	THEME	SPECIFICATION
1.	CE marking	Verification
2.	EU declaration	Conformity
3.	Information of the provider	Same for importers
4.	Documentation	Availability
5.	Instructions for use	Availability
6.	Requirements	Verification
7.	Quality management system	Assessment and conformity
8.	Risk	Information of provider and importer
9.	Responsibility	Storage
10.	Non-conformity	Obligation to provide information Obligation to recall Obligation to withdraw
11.	National competent authority	Information and cooperation

25 ARTICLE 25. RESPONSIBILITIES ALONG THE AI VALUE CHAIN

1. Any distributor, importer, deployer or other third-party shall be considered to be a provider of a high-risk AI system for the purposes of this Regulation and shall be subject to the obligations of the provider under Article 16, in any of the following circumstances:

(a) they put their name or trademark on a high-risk AI system already placed on the market or put into service, without prejudice to contractual arrangements stipulating that the obligations are otherwise allocated;

(b) they make a substantial modification to a high-risk AI system that has already been placed on the market or has already been put into service in such a way that it remains a high-risk AI system pursuant to Article 6;

(c) they modify the intended purpose of an AI system, including a general-purpose AI system, which has not been classified as high-risk and has already been placed on the market or put into service in such a way that the AI system concerned becomes a high-risk AI system in accordance with Article 6.

2. Where the circumstances referred to in paragraph 1 occur, the provider that initially placed the AI system on the market or put it into service shall no longer be considered to be a provider of that specific AI system for the purposes of this Regulation. That initial provider shall closely cooperate with new providers and shall make available the necessary information and provide the reasonably expected technical access and other assistance that are required for the fulfilment of the obligations set out in this Regulation, in particular regarding the compliance with the conformity assessment of high-risk AI systems. This paragraph shall not apply in cases where the initial provider has clearly specified that its AI system is not to be changed into a high-risk AI system and therefore does not fall under the obligation to hand over the documentation.

3. In the case of high-risk AI systems that are safety components of products covered by the Union harmonisation legislation listed in Section A of Annex I, the product manufacturer shall be considered to be the provider of the high-risk AI system, and shall be subject to the obligations under Article 16 under either of the following circumstances:

(a) the high-risk AI system is placed on the market together with the product under the name or trademark of the product manufacturer;

(b) the high-risk AI system is put into service under the name or trademark of the product manufacturer after the product has been placed on the market.

4. The provider of a high-risk AI system and the third party that supplies an AI system, tools, services, components, or processes that are used or integrated in a high-risk AI system shall, by written agreement, specify the necessary information, capabilities, technical access and other assistance based on the generally acknowledged state of the art, in order to enable the provider of the high-risk AI system to fully comply with the obligations set out in this Regulation. This paragraph shall not apply to third parties making accessible to the public tools, services, processes, or components, other than general-purpose AI models, under a free and open-source licence.

The AI Office may develop and recommend voluntary model terms for contracts between providers of high-risk AI systems and third parties that supply tools, services, components or processes that are used for or integrated into high-risk AI systems. When developing those voluntary model terms, the AI Office shall take into account possible contractual requirements applicable in specific sectors or business cases. The voluntary model terms shall be published and be available free of charge in an easily usable electronic format.

5. Paragraphs 2 and 3 are without prejudice to the need to observe and protect intellectual property rights, confidential business information and trade secrets in accordance with Union and national law.

25.1. Recitals

1036. (9) Harmonised rules applicable to the placing on the market, the putting into service and the use of high-risk AI systems should be laid down consistently with Regulation (EC) No 765/2008 of the European Parliament and of the Council,[108] Decision No 768/2008/EC of the European Parliament and of the Council[109] and Regulation (EU) 2019/1020 of the European Parliament and of the Council[110] (New Legislative Framework). The harmonised rules laid down in this Regulation should apply across sectors and, in line with the New Legislative Framework, should be without prejudice to existing Union law, in particular on data protection, consumer protection, fundamental rights, employment, and protection of workers, and product safety, to which this Regulation is complementary. As a consequence, all rights and remedies provided for by such Union law to consumers, and other persons on whom AI systems may have a negative impact, including as regards the compensation of possible damages pursuant to Council Directive 85/374/EEC[111] remain unaffected and

[108] Regulation (EC) No 765/2008 of the European Parliament and of the Council of 9 July 2008 setting out the requirements for accreditation and repealing Regulation (EEC) No 339/93, [2008] OJ L218/30.

[109] Decision No 768/2008/EC of the European Parliament and of the Council of 9 July 2008 on a common framework for the marketing of products, and repealing Council Decision 93/465/EEC, [2008] OJ L218/82.

[110] Regulation (EU) 2019/1020 of the European Parliament and of the Council of 20 June 2019 on market surveillance and compliance of products and amending Directive 2004/42/EC and Regulations (EC) No 765/2008 and (EU) No 305/2011, [2019] OJ L169/1.

[111] Council Directive 85/374/EEC of 25 July 1985 on the approximation of the laws, regulations and administrative provisions of the Member States concerning liability for defective products, [1985] OJ L210/29.

fully applicable. Furthermore, in the context of employment and protection of workers, this Regulation should therefore not affect Union law on social policy and national labour law, in compliance with Union law, concerning employment and working conditions, including health and safety at work and the relationship between employers and workers. This Regulation should also not affect the exercise of fundamental rights as recognised in the Member States and at Union level, including the right or freedom to strike or to take other action covered by the specific industrial relations systems in Member States as well as the right to negotiate, to conclude and enforce collective agreements or to take collective action in accordance with national law. This Regulation should not affect the provisions aiming to improve working conditions in platform work laid down in a Directive of the European Parliament and of the Council on improving working conditions in platform work. Moreover, this Regulation aims to strengthen the effectiveness of such existing rights and remedies by establishing specific requirements and obligations, including in respect of the transparency, technical documentation and record-keeping of AI systems. Furthermore, the obligations placed on various operators involved in the AI value chain under this Regulation should apply without prejudice to national law, in compliance with Union law, having the effect of limiting the use of certain AI systems where such law falls outside the scope of this Regulation or pursues legitimate public interest objectives other than those pursued by this Regulation. For example, national labour law and law on the protection of minors, namely persons below the age of 18, taking into account the UNCRC General Comment No 25 (2021) on children's rights in relation to the digital environment, insofar as they are not specific to AI systems and pursue other legitimate public interest objectives, should not be affected by this Regulation.

1037. (20) In order to obtain the greatest benefits from AI systems while protecting fundamental rights, health and safety and to enable democratic control, AI literacy should equip providers, deployers and affected persons with the necessary notions to make informed decisions regarding AI systems. Those notions may vary with regard to the relevant context and can include understanding the correct application of technical elements during the AI system's development phase, the measures to be applied during its use, the suitable ways in which to interpret the AI system's output, and, in the case of affected persons, the knowledge necessary to understand how decisions taken with the assistance of AI will have an impact on them. In the context of the application this Regulation, AI literacy should provide all relevant actors in the AI value chain with the insights required to ensure the appropriate compliance and its correct enforcement. Furthermore, the wide implementation of AI literacy measures and the introduction of appropriate follow-up actions could contribute to improving working conditions and ultimately sustain the consolidation, and innovation path of trustworthy AI in the Union. The European Artificial Intelligence Board (the 'Board') should support the Commission, to promote AI literacy tools, public awareness and understanding of the benefits, risks, safeguards, rights and obligations in relation to the use of AI systems. In cooperation with the relevant stakeholders, the Commission and the Member States should facilitate the drawing up of voluntary codes of conduct to advance AI literacy among persons dealing with the development, operation and use of AI.

1038. **(83)** In light of the nature and complexity of the value chain for AI systems and in line with the New Legislative Framework, it is essential to ensure legal certainty and facilitate the compliance with this Regulation. Therefore, it is necessary to clarify the role and the specific obligations of relevant operators along that value chain, such as importers and distributors who may contribute to the development of AI systems. In certain situations those operators could act in more than one role at the same time and should therefore fulfil cumulatively all relevant obligations associated with those roles. For example, an operator could act as a distributor and an importer at the same time.

1039. **(85)** General-purpose AI systems may be used as high-risk AI systems by themselves or be components of other high-risk AI systems. Therefore, due to their particular nature and in order to ensure a fair sharing of responsibilities along the AI value chain, the providers of such systems should, irrespective of whether they may be used as high-risk AI systems as such by other providers or as components of high-risk AI systems and unless provided otherwise under this Regulation, closely cooperate with the providers of the relevant high-risk AI systems to enable their compliance with the relevant obligations under this Regulation and with the competent authorities established under this Regulation.

1040. **(88)** Along the AI value chain multiple parties often supply AI systems, tools and services but also components or processes that are incorporated by the provider into the AI system with various objectives, including the model training, model retraining, model testing and evaluation, integration into software, or other aspects of model development. Those parties have an important role to play in the value chain towards the provider of the high-risk AI system into which their AI systems, tools, services, components or processes are integrated, and should provide by written agreement this provider with the necessary information, capabilities, technical access and other assistance based on the generally acknowledged state of the art, in order to enable the provider to fully comply with the obligations set out in this Regulation, without compromising their own intellectual property rights or trade secrets.

1041. **(89)** Third parties making accessible to the public tools, services, processes, or AI components other than general-purpose AI models, should not be mandated to comply with requirements targeting the responsibilities along the AI value chain, in particular towards the provider that has used or integrated them, when those tools, services, processes, or AI components are made accessible under a free and open-source licence. Developers of free and open-source tools, services, processes, or AI components other than general-purpose AI models should be encouraged to implement widely adopted documentation practices, such as model cards and data sheets, as a way to accelerate information sharing along the AI value chain, allowing the promotion of trustworthy AI systems in the Union.

1042. **(90)** The Commission could develop and recommend voluntary model contractual terms between providers of high-risk AI systems and third parties that supply tools, services, components or processes that are used or integrated in high-risk AI systems, to facilitate the cooperation along the value chain. When developing voluntary model contractual terms, the Commission should also take into account possible contractual requirements applicable in specific sectors or business cases.

1043. **(101)** Providers of general-purpose AI models have a particular role and responsibility along the AI value chain, as the models they provide may form the basis for a range of downstream systems, often provided by downstream providers that necessitate a good understanding of the models and their capabilities, both to enable the integration of such models into their products, and to fulfil their obligations under this or other regulations. Therefore, proportionate transparency measures should be laid down, including the drawing up and keeping up to date of documentation, and the provision of information on the general-purpose AI model for its usage by the downstream providers. Technical documentation should be prepared and kept up to date by the general-purpose AI model provider for the purpose of making it available, upon request, to the AI Office and the national competent authorities. The minimal set of elements to be included in such documentation should be set out in specific annexes to this Regulation. The Commission should be empowered to amend those annexes by means of delegated acts in light of evolving technological developments.

1044. **(109)** Compliance with the obligations applicable to the providers of general-purpose AI models should be commensurate and proportionate to the type of model provider, excluding the need for compliance for persons who develop or use models for non-professional or scientific research purposes, who should nevertheless be encouraged to voluntarily comply with these requirements. Without prejudice to Union copyright law, compliance with those obligations should take due account of the size of the provider and allow simplified ways of compliance for SMEs, including start-ups, that should not represent an excessive cost and not discourage the use of such models. In the case of a modification or fine-tuning of a model, the obligations for providers of general-purpose AI models should be limited to that modification or fine-tuning, for example by complementing the already existing technical documentation with information on the modifications, including new training data sources, as a means to comply with the value chain obligations provided in this Regulation.

1045. (114) The providers of general-purpose AI models presenting systemic risks should be subject, in addition to the obligations provided for providers of general-purpose AI models, to obligations aimed at identifying and mitigating those risks and ensuring an adequate level of cybersecurity protection, regardless of whether it is provided as a standalone model or embedded in an AI system or a product. To achieve those objectives, this Regulation should require providers to perform the necessary model evaluations, in particular prior to its first placing on the market, including conducting and documenting adversarial testing of models, also, as appropriate, through internal or independent external testing. In addition, providers of general-purpose AI models with systemic risks should continuously assess and mitigate systemic risks, including for example by putting in place risk-management policies, such as accountability and governance processes, implementing post-market monitoring, taking appropriate measures along the entire model's lifecycle and cooperating with relevant actors along the AI value chain.

1046. (135) Without prejudice to the mandatory nature and full applicability of the transparency obligations, the Commission may also encourage and facilitate the drawing up of codes of practice at Union level to facilitate the effective implementation of the obligations regarding the detection and labelling of artificially generated or manipulated content, including to support practical arrangements for making, as appropriate, the detection mechanisms accessible and facilitating cooperation with other actors along the value chain, disseminating content or checking its authenticity and provenance to enable the public to effectively distinguish AI-generated content.

25.2. General Approach

25.2.1 Preamble

1047. Each operator in the chain plays a role in maintaining trust despite potential risks.

1048. The term 'Responsibilities'[112] should be understood as being tasked with carrying out an action, rather than assuming the consequences of a non-compliance or failure to perform.[113]

[112] Something that it is your job or duty to deal with (Cambridge Dictionary).

[113] In the French version of the Regulation, the English term 'Responsibilities' has been translated into '*Responsabilités*'. However, a more accurate French equivalent would be '*Redevabilité*' in the sense of 'being responsible for the execution' or 'being in charge of execution'.

25.2.2 Guiding Principles

1049. Each organisation assumes the obligations associated with its status throughout the lifecycle of high-risk AI systems.

1050. However, this status can shift to that of a provider in the following cases:

- marketing without a distinct provider trademark;
- substantial modifications to the high-risk AI system.

25.3. Marketing

25.3.1 Conditions

1051. Any importer, distributor, or deployer will be considered to be a provider of a high-risk AI system if they market a high-risk AI system under their name or trademark after it was placed on the market or put into service, and they will therefore have new obligations.

25.3.2 Consequences

1052. In this case, the organisation concerned must implement the following obligations:

NO.	THEME	SPECIFICATION
1.	Obligations	All those referred to in Article 16 of the AIA, concerning the obligations of the provider
2.	Component	The same applies if the high-risk AI system is integrated under the name of the product provider
3.	Cooperation	Initial provider has an obligation to cooperate with the new provider
4.	National competent authority	Information and cooperation

25.4. Substantial Modifications

25.4.1 Conditions

1053. Any importer, distributor, or deployer will be considered to be a provider of a high-risk AI system if they make a substantial modification to that system.

25.4.2 Consequences

1054. In this case, the organisation concerned must implement the following obligations:

NO.	THEME	SPECIFICATION
1.	Obligations	All those referred to in Article 16 of the AIA, concerning the obligations of the provider
2.	Component	The same applies if the high-risk AI system is integrated under the name of the product provider
3.	Cooperation	Initial provider has an obligation to cooperate with the new provider
4.	National competent authority	Information and cooperation

26 ARTICLE 26. OBLIGATIONS OF DEPLOYERS OF HIGH-RISK AI SYSTEMS

1. Deployers of high-risk AI systems shall take appropriate technical and organisational measures to ensure they use such systems in accordance with the instructions for use accompanying the systems, pursuant to paragraphs 3 and 6.

2. Deployers shall assign human oversight to natural persons who have the necessary competence, training and authority, as well as the necessary support.

3. The obligations set out in paragraphs 1 and 2, are without prejudice to other deployer obligations under Union or national law and to the deployer's freedom to organise its own resources and activities for the purpose of implementing the human oversight measures indicated by the provider.

4. Without prejudice to paragraphs 1 and 2, to the extent the deployer exercises control over the input data, that deployer shall ensure that input data is relevant and sufficiently representative in view of the intended purpose of the high-risk AI system.

5. Deployers shall monitor the operation of the high-risk AI system on the basis of the instructions for use and, where relevant, inform providers in accordance with Article 72. Where deployers have reason to consider that the use of the high-risk AI system in accordance with the instructions may result in that AI system presenting a risk within the meaning of Article 79(1), they shall, without undue delay, inform the provider or distributor and the relevant market surveillance authority, and shall suspend the use of that system. Where deployers have identified a serious incident, they shall also immediately inform first the provider, and then the importer or distributor and the relevant market surveillance authorities of that incident. If the deployer is not able to reach the provider, Article 73 shall apply *mutatis mutandis*. This obligation shall not cover sensitive operational data of deployers of AI systems which are law enforcement authorities.

For deployers that are financial institutions subject to requirements regarding their internal governance, arrangements or processes under Union financial services law, the monitoring obligation set out in the first subparagraph shall be deemed to be fulfilled by complying with the rules on internal governance arrangements, processes and mechanisms pursuant to the relevant financial service law.

6. Deployers of high-risk AI systems shall keep the logs automatically generated by that high-risk AI system to the extent such logs are under their control, for a period appropriate to the intended purpose of the high-risk AI system, of at least six months, unless provided otherwise in applicable Union or national law, in particular in Union law on the protection of personal data.

Deployers that are financial institutions subject to requirements regarding their internal governance, arrangements or processes under Union financial services law shall maintain the logs as part of the documentation kept pursuant to the relevant Union financial service law.

7. Before putting into service or using a high-risk AI system at the workplace, deployers who are employers shall inform workers' representatives and the affected workers that they will be subject to the use of the high-risk AI system. This information shall be provided, where applicable, in accordance with the rules and procedures laid down in Union and national law and practice on information of workers and their representatives.

8. Deployers of high-risk AI systems that are public authorities, or Union institutions, bodies, offices or agencies shall comply with the registration obligations referred to in Article 49. When such deployers find that the high-risk AI system that they envisage using has not been registered in the EU database referred to in Article 71, they shall not use that system and shall inform the provider or the distributor.

9. Where applicable, deployers of high-risk AI systems shall use the information provided under Article 13 of this Regulation to comply with their obligation to carry out a data protection impact assessment under Article 35 of Regulation (EU) 2016/679 or Article 27 of Directive (EU) 2016/680.

10. Without prejudice to Directive (EU) 2016/680, in the framework of an investigation for the targeted search of a person suspected or convicted of having committed a criminal offence, the deployer of a high-risk AI system for post-remote biometric identification shall request an authorisation, ex ante, or without undue delay and no later than 48 hours, by a judicial authority or an administrative authority whose decision is binding and subject to judicial review, for the use of that system, except when it is used for the initial identification of a potential suspect based on objective and verifiable facts directly linked to the offence. Each use shall be limited to what is strictly necessary for the investigation of a specific criminal offence.

If the authorisation requested pursuant to the first subparagraph is rejected, the use of the post-remote biometric identification system linked to that requested authorisation shall be stopped with immediate effect and the personal data linked to the use of the high-risk AI system for which the authorisation was requested shall be deleted.

In no case shall such high-risk AI system for post-remote biometric identification be used for law enforcement purposes in an untargeted way, without any link to a criminal offence, a criminal proceeding, a genuine and present or genuine and foreseeable threat of a criminal offence, or the search for a specific missing person. It shall be ensured that no decision that produces an adverse legal effect on a person may be taken by the law enforcement authorities based solely on the output of such post-remote biometric identification systems.

This paragraph is without prejudice to Article 9 of Regulation (EU) 2016/679 and Article 10 of Directive (EU) 2016/680 for the processing of biometric data.

Regardless of the purpose or deployer, each use of such high-risk AI systems shall be documented in the relevant police file and shall be made available to the relevant market surveillance authority and the national data protection authority upon request, excluding the disclosure of sensitive operational data related to law enforcement. This subparagraph shall be without prejudice to the powers conferred by Directive (EU) 2016/680 on supervisory authorities.

Deployers shall submit annual reports to the relevant market surveillance and national data protection authorities on their use of post-remote biometric identification systems, excluding the disclosure of sensitive operational data related to law enforcement. The reports may be aggregated to cover more than one deployment.

Member States may introduce, in accordance with Union law, more restrictive laws on the use of post-remote biometric identification systems.

11. Without prejudice to Article 50 of this Regulation, deployers of high-risk AI systems referred to in Annex III that make decisions or assist in making decisions related to natural persons shall inform the natural persons that they are subject to the use of the high-risk AI system. For high-risk AI systems used for law enforcement purposes Article 13 of Directive (EU) 2016/680 shall apply.

12. Deployers shall cooperate with the relevant competent authorities in any action those authorities take in relation to the high-risk AI system in order to implement this Regulation.

26.1. Recitals

1055. **(10)** The fundamental right to the protection of personal data is safeguarded in particular by Regulations (EU) 2016/679[114] and (EU) 2018/1725[115] of the European Parliament and of the Council and Directive (EU) 2016/680 of the European Parliament and of the Council.[116] Directive 2002/58/EC of the European Parliament and of the Council[117] additionally protects private life and the confidentiality of communications, including by way of providing conditions for any storing of personal and non-personal data in, and access from, terminal equipment. Those Union legal acts provide the basis for sustainable and responsible data processing, including where data sets include a mix of personal and non-personal data. This Regulation does not seek to affect the application of existing Union law governing the processing of personal data, including the tasks and powers of the independent supervisory authorities competent to monitor compliance with those instruments

1056. It also does not affect the obligations of providers and deployers of AI systems in their role as data controllers or processors stemming from Union or national law on the protection of personal data in so far as the design, the development or the use of AI systems involves the processing of personal data. It is also appropriate to clarify that data subjects continue to enjoy all the rights and guarantees awarded to them by such Union law, including the rights related to solely automated individual decision-making, including profiling. Harmonised rules for the placing on the market, the putting into service and the use of AI systems established under this Regulation should facilitate the effective implementation and enable the exercise of the data subjects' rights and other

---

114 Regulation (EU) 2016/679 of the European Parliament and of the Council of 27 April 2016 on the protection of natural persons with regard to the processing of personal data and on the free movement of such data, and repealing Directive 95/46/EC (General Data Protection Regulation), [2016] OJ L119/1.

115 Regulation (EU) 2018/1725 of the European Parliament and of the Council of 23 October 2018 on the protection of natural persons with regard to the processing of personal data by the Union institutions, bodies, offices and agencies and on the free movement of such data, and repealing Regulation (EC) No 45/2001 and Decision No 1247/2002/EC, [2018] OJ L295/39.

116 Directive (EU) 2016/680 of the European Parliament and of the Council of 27 April 2016 on the protection of natural persons with regard to the processing of personal data by competent authorities for the purposes of the prevention, investigation, detection or prosecution of criminal offences or the execution of criminal penalties, and on the free movement of such data, and repealing Council Framework Decision 2008/977/JHA, [2016] OJ L119/89.

117 Directive 2002/58/EC of the European Parliament and of the Council of 12 July 2002 concerning the processing of personal data and the protection of privacy in the electronic communications sector (Directive on privacy and electronic communications), [2002] OJ L201/37.

remedies guaranteed under Union law on the protection of personal data and of other fundamental rights.

1057. **(33)** The use of those systems for the purpose of law enforcement should therefore be prohibited, except in exhaustively listed and narrowly defined situations, where the use is strictly necessary to achieve a substantial public interest, the importance of which outweighs the risks. Those situations involve the search for certain victims of crime including missing persons; certain threats to the life or to the physical safety of natural persons or of a terrorist attack; and the localisation or identification of perpetrators or suspects of the criminal offences listed in an annex to this Regulation, where those criminal offences are punishable in the Member State concerned by a custodial sentence or a detention order for a maximum period of at least four years and as they are defined in the law of that Member State. Such a threshold for the custodial sentence or detention order in accordance with national law contributes to ensuring that the offence should be serious enough to potentially justify the use of 'real-time' remote biometric identification systems. Moreover, the list of criminal offences provided in an annex to this Regulation is based on the 32 criminal offences listed in the Council Framework Decision 2002/584/JHA,[118] taking into account that some of those offences are, in practice, likely to be more relevant than others, in that the recourse to 'real-time' remote biometric identification could, foreseeably, be necessary and proportionate to highly varying degrees for the practical pursuit of the localisation or identification of a perpetrator or suspect of the different criminal offences listed and having regard to the likely differences in the seriousness, probability and scale of the harm or possible negative consequences.

1058. An imminent threat to life or the physical safety of natural persons could also result from a serious disruption of critical infrastructure, as defined in Article 2, point (4) of Directive (EU) 2022/2557 of the European Parliament and of the Council,[119] where the disruption or destruction of such critical infrastructure would result in an imminent threat to life or the physical safety of a person, including through serious harm to the provision of basic supplies to the population or to the exercise of the core function of the State. In addition, this Regulation should preserve the ability for law enforcement, border control, immigration or asylum authorities to carry out identity checks in the presence of the person concerned in accordance with the conditions set out in Union and national law for such checks. In particular, law enforcement, border control, immigration or asylum authorities should be able to use information systems,

118 Council Framework Decision 2002/584/JHA of 13 June 2002 on the European arrest warrant and the surrender procedures between Member States, [2002] OJ L190/1.

119 Directive (EU) 2022/2557 of the European Parliament and of the Council of 14 December 2022 on the resilience of critical entities and repealing Council Directive 2008/114/EC, [2022] OJ L333/164.

in accordance with Union or national law, to identify persons who, during an identity check, either refuse to be identified or are unable to state or prove their identity, without being required by this Regulation to obtain prior authorisation. This could be, for example, a person involved in a crime, being unwilling, or unable due to an accident or a medical condition, to disclose their identity to law enforcement authorities.

1059. (35) Each use of a 'real-time' remote biometric identification system in publicly accessible spaces for the purpose of law enforcement should be subject to an express and specific authorisation by a judicial authority or by an independent administrative authority of a Member State whose decision is binding. Such authorisation should, in principle, be obtained prior to the use of the AI system with a view to identifying a person or persons. Exceptions to that rule should be allowed in duly justified situations on grounds of urgency, namely in situations where the need to use the systems concerned is such as to make it effectively and objectively impossible to obtain an authorisation before commencing the use of the AI system. In such situations of urgency, the use of the AI system should be restricted to the absolute minimum necessary and should be subject to appropriate safeguards and conditions, as determined in national law and specified in the context of each individual urgent use case by the law enforcement authority itself. In addition, the law enforcement authority should in such situations request such authorisation while providing the reasons for not having been able to request it earlier, without undue delay and at the latest within 24 hours. If such an authorisation is rejected, the use of real-time biometric identification systems linked to that authorisation should cease with immediate effect and all the data related to such use should be discarded and deleted. Such data includes input data directly acquired by an AI system in the course of the use of such system as well as the results and outputs of the use linked to that authorisation. It should not include input that is legally acquired in accordance with another Union or national law. In any case, no decision producing an adverse legal effect on a person should be taken based solely on the output of the remote biometric identification system.

1060. (36) In order to carry out their tasks in accordance with the requirements set out in this Regulation as well as in national rules, the relevant market surveillance authority and the national data protection authority should be notified of each use of the real-time biometric identification system. Market surveillance authorities and the national data protection authorities that have been notified should submit to the Commission an annual report on the use of real-time biometric identification systems.

1061. (37) Furthermore, it is appropriate to provide, within the exhaustive framework set by this Regulation that such use in the territory of a Member State in accordance with this Regulation should only be possible where and in as far as the Member State concerned has decided to expressly provide for the possibility to authorise such use in its detailed rules of national law. Consequently, Member States remain free under this Regulation not to provide for such a possibility at all or to only provide for such a possibility in respect of some of the objectives capable of justifying authorised use identified in this Regulation. Such national rules should be notified to the Commission within 30 days of their adoption.

1062. **(59)** Given their role and responsibility, actions by law enforcement authorities involving certain uses of AI systems are characterised by a significant degree of power imbalance and may lead to surveillance, arrest or deprivation of a natural person's liberty as well as other adverse impacts on fundamental rights guaranteed in the Charter. In particular, if the AI system is not trained with high-quality data, does not meet adequate requirements in terms of its performance, its accuracy or robustness, or is not properly designed and tested before being put on the market or otherwise put into service, it may single out people in a discriminatory or otherwise incorrect or unjust manner. Furthermore, the exercise of important procedural fundamental rights, such as the right to an effective remedy and to a fair trial as well as the right of defence and the presumption of innocence, could be hampered, in particular, where such AI systems are not sufficiently transparent, explainable and documented. It is therefore appropriate to classify as high-risk, insofar as their use is permitted under relevant Union and national law, a number of AI systems intended to be used in the law enforcement context where accuracy, reliability and transparency is particularly important to avoid adverse impacts, retain public trust and ensure accountability and effective redress. In view of the nature of the activities and the risks relating thereto, those high-risk AI systems should include in particular AI systems intended to be used by or on behalf of law enforcement authorities or by Union institutions, bodies, offices, or agencies in support of law enforcement authorities for assessing the risk of a natural person to become a victim of criminal offences, as polygraphs and similar tools, for the evaluation of the reliability of evidence in in the course of investigation or prosecution of criminal offences, and, insofar as not prohibited under this Regulation, for assessing the risk of a natural person offending or reoffending not solely on the basis of the profiling of natural persons or the assessment of personality traits and characteristics or the past criminal behaviour of natural persons or groups, for profiling in the course of detection, investigation or prosecution of criminal offences. AI systems specifically intended to be used for administrative proceedings by tax and customs authorities as well as by financial intelligence units carrying out administrative tasks analysing information pursuant to Union anti-money laundering law should not be classified as high-risk AI systems used by law enforcement authorities for the purpose of prevention, detection, investigation and prosecution of criminal offences. The use of AI tools by law enforcement and other relevant authorities should not become a factor of inequality, or exclusion. The impact of the use of AI tools on the defence rights of suspects should not be ignored, in particular the difficulty in obtaining meaningful information on the functioning of those systems and the resulting difficulty in challenging their results in court, in particular by natural persons under investigation.

1063. (72) To address concerns related to opacity and complexity of certain AI systems and help deployers to fulfil their obligations under this Regulation, transparency should be required for high-risk AI systems before they are placed on the market or put it into service. High-risk AI systems should be designed in a manner to enable deployers to understand how the AI system works, evaluate its functionality, and comprehend its strengths and limitations. High-risk AI systems should be accompanied by appropriate information in the form of instructions of use. Such information should include the characteristics, capabilities and limitations of performance of the AI system. Those would cover information on possible known and foreseeable circumstances related to the use of the high-risk AI system, including deployer action that may influence system behaviour and performance, under which the AI system can lead to risks to health, safety, and fundamental rights, on the changes that have been pre-determined and assessed for conformity by the provider and on the relevant human oversight measures, including the measures to facilitate the interpretation of the outputs of the AI system by the deployers. Transparency, including the accompanying instructions for use, should assist deployers in the use of the system and support informed decision making by them. Deployers should, inter alia, be in a better position to make the correct choice of the system that they intend to use in light of the obligations applicable to them, be educated about the intended and precluded uses, and use the AI system correctly and as appropriate. In order to enhance legibility and accessibility of the information included in the instructions of use, where appropriate, illustrative examples, for instance on the limitations and on the intended and precluded uses of the AI system, should be included. Providers should ensure that all documentation, including the instructions for use, contains meaningful, comprehensive, accessible and understandable information, taking into account the needs and foreseeable knowledge of the target deployers. Instructions for use should be made available in a language which can be easily understood by target deployers, as determined by the Member State concerned.

1064. (73) High-risk AI systems should be designed and developed in such a way that natural persons can oversee their functioning, ensure that they are used as intended and that their impacts are addressed over the system's lifecycle. To that end, appropriate human oversight measures should be identified by the provider of the system before its placing on the market or putting into service. In particular, where appropriate, such measures should guarantee that the system is subject to in-built operational constraints that cannot be overridden by the system itself and is responsive to the human operator, and that the natural persons to whom human oversight has been assigned have the necessary competence, training and authority to carry out that role. It is also essential, as appropriate, to ensure that high-risk AI systems include mechanisms to guide and inform a natural person to whom human oversight has been assigned to make informed decisions if, when and how to intervene in order to avoid negative consequences or risks, or stop the system if it does not perform as intended. Considering the significant consequences for persons in the case of an incorrect match by certain biometric identification systems, it is appropriate to provide for an enhanced human oversight requirement for those systems so that no action or decision may be taken by the deployer on the basis of the identification resulting from the system unless this has been separately verified and confirmed by at least two natural persons. Those persons could be from one or more entities and include the person operating or using the system. This requirement should not pose unnecessary burden or delays and it could be sufficient that the separate verifications by the different persons are automatically recorded in the logs generated by the system. Given the specificities of the areas of law enforcement, migration, border control and asylum, this requirement should not apply where Union or national law considers the application of that requirement to be disproportionate.

1065. **(84)** To ensure legal certainty, it is necessary to clarify that, under certain specific conditions, any distributor, importer, deployer or other third-party should be considered to be a provider of a high-risk AI system and therefore assume all the relevant obligations. This would be the case if that party puts its name or trademark on a high-risk AI system already placed on the market or put into service, without prejudice to contractual arrangements stipulating that the obligations are allocated otherwise. This would also be the case if that party makes a substantial modification to a high-risk AI system that has already been placed on the market or has already been put into service in a way that it remains a high-risk AI system in accordance with this Regulation, or if it modifies the intended purpose of an AI system, including a general-purpose AI system, which has not been classified as high-risk and has already been placed on the market or put into service, in a way that the AI system becomes a high-risk AI system in accordance with this Regulation. Those provisions should apply without prejudice to more specific provisions established in certain Union harmonisation legislation based on the New Legislative Framework, together with which this Regulation should apply. For example, Article 16(2) of Regulation (EU) 2017/745, establishing that certain changes should not be considered to be modifications of a device that could affect its compliance with the applicable requirements, should continue to apply to high-risk AI systems that are medical devices within the meaning of that Regulation.

1066. **(91)** Given the nature of AI systems and the risks to safety and fundamental rights possibly associated with their use, including as regards the need to ensure proper monitoring of the performance of an AI system in a real-life setting, it is appropriate to set specific responsibilities for deployers. Deployers should in particular take appropriate technical and organisational measures to ensure they use high-risk AI systems in accordance with the instructions of use and certain other obligations should be provided for with regard to monitoring of the functioning of the AI systems and with regard to record-keeping, as appropriate. Furthermore, deployers should ensure that the persons assigned to implement the instructions for use and human oversight as set out in this Regulation have the necessary competence, in particular an adequate level of AI literacy, training and authority to properly fulfil those tasks. Those obligations should be without prejudice to other deployer obligations in relation to high-risk AI systems under Union or national law.

1067. **(93)** Whilst risks related to AI systems can result from the way such systems are designed, risks can as well stem from how such AI systems are used. Deployers of high-risk AI system therefore play a critical role in ensuring that fundamental rights are protected, complementing the obligations of the provider when developing the AI system. Deployers are best placed to understand how the high-risk AI system will be used concretely and can therefore identify potential significant risks that were not foreseen in the development phase, due to a more precise knowledge of the context of use, the persons or groups of persons likely to be affected, including vulnerable groups. Deployers of high-risk AI systems listed in an annex to this Regulation also play a critical role in informing natural persons and should, when they make decisions or assist in making decisions related to natural persons, where applicable, inform the natural persons that they are subject to the use of the high-risk AI system. This information should include the intended purpose and the type of decisions it makes. The deployer should also inform the natural persons about their right to an explanation provided under this Regulation. With regard to high-risk AI systems used for law enforcement purposes, that obligation should be implemented in accordance with Article 13 of Directive (EU) 2016/680.

1068. **(95)** Without prejudice to applicable Union law, in particular Regulation (EU) 2016/679 and Directive (EU) 2016/680, considering the intrusive nature of post-remote biometric identification systems, the use of post-remote biometric identification systems should be subject to safeguards. Post-remote biometric identification systems should always be used in a way that is proportionate, legitimate and strictly necessary, and thus targeted, in terms of the individuals to be identified, the location, temporal scope and based on a closed data set of legally acquired video footage. In any case, post-remote biometric identification systems should not be used in the framework of law enforcement to lead to indiscriminate surveillance. The conditions for post-remote biometric identification should in any case not provide a basis to circumvent the conditions of the prohibition and strict exceptions for real time remote biometric identification.

1069. **(96)** In order to efficiently ensure that fundamental rights are protected, deployers of high-risk AI systems that are bodies governed by public law, or private entities providing public services and deployers of certain high-risk AI systems listed in an annex to this Regulation, such as banking or insurance entities, should carry out a fundamental rights impact assessment prior to putting it into use. Services important for individuals that are of public nature may also be provided by private entities. Private entities providing such public services are linked to tasks in the public interest such as in the areas of education, healthcare, social services, housing, administration of justice. The aim of the fundamental rights impact assessment is for the deployer to identify the specific risks to the rights of individuals or groups of individuals likely to be affected, identify measures to be taken in the case of a materialisation of those risks. The impact assessment should be performed prior to deploying the high-risk AI system, and should be updated when the deployer considers that any of the relevant factors have changed. The impact assessment should identify the deployer's relevant processes in which the high-risk AI system will be used in line with its intended purpose, and should include a description of the period of time and frequency in which the system is intended to be used as well as of specific categories of natural persons and groups who are likely to be affected in the specific context of use. The assessment should also include the identification of specific risks of harm likely to have an impact on the fundamental rights of those persons or groups. While performing this assessment, the deployer should take into account information relevant to a proper assessment of the impact, including but not limited to the information given by the provider of the high-risk AI system in the instructions for use. In light of the risks identified, deployers should determine measures to be taken in the case of a materialisation of those risks, including for example governance arrangements in that specific context of use, such as arrangements for human oversight according to the instructions of use or, complaint handling and redress procedures, as they could be instrumental in mitigating risks to fundamental rights in concrete use-cases. After performing that impact assessment, the deployer should notify the relevant market surveillance authority. Where appropriate, to collect relevant information necessary to perform the impact assessment, deployers of high-risk AI system, in particular when AI systems are used in the public sector, could involve relevant stakeholders, including the representatives of groups of persons likely to be affected by the AI system, independent experts, and civil society organisations in conducting such impact assessments and designing measures to be taken in the case of materialisation of the risks. The European Artificial Intelligence Office (AI Office) should develop a template for a questionnaire in order to facilitate compliance and reduce the administrative burden for deployers.

1070. (120) Furthermore, obligations placed on providers and deployers of certain AI systems in this Regulation to enable the detection and disclosure that the outputs of those systems are artificially generated or manipulated are particularly relevant to facilitate the effective implementation of Regulation (EU) 2022/2065. This applies in particular as regards the obligations of providers of very large online platforms or very large online search engines to identify and mitigate systemic risks that may arise from the dissemination of content that has been artificially generated or manipulated, in particular risk of the actual or foreseeable negative effects on democratic processes, civic discourse and electoral processes, including through disinformation.

1071. **(131)** In order to facilitate the work of the Commission and the Member States in the AI field as well as to increase the transparency towards the public, providers of high-risk AI systems other than those related to products falling within the scope of relevant existing Union harmonisation legislation, as well as providers who consider that an AI system listed in the high-risk use cases in an annex to this Regulation is not high-risk on the basis of a derogation, should be required to register themselves and information about their AI system in an EU database, to be established and managed by the Commission. Before using an AI system listed in the high-risk use cases in an annex to this Regulation, deployers of high-risk AI systems that are public authorities, agencies or bodies, should register themselves in such database and select the system that they envisage to use. Other deployers should be entitled to do so voluntarily. This section of the EU database should be publicly accessible, free of charge, the information should be easily navigable, understandable and machine-readable. The EU database should also be user-friendly, for example by providing search functionalities, including through keywords, allowing the general public to find relevant information to be submitted upon the registration of high-risk AI systems and on the use case of high-risk AI systems, set out in an annex to this Regulation, to which the high-risk AI systems correspond. Any substantial modification of high-risk AI systems should also be registered in the EU database. For high-risk AI systems in the area of law enforcement, migration, asylum and border control management, the registration obligations should be fulfilled in a secure non-public section of the EU database. Access to the secure non-public section should be strictly limited to the Commission as well as to market surveillance authorities with regard to their national section of that database. High-risk AI systems in the area of critical infrastructure should only be registered at national level. The Commission should be the controller of the EU database, in accordance with Regulation (EU) 2018/1725. In order to ensure the full functionality of the EU database, when deployed, the procedure for setting the database should include the development of functional specifications by the Commission and an independent audit report. The Commission should take into account cybersecurity risks when carrying out its tasks as data controller on the EU database. In order to maximise the availability and use of the EU database by the public, the EU database, including the information made available through it, should comply with requirements under the Directive (EU) 2019/882.

1072. **(134)** Further to the technical solutions employed by the providers of the AI system, deployers who use an AI system to generate or manipulate image, audio or video content that appreciably resembles existing persons, objects, places, entities or events and would falsely appear to a person to be authentic or truthful (deep fakes), should also clearly and distinguishably disclose that the content has been artificially created or manipulated by labelling the AI output accordingly and disclosing its artificial origin. Compliance with this transparency obligation should not be interpreted as indicating that the use of the AI system or its output impedes the right to freedom of expression and the right to freedom of the arts and sciences guaranteed in the Charter, in particular where the content is part of an evidently creative, satirical, artistic, fictional or analogous work or programme, subject to appropriate safeguards for the rights and freedoms of third parties. In those cases, the transparency obligation for deep fakes set out in this Regulation is limited to disclosure of the existence of such generated or manipulated content in an appropriate manner that does not hamper the display or enjoyment of the work, including its normal exploitation and use, while maintaining the utility and quality of the work. In addition, it is also appropriate to envisage a similar disclosure obligation in relation to AI-generated or manipulated text to the extent it is published with the purpose of informing the public on matters of public interest unless the AI-generated content has undergone a process of human review or editorial control and a natural or legal person holds editorial responsibility for the publication of the content.

1073. (136) The obligations placed on providers and deployers of certain AI systems in this Regulation to enable the detection and disclosure that the outputs of those systems are artificially generated or manipulated are particularly relevant to facilitate the effective implementation of Regulation (EU) 2022/2065. This applies in particular as regards the obligations of providers of very large online platforms or very large online search engines to identify and mitigate systemic risks that may arise from the dissemination of content that has been artificially generated or manipulated, in particular the risk of the actual or foreseeable negative effects on democratic processes, civic discourse and electoral processes, including through disinformation. The requirement to label content generated by AI systems under this Regulation is without prejudice to the obligation in Article 16(6) of Regulation (EU) 2022/2065 for providers of hosting services to process notices on illegal content received pursuant to Article 16(1) of that Regulation and should not influence the assessment and the decision on the illegality of the specific content. That assessment should be performed solely with reference to the rules governing the legality of the content.

1074. (137) Compliance with the transparency obligations for the AI systems covered by this Regulation should not be interpreted as indicating that the use of the AI system or its output is lawful under this Regulation or other Union and Member State law and should be without prejudice to other transparency obligations for deployers of AI systems laid down in Union or national law.

1075. (141) In order to accelerate the process of development and the placing on the market of the high-risk AI systems listed in an annex to this Regulation, it is important that providers or prospective providers of such systems may also benefit from a specific regime for testing those systems in real world conditions, without participating in an AI regulatory sandbox. However, in such cases, taking into account the possible consequences of such testing on individuals, it should be ensured that appropriate and sufficient guarantees and conditions are introduced by this Regulation for providers or prospective providers. Such guarantees should include, inter alia, requesting informed consent of natural persons to participate in testing in real world conditions, with the exception of law enforcement where the seeking of informed consent would prevent the AI system from being tested. Consent of subjects to participate in such testing under this Regulation is distinct from, and without prejudice to, consent of data subjects for the processing of their personal data under the relevant data protection law. It is also important to minimise the risks and enable oversight by competent authorities and therefore require prospective providers to have a real-world testing plan submitted to competent market surveillance authority, register the testing in dedicated sections in the EU database subject to some limited exceptions, set limitations on the period for which the testing can be done and require additional safeguards for persons belonging to certain vulnerable groups, as well as a written agreement defining the roles and responsibilities of prospective providers and deployers and effective oversight by competent personnel involved in the real world testing. Furthermore, it is appropriate to envisage additional safeguards to ensure that the predictions, recommendations or decisions of the AI system can be effectively reversed and disregarded and that personal data is protected and is deleted when the subjects have withdrawn their consent to participate in the testing without prejudice to their rights as data subjects under the Union data protection law. As regards transfer of data, it is also appropriate to envisage that data collected and processed for the purpose of testing in real-world conditions should be transferred to third countries only where appropriate and applicable safeguards under Union law are implemented, in particular in accordance with bases for transfer of personal data under Union law on data protection, while for non-personal data appropriate safeguards are put in place in accordance with Union law, such as Regulations (EU) 2022/868[120] and (EU) 2023/2854[121] of the European Parliament and of the Council.

---

120 Regulation (EU) 2022/868 of the European Parliament and of the Council of 30 May 2022 on European data governance and amending Regulation (EU) 2018/1724 (Data Governance Act), [2022] OJ L152/1.

121 Regulation (EU) 2023/2854 of the European Parliament and of the Council of 13 December 2023 on harmonised rules on fair access to and use of data and amending Regulation (EU) 2017/2394 and Directive (EU) 2020/1828 (Data Act), [2023] OJ L, 2023/2854.

1076. (143) In order to promote and protect innovation, it is important that the interests of SMEs, including start-ups, that are providers or deployers of AI systems are taken into particular account. To that end, Member States should develop initiatives, which are targeted at those operators, including on awareness raising and information communication. Member States should provide SMEs, including start-ups, that have a registered office or a branch in the Union, with priority access to the AI regulatory sandboxes provided that they fulfil the eligibility conditions and selection criteria and without precluding other providers and prospective providers to access the sandboxes provided the same conditions and criteria are fulfilled. Member States should utilise existing channels and where appropriate, establish new dedicated channels for communication with SMEs, including start-ups, deployers, other innovators and, as appropriate, local public authorities, to support SMEs throughout their development path by providing guidance and responding to queries about the implementation of this Regulation. Where appropriate, these channels should work together to create synergies and ensure homogeneity in their guidance to SMEs, including start-ups, and deployers. Additionally, Member States should facilitate the participation of SMEs and other relevant stakeholders in the standardisation development processes. Moreover, the specific interests and needs of providers that are SMEs, including start-ups, should be taken into account when notified bodies set conformity assessment fees. The Commission should regularly assess the certification and compliance costs for SMEs, including start-ups, through transparent consultations and should work with Member States to lower such costs. For example, translation costs related to mandatory documentation and communication with authorities may constitute a significant cost for providers and other operators, in particular those of a smaller scale. Member States should possibly ensure that one of the languages determined and accepted by them for relevant providers' documentation and for communication with operators is one which is broadly understood by the largest possible number of cross-border deployers. In order to address the specific needs of SMEs, including start-ups, the Commission should provide standardised templates for the areas covered by this Regulation, upon request of the Board. Additionally, the Commission should complement Member States' efforts by providing a single information platform with easy-to-use information with regards to this Regulation for all providers and deployers, by organising appropriate communication campaigns to raise awareness about the obligations arising from this Regulation, and by evaluating and promoting the convergence of best practices in public procurement procedures in relation to AI systems. Medium-sized enterprises which until recently qualified as small enterprises within the meaning of the Annex to Commission Recommendation 2003/361/EC[122] should have access to

[122] Commission Recommendation of 6 May 2003 concerning the definition of micro, small and medium-sized enterprises, [2003] OJ L124/36.

those support measures, as those new medium-sized enterprises may sometimes lack the legal resources and training necessary to ensure proper understanding of, and compliance with, this Regulation.

1077. (158) Union financial services law includes internal governance and risk-management rules and requirements which are applicable to regulated financial institutions in the course of provision of those services, including when they make use of AI systems. In order to ensure coherent application and enforcement of the obligations under this Regulation and relevant rules and requirements of the Union financial services legal acts, the competent authorities for the supervision and enforcement of those legal acts, in particular competent authorities as defined in Regulation (EU) No 575/2013 of the European Parliament and of the Council[123] and Directives 2008/48/EC,[124] 2009/138/EC,[125] 2013/36/EU,[126] 2014/17/EU[127] and (EU) 2016/97[128] of the European Parliament and of the Council, should be designated, within their respective competences, as competent authorities for the purpose of supervising the implementation of this Regulation, including for market surveillance activities, as regards AI systems provided or used by regulated and supervised financial institutions unless Member States decide to designate another authority to fulfil these market surveillance tasks. Those competent authorities should have all powers under this Regulation and Regulation (EU) 2019/1020 to enforce the requirements and obligations of this Regulation, including powers to carry our *ex post* market surveillance activities that can be integrated, as appropriate, into their existing supervisory mechanisms and procedures under the relevant Union financial services law. It is appropriate to envisage that, when acting as market surveillance authorities under this Regulation, the national authorities responsible for the supervision of credit institutions regulated under Directive 2013/36/EU,

---

[123] Regulation (EU) No 575/2013 of the European Parliament and of the Council of 26 June 2013 on prudential requirements for credit institutions and investment firms and amending Regulation (EU) No 648/2012, [2013] OJ L176/1.

[124] Directive 2008/48/EC of the European Parliament and of the Council of 23 April 2008 on credit agreements for consumers and repealing Council Directive 87/102/EEC, [2008] OJ L133/66.

[125] Directive 2009/138/EC of the European Parliament and of the Council of 25 November 2009 on the taking-up and pursuit of the business of Insurance and Reinsurance (Solvency II), [2009] OJ L335/1.

[126] Directive 2013/36/EU of the European Parliament and of the Council of 26 June 2013 on access to the activity of credit institutions and the prudential supervision of credit institutions and investment firms, amending Directive 2002/87/EC and repealing Directives 2006/48/EC and 2006/49/EC, [2013] OJ L176/338.

[127] Directive 2014/17/EU of the European Parliament and of the Council of 4 February 2014 on credit agreements for consumers relating to residential immovable property and amending Directives 2008/48/EC and 2013/36/EU and Regulation (EU) No 1093/2010, [2014] OJ L60/34.

[128] Directive (EU) 2016/97 of the European Parliament and of the Council of 20 January 2016 on insurance distribution, [2016] OJ L26/19.

which are participating in the Single Supervisory Mechanism established by Council Regulation (EU) No 1024/2013,[129] should report, without delay, to the European Central Bank any information identified in the course of their market surveillance activities that may be of potential interest for the European Central Bank's prudential supervisory tasks as specified in that Regulation. To further enhance the consistency between this Regulation and the rules applicable to credit institutions regulated under Directive 2013/36/EU, it is also appropriate to integrate some of the providers' procedural obligations in relation to risk management, post marketing monitoring and documentation into the existing obligations and procedures under Directive 2013/36/EU. In order to avoid overlaps, limited derogations should also be envisaged in relation to the quality management system of providers and the monitoring obligation placed on deployers of high-risk AI systems to the extent that these apply to credit institutions regulated by Directive 2013/36/EU. The same regime should apply to insurance and re-insurance undertakings and insurance holding companies under Directive 2009/138/EC and the insurance intermediaries under Directive (EU) 2016/97 and other types of financial institutions subject to requirements regarding internal governance, arrangements or processes established pursuant to the relevant Union financial services law to ensure consistency and equal treatment in the financial sector.

26.2. General Approach

26.2.1 Preamble

1078. The final link in the chain is equally involved in maintaining trust.

26.2.2 Guiding Principles

1079. 'Deployer' means 'a natural or legal person, public authority, agency or other body using an AI system under its authority except where the AI system is used in the course of a personal non-professional activity'.[130]

1080. The deployer must use the system in a way that maintains risks at the initial level determined by the provider before it was placed on the market.

---

129 Council Regulation (EU) No 1024/2013 of 15 October 2013 conferring specific tasks on the European Central Bank concerning policies relating to the prudential supervision of credit institutions, [2013] OJ L287/63.

130 AI Act, Art. 3(4).

26.3. Obligations

1081. They are as follows:

NO.	THEME	SPECIFICATION
1.	Guarantee	Technical and organisational measures to keep the high-risk AI system within the sphere of conformity
2.	Human oversight	Application of requirements
3.	Data	Accurate and relevant
4.	Monitoring	In accordance with the instructions for use
5.	Information	In the event of risk: all persons upstream
6.	Incident	Obligation to intervene
7.	Logs	Archiving and traceability of logs under its responsibility
8.	Impact assessment	Transparency and information

27 ARTICLE 27. FUNDAMENTAL RIGHTS IMPACT ASSESSMENT FOR HIGH-RISK AI SYSTEMS

1. Prior to deploying a high-risk AI system referred to in Article 6(2), with the exception of high-risk AI systems intended to be used in the area listed in point 2 of Annex III, deployers that are bodies governed by public law, or are private entities providing public services, and deployers of high-risk AI systems referred to in points 5 (b) and (c) of Annex III, shall perform an assessment of the impact on fundamental rights that the use of such system may produce. For that purpose, deployers shall perform an assessment consisting of:

(a) a description of the deployer's processes in which the high-risk AI system will be used in line with its intended purpose;

(b) a description of the period of time within which, and the frequency with which, each high-risk AI system is intended to be used;

(c) the categories of natural persons and groups likely to be affected by its use in the specific context;

(d) the specific risks of harm likely to have an impact on the categories of natural persons or groups of persons identified pursuant to point (c) of this paragraph, taking into account the information given by the provider pursuant to Article 13;

(e) a description of the implementation of human oversight measures, according to the instructions for use;

(f) the measures to be taken in the case of the materialisation of those risks, including the arrangements for internal governance and complaint mechanisms.

2. The obligation laid down in paragraph 1 applies to the first use of the high-risk AI system. The deployer may, in similar cases, rely on previously conducted fundamental rights impact assessments or existing impact assessments carried out by provider. If, during the use of the high-risk AI system, the deployer considers that any of the elements listed in paragraph 1 has changed or is no longer up to date, the deployer shall take the necessary steps to update the information.

3. Once the assessment referred to in paragraph 1 of this Article has been performed, the deployer shall notify the market surveillance authority of its results, submitting the filled-out template referred to in paragraph 5 of this Article as part of the notification. In the case referred to in Article 46(1), deployers may be exempt from that obligation to notify.

4. If any of the obligations laid down in this Article is already met through the data protection impact assessment conducted pursuant to Article 35 of Regulation (EU) 2016/679 or Article 27 of Directive (EU) 2016/680, the fundamental rights impact assessment referred to in paragraph 1 of this Article shall complement that data protection impact assessment.

5. The AI Office shall develop a template for a questionnaire, including through an automated tool, to facilitate deployers in complying with their obligations under this Article in a simplified manner.

27.1. Recitals

1082. (34) In order to ensure that those systems are used in a responsible and proportionate manner, it is also important to establish that, in each of those exhaustively listed and narrowly defined situations, certain elements should be taken into account, in particular as regards the nature of the situation giving rise to the request and the consequences of the use for the rights and freedoms of all persons concerned and the safeguards and conditions provided for with the use. In addition, the use of 'real-time' remote biometric identification systems in publicly accessible spaces for the purpose of law enforcement should be deployed only to confirm the specifically targeted individual's identity and should be limited to what is strictly necessary concerning the period of time, as well as the geographic and personal scope, having regard in particular to the evidence or indications regarding the threats, the victims or perpetrator. The use of the real-time remote biometric identification system in publicly accessible spaces should be authorised only if the relevant law enforcement authority has completed a fundamental rights impact assessment and, unless provided otherwise in this Regulation, has registered the system in the database as set out in this Regulation.

The reference database of persons should be appropriate for each use case in each of the situations mentioned above.

1083. (96) In order to efficiently ensure that fundamental rights are protected, deployers of high-risk AI systems that are bodies governed by public law, or private entities providing public services and deployers of certain high-risk AI systems listed in an annex to this Regulation, such as banking or insurance entities, should carry out a fundamental rights impact assessment prior to putting it into use. Services important for individuals that are of public nature may also be provided by private entities. Private entities providing such public services are linked to tasks in the public interest such as in the areas of education, healthcare, social services, housing, administration of justice. The aim of the fundamental rights impact assessment is for the deployer to identify the specific risks to the rights of individuals or groups of individuals likely to be affected, identify measures to be taken in the case of a materialisation of those risks. The impact assessment should be performed prior to deploying the high-risk AI system, and should be updated when the deployer considers that any of the relevant factors have changed. The impact assessment should identify the deployer's relevant processes in which the high-risk AI system will be used in line with its intended purpose, and should include a description of the period of time and frequency in which the system is intended to be used as well as of specific categories of natural persons and groups who are likely to be affected in the specific context of use. The assessment should also include the identification of specific risks of harm likely to have an impact on the fundamental rights of those persons or groups. While performing this assessment, the deployer should take into account information relevant to a proper assessment of the impact, including but not limited to the information given by the provider of the high-risk AI system in the instructions for use. In light of the risks identified, deployers should determine measures to be taken in the case of a materialisation of those risks, including for example governance arrangements in that specific context of use, such as arrangements for human oversight according to the instructions of use or, complaint handling and redress procedures, as they could be instrumental in mitigating risks to fundamental rights in concrete use-cases. After performing that impact assessment, the deployer should notify the relevant market surveillance authority. Where appropriate, to collect relevant information necessary to perform the impact assessment, deployers of high-risk AI system, in particular when AI systems are used in the public sector, could involve relevant stakeholders, including the representatives of groups of persons likely to be affected by the AI system, independent experts, and civil society organisations in conducting such impact assessments and designing measures to be taken in the case of materialisation of the risks. The European Artificial Intelligence Office (AI Office) should develop a template for a questionnaire in order to facilitate compliance and reduce the administrative burden for deployers.

27.2. General Approach

27.2.1 Preamble

1084. The purpose of the impact assessment is to manage risks during the use phase.

27.2.2 Guiding Principles

1085. This obligation is limited according to the following criteria:
- the deployer's legal status;
- the nature of the activities.

27.3. Stakeholders Acting as Deployers

1086. These include:
- bodies governed by public law;
- private entities providing public services;
- deployers s of high-risk AI systems in the following areas:
  - AI systems intended to be used to evaluate the creditworthiness of natural persons or establish their credit score, with the exception of AI systems used for the purpose of detecting financial fraud;[131]
  - AI systems intended to be used for risk assessment and pricing in relation to natural persons in the case of life and health insurance.[132]

27.4. Activities

1087. The impact assessment covers the deployment phase in a body or entity, and the implementation phase by end users.

27.5. Composition

1088. The impact assessment includes the following requirements

NO.	THEME	SPECIFICATION
1.	Impact	Only on fundamental rights, not health, safety, environmental protection, the rule of law or democracy
2.	Process	Use cases

[131] AI Act, Annex III, 5(b).
[132] AI Act, Annex III, 5(c).

NO.	THEME	SPECIFICATION
3.	Duration	Period and frequency of use
4.	Natural persons	Persons or group of persons concerned in the specific context of use
5.	Assessment	Associated risks and harm
6.	Human oversight	Preventive measures and conditions of implementation
7.	Reaction plan	Measures to be taken in the case of the materialisation of the risk Mechanism for implementing internal governance Internal complaints mechanism

27.6. Application

1089. The conditions for implementation are as follows:

NO.	THEME	SPECIFICATION
1.	Period	First use
2.	Cooperation	Notification of results to the national competent authority
3.	Exemption	Derogation by special authority of the national competent authority[133]
4.	Complementarity	Combination with data protection impact assessment[134]
5.	Template	Questionnaires and tools developed by the AI Office

SECTION 4. NOTIFYING AUTHORITIES AND NOTIFIED BODIES

28 ARTICLE 28. NOTIFYING AUTHORITIES

1. Each Member State shall designate or establish at least one notifying authority responsible for setting up and carrying out the necessary procedures for the assessment, designation and notification of conformity assessment bodies and for their monitoring. Those procedures shall be developed in cooperation between the notifying authorities of all Member States.

133 AI Act, Art. 46(1).
134 GDPR (EU) 2016/679, Art. 35.

> **2.** Member States may decide that the assessment and monitoring referred to in paragraph 1 is to be carried out by a national accreditation body within the meaning of, and in accordance with, Regulation (EC) No 765/2008.
>
> **3.** Notifying authorities shall be established, organised and operated in such a way that No conflict of interest arises with conformity assessment bodies, and that the objectivity and impartiality of their activities are safeguarded.
>
> **4.** Notifying authorities shall be organised in such a way that decisions relating to the notification of conformity assessment bodies are taken by competent persons different from those who carried out the assessment of those bodies.
>
> **5.** Notifying authorities shall offer or provide neither any activities that conformity assessment bodies perform, nor any consultancy services on a commercial or competitive basis.
>
> **6.** Notifying authorities shall safeguard the confidentiality of the information that they obtain, in accordance with Article 78.
>
> **7.** Notifying authorities shall have an adequate number of competent personnel at their disposal for the proper performance of their tasks. Competent personnel shall have the necessary expertise, where applicable, for their function, in fields such as information technologies, AI and law, including the supervision of fundamental rights.

28.1. Recitals

1090. (153) Member States hold a key role in the application and enforcement of this Regulation. In that respect, each Member State should designate at least one notifying authority and at least one market surveillance authority as national competent authorities for the purpose of supervising the application and implementation of this Regulation. Member States may decide to appoint any kind of public entity to perform the tasks of the national competent authorities within the meaning of this Regulation, in accordance with their specific national organisational characteristics and needs. In order to increase organisation efficiency on the side of Member States and to set a single point of contact vis-à-vis the public and other counterparts at Member State and Union levels, each Member State should designate a market surveillance authority to act as a single point of contact.

28.2. General Approach

28.2.1 Preamble

1091. The management of risks associated with high-risk AI systems is based on a certification mechanism organised at two levels:

- notifying authorities;
- notified bodies.

28.2.2 Guiding Principles

1092. The chain of trust and risk management are founded on the following three pillars:

28.3. Definition

1093. 'Notifying authority' means 'the national authority responsible for setting up and carrying out the necessary procedures for the assessment, designation and notification of conformity assessment bodies and for their monitoring'.[135]

28.4. Characteristics

1094. They are as follows:

NO.	THEME	SPECIFICATION
1.	Designation	Member States
2.	Number	At least one
3.	Accreditation	Option left to Member States
4.	Conflicts of interest	No link with notified bodies No commercial interests
5.	Quality	Objectivity Impartiality
6.	Confidentiality	Protection
7.	Expertise	Technical and legal

135 AI Act, Art. 3(19).

29 ARTICLE 29. APPLICATION OF A CONFORMITY ASSESSMENT BODY FOR NOTIFICATION

1. Conformity assessment bodies shall submit an application for notification to the notifying authority of the Member State in which they are established.

2. The application for notification shall be accompanied by a description of the conformity assessment activities, the conformity assessment module or modules and the types of AI systems for which the conformity assessment body claims to be competent, as well as by an accreditation certificate, where one exists, issued by a national accreditation body attesting that the conformity assessment body fulfils the requirements laid down in Article 31.

Any valid document related to existing designations of the applicant notified body under any other Union harmonisation legislation shall be added.

3. Where the conformity assessment body concerned cannot provide an accreditation certificate, it shall provide the notifying authority with all the documentary evidence necessary for the verification, recognition and regular monitoring of its compliance with the requirements laid down in Article 31.

4. For notified bodies which are designated under any other Union harmonisation legislation, all documents and certificates linked to those designations may be used to support their designation procedure under this Regulation, as appropriate. The notified body shall update the documentation referred to in paragraphs 2 and 3 of this Article whenever relevant changes occur, in order to enable the authority responsible for notified bodies to monitor and verify continuous compliance with all the requirements laid down in Article 31.

29.1. Recitals

1095. (9) Harmonised rules applicable to the placing on the market, the putting into service and the use of high-risk AI systems should be laid down consistently with Regulation (EC) No 765/2008 of the European Parliament and of the Council,[136] Decision No 768/2008/EC of the European Parliament and of the Council[137] and Regulation (EU) 2019/1020 of the European Parliament and of the Council[138] (New Legislative Framework). The harmonised rules laid down in

---

136 Regulation (EC) No 765/2008 of the European Parliament and of the Council of 9 July 2008 setting out the requirements for accreditation and repealing Regulation (EEC) No 339/93, [2008] OJ L218/30.

137 Decision No 768/2008/EC of the European Parliament and of the Council of 9 July 2008 on a common framework for the marketing of products, and repealing Council Decision 93/465/EEC, [2008] OJ L218/82.

138 Regulation (EU) 2019/1020 of the European Parliament and of the Council of 20 June 2019 on market surveillance and compliance of products and amending Directive 2004/42/EC and Regulations (EC) No 765/2008 and (EU) No 305/2011, [2019] OJ L169/1.

this Regulation should apply across sectors and, in line with the New Legislative Framework, should be without prejudice to existing Union law, in particular on data protection, consumer protection, fundamental rights, employment, and protection of workers, and product safety, to which this Regulation is complementary. As a consequence, all rights and remedies provided for by such Union law to consumers, and other persons on whom AI systems may have a negative impact, including as regards the compensation of possible damages pursuant to Council Directive 85/374/EEC[139] remain unaffected and fully applicable. Furthermore, in the context of employment and protection of workers, this Regulation should therefore not affect Union law on social policy and national labour law, in compliance with Union law, concerning employment and working conditions, including health and safety at work and the relationship between employers and workers. This Regulation should also not affect the exercise of fundamental rights as recognised in the Member States and at Union level, including the right or freedom to strike or to take other action covered by the specific industrial relations systems in Member States as well as the right to negotiate, to conclude and enforce collective agreements or to take collective action in accordance with national law. This Regulation should not affect the provisions aiming to improve working conditions in platform work laid down in a Directive of the European Parliament and of the Council on improving working conditions in platform work. Moreover, this Regulation aims to strengthen the effectiveness of such existing rights and remedies by establishing specific requirements and obligations, including in respect of the transparency, technical documentation and record-keeping of AI systems. Furthermore, the obligations placed on various operators involved in the AI value chain under this Regulation should apply without prejudice to national law, in compliance with Union law, having the effect of limiting the use of certain AI systems where such law falls outside the scope of this Regulation or pursues legitimate public interest objectives other than those pursued by this Regulation. For example, national labour law and law on the protection of minors, namely persons below the age of 18, taking into account the UNCRC General Comment No 25 (2021) on children's rights in relation to the digital environment, insofar as they are not specific to AI systems and pursue other legitimate public interest objectives, should not be affected by this Regulation.

1096. (153) Member States hold a key role in the application and enforcement of this Regulation. In that respect, each Member State should designate at least one notifying authority and at least one market surveillance authority as national competent authorities for the purpose of supervising the application and implementation of this Regulation. Member States may decide to appoint any

---

139 Council Directive 85/374/EEC of 25 July 1985 on the approximation of the laws, regulations and administrative provisions of the Member States concerning liability for defective products, [1985] OJ L210/29.

kind of public entity to perform the tasks of the national competent authorities within the meaning of this Regulation, in accordance with their specific national organisational characteristics and needs. In order to increase organisation efficiency on the side of Member States and to set a single point of contact vis-à-vis the public and other counterparts at Member State and Union levels, each Member State should designate a market surveillance authority to act as a single point of contact.

29.2. General Approach

29.2.1 Preamble

1097. Notified bodies are in charge of assessing conformity, which is the foundation of risk management to enable a trustworthy AI ecosystem.

29.2.2 Guiding Principles

1098. Notified bodies certify all requirements necessary for:

- the issuance of an EU declaration of conformity;
- CE marking.

29.3. Definition

1099. A 'notified body' means 'a conformity assessment body notified in accordance with this Regulation and other relevant Union harmonisation legislation'.[140]

29.3.1 Status

1100. Such status is granted by the notifying authority.

29.3.2 Roles and Responsibilities

1101. 'Notified bodies are free to offer their conformity assessment services, within their scope of notification, to any economic operator established either inside or outside the Union. They may carry out these activities also on the territory of other Member States or of third countries.

1102. Notified bodies must provide relevant information to their notifying authority, the market surveillance authorities and other notified bodies.

---

[140] AI Act, Art. 3(22).

1103. Notified bodies must operate in a competent, non-discriminatory, transparent, neutral, independent and impartial manner.

1104. Notified bodies must have at their disposal the necessary personnel, who have sufficient and relevant knowledge and experience to carry out conformity assessment in accordance with Union harmonisation legislation in question.

1105. Notified bodies must make adequate arrangements to ensure confidentiality of the information obtained in the course of conformity assessment.

1106. Notified bodies must be adequately insured to cover their professional activities, unless liability is assured under the national legislation of the notifying Member State.

1107. Notified bodies may demonstrate their competence through accreditation, which is the preferred way to assess their technical competence.'[141]

30 ARTICLE 30. NOTIFICATION PROCEDURE

1. Notifying authorities may notify only conformity assessment bodies which have satisfied the requirements laid down in Article 31.

2. Notifying authorities shall notify the Commission and the other Member States, using the electronic notification tool developed and managed by the Commission, of each conformity assessment body referred to in paragraph 1.

3. The notification referred to in paragraph 2 of this Article shall include full details of the conformity assessment activities, the conformity assessment module or modules, the types of AI systems concerned, and the relevant attestation of competence. Where a notification is not based on an accreditation certificate as referred to in Article 29(2), the notifying authority shall provide the Commission and the other Member States with documentary evidence which attests to the competence of the conformity assessment body and to the arrangements in place to ensure that that body will be monitored regularly and will continue to satisfy the requirements laid down in Article 31.

4. The conformity assessment body concerned may perform the activities of a notified body only where no objections are raised by the Commission or the other Member States within two weeks of a notification by a notifying authority where it includes an accreditation certificate referred to in Article 29(2), or within two months of a notification by the notifying authority where it includes documentary evidence referred to in Article 29(3).

[141] 'The "Blue Guide" on the implementation of EU product rules 2022', [2022] OJ C247/1, para. 5.2.2., p. 81.

5. Where objections are raised, the Commission shall, without delay, enter into consultations with the relevant Member States and the conformity assessment body. In view thereof, the Commission shall decide whether the authorisation is justified. The Commission shall address its decision to the Member State concerned and to the relevant conformity assessment body.

30.1. Recitals

1108. (125) Given the complexity of high-risk AI systems and the risks that are associated with them, it is important to develop an adequate conformity assessment procedure for high-risk AI systems involving notified bodies, so-called third party conformity assessment. However, given the current experience of professional pre-market certifiers in the field of product safety and the different nature of risks involved, it is appropriate to limit, at least in an initial phase of application of this Regulation, the scope of application of third-party conformity assessment for high-risk AI systems other than those related to products. Therefore, the conformity assessment of such systems should be carried out as a general rule by the provider under its own responsibility, with the only exception of AI systems intended to be used for biometrics.

1109. (126) In order to carry out third-party conformity assessments when so required, notified bodies should be notified under this Regulation by the national competent authorities, provided that they comply with a set of requirements, in particular on independence, competence, absence of conflicts of interests and suitable cybersecurity requirements. Notification of those bodies should be sent by national competent authorities to the Commission and the other Member States by means of the electronic notification tool developed and managed by the Commission pursuant to Article R23 of Annex I to Decision No 768/2008/EC.

1110. (127) In line with Union commitments under the World Trade Organization Agreement on Technical Barriers to Trade, it is adequate to facilitate the mutual recognition of conformity assessment results produced by competent conformity assessment bodies, independent of the territory in which they are established, provided that those conformity assessment bodies established under the law of a third country meet the applicable requirements of this Regulation and the Union has concluded an agreement to that extent. In this context, the Commission should actively explore possible international instruments for that purpose and in particular pursue the conclusion of mutual recognition agreements with third countries.

1111. (161) It is necessary to clarify the responsibilities and competences at Union and national level as regards AI systems that are built on general-purpose AI models. To avoid overlapping competences, where an AI system is based on a general-purpose AI model and the model and system are provided by the same provider, the supervision should take place at Union level through the AI Office, which should have the powers of a market surveillance authority within the meaning of Regulation (EU) 2019/1020 for this purpose. In all other cases, national market surveillance authorities remain responsible for the supervision of AI systems. However, for general-purpose AI systems that can be used directly by deployers for at least one purpose that is classified as high-risk, market surveillance authorities should cooperate with the AI Office to carry out evaluations of compliance and inform the Board and other market surveillance authorities accordingly. Furthermore, market surveillance authorities should be able to request assistance from the AI Office where the market surveillance authority is unable to conclude an investigation on a high-risk AI system because of its inability to access certain information related to the general-purpose AI model on which the high-risk AI system is built. In such cases, the procedure regarding mutual assistance in cross-border cases in Chapter VI of Regulation (EU) 2019/1020 should apply *mutatis mutandis*.

30.2. General Approach

30.2.1 Preamble

1112. The procedure applies to:

- accredited bodies;
- bodies specifically requesting the status of a notified body.

30.2.2 Guiding Principles

1113. The objective is to create a European market for compliance assessment activities related to high-risk AI systems.

30.3. Procedure

1114. The characteristics are as follows:

NO.	THEME	SPECIFICATION
1.	Requirement	Compliance with the obligations laid down in Art. 31
2.	Knowledge	Communication of notified activities to the European Commission
3.	Documentation	Description of competences Assessment methods Type of high-risk AI systems
4.	Objections	European Commission and other Member States may raise objections Deadline: Two weeks if there is an accreditation certificate Two months in other cases

31 ARTICLE 31. REQUIREMENTS RELATING TO NOTIFIED BODIES

1. A notified body shall be established under the national law of a Member State and shall have legal personality.

2. Notified bodies shall satisfy the organisational, quality management, resources and process requirements that are necessary to fulfil their tasks, as well as suitable cybersecurity requirements.

3. The organisational structure, allocation of responsibilities, reporting lines and operation of notified bodies shall ensure confidence in their performance, and in the results of the conformity assessment activities that the notified bodies conduct.

4. Notified bodies shall be independent of the provider of a high-risk AI system in relation to which they perform conformity assessment activities. Notified bodies shall also be independent of any other operator having an economic interest in high-risk AI systems assessed, as well as of any competitors of the provider. This shall not preclude the use of assessed high-risk AI systems that are necessary for the operations of the conformity assessment body, or the use of such high-risk AI systems for personal purposes.

5. Neither a conformity assessment body, its top-level management nor the personnel responsible for carrying out its conformity assessment tasks shall be directly involved in the design, development, marketing or use of high-risk AI systems, nor shall they represent the parties engaged in those activities. They shall not engage in any activity that might conflict with their independence of judgement or integrity in relation to conformity assessment activities for which they are notified. This shall, in particular, apply to consultancy services.

6. Notified bodies shall be organised and operated so as to safeguard the independence, objectivity and impartiality of their activities. Notified bodies shall document and implement a structure and procedures to safeguard impartiality and to promote and apply the principles of impartiality throughout their organisation, personnel and assessment activities.

7. Notified bodies shall have documented procedures in place ensuring that their personnel, committees, subsidiaries, subcontractors and any associated body or personnel of external bodies maintain, in accordance with Article 78, the confidentiality of the information which comes into their possession during the performance of conformity assessment activities, except when its disclosure is required by law. The staff of notified bodies shall be bound to observe professional secrecy with regard to all information obtained in carrying out their tasks under this Regulation, except in relation to the notifying authorities of the Member State in which their activities are carried out.

8. Notified bodies shall have procedures for the performance of activities which take due account of the size of a provider, the sector in which it operates, its structure, and the degree of complexity of the AI system concerned.

9. Notified bodies shall take out appropriate liability insurance for their conformity assessment activities, unless liability is assumed by the Member State in which they are established in accordance with national law or that Member State is itself directly responsible for the conformity assessment.

10. Notified bodies shall be capable of carrying out all their tasks under this Regulation with the highest degree of professional integrity and the requisite competence in the specific field, whether those tasks are carried out by notified bodies themselves or on their behalf and under their responsibility.

11. Notified bodies shall have sufficient internal competences to be able effectively to evaluate the tasks conducted by external parties on their behalf. The notified body shall have permanent availability of sufficient administrative, technical, legal and scientific personnel who possess experience and knowledge relating to the relevant types of AI systems, data and data computing, and relating to the requirements set out in Section 2.

12. Notified bodies shall participate in coordination activities as referred to in Article 38. They shall also take part directly, or be represented in, European standardisation organisations, or ensure that they are aware and up to date in respect of relevant standards.

31.1. Recitals

1115. **(68)** For the development and assessment of high-risk AI systems, certain actors, such as providers, notified bodies and other relevant entities, such as European Digital Innovation Hubs, testing experimentation facilities and researchers, should be able to access and use high-quality data sets within the fields of activities of those actors which are related to this Regulation. European common data spaces established by the Commission and the facilitation of data sharing between businesses and with government in the public interest will be instrumental to provide trustful, accountable and non-discriminatory access to high-quality data for the training, validation and testing of AI systems. For example, in health, the European health data space will facilitate non-discriminatory access to health data and the training of AI algorithms on those data sets, in a privacy-preserving, secure, timely, transparent and trustworthy manner, and with an appropriate institutional governance. Relevant competent authorities, including sectoral ones, providing or supporting the access to data may also support the provision of high-quality data for the training, validation and testing of AI systems.

1116. **(125)** Given the complexity of high-risk AI systems and the risks that are associated with them, it is important to develop an adequate conformity assessment procedure for high-risk AI systems involving notified bodies, so-called third party conformity assessment. However, given the current experience of professional pre-market certifiers in the field of product safety and the different nature of risks involved, it is appropriate to limit, at least in an initial phase of application of this Regulation, the scope of application of third-party conformity assessment for high-risk AI systems other than those related to products. Therefore, the conformity assessment of such systems should be carried out as a general rule by the provider under its own responsibility, with the only exception of AI systems intended to be used for biometrics.

1117. **(126)** In order to carry out third-party conformity assessments when so required, notified bodies should be notified under this Regulation by the national competent authorities, provided that they comply with a set of requirements, in particular on independence, competence, absence of conflicts of interests and suitable cybersecurity requirements. Notification of those bodies should be sent by national competent authorities to the Commission and the other Member States by means of the electronic notification tool developed and managed by the Commission pursuant to Article R23 of Annex I to Decision No 768/2008/EC.

31.2. General Approach

31.2.1 Preamble

1118. Notified bodies must comply with a list of requirements to ensure the effectiveness of compliance assessments.

31.2.2 Guiding Principles

1119. They are defined as follows: 'The assessment of a conformity assessment body seeking notification determines if it is technically competent and capable of carrying out the conformity assessment procedures in question, and if it can demonstrate the necessary level of independence, impartiality and integrity'.

1120. Member States take the final responsibility for the competence of their notified bodies with respect to the other Member States and the EU institutions. They must therefore verify the competence of the bodies seeking notification, based on the criteria laid down in the applicable Union harmonisation legislation in conjunction with essential requirements and the conformity assessment procedure(s) in question. In general, the competence criteria set out in the Union harmonisation acts cover:

- availability of personnel and equipment;
- independence and impartiality in relation to those directly or indirectly concerned with the product (such as the designer, the manufacturer, the

manufacturer's authorised representative, the provider, the assembler, the installer, the user);

- technical competence of personnel that is relevant to the products and conformity assessment procedure in question;
- maintenance of professional secrecy and integrity; and
- subscription to civil liability insurance, unless that liability is covered by the state under national law.

1121. Notifying authorities or accreditation bodies must carry out periodic monitoring to assess the continuity of the competence of notified bodies after they are notified.

1122. Notified Bodies may have activities or personnel outside the Member State where they are legally established, or even outside the Union. However, the notifying authority of this Member State must be capable of ensuring the monitoring of the whole Notified Body (not only the head office). Having all the testing facilities in another Member State or even outside the EU would make it almost impossible for the notifying authority to monitor the operations of the whole Notified Body.

1123. The supervision of multi-site conformity assessment bodies is done under the cross-border cooperation among the national accreditation bodies and notifying authorities; however, the responsibility remains with the notifying authority of the Member State in which the conformity assessment body is established. The conformity assessment body as the main entity to be notified must have itself the means and the competence to carry out the tasks required for the notification. While it may have recourse to subsidiaries/subcontracting, it should not rely for all test and evaluations on subsidiaries/ subcontractors.[142]

1124. The notified body may subcontract specific tasks connected with the conformity assessment, has to ensure that the subcontractor meets the same requirements that are applicable to the notified body itself and may subcontract specific activities only with the agreement of the client. Thus, structures where the head office of the candidate-notified body in the Member State of notification consists of very few staff performing only commercial tasks but none of the conformity assessment tasks for which the body is (to be) notified would be carried out in that Member State, cannot be accepted.'[143]

---

[142] Article R20(1) of Annex I of Decision No 768/2008/EC sets out the obligations of the notified body when it subcontracts specific tasks connected with conformity assessment or has recourse to a subsidiary.

[143] 'The "Blue Guide" on the implementation of EU product rules 2022', [2022] OJ C247/1, para. 5.3.2.2., p. 89.

31.3. *Characteristics*

1125. They are as follows:

NO.	THEME	SPECIFICATION
1.	Activity	Conformity control and cybersecurity
2.	Guarantee	Confidence in the performance and results
3.	Independence	Presence of AI systems and absence of conflict of interest
4.	Impartiality	Absence of conflict of interest

32 ARTICLE 32. PRESUMPTION OF CONFORMITY WITH REQUIREMENTS RELATING TO NOTIFIED BODIES

Where a conformity assessment body demonstrates its conformity with the criteria laid down in the relevant harmonised standards or parts thereof, the references of which have been published in the Official Journal of the European Union, it shall be presumed to comply with the requirements set out in Article 31 in so far as the applicable harmonised standards cover those requirements.

32.1. *Recitals*

1126. **(117)** The codes of practice should represent a central tool for the proper compliance with the obligations provided for under this Regulation for providers of general-purpose AI models. Providers should be able to rely on codes of practice to demonstrate compliance with the obligations. By means of implementing acts, the Commission may decide to approve a code of practice and give it a general validity within the Union, or, alternatively, to provide common rules for the implementation of the relevant obligations, if, by the time this Regulation becomes applicable, a code of practice cannot be finalised or is not deemed adequate by the AI Office. Once a harmonised standard is published and assessed as suitable to cover the relevant obligations by the AI Office, compliance with a European harmonised standard should grant providers the presumption of conformity. Providers of general-purpose AI models should furthermore be able to demonstrate compliance using alternative adequate means, if codes of practice or harmonised standards are not available, or they choose not to rely on those.

32.2. General Approach

1127. In order to facilitate a single market, accredited notified bodies (such as Cofrac accreditation in France) benefit from a rebuttable presumption of conformity.

33 ARTICLE 33. SUBSIDIARIES OF NOTIFIED BODIES AND SUBCONTRACTING

1. Where a notified body subcontracts specific tasks connected with the conformity assessment or has recourse to a subsidiary, it shall ensure that the subcontractor or the subsidiary meets the requirements laid down in Article 31, and shall inform the notifying authority accordingly.

2. Notified bodies shall take full responsibility for the tasks performed by any subcontractors or subsidiaries.

3. Activities may be subcontracted or carried out by a subsidiary only with the agreement of the provider. Notified bodies shall make a list of their subsidiaries publicly available.

4. The relevant documents concerning the assessment of the qualifications of the subcontractor or the subsidiary and the work carried out by them under this Regulation shall be kept at the disposal of the notifying authority for a period of five years from the termination date of the subcontracting.

33.1. General Approach

1128. This Article organises the subcontracting activities of notified bodies. It does not contain any specific provisions related to AI technologies.

34 ARTICLE 34. OPERATIONAL OBLIGATIONS OF NOTIFIED BODIES

1. Notified bodies shall verify the conformity of high-risk AI systems in accordance with the conformity assessment procedures set out in Article 43.

2. Notified bodies shall avoid unnecessary burdens for providers when performing their activities, and take due account of the size of the provider, the sector in which it operates, its structure and the degree of complexity of the high-risk AI system concerned, in particular in view of minimising administrative burdens and compliance costs for micro- and small enterprises within the meaning of Recommendation 2003/361/EC. The notified body shall, nevertheless, respect the degree of rigour and the level of protection required for the compliance of the high-risk AI system with the requirements of this Regulation.

3. Notified bodies shall make available and submit upon request all relevant documentation, including the providers' documentation, to the notifying authority referred to in Article 28 to allow that authority to conduct its assessment, designation, notification and monitoring activities, and to facilitate the assessment outlined in this Section.

34.1. Recitals

1129. (64) To mitigate the risks from high-risk AI systems placed on the market or put into service and to ensure a high level of trustworthiness, certain mandatory requirements should apply to high-risk AI systems, taking into account the intended purpose and the context of use of the AI system and according to the risk-management system to be established by the provider. The measures adopted by the providers to comply with the mandatory requirements of this Regulation should take into account the generally acknowledged state of the art on AI, be proportionate and effective to meet the objectives of this Regulation. Based on the New Legislative Framework, as clarified in Commission notice 'The "Blue Guide" on the implementation of EU product rules 2022', the general rule is that more than one legal act of Union harmonisation legislation may be applicable to one product, since the making available or putting into service can take place only when the product complies with all applicable Union harmonisation legislation. The hazards of AI systems covered by the requirements of this Regulation concern different aspects than the existing Union harmonisation legislation and therefore the requirements of this Regulation would complement the existing body of the Union harmonisation legislation. For example, machinery or medical devices products incorporating an AI system might present risks not addressed by the essential health and safety requirements set out in the relevant Union harmonised legislation, as that sectoral law does not deal with risks specific to AI systems. This calls for a simultaneous and complementary application of the various legislative acts. To ensure consistency and to avoid an unnecessary administrative burden and unnecessary costs, providers of a product that contains one or more high-risk AI system, to which the requirements of this Regulation and of the Union harmonisation legislation based on the New Legislative Framework and listed in an annex to this Regulation apply, should have flexibility with regard to operational decisions on how to ensure compliance of a product that contains one or more AI systems with all the applicable requirements of that Union harmonised legislation in an optimal manner. That flexibility could mean, for example a decision by the provider to integrate a part of the necessary testing and reporting processes, information and documentation required under this Regulation into already existing documentation and procedures required under existing Union harmonisation legislation based on the New Legislative

Framework and listed in an annex to this Regulation. This should not, in any way, undermine the obligation of the provider to comply with all the applicable requirements.

1130. **(124)** It is appropriate that, in order to minimise the burden on operators and avoid any possible duplication, for high-risk AI systems related to products which are covered by existing Union harmonisation legislation based on the New Legislative Framework, the compliance of those AI systems with the requirements of this Regulation should be assessed as part of the conformity assessment already provided for in that law. The applicability of the requirements of this Regulation should thus not affect the specific logic, methodology or general structure of conformity assessment under the relevant Union harmonisation legislation.

1131. **(146)** Moreover, in light of the very small size of some operators and in order to ensure proportionality regarding costs of innovation, it is appropriate to allow microenterprises to fulfil one of the most costly obligations, namely to establish a quality management system, in a simplified manner which would reduce the administrative burden and the costs for those enterprises without affecting the level of protection and the need for compliance with the requirements for high-risk AI systems. The Commission should develop guidelines to specify the elements of the quality management system to be fulfilled in this simplified manner by microenterprises.

34.2. General Approach

34.2.1 Preamble

1132. Notified bodies must:

- limit their verifications to the requirements for high-risk AI systems only;
- conduct assessments in compliance with the Regulation;[144]
- minimise unnecessary burdens;
- collaborate with notifying authorities.

34.2.2 Limitation of Verifications

1133. The elements to be verified are those required by Articles 6 to 15 of the Regulation.

[144] AI Act, Art. 43.

34.3. *Evaluation Methodology*

1134. It is set out in Article 43 of the Regulation.

34.4. *Minimisation of Burdens*

1135. Notified bodies must avoid unnecessary burdens and adapt their verifications according to the following:

NO.	THEME	SPECIFICATION
1.	AI system	Level of risk
		Degree of complexity
2.	Provider	Size and sector in which it operates
3.	Process	Minimisation of administrative burdens and costs
4.	Guarantee	Commitment to compliance

34.5. *Collaboration*

1136. All certificates, documentation, and compliance assessment records must be made available to the notifying authorities.

35 ARTICLE 35. IDENTIFICATION NUMBERS AND LISTS OF NOTIFIED BODIES

> **1.** The Commission shall assign a single identification number to each notified body, even where a body is notified under more than one Union act.
> **2.** The Commission shall make publicly available the list of the bodies notified under this Regulation, including their identification numbers and the activities for which they have been notified. The Commission shall ensure that the list is kept up to date.

35.1. *General Approach*

1137. This Article does not contain any specific provisions related to AI technologies.

36 ARTICLE 36. CHANGES TO NOTIFICATIONS

1. The notifying authority shall notify the Commission and the other Member States of any relevant changes to the notification of a notified body via the electronic notification tool referred to in Article 30(2).

2. The procedures laid down in Articles 29 and 30 shall apply to extensions of the scope of the notification.

For changes to the notification other than extensions of its scope, the procedures laid down in paragraphs (3) to (9) shall apply.

3. Where a notified body decides to cease its conformity assessment activities, it shall inform the notifying authority and the providers concerned as soon as possible and, in the case of a planned cessation, at least one year before ceasing its activities. The certificates of the notified body may remain valid for a period of nine months after cessation of the notified body's activities, on condition that another notified body has confirmed in writing that it will assume responsibilities for the high-risk AI systems covered by those certificates. The latter notified body shall complete a full assessment of the high-risk AI systems affected by the end of that nine-month-period before issuing new certificates for those systems. Where the notified body has ceased its activity, the notifying authority shall withdraw the designation.

4. Where a notifying authority has sufficient reason to consider that a notified body no longer meets the requirements laid down in Article 31, or that it is failing to fulfil its obligations, the notifying authority shall without delay investigate the matter with the utmost diligence. In that context, it shall inform the notified body concerned about the objections raised and give it the possibility to make its views known. If the notifying authority comes to the conclusion that the notified body no longer meets the requirements laid down in Article 31 or that it is failing to fulfil its obligations, it shall restrict, suspend or withdraw the designation as appropriate, depending on the seriousness of the failure to meet those requirements or fulfil those obligations. It shall immediately inform the Commission and the other Member States accordingly.

5. Where its designation has been suspended, restricted, or fully or partially withdrawn, the notified body shall inform the providers concerned within 10 days.

6. In the event of the restriction, suspension or withdrawal of a designation, the notifying authority shall take appropriate steps to ensure that the files of the notified body concerned are kept, and to make them available to notifying authorities in other Member States and to market surveillance authorities at their request.

7. In the event of the restriction, suspension or withdrawal of a designation, the notifying authority shall:

(a) assess the impact on the certificates issued by the notified body;

(b) submit a report on its findings to the Commission and the other Member States within three months of having notified the changes to the designation;

(c) require the notified body to suspend or withdraw, within a reasonable period of time determined by the authority, any certificates which were unduly issued, in order to ensure the continuing conformity of high-risk AI systems on the market;

(d) inform the Commission and the Member States about certificates the suspension or withdrawal of which it has required;

(e) provide the national competent authorities of the Member State in which the provider has its registered place of business with all relevant information about the certificates of which it has required the suspension or withdrawal; that authority shall take the appropriate measures, where necessary, to avoid a potential risk to health, safety or fundamental rights.

8. With the exception of certificates unduly issued, and where a designation has been suspended or restricted, the certificates shall remain valid in one of the following circumstances:

(a) the notifying authority has confirmed, within one month of the suspension or restriction, that there is no risk to health, safety or fundamental rights in relation to certificates affected by the suspension or restriction, and the notifying authority has outlined a timeline for actions to remedy the suspension or restriction; or

(b) the notifying authority has confirmed that no certificates relevant to the suspension will be issued, amended or re-issued during the course of the suspension or restriction, and states whether the notified body has the capability of continuing to monitor and remain responsible for existing certificates issued for the period of the suspension or restriction; in the event that the notifying authority determines that the notified body does not have the capability to support existing certificates issued, the provider of the system covered by the certificate shall confirm in writing to the national competent authorities of the Member State in which it has its registered place of business, within three months of the suspension or restriction, that another qualified notified body is temporarily assuming the functions of the notified body to monitor and remain responsible for the certificates during the period of suspension or restriction.

9. With the exception of certificates unduly issued, and where a designation has been withdrawn, the certificates shall remain valid for a period of nine months under the following circumstances:

(a) the national competent authority of the Member State in which the provider of the high-risk AI system covered by the certificate has its registered place of business has confirmed that there is no risk to health, safety or fundamental rights associated with the high-risk AI systems concerned; and

(b) another notified body has confirmed in writing that it will assume immediate responsibility for those AI systems and completes its assessment within 12 months of the withdrawal of the designation.

In the circumstances referred to in the first subparagraph, the national competent authority of the Member State in which the provider of the system covered by the certificate has its place of business may extend the provisional validity of the certificates for additional periods of three months, which shall not exceed 12 months in total.

The national competent authority or the notified body assuming the functions of the notified body affected by the change of designation shall immediately inform the Commission, the other Member States and the other notified bodies thereof.

36.1. General Approach

1138. The rules for making changes to notifications are organised as follows:

NO.	THEME	SPECIFICATION
1.	Modification	Notification by the notifying authority to the European Commission
2.	Technical details	Notification platform (Art. 30(2))
3.	Cessation of activities	Notification by the notified body to the notifying authority and the providers concerned
4.	Breach of obligations	If the notified body fails to fulfil its obligations, notification by the notifying authority Notification to the European Commission

37 ARTICLE 37. CHALLENGE TO THE COMPETENCE OF NOTIFIED BODIES

1. The Commission shall, where necessary, investigate all cases where there are reasons to doubt the competence of a notified body or the continued fulfilment by a notified body of the requirements laid down in Article 31 and of its applicable responsibilities.

2. The notifying authority shall provide the Commission, on request, with all relevant information relating to the notification or the maintenance of the competence of the notified body concerned.

3. The Commission shall ensure that all sensitive information obtained in the course of its investigations pursuant to this Article is treated confidentially in accordance with Article 78.

4. Where the Commission ascertains that a notified body does not meet or no longer meets the requirements for its notification, it shall inform the notifying Member State accordingly and request it to take the necessary corrective measures, including the suspension or withdrawal of the notification if necessary. Where the Member State fails to take the necessary corrective measures, the Commission may, by means of an implementing act, suspend, restrict or withdraw the designation. That implementing act shall be adopted in accordance with the examination procedure referred to in Article 98(2).

37.1. Recitals

1139. (126) In order to carry out third-party conformity assessments when so required, notified bodies should be notified under this Regulation by the national competent authorities, provided that they comply with a set of requirements, in particular on independence, competence, absence of conflicts of interests and suitable cybersecurity requirements. Notification of those bodies should be sent by national competent authorities to the Commission and the other Member States by means of the electronic notification tool developed and managed by the Commission pursuant to Article R23 of Annex I to Decision No 768/2008/EC.

1140. (157) This Regulation is without prejudice to the competences, tasks, powers and independence of relevant national public authorities or bodies which supervise the application of Union law protecting fundamental rights, including equality bodies and data protection authorities. Where necessary for their mandate, those national public authorities or bodies should also have access to any documentation created under this Regulation. A specific safeguard procedure should be set for ensuring adequate and timely enforcement against AI systems presenting a risk to health, safety and fundamental rights. The procedure for such AI systems presenting a risk should be applied to high-risk AI systems presenting a risk, prohibited systems which have been placed on the market, put into service or used in violation of the prohibited practices laid down in this Regulation and AI systems which have been made available in violation of the transparency requirements laid down in this Regulation and present a risk.

37.2. General Approach

1141. This Article does not contain any specific provisions related to AI technologies.

38 ARTICLE 38. COORDINATION OF NOTIFIED BODIES

1. The Commission shall ensure that, with regard to high-risk AI systems, appropriate coordination and cooperation between notified bodies active in the conformity assessment procedures pursuant to this Regulation are put in place and properly operated in the form of a sectoral group of notified bodies.

2. Each notifying authority shall ensure that the bodies notified by it participate in the work of a group referred to in paragraph 1, directly or through designated representatives.

3. The Commission shall provide for the exchange of knowledge and best practices between notifying authorities.

38.1. Recitals

1142. **(167)** In order to ensure trustful and constructive cooperation of competent authorities on Union and national level, all parties involved in the application of this Regulation should respect the confidentiality of information and data obtained in carrying out their tasks, in accordance with Union or national law. They should carry out their tasks and activities in such a manner as to protect, in particular, intellectual property rights, confidential business information and trade secrets, the effective implementation of this Regulation, public and national security interests, the integrity of criminal and administrative proceedings, and the integrity of classified information.

38.2. General Approach

1143. This Article does not contain any specific provisions related to AI technologies.

39 ARTICLE 39. CONFORMITY ASSESSMENT BODIES OF THIRD COUNTRIES

Conformity assessment bodies established under the law of a third country with which the Union has concluded an agreement may be authorised to carry out the activities of notified bodies under this Regulation, provided that they meet the requirements laid down in Article 31 or they ensure an equivalent level of compliance.

39.1. Recitals

1144. **(127)** In line with Union commitments under the World Trade Organization Agreement on Technical Barriers to Trade, it is adequate to facilitate the mutual recognition of conformity assessment results produced by competent conformity assessment bodies, independent of the territory in which they are established, provided that those conformity assessment bodies established under the law of a third country meet the applicable requirements of this Regulation and the Union has concluded an agreement to that extent. In this context, the Commission should actively explore possible international instruments for that purpose and in particular pursue the conclusion of mutual recognition agreements with third countries.

39.2. General Approach

1145. This Article does not contain any specific provisions related to AI technologies.

SECTION 5. STANDARDS, CONFORMITY ASSESSMENT, CERTIFICATES, REGISTRATION

40 ARTICLE 40. HARMONISED STANDARDS AND STANDARDISATION DELIVERABLES

1. High-risk AI systems or general-purpose AI models which are in conformity with harmonised standards or parts thereof the references of which have been published in the Official Journal of the European Union in accordance with Regulation (EU) No 1025/2012 shall be presumed to be in conformity with the requirements set out in Section 2 of this Chapter or, as applicable, with the obligations set out in of Chapter V, Sections 2 and 3, of this Regulation, to the extent that those standards cover those requirements or obligations.

2. In accordance with Article 10 of Regulation (EU) No 1025/2012, the Commission shall issue, without undue delay, standardisation requests covering all requirements set out in Section 2 of this Chapter and, as applicable, standardisation requests covering obligations set out in Chapter V, Sections 2 and 3, of this Regulation. The standardisation request shall also ask for deliverables on reporting and documentation processes to improve AI systems' resource performance, such as reducing the high-risk AI system's consumption of energy and of other resources during its lifecycle, and on the energy-efficient development of general-purpose AI models. When preparing a standardisation request, the Commission shall consult the Board and relevant stakeholders, including the advisory forum.

When issuing a standardisation request to European standardisation organisations, the Commission shall specify that standards have to be clear, consistent, including with the standards developed in the various sectors for products covered by the existing Union harmonisation legislation listed in Annex I, and aiming to ensure that high-risk AI systems or general-purpose AI models placed on the market or put into service in the Union meet the relevant requirements or obligations laid down in this Regulation.

The Commission shall request the European standardisation organisations to provide evidence of their best efforts to fulfil the objectives referred to in the first and the second subparagraph of this paragraph in accordance with Article 24 of Regulation (EU) No 1025/2012.

3. The participants in the standardisation process shall seek to promote investment and innovation in AI, including through increasing legal certainty, as well as the competitiveness and growth of the Union market, to contribute to strengthening global cooperation on standardisation and taking into account existing international standards in the field of AI that are consistent with Union values, fundamental rights and interests, and to enhance multi-stakeholder governance ensuring a balanced representation of interests and the effective participation of all relevant stakeholders in accordance with Articles 5, 6, and 7 of Regulation (EU) No 1025/2012.

40.1. Recitals

1146. (27) While the risk-based approach is the basis for a proportionate and effective set of binding rules, it is important to recall the 2019 Ethics guidelines for trustworthy AI developed by the independent AI HLEG appointed by the Commission. In those guidelines, the AI HLEG developed seven non-binding ethical principles for AI which are intended to help ensure that AI is trustworthy and ethically sound. The seven principles include human agency and oversight; technical robustness and safety; privacy and data governance; transparency; diversity, non-discrimination and fairness; societal and environmental well-being and accountability. Without prejudice to the legally binding requirements of this Regulation and any other applicable Union law, those guidelines contribute to the design of coherent, trustworthy and human-centric AI, in line with the Charter and with the values on which the Union is founded. According to the guidelines of the AI HLEG, human agency and oversight means that AI systems are developed and used as a tool that serves people, respects human dignity and personal autonomy, and that is functioning in a way that can be appropriately controlled and overseen by humans. Technical robustness and safety means that AI systems are developed and used in a way that allows robustness in the case of problems and resilience against attempts to alter the use or performance of the AI system so as to allow unlawful use by third parties, and minimise unintended harm. Privacy and data governance means that AI systems are developed and used in accordance with privacy and data protection rules, while processing data that meets high standards in terms of quality and integrity. Transparency means that AI systems are developed and used in a way that allows appropriate traceability and explainability, while making humans aware that they communicate or interact with an AI system, as well as duly informing deployers of the capabilities and limitations of that AI system and affected persons about their rights. Diversity, non-discrimination and fairness means that AI systems are developed and used in a way that includes diverse actors and promotes equal access, gender equality and cultural diversity, while avoiding discriminatory impacts and unfair biases that are prohibited by Union or national law. Social and environmental well-being means that AI systems are developed and used in a sustainable and environmentally friendly manner as well as in a way to benefit all human beings, while monitoring and assessing the long-term impacts on the individual, society and democracy. The application of those principles should be translated, when possible, in the design and use of AI models. They should in any case serve as a basis for the drafting of codes of conduct under this Regulation. All stakeholders, including industry, academia, civil society and standardisation organisations, are encouraged to take into account, as appropriate, the ethical principles for the development of voluntary best practices and standards.

1147. **(81)** The provider should establish a sound quality management system, ensure the accomplishment of the required conformity assessment procedure, draw up the relevant documentation and establish a robust post-market monitoring system. Providers of high-risk AI systems that are subject to obligations regarding quality management systems under relevant sectoral Union law should have the possibility to include the elements of the quality management system provided for in this Regulation as part of the existing quality management system provided for in that other sectoral Union law. The complementarity between this Regulation and existing sectoral Union law should also be taken into account in future standardisation activities or guidance adopted by the Commission. Public authorities which put into service high-risk AI systems for their own use may adopt and implement the rules for the quality management system as part of the quality management system adopted at a national or regional level, as appropriate, taking into account the specificities of the sector and the competences and organisation of the public authority concerned.

1148. **(117)** The codes of practice should represent a central tool for the proper compliance with the obligations provided for under this Regulation for providers of general-purpose AI models. Providers should be able to rely on codes of practice to demonstrate compliance with the obligations. By means of implementing acts, the Commission may decide to approve a code of practice and give it a general validity within the Union, or, alternatively, to provide common rules for the implementation of the relevant obligations, if, by the time this Regulation becomes applicable, a code of practice cannot be finalised or is not deemed adequate by the AI Office. Once a harmonised standard is published and assessed as suitable to cover the relevant obligations by the AI Office, compliance with a European harmonised standard should grant providers the presumption of conformity. Providers of general-purpose AI models should furthermore be able to demonstrate compliance using alternative adequate means, if codes of practice or harmonised standards are not available, or they choose not to rely on those.

1149. (121) Standardisation should play a key role to provide technical solutions to providers to ensure compliance with this Regulation, in line with the state of the art, to promote innovation as well as competitiveness and growth in the single market. Compliance with harmonised standards as defined in Article 2, point (1)(c), of Regulation (EU) No 1025/2012 of the European Parliament and of the Council,[145] which are normally expected to reflect the state of the art, should be a means for providers to demonstrate conformity with the requirements of this Regulation. A balanced representation of interests involving all relevant stakeholders in the development of standards, in particular SMEs, consumer organisations and environmental and social stakeholders in accordance with Articles 5 and 6 of Regulation (EU) No 1025/2012 should therefore be encouraged. In order to facilitate compliance, the standardisation requests should be issued by the Commission without undue delay. When preparing the standardisation request, the Commission should consult the advisory forum and the Board in order to collect relevant expertise. However, in the absence of relevant references to harmonised standards, the Commission should be able to establish, via implementing acts, and after consultation of the advisory forum, common specifications for certain requirements under this Regulation. The common specification should be an exceptional fall back solution to facilitate the provider's obligation to comply with the requirements of this Regulation, when the standardisation request has not been accepted by any of the European standardisation organisations, or when the relevant harmonised standards insufficiently address fundamental rights concerns, or when the harmonised standards do not comply with the request, or when there are delays in the adoption of an appropriate harmonised standard. Where such a delay in the adoption of a harmonised standard is due to the technical complexity of that standard, this should be considered by the Commission before contemplating the establishment of common specifications. When developing common specifications, the Commission is encouraged to cooperate with international partners and international standardisation bodies.

---

145 Regulation (EU) No 1025/2012 of the European Parliament and of the Council of 25 October 2012 on European standardisation, amending Council Directives 89/686/EEC and 93/15/EEC and Directives 94/9/EC, 94/25/EC, 95/16/EC, 97/23/EC, 98/34/EC, 2004/22/EC, 2007/23/EC, 2009/23/EC and 2009/105/EC of the European Parliament and of the Council and repealing Council Decision 87/95/EEC and Decision No 1673/2006/EC of the European Parliament and of the Council, [2012] OJ L316/12.

1150. **(122)** It is appropriate that, without prejudice to the use of harmonised standards and common specifications, providers of a high-risk AI system that has been trained and tested on data reflecting the specific geographical, behavioural, contextual or functional setting within which the AI system is intended to be used, should be presumed to comply with the relevant measure provided for under the requirement on data governance set out in this Regulation. Without prejudice to the requirements related to robustness and accuracy set out in this Regulation, in accordance with Article 54(3) of Regulation (EU) 2019/881, high-risk AI systems that have been certified or for which a statement of conformity has been issued under a cybersecurity scheme pursuant to that Regulation and the references of which have been published in the Official Journal of the European Union should be presumed to comply with the cybersecurity requirement of this Regulation in so far as the cybersecurity certificate or statement of conformity or parts thereof cover the cybersecurity requirement of this Regulation. This remains without prejudice to the voluntary nature of that cybersecurity scheme.

40.2. General Approach

1151. The regulatory approach is a crucial component in the creation of an artificial intelligence market built on trust.

40.3. Architecture

1152. It is organised as follows:

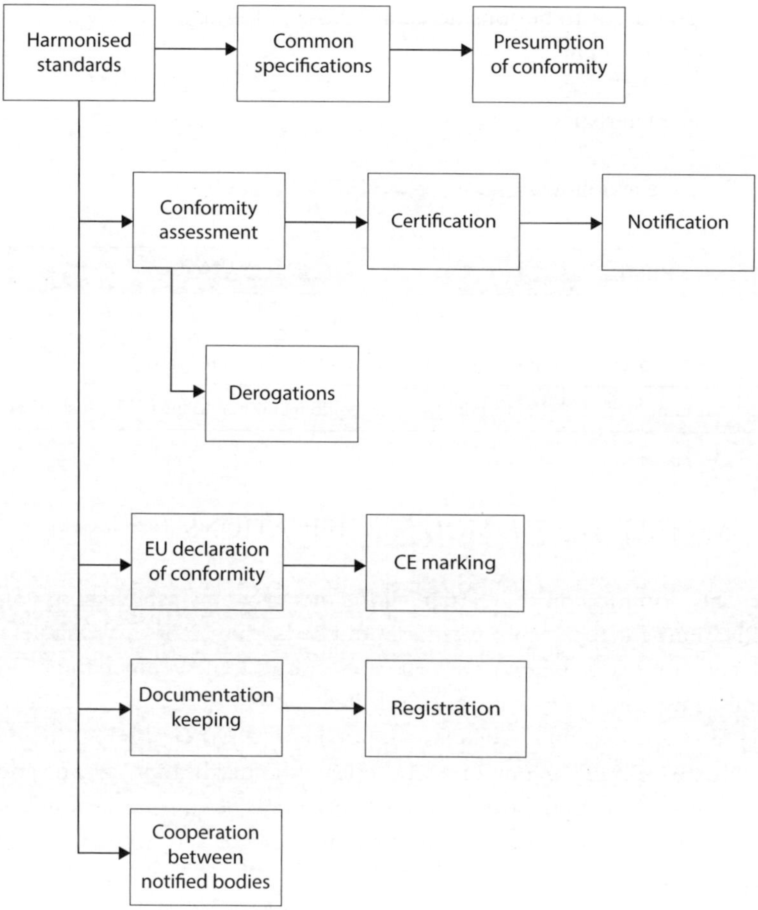

40.4. Definition

1153. 'Harmonised standard' means 'a harmonised standard as defined in Article 2(1), point (c), of Regulation (EU) No 1025/2012',[146] which is follows:

- '"harmonised standard" means a European standard adopted on the basis of a request made by the Commission for the application of Union harmonisation legislation.'

[146] AI Act, Art. 3(27).

40.5. Standards

40.5.1 Typology

1154. The standards to be considered are those published in the *Official Journal of the European Union.*

40.5.2 Characteristics

1155. They are as follows:

NO.	THEME	SPECIFICATION
1.	Full coverage	By a standard or parts thereof
2.	Partial coverage	In this case, the presumption does not apply
3.	Presumption	Conformity with the requirements applicable to high-risk AI systems

41 ARTICLE 41. COMMON SPECIFICATIONS

1. The Commission may adopt, implementing acts establishing common specifications for the requirements set out in Section 2 of this Chapter or, as applicable, for the obligations set out in Sections 2 and 3 of Chapter V where the following conditions have been fulfilled:

(a) the Commission has requested, pursuant to Article 10(1) of Regulation (EU) No 1025/2012, one or more European standardisation organisations to draft a harmonised standard for the requirements set out in Section 2 of this Chapter, or, as applicable, for the obligations set out in Sections 2 and 3 of Chapter V, and:

(i) the request has not been accepted by any of the European standardisation organisations; or

(ii) the harmonised standards addressing that request are not delivered within the deadline set in accordance with Article 10(1) of Regulation (EU) No 1025/2012; or

(iii) the relevant harmonised standards insufficiently address fundamental rights concerns; or

(iv) the harmonised standards do not comply with the request; and

(b) No reference to harmonised standards covering the requirements referred to in Section 2 of this Chapter or, as applicable, the obligations referred to in Sections 2 and 3 of Chapter V has been published in the Official Journal of the European Union in accordance with Regulation (EU) No 1025/2012, and no such reference is expected to be published within a reasonable period.

When drafting the common specifications, the Commission shall consult the advisory forum referred to in Article 67.

The implementing acts referred to in the first subparagraph of this paragraph shall be adopted in accordance with the examination procedure referred to in Article 98(2).

2. Before preparing a draft implementing act, the Commission shall inform the committee referred to in Article 22 of Regulation (EU) No 1025/2012 that it considers the conditions laid down in paragraph 1 of this Article to be fulfilled.

3. High-risk AI systems or general-purpose AI models which are in conformity with the common specifications referred to in paragraph 1, or parts of those specifications, shall be presumed to be in conformity with the requirements set out in Section 2 of this Chapter or, as applicable, to comply with the obligations referred to in Sections 2 and 3 of Chapter V, to the extent those common specifications cover those requirements or those obligations.

4. Where a harmonised standard is adopted by a European standardisation organisation and proposed to the Commission for the publication of its reference in the Official Journal of the European Union, the Commission shall assess the harmonised standard in accordance with Regulation (EU) No 1025/2012. When reference to a harmonised standard is published in the Official Journal of the European Union, the Commission shall repeal the implementing acts referred to in paragraph 1, or parts thereof which cover the same requirements set out in Section 2 of this Chapter or, as applicable, the same obligations set out in Sections 2 and 3 of Chapter V.

5. Where providers of high-risk AI systems or general-purpose AI models do not comply with the common specifications referred to in paragraph 1, they shall duly justify that they have adopted technical solutions that meet the requirements referred to in Section 2 of this Chapter or, as applicable, comply with the obligations set out in Sections 2 and 3 of Chapter V to a level at least equivalent thereto.

6. Where a Member State considers that a common specification does not entirely meet the requirements set out in Section 2 or, as applicable, comply with obligations set out in Sections 2 and 3 of Chapter V, it shall inform the Commission thereof with a detailed explanation. The Commission shall assess that information and, if appropriate, amend the implementing act establishing the common specification concerned.

41.1. Recitals

1156. (121) Standardisation should play a key role to provide technical solutions to providers to ensure compliance with this Regulation, in line with the state of the art, to promote innovation as well as competitiveness and growth in the single market. Compliance with harmonised standards as defined in Article 2, point (1)(c), of Regulation (EU) No 1025/2012 of the European Parliament and of the Council,[147] which are normally expected to reflect the state of the art, should be a means for providers to demonstrate conformity with the requirements of this Regulation. A balanced representation of interests involving all relevant stakeholders in the development of standards, in particular SMEs, consumer organisations and environmental and social stakeholders in accordance with Articles 5 and 6 of Regulation (EU) No 1025/2012 should therefore be encouraged. In order to facilitate compliance, the standardisation requests should be issued by the Commission without undue delay. When preparing the standardisation request, the Commission should consult the advisory forum and the Board in order to collect relevant expertise. However, in the absence of relevant references to harmonised standards, the Commission should be able to establish, via implementing acts, and after consultation of the advisory forum, common specifications for certain requirements under this Regulation. The common specification should be an exceptional fall back solution to facilitate the provider's obligation to comply with the requirements of this Regulation, when the standardisation request has not been accepted by any of the European standardisation organisations, or when the relevant harmonised standards insufficiently address fundamental rights concerns, or when the harmonised standards do not comply with the request, or when there are delays in the adoption of an appropriate harmonised standard. Where such a delay in the adoption of a harmonised standard is due to the technical complexity of that standard, this should be considered by the Commission before contemplating the establishment of common specifications. When developing common specifications, the Commission is encouraged to cooperate with international partners and international standardisation bodies.

1157. (122) It is appropriate that, without prejudice to the use of harmonised standards and common specifications, providers of a high-risk AI system that has been trained and tested on data reflecting the specific geographical, behavioural, contextual or functional setting within which the AI system is intended to be used, should be presumed to comply with the relevant measure provided for under the requirement on data governance set out in this Regulation. Without prejudice to the requirements related to robustness and accuracy set out in this Regulation, in accordance with Article 54(3) of Regulation (EU) 2019/881, high-risk AI systems that have been certified or for which a statement of conformity has been issued under a cybersecurity scheme pursuant to that Regulation and the references of which have been published in the Official Journal of the European

[147] Regulation (EU) No 1025/2012 of the European Parliament and of the Council of 25 October 2012 on European standardisation, amending Council Directives 89/686/EEC and 93/15/EEC and Directives 94/9/EC, 94/25/EC, 95/16/EC, 97/23/EC, 98/34/EC, 2004/22/EC, 2007/23/EC, 2009/23/EC and 2009/105/EC of the European Parliament and of the Council and repealing Council Decision 87/95/EEC and Decision No 1673/2006/EC of the European Parliament and of the Council, [2012] OJ L316/12.

Union should be presumed to comply with the cybersecurity requirement of this Regulation in so far as the cybersecurity certificate or statement of conformity or parts thereof cover the cybersecurity requirement of this Regulation. This remains without prejudice to the voluntary nature of that cybersecurity scheme.

41.2. General Approach

41.2.1 Preamble

1158. Common specifications serve as alternatives to technical regulation through harmonised standards. The standard framework is the deployment of high-risk AI systems in compliance with harmonised standards.[148]

41.2.2 Definition

1159. 'Common specification' means 'a set of technical specifications as defined in Article 2, point (4) of Regulation (EU) No 1025/2012, providing means to comply with certain requirements established under this Regulation'.[149]

41.3. Formalities And Procedure

1160. Common specifications are:

- drafted by the European Commission;
- after consultation of the advisory forum.[150]

41.4. Characteristics

1161. They are as follows:

NO.	THEME	SPECIFICATION
1.	Coverage	Requirements for high-risk AI systems
2.	Impact	Rebuttable presumption of conformity
3.	Adequacy	Technical solutions are "at least equivalent" to the common specifications

148 AI Act, Art. 40.
149 AI Act, Art. 3(28).
150 AI Act, Art. 67.

42 ARTICLE 42. PRESUMPTION OF CONFORMITY WITH CERTAIN REQUIREMENTS

1. High-risk AI systems that have been trained and tested on data reflecting the specific geographical, behavioural, contextual or functional setting within which they are intended to be used shall be presumed to comply with the relevant requirements laid down in Article 10(4).

2. High-risk AI systems that have been certified or for which a statement of conformity has been issued under a cybersecurity scheme pursuant to Regulation (EU) 2019/881 and the references of which have been published in the Official Journal of the European Union shall be presumed to comply with the cybersecurity requirements set out in Article 15 of this Regulation in so far as the cybersecurity certificate or statement of conformity or parts thereof cover those requirements.

42.1. Recitals

1162. (122) It is appropriate that, without prejudice to the use of harmonised standards and common specifications, providers of a high-risk AI system that has been trained and tested on data reflecting the specific geographical, behavioural, contextual or functional setting within which the AI system is intended to be used, should be presumed to comply with the relevant measure provided for under the requirement on data governance set out in this Regulation. Without prejudice to the requirements related to robustness and accuracy set out in this Regulation, in accordance with Article 54(3) of Regulation (EU) 2019/881, high-risk AI systems that have been certified or for which a statement of conformity has been issued under a cybersecurity scheme pursuant to that Regulation and the references of which have been published in the Official Journal of the European Union should be presumed to comply with the cybersecurity requirement of this Regulation in so far as the cybersecurity certificate or statement of conformity or parts thereof cover the cybersecurity requirement of this Regulation. This remains without prejudice to the voluntary nature of that cybersecurity scheme.

42.2. General Approach

42.2.1 Preamble

1163. Specific presumptions of conformity are provided for:

- data and uses within a high-risk AI system;
- cybersecurity requirements.

42.2.2 Guiding Principles

1164. The purpose of such presumptions is to:
- avoid duplication of conformity monitoring processes;
- limit the budgetary cost of such processes.

42.3. Data

1165. They include:
- training data;[151]
- testing data;[152]
- validation data;[153]
- input data.[154]

42.4. Characteristics

1166. They are as follows:

NO.	THEME	SPECIFICATION
1.	Purpose	Training and testing
2.	Setting	Geographical, behavioural and functional
3.	Effect	Presumption of conformity with data requirement[155]

42.5. Presumption Regarding Cybersecurity

1167. The presumption applies in the following two cases:
- the high-risk AI system has been issued a statement of conformity under a cybersecurity scheme;[156]
- the high-risk AI system has been certified.

---

151 AI Act, Art. 3(29).
152 AI Act, Art. 3(32).
153 AI Act, Art. 3(30).
154 AI Act, Art. 3(33).
155 Requirements set out in Art. 10(4) of the AI Act.
156 Regulation (EU) 2019/881 of the European Parliament and of the Council of 17 April 2019 on ENISA (the European Union Agency for Cybersecurity) and on information and communications technology cybersecurity certification and repealing Regulation (EU) No 526/2013 (Cybersecurity Act), [2019] OJ L151/15.

1168. They characteristics are as follows:

NO.	THEME	SPECIFICATION
1.	Requirement	Article 15 on cybersecurity
2.	Effect	Rebuttable presumption

43 ARTICLE 43. CONFORMITY ASSESSMENT

1. For high-risk AI systems listed in point 1 of Annex III, where, in demonstrating the compliance of a high-risk AI system with the requirements set out in Section 2, the provider has applied harmonised standards referred to in Article 40, or, where applicable, common specifications referred to in Article 41, the provider shall opt for one of the following conformity assessment procedures based on:

(a) the internal control referred to in Annex VI; or

(b) the assessment of the quality management system and the assessment of the technical documentation, with the involvement of a notified body, referred to in Annex VII.

In demonstrating the compliance of a high-risk AI system with the requirements set out in Section 2, the provider shall follow the conformity assessment procedure set out in Annex VII where:

(a) harmonised standards referred to in Article 40 do not exist, and common specifications referred to in Article 41 are not available;

(b) the provider has not applied, or has applied only part of, the harmonised standard;

(c) the common specifications referred to in point (a) exist, but the provider has not applied them;

(d) one or more of the harmonised standards referred to in point (a) has been published with a restriction, and only on the part of the standard that was restricted.

For the purposes of the conformity assessment procedure referred to in Annex VII, the provider may choose any of the notified bodies. However, where the high-risk AI system is intended to be put into service by law enforcement, immigration or asylum authorities or by Union institutions, bodies, offices or agencies, the market surveillance authority referred to in Article 74(8) or (9), as applicable, shall act as a notified body.

2. For high-risk AI systems referred to in points 2 to 8 of Annex III, providers shall follow the conformity assessment procedure based on internal control as referred to in Annex VI, which does not provide for the involvement of a notified body.

3. For high-risk AI systems covered by the Union harmonisation legislation listed in Section A of Annex I, the provider shall follow the relevant conformity assessment procedure as required under those legal acts. The requirements set out in Section 2 of this Chapter shall apply to those high-risk AI systems and shall be part of that assessment. Points 4.3., 4.4., 4.5. and the fifth paragraph of point 4.6 of Annex VII shall also apply.

For the purposes of that assessment, notified bodies which have been notified under those legal acts shall be entitled to control the conformity of the high-risk AI systems with the requirements set out in Section 2, provided that the compliance of those notified bodies with requirements laid down in Article 31(4), (5), (10) and (11) has been assessed in the context of the notification procedure under those legal acts.

Where a legal act listed in Section A of Annex I enables the product manufacturer to opt out from a third-party conformity assessment, provided that that manufacturer has applied all harmonised standards covering all the relevant requirements, that manufacturer may use that option only if it has also applied harmonised standards or, where applicable, common specifications referred to in Article 41, covering all requirements set out in Section 2 of this Chapter.

4. High-risk AI systems that have already been subject to a conformity assessment procedure shall undergo a new conformity assessment procedure in the event of a substantial modification, regardless of whether the modified system is intended to be further distributed or continues to be used by the current deployer.

For high-risk AI systems that continue to learn after being placed on the market or put into service, changes to the high-risk AI system and its performance that have been pre-determined by the provider at the moment of the initial conformity assessment and are part of the information contained in the technical documentation referred to in point 2(f) of Annex IV, shall not constitute a substantial modification.

5. The Commission is empowered to adopt delegated acts in accordance with Article 97 in order to amend Annexes VI and VII by updating them in light of technical progress.

6. The Commission is empowered to adopt delegated acts in accordance with Article 97 in order to amend paragraphs 1 and 2 of this Article in order to subject high-risk AI systems referred to in points 2 to 8 of Annex III to the conformity assessment procedure referred to in Annex VII or parts thereof. The Commission shall adopt such delegated acts taking into account the effectiveness of the conformity assessment procedure based on internal control referred to in Annex VI in preventing or minimising the risks to health and safety and protection of fundamental rights posed by such systems, as well as the availability of adequate capacities and resources among notified bodies.

43.1. Recitals

1169. (49) As regards high-risk AI systems that are safety components of products or systems, or which are themselves products or systems falling within the scope of Regulation (EC) No 300/2008 of the European Parliament and of the Council,[157] Regulation (EU) No 167/2013 of the European Parliament and of the Council,[158] Regulation (EU) No 168/2013 of the European Parliament and of the Council,[159] Directive 2014/90/EU of the European Parliament and of the Council,[160] Directive (EU) 2016/797 of the European Parliament and of the Council,[161] Regulation (EU) 2018/858 of the European Parliament and of the Council,[162] Regulation (EU) 2018/1139 of the European Parliament and of the Council,[163] and Regulation (EU) 2019/2144 of the European Parliament and of the Council,[164] it is appropriate to amend those acts to ensure that the

---

157 Regulation (EC) No 300/2008 of the European Parliament and of the Council of 11 March 2008 on common rules in the field of civil aviation security and repealing Regulation (EC) No 2320/2002, [2008] OJ L97/72.

158 Regulation (EU) No 167/2013 of the European Parliament and of the Council of 5 February 2013 on the approval and market surveillance of agricultural and forestry vehicles, [2013] OJ L60/1.

159 Regulation (EU) No 168/2013 of the European Parliament and of the Council of 15 January 2013 on the approval and market surveillance of two- or three-wheel vehicles and quadricycles, [2013] OJ L60/52.

160 Directive 2014/90/EU of the European Parliament and of the Council of 23 July 2014 on marine equipment and repealing Council Directive 96/98/EC, [2014] OJ L257/146.

161 Directive (EU) 2016/797 of the European Parliament and of the Council of 11 May 2016 on the interoperability of the rail system within the European Union, [2016] O L138/44.

162 Regulation (EU) 2018/858 of the European Parliament and of the Council of 30 May 2018 on the approval and market surveillance of motor vehicles and their trailers, and of systems, components and separate technical units intended for such vehicles, amending Regulations (EC) No 715/2007 and (EC) No 595/2009 and repealing Directive 2007/46/EC, [2018] OJ L151/1.

163 Regulation (EU) 2018/1139 of the European Parliament and of the Council of 4 July 2018 on common rules in the field of civil aviation and establishing a European Union Aviation Safety Agency, and amending Regulations (EC) No 2111/2005, (EC) No 1008/2008, (EU) No 996/2010, (EU) No 376/2014 and Directives 2014/30/EU and 2014/53/EU of the European Parliament and of the Council, and repealing Regulations (EC) No 552/2004 and (EC) No 216/2008 of the European Parliament and of the Council and Council Regulation (EEC) No 3922/91, [2018] OJ L212/1.

164 Regulation (EU) 2019/2144 of the European Parliament and of the Council of 27 November 2019 on type-approval requirements for motor vehicles and their trailers, and systems, components and separate technical units intended for such vehicles, as regards their general safety and the protection of vehicle occupants and vulnerable road users, amending Regulation (EU) 2018/858 of the European Parliament and of the Council and repealing Regulations (EC) No 78/2009, (EC) No 79/2009 and (EC) No 661/2009 of the European Parliament and of the Council and Commission Regulations (EC) No 631/2009, (EU) No 406/2010, (EU) No 672/2010, (EU) No 1003/2010, (EU) No 1005/2010, (EU) No 1008/2010, (EU) No 1009/2010, (EU) No 19/2011, (EU) No 109/2011, (EU) No 458/2011, (EU) No 65/2012, (EU) No 130/2012, (EU) No 347/2012, (EU) No 351/2012, (EU) No 1230/2012 and (EU) 2015/166, [2019] OJ L325/1.

Commission takes into account, on the basis of the technical and regulatory specificities of each sector, and without interfering with existing governance, conformity assessment and enforcement mechanisms and authorities established therein, the mandatory requirements for high-risk AI systems laid down in this Regulation when adopting any relevant delegated or implementing acts on the basis of those acts.

1170. **(50)** As regards AI systems that are safety components of products, or which are themselves products, falling within the scope of certain Union harmonisation legislation listed in an annex to this Regulation, it is appropriate to classify them as high-risk under this Regulation if the product concerned undergoes the conformity assessment procedure with a third-party conformity assessment body pursuant to that relevant Union harmonisation legislation. In particular, such products are machinery, toys, lifts, equipment and protective systems intended for use in potentially explosive atmospheres, radio equipment, pressure equipment, recreational craft equipment, cableway installations, appliances burning gaseous fuels, medical devices, in vitro diagnostic medical devices, automotive and aviation.

1171. **(51)** The classification of an AI system as high-risk pursuant to this Regulation should not necessarily mean that the product whose safety component is the AI system, or the AI system itself as a product, is considered to be high-risk under the criteria established in the relevant Union harmonisation legislation that applies to the product. This is, in particular, the case for Regulations (EU) 2017/745 and (EU) 2017/746, where a third-party conformity assessment is provided for medium-risk and high-risk products.

1172. **(59)** Given their role and responsibility, actions by law enforcement authorities involving certain uses of AI systems are characterised by a significant degree of power imbalance and may lead to surveillance, arrest or deprivation of a natural person's liberty as well as other adverse impacts on fundamental rights guaranteed in the Charter. In particular, if the AI system is not trained with high-quality data, does not meet adequate requirements in terms of its performance, its accuracy or robustness, or is not properly designed and tested before being put on the market or otherwise put into service, it may single out people in a discriminatory or otherwise incorrect or unjust manner. Furthermore, the exercise of important procedural fundamental rights, such as the right to an effective remedy and to a fair trial as well as the right of defence and the presumption of innocence, could be hampered, in particular, where such AI systems are not sufficiently transparent, explainable and documented. It is therefore appropriate to classify as high-risk, insofar as their use is permitted under relevant Union and national law, a number of AI systems intended to be used in the law enforcement context where accuracy, reliability and transparency is particularly important to avoid adverse impacts, retain public trust and ensure accountability and effective redress. In view of the nature of the activities and the risks relating thereto, those high-risk AI systems should include in particular AI systems intended to be used by or on behalf of law enforcement authorities or by Union institutions, bodies, offices, or agencies in support of law enforcement authorities for assessing the risk of a natural person to become a victim of criminal offences, as polygraphs and similar tools, for the evaluation of the reliability of evidence in in the course of investigation or prosecution of criminal offences, and, insofar as not prohibited under this Regulation, for assessing the risk of a natural person offending or reoffending not solely on the basis of the profiling of natural persons or the assessment of personality traits and characteristics or the past criminal behaviour of natural persons or groups, for profiling in the course of detection, investigation or prosecution of criminal offences. AI systems specifically intended to be used for administrative proceedings by tax and customs authorities as well as by financial intelligence units carrying out administrative tasks analysing information pursuant to Union anti-money laundering law should not be classified as high-risk AI systems used by law enforcement authorities for the purpose of prevention, detection, investigation and prosecution of criminal offences. The use of AI tools by law enforcement and other relevant authorities should not become a factor of inequality, or exclusion. The impact of the use of AI tools on the defence rights of suspects should not be ignored, in particular the difficulty in obtaining meaningful information on the functioning of those systems and the resulting difficulty in challenging their results in court, in particular by natural persons under investigation.

1173. (78) The conformity assessment procedure provided by this Regulation should apply in relation to the essential cybersecurity requirements of a product with digital elements covered by a regulation of the European Parliament and of the Council on horizontal cybersecurity requirements for products with digital elements and classified as a high-risk AI system under this Regulation. However, this rule should not result in reducing the necessary level of assurance for critical products with digital elements covered by a regulation of the European Parliament and of the Council on horizontal cybersecurity requirements for products with digital elements. Therefore, by way of derogation from this rule, high-risk AI systems that fall within the scope of this Regulation and are also qualified as important and critical products with digital elements pursuant to a regulation of the European Parliament and of the Council on horizontal cybersecurity requirements for products with digital elements and to which the conformity assessment procedure based on internal control set out in an annex to this Regulation applies, are subject to the conformity assessment provisions of a regulation of the European Parliament and of the Council on horizontal cybersecurity requirements for products with digital elements insofar as the essential cybersecurity requirements of that regulation are concerned. In this case, for all the other aspects covered by this Regulation the respective provisions on conformity assessment based on internal control set out in an annex to this Regulation should apply. Building on the knowledge and expertise of ENISA on the cybersecurity policy and tasks assigned to ENISA under the Regulation (EU) 2019/881 of the European Parliament and of the Council,[165] the Commission should cooperate with ENISA on issues related to cybersecurity of AI systems.

1174. (81) The provider should establish a sound quality management system, ensure the accomplishment of the required conformity assessment procedure, draw up the relevant documentation and establish a robust post-market monitoring system. Providers of high-risk AI systems that are subject to obligations regarding quality management systems under relevant sectoral Union law should have the possibility to include the elements of the quality management system provided for in this Regulation as part of the existing quality management system provided for in that other sectoral Union law. The complementarity between this Regulation and existing sectoral Union law should also be taken into account in future standardisation activities or guidance adopted by the Commission. Public authorities which put into service high-risk AI systems for their own use may adopt and implement the rules for the quality management system as part of the quality management system adopted at a national or regional level, as appropriate, taking into account the specificities of the sector and the competences and organisation of the public authority concerned.

1175. (86) Where, under the conditions laid down in this Regulation, the provider that initially placed the AI system on the market or put it into service should no longer be considered to be the provider for the purposes of this Regulation, and when that provider has not expressly excluded the change of the AI system into a high-risk AI system, the former provider should nonetheless closely cooperate and make available the necessary information and provide the reasonably expected technical access and other assistance that are required for the fulfilment of the obligations set out in this Regulation, in particular regarding the compliance with the conformity assessment of high-risk AI systems.

1176. (123) In order to ensure a high level of trustworthiness of high-risk AI systems, those systems should be subject to a conformity assessment prior to their placing on the market or putting into service.

1177. (124) It is appropriate that, in order to minimise the burden on operators and avoid any possible duplication, for high-risk AI systems related to products which are covered by existing Union harmonisation legislation based on the New Legislative Framework, the compliance of those AI systems with the requirements of this Regulation should be assessed as part of the conformity assessment already provided for in that law. The applicability of the requirements of this Regulation

---

165 Regulation (EU) 2019/881 of the European Parliament and of the Council of 17 April 2019 on ENISA (the European Union Agency for Cybersecurity) and on information and communications technology cybersecurity certification and repealing Regulation (EU) No 526/2013 (Cybersecurity Act), [2019] OJ L151/15.

should thus not affect the specific logic, methodology or general structure of conformity assessment under the relevant Union harmonisation legislation.

1178. **(125)** Given the complexity of high-risk AI systems and the risks that are associated with them, it is important to develop an adequate conformity assessment procedure for high-risk AI systems involving notified bodies, so-called third party conformity assessment. However, given the current experience of professional pre-market certifiers in the field of product safety and the different nature of risks involved, it is appropriate to limit, at least in an initial phase of application of this Regulation, the scope of application of third-party conformity assessment for high-risk AI systems other than those related to products. Therefore, the conformity assessment of such systems should be carried out as a general rule by the provider under its own responsibility, with the only exception of AI systems intended to be used for biometrics.

1179. **(127)** In line with Union commitments under the World Trade Organization Agreement on Technical Barriers to Trade, it is adequate to facilitate the mutual recognition of conformity assessment results produced by competent conformity assessment bodies, independent of the territory in which they are established, provided that those conformity assessment bodies established under the law of a third country meet the applicable requirements of this Regulation and the Union has concluded an agreement to that extent. In this context, the Commission should actively explore possible international instruments for that purpose and in particular pursue the conclusion of mutual recognition agreements with third countries.

1180. **(128)** In line with the commonly established notion of substantial modification for products regulated by Union harmonisation legislation, it is appropriate that whenever a change occurs which may affect the compliance of a high-risk AI system with this Regulation (e.g. change of operating system or software architecture), or when the intended purpose of the system changes, that AI system should be considered to be a new AI system which should undergo a new conformity assessment. However, changes occurring to the algorithm and the performance of AI systems which continue to 'learn' after being placed on the market or put into service, namely automatically adapting how functions are carried out, should not constitute a substantial modification, provided that those changes have been pre-determined by the provider and assessed at the moment of the conformity assessment.

1181. **(139)** The objectives of the AI regulatory sandboxes should be to foster AI innovation by establishing a controlled experimentation and testing environment in the development and pre-marketing phase with a view to ensuring compliance of the innovative AI systems with this Regulation and other relevant Union and national law. Moreover, the AI regulatory sandboxes should aim to enhance legal certainty for innovators and the competent authorities' oversight and understanding of the opportunities, emerging risks and the impacts of AI use, to facilitate regulatory learning for authorities and undertakings, including with a view to future adaptions of the legal framework, to support cooperation and the sharing of best practices with the authorities involved in the AI regulatory sandbox, and to accelerate access to markets, including by removing barriers for SMEs, including start-ups. AI regulatory sandboxes should be widely available throughout the Union, and particular attention should be given to their accessibility for SMEs, including start-ups. The participation in the AI regulatory sandbox should focus on issues that raise legal uncertainty for providers and prospective providers to innovate, experiment with AI in the Union and contribute to evidence-based regulatory learning. The supervision of the AI systems in the AI regulatory sandbox should therefore cover their development, training, testing and validation before the systems are placed on the market or put into service, as well as the notion and occurrence of substantial modification that may require a new conformity assessment procedure. Any significant risks identified during the development and testing of such AI systems should result in adequate mitigation and, failing that, in the suspension of the development and testing process. Where appropriate, national competent authorities establishing AI regulatory sandboxes should cooperate with other relevant authorities, including those supervising the protection of fundamental rights, and could allow for the involvement of other actors within the AI ecosystem such as national or European standardisation organisations, notified bodies, testing and experimentation facilities, research and experimentation labs, European Digital Innovation Hubs and relevant stakeholder and civil society organisations. To ensure uniform implementation across the Union and economies of scale, it is appropriate to establish common rules for the AI regulatory sandboxes' implementation and a framework for cooperation between the relevant authorities involved in the supervision of the sandboxes. AI regulatory sandboxes established under this Regulation should be without prejudice to other law allowing for the establishment of other sandboxes aiming to ensure compliance with law other than this Regulation. Where appropriate, relevant competent authorities in charge of those other regulatory sandboxes should consider the benefits of using those sandboxes also for the purpose of ensuring compliance of AI systems with this Regulation. Upon agreement between the national competent authorities and the participants in the AI regulatory sandbox, testing in real world conditions may also be operated and supervised in the framework of the AI regulatory sandbox.

1182. **(143)** In order to promote and protect innovation, it is important that the interests of SMEs, including start-ups, that are providers or deployers of AI systems are taken into particular account. To that end, Member States should develop initiatives, which are targeted at those operators, including on awareness raising and information communication. Member States should provide SMEs, including start-ups, that have a registered office or a branch in the Union, with priority access to the AI regulatory sandboxes provided that they fulfil the eligibility conditions and selection criteria and without precluding other providers and prospective providers to access the sandboxes provided the same conditions and criteria are fulfilled. Member States should utilise existing channels and where appropriate, establish new dedicated channels for communication with SMEs, including start-ups, deployers, other innovators and, as appropriate, local public authorities, to support SMEs throughout their development path by providing guidance and responding to queries about the implementation of this Regulation. Where appropriate, these channels should work together to create synergies and ensure homogeneity in their guidance to SMEs, including start-ups, and deployers. Additionally, Member States should facilitate the participation of SMEs and other relevant stakeholders in the standardisation development processes. Moreover, the specific interests and needs of providers that are SMEs, including start-ups, should be taken into account when notified bodies set conformity assessment fees. The Commission should regularly assess the certification and compliance costs for SMEs, including start-ups, through transparent consultations and should work with Member States to lower such costs. For example, translation costs related to mandatory documentation and communication with authorities may constitute a significant cost for providers and other operators, in particular those of a smaller scale. Member States should possibly ensure that one of the languages determined and accepted by them for relevant providers' documentation and for communication with operators is one which is broadly understood by the largest possible number of cross-border deployers. In order to address the specific needs of SMEs, including start-ups, the Commission should provide standardised templates for the areas covered by this Regulation, upon request of the Board. Additionally, the Commission should complement Member States' efforts by providing a single information platform with easy-to-use information with regards to this Regulation for all providers and deployers, by organising appropriate communication campaigns to raise awareness about the obligations arising from this Regulation, and by evaluating and promoting the convergence of best practices in public procurement procedures in relation to AI systems. Medium-sized enterprises which until recently qualified as small enterprises within the meaning of the Annex to Commission Recommendation 2003/361/EC[166] should have access to those support measures, as those new medium-sized enterprises may sometimes lack the legal resources and training necessary to ensure proper understanding of, and compliance with, this Regulation.

1183. **(147)** It is appropriate that the Commission facilitates, to the extent possible, access to testing and experimentation facilities to bodies, groups or laboratories established or accredited pursuant to any relevant Union harmonisation

166 Commission Recommendation of 6 May 2003 concerning the definition of micro, small and medium-sized enterprises, [2003] OJ L124/36.

legislation and which fulfil tasks in the context of conformity assessment of products or devices covered by that Union harmonisation legislation. This is, in particular, the case as regards expert panels, expert laboratories and reference laboratories in the field of medical devices pursuant to Regulations (EU) 2017/745 and (EU) 2017/746.

1184. **(173)** In order to ensure that the regulatory framework can be adapted where necessary, the power to adopt acts in accordance with Article 290 TFEU should be delegated to the Commission to amend the conditions under which an AI system is not to be considered to be high-risk, the list of high-risk AI systems, the provisions regarding technical documentation, the content of the EU declaration of conformity the provisions regarding the conformity assessment procedures, the provisions establishing the high-risk AI systems to which the conformity assessment procedure based on assessment of the quality management system and assessment of the technical documentation should apply, the threshold, benchmarks and indicators, including by supplementing those benchmarks and indicators, in the rules for the classification of general-purpose AI models with systemic risk, the criteria for the designation of general-purpose AI models with systemic risk, the technical documentation for providers of general-purpose AI models and the transparency information for providers of general-purpose AI models. It is of particular importance that the Commission carry out appropriate consultations during its preparatory work, including at expert level, and that those consultations be conducted in accordance with the principles laid down in the Interinstitutional Agreement of 13 April 2016 on Better Law-Making.[167] In particular, to ensure equal participation in the preparation of delegated acts, the European Parliament and the Council receive all documents at the same time as Member States' experts, and their experts systematically have access to meetings of Commission expert groups dealing with the preparation of delegated acts.

1185. **(179)** This Regulation should apply from 2 August 2026. However, taking into account the unacceptable risk associated with the use of AI in certain ways, the prohibitions as well as the general provisions of this Regulation should already apply from 2 February 2025. While the full effect of those prohibitions follows with the establishment of the governance and enforcement of this Regulation, anticipating the application of the prohibitions is important to take account of unacceptable risks and to have an effect on other procedures, such as in civil law. Moreover, the infrastructure related to the governance and the conformity assessment system should be operational before 2 August 2026, therefore the provisions on notified bodies and governance structure should apply from 2 August 2025. Given the rapid pace of technological advancements and adoption of general-purpose AI models, obligations for providers of general-purpose AI models should apply from 2 August 2025. Codes of practice should be ready by 2 May 2025 in view of enabling providers

---

[167] [2016] OJ L123/1.

to demonstrate compliance on time. The AI Office should ensure that classification rules and procedures are up to date in light of technological developments. In addition, Member States should lay down and notify to the Commission the rules on penalties, including administrative fines, and ensure that they are properly and effectively implemented by the date of application of this Regulation. Therefore the provisions on penalties should apply from 2 August 2025.

43.2. General Approach

43.2.1 Preamble

1186. AI system conformity corresponds to two very different concepts:

- the conformity of the AI system with its intended purpose;
- the conformity of the AI system with the requirements of trustworthy AI.

43.2.2 Guiding Principles

1187. The assessment of high-risk AI system conformity does not follow a one-size-fits-all approach.

1188. It is determined based on the following elements

- the types of high-risk AI systems;
- the presence or absence of harmonised standards.

43.3. Definition

1189. 'Conformity assessment' means 'the process of demonstrating whether the requirements set out in Chapter III, Section 2 relating to a high-risk AI system have been fulfilled'.[168]

43.3.1 Conformity Items

1190. The conformity assessment covers the following items:

NO.	THEME	SPECIFICATION	REFERENCES
1.	Requirements	Compliance with the requirements according to the intended purpose	AIA, Art. 8
2.	Risk management system	Approach	AIA, Art. 9

168 AI Act, Art. 3(20).

NO.	THEME	SPECIFICATION	REFERENCES
3.	Data and data governance	Training data	AIA, Art. 10
4.	Technical documentation	Demonstration of compliance	AIA, Art. 11
5.	Record-keeping	Technical specifications	AIA, Art. 12
6.	Transparency	Provision of information to deployers	AIA, Art. 13
7.	Human	Human oversight and 'stop' button	AIA, Art. 14
8.	Accuracy	Output	AIA, Art. 15
9.	Robustness	Resilience	AIA, Art. 15
10.	Cybersecurity	Anti-fraud measures and surveillance	AIA, Art. 15

43.4. Classification

1191. The types of assessment procedures concern the following:

NO.	THEME	SPECIFICATION	REFERENCE
1.	Biometrics	Remote biometric identification (in real time or post-remote)	AIA, Annex III(1)
		Biometric categorisation	AIA, Annex III(1)
		Emotion recognition	AIA, Annex III(1)
2.	Critical infrastructure; education and vocational training; employment, workers' management and access to self-employment; access to and enjoyment of essential private services and essential public services and benefits; law enforcement; migration, asylum and border control management; administration of justice and democratic processes	Conformity assessment procedure based on internal control as referred to in Annex IV, which does not provide for the involvement of a notified body	AIA, Annex III(2)–(8)
3.	AI systems listed in Section A of Annex I	Application of requirements set out in: • Articles 6 to 15 • Annex VII, points 4.3, 4.4, 4.5 and 4.6(5).	AIA, Annex I, Section A

43.5. *Conformity of High-Risk Biometric AI Systems*

43.5.1 Typology

1192. Among all biometric identification systems for natural persons, a specific conformity assessment is provided for a particular category of biometric identification systems based on the characteristics defined below.

43.5.2 Characteristics

1193. They are as follows:

NO.	THEME	SPECIFICATION	COMMENT
1.	Technology	All types of identification and categorisation	
2.	Affected person	Natural persons only	
3.	Place	Publicly accessible space Prohibited	Special rules for high-risk AI systems for law enforcement purposes On an *ad hoc* basis in this type of space for post-remote identification
4.	Medium	Remote	
5.	Timeframe	Real-time or post-remote	
6.	Reference framework	Harmonised standards or common specifications	
7.	General procedure	Either: 1. Assessment based on internal control; or 2. Assessment by a notified body	
8.	Derogation	In the absence of harmonised standards or common specifications, conformity is assessed in accordance with Annex VII, with the involvement of a notified body	Special case: law enforcement, immigration or asylum authorities or by Union institutions, bodies, offices or agencies[169]

[169] In these cases, the notified body is the market surveillance authority. AI Act, Art. 43(1).

43.6. *Conformity of High-Risk AI Systems – List of Annex III (Points 2 to 8)*

43.6.1 Typology

1194. This second category includes high-risk AI systems that do not fall under:
- classification based on criteria;[170] or
- specific biometric identification systems.[171]

43.6.2 Classification

1195. The systems concerned relate to the following areas:
- critical infrastructure (management and operation);
- education and vocational training;
- employment, workers' management and access to self-employment;
- access to and enjoyment of essential private services and essential public services and benefits;
- law enforcement;
- migration, asylum and border control management;
- administration of justice and democratic processes.

43.6.3 Characteristics

1196. They are as follows:

NO.	THEME	SPECIFICATION
1.	Procedure	Internal control
2.	Scope	Compliance of the quality management system[172]
3.	Technical documentation	AIA, Art. 11
4.	Technical documentation	Design and development

[170] AI Act, Art. 6.
[171] AI Act, Annex III, points 2–8.
[172] AI Act, Art. 17.

43.7. *Conformity of High-Risk AI Systems – List of Annex I, Section A*

43.7.1 Typology

1197. This conformity assessment applies to a series of technical fields corresponding to specific legal acts, which are exhaustively listed below.

43.7.2 Classification

1198. The systems concerned are as follows:

- Directive 2006/42/EC of 17 May 2006 on machinery, and amending Directive 95/16/EC, [2006] OJ L157/24;[173]
- Directive 2009/48/EC of 18 June 2009 on the safety of toys, [2009] OJ L170/1;
- Directive 2013/53/EU of 20 November 2013 on recreational craft and personal watercraft and repealing Directive 94/25/EC, [2013] OJ L354/90;
- Directive 2014/33/EU of 26 February 2014 on the harmonisation of the laws of the Member States relating to lifts and safety components for lifts, [2014] OJ L96/251;
- Directive 2014/34/EU of 26 February 2014 on the harmonisation of the laws of the Member States relating to equipment and protective systems intended for use in potentially explosive atmospheres, [2014] OJ L96/309;
- Directive 2014/53/EU of 16 April 2014 on the harmonisation of the laws of the Member States relating to the making available on the market of radio equipment and repealing Directive 1999/5/EC, [2014] OJ L153/62;
- Directive 2014/68/EU of 15 May 2014 on the harmonisation of the laws of the Member States relating to the making available on the market of pressure equipment, [2014] OJ L189/164;
- Regulation (EU) 2016/424 of 9 March 2016 on cableway installations and repealing Directive 2000/9/EC, [2016] OJ L81/1;
- Regulation (EU) 2016/425 of 9 March 2016 on personal protective equipment and repealing Council Directive 89/686/EEC, [2016] OJ L81/51;
- Regulation (EU) 2016/426 of 9 March 2016 on appliances burning gaseous fuels and repealing Directive 2009/142/EC, [2016] OJ L81/99;
- Regulation (EU) 2017/745 of 5 April 2017 on medical devices, amending Directive 2001/83/EC, Regulation (EC) No 178/2002 and Regulation (EC)

[173] This directive, which is still in force, will gradually be replaced by Regulation (EU) 2023/1230 of the European Parliament and of the Council of 14 June 2023 on machinery and repealing Directive 2006/42/EC of the European Parliament and of the Council and Council Directive 73/361/EEC (*OJEU*, L 165, 29 June 2023, p. 1), which will apply from 14 January 2027.

No 1223/2009 and repealing Council Directives 90/385/EEC and 93/42/EEC, [2017] OJ L117/1;

- Regulation (EU) 2017/746 of 5 April 2017 on in vitro diagnostic medical devices and repealing Directive 98/79/EC and Commission Decision 2010/227/EU, [2017] OJ L117/176.

43.7.3 Characteristics

1199. They are as follows:

NO.	THEME	SPECIFICATION	COMMENT
1.	General procedure	Assessment rules for listed systems	
2.	Supplementary procedure	• risk management system, data and technical documentation • transparency, accuracy, robustness, cybersecurity and record-keeping requirements • the requirement for human oversight to ensure control over high-risk AI systems in all circumstances • the technical documentation shall be examined by the notified body. Where relevant, and limited to what is necessary to fulfil its tasks, the notified body shall be granted full access to the training, validation, and testing data sets used, including, where appropriate and subject to security safeguards, through API or other relevant technical means and tools enabling remote access • in examining the technical documentation, the notified body may require that the provider supply further evidence or carry out further tests so as to enable a proper assessment of the conformity of the AI system with the requirements set out in Chapter III, Section 2. Where the notified body is not satisfied with the tests carried out by the provider, the notified body shall itself directly carry out adequate tests, as appropriate • where necessary to assess the conformity of the high-risk AI system with the requirements set out in Chapter III, Section 2, after all other reasonable means to verify conformity have been exhausted and have proven to be insufficient, and upon a reasoned request, the notified body shall also be granted access to the training and trained models of the AI system, including its relevant parameters. Such access shall be subject to existing Union law on the protection of intellectual property and trade secrets • where the AI system does not meet the requirement relating to the data used to train it, re-training of the AI system will be needed prior to the application for a new conformity assessment. In this case, the reasoned assessment decision of the notified body refusing to issue the Union technical documentation assessment certificate shall contain specific considerations on the quality data used to train the AI system, in particular on the reasons for non-compliance	To be associated with the general procedure

44 ARTICLE 44. CERTIFICATES

1. Certificates issued by notified bodies in accordance with Annex VII shall be drawn-up in a language which can be easily understood by the relevant authorities in the Member State in which the notified body is established.

2. Certificates shall be valid for the period they indicate, which shall not exceed five years for AI systems covered by Annex I, and four years for AI systems covered by Annex III. At the request of the provider, the validity of a certificate may be extended for further periods, each not exceeding five years for AI systems covered by Annex I, and four years for AI systems covered by Annex III, based on a re-assessment in accordance with the applicable conformity assessment procedures. Any supplement to a certificate shall remain valid, provided that the certificate which it supplements is valid.

3. Where a notified body finds that an AI system no longer meets the requirements set out in Section 2, it shall, taking account of the principle of proportionality, suspend or withdraw the certificate issued or impose restrictions on it, unless compliance with those requirements is ensured by appropriate corrective action taken by the provider of the system within an appropriate deadline set by the notified body. The notified body shall give reasons for its decision.

An appeal procedure against decisions of the notified bodies, including on conformity certificates issued, shall be available.

44.1. General Approach

44.1.1 Preamble

1200. The purpose of the certificates is to:

- ensure the conformity procedure;
- enable trust in said high-risk AI systems.

44.1.2 Guiding Principles

1201. They are as follows:

NO.	THEME	SPECIFICATION
1.	Notifications	By the notified authority
2.	Validity	Five years maximum
3.	Renewal	Five years after re-assessment
4.	Suspension or withdrawal	Appropriate corrective action within an appropriate deadline

45 ARTICLE 45. INFORMATION OBLIGATIONS OF NOTIFIED BODIES

1. Notified bodies shall inform the notifying authority of the following:

(a) any Union technical documentation assessment certificates, any supplements to those certificates, and any quality management system approvals issued in accordance with the requirements of Annex VII;

(b) any refusal, restriction, suspension or withdrawal of a Union technical documentation assessment certificate or a quality management system approval issued in accordance with the requirements of Annex VII;

(c) any circumstances affecting the scope of or conditions for notification;

(d) any request for information which they have received from market surveillance authorities regarding conformity assessment activities;

(e) on request, conformity assessment activities performed within the scope of their notification and any other activity performed, including cross-border activities and subcontracting.

2. Each notified body shall inform the other notified bodies of:

(a) quality management system approvals which it has refused, suspended or withdrawn, and, upon request, of quality system approvals which it has issued;

(b) Union technical documentation assessment certificates or any supplements thereto which it has refused, withdrawn, suspended or otherwise restricted, and, upon request, of the certificates and/or supplements thereto which it has issued.

3. Each notified body shall provide the other notified bodies carrying out similar conformity assessment activities covering the same types of AI systems with relevant information on issues relating to negative and, on request, positive conformity assessment results.

4. Notified bodies shall safeguard the confidentiality of the information that they obtain, in accordance with Article 78.

45.1. General Approach

45.1.1 Preamble

1202. To enable harmonised application of the requirements, a common approach to market surveillance activities is needed.

45.1.2 Guiding Principles

1203. The Regulation imposes essential requirements without defining technical solutions. To create a trust-based market, notified bodies should assess the conformity of each solution according to common objective criteria.

45.2. *Notifications*

1204. Notified bodies must provide the notifying authority with information enabling it to:

- identify high-risk AI systems;
- monitor their developments;
- track incidents.

45.3. *Information*

1205. General communication on high-risk AI systems must take place among notified bodies to ensure transparency regarding:

- refusals;
- suspensions;
- withdrawals.

1206. The approvals and certificates issued may be communicated upon request.

45.4. *Cooperation*

1207. With the same objective of increasing the level of trust, notified bodies must share relevant information related to:

- negative conformity assessment results;
- and, on request, positive conformity assessment results.

46 ARTICLE 46. DEROGATION FROM CONFORMITY ASSESSMENT PROCEDURE

1. By way of derogation from Article 43 and upon a duly justified request, any market surveillance authority may authorise the placing on the market or the putting into service of specific high-risk AI systems within the territory of the Member State concerned, for exceptional reasons of public security or the protection of life and health of persons, environmental protection or the protection of key industrial and infrastructural assets. That authorisation shall be for a limited period while the necessary conformity assessment procedures are being carried out, taking into account the exceptional reasons justifying the derogation. The completion of those procedures shall be undertaken without undue delay.

2. In a duly justified situation of urgency for exceptional reasons of public security or in the case of specific, substantial and imminent threat to the life or physical safety of natural persons, law-enforcement authorities or civil protection authorities may put a specific high-risk AI system into service without the authorisation referred to in paragraph 1, provided that such authorisation is requested during or after the use without undue delay. If the authorisation referred to in paragraph 1 is refused, the use of the high-risk AI system shall be stopped with immediate effect and all the results and outputs of such use shall be immediately discarded.

3. The authorisation referred to in paragraph 1 shall be issued only if the market surveillance authority concludes that the high-risk AI system complies with the requirements of Section 2. The market surveillance authority shall inform the Commission and the other Member States of any authorisation issued pursuant to paragraphs 1 and 2. This obligation shall not cover sensitive operational data in relation to the activities of law-enforcement authorities.

4. Where, within 15 calendar days of receipt of the information referred to in paragraph 3, no objection has been raised by either a Member State or the Commission in respect of an authorisation issued by a market surveillance authority of a Member State in accordance with paragraph 1, that authorisation shall be deemed justified.

5. Where, within 15 calendar days of receipt of the notification referred to in paragraph 3, objections are raised by a Member State against an authorisation issued by a market surveillance authority of another Member State, or where the Commission considers the authorisation to be contrary to Union law, or the conclusion of the Member States regarding the compliance of the system as referred to in paragraph 3 to be unfounded, the Commission shall, without delay, enter into consultations with the relevant Member State. The operators concerned shall be consulted and have the possibility to present their views. Having regard thereto, the Commission shall decide whether the authorisation is justified. The Commission shall address its decision to the Member State concerned and to the relevant operators.

6. Where the Commission considers the authorisation unjustified, it shall be withdrawn by the market surveillance authority of the Member State concerned.

7. For high-risk AI systems related to products covered by Union harmonisation legislation listed in Section A of Annex I, only the derogations from the conformity assessment established in that Union harmonisation legislation shall apply.

46.1. Recitals

1208. **(22)** In light of their digital nature, certain AI systems should fall within the scope of this Regulation even when they are not placed on the market, put into service, or used in the Union. This is the case, for example, where an operator established in the Union contracts certain services to an operator established in a third country in relation to an activity to be performed by an AI system that would qualify as high-risk. In those circumstances, the AI system used in a third country by the operator could process data lawfully collected in and transferred from the Union, and provide to the contracting operator in the Union the output of that AI system resulting from that processing, without that AI system being placed on the market, put into service or used in the Union. To prevent the circumvention of this Regulation and to ensure an effective protection of natural persons located in the Union, this Regulation should also apply to providers and deployers of AI systems that are established in a third country, to the extent the output produced by those systems is intended to be used in the Union. Nonetheless, to take into account existing arrangements and special needs for future cooperation with foreign partners with whom information and evidence is exchanged, this Regulation should not apply to public authorities of a third country and international organisations when acting in the framework of cooperation or international agreements concluded at Union or national level for law enforcement and judicial cooperation with the Union or the Member States, provided that the relevant third country or international organisation provides adequate safeguards with respect to the protection of fundamental rights and freedoms of individuals. Where relevant, this may cover activities of entities entrusted by the third countries to carry out specific tasks in support of such law enforcement and judicial cooperation. Such framework for cooperation or agreements have been established bilaterally between Member States and third countries or between the European Union, Europol and other Union agencies and third countries and international organisations. The authorities competent for supervision of the law enforcement and judicial authorities under this Regulation should assess whether those frameworks for cooperation or international agreements include adequate safeguards with respect to the protection of fundamental rights and freedoms of individuals. Recipient national authorities and Union institutions, bodies, offices and agencies making use of such outputs in the Union remain accountable to ensure their use complies with Union law. When those international agreements are revised or new ones are concluded in the future, the contracting parties should make utmost efforts to align those agreements with the requirements of this Regulation.

1209. **(50)** As regards AI systems that are safety components of products, or which are themselves products, falling within the scope of certain Union harmonisation legislation listed in an annex to this Regulation, it is appropriate to classify them as high-risk under this Regulation if the product concerned undergoes the conformity assessment procedure with a third-party conformity assessment body pursuant to that relevant Union harmonisation legislation. In particular, such products are machinery, toys, lifts, equipment and protective systems intended for use in potentially explosive atmospheres, radio equipment, pressure equipment, recreational craft equipment, cableway installations, appliances burning gaseous fuels, medical devices, in vitro diagnostic medical devices, automotive and aviation.

1210. **(51)** The classification of an AI system as high-risk pursuant to this Regulation should not necessarily mean that the product whose safety component is the AI system, or the AI system itself as a product, is considered to be high-risk under the criteria established in the relevant Union harmonisation legislation that applies to the product. This is, in particular, the case for Regulations (EU) 2017/745 and (EU) 2017/746, where a third-party conformity assessment is provided for medium-risk and high-risk products.

1211. **(59)** Given their role and responsibility, actions by law enforcement authorities involving certain uses of AI systems are characterised by a significant degree of power imbalance and may lead to surveillance, arrest or deprivation of a natural person's liberty as well as other adverse impacts on fundamental rights guaranteed in the Charter. In particular, if the AI system is not trained with high-quality data, does not meet adequate requirements in terms of its performance, its accuracy or robustness, or is not properly designed and tested before being put on the market or otherwise put into service, it may single out people in a discriminatory or otherwise incorrect or unjust manner. Furthermore, the exercise of important procedural fundamental rights, such as the right to an effective remedy and to a fair trial as well as the right of defence and the presumption of innocence, could be hampered, in particular, where such AI systems are not sufficiently transparent, explainable and documented. It is therefore appropriate to classify as high-risk, insofar as their use is permitted under relevant Union and national law, a number of AI systems intended to be used in the law enforcement context where accuracy, reliability and transparency is particularly important to avoid adverse impacts, retain public trust and ensure accountability and effective redress. In view of the nature of the activities and the risks relating thereto, those high-risk AI systems should include in particular AI systems intended to be used by or on behalf of law enforcement authorities or by Union institutions, bodies, offices, or agencies in support of law enforcement authorities for assessing the risk of a natural person to become a victim of criminal offences, as polygraphs and similar tools, for the evaluation of the reliability of evidence in in the course of investigation or prosecution of criminal offences, and, insofar as not prohibited under this Regulation, for assessing the risk of a natural person offending or reoffending not solely on the basis of the profiling of natural persons or the assessment of personality traits and characteristics or the past criminal behaviour of natural persons or groups, for profiling in the course of detection, investigation or prosecution of criminal offences. AI systems specifically intended to be used for administrative proceedings by tax and customs authorities as well as by financial intelligence units carrying out administrative tasks analysing information pursuant to Union anti-money laundering law should not be classified as high-risk AI systems used by law enforcement authorities for the purpose of prevention, detection, investigation and prosecution of criminal offences. The use of AI tools by law enforcement and other relevant authorities should not become a factor of inequality, or exclusion.

The impact of the use of AI tools on the defence rights of suspects should not be ignored, in particular the difficulty in obtaining meaningful information on the functioning of those systems and the resulting difficulty in challenging their results in court, in particular by natural persons under investigation.

1212. **(78)** The conformity assessment procedure provided by this Regulation should apply in relation to the essential cybersecurity requirements of a product with digital elements covered by a regulation of the European Parliament and of the Council on horizontal cybersecurity requirements for products with digital elements and classified as a high-risk AI system under this Regulation. However, this rule should not result in reducing the necessary level of assurance for critical products with digital elements covered by a regulation of the European Parliament and of the Council on horizontal cybersecurity requirements for products with digital elements. Therefore, by way of derogation from this rule, high-risk AI systems that fall within the scope of this Regulation and are also qualified as important and critical products with digital elements pursuant to a regulation of the European Parliament and of the Council on horizontal cybersecurity requirements for products with digital elements and to which the conformity assessment procedure based on internal control set out in an annex to this Regulation applies, are subject to the conformity assessment provisions of a regulation of the European Parliament and of the Council on horizontal cybersecurity requirements for products with digital elements insofar as the essential cybersecurity requirements of that regulation are concerned. In this case, for all the other aspects covered by this Regulation the respective provisions on conformity assessment based on internal control set out in an annex to this Regulation should apply. Building on the knowledge and expertise of ENISA on the cybersecurity policy and tasks assigned to ENISA under the Regulation (EU) 2019/881 of the European Parliament and of the Council,[174] the Commission should cooperate with ENISA on issues related to cybersecurity of AI systems.

46.2. General Approach

46.2.1 Preamble

1213. For high-risk AI systems, there is a derogation system, but it is very limited due to the hazardous nature of such systems.

[174] Regulation (EU) 2019/881 of the European Parliament and of the Council of 17 April 2019 on ENISA (the European Union Agency for Cybersecurity) and on information and communications technology cybersecurity certification and repealing Regulation (EU) No 526/2013 (Cybersecurity Act), *OJEU*, L 151, 7 June 2019, p. 15.

46.2.2 Guiding Principles

1214. The idea is to limit risk management obligations in the event of urgent and severe crises affecting the safety of persons.

46.2.3 Characteristics

1215. The derogation is subject to the following rules:

NO.	THEME	SPECIFICATION
1.	Competence	Market surveillance authority
2.	Objectives	Public security (exceptional reasons) Protection of life of persons Protection of health of persons Environmental protection Protection of key industrial assets Protection of key infrastructural assets
3.	Authorisation	Placing on the market Putting into service
4.	Geographical scope	Within the territory of the Member State concerned
5.	Duration	Limited
6.	Conformity	The derogation only concerns the compliance period and not the compliance requirement The derogation implies that the market surveillance authority must verify compliance with the main requirements of high-risk AI systems

1216. To avoid conflicting positions, a cooperation mechanism is established with:

- the European Commission;
- the other Member States.

47 ARTICLE 47. EU DECLARATION OF CONFORMITY

1. The provider shall draw up a written machine readable, physical or electronically signed EU declaration of conformity for each high-risk AI system, and keep it at the disposal of the national competent authorities for 10 years after the high-risk AI system has been placed on the market or put into service. The EU declaration of conformity shall identify the high-risk AI system for which it has been drawn up. A copy of the EU declaration of conformity shall be submitted to the relevant national competent authorities upon request.

2. The EU declaration of conformity shall state that the high-risk AI system concerned meets the requirements set out in Section 2. The EU declaration of conformity shall contain the information set out in Annex V, and shall be translated into a language that can be easily understood by the national competent authorities of the Member States in which the high-risk AI system is placed on the market or made available.

3. Where high-risk AI systems are subject to other Union harmonisation legislation which also requires an EU declaration of conformity, a single EU declaration of conformity shall be drawn up in respect of all Union law applicable to the high-risk AI system. The declaration shall contain all the information required to identify the Union harmonisation legislation to which the declaration relates.

4. By drawing up the EU declaration of conformity, the provider shall assume responsibility for compliance with the requirements set out in Section 2. The provider shall keep the EU declaration of conformity up-to-date as appropriate.

5. The Commission is empowered to adopt delegated acts in accordance with Article 97 in order to amend Annex V by updating the content of the EU declaration of conformity set out in that Annex, in order to introduce elements that become necessary in light of technical progress.

47.1. Recitals

1217. (77) Without prejudice to the requirements related to robustness and accuracy set out in this Regulation, high-risk AI systems which fall within the scope of a regulation of the European Parliament and of the Council on horizontal cybersecurity requirements for products with digital elements, in accordance with that regulation may demonstrate compliance with the cybersecurity requirements of this Regulation by fulfilling the essential cybersecurity requirements set out in that regulation. When high-risk AI systems fulfil the essential requirements of a regulation of the European Parliament and of the Council on horizontal cybersecurity requirements for products with digital elements, they should be deemed compliant with the cybersecurity requirements set out in this Regulation in so far as the achievement of those requirements is demonstrated in the EU declaration of conformity or parts thereof issued under that regulation. To that end, the assessment of the cybersecurity risks, associated to a product with digital elements classified as high-risk AI system according to this Regulation, carried out under a regulation of the European Parliament and of the Council on horizontal cybersecurity requirements for products with digital elements, should consider risks to the cyber resilience of an AI system as regards attempts by unauthorised third parties to alter its use, behaviour or performance, including AI specific vulnerabilities such as data poisoning or adversarial attacks, as well as, as relevant, risks to fundamental rights as required by this Regulation.

47.2. *General Approach*

47.2.1 Preamble

1218. Risk management primarily rests with the provider. Therefore, it is the provider's responsibility to draw up the declaration of conformity at its own risk.

47.2.2 Characteristics

1219. They are as follows:

NO.	THEME	SPECIFICATION	COMMENT
1.	Certificate	For each high-risk AI system	
2.	Provision	At the request of national authorities	
3.	Duration	10 years after the placing on the market or putting into service	
4.	Copy	At the request of national authorities	

47.2.3 Personal Data

1220. According to the EDPS, 'insofar as high-risk AI systems require the processing of personal data or process personal data to fulfil their task, the certification of these AI systems in the context of the CE marking should expressly include a verification of compliance, among others, with the data protection by design and by default, given the possible high level of interference of the high-risk AI systems with the fundamental rights to privacy and to the protection of personal data, as well as the need to ensure a high level of trust in the AI system'.[175]

1221. Notes:

- (1) The above proposal from the EDPS has not been incorporated into the Regulation as such.
- (2) However, it appears that a compliance analysis requires consideration of data protection regulations for requirements related to the protection of fundamental rights.

[175] EDPS, Opinion 44/2023 of 23 October 2023, para. 27.

48 ARTICLE 48. CE MARKING

1. The CE marking shall be subject to the general principles set out in Article 30 of Regulation (EC) No 765/2008.

2. For high-risk AI systems provided digitally, a digital CE marking shall be used, only if it can easily be accessed via the interface from which that system is accessed or via an easily accessible machine-readable code or other electronic means.

3. The CE marking shall be affixed visibly, legibly and indelibly for high-risk AI systems. Where that is not possible or not warranted on account of the nature of the high-risk AI system, it shall be affixed to the packaging or to the accompanying documentation, as appropriate.

4. Where applicable, the CE marking shall be followed by the identification number of the notified body responsible for the conformity assessment procedures set out in Article 43. The identification number of the notified body shall be affixed by the body itself or, under its instructions, by the provider or by the provider's authorised representative. The identification number shall also be indicated in any promotional material which mentions that the high-risk AI system fulfils the requirements for CE marking.

5. Where high-risk AI systems are subject to other Union law which also provides for the affixing of the CE marking, the CE marking shall indicate that the high-risk AI system also fulfil the requirements of that other law.

48.1. Recitals

1222. **(129)** High-risk AI systems should bear the CE marking to indicate their conformity with this Regulation so that they can move freely within the internal market. For high-risk AI systems embedded in a product, a physical CE marking should be affixed, and may be complemented by a digital CE marking. For high-risk AI systems only provided digitally, a digital CE marking should be used. Member States should not create unjustified obstacles to the placing on the market or the putting into service of high-risk AI systems that comply with the requirements laid down in this Regulation and bear the CE marking.

48.2. General Approach

48.2.1 Preamble

1223. As the first visual indicator of trust, the CE marking demonstrates compliance with the requirements.

48.2.2 Definition

1224. 'CE marking' means 'a marking by which a provider indicates that an AI system is in conformity with the requirements set out in Chapter III, Section 2 and other applicable Union harmonisation legislation providing for its affixing'.[176]

48.2.3 Legal Framework

1225. The CE marking under the AI Act is subject to the general principles set out in Article 30 of Regulation (EC) No. 765/2008.

48.3. Characteristics

1226. They are as follows:

NO.	THEME	SPECIFICATION
1.	Scope	High-risk AI system
2.	Form	Visible Legible Indelible
3.	Alternative, where that is not possible	Affixed to the packaging or to the accompanying documentation
4.	Reference of the notified body	Identification number of the notified body on CE marking and on promotional material

49 ARTICLE 49. REGISTRATION

1. Before placing on the market or putting into service a high-risk AI system listed in Annex III, with the exception of high-risk AI systems referred to in point 2 of Annex III, the provider or, where applicable, the authorised representative shall register themselves and their system in the EU database referred to in Article 71.

2. Before placing on the market or putting into service an AI system for which the provider has concluded that it is not high-risk according to Article 6(3), that provider or, where applicable, the authorised representative shall register themselves and that system in the EU database referred to in Article 71.

[176] AI Act, Art. 3(24).

3. Before putting into service or using a high-risk AI system listed in Annex III, with the exception of high-risk AI systems listed in point 2 of Annex III, deployers that are public authorities, Union institutions, bodies, offices or agencies or persons acting on their behalf shall register themselves, select the system and register its use in the EU database referred to in Article 71.

4. For high-risk AI systems referred to in points 1, 6 and 7 of Annex III, in the areas of law enforcement, migration, asylum and border control management, the registration referred to in paragraphs 1, 2 and 3 of this Article shall be in a secure non-public section of the EU database referred to in Article 71 and shall include only the following information, as applicable, referred to in:

(a) Section A, points 1 to 10, of Annex VIII, with the exception of points 6, 8 and 9;

(b) Section B, points 1 to 5, and points 8 and 9 of Annex VIII;

(c) Section C, points 1 to 3, of Annex VIII;

(d) points 1, 2, 3 and 5, of Annex IX.

Only the Commission and national authorities referred to in Article 74(8) shall have access to the respective restricted sections of the EU database listed in the first subparagraph of this paragraph.

5. High-risk AI systems referred to in point 2 of Annex III shall be registered at national level.

49.1. Recitals

1227. **(131)** In order to facilitate the work of the Commission and the Member States in the AI field as well as to increase the transparency towards the public, providers of high-risk AI systems other than those related to products falling within the scope of relevant existing Union harmonisation legislation, as well as providers who consider that an AI system listed in the high-risk use cases in an annex to this Regulation is not high-risk on the basis of a derogation, should be required to register themselves and information about their AI system in an EU database, to be established and managed by the Commission. Before using an AI system listed in the high-risk use cases in an annex to this Regulation, deployers of high-risk AI systems that are public authorities, agencies or bodies, should register themselves in such database and select the system that they envisage to use. Other deployers should be entitled to do so voluntarily. This section of the EU database should be publicly accessible, free of charge, the information should be easily navigable, understandable and machine-readable. The EU database should also be user-friendly, for example by providing search functionalities, including through keywords, allowing the general public to find relevant information to be submitted upon the registration of high-risk AI systems and on the use case of high-risk AI systems, set out in an annex to this Regulation, to which the high-risk AI systems correspond. Any substantial modification of high-risk AI systems should also be registered in the EU database. For high-risk AI systems in the area of law enforcement, migration, asylum and border control management, the registration obligations should be fulfilled in a secure non-public section of the EU database. Access to the secure non-public section should be strictly limited to the Commission as well as to market surveillance authorities with regard to their national section of that database. High-risk AI systems in the area of critical infrastructure should only be registered at national level. The Commission should be the controller of the EU database, in accordance with Regulation (EU) 2018/1725. In order to ensure the full functionality of the EU database, when deployed, the procedure for setting the database should include the development of functional specifications by the Commission and an independent audit report. The Commission should take into account cybersecurity risks when carrying out its tasks as data controller on the EU database. In order to maximise the availability and use of the EU database by the public, the EU database, including the information made available through it, should comply with requirements under the Directive (EU) 2019/882.

49.2. General Approach

49.2.1 Preamble

1228. During this initial phase, which marks the advent of a third digital revolution, a system is planned for centralising key information on certain high-risk AI systems.

49.2.2 Actors

1229. The registration obligation applies to:

- providers or authorised representatives;
- deployers.

49.2.3 High-Risk AI System

1230. The systems concerned are as follows:

NO.	THEME	REFERENCE
1.	Biometrics	AIA, Annex III(1)
2.	Critical infrastructure It is excluded from the registration obligation in the EU database	AIA, Annex III(2)
3.	Education and vocational training	AIA, Annex III(3)

NO.	THEME	REFERENCE
4.	Employment, workers' management and access to self-employment	AIA, Annex III(4)
5.	Access to and enjoyment of essential private services and essential public services and benefits	AIA, Annex III(5)
6.	Law enforcement, in so far as their use is permitted under relevant Union or national law	AIA, Annex III(6)
7.	Migration, asylum and border control management, in so far as their use is permitted under relevant Union or national law	AIA, Annex III(7)
8.	Administration of justice and democratic processes	AIA, Annex III(8)

1231. Notes:

- (1) All systems concerned are listed in Annex III.
- (2) The registration specifications in the database are detailed in Article 71.
- (3) High-risk AI systems related to critical infrastructure are registered at national level.
- (4) For high-risk AI systems in the areas of biometrics,[177] law enforcement,[178] migration, asylum, and border control management,[179] high-risk AI systems are registered in a secure non-public section of the EU database.

49.2.4 Obligations of Providers

1232. They are as follows:

NO.	THEME	SPECIFICATION
1.	Identity	References of the provider or authorised representative
2.	Type	Characteristics of the high-risk AI system
3.	Activities	Before the placing on the market or putting into service
4.	Derogation	AI systems declared as non-high-risk must be registered as such.

177 AI Act, Annex III(1).
178 AI Act, Annex III(6).
179 AI Act, Annex III(7).

49.2.5 Obligations of Deployers

1233. They are as follows:

NO.	THEME	SPECIFICATION
1.	Deployers concerned	Public authorities Union institutions, bodies, offices or agencies or persons acting on their behalf
2.	Identity	References of the deployer
3.	Type	Selection of the systems registered by the providers
4.	Activities	Before the putting into service or use
5.	Derogation	No derogation

49.2.6 Summary Chart

1234. The regulation of high-risk AI systems can be summarised as follows in the form of a macroscopic legal algorithm:

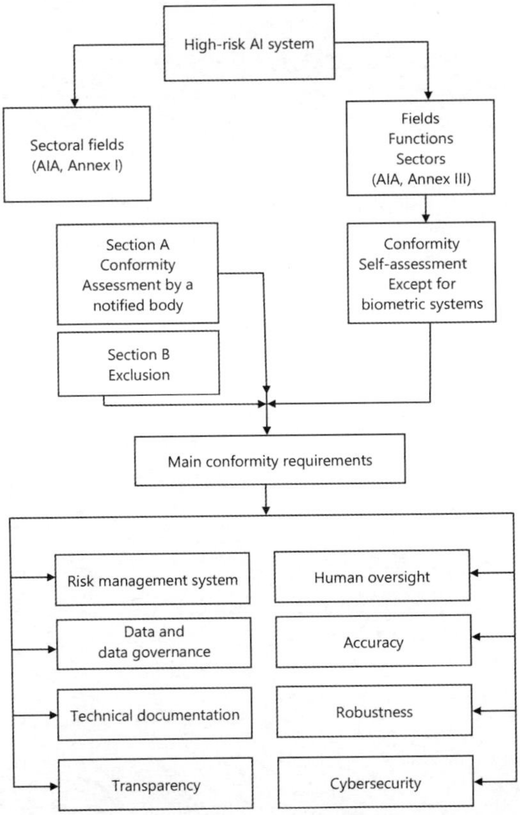

CHAPTER IV

TRANSPARENCY OBLIGATIONS FOR PROVIDERS AND DEPLOYERS OF CERTAIN AI SYSTEMS

1235. **Key takeaways:** Comprising a single article, this Chapter covers most of the AI systems deployed for everyday use.

50 ARTICLE 50. TRANSPARENCY OBLIGATIONS FOR PROVIDERS AND DEPLOYERS OF CERTAIN AI SYSTEMS

1. Providers shall ensure that AI systems intended to interact directly with natural persons are designed and developed in such a way that the natural persons concerned are informed that they are interacting with an AI system, unless this is obvious from the point of view of a natural person who is reasonably well-informed, observant and circumspect, taking into account the circumstances and the context of use. This obligation shall not apply to AI systems authorised by law to detect, prevent, investigate or prosecute criminal offences, subject to appropriate safeguards for the rights and freedoms of third parties, unless those systems are available for the public to report a criminal offence.

2. Providers of AI systems, including general-purpose AI systems, generating synthetic audio, image, video or text content, shall ensure that the outputs of the AI system are marked in a machine-readable format and detectable as artificially generated or manipulated. Providers shall ensure their technical solutions are effective, interoperable, robust and reliable as far as this is technically feasible, taking into account the specificities and limitations of various types of content, the costs of implementation and the generally acknowledged state of the art, as may be reflected in relevant technical standards. This obligation shall not apply to the extent the AI systems perform an assistive function for standard editing or do not substantially alter the input data provided by the deployer or the semantics thereof, or where authorised by law to detect, prevent, investigate or prosecute criminal offences.

3. Deployers of an emotion recognition system or a biometric categorisation system shall inform the natural persons exposed thereto of the operation of the system, and shall process the personal data in accordance with Regulations (EU) 2016/679 and (EU) 2018/1725 and Directive (EU) 2016/680, as applicable. This obligation shall not apply to AI systems used for biometric categorisation and emotion recognition, which are permitted by law to detect, prevent or investigate criminal offences, subject to appropriate safeguards for the rights and freedoms of third parties, and in accordance with Union law.

4. Deployers of an AI system that generates or manipulates image, audio or video content constituting a deep fake, shall disclose that the content has been artificially generated or manipulated. This obligation shall not apply where the use is authorised by law to detect, prevent, investigate or prosecute criminal offence. Where the content forms part of an evidently artistic, creative, satirical, fictional or analogous work or programme, the transparency obligations set out in this paragraph are limited to disclosure of the existence of such generated or manipulated content in an appropriate manner that does not hamper the display or enjoyment of the work.

Deployers of an AI system that generates or manipulates text which is published with the purpose of informing the public on matters of public interest shall disclose that the text has been artificially generated or manipulated. This obligation shall not apply where the use is authorised by law to detect, prevent, investigate or prosecute criminal offences or where the AI-generated content has undergone a process of human review or editorial control and where a natural or legal person holds editorial responsibility for the publication of the content.

5. The information referred to in paragraphs 1 to 4 shall be provided to the natural persons concerned in a clear and distinguishable manner at the latest at the time of the first interaction or exposure. The information shall conform to the applicable accessibility requirements.

6. Paragraphs 1 to 4 shall not affect the requirements and obligations set out in Chapter III, and shall be without prejudice to other transparency obligations laid down in Union or national law for deployers of AI systems.

7. The AI Office shall encourage and facilitate the drawing up of codes of practice at Union level to facilitate the effective implementation of the obligations regarding the detection and labelling of artificially generated or manipulated content. The Commission may adopt implementing acts to approve those codes of practice in accordance with the procedure laid down in Article 56 (6). If it deems the code is not adequate, the Commission may adopt an implementing act specifying common rules for the implementation of those obligations in accordance with the examination procedure laid down in Article 98(2).

50.1. Recitals

1236. **(26)** In order to introduce a proportionate and effective set of binding rules for AI systems, a clearly defined risk-based approach should be followed. That approach should tailor the type and content of such rules to the intensity and scope of the risks that AI systems can generate. It is therefore necessary to prohibit certain unacceptable AI practices, to lay down requirements for high-risk AI systems and obligations for the relevant operators, and to lay down transparency obligations for certain AI systems.

1237. **(27)** While the risk-based approach is the basis for a proportionate and effective set of binding rules, it is important to recall the 2019 Ethics guidelines for trustworthy AI developed by the independent AI HLEG appointed by the Commission. In those guidelines, the AI HLEG developed seven non-binding ethical principles for AI which are intended to help ensure that AI is trustworthy and ethically sound. The seven principles include human agency and oversight; technical robustness and safety; privacy and data governance; transparency; diversity, non-discrimination and fairness; societal and environmental well-being and accountability. Without prejudice to the legally binding requirements of this Regulation and any other applicable Union law, those guidelines contribute to the design of coherent, trustworthy and human-centric AI, in line with the Charter and with the values on which the Union is founded. According to the guidelines of the AI HLEG, human agency and oversight means that AI systems are developed and used as a tool that serves people, respects human dignity and personal autonomy, and that is functioning in a way that can be appropriately controlled and overseen by humans. Technical robustness and safety means that AI systems are developed and used in a way that allows robustness in the case of problems and resilience against attempts to alter the use or performance of the AI system so as to allow unlawful use by third parties, and minimise unintended harm. Privacy and data governance means that AI systems are developed and used in accordance with privacy and data protection rules, while processing data that meets high standards in terms of quality and integrity. Transparency means that AI systems are developed and used in a way that allows appropriate traceability and explainability, while making humans aware that they communicate or interact with an AI system, as well as duly informing deployers of the capabilities and limitations of that AI system and affected persons about their rights. Diversity, non-discrimination and fairness means that AI systems are developed and used in a way that includes diverse actors and promotes equal access, gender equality and cultural diversity, while avoiding discriminatory impacts and unfair biases that are prohibited by Union or national law. Social and environmental well-being means that AI systems are developed and used in a sustainable and environmentally friendly manner as well as in a way to benefit all human beings, while monitoring and assessing the long-term impacts on the individual, society and democracy. The application of those principles should be translated, when possible, in the design and use of AI models. They should in any case serve as a basis for the drafting of codes of conduct under this Regulation. All stakeholders, including industry, academia, civil society and standardisation organisations, are encouraged to take into account, as appropriate, the ethical principles for the development of voluntary best practices and standards.

1238. **(72)** To address concerns related to opacity and complexity of certain AI systems and help deployers to fulfil their obligations under this Regulation, transparency should be required for high-risk AI systems before they are placed on the market or put it into service. High-risk AI systems should be designed in a manner to enable deployers to understand how the AI system works, evaluate its functionality, and comprehend its strengths and limitations. High-risk AI systems should be accompanied by appropriate information in the form of instructions of use. Such information should include the characteristics, capabilities and limitations of performance of the AI system. Those would cover information on possible known and foreseeable circumstances related to the use of the high-risk AI system, including deployer action that may influence system behaviour and performance, under which the AI system can lead to risks to health, safety, and fundamental rights, on the changes that have been pre-determined and assessed for conformity by the provider and on the relevant human oversight measures, including the measures to facilitate the interpretation of the outputs of the AI system by the deployers. Transparency, including the accompanying instructions for use, should assist deployers in the use of the system and support informed decision making by them. Deployers should, inter alia, be in a better position to make the correct choice of the system that they intend to use in light of the obligations applicable to them, be educated about the intended and precluded uses, and use the AI system correctly and as appropriate. In order to enhance legibility and accessibility of the information included in the instructions of use, where appropriate, illustrative examples, for instance on the limitations and on the intended and precluded uses of the AI system, should be included. Providers should ensure that all documentation, including the instructions for use, contains meaningful, comprehensive, accessible and understandable information, taking into account the needs and foreseeable knowledge of the target deployers. Instructions for use should be made available in a language which can be easily understood by target deployers, as determined by the Member State concerned.

1239. **(125)** Given the complexity of high-risk AI systems and the risks that are associated with them, it is important to develop an adequate conformity assessment procedure for high-risk AI systems involving notified bodies, so-called third party conformity assessment. However, given the current experience of professional pre-market certifiers in the field of product safety and the different nature of risks involved, it is appropriate to limit, at least in an initial phase of application of this Regulation, the scope of application of third-party conformity assessment for high-risk AI systems other than those related to products. Therefore, the conformity assessment of such systems should be carried out as a general rule by the provider under its own responsibility, with the only exception of AI systems intended to be used for biometrics.

1240. (132) Certain AI systems intended to interact with natural persons or to generate content may pose specific risks of impersonation or deception irrespective of whether they qualify as high-risk or not. In certain circumstances, the use of these systems should therefore be subject to specific transparency obligations without prejudice to the requirements and obligations for high-risk AI systems and subject to targeted exceptions to take into account the special need of law enforcement. In particular, natural persons should be notified that they are interacting with an AI system, unless this is obvious from the point of view of a natural person who is reasonably well-informed, observant and circumspect taking into account the circumstances and the context of use. When implementing that obligation, the characteristics of natural persons belonging to vulnerable groups due to their age or disability should be taken into account to the extent the AI system is intended to interact with those groups as well. Moreover, natural persons should be notified when they are exposed to AI systems that, by processing their biometric data, can identify or infer the emotions or intentions of those persons or assign them to specific categories. Such specific categories can relate to aspects such as sex, age, hair colour, eye colour, tattoos, personal traits, ethnic origin, personal preferences and interests. Such information and notifications should be provided in accessible formats for persons with disabilities.

1241. (134) Further to the technical solutions employed by the providers of the AI system, deployers who use an AI system to generate or manipulate image, audio or video content that appreciably resembles existing persons, objects, places, entities or events and would falsely appear to a person to be authentic or truthful (deep fakes), should also clearly and distinguishably disclose that the content has been artificially created or manipulated by labelling the AI output accordingly and disclosing its artificial origin. Compliance with this transparency obligation should not be interpreted as indicating that the use of the AI system or its output impedes the right to freedom of expression and the right to freedom of the arts and sciences guaranteed in the Charter, in particular where the content is part of an evidently creative, satirical, artistic, fictional or analogous work or programme, subject to appropriate safeguards for the rights and freedoms of third parties. In those cases, the transparency obligation for deep fakes set out in this Regulation is limited to disclosure of the existence of such generated or manipulated content in an appropriate manner that does not hamper the display or enjoyment of the work, including its normal exploitation and use, while maintaining the utility and quality of the work. In addition, it is also appropriate to envisage a similar disclosure obligation in relation to AI-generated or manipulated text to the extent it is published with the purpose of informing the public on matters of public interest unless the AI-generated content has undergone a process of human review or editorial control and a natural or legal person holds editorial responsibility for the publication of the content.

1242. **(135)** Without prejudice to the mandatory nature and full applicability of the transparency obligations, the Commission may also encourage and facilitate the drawing up of codes of practice at Union level to facilitate the effective implementation of the obligations regarding the detection and labelling of artificially generated or manipulated content, including to support practical arrangements for making, as appropriate, the detection mechanisms accessible and facilitating cooperation with other actors along the value chain, disseminating content or checking its authenticity and provenance to enable the public to effectively distinguish AI-generated content.

1243. **(137)** Compliance with the transparency obligations for the AI systems covered by this Regulation should not be interpreted as indicating that the use of the AI system or its output is lawful under this Regulation or other Union and Member State law and should be without prejudice to other transparency obligations for deployers of AI systems laid down in Union or national law.

50.2. General Approach

50.2.1 Preamble

1244. Collaboration with artificial intelligence requires that humans keep the upper hand.

1245. Distinguishing what is human from what is done by machines is an ethical imperative.[1]

50.2.2 Classification

1246. Keeping the upper hand requires the organisation of 'transparency', allowing individuals to understand their 'artificial counterparts'.

1 Quote by Alexei Grinbaum, taken up by A. Piquard in 'Intelligences artificielles le défi de rendre détectables les contenus générés par des IA' ['Artificial intelligence: The challenge of making AI-generated content detectable'], *Le Monde*, 25 May 2023.

1247. Human-machine dialogue is structured around the following situations:

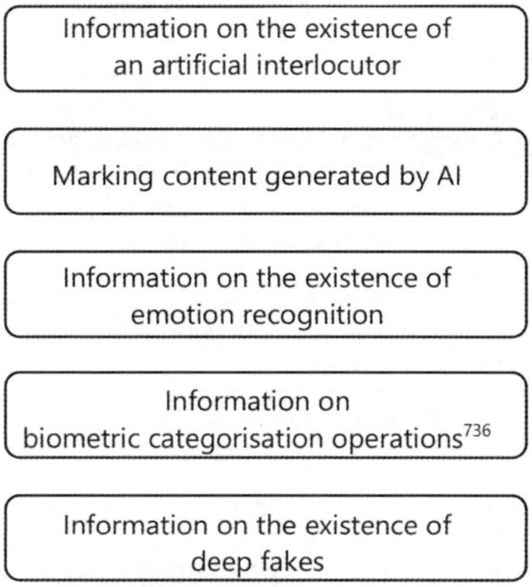

50.3. Human-Artificial Intelligence Interface[2]

50.3.1 Introduction

1248. The objective is to require providers to design and develop AI systems in such a way that natural persons are able to recognize when they are interacting with non-humans.

50.3.2 Characteristics

1249. They are as follows:

NO.	THEME	SPECIFICATION
1.	Actor	Provider Note: • (1) Deployers are not concerned by this obligation; this obligation is binding on the provider with regard to natural persons who interact with the transparent AI system placed on the market or put into service

[2] AI Act, Art. 50(1).

NO.	THEME	SPECIFICATION
2.	Technology	AI system intended to interact with natural persons Notes: • (1) It is the purpose that characterises the AI system and not its category • (2) Presumably this also applies to general-purpose AI systems, despite the fact that Article 50(1) on the interaction with AI systems does not refer to general-purpose systems as does Article 50(2) with regard to the marking of content
3.	Modalities	Deciding to make an interaction with an artificial agent apparent Compliance with accessibility requirements Direct interaction
4.	Period	At the time of the first interaction
5.	Format	In a clear manner
6.	Derogation	Unless this is obvious from the point of view of a natural person who is reasonably well-informed, observant and circumspect or Use is authorised by law to detect, prevent, investigate or prosecute criminal offences
7.	Transparency (Cumulation)	Obligations that apply in addition to: • the obligations relating to high-risk AI systems when they interact with humans • the transparency obligations of deployers laid down in Union or national law for deployers

50.4. Marking Content[3]

50.4.1 Introduction

1250. The transparency obligation requires distinguishing between human-origin data and synthetic or artificial data.

50.4.2 Characteristics

1251. The marking obligation applies to the following:

NO.	THEME	SPECIFICATION
1.	Actor	Provider
2.	AI technology	AI system and general-purpose AI system

[3] AI Act, Art. 50(2).

NO.	THEME	SPECIFICATION
3.	Artificial content	Audio Text Image Video
4.	Format	Machine-readable Detectable as artificial
5.	Operation	Generation Manipulation
6.	Method	Information should be provided in a clear manner Interoperability Reliability Taking into account: • the state of the art • the costs of implementation • relevant standards Compliance with accessibility requirements
7.	Period	At the time of the first interaction or exposure[4]
8.	Derogation	AI systems performing an assistive function for standard editing AI systems not substantially altering the input data provided by the deployer AI systems not substantially altering the semantics of the input data Use is authorised by law to detect, prevent, investigate or prosecute criminal offences
9.	AI Office	Identification format Code of practice
10.	Transparency (Cumulation)	Obligations that apply in addition to: • the obligations relating to high-risk AI systems when they interact with humans • the transparency obligations of deployers laid down in Union or national law

50.5. Emotions Recognition[5]

50.5.1 Introduction

1252. All AI systems intended to be used for recognising a natural person's emotions must provide information on how they operate.

---

4 AI Act, Art. 50(5).
5 AI Act, Art. 50(3).

50.5.2 Characteristics

1253. They are as follows:

NO.	THEME	SPECIFICATION
1.	Actor	Deployer
2.	Technology	AI system and general-purpose AI system
3.	Information	Interaction with artificial intelligence
4.	Form	Information to be provided to natural persons In a clear and distinguishable manner Compliance with accessibility requirements
5.	Period	At the time of the first interaction or exposure
6.	Derogation	The interaction with an AI is obvious and clear taking into account the context of use Use permitted by law to detect, prevent or investigate criminal offences
7.	Transparency (Cumulation)	Obligations that apply in addition to: • the obligations relating to high-risk AI systems when they interact with humans • the transparency obligations of deployers laid down in Union or national law

50.6. Biometric Categorisations

50.6.1 Introduction

1254. All AI systems intended to be used for biometric categorisation must provide information on how they operate.

50.6.2 Characteristics

1255. They are as follows:

NO.	THEME	SPECIFICATION
1.	Actor	Deployer
2.	Technology	AI system and general-purpose AI system
3.	Purpose	Biometric categorisation
4.	Information	Exposure, operation

NO.	THEME	SPECIFICATION
5.	Form	Information to be provided to natural persons In a clear and distinguishable manner Compliance with accessibility requirements
6.	Period	At the time of the first interaction or exposure
7.	Derogation	Use permitted by law to detect, prevent or investigate criminal offences
8.	Transparency (Cumulation)	Obligations that apply in addition to: • the obligations relating to high-risk AI systems when they interact with humans • the transparency obligations of deployers laid down in Union or national law

50.7. Multimedia Deep Fakes

50.7.1 Introduction

1256. The manipulations performed by AI are now hyper-realistic.

1257. The objective is to combat all artificial fakes that may appear to be authentic or truthful.

50.7.2 Definition

1258. 'Deep fake' means 'AI-generated or manipulated image, audio or video content that resembles existing persons, objects, places, entities or events and would falsely appear to a person to be authentic or truthful'.[6]

50.7.3 Characteristics

1259. They are as follows:

NO.	THEME	SPECIFICATION
1.	Actor	Deployer
2.	Technology	AI system Note: • Presumably this also applies to general-purpose AI systems, despite the fact that Article 50(4) on artificially generated or manipulated does not refer to general-purpose systems as does Article 50(2) with regard to the marking of content

6 AI Act, Art. 3(60).

NO.	THEME	SPECIFICATION
3.	Medium	Image Audio Video
4.	Purpose	Resemblance to real people, objects, places, entities or events
5.	Information	Artificially generated or manipulated
6.	Form	Information to be provided to natural persons In a clear and distinguishable manner Compliance with accessibility requirements
7.	Period	At the time of the first interaction or exposure
8.	Derogation	Use is authorised by law to detect, prevent, investigate or prosecute criminal offences Artistic works: transparency obligation is limited to disclosure of the existence of such generated or manipulated content that does not hamper the display or enjoyment of the work Informing the public on matters of public interest The AI-generated content has undergone a process of editorial control and a natural or legal person holds editorial responsibility for the publication of the content
9.	AI Office	Identification format Code of practice
10.	Transparency (Cumulation)	Obligations that apply in addition to: • the obligations relating to high-risk AI systems when they interact with humans; • the transparency obligations of deployers laid down in Union or national law.

50.8. Find Out More

50.8.1 Toolbox

1260. Enkaoua, C. 'L'utilisation d'une IA comme ChatGPT ne remplace pas spécialiste; elle complète l'expertise humaine', Entretien avec Alain Bensoussan, avocat au barreau de Paris, spécialiste Droit du numérique et des communications ['The use of an AI like ChatGPT does not replace a specialist; it complements human expertise', Interview with Alain Bensoussan, lawyer at the Paris Bar, specialist in digital and communications law], *Gaz. Pal.*, 14 November 2023, no. 37, Actualité, p. 7.

50.9. *Final Provisions*

50.9.1 Coordinated Texts

1261. Compliance with the transparency requirements for the AI systems covered by the AI Act should not be interpreted as indicating that such systems are lawful as such under other EU or national law.[7]

[7] AI Act, Rec. 137.

CHAPTER V
GENERAL-PURPOSE AI MODELS

1262. Key takeaways: Following the 'colonisation of the planet' by OpenAI's ChatGPT, the European Commission hastily introduced rules for generative artificial intelligence.

1263. The Regulation applies to:

- providers of general-purpose AI models and their authorised representatives;
- specific rules for such models that may present systemic risk;
- general-purpose AI systems.

SECTION 1. CLASSIFICATION RULES

51 ARTICLE 51. CLASSIFICATION OF GENERAL-PURPOSE AI MODELS AS GENERAL-PURPOSE AI MODELS WITH SYSTEMIC RISK

1. A general-purpose AI model shall be classified as a general-purpose AI model with systemic risk if it meets any of the following conditions:

(a) it has high impact capabilities evaluated on the basis of appropriate technical tools and methodologies, including indicators and benchmarks;

(b) based on a decision of the Commission, ex officio or following a qualified alert from the scientific panel, it has capabilities or an impact equivalent to those set out in point (a) having regard to the criteria set out in Annex XIII.

2. A general-purpose AI model shall be presumed to have high impact capabilities pursuant to paragraph 1, point (a), when the cumulative amount of computation used for its training measured in floating point operations is greater than 10^{25}.

3. The Commission shall adopt delegated acts in accordance with Article 97 to amend the thresholds listed in paragraphs 1 and 2 of this Article, as well as to supplement benchmarks and indicators in light of evolving technological developments, such as algorithmic improvements or increased hardware efficiency, when necessary, for these thresholds to reflect the state of the art.

51.1. Recitals

1264. **(111)** It is appropriate to establish a methodology for the classification of general-purpose AI models as general-purpose AI model with systemic risks. Since systemic risks result from particularly high capabilities, a general-purpose AI model should be considered to present systemic risks if it has high-impact capabilities, evaluated on the basis of appropriate technical tools and methodologies, or significant impact on the internal market due to its reach. High-impact capabilities in general-purpose AI models means capabilities that match or exceed the capabilities recorded in the most advanced general-purpose AI models. The full range of capabilities in a model could be better understood after its placing on the market or when deployers interact with the model. According to the state of the art at the time of entry into force of this Regulation, the cumulative amount of computation used for the training of the general-purpose AI model measured in floating point operations is one of the relevant approximations for model capabilities. The cumulative amount of computation used for training includes the computation used across the activities and methods that are intended to enhance the capabilities of the model prior to deployment, such as pre-training, synthetic data generation and fine-tuning. Therefore, an initial threshold of floating point operations should be set, which, if met by a general-purpose AI model, leads to a presumption that the model is a general-purpose AI model with systemic risks. This threshold should be adjusted over time to reflect technological and industrial changes, such as algorithmic improvements or increased hardware efficiency, and should be supplemented with benchmarks and indicators for model capability. To inform this, the AI Office should engage with the scientific community, industry, civil society and other experts. Thresholds, as well as tools and benchmarks for the assessment of high-impact capabilities, should be strong predictors of generality, its capabilities and associated systemic risk of general-purpose AI models, and could take into account the way the model will be placed on the market or the number of users it may affect. To complement this system, there should be a possibility for the Commission to take individual decisions designating a general-purpose AI model as a general-purpose AI model with systemic risk if it is found that such model has capabilities or an impact equivalent to those captured by the set threshold. That decision should be taken on the basis of an overall assessment of the criteria for the designation of a general-purpose AI model with systemic risk set out in an annex to this Regulation, such as quality or size of the training data set, number of business and end users, its input and output modalities, its level of autonomy and scalability, or the tools it has access to. Upon a reasoned request of a provider whose model has been designated as a general-purpose AI model with systemic risk, the Commission should take the request into account and may decide to reassess whether the general-purpose AI model can still be considered to present systemic risks.

1265. **(112)** It is also necessary to clarify a procedure for the classification of a general-purpose AI model with systemic risks. A general-purpose AI model that meets the applicable threshold for high-impact capabilities should be presumed to be a general-purpose AI models with systemic risk. The provider should notify the AI Office at the latest two weeks after the requirements are met or it becomes known that a general-purpose AI model will meet the requirements that lead to the presumption. This is especially relevant in relation to the threshold of floating point operations because training of general-purpose AI models takes considerable planning which includes the upfront allocation of compute resources and, therefore, providers of general-purpose AI models are able to know if their model would meet the threshold before the training is completed. In the context of that notification, the provider should be able to demonstrate that, because of its specific characteristics, a general-purpose AI model exceptionally does not present systemic risks, and that it thus should not be classified as a general-purpose AI model with systemic risks. That information is valuable for the AI Office to anticipate the placing on the market of general-purpose AI models with systemic risks and the providers can start to engage with the AI Office early on. That information is especially important with regard to general-purpose AI models that are planned to be released as open-source, given that, after the open-source model release, necessary measures to ensure compliance with the obligations under this Regulation may be more difficult to implement.

1266. **(113)** If the Commission becomes aware of the fact that a general-purpose AI model meets the requirements to classify as a general-purpose AI model with systemic risk, which previously had either not been known or of which the relevant provider has failed to notify the Commission, the Commission should be empowered to designate it so. A system of qualified alerts should ensure that the AI Office is made aware by the scientific panel of general-purpose AI models that should possibly be classified as general-purpose AI models with systemic risk, in addition to the monitoring activities of the AI Office.

1267. **(163)** With a view to complementing the governance systems for general-purpose AI models, the scientific panel should support the monitoring activities of the AI Office and may, in certain cases, provide qualified alerts to the AI Office which trigger follow-ups, such as investigations. This should be the case where the scientific panel has reason to suspect that a general-purpose AI model poses a concrete and identifiable risk at Union level. Furthermore, this should be the case where the scientific panel has reason to suspect that a general-purpose AI model meets the criteria that would lead to a classification as general-purpose AI model with systemic risk. To equip the scientific panel with the information necessary for the performance of those tasks, there should be a mechanism whereby the scientific panel can request the Commission to require documentation or information from a provider.

1268. **(173)** In order to ensure that the regulatory framework can be adapted where necessary, the power to adopt acts in accordance with Article 290 TFEU should be delegated to the Commission to amend the conditions under which an AI system is not to be considered to be high-risk, the list of high-risk AI systems, the provisions regarding technical documentation, the content of the EU declaration of conformity the provisions regarding the conformity assessment procedures, the provisions establishing the high-risk AI systems to which the conformity assessment procedure based on assessment of the quality management system and assessment of the technical documentation should apply, the threshold, benchmarks and indicators, including by supplementing those benchmarks and indicators, in the rules for the classification of general-purpose AI models with systemic risk, the criteria for the designation of general-purpose AI models with systemic risk, the technical documentation for providers of general-purpose AI models and the transparency information for providers of general-purpose AI models. It is of particular importance that the Commission carry out appropriate consultations during its preparatory work, including at expert level, and that those consultations be conducted in accordance with the principles laid down in the Interinstitutional Agreement of 13 April 2016 on Better Law-Making.[1] In particular, to ensure equal participation in the preparation of delegated acts, the European Parliament and the Council receive all documents at the same time as Member States' experts, and their experts systematically have access to meetings of Commission expert groups dealing with the preparation of delegated acts.

51.2. General Approach

51.2.1 Preamble

1269. General-purpose AI models enable a range of operations (texts, sounds, images, and videos) in numerous contexts.

51.2.2 Guiding Principles

1270. The objective is to create a special category within AI systems for general-purpose AI models, taking into account:

- their specific characteristics;
- the associated systemic risks.

[1] [2016] OJ L123/1.

51.2.3 Actors

1271. Obligations concern providers and their authorised representatives.

51.2.4 Definitions

1272. 'General-purpose AI model' means 'an AI model, including where such an AI model is trained with a large amount of data using self-supervision at scale, that displays significant generality and is capable of competently performing a wide range of distinct tasks regardless of the way the model is placed on the market and that can be integrated into a variety of downstream systems or applications, except AI models that are used for research, development or prototyping activities before they are placed on the market'.[2]

1273. 'General-purpose AI system' means 'an AI system which is based on a general-purpose AI model and which has the capability to serve a variety of purposes, both for direct use as well as for integration in other AI systems'.[3]

51.3. General-Purpose AI Model with Systemic Risk

51.3.1 Notion of Systemic Risk

1274. 'Systemic risk'[4] means 'a risk that is specific to the high-impact capabilities of general-purpose AI models, having a significant impact on the Union market due to their reach, or due to actual or reasonably foreseeable negative effects on public health, safety, public security, fundamental rights, or the society as a whole, that can be propagated at scale across the value chain'.

51.3.2 Criteria

1275. Applicable alternatively, they correspond to the following model types:

NO.	MODEL	SPECIFICATION
1.	High impact capabilities	Heavy damaging consequences
2.	Decision of the European Commission	Model with high impact capabilities
3.	Qualified alert	From the scientific panel of independent experts[5]

[2] AI Act, Art. 3(63).
[3] AI Act, Art. 3(66).
[4] AI Act, Art. 3(65).
[5] AI Act, Art. 68.

51.3.3 Qualification

1276. To classify a general-purpose AI model as potentially presenting a systemic risk, the European Commission apply the following criteria, set out in Annex XIII:

NO.	MODEL	SPECIFICATION	REFERENCES
1.	Parameters of the model	E.g. OpenAI's GPT model has at least 175 billion parameters	AIA, Annex XIII(a)
2.	Quality	E.g. data set measured through tokens.	AIA, Annex XIII(b)
3.	Quantity	E.g. data set measured through tokens	AIA, Annex XIII(b)
4.	Computation	Amount of computation used for training the model, measured in floating point operations Taking into account the number of tasks or the ability to learn new tasks. High impact with at least 10,000 registered professional users in the EU	AIA, Annex XIII(c)
5.	Data	The input and output modalities of the model with high impact capabilities	AIA, Annex XIII(d)
6.	Capability	Number of tasks, adaptability to learn new tasks	AIA, Annex XIII(e)
7.	Market	High impact on the internal market with at least 10,000 registered business users established in the EU	AIA, Annex XIII(f)
8.	End-users	Number of registered end-users	AIA, Annex XIII(g)

51.3.4 Presumption

1277. A general-purpose AI model is presumed to present systemic risk when the amount of computation used for its training measured in floating point operations is greater than 10^{25}.

51.3.5 Evolution

1278. It is decided in the light of:

- algorithmic improvements;
- increased hardware efficiency.

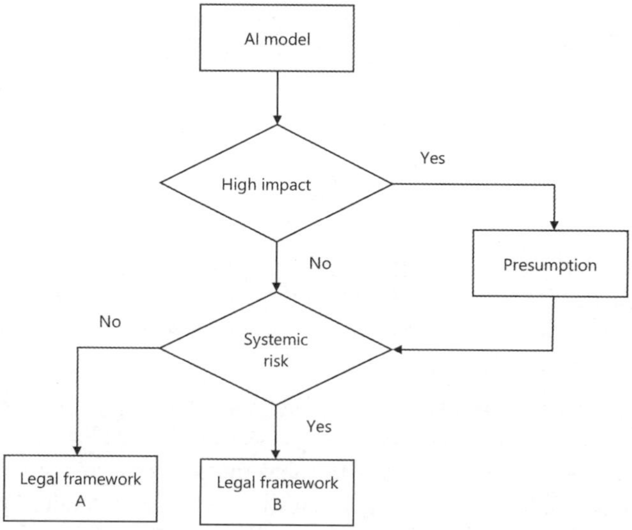

52 ARTICLE 52. PROCEDURE

1. Where a general-purpose AI model meets the condition referred to in Article 51(1), point (a), the relevant provider shall notify the Commission without delay and in any event within two weeks after that requirement is met or it becomes known that it will be met. That notification shall include the information necessary to demonstrate that the relevant requirement has been met. If the Commission becomes aware of a general-purpose AI model presenting systemic risks of which it has not been notified, it may decide to designate it as a model with systemic risk.

2. The provider of a general-purpose AI model that meets the condition referred to in Article 51(1), point (a), may present, with its notification, sufficiently substantiated arguments to demonstrate that, exceptionally, although it meets that requirement, the general-purpose AI model does not present, due to its specific characteristics, systemic risks and therefore should not be classified as a general-purpose AI model with systemic risk.

3. Where the Commission concludes that the arguments submitted pursuant to paragraph 2 are not sufficiently substantiated and the relevant provider was not able to demonstrate that the general-purpose AI model does not present, due to its specific characteristics, systemic risks, it shall reject those arguments, and the general-purpose AI model shall be considered to be a general-purpose AI model with systemic risk.

4. The Commission may designate a general-purpose AI model as presenting systemic risks, ex officio or following a qualified alert from the scientific panel pursuant to Article 90(1), point (a), on the basis of criteria set out in Annex XIII.

The Commission is empowered to adopt delegated acts in accordance with Article 97 in order to amend Annex XIII by specifying and updating the criteria set out in that Annex.

5. Upon a reasoned request of a provider whose model has been designated as a general-purpose AI model with systemic risk pursuant to paragraph 4, the Commission shall take the request into account and may decide to reassess whether the general-purpose AI model can still be considered to present systemic risks on the basis of the criteria set out in Annex XIII. Such a request shall contain objective, detailed and new reasons that have arisen since the designation decision. Providers may request reassessment at the earliest six months after the designation decision. Where the Commission, following its reassessment, decides to maintain the designation as a general-purpose AI model with systemic risk, providers may request reassessment at the earliest six months after that decision.

6. The Commission shall ensure that a list of general-purpose AI models with systemic risk is published and shall keep that list up to date, without prejudice to the need to observe and protect intellectual property rights and confidential business information or trade secrets in accordance with Union and national law.

52.1. Recitals

1279. **(111)** It is appropriate to establish a methodology for the classification of general-purpose AI models as general-purpose AI model with systemic risks. Since systemic risks result from particularly high capabilities, a general-purpose AI model should be considered to present systemic risks if it has high-impact capabilities, evaluated on the basis of appropriate technical tools and methodologies, or significant impact on the internal market due to its reach. High-impact capabilities in general-purpose AI models means capabilities that match or exceed the capabilities recorded in the most advanced general-purpose AI models. The full range of capabilities in a model could be better understood after its placing on the market or when deployers interact with the model. According to the state of the art at the time of entry into force of this Regulation, the cumulative amount of computation used for the training of the general-purpose AI model measured in floating point operations is one of the relevant approximations for model capabilities. The cumulative amount of computation used for training includes the computation used across the activities and methods that are intended to enhance the capabilities of the model prior to deployment, such as pre-training, synthetic data generation and fine-tuning. Therefore, an initial threshold of floating point operations should be set, which, if met by a general-purpose AI model, leads to a presumption that the model is a general-purpose AI model with systemic risks. This threshold should be adjusted over time to reflect technological and industrial changes, such as algorithmic improvements or increased hardware efficiency, and should be supplemented with benchmarks and indicators for model capability. To inform this, the AI Office should engage with the scientific community, industry, civil society and other experts. Thresholds, as well as tools and benchmarks for the assessment of high-impact capabilities, should be strong predictors of generality, its capabilities and associated systemic risk of general-purpose AI models, and could take into account the way the model will be placed on the market or the number of users it may affect. To complement this system, there should be a possibility for the Commission to take individual decisions designating a general-purpose AI model as a general-purpose AI model with systemic risk if it is found that such model has capabilities or an impact equivalent to those captured by the set threshold. That decision should be taken on the basis of an overall assessment of the criteria for the designation of a general-purpose AI model with systemic risk set out in an annex to this Regulation, such as quality or size of the training data set, number of business and end users, its input and output modalities, its level of autonomy and scalability, or the tools it has access to. Upon a reasoned request of a provider whose model has been designated as a general-purpose AI model with systemic risk, the Commission should take the request into account and may decide to reassess whether the general-purpose AI model can still be considered to present systemic risks.

1280. (112) It is also necessary to clarify a procedure for the classification of a general-purpose AI model with systemic risks. A general-purpose AI model that meets the applicable threshold for high-impact capabilities should be presumed to be a general-purpose AI models with systemic risk. The provider should notify the AI Office at the latest two weeks after the requirements are met or it becomes known that a general-purpose AI model will meet the requirements that lead to the presumption. This is especially relevant in relation to the threshold of floating point operations because training of general-purpose AI models takes considerable planning which includes the upfront allocation of compute resources and, therefore, providers of general-purpose AI models are able to know if their model would meet the threshold before the training is completed. In the context of that notification, the provider should be able to demonstrate that, because of its specific characteristics, a general-purpose AI model exceptionally does not present systemic risks, and that it thus should not be classified as a general-purpose AI model with systemic risks. That information is valuable for the AI Office to anticipate the placing on the market of general-purpose AI models with systemic risks and the providers can start to engage with the AI Office early on. That information is especially important with regard to general-purpose AI models that are planned to be released as open-source, given that, after the open-source model release, necessary measures to ensure compliance with the obligations under this Regulation may be more difficult to implement.

1281. (113) If the Commission becomes aware of the fact that a general-purpose AI model meets the requirements to classify as a general-purpose AI model with systemic risk, which previously had either not been known or of which the relevant provider has failed to notify the Commission, the Commission should be empowered to designate it so. A system of qualified alerts should ensure that the AI Office is made aware by the scientific panel of general-purpose AI models that should possibly be classified as general-purpose AI models with systemic risk, in addition to the monitoring activities of the AI Office.

1282. (163) With a view to complementing the governance systems for general-purpose AI models, the scientific panel should support the monitoring activities of the AI Office and may, in certain cases, provide qualified alerts to the AI Office which trigger follow-ups, such as investigations. This should be the case where the scientific panel has reason to suspect that a general-purpose AI model poses a concrete and identifiable risk at Union level. Furthermore, this should be the case where the scientific panel has reason to suspect that a general-purpose AI model meets the criteria that would lead to a classification as general-purpose AI model with systemic risk. To equip the scientific panel with the information necessary for the performance of those tasks, there should be a mechanism whereby the scientific panel can request the Commission to require documentation or information from a provider.

1283. (173) In order to ensure that the regulatory framework can be adapted where necessary, the power to adopt acts in accordance with Article 290 TFEU should be delegated to the Commission to amend the conditions under which an AI system is not to be considered to be high-risk, the list of high-risk AI systems, the provisions regarding technical documentation, the content of the EU declaration of conformity the provisions regarding the conformity assessment procedures, the provisions establishing the high-risk AI systems to which the conformity assessment procedure based on assessment of the quality management system and assessment of the technical documentation should apply, the threshold, benchmarks and indicators, including by supplementing those benchmarks and indicators, in the rules for the classification of general-purpose AI models with systemic risk, the criteria for the designation of general-purpose AI models with systemic risk, the technical documentation for providers of general-purpose AI models and the transparency information for providers of general-purpose AI models. It is of particular importance that the Commission carry out appropriate consultations during its preparatory work, including at expert level, and that those consultations be conducted in accordance with the principles laid down in the Interinstitutional Agreement of 13 April 2016 on Better Law-Making.[6] In particular, to ensure equal participation in the preparation of delegated acts, the European Parliament and the Council receive all documents at the same time as Member States' experts, and their experts systematically have access to meetings of Commission expert groups dealing with the preparation of delegated acts.

52.2. General Approach

52.2.1 Preamble

1284. The objective is to identify and monitor the evolution of general-purpose models presenting systemic risks.

52.2.2 Actors

1285. This requirement is provided for providers.

52.2.3 Deadline

1286. Two weeks after:

- the system met the systemic risk conditions; or
- it becomes known that they will be met.

52.2.4 Activity

1287. The deadline is counted during the design phase, independently of its placing on the market.

52.2.5 Modalities

1288. The notification includes the systemic risk classification dossier.

1289. Note:

- (1) In the absence of notification, the European Commission may officially declare that a general-purpose AI model presents systemic risks.

52.2.6 Derogations

1290. The provider may request a derogation by presenting a dossier demonstrating that despite its specifications leading to such classification, the systemic risks in question do not justify the classification.

---

6 [2016] OJ L123/1.

52.2.7 *Ex Officio* Classification

1291. The European Commission may designate a general-purpose AI model as presenting systemic risks, *ex officio* or following a qualified alert from the scientific panel. In this case, it must implement the criteria set out in Annex XIII.

52.2.8 Publication

1292. The European Commission must implement a transparency policy regarding systemic risk by adhering to the following guiding principles:

NO.	THEME	SPECIFICATION
1.	List of models	Publication
2.	Update	Regularly
3.	Information	General
4.	Protection	Respect for: • intellectual property rights • confidential business information • trade secrets

SECTION 2. OBLIGATIONS FOR PROVIDERS OF GENERAL-PURPOSE AI MODELS

53 ARTICLE 53. OBLIGATIONS FOR PROVIDERS OF GENERAL-PURPOSE AI MODELS

1. Providers of general-purpose AI models shall:

(a) draw up and keep up-to-date the technical documentation of the model, including its training and testing process and the results of its evaluation, which shall contain, at a minimum, the information set out in Annex XI for the purpose of providing it, upon request, to the AI Office and the national competent authorities;

(b) draw up, keep up-to-date and make available information and documentation to providers of AI systems who intend to integrate the general-purpose AI model into their AI systems. Without prejudice to the need to observe and protect intellectual property rights and confidential business information or trade secrets in accordance with Union and national law, the information and documentation shall:

(i) enable providers of AI systems to have a good understanding of the capabilities and limitations of the general-purpose AI model and to comply with their obligations pursuant to this Regulation; and

(ii) contain, at a minimum, the elements set out in Annex XII;

(c) put in place a policy to comply with Union law on copyright and related rights, and in particular to identify and comply with, including through state-of-the-art technologies, a reservation of rights expressed pursuant to Article 4(3) of Directive (EU) 2019/79;

(d) draw up and make publicly available a sufficiently detailed summary about the content used for training of the general-purpose AI model, according to a template provided by the AI Office.

2. The obligations set out in paragraph 1, points (a) and (b), shall not apply to providers of AI models that are released under a free and open-source licence that allows for the access, usage, modification, and distribution of the model, and whose parameters, including the weights, the information on the model architecture, and the information on model usage, are made publicly available. This exception shall not apply to general-purpose AI models with systemic risks.

3. Providers of general-purpose AI models shall cooperate as necessary with the Commission and the national competent authorities in the exercise of their competences and powers pursuant to this Regulation.

4. Providers of general-purpose AI models may rely on codes of practice within the meaning of Article 56 to demonstrate compliance with the obligations set out in paragraph 1 of this Article, until a harmonised standard is published. Compliance with European harmonised standards grants providers the presumption of conformity to the extent that those standards cover those obligations. Providers of general-purpose AI models who do not adhere to an approved code of practice or do not comply with a European harmonised standard shall demonstrate alternative adequate means of compliance for assessment by the Commission.

5. For the purpose of facilitating compliance with Annex XI, in particular points 2 (d) and (e) thereof, the Commission is empowered to adopt delegated acts in accordance with Article 97 to detail measurement and calculation methodologies with a view to allowing for comparable and verifiable documentation.

6. The Commission is empowered to adopt delegated acts in accordance with Article 97(2) to amend Annexes XI and XII in light of evolving technological developments.

7. Any information or documentation obtained pursuant to this Article, including trade secrets, shall be treated in accordance with the confidentiality obligations set out in Article 78.

53.1. *Recitals*

1293. **(97)** The notion of general-purpose AI models should be clearly defined and set apart from the notion of AI systems to enable legal certainty. The definition should be based on the key functional characteristics of a general-purpose AI model, in particular the generality and the capability to competently perform a wide range of distinct tasks. These models are typically trained on large amounts of data, through various methods, such as self-supervised, unsupervised or reinforcement learning. General-purpose AI models may be placed on the market in various ways, including through libraries, application programming interfaces (APIs), as direct download, or as physical copy. These models may be further modified or fine-tuned into new models. Although AI models are essential components of AI systems, they do not constitute AI systems on their own. AI models require the addition of further components, such as for example a user interface, to become AI systems. AI models are typically integrated into and form part of AI systems. This Regulation provides specific rules for general-purpose AI models and for general-purpose AI models that pose systemic risks, which should apply also when these models are integrated or form part of an AI system. It should be understood that the obligations for the providers of general-purpose AI models should apply once the general-purpose AI models are placed on the market. When the provider of a general-purpose AI model integrates an own model into its own AI system that is made available on the market or put into service, that model should be considered to be placed on the market and, therefore, the obligations in this Regulation for models should continue to apply in addition to those for AI systems. The obligations laid down for models should in any case not apply when an own model is used for purely internal processes that are not essential for providing a product or a service to third parties and the rights of natural persons are not affected. Considering their potential significantly negative effects, the general-purpose AI models with systemic risk should always be subject to the relevant obligations under this Regulation. The definition should not cover AI models used before their placing on the market for the sole purpose of research, development and prototyping activities. This is without prejudice to the obligation to comply with this Regulation when, following such activities, a model is placed on the market.

1294. **(98)** Whereas the generality of a model could, inter alia, also be determined by a number of parameters, models with at least a billion of parameters and trained with a large amount of data using self-supervision at scale should be considered to display significant generality and to competently perform a wide range of distinctive tasks.

1295. **(99)** Large generative AI models are a typical example for a general-purpose AI model, given that they allow for flexible generation of content, such as in the form of text, audio, images or video, that can readily accommodate a wide range of distinctive tasks.

1296. **(100)** When a general-purpose AI model is integrated into or forms part of an AI system, this system should be considered to be general-purpose AI system when, due to this integration, this system has the capability to serve a variety of purposes. A general-purpose AI system can be used directly, or it may be integrated into other AI systems.

1297. **(101)** Providers of general-purpose AI models have a particular role and responsibility along the AI value chain, as the models they provide may form the basis for a range of downstream systems, often provided by downstream providers that necessitate a good understanding of the models and their capabilities, both to enable the integration of such models into their products, and to fulfil their obligations under this or other regulations. Therefore, proportionate transparency measures should be laid down, including the drawing up and keeping up to date of documentation, and the provision of information on the general-purpose AI model for its usage by the downstream providers. Technical documentation should be prepared and kept up to date by the general-purpose AI model provider for the purpose of making it available, upon request, to the AI Office and the national competent authorities. The minimal set of elements to be included in such documentation should be set out in specific annexes to this Regulation. The Commission should be empowered to amend those annexes by means of delegated acts in light of evolving technological developments.

1298. **(102)** Software and data, including models, released under a free and open-source licence that allows them to be openly shared and where users can freely access, use, modify and redistribute them or modified versions thereof, can contribute to research and innovation in the market and can provide significant growth opportunities for the Union economy. General-purpose AI models released under free and open-source licences should be considered to ensure high levels of transparency and openness if their parameters, including the weights, the information on the model architecture, and the information on model usage are made publicly available. The licence should be considered to be free and open-source also when it allows users to run, copy, distribute, study, change and improve software and data, including models under the condition that the original provider of the model is credited, the identical or comparable terms of distribution are respected.

1299. **(103)** Free and open-source AI components covers the software and data, including models and general-purpose AI models, tools, services or processes of an AI system. Free and open-source AI components can be provided through different channels, including their development on open repositories. For the purposes of this Regulation, AI components that are provided against a price or otherwise monetised, including through the provision of technical support or other services, including through a software platform, related to the AI component, or the use of personal data for reasons other than exclusively for improving the security, compatibility or interoperability of the software, with the exception of transactions between microenterprises, should not benefit from the exceptions provided to free and open-source AI components. The fact of making AI components available through open repositories should not, in itself, constitute a monetisation.

1300. (104) The providers of general-purpose AI models that are released under a free and open-source licence, and whose parameters, including the weights, the information on the model architecture, and the information on model usage, are made publicly available should be subject to exceptions as regards the transparency-related requirements imposed on general-purpose AI models, unless they can be considered to present a systemic risk, in which case the circumstance that the model is transparent and accompanied by an open-source license should not be considered to be a sufficient reason to exclude compliance with the obligations under this Regulation. In any case, given that the release of general-purpose AI models under free and open-source licence does not necessarily reveal substantial information on the data set used for the training or fine-tuning of the model and on how compliance of copyright law was thereby ensured, the exception provided for general-purpose AI models from compliance with the transparency-related requirements should not concern the obligation to produce a summary about the content used for model training and the obligation to put in place a policy to comply with Union copyright law, in particular to identify and comply with the reservation of rights pursuant to Article 4(3) of Directive (EU) 2019/790 of the European Parliament and of the Council.[7]

1301. (105) General-purpose AI models, in particular large generative AI models, capable of generating text, images, and other content, present unique innovation opportunities but also challenges to artists, authors, and other creators and the way their creative content is created, distributed, used and consumed. The development and training of such models require access to vast amounts of text, images, videos and other data. Text and data mining techniques may be used extensively in this context for the retrieval and analysis of such content, which may be protected by copyright and related rights. Any use of copyright protected content requires the authorisation of the rightsholder concerned unless relevant copyright exceptions and limitations apply. Directive (EU) 2019/790 introduced exceptions and limitations allowing reproductions and extractions of works or other subject matter, for the purpose of text and data mining, under certain

7 Directive (EU) 2019/790 of the European Parliament and of the Council of 17 April 2019 on copyright and related rights in the Digital Single Market and amending Directives 96/9/EC and 2001/29/EC, [2019] OJ L130/92.

conditions. Under these rules, rightsholders may choose to reserve their rights over their works or other subject matter to prevent text and data mining, unless this is done for the purposes of scientific research. Where the rights to opt out has been expressly reserved in an appropriate manner, providers of general-purpose AI models need to obtain an authorisation from rightsholders if they want to carry out text and data mining over such works.

1302. **(106)** Providers that place general-purpose AI models on the Union market should ensure compliance with the relevant obligations in this Regulation. To that end, providers of general-purpose AI models should put in place a policy to comply with Union law on copyright and related rights, in particular to identify and comply with the reservation of rights expressed by rightsholders pursuant to Article 4(3) of Directive (EU) 2019/790. Any provider placing a general-purpose AI model on the Union market should comply with this obligation, regardless of the jurisdiction in which the copyright-relevant acts underpinning the training of those general-purpose AI models take place. This is necessary to ensure a level playing field among providers of general-purpose AI models where no provider should be able to gain a competitive advantage in the Union market by applying lower copyright standards than those provided in the Union.

1303. **(108)** With regard to the obligations imposed on providers of general-purpose AI models to put in place a policy to comply with Union copyright law and make publicly available a summary of the content used for the training, the AI Office should monitor whether the provider has fulfilled those obligations without verifying or proceeding to a work-by-work assessment of the training data in terms of copyright compliance. This Regulation does not affect the enforcement of copyright rules as provided for under Union law.

1304. **(109)** Compliance with the obligations applicable to the providers of general-purpose AI models should be commensurate and proportionate to the type of model provider, excluding the need for compliance for persons who develop or use models for non-professional or scientific research purposes, who should nevertheless be encouraged to voluntarily comply with these requirements. Without prejudice to Union copyright law, compliance with those obligations should take due account of the size of the provider and allow simplified ways of compliance for SMEs, including start-ups, that should not represent an excessive cost and not discourage the use of such models. In the case of a modification or fine-tuning of a model, the obligations for providers of general-purpose AI models should be limited to that modification or fine-tuning, for example by complementing the already existing technical documentation with information on the modifications, including new training data sources, as a means to comply with the value chain obligations provided in this Regulation.

1305. **(111)** It is appropriate to establish a methodology for the classification of general-purpose AI models as general-purpose AI model with systemic risks. Since systemic risks result from particularly high capabilities, a general-purpose AI model should be considered to present systemic risks if it has high-impact capabilities, evaluated on the basis of appropriate technical tools and methodologies, or significant impact on the internal market due to its reach. High-impact capabilities in general-purpose AI models means capabilities that match or exceed the capabilities recorded in the most advanced general-purpose AI models. The full range of capabilities in a model could be better understood after its placing on the market or when deployers interact with the model. According to the state of the art at the time of entry into force of this Regulation, the cumulative amount of computation used for the training of the general-purpose AI model measured in floating point operations is one of the relevant approximations for model capabilities. The cumulative amount of computation used for training includes the computation used across the activities and methods that are intended to enhance the capabilities of the model prior to deployment, such as pre-training, synthetic data generation and fine-tuning. Therefore, an initial threshold of floating point operations should be set, which, if met by a general-purpose AI model, leads to a presumption that the model is a general-purpose AI model with systemic risks. This threshold should be adjusted over time to reflect technological and industrial changes, such as algorithmic improvements or increased hardware efficiency, and should be supplemented with benchmarks and indicators for model capability. To inform this, the AI Office should engage with the scientific community, industry, civil society and other experts. Thresholds, as well as tools and benchmarks for the assessment of high-impact capabilities, should be strong predictors of generality, its capabilities and associated systemic risk of general-purpose AI models, and could take into account the way the model will be placed on the market or the number of users it may affect. To complement this system, there should be a possibility for the Commission to take individual decisions designating a general-purpose AI model as a general-purpose AI model with systemic risk if it is found that such model has capabilities or an impact equivalent to those captured by the set threshold. That decision should be taken on the basis of an overall assessment of the criteria for the designation of a general-purpose AI model with systemic risk set out in an annex to this Regulation, such as quality or size of the training data set, number of business and end users, its input and output modalities, its level of autonomy and scalability, or the tools it has access to. Upon a reasoned request of a provider whose model has been designated as a general-purpose AI model with systemic risk, the Commission should take the request into account and may decide to reassess whether the general-purpose AI model can still be considered to present systemic risks.

1306. **(112)** It is also necessary to clarify a procedure for the classification of a general-purpose AI model with systemic risks. A general-purpose AI model that meets the applicable threshold for high-impact capabilities should be presumed to be a general-purpose AI models with systemic risk. The provider should notify the AI Office at the latest two weeks after the requirements are met or it becomes known that a general-purpose AI model will meet the requirements that lead to the presumption. This is especially relevant in relation to the threshold of floating point operations because training of general-purpose AI models takes considerable planning which includes the upfront allocation of compute resources and, therefore, providers of general-purpose AI models are able to know if their model would meet the threshold before the training is completed. In the context of that notification, the provider should be able to demonstrate that, because of its specific characteristics, a general-purpose AI model exceptionally does not present systemic risks, and that it thus should not be classified as a general-purpose AI model with systemic risks. That information is valuable for the AI Office to anticipate the placing on the market of general-purpose AI models with systemic risks and the providers can start to engage with the AI Office early on. That information is especially important with regard to general-purpose AI models that are planned to be released as open-source, given that, after the open-source model release, necessary measures to ensure compliance with the obligations under this Regulation may be more difficult to implement.

1307. (113) If the Commission becomes aware of the fact that a general-purpose AI model meets the requirements to classify as a general-purpose AI model with systemic risk, which previously had either not been known or of which the relevant provider has failed to notify the Commission, the Commission should be empowered to designate it so. A system of qualified alerts should ensure that the AI Office is made aware by the scientific panel of general-purpose AI models that should possibly be classified as general-purpose AI models with systemic risk, in addition to the monitoring activities of the AI Office.

1308. (116) The AI Office should encourage and facilitate the drawing up, review and adaptation of codes of practice, taking into account international approaches. All providers of general-purpose AI models could be invited to participate. To ensure that the codes of practice reflect the state of the art and duly take into account a diverse set of perspectives, the AI Office should collaborate with relevant national competent authorities, and could, where appropriate, consult with civil society organisations and other relevant stakeholders and experts, including the Scientific Panel, for the drawing up of such codes. Codes of practice should cover obligations for providers of general-purpose AI models and of general-purpose AI models presenting systemic risks. In addition, as regards systemic risks, codes of practice should help to establish a risk taxonomy of the type and nature of the systemic risks at Union level, including their sources. Codes of practice should also be focused on specific risk assessment and mitigation measures.

53.2. *General Approach*

53.2.1 Preamble

1309. The Regulation:

- applies to all general-purpose AI models;
- defines general requirements;
- specifies particular requirements for general-purpose AI models with systemic risks.

53.2.2 Actors

1310. The obligations concern providers and authorised representatives.

53.2.3 Activities

1311. All requirements must be met before the placing on the market.

53.2.4 Classification

1312. It is divided into two categories:

- the technical documentation of the general-purpose AI model;
- the documentation for providers of AI systems.

1313. Note:

- (1) This documentation is distinct from the instructions of use, which include information[8] provided by the provider to inform the deployer of, in particular an AI system's, intended purpose and proper use.

53.2.5 Technical Documentation of the Model

1314. It includes the following:

NO.	AREA	SPECIFICATION	REFERENCES
1.	AI system	List of AI systems (type and nature) in which the model can be integrated	AIA, Annex XI(1)(a)
2.	Architecture	General description and number of parameters	AIA, Annex XI(1)(d)

[8] AI Act, Art. 3(15).

NO.	AREA	SPECIFICATION	REFERENCES
3.	Tasks	Description of the tasks that the model can perform	AIA, Annex XI(1)(a)
4.	Inputs and outputs	Type and format	AIA, Annex XI(1)(e)
5.	Results	Quality evaluation and qualification	AIA, Art. 53
6.	Testing	Methods (test sets)	AIA, Art. 53
7.	Training	Description of processes	AIA, Art. 53
8.	Policy	Description of acceptable uses	AIA, Annex XI(1)(b)
9.	Distribution	Model date of release and methods of distribution	AIA, Annex XI(1)(c)
10.	Licence	Draft contract	AIA, Annex XI(1)(f)

53.2.6 Documentation for Providers of AI Systems

53.2.6.1 *Introduction*

1315. This second documentation, correlated with the first, is intended for providers of AI systems.

53.2.6.2 *Actors*

1316. It concerns providers of models as such.

53.2.6.3 *Activity*

1317. Access to this documentation requires that the model has been placed on the market.

53.2.6.4 *Composition*

1318. It is as follows:

NO.	AREA	SPECIFICATION	REFERENCES
1.	Capabilities	Have a good understanding	AIA, Art. 53
2.	Limitation	Description of limitations and consequences	AIA, Art. 53
3.	Process	Description of development steps	AIA, Art. 53
4.	Tasks	List	AIA, Annex XII(1)(a)
5.	AI system	AI systems (type and nature) in which the model can be integrated	AIA, Annex XII(1)(a)

NO.	AREA	SPECIFICATION	REFERENCES
6.	Policy	Description of acceptable uses	AIA, Annex XII(1)(b)
7.	Publication	Date	AIA, Annex XII(1)(c)
8.	Distribution	Methods	AIA, Annex XII(1)(c)
9.	Technical specifications	How the model interacts with hardware or software	AIA, Annex XII(1)(d)
10.	Software	Versions related to the use of the model	AIA, Annex XII(1)(e)
11.	Protection	Intellectual property rights Confidential business information Trade secrets	AIA, Art. 53(1)(b)

53.2.6.5 *Derogation*

1319. Derogations from these obligations are possible as follows:

NO.	THEME	SPECIFICATION
1.	Contract	Free and open-source licence
2.	Characteristics of the licence	Allows for: • access • usage • modification • distribution
3.	Communication of specifications	Architecture of the model Parameters (including the weights) Usage of the model

1320. Note:

- (1) This derogation does not apply to general-purpose AI models with systemic risks.

53.2.7 Policy and Copyright

1321. The provider must present its policy to comply with copyright law, including:

- training modalities;
- respect for copyrighted works.[9]

9 Directive (EU) 2019/790, Art. 4(3).

53.2.8 Publicly Available Information

1322. The provider must make publicly available a detailed summary about the content used for training of the general-purpose AI model.

1323. Note:
- (1) This summary should be based on a template provided by the AI Office.

53.2.9 Operations on Models

53.2.9.1 *Introduction*

1324. The notion of operations includes:
- retraining of models;
- fine-tuning of responses.

53.2.9.2 *Qualification*

1325. According to the European Data Protection Supervisor (EDPS), 'the emergence of AI system training techniques such as Parameter Efficient Fine-Tuning (PEFT) have significantly decreased the cost, and thus made broadly available, the retraining of foundation models'.

1326. In the absence of clarification, the 're-trainer' should be considered as a provider when the model's behaviour is substantially modified.

1327. In this context, it specifies the following:
- 'Given the impact that the retraining of AI systems can have on their performance, purpose and their compliance with legal requirements, the EDPS considers necessary to clarify the role of AI operators retraining AI systems, specifying whether the 're-trainers' are providers. The EDPS understands that AI operators retraining pre-trained AI systems should be qualified as 'providers' in order to guarantee that compliance the requirements of the AI Act remains ensured. The EDPS recommends the co-legislators to clarify this aspect in the AI Act beyond any doubt.'[10]

---

[10] EDPS, Opinion 44/2023 of 23 October 2023.

54 ARTICLE 54. AUTHORISED REPRESENTATIVES OF PROVIDERS OF GENERAL-PURPOSE AI MODELS

1. Prior to placing a general-purpose AI model on the Union market, providers established in third countries shall, by written mandate, appoint an authorised representative which is established in the Union.

2. The provider shall enable its authorised representative to perform the tasks specified in the mandate received from the provider.

3. The authorised representative shall perform the tasks specified in the mandate received from the provider. It shall provide a copy of the mandate to the AI Office upon request, in one of the official languages of the institutions of the Union. For the purposes of this Regulation, the mandate shall empower the authorised representative to carry out the following tasks:

(a) verify that the technical documentation specified in Annex XI has been drawn up and all obligations referred to in Article 53 and, where applicable, Article 55 have been fulfilled by the provider;

(b) keep a copy of the technical documentation specified in Annex XI at the disposal of the AI Office and national competent authorities, for a period of 10 years after the general-purpose AI model has been placed on the market, and the contact details of the provider that appointed the authorised representative;

(c) provide the AI Office, upon a reasoned request, with all the information and documentation, including that referred to in point (b), necessary to demonstrate compliance with the obligations in this Chapter;

(d) cooperate with the AI Office and competent authorities, upon a reasoned request, in any action they take in relation to the general-purpose AI model, including when the model is integrated into AI systems placed on the market or put into service in the Union.

4. The mandate shall empower the authorised representative to be addressed, in addition to or instead of the provider, by the AI Office or the competent authorities, on all issues related to ensuring compliance with this Regulation.

5. The authorised representative shall terminate the mandate if it considers or has reason to consider the provider to be acting contrary to its obligations pursuant to this Regulation. In such a case, it shall also immediately inform the AI Office about the termination of the mandate and the reasons therefor.

6. The obligation set out in this Article shall not apply to providers of general-purpose AI models that are released under a free and open-source licence that allows for the access, usage, modification, and distribution of the model, and whose parameters, including the weights, the information on the model architecture, and the information on model usage, are made publicly available, unless the general-purpose AI models present systemic risks.

54.1. Recitals

1328. **(82)** To enable enforcement of this Regulation and create a level playing field for operators, and, taking into account the different forms of making available of digital products, it is important to ensure that, under all circumstances, a person established in the Union can provide authorities with all the necessary information on the compliance of an AI system. Therefore, prior to making their AI systems available in the Union, providers established in third countries should, by written mandate, appoint an authorised representative established in the Union. This authorised representative plays a pivotal role in ensuring the compliance of the high-risk AI systems placed on the market or put into service in the Union by those providers who are not established in the Union and in serving as their contact person established in the Union.

54.2. General Approach

54.2.1 Preamble

1329. An authorised representative is required for general-purpose AI models when the provider is established in a third country outside the European Union.

54.2.2 Guiding Principles

1330. The authorised representative acts on behalf of the third-country provider.

1331. The authorised representative must be established in the EU and be appointed by written mandate.

1332. The mandate specifies the provider tasks that are delegated to the authorised representative.

1333. Notes:

- (1) The authorised representative terminates the mandate if the provider fails to meet its obligations.
- (2) In such a case, the authorised representative must inform the AI Office about the termination of the mandate and the reasons therefor.

54.2.3 Obligations

1334. They are as follows:

NO.	THEME	SPECIFICATION
1.	Provider	Contact details
2.	Technical documentation	Verification that all obligations have been fulfilled (Annex XI and Article 53 and, where applicable, Article 55)
3.	Duration	10 years
4.	Communication	AI Office upon request
5.	Demonstration of requirements	AI Office upon reasoned request
6.	Cooperation	National competent authority and AI Office
7.	Representation	Empowerment by the provider in the mandate

SECTION 3. OBLIGATIONS OF PROVIDERS OF GENERAL-PURPOSE AI MODELS WITH SYSTEMIC RISK

55 ARTICLE 55. OBLIGATIONS OF PROVIDERS OF GENERAL-PURPOSE AI MODELS WITH SYSTEMIC RISK

1. In addition to the obligations listed in Articles 53 and 54, providers of general-purpose AI models with systemic risk shall:

(a) perform model evaluation in accordance with standardised protocols and tools reflecting the state of the art, including conducting and documenting adversarial testing of the model with a view to identifying and mitigating systemic risks;

(b) assess and mitigate possible systemic risks at Union level, including their sources, that may stem from the development, the placing on the market, or the use of general-purpose AI models with systemic risk;

(c) keep track of, document, and report, without undue delay, to the AI Office and, as appropriate, to national competent authorities, relevant information about serious incidents and possible corrective measures to address them;

(d) ensure an adequate level of cybersecurity protection for the general-purpose AI model with systemic risk and the physical infrastructure of the model.

2. Providers of general-purpose AI models with systemic risk may rely on codes of practice within the meaning of Article 56 to demonstrate compliance with the obligations set out in paragraph 1 of this Article, until a harmonised standard is published. Compliance with European harmonised standards grants providers the presumption of conformity to the extent that those standards cover those obligations. Providers of general-purpose AI models with systemic risks who do not adhere to an approved code of practice or do not comply with a European harmonised standard shall demonstrate alternative adequate means of compliance for assessment by the Commission.

3. Any information or documentation obtained pursuant to this Article, including trade secrets, shall be treated in accordance with the confidentiality obligations set out in Article 78.

55.1. Recitals

1335. **(114)** The providers of general-purpose AI models presenting systemic risks should be subject, in addition to the obligations provided for providers of general-purpose AI models, to obligations aimed at identifying and mitigating those risks and ensuring an adequate level of cybersecurity protection, regardless of whether it is provided as a standalone model or embedded in an AI system or a product. To achieve those objectives, this Regulation should require providers to perform the necessary model evaluations, in particular prior to its first placing on the market, including conducting and documenting adversarial testing of models, also, as appropriate, through internal or independent external testing. In addition, providers of general-purpose AI models with systemic risks should continuously assess and mitigate systemic risks, including for example by putting in place risk-management policies, such as accountability and governance processes, implementing post-market monitoring, taking appropriate measures along the entire model's lifecycle and cooperating with relevant actors along the AI value chain.

1336. **(115)** Providers of general-purpose AI models with systemic risks should assess and mitigate possible systemic risks. If, despite efforts to identify and prevent risks related to a general-purpose AI model that may present systemic risks, the development or use of the model causes a serious incident, the general-purpose AI model provider should without undue delay keep track of the incident and report any relevant information and possible corrective measures to the Commission and national competent authorities. Furthermore, providers should ensure an adequate level of cybersecurity protection for the model and its physical infrastructure, if appropriate, along the entire model lifecycle. Cybersecurity protection related to systemic risks associated with malicious use or attacks should duly consider accidental model leakage, unauthorised releases, circumvention of safety measures, and defence against cyberattacks, unauthorised access or model theft. That protection could be facilitated by securing model weights, algorithms, servers, and data sets, such as through operational security measures for information security, specific cybersecurity policies, adequate technical and established solutions, and cyber and physical access controls, appropriate to the relevant circumstances and the risks involved.

1337. **(116)** The AI Office should encourage and facilitate the drawing up, review and adaptation of codes of practice, taking into account international approaches. All providers of general-purpose AI models could be invited to participate. To ensure that the codes of practice reflect the state of the art and duly take into account a diverse set of perspectives, the AI Office should collaborate with relevant national competent authorities, and could, where appropriate, consult with civil society organisations and other relevant stakeholders and experts, including the Scientific Panel, for the drawing up of such codes. Codes of practice should cover obligations for providers of general-purpose AI models and of general-purpose AI models presenting systemic risks. In addition, as regards systemic risks, codes of practice should help to establish a risk taxonomy of the type and nature of the systemic risks at Union level, including their sources. Codes of practice should also be focused on specific risk assessment and mitigation measures.

55.2. General Approach

55.2.1 Preamble

1338. General-purpose AI models presenting systemic risks are subject to additional requirements.

55.2.2 Actors

1339. The concerned operators are:

- providers;
- authorised representatives.

55.2.3 Obligations

1340. They include the following requirements:

NO.	THEME	SPECIFICATION
1.	Risks	Evaluation
2.	Measures	Mitigation policy

NO.	THEME	SPECIFICATION
3.	Activities	Development Placing on the market Use
4.	Serious incidents	Obligation to report
5.	Corrective measures for serious incidents	Notification
6.	Cybersecurity	Adequate level of protection
7.	Code of practice	Recommended Otherwise, alternative means should be subject to European Commission's assessment
8.	Protection	Trade secrets

56 ARTICLE 56. CODES OF PRACTICE

1. The AI Office shall encourage and facilitate the drawing up of codes of practice at Union level in order to contribute to the proper application of this Regulation, taking into account international approaches.

2. The AI Office and the Board shall aim to ensure that the codes of practice cover at least the obligations provided for in Articles 53 and 55, including the following issues:

(a) the means to ensure that the information referred to in Article 53(1), points (a) and (b), is kept up to date in light of market and technological developments;

(b) the adequate level of detail for the summary about the content used for training;

(c) the identification of the type and nature of the systemic risks at Union level, including their sources, where appropriate;

(d) the measures, procedures and modalities for the assessment and management of the systemic risks at Union level, including the documentation thereof, which shall be proportionate to the risks, take into consideration their severity and probability and take into account the specific challenges of tackling those risks in light of the possible ways in which such risks may emerge and materialise along the AI value chain.

3. The AI Office may invite all providers of general-purpose AI models, as well as relevant national competent authorities, to participate in the drawing-up of codes of practice. Civil society organisations, industry, academia and other relevant stakeholders, such as downstream providers and independent experts, may support the process.

4. The AI Office and the Board shall aim to ensure that the codes of practice clearly set out their specific objectives and contain commitments or measures, including key performance indicators as appropriate, to ensure the achievement of those objectives, and that they take due account of the needs and interests of all interested parties, including affected persons, at Union level.

5. The AI Office shall aim to ensure that participants to the codes of practice report regularly to the AI Office on the implementation of the commitments and the measures taken and their outcomes, including as measured against the key performance indicators as appropriate. Key performance indicators and reporting commitments shall reflect differences in size and capacity between various participants.

6. The AI Office and the Board shall regularly monitor and evaluate the achievement of the objectives of the codes of practice by the participants and their contribution to the proper application of this Regulation. The AI Office and the Board shall assess whether the codes of practice cover the obligations provided for in Articles 53 and 55, and shall regularly monitor and evaluate the achievement of their objectives. They shall publish their assessment of the adequacy of the codes of practice.

The Commission may, by way of an implementing act, approve a code of practice and give it a general validity within the Union. That implementing act shall be adopted in accordance with the examination procedure referred to in Article 98(2).

7. The AI Office may invite all providers of general-purpose AI models to adhere to the codes of practice. For providers of general-purpose AI models not presenting systemic risks this adherence may be limited to the obligations provided for in Article 53, unless they declare explicitly their interest to join the full code.

8. The AI Office shall, as appropriate, also encourage and facilitate the review and adaptation of the codes of practice, in particular in light of emerging standards. The AI Office shall assist in the assessment of available standards.

9. Codes of practice shall be ready at the latest by 2 May 2025. The AI Office shall take the necessary steps, including inviting providers pursuant to paragraph 7.

If, by 2 August 2025, a code of practice cannot be finalised, or if the AI Office deems it is not adequate following its assessment under paragraph 6 of this Article, the Commission may provide, by means of implementing acts, common rules for the implementation of the obligations provided for in Articles 53 and 55, including the issues set out in paragraph 2 of this Article. Those implementing acts shall be adopted in accordance with the examination procedure referred to in Article 98(2).

56.1. Recitals

1341. (116) The AI Office should encourage and facilitate the drawing up, review and adaptation of codes of practice, taking into account international approaches. All providers of general-purpose AI models could be invited to participate. To ensure that the codes of practice reflect the state of the art and duly take into account a diverse set of perspectives, the AI Office should collaborate with relevant national competent authorities, and could, where appropriate, consult with civil society organisations and other relevant stakeholders and experts, including the Scientific Panel, for the drawing up of such codes. Codes of practice should cover obligations for providers of general-purpose AI models and of general-purpose AI models presenting systemic risks. In addition, as regards systemic risks, codes of practice should help to establish a risk taxonomy of the type and nature of the systemic risks at Union level, including their sources. Codes of practice should also be focused on specific risk assessment and mitigation measures.

1342. (117) The codes of practice should represent a central tool for the proper compliance with the obligations provided for under this Regulation for providers of general-purpose AI models. Providers should be able to rely on codes of practice to demonstrate compliance with the obligations. By means of implementing acts, the Commission may decide to approve a code of practice and give it a general validity within the Union, or, alternatively, to provide common rules for the implementation of the relevant obligations, if, by the time this Regulation becomes applicable, a code of practice cannot be finalised or is not deemed adequate by the AI Office. Once a harmonised standard is published and assessed as suitable to cover the relevant obligations by the AI Office, compliance with a European harmonised standard should grant providers the presumption of conformity. Providers of general-purpose AI models should furthermore be able to demonstrate compliance using alternative adequate means, if codes of practice or harmonised standards are not available, or they choose not to rely on those.

1343. (135) Without prejudice to the mandatory nature and full applicability of the transparency obligations, the Commission may also encourage and facilitate the drawing up of codes of practice at Union level to facilitate the effective implementation of the obligations regarding the detection and labelling of artificially generated or manipulated content, including to support practical arrangements for making, as appropriate, the detection mechanisms accessible and facilitating cooperation with other actors along the value chain, disseminating content or checking its authenticity and provenance to enable the public to effectively distinguish AI-generated content.

1344. (165) The development of AI systems other than high-risk AI systems in accordance with the requirements of this Regulation may lead to a larger uptake of ethical and trustworthy AI in the Union. Providers of AI systems that are not high-risk should be encouraged to create codes of conduct, including related governance mechanisms, intended to foster the voluntary application of some or all of the mandatory requirements applicable to high-risk AI systems, adapted in light of the intended purpose of the systems and the lower risk involved and taking into account the available technical solutions and industry best practices such as model and data cards. Providers and, as appropriate, deployers of all AI systems, high-risk or not, and AI models should also be encouraged to apply on a voluntary basis additional requirements related, for example, to the elements of the Union's Ethics Guidelines for Trustworthy AI, environmental sustainability, AI literacy measures, inclusive and diverse design and development of AI systems, including attention to vulnerable persons and accessibility to persons with disability, stakeholders' participation with the involvement, as appropriate, of relevant stakeholders such as business and civil society organisations, academia, research organisations, trade unions and consumer protection organisations in the design and development of AI systems, and diversity of the development teams, including gender balance. To ensure that the voluntary codes of conduct are effective, they should be based on clear objectives and key performance indicators to measure the achievement of those objectives. They should also be developed in an inclusive way, as appropriate, with the involvement of relevant stakeholders such as business and civil society organisations, academia, research organisations, trade unions and consumer protection organisation. The Commission may develop initiatives, including of a sectoral nature, to facilitate the lowering of technical barriers hindering cross-border exchange of data for AI development, including on data access infrastructure, semantic and technical interoperability of different types of data.

56.2. General Approach

56.2.1 Preamble

1345. Codes of practice formalise a voluntary harmonisation policy within the EU.

56.2.2 Guiding Principles

1346. The AI Office is responsible for:

- encouraging the development of generic and sector-specific codes;
- ensuring the harmonisation of approaches and associated requirements;
- providing elements for developing such codes;
- assessing the codes over time.

56.2.3 Modalities

1347. A code of practice must specify the following:

NO.	THEME	SPECIFICATION
1.	Technical documentation	Updated in light of market and technological developments
2.	Systemic risks	Origin and nature
3.	Risk management	Assessment Method Proportionality

56.2.4 Deadline

1348. Codes of practice must be operational by 2 August 2025.

1349. Note:

- (1) The European Commission may approve, by means of an implementing act, a code of practice, and generalise it within the EU.

56.3. Find Out More

56.3.1 Toolbox

1350. ISED-ISDE, 'Voluntary Code of Conduct on the Responsible Development and Management of Advanced Generative AI Systems', *Innovation, Science and Economic Development Canada*, September 2023.

CHAPTER VI

MEASURES IN SUPPORT OF INNOVATION

1351. Key takeaways: Measures are taken to support innovation in AI technologies, focused primarily on the following areas:

- regulatory sandboxes;
- support policies;
- derogations for SMEs, startups, or microenterprises.

57 ARTICLE 57. AI REGULATORY SANDBOXES

1. Member States shall ensure that their competent authorities establish at least one AI regulatory sandbox at national level, which shall be operational by 2 August 2026. That sandbox may also be established jointly with the competent authorities of other Member States. The Commission may provide technical support, advice and tools for the establishment and operation of AI regulatory sandboxes.

The obligation under the first subparagraph may also be fulfilled by participating in an existing sandbox in so far as that participation provides an equivalent level of national coverage for the participating Member States.

2. Additional AI regulatory sandboxes at regional or local level, or established jointly with the competent authorities of other Member States may also be established.

3. The European Data Protection Supervisor may also establish an AI regulatory sandbox for Union institutions, bodies, offices and agencies, and may exercise the roles and the tasks of national competent authorities in accordance with this Chapter.

4. Member States shall ensure that the competent authorities referred to in paragraphs 1 and 2 allocate sufficient resources to comply with this Article effectively and in a timely manner. Where appropriate, national competent authorities shall cooperate with other relevant authorities, and may allow for the involvement of other actors within the AI ecosystem. This Article shall not affect other regulatory sandboxes established under Union or national law. Member States shall ensure an appropriate level of cooperation between the authorities supervising those other sandboxes and the national competent authorities.

5. AI regulatory sandboxes established under paragraph 1 shall provide for a controlled environment that fosters innovation and facilitates the development, training, testing and validation of innovative AI systems for a limited time before their being placed on the market or put into service pursuant to a specific sandbox plan agreed between the providers or prospective providers and the competent authority. Such sandboxes may include testing in real world conditions supervised therein.

6. Competent authorities shall provide, as appropriate, guidance, supervision and support within the AI regulatory sandbox with a view to identifying risks, in particular to fundamental rights, health and safety, testing, mitigation measures, and their effectiveness in relation to the obligations and requirements of this Regulation and, where relevant, other Union and national law supervised within the sandbox.

7. Competent authorities shall provide providers and prospective providers participating in the AI regulatory sandbox with guidance on regulatory expectations and how to fulfil the requirements and obligations set out in this Regulation.

Upon request of the provider or prospective provider of the AI system, the competent authority shall provide a written proof of the activities successfully carried out in the sandbox. The competent authority shall also provide an exit report detailing the activities carried out in the sandbox and the related results and learning outcomes. Providers may use such documentation to demonstrate their compliance with this Regulation through the conformity assessment process or relevant market surveillance activities. In this regard, the exit reports and the written proof provided by the national competent authority shall be taken positively into account by market surveillance authorities and notified bodies, with a view to accelerating conformity assessment procedures to a reasonable extent.

8. Subject to the confidentiality provisions in Article 78, and with the agreement of the provider or prospective provider, the Commission and the Board shall be authorised to access the exit reports and shall take them into account, as appropriate, when exercising their tasks under this Regulation. If both the provider or prospective provider and the national competent authority explicitly agree, the exit report may be made publicly available through the single information platform referred to in this Article.

9. The establishment of AI regulatory sandboxes shall aim to contribute to the following objectives:

(a) improving legal certainty to achieve regulatory compliance with this Regulation or, where relevant, other applicable Union and national law;

(b) supporting the sharing of best practices through cooperation with the authorities involved in the AI regulatory sandbox;

(c) fostering innovation and competitiveness and facilitating the development of an AI ecosystem;

(d) contributing to evidence-based regulatory learning;

(e) facilitating and accelerating access to the Union market for AI systems, in particular when provided by SMEs, including start-ups.

10. National competent authorities shall ensure that, to the extent the innovative AI systems involve the processing of personal data or otherwise fall under the supervisory remit of other national authorities or competent authorities providing or supporting access to data, the national data protection authorities and those other national or competent authorities are associated with the operation of the AI regulatory sandbox and involved in the supervision of those aspects to the extent of their respective tasks and powers.

11. The AI regulatory sandboxes shall not affect the supervisory or corrective powers of the competent authorities supervising the sandboxes, including at regional or local level. Any significant risks to health and safety and fundamental rights identified during the development and testing of such AI systems shall result in an adequate mitigation. National competent authorities shall have the power to temporarily or permanently suspend the testing process, or the participation in the sandbox if no effective mitigation is possible, and shall inform the AI Office of such decision. National competent authorities shall exercise their supervisory powers within the limits of the relevant law, using their discretionary powers when implementing legal provisions in respect of a specific AI regulatory sandbox project, with the objective of supporting innovation in AI in the Union.

12. Providers and prospective providers participating in the AI regulatory sandbox shall remain liable under applicable Union and national liability law for any damage inflicted on third parties as a result of the experimentation taking place in the sandbox. However, provided that the prospective providers observe the specific plan and the terms and conditions for their participation and follow in good faith the guidance given by the national competent authority, no administrative fines shall be imposed by the authorities for infringements of this Regulation. Where other competent authorities responsible for other Union and national law were actively involved in the supervision of the AI system in the sandbox and provided guidance for compliance, no administrative fines shall be imposed regarding that law.

13. The AI regulatory sandboxes shall be designed and implemented in such a way that, where relevant, they facilitate cross-border cooperation between national competent authorities.

14. National competent authorities shall coordinate their activities and cooperate within the framework of the Board.

15. National competent authorities shall inform the AI Office and the Board of the establishment of a sandbox, and may ask them for support and guidance. The AI Office shall make publicly available a list of planned and existing sandboxes and keep it up to date in order to encourage more interaction in the AI regulatory sandboxes and cross-border cooperation.

16. National competent authorities shall submit annual reports to the AI Office and to the Board, from one year after the establishment of the AI regulatory sandbox and every year thereafter until its termination, and a final report. Those reports shall provide information on the progress and results of the implementation of those sandboxes, including best practices, incidents, lessons learnt and recommendations on their setup and, where relevant, on the application and possible revision of this Regulation, including its delegated and implementing acts, and on the application of other Union law supervised by the competent authorities within the sandbox. The national competent authorities shall make those annual reports or abstracts thereof available to the public, online. The Commission shall, where appropriate, take the annual reports into account when exercising its tasks under this Regulation.

17. The Commission shall develop a single and dedicated interface containing all relevant information related to AI regulatory sandboxes to allow stakeholders to interact with AI regulatory sandboxes and to raise enquiries with competent authorities, and to seek non-binding guidance on the conformity of innovative products, services, business models embedding AI technologies, in accordance with Article 62(1), point (c). The Commission shall proactively coordinate with national competent authorities, where relevant.

57.1. Recitals

1352. (25) This Regulation should support innovation, should respect freedom of science, and should not undermine research and development activity. It is therefore necessary to exclude from its scope AI systems and models specifically developed and put into service for the sole purpose of scientific research and development. Moreover, it is necessary to ensure that this Regulation does not otherwise affect scientific research and development activity on AI systems or models prior to being placed on the market or put into service. As regards product-oriented research, testing and development activity regarding AI systems or models, the provisions of this Regulation should also not apply prior to those systems and models being put into service or placed on the market. That exclusion is without prejudice to the obligation to comply with this Regulation where an AI system falling into the scope of this Regulation is placed on the market or put into service as a result of such research and development activity and to the application of provisions on AI regulatory sandboxes and testing in real world conditions. Furthermore, without prejudice to the exclusion of AI systems specifically developed and put into service for the sole purpose of scientific research and development, any other AI system that may be used for the conduct of any research and development activity should remain subject to the provisions of this Regulation. In any event, any research and development activity should be carried out in accordance with recognised ethical and professional standards for scientific research and should be conducted in accordance with applicable Union law.

1353. **(138)** AI is a rapidly developing family of technologies that requires regulatory oversight and a safe and controlled space for experimentation, while ensuring responsible innovation and integration of appropriate safeguards and risk mitigation measures. To ensure a legal framework that promotes innovation, is future-proof and resilient to disruption, Member States should ensure that their national competent authorities establish at least one AI regulatory sandbox at national level to facilitate the development and testing of innovative AI systems under strict regulatory oversight before these systems are placed on the market or otherwise put into service. Member States could also fulfil this obligation through participating in already existing regulatory sandboxes or establishing jointly a sandbox with one or more Member States' competent authorities, insofar as this participation provides equivalent level of national coverage for the participating Member States. AI regulatory sandboxes could be established in physical, digital or hybrid form and may accommodate physical as well as digital products. Establishing authorities should also ensure that the AI regulatory sandboxes have the adequate resources for their functioning, including financial and human resources.

1354. **(139)** The objectives of the AI regulatory sandboxes should be to foster AI innovation by establishing a controlled experimentation and testing environment in the development and pre-marketing phase with a view to ensuring compliance of the innovative AI systems with this Regulation and other relevant Union and national law. Moreover, the AI regulatory sandboxes should aim to enhance legal certainty for innovators and the competent authorities' oversight and understanding of the opportunities, emerging risks and the impacts of AI use, to facilitate regulatory learning for authorities and undertakings, including with a view to future adaptions of the legal framework, to support cooperation and the sharing of best practices with the authorities involved in the AI regulatory sandbox, and to accelerate access to markets, including by removing barriers for SMEs, including start-ups. AI regulatory sandboxes should be widely available throughout the Union, and particular attention should be given to their accessibility for SMEs, including start-ups. The participation in the AI regulatory sandbox should focus on issues that raise legal uncertainty for providers and prospective providers to innovate, experiment with AI in the Union and contribute to evidence-based regulatory learning. The supervision of the AI systems in the AI regulatory sandbox should therefore cover their development, training, testing and validation before the systems are placed on the market or put into service, as well as the notion and occurrence of substantial modification that may require a new conformity assessment procedure. Any significant risks identified during the development and testing of such AI systems should result in adequate mitigation and, failing that, in the suspension of the development and testing process. Where appropriate, national competent authorities establishing AI regulatory sandboxes should cooperate with other relevant authorities, including those supervising the protection of fundamental rights, and could allow for the involvement of other actors within the AI ecosystem such as national or European standardisation organisations, notified bodies, testing and experimentation facilities, research and experimentation labs, European Digital Innovation Hubs and relevant stakeholder and civil society organisations. To ensure uniform implementation across the Union and economies of scale, it is appropriate to establish common rules for the AI regulatory sandboxes' implementation and a framework for cooperation between the relevant authorities involved in the supervision of the sandboxes. AI regulatory sandboxes established under this Regulation should be without prejudice to other law allowing for the establishment of other sandboxes aiming to ensure compliance with law other than this Regulation. Where appropriate, relevant competent authorities in charge of those other regulatory sandboxes should consider the benefits of using those sandboxes also for the purpose of ensuring compliance of AI systems with this Regulation. Upon agreement between the national competent authorities and the participants in the AI regulatory sandbox, testing in real world conditions may also be operated and supervised in the framework of the AI regulatory sandbox.

1355. (140) This Regulation should provide the legal basis for the providers and prospective providers in the AI regulatory sandbox to use personal data collected for other purposes for developing certain AI systems in the public interest within the AI regulatory sandbox, only under specified conditions, in accordance with Article 6(4) and Article 9(2), point (g), of Regulation (EU) 2016/679, and Articles 5, 6 and 10 of Regulation (EU) 2018/1725, and without prejudice to Article 4(2) and Article 10 of Directive (EU) 2016/680. All other obligations of data controllers and rights of data subjects under Regulations (EU) 2016/679 and (EU) 2018/1725 and Directive (EU) 2016/680 remain applicable. In particular, this Regulation should not provide a legal basis in the meaning of Article 22(2), point (b) of Regulation (EU) 2016/679 and Article 24(2), point (b) of Regulation (EU) 2018/1725. Providers and prospective providers in the AI regulatory sandbox should ensure appropriate safeguards and cooperate with the competent authorities, including by following their guidance and acting expeditiously and in good faith to adequately mitigate any identified significant risks to safety, health, and fundamental rights that may arise during the development, testing and experimentation in that sandbox.

1356. (141) In order to accelerate the process of development and the placing on the market of the high-risk AI systems listed in an annex to this Regulation, it is important that providers or prospective providers of such systems may also benefit from a specific regime for testing those systems in real world conditions, without participating in an AI regulatory sandbox. However, in such cases, taking into account the possible consequences of such testing on individuals, it should be ensured that appropriate and sufficient guarantees and conditions are introduced by this Regulation for providers or prospective providers. Such guarantees should include, inter alia, requesting informed consent of natural persons to participate in testing in real world conditions, with the exception of law enforcement where the seeking of informed consent would prevent the AI system from being tested. Consent of subjects to participate in such testing under this Regulation is distinct from, and without prejudice to, consent of data subjects for the processing of their personal data under the relevant data protection law. It is also important to minimise the risks and enable oversight by competent authorities and therefore require prospective providers to have a real-world testing plan submitted to competent market surveillance authority, register the testing in dedicated sections in the EU database subject to some limited exceptions, set limitations on the period for which the testing can be done and require additional safeguards for persons belonging to certain vulnerable groups, as well as a written agreement defining the roles and responsibilities of prospective providers and deployers and effective oversight by competent personnel involved in the real world testing. Furthermore, it is appropriate to envisage additional safeguards to ensure that the predictions, recommendations or decisions of the AI system can be effectively reversed and disregarded and that personal data is protected and is deleted when the subjects have withdrawn their consent to participate in the testing without prejudice to their rights as data subjects under the Union data protection law. As regards transfer of data, it is also appropriate to envisage that data collected and processed for the purpose of testing in real-world conditions should be transferred to third countries only where appropriate and applicable safeguards under Union law are implemented, in particular in accordance with bases for transfer of personal data under Union law on data protection, while for non-personal data appropriate safeguards are put in place in accordance with Union law, such as Regulations (EU) 2022/868[1] and (EU) 2023/2854[2] of the European Parliament and of the Council.

---

1 Regulation (EU) 2022/868 of the European Parliament and of the Council of 30 May 2022 on European data governance and amending Regulation (EU) 2018/1724 (Data Governance Act), [2022] OJ L152/1.

2 Regulation (EU) 2023/2854 of the European Parliament and of the Council of 13 December 2023 on harmonised rules on fair access to and use of data and amending Regulation (EU) 2017/2394 and Directive (EU) 2020/1828 (Data Act), [2023] OJ L, 2023/2854.

1357. (142) To ensure that AI leads to socially and environmentally beneficial outcomes, Member States are encouraged to support and promote research and development of AI solutions in support of socially and environmentally beneficial outcomes, such as AI-based solutions to increase accessibility for persons with disabilities, tackle socio-economic inequalities, or meet environmental targets, by allocating sufficient resources, including public and Union funding, and, where appropriate and provided that the eligibility and selection criteria are fulfilled, considering in particular projects which pursue such objectives. Such projects should be based on the principle of interdisciplinary cooperation between AI developers, experts on inequality and non-discrimination, accessibility, consumer, environmental, and digital rights, as well as academics.

1358. (143) In order to promote and protect innovation, it is important that the interests of SMEs, including start-ups, that are providers or deployers of AI systems are taken into particular account. To that end, Member States should develop initiatives, which are targeted at those operators, including on awareness raising and information communication. Member States should provide SMEs, including start-ups, that have a registered office or a branch in the Union, with priority access to the AI regulatory sandboxes provided that they fulfil the eligibility conditions and selection criteria and without precluding other providers and prospective providers to access the sandboxes provided the same conditions and criteria are fulfilled. Member States should utilise existing channels and where appropriate, establish new dedicated channels for communication with SMEs, including start-ups, deployers, other innovators and, as appropriate, local public authorities, to support SMEs throughout their development path by providing guidance and responding to queries about the implementation of this Regulation. Where appropriate, these channels should work together to create synergies and ensure homogeneity in their guidance to SMEs, including start-ups, and deployers. Additionally, Member States should facilitate the participation of SMEs and other relevant stakeholders in the standardisation development processes. Moreover, the specific interests and needs of providers that are SMEs, including start-ups, should be taken into account when notified bodies set conformity assessment fees. The Commission should regularly assess the certification and compliance costs for SMEs, including start-ups, through transparent consultations and should work with Member States to lower such costs. For example, translation costs related to mandatory documentation and communication with authorities may constitute a significant cost for providers and other operators, in particular those of a smaller scale. Member States should possibly ensure that one of the languages determined and accepted by them for relevant providers' documentation and for communication with operators is one which is broadly understood by the largest possible number of cross-border deployers. In order to address the specific needs of SMEs, including start-ups, the Commission should provide standardised templates for the areas covered by this Regulation, upon request of the Board. Additionally, the Commission should complement Member States' efforts by providing a single information platform with easy-to-use information with regards to this Regulation for all providers and deployers, by organising appropriate communication campaigns to raise awareness about the obligations arising from this Regulation, and by evaluating and promoting the convergence of best practices in public procurement procedures in relation to AI systems. Medium-sized enterprises which until recently qualified as small enterprises within the meaning of the Annex to Commission Recommendation 2003/361/EC[3] should have access to those support measures, as those new medium-sized enterprises may sometimes lack the legal resources and training necessary to ensure proper understanding of, and compliance with, this Regulation.

57.2. General Approach

1359. Measures in support of innovation concern the following:

- Regulatory sandboxes
- Personal data
- Measures for SMEs
- Measures for deployers

57.3. Regulatory Sandboxes

57.3.1 Definition

1360. 'AI regulatory sandbox' means 'a controlled framework set up by a competent authority which offers providers or prospective providers of AI systems the possibility to develop, train, validate and test, where appropriate in real-world conditions, an innovative AI system, pursuant to a sandbox plan for a limited time under regulatory supervision'.[4]

---

3 Commission Recommendation of 6 May 2003 concerning the definition of micro, small and medium-sized enterprises, [2003] OJ L124/36.

4 AI Act, Art. 3(55).

57.3.2 Authorities

1361. Regulatory sandboxes are established by:

- one or more national competent authorities of Member States;
- the European Data Protection Supervisor (EDPS).

57.3.3 Characteristics

1362. They are as follows:

NO.	THEME	SPECIFICATION
1.	Innovation	State-of-the-art approach
2.	Purpose	Development Training Testing Validation
3.	Period	Before the placing on the market or putting into service
4.	Procedure	Specific sandbox plan
5.	Duration	Limited according to purposes
6.	Control	National competent authority
7.	Supervision	National competent authority
8.	Requirements	Compliance with the obligations of the AIA
9.	Involvement of the relevant authorities	In the event of significant risks to health and safety and fundamental rights Suspension if no effective mitigation is possible
10.	Liability	Participants in the sandboxes remain liable for any damage inflicted on third parties

57.3.4 Cooperation

1363. A cooperation is organised between:

- the national competent authorities;
- the AI Board;
- competent authorities where personal data are used.

1364. Cooperation concerns

- information on regulatory sandboxes;
- terms of control and supervision;
- results;
- incidents.

57.3.5 Application

1365. Arrangements for the implementation of AI regulatory sandboxes are defined by the European Commission by means of implementing acts.

58 ARTICLE 58. DETAILED ARRANGEMENTS FOR, AND FUNCTIONING OF, AI REGULATORY SANDBOXES

1. In order to avoid fragmentation across the Union, the Commission shall adopt implementing acts specifying the detailed arrangements for the establishment, development, implementation, operation and supervision of the AI regulatory sandboxes. The implementing acts shall include common principles on the following issues:

(a) eligibility and selection criteria for participation in the AI regulatory sandbox;

(b) procedures for the application, participation, monitoring, exiting from and termination of the AI regulatory sandbox, including the sandbox plan and the exit report;

(c) the terms and conditions applicable to the participants.

Those implementing acts shall be adopted in accordance with the examination procedure referred to in Article 98(2).

2. The implementing acts referred to in paragraph 1 shall ensure:

(a) that AI regulatory sandboxes are open to any applying provider or prospective provider of an AI system who fulfils eligibility and selection criteria, which shall be transparent and fair, and that national competent authorities inform applicants of their decision within three months of the application;

(b) that AI regulatory sandboxes allow broad and equal access and keep up with demand for participation; providers and prospective providers may also submit applications in partnerships with deployers and other relevant third parties;

(c) that the detailed arrangements for, and conditions concerning AI regulatory sandboxes support, to the best extent possible, flexibility for national competent authorities to establish and operate their AI regulatory sandboxes;

(d) that access to the AI regulatory sandboxes is free of charge for SMEs, including start-ups, without prejudice to exceptional costs that national competent authorities may recover in a fair and proportionate manner;

(e) that they facilitate providers and prospective providers, by means of the learning outcomes of the AI regulatory sandboxes, in complying with conformity assessment obligations under this Regulation and the voluntary application of the codes of conduct referred to in Article 95;

(f) that AI regulatory sandboxes facilitate the involvement of other relevant actors within the AI ecosystem, such as notified bodies and standardisation organisations, SMEs, including start-ups, enterprises, innovators, testing and experimentation facilities, research and experimentation labs and European Digital Innovation Hubs, centres of excellence, individual researchers, in order to allow and facilitate cooperation with the public and private sectors;

(g) that procedures, processes and administrative requirements for application, selection, participation and exiting the AI regulatory sandbox are simple, easily intelligible, and clearly communicated in order to facilitate the participation of SMEs, including start-ups, with limited legal and administrative capacities and are streamlined across the Union, in order to avoid fragmentation and that participation in an AI regulatory sandbox established by a Member State, or by the European Data Protection Supervisor is mutually and uniformly recognised and carries the same legal effects across the Union;

(h) that participation in the AI regulatory sandbox is limited to a period that is appropriate to the complexity and scale of the project and that may be extended by the national competent authority;

(i) that AI regulatory sandboxes facilitate the development of tools and infrastructure for testing, benchmarking, assessing and explaining dimensions of AI systems relevant for regulatory learning, such as accuracy, robustness and cybersecurity, as well as measures to mitigate risks to fundamental rights and society at large.

3. Prospective providers in the AI regulatory sandboxes, in particular SMEs and start-ups, shall be directed, where relevant, to pre-deployment services such as guidance on the implementation of this Regulation, to other value-adding services such as help with standardisation documents and certification, testing and experimentation facilities, European Digital Innovation Hubs and centres of excellence.

4. Where national competent authorities consider authorising testing in real world conditions supervised within the framework of an AI regulatory sandbox to be established under this Article, they shall specifically agree the terms and conditions of such testing and, in particular, the appropriate safeguards with the participants, with a view to protecting fundamental rights, health and safety. Where appropriate, they shall cooperate with other national competent authorities with a view to ensuring consistent practices across the Union.

58.1. Recitals

1366. **(25)** This Regulation should support innovation, should respect freedom of science, and should not undermine research and development activity. It is therefore necessary to exclude from its scope AI systems and models specifically developed and put into service for the sole purpose of scientific research and development. Moreover, it is necessary to ensure that this Regulation does not otherwise affect scientific research and development activity on AI systems or models prior to being placed on the market or put into service. As regards product-oriented research, testing and development activity regarding AI systems or models, the provisions of this Regulation should also not apply prior to those systems and models being put into service or placed on the market. That exclusion is without prejudice to the obligation to comply with this Regulation where an AI system falling into the scope of this Regulation is placed on the market or put into service as a result of such research and development activity and to the application of provisions on AI regulatory sandboxes and testing in real world conditions. Furthermore, without prejudice to the exclusion of AI systems specifically developed and put into service for the sole purpose of scientific research and development, any other AI system that may be used for the conduct of any research and development activity should remain subject to the provisions of this Regulation. In any event, any research and development activity should be carried out in accordance with recognised ethical and professional standards for scientific research and should be conducted in accordance with applicable Union law.

1367. **(138)** AI is a rapidly developing family of technologies that requires regulatory oversight and a safe and controlled space for experimentation, while ensuring responsible innovation and integration of appropriate safeguards and risk mitigation measures. To ensure a legal framework that promotes innovation, is future-proof and resilient to disruption, Member States should ensure that their national competent authorities establish at least one AI regulatory sandbox at national level to facilitate the development and testing of innovative AI systems under strict regulatory oversight before these systems are placed on the market or otherwise put into service. Member States could also fulfil this obligation through participating in already existing regulatory sandboxes or establishing jointly a sandbox with one or more Member States' competent authorities, insofar as this participation provides equivalent level of national coverage for the participating Member States. AI regulatory sandboxes could be established in physical, digital or hybrid form and may accommodate physical as well as digital products. Establishing authorities should also ensure that the AI regulatory sandboxes have the adequate resources for their functioning, including financial and human resources.

1368. **(139)** The objectives of the AI regulatory sandboxes should be to foster AI innovation by establishing a controlled experimentation and testing environment in the development and pre-marketing phase with a view to ensuring compliance of the innovative AI systems with this Regulation and other relevant Union and national law. Moreover, the AI regulatory sandboxes should aim to enhance legal certainty for innovators and the competent authorities' oversight and understanding of the opportunities, emerging risks and the impacts of AI use, to facilitate regulatory learning for authorities and undertakings, including with a view to future adaptions of the legal framework, to support cooperation and the sharing of best practices with the authorities involved in the AI regulatory sandbox, and to accelerate access to markets, including by removing barriers for SMEs, including start-ups. AI regulatory sandboxes should be widely available throughout the Union, and particular attention should be given to their accessibility for SMEs, including start-ups. The participation in the AI regulatory sandbox should focus on issues that raise legal uncertainty for providers and prospective providers to innovate, experiment with AI in the Union and contribute to evidence-based regulatory learning. The supervision of the AI systems in the AI regulatory sandbox should therefore cover their development, training, testing and validation before the systems are placed on the market or put into service, as well as the notion and occurrence of substantial modification that may require a new conformity assessment procedure. Any significant risks identified during the development and testing of such AI systems should result in adequate mitigation and, failing that, in the suspension of the development and testing process. Where appropriate, national competent authorities establishing AI regulatory sandboxes should cooperate with other relevant authorities, including those supervising the protection of fundamental rights, and could allow for the involvement of other actors within the AI ecosystem such as national or European standardisation organisations, notified bodies, testing and experimentation facilities, research and experimentation labs, European Digital Innovation Hubs and relevant stakeholder and civil society organisations. To ensure uniform implementation across the Union and economies of scale, it is appropriate to establish common rules for the AI regulatory sandboxes' implementation and a framework for cooperation between the relevant authorities involved in the supervision of the sandboxes. AI regulatory sandboxes established under this Regulation should be without prejudice to other law allowing for the establishment of other sandboxes aiming to ensure compliance with law other than this Regulation. Where appropriate, relevant competent authorities in charge of those other regulatory sandboxes should consider the benefits of using those sandboxes also for the purpose of ensuring compliance of AI systems with this Regulation. Upon agreement between the national competent authorities and the participants in the AI regulatory sandbox, testing in real world conditions may also be operated and supervised in the framework of the AI regulatory sandbox.

1369. **(143)** In order to promote and protect innovation, it is important that the interests of SMEs, including start-ups, that are providers or deployers of AI systems are taken into particular account. To that end, Member States should develop initiatives, which are targeted at those operators, including on awareness raising and information communication. Member States should provide SMEs, including start-ups, that have a registered office or a branch in the Union, with priority access to the AI regulatory sandboxes provided that they fulfil the eligibility conditions and selection criteria and without precluding other providers and prospective providers to access the sandboxes provided the same conditions and criteria are fulfilled. Member States should utilise existing channels and where appropriate, establish new dedicated channels for communication with SMEs, including start-ups, deployers, other innovators and, as appropriate, local public authorities, to support SMEs throughout their development path by providing guidance and responding to queries about the implementation of this Regulation. Where appropriate, these channels should work together to create synergies and ensure homogeneity in their guidance to SMEs, including start-ups, and deployers. Additionally, Member States should facilitate the participation of SMEs and other relevant stakeholders in the standardisation development processes. Moreover, the specific interests and needs of providers that are SMEs, including start-ups, should be taken into account when notified bodies set conformity assessment fees. The Commission should regularly assess the certification and compliance costs for SMEs, including start-ups, through transparent consultations and should work with Member States to lower such costs. For example, translation costs related to mandatory documentation and communication with authorities may constitute a significant cost for providers and other operators, in particular those of a smaller scale. Member States should possibly ensure that one of the languages determined and accepted by them for relevant providers' documentation and for communication with operators is one which is broadly understood by the largest possible number of cross-border deployers. In order to address the specific needs of SMEs, including start-ups, the Commission should provide standardised templates for the areas covered by this Regulation, upon request of the Board. Additionally, the Commission should complement Member States' efforts by providing a single information platform with easy-to-use information with regards to this Regulation for all providers and deployers, by organising appropriate communication campaigns to raise awareness about the obligations arising from this Regulation, and by evaluating and promoting the convergence of best practices in public procurement procedures in relation to AI systems. Medium-sized enterprises which until recently qualified as small enterprises within the meaning of the Annex to Commission Recommendation 2003/361/EC[5] should have access to those support measures, as those new medium-sized enterprises may sometimes lack the legal resources and training necessary to ensure proper understanding of, and compliance with, this Regulation.

58.2. General Approach

58.2.1 Preamble

1370. The possibilities for organising a regulatory sandbox are strictly regulated.

5 Commission Recommendation of 6 May 2003 concerning the definition of micro, small and medium-sized enterprises, [2003] OJ L124/36.

58.2.2 Definition

1371. 'AI regulatory sandbox' means 'a controlled framework set up by a competent authority which offers providers or prospective providers of AI systems the possibility to develop, train, validate and test, where appropriate in real-world conditions, an innovative AI system, pursuant to a sandbox plan for a limited time under regulatory supervision'.[6]

1372. 'Sandbox plan' means a 'document agreed between the participating provider and the competent authority describing the objectives, conditions, timeframe, methodology and requirements for the activities carried out within the sandbox'.[7]

58.2.3 Guiding Principles

1373. A sandbox enables to support innovation by organising, within a specific environment, derogations from the regulatory rules governing AI systems.

58.2.4 Modalities

1374. They are as follows:

NO.	THEME	SPECIFICATION
1.	EU authority	European Commission
2.	Form	Implementing act
3.	Criteria	Eligibility Selection
4.	Procedure	Application Monitoring Exit Termination
5.	Content	Sandbox plan
6.	Participants	Contact details
7.	Application	National competent authority
8.	Costs	Free of charge for SMEs
9.	Cooperation	Public and private sectors
10.	Duration	According to the experimentation

6 AI Act, Art. 3(55).
7 AI Act, Art. 3(54).

59 ARTICLE 59. FURTHER PROCESSING OF PERSONAL DATA FOR DEVELOPING CERTAIN AI SYSTEMS IN THE PUBLIC INTEREST IN THE AI REGULATORY SANDBOX

1. In the AI regulatory sandbox, personal data lawfully collected for other purposes may be processed solely for the purpose of developing, training and testing certain AI systems in the sandbox when all of the following conditions are met:

(a) AI systems shall be developed for safeguarding substantial public interest by a public authority or another natural or legal person and in one or more of the following areas:

(i) public safety and public health, including disease detection, diagnosis prevention, control and treatment and improvement of health care systems;

(ii) a high level of protection and improvement of the quality of the environment, protection of biodiversity, protection against pollution, green transition measures, climate change mitigation and adaptation measures;

(iii) energy sustainability;

(iv) safety and resilience of transport systems and mobility, critical infrastructure and networks;

(v) efficiency and quality of public administration and public services;

(b) the data processed are necessary for complying with one or more of the requirements referred to in Chapter III, Section 2 where those requirements cannot effectively be fulfilled by processing anonymised, synthetic or other non-personal data;

(c) there are effective monitoring mechanisms to identify if any high risks to the rights and freedoms of the data subjects, as referred to in Article 35 of Regulation (EU) 2016/679 and in Article 39 of Regulation (EU) 2018/1725, may arise during the sandbox experimentation, as well as response mechanisms to promptly mitigate those risks and, where necessary, stop the processing;

(d) any personal data to be processed in the context of the sandbox are in a functionally separate, isolated and protected data processing environment under the control of the prospective provider and only authorised persons have access to those data;

(e) providers can further share the originally collected data only in accordance with Union data protection law; any personal data created in the sandbox cannot be shared outside the sandbox;

(f) any processing of personal data in the context of the sandbox neither leads to measures or decisions affecting the data subjects nor does it affect the application of their rights laid down in Union law on the protection of personal data;

(g) any personal data processed in the context of the sandbox are protected by means of appropriate technical and organisational measures and deleted once the participation in the sandbox has terminated or the personal data has reached the end of its retention period;

(h) the logs of the processing of personal data in the context of the sandbox are kept for the duration of the participation in the sandbox, unless provided otherwise by Union or national law;

(i) a complete and detailed description of the process and rationale behind the training, testing and validation of the AI system is kept together with the testing results as part of the technical documentation referred to in Annex IV;

(j) a short summary of the AI project developed in the sandbox, its objectives and expected results is published on the website of the competent authorities; this obligation shall not cover sensitive operational data in relation to the activities of law enforcement, border control, immigration or asylum authorities.

2. For the purposes of the prevention, investigation, detection or prosecution of criminal offences or the execution of criminal penalties, including safeguarding against and preventing threats to public security, under the control and responsibility of law enforcement authorities, the processing of personal data in AI regulatory sandboxes shall be based on a specific Union or national law and subject to the same cumulative conditions as referred to in paragraph 1.

3. Paragraph 1 is without prejudice to Union or national law which excludes processing of personal data for other purposes than those explicitly mentioned in that law, as well as to Union or national law laying down the basis for the processing of personal data which is necessary for the purpose of developing, testing or training of innovative AI systems or any other legal basis, in compliance with Union law on the protection of personal data.

59.1. Recitals

1375. (25) This Regulation should support innovation, should respect freedom of science, and should not undermine research and development activity. It is therefore necessary to exclude from its scope AI systems and models specifically developed and put into service for the sole purpose of scientific research and development. Moreover, it is necessary to ensure that this Regulation does not otherwise affect scientific research and development activity on AI systems or models prior to being placed on the market or put into service. As regards product-oriented research, testing and development activity regarding AI systems or models, the provisions of this Regulation should also not apply prior to those systems and models being put into service or placed on the market. That exclusion is without prejudice to the obligation to comply with this Regulation where an AI system falling into the scope of this Regulation is placed on the market or put into service as a result of such research and development activity and to the application of provisions on AI regulatory sandboxes and testing in real world conditions. Furthermore, without prejudice to the exclusion of AI systems specifically developed and put into service for the sole purpose of scientific research and development, any other AI system that may be used for the conduct of any research and development activity should remain subject to the provisions of this Regulation. In any event, any research and development activity should be carried out in accordance with recognised ethical and professional standards for scientific research and should be conducted in accordance with applicable Union law.

1376. (63) The fact that an AI system is classified as a high-risk AI system under this Regulation should not be interpreted as indicating that the use of the system is lawful under other acts of Union law or under national law compatible with Union law, such as on the protection of personal data, on the use of polygraphs and similar tools or other systems to detect the emotional state of natural persons. Any such use should continue to occur solely in accordance with the applicable requirements resulting from the Charter and from the applicable acts of secondary Union law and national law. This Regulation should not be understood as providing for the legal ground for processing of personal data, including special categories of personal data, where relevant, unless it is specifically otherwise provided for in this Regulation.

1377. (138) AI is a rapidly developing family of technologies that requires regulatory oversight and a safe and controlled space for experimentation, while ensuring responsible innovation and integration of appropriate safeguards and risk mitigation measures. To ensure a legal framework that promotes innovation, is future-proof and resilient to disruption, Member States should ensure that their national competent authorities establish at least one AI regulatory sandbox at national level to facilitate the development and testing of innovative AI systems under strict regulatory oversight before these systems are placed on the market or otherwise put into service. Member States could also fulfil this obligation through participating in already existing regulatory sandboxes or establishing jointly a sandbox with one or more Member States' competent authorities, insofar as this participation provides equivalent level of national coverage for the participating Member States. AI regulatory sandboxes could be established in physical, digital or hybrid form and may accommodate physical as well as digital products. Establishing authorities should also ensure that the AI regulatory sandboxes have the adequate resources for their functioning, including financial and human resources.

1378. (139) The objectives of the AI regulatory sandboxes should be to foster AI innovation by establishing a controlled experimentation and testing environment in the development and pre-marketing phase with a view to ensuring compliance of the innovative AI systems with this Regulation and other relevant Union and national law. Moreover, the AI regulatory sandboxes should aim to enhance legal certainty for innovators and the competent authorities' oversight and understanding of the opportunities, emerging risks and the impacts of AI use, to facilitate regulatory learning for authorities and undertakings, including with a view to future adaptions of the legal framework, to support cooperation and the sharing of best practices with the authorities involved in the AI regulatory sandbox, and to accelerate access to markets, including by removing barriers for SMEs, including start-ups. AI regulatory sandboxes should be widely available throughout the Union, and particular attention should be given to their accessibility for SMEs, including start-ups. The participation in the AI regulatory sandbox should focus on issues that raise legal uncertainty for providers and prospective providers to innovate, experiment with AI in the Union and contribute to evidence-based regulatory learning. The supervision of the AI systems in the AI regulatory sandbox should therefore cover their development, training, testing and validation before the systems are placed on the market or put into service, as well as the notion and occurrence of substantial modification that may require a new conformity assessment procedure. Any significant risks identified during the development and testing of such AI systems should result in adequate mitigation and, failing that, in the suspension of the development and testing process. Where appropriate, national competent authorities establishing AI regulatory sandboxes should cooperate with other relevant authorities, including those supervising the protection of fundamental rights, and could allow for the involvement of other actors within the AI ecosystem such as national or European standardisation organisations, notified bodies, testing and experimentation facilities, research and experimentation labs, European Digital Innovation Hubs and relevant stakeholder and civil society organisations. To ensure uniform implementation across the Union and economies of scale, it is appropriate to establish common rules for the AI regulatory sandboxes' implementation and a framework for cooperation between the relevant authorities involved in the supervision of the sandboxes. AI regulatory sandboxes established under this Regulation should be without prejudice to other law allowing for the establishment of other sandboxes aiming to ensure compliance with law other than this Regulation. Where appropriate, relevant competent authorities in charge of those other regulatory sandboxes should consider the benefits of using those sandboxes also for the purpose of ensuring compliance of AI systems with this Regulation. Upon agreement between the national competent authorities and the participants in the AI regulatory sandbox, testing in real world conditions may also be operated and supervised in the framework of the AI regulatory sandbox.

1379. (143) In order to promote and protect innovation, it is important that the interests of SMEs, including start-ups, that are providers or deployers of AI systems are taken into particular account. To that end, Member States should develop initiatives, which are targeted at those operators, including on awareness raising and information communication. Member States should provide SMEs, including start-ups, that have a registered office or a branch in the Union, with priority access to the AI regulatory sandboxes provided that they fulfil the eligibility conditions and selection criteria and without precluding other providers and prospective providers to access the sandboxes provided the same conditions and criteria are fulfilled. Member States should utilise existing channels and where appropriate, establish new dedicated channels for communication with SMEs, including start-ups, deployers, other innovators and, as appropriate, local public authorities, to support SMEs throughout their development path by providing guidance and responding to queries about the implementation of this Regulation. Where appropriate, these channels should work together to create synergies and ensure homogeneity in their guidance to SMEs, including start-ups, and deployers. Additionally, Member States should facilitate the participation of SMEs and other relevant stakeholders in the standardisation development processes. Moreover, the specific interests and needs of providers that are SMEs, including start-ups, should be taken into account when notified bodies set conformity assessment fees. The Commission should regularly assess the certification and compliance costs for SMEs, including start-ups, through transparent consultations and should work with Member States to lower such costs. For example, translation costs related to mandatory documentation and communication with authorities may constitute a significant cost for providers and other operators, in particular those of a smaller scale. Member States should possibly ensure that one of the languages determined and accepted by them for relevant providers' documentation and for communication with operators is one which is broadly understood by the largest possible number of cross-border deployers. In order to address the specific needs of SMEs, including start-ups, the Commission should provide standardised templates for the areas covered by this Regulation, upon request of the Board. Additionally, the Commission should complement Member States' efforts by providing a single information platform with easy-to-use information with regards to this Regulation for all providers and deployers, by organising appropriate communication campaigns to raise awareness about the obligations arising from this Regulation, and by evaluating and promoting the convergence of best practices in public procurement procedures in relation to AI systems. Medium-sized enterprises which until recently qualified as small enterprises within the meaning of the Annex to Commission Recommendation 2003/361/EC[8] should have access to those support measures, as those new medium-sized enterprises may sometimes lack the legal resources and training necessary to ensure proper understanding of, and compliance with, this Regulation.

[8] Commission Recommendation of 6 May 2003 concerning the definition of micro, small and medium-sized enterprises, [2003] OJ L124/36.

59.2. *General Approach*

1380. Many technologies require large databases, particularly those containing personal data.

1381. The objective of this Article is to enable such databases within the framework of derogations.

59.3. *Personal Data*

1382. In that context, personal data are used as follows:

NO.	THEME	SPECIFICATION
1.	Area	In an AI regulatory sandbox
2.	Orientation	Substantial public interest
3.	Use	Development Training Testing
4.	Purpose	Distinction of the initial purposes of the initial collection
5.	Area	Public safety Public health Environmental protection Energy sustainability Critical infrastructure Networks Public administration Public services
6.	Application	Requirements specific to high-risk AI systems, such as: • risk management system, data and technical documentation • transparency, accuracy, robustness, cybersecurity and record-keeping • human oversight to ensure control over high-risk AI systems in all circumstances
7.	Procedure	Effective monitoring mechanisms to identify high risks to the fundamental rights of data subjects. Data used in a separate, isolated and protected environment. Deletion at the end of the experimentation
8.	Limitation	No sharing outside the authorised experimentation
9.	Logs	Kept for the duration of the experimentation
10.	Documentation	The documentation of the experimentation is part of the technical documentation
11.	Public information	Measures, objectives and expected results are published on the website of the national competent authorities

60 ARTICLE 60. TESTING OF HIGH-RISK AI SYSTEMS IN REAL WORLD CONDITIONS OUTSIDE AI REGULATORY SANDBOXES

1. Testing of high-risk AI systems in real world conditions outside AI regulatory sandboxes may be conducted by providers or prospective providers of high-risk AI systems listed in Annex III, in accordance with this Article and the real-world testing plan referred to in this Article, without prejudice to the prohibitions under Article 5.

The Commission shall, by means of implementing acts, specify the detailed elements of the real-world testing plan. Those implementing acts shall be adopted in accordance with the examination procedure referred to in Article 98(2).

This paragraph shall be without prejudice to Union or national law on the testing in real world conditions of high-risk AI systems related to products covered by Union harmonisation legislation listed in Annex I.

2. Providers or prospective providers may conduct testing of high-risk AI systems referred to in Annex III in real world conditions at any time before the placing on the market or the putting into service of the AI system on their own or in partnership with one or more deployers or prospective deployers.

3. The testing of high-risk AI systems in real world conditions under this Article shall be without prejudice to any ethical review that is required by Union or national law.

4. Providers or prospective providers may conduct the testing in real world conditions only where all of the following conditions are met:

(a) the provider or prospective provider has drawn up a real-world testing plan and submitted it to the market surveillance authority in the Member State where the testing in real world conditions is to be conducted;

(b) the market surveillance authority in the Member State where the testing in real world conditions is to be conducted has approved the testing in real world conditions and the real-world testing plan; where the market surveillance authority has not provided an answer within 30 days, the testing in real world conditions and the real-world testing plan shall be understood to have been approved; where national law does not provide for a tacit approval, the testing in real world conditions shall remain subject to an authorisation;

(c) the provider or prospective provider, with the exception of providers or prospective providers of high-risk AI systems referred to in points 1, 6 and 7 of Annex III in the areas of law enforcement, migration, asylum and border control management, and high-risk AI systems referred to in point 2 of Annex III has registered the testing in real world conditions in accordance with Article 71(4) with a Union-wide unique single identification number and with the information specified in Annex IX; the provider or prospective provider of high-risk AI systems referred to in points 1, 6 and 7 of Annex III in the areas of law enforcement, migration, asylum and border control management, has registered the testing in real-world conditions in the secure non-public section of the EU database according to Article 49(4), point (d), with a Union-wide unique single identification number and with the information specified therein; the provider or prospective provider of high-risk AI systems referred to in point 2 of Annex III has registered the testing in real-world conditions in accordance with Article 49(5);

(d) the provider or prospective provider conducting the testing in real world conditions is established in the Union or has appointed a legal representative who is established in the Union;

(e) data collected and processed for the purpose of the testing in real world conditions shall be transferred to third countries only provided that appropriate and applicable safeguards under Union law are implemented;

(f) the testing in real world conditions does not last longer than necessary to achieve its objectives and in any case not longer than six months, which may be extended for an additional period of six months, subject to prior notification by the provider or prospective provider to the market surveillance authority, accompanied by an explanation of the need for such an extension;

(g) the subjects of the testing in real world conditions who are persons belonging to vulnerable groups due to their age or disability, are appropriately protected;

(h) where a provider or prospective provider organises the testing in real world conditions in cooperation with one or more deployers or prospective deployers, the latter have been informed of all aspects of the testing that are relevant to their decision to participate, and given the relevant instructions for use of the AI system referred to in Article 13; the provider or prospective provider and the deployer or prospective deployer shall conclude an agreement specifying their roles and responsibilities with a view to ensuring compliance with the provisions for testing in real world conditions under this Regulation and under other applicable Union and national law;

(i) the subjects of the testing in real world conditions have given informed consent in accordance with Article 61, or in the case of law enforcement, where the seeking of informed consent would prevent the AI system from being tested, the testing itself and the outcome of the testing in the real world conditions shall not have any negative effect on the subjects, and their personal data shall be deleted after the test is performed;

(j) the testing in real world conditions is effectively overseen by the provider or prospective provider, as well as by deployers or prospective deployers through persons who are suitably qualified in the relevant field and have the necessary capacity, training and authority to perform their tasks;

(k) the predictions, recommendations or decisions of the AI system can be effectively reversed and disregarded.

5. Any subjects of the testing in real world conditions, or their legally designated representative, as appropriate, may, without any resulting detriment and without having to provide any justification, withdraw from the testing at any time by revoking their informed consent and may request the immediate and permanent deletion of their personal data. The withdrawal of the informed consent shall not affect the activities already carried out.

6. In accordance with Article 75, Member States shall confer on their market surveillance authorities the powers of requiring providers and prospective providers to provide information, of carrying out unannounced remote or on-site inspections, and of performing checks on the conduct of the testing in real world conditions and the related high-risk AI systems. Market surveillance authorities shall use those powers to ensure the safe development of testing in real world conditions.

7. Any serious incident identified in the course of the testing in real world conditions shall be reported to the national market surveillance authority in accordance with Article 73. The provider or prospective provider shall adopt immediate mitigation measures or, failing that, shall suspend the testing in real world conditions until such mitigation takes place, or otherwise terminate it. The provider or prospective provider shall establish a procedure for the prompt recall of the AI system upon such termination of the testing in real world conditions.

8. Providers or prospective providers shall notify the national market surveillance authority in the Member State where the testing in real world conditions is to be conducted of the suspension or termination of the testing in real world conditions and of the final outcomes.

9. The provider or prospective provider shall be liable under applicable Union and national liability law for any damage caused in the course of their testing in real world conditions.

60.1. Recitals

1383. (141) In order to accelerate the process of development and the placing on the market of the high-risk AI systems listed in an annex to this Regulation, it is important that providers or prospective providers of such systems may also benefit from a specific regime for testing those systems in real world conditions, without participating in an AI regulatory sandbox. However, in such cases, taking into account the possible consequences of such testing on individuals, it should be ensured that appropriate and sufficient guarantees and conditions are introduced by this Regulation for providers or prospective providers. Such guarantees should include, inter alia, requesting informed consent of natural persons to participate in testing in real world conditions, with the exception of law enforcement where the seeking of informed consent would prevent the AI system from being tested. Consent of subjects to participate in such testing under this Regulation is distinct from, and without prejudice to, consent of data subjects for the processing of their personal data under the relevant data protection law. It is also important to minimise the risks and enable oversight by competent authorities and therefore require prospective providers to have a real-world testing plan submitted to competent market surveillance authority, register the testing in dedicated sections in the EU database subject to some limited exceptions, set limitations on the period for which the testing can be done and require additional safeguards for persons belonging to certain vulnerable groups, as well as a written agreement defining the roles and responsibilities of prospective providers and deployers and effective oversight by competent personnel involved in the real world testing. Furthermore, it is appropriate to envisage additional safeguards to ensure that the predictions, recommendations or decisions of the AI system can be effectively reversed and disregarded and that personal data is protected and is deleted when the subjects have withdrawn their consent to participate in the testing without prejudice to their rights as data subjects under the Union data protection law. As regards transfer of data, it is also appropriate to envisage that data collected and processed for the purpose of testing in real-world conditions should be transferred to third countries only where appropriate and applicable safeguards under Union law are implemented, in particular in accordance with bases for transfer of personal data under Union law on data protection, while for non-personal data appropriate safeguards are put in place in accordance with Union law, such as Regulations (EU) 2022/868[9] and (EU) 2023/2854[10] of the European Parliament and of the Council.

60.2. General Approach

60.2.1 Preamble

1384. It is possible to conduct testing in real conditions outside regulatory sandboxes within a very strict framework.

1385. 'Testing in real-world conditions' means the temporary testing of an AI system for its intended purpose in real-world conditions outside a laboratory or otherwise simulated environment, with a view to gathering reliable and robust data and to assessing and verifying the conformity of the AI system with the requirements of this Regulation.[11]

---

9 Regulation (EU) 2022/868 of the European Parliament and of the Council of 30 May 2022 on European data governance and amending Regulation (EU) 2018/1724 (Data Governance Act), [2022] OJ L152/1.

10 Regulation (EU) 2023/2854 of the European Parliament and of the Council of 13 December 2023 on harmonised rules on fair access to and use of data and amending Regulation (EU) 2017/2394 and Directive (EU) 2020/1828 (Data Act), [2023] OJ L, 2023/2854.

11 AI Act, Art. 3(57).

60.2.2 Guiding Principles

1386. These tests may concern the high-risk AI systems listed in Annex III, which are as follows:

NO.	THEME	SPECIFICATION	REFERENCE
1.	Access to self-employment		AIA, Annex III(4)
2.	Asylum	In so far as use is permitted under relevant Union or national law	AIA, Annex III(7)
3.	Biometrics	In so far as use is permitted under relevant Union or national law	AIA, Annex III(1)
4.	Border control management	In so far as use is permitted under relevant Union or national law	AIA, Annex III(7)
5.	Critical infrastructure	E.g. road traffic, supply of water, gas, heating or electricity	AIA, Annex III(2)
6.	Democracy	Democratic processes	AIA, Annex III(8)
7.	Education		AIA, Annex III(3)
8.	Employment		AIA, Annex III(4)
9.	Essential private services	Access and enjoyment	AIA, Annex III(5)
10.	Essential public benefits	Access and enjoyment	AIA, Annex III(5)
11.	Essential public services	Access and enjoyment	AIA, Annex III(5)
12.	Justice	Administration of justice	AIA, Annex III(8)
13.	Law enforcement	In so far as use is permitted under relevant Union or national law	AIA, Annex III(6)
14.	Migration	In so far as use is permitted under relevant Union or national law	AIA, Annex III(7)
15.	Training		AIA, Annex III(3)
16.	Workers' management		AIA, Annex III(4)

60.2.3 Modalities

1387. They are as follows:

NO.	THEME	SPECIFICATION
1.	Authority	Commission
2.	Form	Implementing act
3.	Procedure	Assistance by a committee[12]
4.	High-risk system under Annex I	Testing should follow the harmonisation legislation listed in the said Annex
5.	High-risk system under Annex III	The system concerned by the testing under Article 60
6.	Actors	Providers on their own or in partnership with deployers
7.	Activity	Before the placing on the market or putting into service
8.	Fundamental freedom	Prior ethical review Compliance with prohibitions on AI systems[13]
9.	Conditions	Testing plan Approval by the market surveillance authority
10.	Duration	6 months, which may be extended once for the same duration
11.	Subjects (natural persons)	Informed consent Possibility of revoking consent with deletion of personal data; withdrawal of consent does not affect the activities already carried out
12.	Oversight	Suitably qualified internal or external staff
13.	Serious incidents	Notification to the national market surveillance authority Mitigation measures Recall of AI systems Termination
14.	Liability	Any damage caused

[12] AI Act, Art. 98.
[13] AI Act, Art. 5.

61 ARTICLE 61. INFORMED CONSENT TO PARTICIPATE IN TESTING IN REAL WORLD CONDITIONS OUTSIDE AI REGULATORY SANDBOXES

1. For the purpose of testing in real world conditions under Article 60, freely-given informed consent shall be obtained from the subjects of testing prior to their participation in such testing and after their having been duly informed with concise, clear, relevant, and understandable information regarding:

(a) the nature and objectives of the testing in real world conditions and the possible inconvenience that may be linked to their participation;

(b) the conditions under which the testing in real world conditions is to be conducted, including the expected duration of the subject or subjects' participation;

(c) their rights, and the guarantees regarding their participation, in particular their right to refuse to participate in, and the right to withdraw from, testing in real world conditions at any time without any resulting detriment and without having to provide any justification;

(d) the arrangements for requesting the reversal or the disregarding of the predictions, recommendations or decisions of the AI system;

(e) the Union-wide unique single identification number of the testing in real world conditions in accordance with Article 60(4) point (c), and the contact details of the provider or its legal representative from whom further information can be obtained.

2. The informed consent shall be dated and documented and a copy shall be given to the subjects of testing or their legal representative.

61.1. Recitals

1388. (25) This Regulation should support innovation, should respect freedom of science, and should not undermine research and development activity. It is therefore necessary to exclude from its scope AI systems and models specifically developed and put into service for the sole purpose of scientific research and development. Moreover, it is necessary to ensure that this Regulation does not otherwise affect scientific research and development activity on AI systems or models prior to being placed on the market or put into service. As regards product-oriented research, testing and development activity regarding AI systems or models, the provisions of this Regulation should also not apply prior to those systems and models being put into service or placed on the market. That exclusion is without prejudice to the obligation to comply with this Regulation where an AI system falling into the scope of this Regulation is placed on the market or put into service as a result of such research and development activity and to the application of provisions on AI regulatory sandboxes and testing in real world conditions. Furthermore, without prejudice to the exclusion of AI systems specifically developed and put into service for the sole purpose of scientific research and development, any other AI system that may be used for the conduct of any research and development activity should remain subject to the provisions of this Regulation. In any event, any research and development activity should be carried out in accordance with recognised ethical and professional standards for scientific research and should be conducted in accordance with applicable Union law.

1389. **(141)** In order to accelerate the process of development and the placing on the market of the high-risk AI systems listed in an annex to this Regulation, it is important that providers or prospective providers of such systems may also benefit from a specific regime for testing those systems in real world conditions, without participating in an AI regulatory sandbox. However, in such cases, taking into account the possible consequences of such testing on individuals, it should be ensured that appropriate and sufficient guarantees and conditions are introduced by this Regulation for providers or prospective providers. Such guarantees should include, inter alia, requesting informed consent of natural persons to participate in testing in real world conditions, with the exception of law enforcement where the seeking of informed consent would prevent the AI system from being tested. Consent of subjects to participate in such testing under this Regulation is distinct from, and without prejudice to, consent of data subjects for the processing of their personal data under the relevant data protection law. It is also important to minimise the risks and enable oversight by competent authorities and therefore require prospective providers to have a real-world testing plan submitted to competent market surveillance authority, register the testing in dedicated sections in the EU database subject to some limited exceptions, set limitations on the period for which the testing can be done and require additional safeguards for persons belonging to certain vulnerable groups, as well as a written agreement defining the roles and responsibilities of prospective providers and deployers and effective oversight by competent personnel involved in the real world testing. Furthermore, it is appropriate to envisage additional safeguards to ensure that the predictions, recommendations or decisions of the AI system can be effectively reversed and disregarded and that personal data is protected and is deleted when the subjects have withdrawn their consent to participate in the testing without prejudice to their rights as data subjects under the Union data protection law. As regards transfer of data, it is also appropriate to envisage that data collected and processed for the purpose of testing in real-world conditions should be transferred to third countries only where appropriate and applicable safeguards under Union law are implemented, in particular in accordance with bases for transfer of personal data under Union law on data protection, while for non-personal data appropriate safeguards are put in place in accordance with Union law, such as Regulations (EU) 2022/868[14] and (EU) 2023/2854[15] of the European Parliament and of the Council.

61.2. General Approach

61.2.1 Preamble

1390. In view of the risks involved, natural persons may only participate in testing in real-world conditions if their freely given and informed consent is obtained.

61.2.2 Definition

1391. 'Informed consent' means a subject's freely given, specific, unambiguous and voluntary expression of his or her willingness to participate in a particular testing in real-world conditions, after having been informed of all aspects of the testing that are relevant to the subject's decision to participate.[16]

61.2.3 Guiding Principles

1392. This consent must be consistent with that relating to the processing of personal data covered by the GDPR.[17]

61.3. Modalities

1393. They are as follows:

NO.	THEME	SPECIFICATION
1.	Provider	Contact details
2.	Identification	Union-wide unique single identification number
3.	Form	Written Copy given to the subjects

14 Regulation (EU) 2022/868 of the European Parliament and of the Council of 30 May 2022 on European data governance and amending Regulation (EU) 2018/1724 (Data Governance Act), [2022] OJ L152/1.

15 Regulation (EU) 2023/2854 of the European Parliament and of the Council of 13 December 2023 on harmonised rules on fair access to and use of data and amending Regulation (EU) 2017/2394 and Directive (EU) 2020/1828 (Data Act), [2023] OJ L, 2023/2854.

16 AI Act, Art. 3(59).

17 GDPR (EU) 2016/679, Art. 7.

NO.	THEME	SPECIFICATION
4.	Testing	Objectives Nature
5.	Impact	Inconvenience
6.	Conditions	List
7.	Duration	Expected duration
8.	Protection	Rights Associated guarantees
9.	Results	Influence on the predictions, recommendations or decisions, including withdrawal options

62 ARTICLE 62. MEASURES FOR PROVIDERS AND DEPLOYERS, IN PARTICULAR SMES, INCLUDING START-UPS

1. Member States shall undertake the following actions:

(a) provide SMEs, including start-ups, having a registered office or a branch in the Union, with priority access to the AI regulatory sandboxes, to the extent that they fulfil the eligibility conditions and selection criteria; the priority access shall not preclude other SMEs, including start-ups, other than those referred to in this paragraph from access to the AI regulatory sandbox, provided that they also fulfil the eligibility conditions and selection criteria;

(b) organise specific awareness raising and training activities on the application of this Regulation tailored to the needs of SMEs including start-ups, deployers and, as appropriate, local public authorities;

(c) utilise existing dedicated channels and where appropriate, establish new ones for communication with SMEs including start-ups, deployers, other innovators and, as appropriate, local public authorities to provide advice and respond to queries about the implementation of this Regulation, including as regards participation in AI regulatory sandboxes;

(d) facilitate the participation of SMEs and other relevant stakeholders in the standardisation development process.

2. The specific interests and needs of the SME providers, including start-ups, shall be taken into account when setting the fees for conformity assessment under Article 43, reducing those fees proportionately to their size, market size and other relevant indicators.

3. The AI Office shall undertake the following actions:

(a) provide standardised templates for areas covered by this Regulation, as specified by the Board in its request;

(b) develop and maintain a single information platform providing easy to use information in relation to this Regulation for all operators across the Union;

(c) organise appropriate communication campaigns to raise awareness about the obligations arising from this Regulation;

(d) evaluate and promote the convergence of best practices in public procurement procedures in relation to AI systems.

62.1. Recitals

1394. (8) A Union legal framework laying down harmonised rules on AI is therefore needed to foster the development, use and uptake of AI in the internal market that at the same time meets a high level of protection of public interests, such as health and safety and the protection of fundamental rights, including democracy, the rule of law and environmental protection as recognised and protected by Union law. To achieve that objective, rules regulating the placing on the market, the putting into service and the use of certain AI systems should be laid down, thus ensuring the smooth functioning of the internal market and allowing those systems to benefit from the principle of free movement of goods and services. Those rules should be clear and robust in protecting fundamental rights, supportive of new innovative solutions, enabling a European ecosystem of public and private actors creating AI systems in line with Union values and unlocking the potential of the digital transformation across all regions of the Union. By laying down those rules as well as measures in support of innovation with a particular focus on small and medium enterprises (SMEs), including startups, this Regulation supports the objective of promoting the European human-centric approach to AI and being a global leader in the development of secure, trustworthy and ethical AI as stated by the European Council,[18] and it ensures the protection of ethical principles, as specifically requested by the European Parliament.[19]

1395. (109) Compliance with the obligations applicable to the providers of general-purpose AI models should be commensurate and proportionate to the type of model provider, excluding the need for compliance for persons who develop or use models for non-professional or scientific research purposes, who should nevertheless be encouraged to voluntarily comply with these requirements. Without prejudice to Union copyright law, compliance with those obligations should take due account of the size of the provider and allow simplified ways of

---

18 European Council, Special meeting of the European Council (1 and 2 October 2020) — Conclusions, EUCO 13/20, 2020, p. 6.

19 European Parliament resolution of 20 October 2020 with recommendations to the Commission on a framework of ethical aspects of artificial intelligence, robotics and related technologies, 2020/2012(INL).

compliance for SMEs, including start-ups, that should not represent an excessive cost and not discourage the use of such models. In the case of a modification or fine-tuning of a model, the obligations for providers of general-purpose AI models should be limited to that modification or fine-tuning, for example by complementing the already existing technical documentation with information on the modifications, including new training data sources, as a means to comply with the value chain obligations provided in this Regulation.

1396. **(139)** The objectives of the AI regulatory sandboxes should be to foster AI innovation by establishing a controlled experimentation and testing environment in the development and pre-marketing phase with a view to ensuring compliance of the innovative AI systems with this Regulation and other relevant Union and national law. Moreover, the AI regulatory sandboxes should aim to enhance legal certainty for innovators and the competent authorities' oversight and understanding of the opportunities, emerging risks and the impacts of AI use, to facilitate regulatory learning for authorities and undertakings, including with a view to future adaptions of the legal framework, to support cooperation and the sharing of best practices with the authorities involved in the AI regulatory sandbox, and to accelerate access to markets, including by removing barriers for SMEs, including start-ups. AI regulatory sandboxes should be widely available throughout the Union, and particular attention should be given to their accessibility for SMEs, including start-ups. The participation in the AI regulatory sandbox should focus on issues that raise legal uncertainty for providers and prospective providers to innovate, experiment with AI in the Union and contribute to evidence-based regulatory learning. The supervision of the AI systems in the AI regulatory sandbox should therefore cover their development, training, testing and validation before the systems are placed on the market or put into service, as well as the notion and occurrence of substantial modification that may require a new conformity assessment procedure. Any significant risks identified during the development and testing of such AI systems should result in adequate mitigation and, failing that, in the suspension of the development and testing process. Where appropriate, national competent authorities establishing AI regulatory sandboxes should cooperate with other relevant authorities, including those supervising the protection of fundamental rights, and could allow for the involvement of other actors within the AI ecosystem such as national or European standardisation organisations, notified bodies, testing and experimentation facilities, research and experimentation labs, European Digital Innovation Hubs and relevant stakeholder and civil society organisations. To ensure uniform implementation across the Union and economies of scale, it is appropriate to establish common rules for the AI regulatory sandboxes' implementation and a framework for cooperation between the relevant authorities involved in the supervision of the sandboxes. AI regulatory sandboxes established under this Regulation should be without prejudice to other law allowing for the establishment of other sandboxes aiming to ensure compliance with law other than this Regulation. Where appropriate, relevant competent authorities in charge of those other regulatory sandboxes should consider the benefits of using those sandboxes also for the purpose of ensuring compliance of AI systems with this Regulation. Upon agreement between the national competent authorities and the participants in the AI regulatory sandbox, testing in real world conditions may also be operated and supervised in the framework of the AI regulatory sandbox.

1397. **(143)** In order to promote and protect innovation, it is important that the interests of SMEs, including start-ups, that are providers or deployers of AI systems are taken into particular account. To that end, Member States should develop initiatives, which are targeted at those operators, including on awareness raising and information communication. Member States should provide SMEs, including start-ups, that have a registered office or a branch in the Union, with priority access to the AI regulatory sandboxes provided that they fulfil the eligibility conditions and selection criteria and without precluding other providers and prospective providers to access the sandboxes provided the same conditions and criteria are fulfilled. Member States should utilise existing channels and where appropriate, establish new dedicated channels for communication with SMEs, including start-ups, deployers, other innovators and, as appropriate, local public authorities, to support SMEs throughout their development path by providing guidance and responding to queries about the implementation of this Regulation. Where appropriate, these channels should work together to create synergies and ensure homogeneity in their guidance to SMEs, including start-ups, and deployers. Additionally, Member States should facilitate the participation of SMEs and other relevant stakeholders in the standardisation development processes. Moreover, the specific interests and needs of providers that are SMEs, including start-ups, should be taken into account when notified bodies set conformity assessment fees. The Commission should regularly assess the certification and compliance costs for SMEs, including start-ups, through transparent consultations and should work with Member States to lower such costs.

1398. For example, translation costs related to mandatory documentation and communication with authorities may constitute a significant cost for providers and other operators, in particular those of a smaller scale. Member States should possibly ensure that one of the languages determined and accepted by them for relevant providers' documentation and for communication with operators is one which is broadly understood by the largest possible number of cross-border deployers. In order to address the specific needs of SMEs, including start-ups, the Commission should provide standardised templates for the areas covered by this Regulation, upon request of the Board. Additionally, the Commission should complement Member States' efforts by providing a single information platform with easy-to-use information with regards to this Regulation for all providers and deployers, by organising appropriate communication campaigns to raise awareness about the obligations arising from this Regulation, and by evaluating and promoting the convergence of best practices in public procurement procedures in relation to AI systems. Medium-sized enterprises which until recently qualified as small enterprises within the meaning of the Annex to Commission Recommendation 2003/361/EC[20] should have access to those support measures, as those new medium-sized enterprises may sometimes lack the legal resources and training necessary to ensure proper understanding of, and compliance with, this Regulation.

1399. (144) In order to promote and protect innovation, the AI-on-demand platform, all relevant Union funding programmes and projects, such as Digital Europe Programme, Horizon Europe, implemented by the Commission and the Member States at Union or national level should, as appropriate, contribute to the achievement of the objectives of this Regulation.

1400. (145) In order to minimise the risks to implementation resulting from lack of knowledge and expertise in the market as well as to facilitate compliance of providers, in particular SMEs, including start-ups, and notified bodies with their obligations under this Regulation, the AI-on-demand platform, the European Digital Innovation Hubs and the testing and experimentation facilities established by the Commission and the Member States at Union or national level should contribute to the implementation of this Regulation. Within their respective mission and fields of competence, the AI-on-demand platform, the European Digital Innovation Hubs and the testing and experimentation Facilities are able to provide in particular technical and scientific support to providers and notified bodies.

1401. (150) With a view to ensuring the involvement of stakeholders in the implementation and application of this Regulation, an advisory forum should be established to advise and provide technical expertise to the Board and the Commission. To ensure a varied and balanced stakeholder representation between commercial and non-commercial interest and, within the category of commercial interests, with regards to SMEs and other undertakings, the advisory forum should comprise inter alia industry, start-ups, SMEs, academia, civil society, including the social partners, as well as the Fundamental Rights Agency, ENISA, the European Committee for Standardization (CEN), the European Committee for Electrotechnical Standardization (CENELEC) and the European Telecommunications Standards Institute (ETSI).

1402. (168) Compliance with this Regulation should be enforceable by means of the imposition of penalties and other enforcement measures. Member

---

[20] Commission Recommendation of 6 May 2003 concerning the definition of micro, small and medium-sized enterprises, [2003] OJ L124/36.

States should take all necessary measures to ensure that the provisions of this Regulation are implemented, including by laying down effective, proportionate and dissuasive penalties for their infringement, and to respect the ne bis in idem principle. In order to strengthen and harmonise administrative penalties for infringement of this Regulation, the upper limits for setting the administrative fines for certain specific infringements should be laid down. When assessing the amount of the fines, Member States should, in each individual case, take into account all relevant circumstances of the specific situation, with due regard in particular to the nature, gravity and duration of the infringement and of its consequences and to the size of the provider, in particular if the provider is an SME, including a start-up. The European Data Protection Supervisor should have the power to impose fines on Union institutions, agencies and bodies falling within the scope of this Regulation.

62.2. General Approach

62.2.1 Preamble

1403. Under the Regulation, Member States must take measures to support:

- SME providers;
- start-ups.

62.2.2 Guiding Principles

1404. The support measures are to be provided by the Member States and the AI Office.

1405. They cover:

- training and awareness raising;
- SME participation.

62.3. *Measures to Be Taken by Member States*

1406. They are as follows:

NO.	MEASURE	SPECIFICATION
1.	Regulatory sandboxes	Priority access[1]
2.	Information on the AI Act	Awareness raising Training[2]
3.	Communication about the AI Act	Dedicated channels[3]
4.	Standardisation	Facilitating SME participation in standardisation bodies[4]
5.	Conformity	Minimising costs for conformity assessment[5]

62.4. *Measures to Be Taken by the AI Office*

1407. They are as follows:

NO.	MEASURE	SPECIFICATION
1.	Assistance	Standardised templates[1]
2.	Information on the AI Act	Single information platform[2]
3.	Awareness raising	Communication campaigns[3]
4.	Code of practice	Public procurement procedures in relation to AI systems[4]

[1] AI Act, Art. 62(1)(a).
[2] AI Act, Art. 62(1)(b).
[3] AI Act, Art. 62(1)(c).
[4] AI Act, Art. 62(1)(d).
[5] AI Act, Art. 62(2).
[1] AI Act, Art. 62(3)(a).
[2] AI Act, Art. 62(3)(b).
[3] AI Act, Art. 62(3)(c).
[4] AI Act, Art. 62(3)(d).

62.5. *Find Out More*

62.5.1 Toolbox

1408. Bradford, A., 'The False Choice Between Digital Regulation and Innovation', (2024) 118(2) *Nw. U. L. Rev.*

62.6. *Final Provisions*

62.6.1 Coordinated Texts

1409. Measures for start-ups in the field of AI-optimised supercomputers.[5]

63 ARTICLE 63. DEROGATIONS FOR SPECIFIC OPERATORS

1. Microenterprises within the meaning of Recommendation 2003/361/EC may comply with certain elements of the quality management system required by Article 17 of this Regulation in a simplified manner, provided that they do not have partner enterprises or linked enterprises within the meaning of that Recommendation. For that purpose, the Commission shall develop guidelines on the elements of the quality management system which may be complied with in a simplified manner considering the needs of microenterprises, without affecting the level of protection or the need for compliance with the requirements in respect of high-risk AI systems.

2. Paragraph 1 of this Article shall not be interpreted as exempting those operators from fulfilling any other requirements or obligations laid down in this Regulation, including those established in Articles 9, 10, 11, 12, 13, 14, 15, 72 and 73.

63.1. *Recitals*

1410. (146) Moreover, in light of the very small size of some operators and in order to ensure proportionality regarding costs of innovation, it is appropriate to allow microenterprises to fulfil one of the most costly obligations, namely to establish a quality management system, in a simplified manner which would reduce the administrative burden and the costs for those enterprises without affecting the level of protection and the need for compliance with the requirements for high-risk AI systems. The Commission should develop guidelines to specify

[5] Council Regulation (EU) 2024/1732 of 17 June 2024 amending Regulation (EU) 2021/1173 as regards a EuroHPC initiative for start-ups in order to boost European leadership in trustworthy artificial intelligence, [2024] OJ L 2024/1732.

the elements of the quality management system to be fulfilled in this simplified manner by microenterprises.

63.2. General Approach

63.2.1 Preamble

1411. The aim is to encourage the deployment of microenterprises with reasonable risk management by creating derogations from the general rules governing AI technologies.

63.2.2 Guiding Principles

1412. Alleviating requirements must not lead to the development of high-risk AI systems presenting dangers with regard to the protection of the values of the EU establishing a safe and trustworthy AI market.

63.3. Modalities

1413. For high-risk AI systems in particular, the requirements imposed are as follows:

NO.	THEME	REFERENCE
1.	Risk management system	AIA, Art. 9
2.	Data and data governance	AIA, Art. 10
3.	Technical documentation	AIA, Art. 11
4.	Record-keeping	AIA, Art. 12
5.	Transparency and provision of information to deployers	AIA, Art. 13
6.	Human oversight	AIA, Art. 14
7.	Accuracy	AIA, Art. 15
8.	Robustness	AIA, Art. 15
9.	Cybersecurity	AIA, Art. 15
10.	Post-market monitoring by providers and post-market monitoring plan for high-risk AI systems	AIA, Art. 72
11.	Reporting of serious incidents	AIA, Art. 73

CHAPTER VII
GOVERNANCE

1414. Key takeaways: The governance of AI technologies is organised around:
- EU institutions (Commission, AI Office, AI Board, Advisory Forum);
- national competent authorities.

SECTION 1. GOVERNANCE AT UNION LEVEL

64 ARTICLE 64. AI OFFICE

1. The Commission shall develop Union expertise and capabilities in the field of AI through the AI Office.

2. Member States shall facilitate the tasks entrusted to the AI Office, as reflected in this Regulation.

64.1. Recitals

1415. (101) Providers of general-purpose AI models have a particular role and responsibility along the AI value chain, as the models they provide may form the basis for a range of downstream systems, often provided by downstream providers that necessitate a good understanding of the models and their capabilities, both to enable the integration of such models into their products, and to fulfil their obligations under this or other regulations. Therefore, proportionate transparency measures should be laid down, including the drawing up and keeping up to date of documentation, and the provision of information on the general-purpose AI model for its usage by the downstream providers. Technical documentation should be prepared and kept up to date by the general-purpose AI model provider for the purpose of making it available, upon request, to the AI Office and the national competent authorities. The minimal set of elements to be included in such documentation should be set out in specific annexes to this Regulation. The Commission should be empowered to amend those annexes by means of delegated acts in light of evolving technological developments.

1416. (107) In order to increase transparency on the data that is used in the pre-training and training of general-purpose AI models, including text and data protected by copyright law, it is adequate that providers of such models draw up and make publicly available a sufficiently detailed summary of the content used for training the general-purpose AI model. While taking into due account the need to protect trade secrets and confidential business information, this summary should be generally comprehensive in its scope instead of technically detailed to facilitate parties with legitimate interests, including copyright holders, to exercise and enforce their rights under Union law, for example by listing the main data collections or sets that went into training the model, such as large private or public databases or data archives, and by providing a narrative explanation about other data sources used. It is appropriate for the AI Office to provide a template for the summary, which should be simple, effective, and allow the provider to provide the required summary in narrative form.

1417. **(108)** With regard to the obligations imposed on providers of general-purpose AI models to put in place a policy to comply with Union copyright law and make publicly available a summary of the content used for the training, the AI Office should monitor whether the provider has fulfilled those obligations without verifying or proceeding to a work-by-work assessment of the training data in terms of copyright compliance. This Regulation does not affect the enforcement of copyright rules as provided for under Union law.

1418. **(111)** It is appropriate to establish a methodology for the classification of general-purpose AI models as general-purpose AI model with systemic risks. Since systemic risks result from particularly high capabilities, a general-purpose AI model should be considered to present systemic risks if it has high-impact capabilities, evaluated on the basis of appropriate technical tools and methodologies, or significant impact on the internal market due to its reach. High-impact capabilities in general-purpose AI models means capabilities that match or exceed the capabilities recorded in the most advanced general-purpose AI models. The full range of capabilities in a model could be better understood after its placing on the market or when deployers interact with the model. According to the state of the art at the time of entry into force of this Regulation, the cumulative amount of computation used for the training of the general-purpose AI model measured in floating point operations is one of the relevant approximations for model capabilities. The cumulative amount of computation used for training includes the computation used across the activities and methods that are intended to enhance the capabilities of the model prior to deployment, such as pre-training, synthetic data generation and fine-tuning. Therefore, an initial threshold of floating point operations should be set, which, if met by a general-purpose AI model, leads to a presumption that the model is a general-purpose AI model with systemic risks. This threshold should be adjusted over time to reflect technological and industrial changes, such as algorithmic improvements or increased hardware efficiency, and should be supplemented with benchmarks and indicators for model capability. To inform this, the AI Office should engage with the scientific community, industry, civil society and other experts. Thresholds, as well as tools and benchmarks for the assessment of high-impact capabilities, should be strong predictors of generality, its capabilities and associated systemic risk of general-purpose AI models, and could take into account the way the model will be placed on the market or the number of users it may affect. To complement this system, there should be a possibility for the Commission to take individual decisions designating a general-purpose AI model as a general-purpose AI model with systemic risk if it is found that such model has capabilities or an impact equivalent to those captured by the set threshold. That decision should be taken on the basis of an overall assessment of the criteria for the designation of a general-purpose AI model with systemic risk set out in an annex to this Regulation, such as quality or size of the training data set, number of business and end users, its input and output modalities, its level of autonomy and scalability, or the tools it has access to. Upon a reasoned request of a provider whose model has been designated as a general-purpose AI model with systemic risk, the Commission should take the request into account and may decide to reassess whether the general-purpose AI model can still be considered to present systemic risks.

1419. (112) It is also necessary to clarify a procedure for the classification of a general-purpose AI model with systemic risks. A general-purpose AI model that meets the applicable threshold for high-impact capabilities should be presumed to be a general-purpose AI models with systemic risk. The provider should notify the AI Office at the latest two weeks after the requirements are met or it becomes known that a general-purpose AI model will meet the requirements that lead to the presumption. This is especially relevant in relation to the threshold of floating point operations because training of general-purpose AI models takes considerable planning which includes the upfront allocation of compute resources and, therefore, providers of general-purpose AI models are able to know if their model would meet the threshold before the training is completed. In the context of that notification, the provider should be able to demonstrate that, because of its specific characteristics, a general-purpose AI model exceptionally does not present systemic risks, and that it thus should not be classified as a general-purpose AI model with systemic risks. That information is valuable for the AI Office to anticipate the placing on the market of general-purpose AI models with systemic risks and the providers can start to engage with the AI Office early on. That information is especially important with regard to general-purpose AI models that are planned to be released as open-source, given that, after the open-source model release, necessary measures to ensure compliance with the obligations under this Regulation may be more difficult to implement.

1420. (113) If the Commission becomes aware of the fact that a general-purpose AI model meets the requirements to classify as a general-purpose AI model with systemic risk, which previously had either not been known or of which the relevant provider has failed to notify the Commission, the Commission should be empowered to designate it so. A system of qualified alerts should ensure that the AI Office is made aware by the scientific panel of general-purpose AI models that should possibly be classified as general-purpose AI models with systemic risk, in addition to the monitoring activities of the AI Office.

1421. **(116)** The AI Office should encourage and facilitate the drawing up, review and adaptation of codes of practice, taking into account international approaches. All providers of general-purpose AI models could be invited to participate. To ensure that the codes of practice reflect the state of the art and duly take into account a diverse set of perspectives, the AI Office should collaborate with relevant national competent authorities, and could, where appropriate, consult with civil society organisations and other relevant stakeholders and experts, including the Scientific Panel, for the drawing up of such codes. Codes of practice should cover obligations for providers of general-purpose AI models and of general-purpose AI models presenting systemic risks. In addition, as regards systemic risks, codes of practice should help to establish a risk taxonomy of the type and nature of the systemic risks at Union level, including their sources. Codes of practice should also be focused on specific risk assessment and mitigation measures.

1422. **(117)** The codes of practice should represent a central tool for the proper compliance with the obligations provided for under this Regulation for providers of general-purpose AI models. Providers should be able to rely on codes of practice to demonstrate compliance with the obligations. By means of implementing acts, the Commission may decide to approve a code of practice and give it a general validity within the Union, or, alternatively, to provide common rules for the implementation of the relevant obligations, if, by the time this Regulation becomes applicable, a code of practice cannot be finalised or is not deemed adequate by the AI Office. Once a harmonised standard is published and assessed as suitable to cover the relevant obligations by the AI Office, compliance with a European harmonised standard should grant providers the presumption of conformity. Providers of general-purpose AI models should furthermore be able to demonstrate compliance using alternative adequate means, if codes of practice or harmonised standards are not available, or they choose not to rely on those.

1423. **(148)** This Regulation should establish a governance framework that both allows to coordinate and support the application of this Regulation at national level, as well as build capabilities at Union level and integrate stakeholders in the field of AI. The effective implementation and enforcement of this Regulation require a governance framework that allows to coordinate and build up central expertise at Union level. The AI Office was established by Commission Decision[1] and has as its mission to develop Union expertise and capabilities in the field of AI and to contribute to the implementation of Union law on AI. Member States should facilitate the tasks of the AI Office with a view to support the development of Union expertise and capabilities at Union level and to strengthen the functioning of the digital single market. Furthermore, a Board composed of representatives of the Member States, a scientific panel to integrate the scientific community and an advisory forum to contribute stakeholder input to the implementation of this Regulation, at Union and national level, should be established. The development of Union expertise and capabilities should also include making use of existing resources and expertise, in particular through synergies with structures built up in the context of the Union level enforcement of other law and synergies with related initiatives at Union level, such as the EuroHPC Joint Undertaking and the AI testing and experimentation facilities under the Digital Europe Programme.

1424. **(151)** To support the implementation and enforcement of this Regulation, in particular the monitoring activities of the AI Office as regards general-purpose AI models, a scientific panel of independent experts should be established. The independent experts constituting the scientific panel should be selected on the basis of up-to-date scientific or technical expertise in the field of AI and should perform their tasks with impartiality, objectivity and ensure the confidentiality of information and data obtained in carrying out their tasks and activities. To allow the reinforcement of national capacities necessary for the effective enforcement of this Regulation, Member States should be able to request support from the pool of experts constituting the scientific panel for their enforcement activities.

1425. **(160)** The market surveillance authorities and the Commission should be able to propose joint activities, including joint investigations, to be conducted by market surveillance authorities or market surveillance authorities jointly with the Commission, that have the aim of promoting compliance, identifying non-compliance, raising awareness and providing guidance in relation to this Regulation with respect to specific categories of high-risk AI systems that are found to present a serious risk across two or more Member States. Joint activities to promote compliance should be carried out in accordance with Article 9 of Regulation (EU) 2019/1020. The AI Office should provide coordination support for joint investigations.

1426. **(161)** It is necessary to clarify the responsibilities and competences at Union and national level as regards AI systems that are built on general-purpose AI models. To avoid overlapping competences, where an AI system is based on a general-purpose AI model and the model and system are provided

[1] Commission Decision of 24 January 2024 establishing the European Artificial Intelligence Office (C/2024/390).

by the same provider, the supervision should take place at Union level through the AI Office, which should have the powers of a market surveillance authority within the meaning of Regulation (EU) 2019/1020 for this purpose. In all other cases, national market surveillance authorities remain responsible for the supervision of AI systems. However, for general-purpose AI systems that can be used directly by deployers for at least one purpose that is classified as high-risk, market surveillance authorities should cooperate with the AI Office to carry out evaluations of compliance and inform the Board and other market surveillance authorities accordingly. Furthermore, market surveillance authorities should be able to request assistance from the AI Office where the market surveillance authority is unable to conclude an investigation on a high-risk AI system because of its inability to access certain information related to the general-purpose AI model on which the high-risk AI system is built. In such cases, the procedure regarding mutual assistance in cross-border cases in Chapter VI of Regulation (EU) 2019/1020 should apply *mutatis mutandis*.

1427. (162) To make best use of the centralised Union expertise and synergies at Union level, the powers of supervision and enforcement of the obligations on providers of general-purpose AI models should be a competence of the Commission. The AI Office should be able to carry out all necessary actions to monitor the effective implementation of this Regulation as regards general-purpose AI models. It should be able to investigate possible infringements of the rules on providers of general-purpose AI models both on its own initiative, following the results of its monitoring activities, or upon request from market surveillance authorities in line with the conditions set out in this Regulation. To support effective monitoring of the AI Office, it should provide for the possibility that downstream providers lodge complaints about possible infringements of the rules on providers of general-purpose AI models and systems.

1428. (163) With a view to complementing the governance systems for general-purpose AI models, the scientific panel should support the monitoring activities of the AI Office and may, in certain cases, provide qualified alerts to the AI Office which trigger follow-ups, such as investigations. This should be the case where the scientific panel has reason to suspect that a general-purpose AI model poses a concrete and identifiable risk at Union level. Furthermore, this should be the case where the scientific panel has reason to suspect that a general-purpose AI model meets the criteria that would lead to a classification as general-purpose AI model with systemic risk. To equip the scientific panel with the information necessary for the performance of those tasks, there should be a mechanism whereby the scientific panel can request the Commission to require documentation or information from a provider.

1429. (164) The AI Office should be able to take the necessary actions to monitor the effective implementation of and compliance with the obligations for providers of general-purpose AI models laid down in this Regulation. The AI Office should be able to investigate possible infringements in accordance with the powers provided for in this Regulation, including by requesting documentation and information, by conducting evaluations, as well as by requesting measures from providers of general-purpose AI models. When conducting evaluations, in order to make use of independent expertise, the AI Office should be able to involve independent experts to carry out the evaluations on its behalf. Compliance with the obligations should be enforceable, inter alia, through requests to take appropriate measures, including risk mitigation measures in the case of identified systemic risks as well as restricting the making available on the market, withdrawing or recalling the model. As a safeguard, where needed beyond the procedural rights provided for in this Regulation, providers of general-purpose AI models should have the procedural rights provided for in Article 18 of Regulation (EU) 2019/1020, which should apply *mutatis mutandis*, without prejudice to more specific procedural rights provided for by this Regulation.

64.2. General Approach

64.2.1 Preamble

1430. The AI Office is the European Commission's technical arm.

64.2.2 Guiding Principles

1431. The AI Office acts in consultation with the Member States, which must facilitate its tasks.

65 ARTICLE 65. ESTABLISHMENT AND STRUCTURE OF THE EUROPEAN ARTIFICIAL INTELLIGENCE BOARD

1. A European Artificial Intelligence Board (the 'Board') is hereby established.

2. The Board shall be composed of one representative per Member State. The European Data Protection Supervisor shall participate as observer. The AI Office shall also attend the Board's meetings, without taking part in the votes. Other national and Union authorities, bodies or experts may be invited to the meetings by the Board on a case by case basis, where the issues discussed are of relevance for them.

3. Each representative shall be designated by their Member State for a period of three years, renewable once.

4. Member States shall ensure that their representatives on the Board:

(a) have the relevant competences and powers in their Member State so as to contribute actively to the achievement of the Board's tasks referred to in Article 66;

(b) are designated as a single contact point vis-à-vis the Board and, where appropriate, taking into account Member States' needs, as a single contact point for stakeholders;

(c) are empowered to facilitate consistency and coordination between national competent authorities in their Member State as regards the implementation of this Regulation, including through the collection of relevant data and information for the purpose of fulfilling their tasks on the Board.

5. The designated representatives of the Member States shall adopt the Board's rules of procedure by a two-thirds majority. The rules of procedure shall, in particular, lay down procedures for the selection process, the duration of the mandate of, and specifications of the tasks of, the Chair, detailed arrangements for voting, and the organisation of the Board's activities and those of its sub-groups.

6. The Board shall establish two standing sub-groups to provide a platform for cooperation and exchange among market surveillance authorities and notifying authorities about issues related to market surveillance and notified bodies respectively.

The standing sub-group for market surveillance should act as the administrative cooperation group (ADCO) for this Regulation within the meaning of Article 30 of Regulation (EU) 2019/1020.

The Board may establish other standing or temporary sub-groups as appropriate for the purpose of examining specific issues. Where appropriate, representatives of the advisory forum referred to in Article 67 may be invited to such sub-groups or to specific meetings of those subgroups as observers.

7. The Board shall be organised and operated so as to safeguard the objectivity and impartiality of its activities.

8. The Board shall be chaired by one of the representatives of the Member States. The AI Office shall provide the secretariat for the Board, convene the meetings upon request of the Chair, and prepare the agenda in accordance with the tasks of the Board pursuant to this Regulation and its rules of procedure.

65.1. Recitals

1432. **(20)** In order to obtain the greatest benefits from AI systems while protecting fundamental rights, health and safety and to enable democratic control, AI literacy should equip providers, deployers and affected persons with the necessary notions to make informed decisions regarding AI systems. Those notions may vary with regard to the relevant context and can include understanding the correct application of technical elements during the AI system's development phase, the measures to be applied during its use, the suitable ways in which to interpret the AI system's output, and, in the case of affected persons, the knowledge necessary to understand how decisions taken with the assistance of AI will have an impact on them. In the context of the application this Regulation, AI literacy should provide all relevant actors in the AI value chain with the insights required to ensure the appropriate compliance and its correct enforcement. Furthermore, the wide implementation of AI literacy measures and the introduction of appropriate follow-up actions could contribute to improving working conditions and ultimately sustain the consolidation, and innovation path of trustworthy AI in the Union. The European Artificial Intelligence Board (the 'Board') should support the Commission, to promote AI literacy tools, public awareness and understanding of the benefits, risks, safeguards, rights and obligations in relation to the use of AI systems. In cooperation with the relevant stakeholders, the Commission and the Member States should facilitate the drawing up of voluntary codes of conduct to advance AI literacy among persons dealing with the development, operation and use of AI.

65.2. *General Approach*

1433. The Regulation provides for an institutional mechanism for the management of AI technologies similar to that set up for the General Data Protection Regulation.[2]

65.3. *Architecture*

1434. This governance is organised as follows:

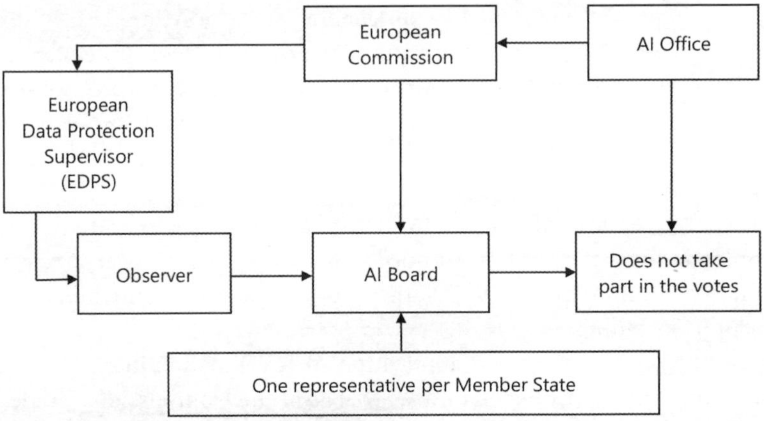

[2] GDPR (2016/679).

65.4. *Characteristics*

1435. They are mainly as follows:

NO.	THEME	SPECIFICATION
1.	Composition	One representative per Member State
2.	Organisation	Rules of procedure
3.	Chairmanship	One of the representatives of the Member States
4.	Secretariat	AI Office

66 ARTICLE 66. TASKS OF THE BOARD

The Board shall advise and assist the Commission and the Member States in order to facilitate the consistent and effective application of this Regulation. To that end, the Board may in particular:

(a) contribute to the coordination among national competent authorities responsible for the application of this Regulation and, in cooperation with and subject to the agreement of the market surveillance authorities concerned, support joint activities of market surveillance authorities referred to in Article 74(11);

(b) collect and share technical and regulatory expertise and best practices among Member States;

(c) provide advice on the implementation of this Regulation, in particular as regards the enforcement of rules on general-purpose AI models;

(d) contribute to the harmonisation of administrative practices in the Member States, including in relation to the derogation from the conformity assessment procedures referred to in Article 46, the functioning of AI regulatory sandboxes, and testing in real world conditions referred to in Articles 57, 59 and 60;

(e) at the request of the Commission or on its own initiative, issue recommendations and written opinions on any relevant matters related to the implementation of this Regulation and to its consistent and effective application, including:

(i) on the development and application of codes of conduct and codes of practice pursuant to this Regulation, as well as of the Commission's guidelines;

(ii) the evaluation and review of this Regulation pursuant to Article 112, including as regards the serious incident reports referred to in Article 73, and the functioning of the EU database referred to in Article 71, the preparation of the delegated or implementing acts, and as regards possible alignments of this Regulation with the Union harmonisation legislation listed in Annex I;

(iii) on technical specifications or existing standards regarding the requirements set out in Chapter III, Section 2;

(iv) on the use of harmonised standards or common specifications referred to in Articles 40 and 41;

(v) trends, such as European global competitiveness in AI, the uptake of AI in the Union, and the development of digital skills;

(vi) trends on the evolving typology of AI value chains, in particular on the resulting implications in terms of accountability;

(vii) on the potential need for amendment to Annex III in accordance with Article 7, and on the potential need for possible revision of Article 5 pursuant to Article 112, taking into account relevant available evidence and the latest developments in technology;

(f) support the Commission in promoting AI literacy, public awareness and understanding of the benefits, risks, safeguards and rights and obligations in relation to the use of AI systems;

(g) facilitate the development of common criteria and a shared understanding among market operators and competent authorities of the relevant concepts provided for in this Regulation, including by contributing to the development of benchmarks;

(h) cooperate, as appropriate, with other Union institutions, bodies, offices and agencies, as well as relevant Union expert groups and networks, in particular in the fields of product safety, cybersecurity, competition, digital and media services, financial services, consumer protection, data and fundamental rights protection;

(i) contribute to effective cooperation with the competent authorities of third countries and with international organisations;

(j) assist national competent authorities and the Commission in developing the organisational and technical expertise required for the implementation of this Regulation, including by contributing to the assessment of training needs for staff of Member States involved in implementing this Regulation;

(k) assist the AI Office in supporting national competent authorities in the establishment and development of AI regulatory sandboxes, and facilitate cooperation and information-sharing among AI regulatory sandboxes;

(l) contribute to, and provide relevant advice on, the development of guidance documents;

(m) advise the Commission in relation to international matters on A;

(n) provide opinions to the Commission on the qualified alerts regarding general-purpose AI models;

(o) receive opinions by the Member States on qualified alerts regarding general-purpose AI models, and on national experiences and practices on the monitoring and enforcement of AI systems, in particular systems integrating the general-purpose AI models.

66.1. *Recitals*

1436. (121) Standardisation should play a key role to provide technical solutions to providers to ensure compliance with this Regulation, in line with the state of the art, to promote innovation as well as competitiveness and growth in the single market. Compliance with harmonised standards as defined in Article 2, point (1)(c), of Regulation (EU) No 1025/2012 of the European Parliament and of the Council,[3] which are normally expected to reflect the state of the art, should be a means for providers to demonstrate conformity with the requirements of this Regulation. A balanced representation of interests involving all relevant stakeholders in the development of standards, in particular SMEs, consumer organisations and environmental and social stakeholders in accordance with Articles 5 and 6 of Regulation (EU) No 1025/2012 should therefore be encouraged. In order to facilitate compliance, the standardisation requests should be issued by the Commission without undue delay. When preparing the standardisation request, the Commission should consult the advisory forum and the Board in order to collect relevant expertise. However, in the absence of relevant references to harmonised standards, the Commission should be able to establish, via implementing acts, and after consultation of the advisory forum, common specifications for certain requirements under this Regulation. The common specification should be an exceptional fall back solution to facilitate the provider's obligation to comply with the requirements of this Regulation, when the standardisation request has not been accepted by any of the European standardisation organisations, or when the relevant harmonised standards insufficiently address fundamental rights concerns, or when the harmonised standards do not comply with the request, or when there are delays in the adoption of an appropriate harmonised standard. Where such a delay in the adoption of a harmonised standard is due to the technical complexity of that standard, this should be considered by the Commission before contemplating the establishment of common specifications. When developing common specifications, the Commission is encouraged to cooperate with international partners and international standardisation bodies.

1437. (143) In order to promote and protect innovation, it is important that the interests of SMEs, including start-ups, that are providers or deployers of AI systems are taken into particular account. To that end, Member States should develop initiatives, which are targeted at those operators, including on awareness

[3] Regulation (EU) No 1025/2012 of the European Parliament and of the Council of 25 October 2012 on European standardisation, amending Council Directives 89/686/EEC and 93/15/EEC and Directives 94/9/EC, 94/25/EC, 95/16/EC, 97/23/EC, 98/34/EC, 2004/22/EC, 2007/23/EC, 2009/23/EC and 2009/105/EC of the European Parliament and of the Council and repealing Council Decision 87/95/EEC and Decision No 1673/2006/EC of the European Parliament and of the Council, [2012] OJ L316/12.

raising and information communication. Member States should provide SMEs, including start-ups, that have a registered office or a branch in the Union, with priority access to the AI regulatory sandboxes provided that they fulfil the eligibility conditions and selection criteria and without precluding other providers and prospective providers to access the sandboxes provided the same conditions and criteria are fulfilled. Member States should utilise existing channels and where appropriate, establish new dedicated channels for communication with SMEs, including start-ups, deployers, other innovators and, as appropriate, local public authorities, to support SMEs throughout their development path by providing guidance and responding to queries about the implementation of this Regulation. Where appropriate, these channels should work together to create synergies and ensure homogeneity in their guidance to SMEs, including start-ups, and deployers. Additionally, Member States should facilitate the participation of SMEs and other relevant stakeholders in the standardisation development processes. Moreover, the specific interests and needs of providers that are SMEs, including start-ups, should be taken into account when notified bodies set conformity assessment fees. The Commission should regularly assess the certification and compliance costs for SMEs, including start-ups, through transparent consultations and should work with Member States to lower such costs. For example, translation costs related to mandatory documentation and communication with authorities may constitute a significant cost for providers and other operators, in particular those of a smaller scale. Member States should possibly ensure that one of the languages determined and accepted by them for relevant providers' documentation and for communication with operators is one which is broadly understood by the largest possible number of cross-border deployers. In order to address the specific needs of SMEs, including start-ups, the Commission should provide standardised templates for the areas covered by this Regulation, upon request of the Board. Additionally, the Commission should complement Member States' efforts by providing a single information platform with easy-to-use information with regards to this Regulation for all providers and deployers, by organising appropriate communication campaigns to raise awareness about the obligations arising from this Regulation, and by evaluating and promoting the convergence of best practices in public procurement procedures in relation to AI systems. Medium-sized enterprises which until recently qualified as small enterprises within the meaning of the Annex to Commission Recommendation 2003/361/EC[4] should have access to those support measures, as those new medium-sized enterprises may sometimes lack the legal resources and training necessary to ensure proper understanding of, and compliance with, this Regulation.

---

[4] Commission Recommendation of 6 May 2003 concerning the definition of micro, small and medium-sized enterprises, [2003] OJ L124/36.

1438. **(148)** This Regulation should establish a governance framework that both allows to coordinate and support the application of this Regulation at national level, as well as build capabilities at Union level and integrate stakeholders in the field of AI. The effective implementation and enforcement of this Regulation require a governance framework that allows to coordinate and build up central expertise at Union level. The AI Office was established by Commission Decision[5] and has as its mission to develop Union expertise and capabilities in the field of AI and to contribute to the implementation of Union law on AI. Member States should facilitate the tasks of the AI Office with a view to support the development of Union expertise and capabilities at Union level and to strengthen the functioning of the digital single market. Furthermore, a Board composed of representatives of the Member States, a scientific panel to integrate the scientific community and an advisory forum to contribute stakeholder input to the implementation of this Regulation, at Union and national level, should be established. The development of Union expertise and capabilities should also include making use of existing resources and expertise, in particular through synergies with structures built up in the context of the Union level enforcement of other law and synergies with related initiatives at Union level, such as the EuroHPC Joint Undertaking and the AI testing and experimentation facilities under the Digital Europe Programme.

1439. **(149)** In order to facilitate a smooth, effective and harmonised implementation of this Regulation a Board should be established. The Board should reflect the various interests of the AI eco-system and be composed of representatives of the Member States. The Board should be responsible for a number of advisory tasks, including issuing opinions, recommendations, advice or contributing to guidance on matters related to the implementation of this Regulation, including on enforcement matters, technical specifications or existing standards regarding the requirements established in this Regulation and providing advice to the Commission and the Member States and their national competent authorities on specific questions related to AI. In order to give some flexibility to Member States in the designation of their representatives in the Board, such representatives may be any persons belonging to public entities who should have the relevant competences and powers to facilitate coordination at national level and contribute to the achievement of the Board's tasks. The Board should establish two standing sub-groups to provide a platform for cooperation and exchange among market surveillance authorities and notifying authorities on issues related, respectively, to market surveillance and notified bodies. The standing subgroup for market surveillance should act as the administrative cooperation group (ADCO) for this Regulation within the meaning of Article 30

---

5 Commission Decision of 24 January 2024 establishing the European Artificial Intelligence Office (C/2024/390).

of Regulation (EU) 2019/1020. In accordance with Article 33 of that Regulation, the Commission should support the activities of the standing subgroup for market surveillance by undertaking market evaluations or studies, in particular with a view to identifying aspects of this Regulation requiring specific and urgent coordination among market surveillance authorities. The Board may establish other standing or temporary sub-groups as appropriate for the purpose of examining specific issues. The Board should also cooperate, as appropriate, with relevant Union bodies, experts groups and networks active in the context of relevant Union law, including in particular those active under relevant Union law on data, digital products and services.

1440. (150) With a view to ensuring the involvement of stakeholders in the implementation and application of this Regulation, an advisory forum should be established to advise and provide technical expertise to the Board and the Commission. To ensure a varied and balanced stakeholder representation between commercial and non-commercial interest and, within the category of commercial interests, with regards to SMEs and other undertakings, the advisory forum should comprise inter alia industry, start-ups, SMEs, academia, civil society, including the social partners, as well as the Fundamental Rights Agency, ENISA, the European Committee for Standardization (CEN), the European Committee for Electrotechnical Standardization (CENELEC) and the European Telecommunications Standards Institute (ETSI).

1441. (161) It is necessary to clarify the responsibilities and competences at Union and national level as regards AI systems that are built on general-purpose AI models. To avoid overlapping competences, where an AI system is based on a general-purpose AI model and the model and system are provided by the same provider, the supervision should take place at Union level through the AI Office, which should have the powers of a market surveillance authority within the meaning of Regulation (EU) 2019/1020 for this purpose. In all other cases, national market surveillance authorities remain responsible for the supervision of AI systems. However, for general-purpose AI systems that can be used directly by deployers for at least one purpose that is classified as high-risk, market surveillance authorities should cooperate with the AI Office to carry out evaluations of compliance and inform the Board and other market surveillance authorities accordingly. Furthermore, market surveillance authorities should be able to request assistance from the AI Office where the market surveillance authority is unable to conclude an investigation on a high-risk AI system because of its inability to access certain information related to the general-purpose AI model on which the high-risk AI system is built. In such cases, the procedure regarding mutual assistance in cross-border cases in Chapter VI of Regulation (EU) 2019/1020 should apply *mutatis mutandis.*

66.2. *General Approach*

66.2.1 Preamble

1442. The European Artificial Intelligence Board has two main tasks beside the European Commission:

- to advise;
- to assist.

66.2.2 Tasks

1443. They are as follows:

NO.	THEME	SPECIFICATION
1.	Coordination	National competent authorities
2.	Cooperation	Market surveillance authority
3.	Expertise State of the art Advice	Technical expertise Legal expertise Best practices Implementation of the AIA
4.	Harmonisation	Administrative practices Conformity assessment procedures Regulatory sandboxes
5.	Recommendations	On its own initiative or at the request of the European Commission

67 ARTICLE 67. ADVISORY FORUM

1. An advisory forum shall be established to provide technical expertise and advise the Board and the Commission, and to contribute to their tasks under this Regulation.

2. The membership of the advisory forum shall represent a balanced selection of stakeholders, including industry, start-ups, SMEs, civil society and academia. The membership of the advisory forum shall be balanced with regard to commercial and non-commercial interests and, within the category of commercial interests, with regard to SMEs and other undertakings.

3. The Commission shall appoint the members of the advisory forum, in accordance with the criteria set out in paragraph 2, from amongst stakeholders with recognised expertise in the field of AI.

4. The term of office of the members of the advisory forum shall be two years, which may be extended by up to no more than four years.

5. The Fundamental Rights Agency, ENISA, the European Committee for Standardization (CEN), the European Committee for Electrotechnical Standardization (CENELEC), and the European Telecommunications Standards Institute (ETSI) shall be permanent members of the advisory forum.

6. The advisory forum shall draw up its rules of procedure. It shall elect two co-chairs from among its members, in accordance with criteria set out in paragraph 2. The term of office of the co-chairs shall be two years, renewable once.

7. The advisory forum shall hold meetings at least twice a year. The advisory forum may invite experts and other stakeholders to its meetings.

8. The advisory forum may prepare opinions, recommendations and written contributions at the request of the Board or the Commission.

9. The advisory forum may establish standing or temporary sub-groups as appropriate for the purpose of examining specific questions related to the objectives of this Regulation.

10. The advisory forum shall prepare an annual report on its activities. That report shall be made publicly available.

67.1. Recitals

1444. (121) Standardisation should play a key role to provide technical solutions to providers to ensure compliance with this Regulation, in line with the state of the art, to promote innovation as well as competitiveness and growth in the single market. Compliance with harmonised standards as defined in Article 2, point (1)(c), of Regulation (EU) No 1025/2012 of the European Parliament and of the Council,[6] which are normally expected to reflect the state of the art, should be a means for providers to demonstrate conformity with the requirements of this Regulation. A balanced representation of interests involving all relevant stakeholders in the development of standards, in particular SMEs, consumer organisations and environmental and social stakeholders in accordance with Articles 5 and 6 of Regulation (EU) No 1025/2012 should therefore be encouraged. In order to facilitate compliance, the standardisation requests should be issued by the Commission without undue delay. When preparing the standardisation request, the Commission should consult the advisory forum

[6] Regulation (EU) No 1025/2012 of the European Parliament and of the Council of 25 October 2012 on European standardisation, amending Council Directives 89/686/EEC and 93/15/EEC and Directives 94/9/EC, 94/25/EC, 95/16/EC, 97/23/EC, 98/34/EC, 2004/22/EC, 2007/23/EC, 2009/23/EC and 2009/105/EC of the European Parliament and of the Council and repealing Council Decision 87/95/EEC and Decision No 1673/2006/EC of the European Parliament and of the Council, [2012] OJ L316/12.

and the Board in order to collect relevant expertise. However, in the absence of relevant references to harmonised standards, the Commission should be able to establish, via implementing acts, and after consultation of the advisory forum, common specifications for certain requirements under this Regulation. The common specification should be an exceptional fall back solution to facilitate the provider's obligation to comply with the requirements of this Regulation, when the standardisation request has not been accepted by any of the European standardisation organisations, or when the relevant harmonised standards insufficiently address fundamental rights concerns, or when the harmonised standards do not comply with the request, or when there are delays in the adoption of an appropriate harmonised standard. Where such a delay in the adoption of a harmonised standard is due to the technical complexity of that standard, this should be considered by the Commission before contemplating the establishment of common specifications. When developing common specifications, the Commission is encouraged to cooperate with international partners and international standardisation bodies.

1445. (148) This Regulation should establish a governance framework that both allows to coordinate and support the application of this Regulation at national level, as well as build capabilities at Union level and integrate stakeholders in the field of AI. The effective implementation and enforcement of this Regulation require a governance framework that allows to coordinate and build up central expertise at Union level. The AI Office was established by Commission Decision[7] and has as its mission to develop Union expertise and capabilities in the field of AI and to contribute to the implementation of Union law on AI. Member States should facilitate the tasks of the AI Office with a view to support the development of Union expertise and capabilities at Union level and to strengthen the functioning of the digital single market. Furthermore, a Board composed of representatives of the Member States, a scientific panel to integrate the scientific community and an advisory forum to contribute stakeholder input to the implementation of this Regulation, at Union and national level, should be established. The development of Union expertise and capabilities should also include making use of existing resources and expertise, in particular through synergies with structures built up in the context of the Union level enforcement of other law and synergies with related initiatives at Union level, such as the EuroHPC Joint Undertaking and the AI testing and experimentation facilities under the Digital Europe Programme.

1446. (150) With a view to ensuring the involvement of stakeholders in the implementation and application of this Regulation, an advisory forum should be established to advise and provide technical expertise to the Board and the

---

[7] Commission Decision of 24 January 2024 establishing the European Artificial Intelligence Office (C/2024/390).

Commission. To ensure a varied and balanced stakeholder representation between commercial and non-commercial interest and, within the category of commercial interests, with regards to SMEs and other undertakings, the advisory forum should comprise inter alia industry, start-ups, SMEs, academia, civil society, including the social partners, as well as the Fundamental Rights Agency, ENISA, the European Committee for Standardization (CEN), the European Committee for Electrotechnical Standardization (CENELEC) and the European Telecommunications Standards Institute (ETSI).

67.2. General Approach

67.2.1 Preamble

1447. The Advisory Forum brings together stakeholders with technical expertise.

67.2.2 Guiding Principles

1448. Its task is to provide the European Commission and the AI Board with:

- technical expertise;
- associated advice.

67.3. Composition

1449. It is composed of representatives from the following sectors:

NO.	THEME	SPECIFICATION
1.	Operators	Providers Authorised representatives Importers Distributors Deployers
2.	Bodies	Industry Start-ups SMEs
3.	Representatives	Civil society Academia
4.	Permanent institutions	Fundamental Rights Agency ENISA European Committee for Standardization (CEN) European Committee for Electrotechnical Standardization (CENELEC) European Telecommunications Standards Institute (ETSI)

67.3.1 Appointment

1450. The appointment procedures are as follows:

NO.	THEME	SPECIFICATION
1.	Criterion	Recognised expertise in the field of AI
2.	Duration	Term of office of 2 years, which may be extended by up to no more than 4 years

67.4. Organisation

1451. It is as follows:

NO.	THEME	SPECIFICATION
1.	Chair	Two co-chairs (Terms of office of 2 years, renewable once)
2.	Organisation	Rules of procedure
3.	Meeting	At least twice a year
4.	Tasks	At the request of the AI Board or the European Commission: • opinions; • recommendations; • contributions.
5.	Sub-groups	Standing or temporary
6.	Report	Annual and public

68 ARTICLE 68. SCIENTIFIC PANEL OF INDEPENDENT EXPERTS

1. The Commission shall, by means of an implementing act, make provisions on the establishment of a scientific panel of independent experts (the 'scientific panel') intended to support the enforcement activities under this Regulation. That implementing act shall be adopted in accordance with the examination procedure referred to in Article 98(2).

2. The scientific panel shall consist of experts selected by the Commission on the basis of up-to-date scientific or technical expertise in the field of AI necessary for the tasks set out in paragraph 3, and shall be able to demonstrate meeting all of the following conditions:

(a) having particular expertise and competence and scientific or technical expertise in the field of AI;

(b) independence from any provider of AI systems or general-purpose AI models;

(c) an ability to carry out activities diligently, accurately and objectively.

The Commission, in consultation with the Board, shall determine the number of experts on the panel in accordance with the required needs and shall ensure fair gender and geographical representation.

3. The scientific panel shall advise and support the AI Office, in particular with regard to the following tasks:

(a) supporting the implementation and enforcement of this Regulation as regards general-purpose AI models and systems, in particular by:

(i) alerting the AI Office of possible systemic risks at Union level of general-purpose AI models, in accordance with Article 90;

(ii) contributing to the development of tools and methodologies for evaluating capabilities of general-purpose AI models and systems, including through benchmarks;

(iii) providing advice on the classification of general-purpose AI models with systemic risk;

(iv) providing advice on the classification of various general-purpose AI models and systems;

(v) contributing to the development of tools and templates;

(b) supporting the work of market surveillance authorities, at their request;

(c) supporting cross-border market surveillance activities as referred to in Article 74(11), without prejudice to the powers of market surveillance authorities;

(d) supporting the AI Office in carrying out its duties in the context of the Union safeguard procedure pursuant to Article 81.

4. The experts on the scientific panel shall perform their tasks with impartiality and objectivity, and shall ensure the confidentiality of information and data obtained in carrying out their tasks and activities. They shall neither seek nor take instructions from anyone when exercising their tasks under paragraph 3. Each expert shall draw up a declaration of interests, which shall be made publicly available. The AI Office shall establish systems and procedures to actively manage and prevent potential conflicts of interest.

5. The implementing act referred to in paragraph 1 shall include provisions on the conditions, procedures and detailed arrangements for the scientific panel and its members to issue alerts, and to request the assistance of the AI Office for the performance of the tasks of the scientific panel.

68.1. Recitals

1452. (96) In order to efficiently ensure that fundamental rights are protected, deployers of high-risk AI systems that are bodies governed by public law, or private entities providing public services and deployers of certain high-risk AI systems listed in an annex to this Regulation, such as banking or insurance entities, should carry out a fundamental rights impact assessment prior to putting it into use. Services important for individuals that are of public nature may also be provided by private entities. Private entities providing such public services are linked to tasks in the public interest such as in the areas of education, healthcare, social services, housing, administration of justice. The aim of the fundamental rights impact assessment is for the deployer to identify the specific risks to the rights of individuals or groups of individuals likely to be affected, identify measures to be taken in the case of a materialisation of those risks. The impact assessment should be performed prior to deploying the high-risk AI system, and should be updated when the deployer considers that any of the relevant factors have changed. The impact assessment should identify the deployer's relevant processes in which the high-risk AI system will be used in line with its intended purpose, and should include a description of the period of time and frequency in which the system is intended to be used as well as of specific categories of natural persons and groups who are likely to be affected in the specific context of use. The assessment should also include the identification of specific risks of harm likely to have an impact on the fundamental rights of those persons or groups. While performing this assessment, the deployer should take into account information relevant to a proper assessment of the impact, including but not limited to the information given by the provider of the high-risk AI system in the instructions for use. In light of the risks identified, deployers should determine measures to be taken in the case of a materialisation of those risks, including for example governance arrangements in that specific context of use, such as arrangements for human oversight according to the instructions of use or, complaint handling and redress procedures, as they could be instrumental in mitigating risks to fundamental rights in concrete use-cases. After performing that impact assessment, the deployer should notify the relevant market surveillance authority. Where appropriate, to collect relevant information necessary to perform the impact assessment, deployers of high-risk AI system, in particular when AI systems are used in the public sector, could involve relevant stakeholders, including the representatives of groups of persons likely to be affected by the AI system, independent experts, and civil society organisations in conducting such impact assessments and designing measures to be taken in the case of materialisation of the risks. The European Artificial Intelligence Office (AI Office) should develop a template for a questionnaire in order to facilitate compliance and reduce the administrative burden for deployers.

1453. (151) To support the implementation and enforcement of this Regulation, in particular the monitoring activities of the AI Office as regards general-purpose AI models, a scientific panel of independent experts should be established. The independent experts constituting the scientific panel should be selected on the basis of up-to-date scientific or technical expertise in the field of AI and should perform their tasks with impartiality, objectivity and ensure the confidentiality of information and data obtained in carrying out their tasks and activities. To allow the reinforcement of national capacities necessary for the effective enforcement of this Regulation, Member States should be able to request support from the pool of experts constituting the scientific panel for their enforcement activities.

1454. (164) The AI Office should be able to take the necessary actions to monitor the effective implementation of and compliance with the obligations for providers of general-purpose AI models laid down in this Regulation. The AI Office should be able to investigate possible infringements in accordance with the powers provided for in this Regulation, including by requesting documentation and information, by conducting evaluations, as well as by requesting measures from providers of general-purpose AI models. When conducting evaluations, in order to make use of independent expertise, the AI Office should be able to involve independent experts to carry out the evaluations on its behalf. Compliance with the obligations should be enforceable, inter alia, through requests to take appropriate measures, including risk mitigation measures in the case of identified systemic risks as well as restricting the making available on the market, withdrawing or recalling the model. As a safeguard, where needed beyond the procedural rights provided for in this Regulation, providers of general-purpose AI models should have the procedural rights provided for in Article 18 of Regulation (EU) 2019/1020, which should apply *mutatis mutandis*, without prejudice to more specific procedural rights provided for by this Regulation.

68.2. General Approach

68.2.1 Preamble

1455. The aim is to provide the European Commission with a group of independent scientific experts whose main activities include:

- providing high-level advice;
- strengthening forward planning capabilities;
- issuing alerts;
- resolving serious situations.

68.2.2 Guiding Principles

1456. Its independence makes it possible to:
- create a scientific counterweight;
- have access to scientific advice from a variety of sources.

68.3. Composition

1457. It is as follows:

NO.	THEME	SPECIFICATION
1.	Expertise	Up-to-date scientific or technical expertise in the field of AI
2.	Independence	From: • providers of AI systems • providers of general-purpose AI models
3.	Activities	Carried out: • diligently • accurately • objectively
4.	Breakdown by gender	Gender equality
5.	Geographical coverage	Fair representation
6.	Number	In accordance with the required needs

68.4. Tasks

1458. They are as follows:

NO.	THEME	SPECIFICATION
1.	Alert	General-purpose AI model with systemic risk
2.	Tools and methodologies	Evaluation of general-purpose AI models
3.	Classification	Advice on general-purpose AI models with systemic risk and other models
4.	Contribution	Development of tools and templates

NO.	THEME	SPECIFICATION
5.	Support	Market surveillance authorities Cross-border market surveillance activities[8]
6.	Contact	AI Office
7.	Appointment	By means of an implementing act

69 ARTICLE 69. ACCESS TO THE POOL OF EXPERTS BY THE MEMBER STATES

1. Member States may call upon experts of the scientific panel to support their enforcement activities under this Regulation.

2. The Member States may be required to pay fees for the advice and support provided by the experts. The structure and the level of fees as well as the scale and structure of recoverable costs shall be set out in the implementing act referred to in Article 68(1), taking into account the objectives of the adequate implementation of this Regulation, cost-effectiveness and the necessity of ensuring effective access to experts for all Member States.

3. The Commission shall facilitate timely access to the experts by the Member States, as needed, and ensure that the combination of support activities carried out by Union AI testing support pursuant to Article 84 and experts pursuant to this Article is efficiently organised and provides the best possible added value.

69.1. Recitals

1459. **(116)** The AI Office should encourage and facilitate the drawing up, review and adaptation of codes of practice, taking into account international approaches. All providers of general-purpose AI models could be invited to participate. To ensure that the codes of practice reflect the state of the art and duly take into account a diverse set of perspectives, the AI Office should collaborate with relevant national competent authorities, and could, where appropriate, consult with civil society organisations and other relevant stakeholders and experts, including the

[8] AI Act, Article 74: "Market surveillance authorities and the Commission shall be able to propose joint activities, including joint investigations, to be conducted by either market surveillance authorities or market surveillance authorities jointly with the Commission, that have the aim of promoting compliance, identifying non-compliance, raising awareness or providing guidance in relation to this Regulation with respect to specific categories of high-risk AI systems that are found to present a serious risk across two or more Member States in accordance with Article 9 of Regulation (EU) 2019/1020. The AI Office shall provide coordination support for joint investigations."

Scientific Panel, for the drawing up of such codes. Codes of practice should cover obligations for providers of general-purpose AI models and of general-purpose AI models presenting systemic risks. In addition, as regards systemic risks, codes of practice should help to establish a risk taxonomy of the type and nature of the systemic risks at Union level, including their sources. Codes of practice should also be focused on specific risk assessment and mitigation measures.

1460. **(148)** This Regulation should establish a governance framework that both allows to coordinate and support the application of this Regulation at national level, as well as build capabilities at Union level and integrate stakeholders in the field of AI. The effective implementation and enforcement of this Regulation require a governance framework that allows to coordinate and build up central expertise at Union level. The AI Office was established by Commission Decision[9] and has as its mission to develop Union expertise and capabilities in the field of AI and to contribute to the implementation of Union law on AI. Member States should facilitate the tasks of the AI Office with a view to support the development of Union expertise and capabilities at Union level and to strengthen the functioning of the digital single market. Furthermore, a Board composed of representatives of the Member States, a scientific panel to integrate the scientific community and an advisory forum to contribute stakeholder input to the implementation of this Regulation, at Union and national level, should be established. The development of Union expertise and capabilities should also include making use of existing resources and expertise, in particular through synergies with structures built up in the context of the Union level enforcement of other law and synergies with related initiatives at Union level, such as the EuroHPC Joint Undertaking and the AI testing and experimentation facilities under the Digital Europe Programme.

1461. **(151)** To support the implementation and enforcement of this Regulation, in particular the monitoring activities of the AI Office as regards general-purpose AI models, a scientific panel of independent experts should be established. The independent experts constituting the scientific panel should be selected on the basis of up-to-date scientific or technical expertise in the field of AI and should perform their tasks with impartiality, objectivity and ensure the confidentiality of information and data obtained in carrying out their tasks and activities. To allow the reinforcement of national capacities necessary for the effective enforcement of this Regulation, Member States should be able to request support from the pool of experts constituting the scientific panel for their enforcement activities.

1462. **(163)** With a view to complementing the governance systems for general-purpose AI models, the scientific panel should support the monitoring activities

9 Commission Decision of 24 January 2024 establishing the European Artificial Intelligence Office (C/2024/390).

of the AI Office and may, in certain cases, provide qualified alerts to the AI Office which trigger follow-ups, such as investigations. This should be the case where the scientific panel has reason to suspect that a general-purpose AI model poses a concrete and identifiable risk at Union level. Furthermore, this should be the case where the scientific panel has reason to suspect that a general-purpose AI model meets the criteria that would lead to a classification as general-purpose AI model with systemic risk. To equip the scientific panel with the information necessary for the performance of those tasks, there should be a mechanism whereby the scientific panel can request the Commission to require documentation or information from a provider.

69.2. Comments

1463. See comments under Article 68.

SECTION 2. NATIONAL COMPETENT AUTHORITIES

70 ARTICLE 70. DESIGNATION OF NATIONAL COMPETENT AUTHORITIES AND SINGLE POINTS OF CONTACT

1. Each Member State shall establish or designate as national competent authorities at least one notifying authority and at least one market surveillance authority for the purposes of this Regulation. Those national competent authorities shall exercise their powers independently, impartially and without bias so as to safeguard the objectivity of their activities and tasks, and to ensure the application and implementation of this Regulation. The members of those authorities shall refrain from any action incompatible with their duties. Provided that those principles are observed, such activities and tasks may be performed by one or more designated authorities, in accordance with the organisational needs of the Member State.

2. Member States shall communicate to the Commission the identity of the notifying authorities and the market surveillance authorities and the tasks of those authorities, as well as any subsequent changes thereto. Member States shall make publicly available information on how competent authorities and single points of contact can be contacted, through electronic communication means by 2 August 2025. Member States shall designate a market surveillance authority to act as the single point of contact for this Regulation, and shall notify the Commission of the identity of the single point of contact. The Commission shall make a list of the single points of contact publicly available.

3. Member States shall ensure that their national competent authorities are provided with adequate technical, financial and human resources, and with infrastructure to fulfil their tasks effectively under this Regulation. In particular, the national competent authorities shall have a sufficient number of personnel permanently available whose competences and expertise shall include an in-depth understanding of AI technologies, data and data computing, personal data protection, cybersecurity, fundamental rights, health and safety risks and knowledge of existing standards and legal requirements. Member States shall assess and, if necessary, update competence and resource requirements referred to in this paragraph on an annual basis.

4. National competent authorities shall take appropriate measures to ensure an adequate level of cybersecurity.

5. When performing their tasks, the national competent authorities shall act in accordance with the confidentiality obligations set out in Article 78.

6. By 2 August 2025, and once every two years thereafter, Member States shall report to the Commission on the status of the financial and human resources of the national competent authorities, with an assessment of their adequacy. The Commission shall transmit that information to the Board for discussion and possible recommendations.

7. The Commission shall facilitate the exchange of experience between national competent authorities.

8. National competent authorities may provide guidance and advice on the implementation of this Regulation, in particular to SMEs including start-ups, taking into account the guidance and advice of the Board and the Commission, as appropriate. Whenever national competent authorities intend to provide guidance and advice with regard to an AI system in areas covered by other Union law, the national competent authorities under that Union law shall be consulted, as appropriate.

9. Where Union institutions, bodies, offices or agencies fall within the scope of this Regulation, the European Data Protection Supervisor shall act as the competent authority for their supervision.

70.1. Recitals

1464. **(53)** It is also important to clarify that there may be specific cases in which AI systems referred to in pre-defined areas specified in this Regulation do not lead to a significant risk of harm to the legal interests protected under those areas because they do not materially influence the decision-making or do not harm those interests substantially. For the purposes of this Regulation, an AI system that does not materially influence the outcome of decision-making should be understood to be an AI system that does not have an impact on the substance, and thereby the outcome, of decision-making, whether human or automated. An AI system that does not materially influence the outcome of decision-making could include situations in which one or more of the following conditions are fulfilled. The first such condition should be that the AI system is intended to perform a narrow procedural task, such as an AI system that transforms unstructured data into structured data, an AI system that classifies incoming documents into categories or an AI system that is used to detect duplicates among a large number of applications. Those tasks are of such narrow and limited nature that they pose only limited risks which are not increased through the use of an AI system in a context that is listed as a high-risk use in an annex to this Regulation. The second condition should be that the task performed by the AI system is intended to improve the result of a previously completed human activity that may be relevant for the purposes of the high-risk uses listed in an annex to this Regulation. Considering those characteristics, the AI system provides only an additional layer to a human activity with consequently lowered risk. That condition would, for example, apply to AI systems that are intended to improve the language used in previously drafted documents, for example in relation to professional tone, academic style of language or by aligning text to a certain brand messaging. The third condition should be that the AI system is intended to detect decision-making patterns or deviations from prior decision-making patterns. The risk would be lowered because the use of the AI system follows a previously completed human assessment which it is not meant to replace or influence, without proper human review. Such AI systems include for instance those that, given a certain grading pattern of a teacher, can be used to check ex post whether the teacher may have deviated from the grading pattern so as to flag potential inconsistencies or anomalies. The fourth condition should be that the AI system is intended to perform a task that is only preparatory to an assessment relevant for the purposes of the AI systems listed in an annex to this Regulation, thus making the possible impact of the output of the system very low in terms of representing a risk for the assessment to follow. That condition covers, inter alia, smart solutions for file handling, which include various functions from indexing, searching, text and speech processing or linking data to other data sources, or AI systems used for translation of initial documents. In any case, AI systems used in high-risk use-cases listed in an annex to this Regulation should be considered to pose significant risks of harm to the health, safety or fundamental rights if the AI system implies profiling within the meaning of Article 4, point (4) of Regulation (EU) 2016/679 or Article 3, point (4) of Directive (EU) 2016/680 or Article 3, point (5) of Regulation (EU) 2018/1725. To ensure traceability and transparency, a provider who considers that an AI system is not high-risk on the basis of the conditions referred to above should draw up documentation of the assessment before that system is placed on the market or put into service and should provide that documentation to national competent authorities upon request. Such a provider should be obliged to register the AI system in the EU database established under this Regulation. With a view to providing further guidance for the practical implementation of the conditions under which the AI systems listed in an annex to this Regulation are, on an exceptional basis, non-high-risk, the Commission should, after consulting the Board, provide guidelines specifying that practical implementation, completed by a comprehensive list of practical examples of use cases of AI systems that are high-risk and use cases that are not.

1465. **(101)** Providers of general-purpose AI models have a particular role and responsibility along the AI value chain, as the models they provide may form the basis for a range of downstream systems, often provided by downstream providers that necessitate a good understanding of the models and their capabilities, both to enable the integration of such models into their products, and to fulfil their obligations under this or other regulations. Therefore, proportionate transparency measures should be laid down, including the drawing up and keeping up to date of documentation, and the provision of information on the general-purpose AI model for its usage by the downstream providers. Technical documentation should be prepared and kept up to date by the general-purpose AI model provider for the purpose of making it available, upon request, to the AI Office and the national competent authorities. The minimal set of elements to be included in such documentation should be set out in specific annexes to this Regulation. The Commission should be empowered to amend those annexes by means of delegated acts in light of evolving technological developments.

1466. **(115)** Providers of general-purpose AI models with systemic risks should assess and mitigate possible systemic risks. If, despite efforts to identify and prevent risks related to a general-purpose AI model that may present systemic risks, the development or use of the model causes a serious incident, the general-purpose AI model provider should without undue delay keep track of the incident and report any relevant information and possible corrective measures to the Commission and national competent authorities. Furthermore, providers should ensure an adequate level of cybersecurity protection for the model and its physical infrastructure, if appropriate, along the entire model lifecycle. Cybersecurity protection related to systemic risks associated with malicious use or attacks should duly consider accidental model leakage, unauthorised releases, circumvention of safety measures, and defence against cyberattacks, unauthorised access or model theft. That protection could be facilitated by securing model weights, algorithms, servers, and data sets, such as through operational security measures for information security, specific cybersecurity policies, adequate technical and established solutions, and cyber and physical access controls, appropriate to the relevant circumstances and the risks involved.

1467. **(116)** The AI Office should encourage and facilitate the drawing up, review and adaptation of codes of practice, taking into account international approaches. All providers of general-purpose AI models could be invited to participate. To ensure that the codes of practice reflect the state of the art and duly take into account a diverse set of perspectives, the AI Office should collaborate with relevant national competent authorities, and could, where appropriate, consult with civil society organisations and other relevant stakeholders and experts, including the Scientific Panel, for the drawing up of such codes. Codes of practice should cover obligations for providers of general-purpose AI models and of general-purpose AI models presenting systemic risks. In addition, as regards systemic risks, codes of practice should help to establish a risk taxonomy of the type and nature of the systemic risks at Union level, including their sources. Codes of practice should also be focused on specific risk assessment and mitigation measures.

1468. **(126)** In order to carry out third-party conformity assessments when so required, notified bodies should be notified under this Regulation by the national competent authorities, provided that they comply with a set of requirements, in particular on independence, competence, absence of conflicts of interests and suitable cybersecurity requirements. Notification of those bodies should be sent by national competent authorities to the Commission and the other Member States by means of the electronic notification tool developed and managed by the Commission pursuant to Article R23 of Annex I to Decision No 768/2008/EC.

1469. **(138)** AI is a rapidly developing family of technologies that requires regulatory oversight and a safe and controlled space for experimentation, while ensuring responsible innovation and integration of appropriate safeguards and risk mitigation measures. To ensure a legal framework that promotes innovation, is future-proof and resilient to disruption, Member States should ensure that their national competent authorities establish at least one AI regulatory sandbox at national level to facilitate the development and testing of innovative AI systems under strict regulatory oversight before these systems are placed on the market or otherwise put into service. Member States could also fulfil this obligation through participating in already existing regulatory sandboxes or establishing jointly a sandbox with one or more Member States' competent authorities, insofar as this participation provides equivalent level of national coverage for the participating Member States. AI regulatory sandboxes could be established in physical, digital or hybrid form and may accommodate physical as well as digital products. Establishing authorities should also ensure that the AI regulatory sandboxes have the adequate resources for their functioning, including financial and human resources.

1470. **(139)** The objectives of the AI regulatory sandboxes should be to foster AI innovation by establishing a controlled experimentation and testing environment in the development and pre-marketing phase with a view to ensuring compliance of the innovative AI systems with this Regulation and other relevant Union and national law. Moreover, the AI regulatory sandboxes should aim to enhance legal certainty for innovators and the competent authorities' oversight and understanding of the opportunities, emerging risks and the impacts of AI use, to facilitate regulatory learning for authorities and undertakings, including with a view to future adaptions of the legal framework, to support cooperation and the sharing of best practices with the authorities involved in the AI regulatory sandbox, and to accelerate access to markets, including by removing barriers for SMEs, including start-ups. AI regulatory sandboxes should be widely available throughout the Union, and particular attention should be given to their accessibility for SMEs, including start-ups. The participation in the AI regulatory sandbox should focus on issues that raise legal uncertainty for providers and prospective providers to innovate, experiment with AI in the Union and contribute to evidence-based regulatory learning. The supervision of the AI systems in the AI regulatory sandbox should therefore cover their development, training, testing and validation before the systems are placed on the market or put into service, as well as the notion and occurrence of substantial modification that may require a new conformity assessment procedure. Any significant risks identified during the development and testing of such AI systems should result in adequate mitigation and, failing that, in the suspension of the development and testing process. Where appropriate, national competent authorities establishing AI regulatory sandboxes should cooperate with other relevant authorities, including those supervising the protection of fundamental rights, and could allow for the involvement of other actors within the AI ecosystem such as national or European standardisation organisations, notified bodies, testing and experimentation facilities, research and experimentation labs, European Digital Innovation Hubs and relevant stakeholder and civil society organisations. To ensure uniform implementation across the Union and economies of scale, it is appropriate to establish common rules for the AI regulatory sandboxes' implementation and a framework for cooperation between the relevant authorities involved in the supervision of the sandboxes. AI regulatory sandboxes established under this Regulation should be without prejudice to other law allowing for the establishment of other sandboxes aiming to ensure compliance with law other than this Regulation. Where appropriate, relevant competent authorities in charge of those other regulatory sandboxes should consider the benefits of using those sandboxes also for the purpose of ensuring compliance of AI systems with this Regulation. Upon agreement between the national competent authorities and the participants in the AI regulatory sandbox, testing in real world conditions may also be operated and supervised in the framework of the AI regulatory sandbox.

1471. (149) In order to facilitate a smooth, effective and harmonised implementation of this Regulation a Board should be established. The Board should reflect the various interests of the AI eco-system and be composed of representatives of the Member States. The Board should be responsible for a number of advisory tasks, including issuing opinions, recommendations, advice or contributing to guidance on matters related to the implementation of this Regulation, including on enforcement matters, technical specifications or existing standards regarding the requirements established in this Regulation and providing advice to the Commission and the Member States and their national competent authorities on specific questions related to AI. In order to give some flexibility to Member States in the designation of their representatives in the

Board, such representatives may be any persons belonging to public entities who should have the relevant competences and powers to facilitate coordination at national level and contribute to the achievement of the Board's tasks. The Board should establish two standing sub-groups to provide a platform for cooperation and exchange among market surveillance authorities and notifying authorities on issues related, respectively, to market surveillance and notified bodies. The standing subgroup for market surveillance should act as the administrative cooperation group (ADCO) for this Regulation within the meaning of Article 30 of Regulation (EU) 2019/1020. In accordance with Article 33 of that Regulation, the Commission should support the activities of the standing subgroup for market surveillance by undertaking market evaluations or studies, in particular with a view to identifying aspects of this Regulation requiring specific and urgent coordination among market surveillance authorities. The Board may establish other standing or temporary sub-groups as appropriate for the purpose of examining specific issues. The Board should also cooperate, as appropriate, with relevant Union bodies, experts groups and networks active in the context of relevant Union law, including in particular those active under relevant Union law on data, digital products and services.

1472. (153) Member States hold a key role in the application and enforcement of this Regulation. In that respect, each Member State should designate at least one notifying authority and at least one market surveillance authority as national competent authorities for the purpose of supervising the application and implementation of this Regulation. Member States may decide to appoint any kind of public entity to perform the tasks of the national competent authorities within the meaning of this Regulation, in accordance with their specific national organisational characteristics and needs. In order to increase organisation efficiency on the side of Member States and to set a single point of contact vis-à-vis the public and other counterparts at Member State and Union levels, each Member State should designate a market surveillance authority to act as a single point of contact.

1473. (154) The national competent authorities should exercise their powers independently, impartially and without bias, so as to safeguard the principles of objectivity of their activities and tasks and to ensure the application and implementation of this Regulation. The members of these authorities should refrain from any action incompatible with their duties and should be subject to confidentiality rules under this Regulation.

1474. (156) In order to ensure an appropriate and effective enforcement of the requirements and obligations set out by this Regulation, which is Union harmonisation legislation, the system of market surveillance and compliance of products established by Regulation (EU) 2019/1020 should apply in its entirety. Market surveillance authorities designated pursuant to this Regulation should have all enforcement powers laid down in this Regulation and in Regulation

(EU) 2019/1020 and should exercise their powers and carry out their duties independently, impartially and without bias. Although the majority of AI systems are not subject to specific requirements and obligations under this Regulation, market surveillance authorities may take measures in relation to all AI systems when they present a risk in accordance with this Regulation. Due to the specific nature of Union institutions, agencies and bodies falling within the scope of this Regulation, it is appropriate to designate the European Data Protection Supervisor as a competent market surveillance authority for them. This should be without prejudice to the designation of national competent authorities by the Member States. Market surveillance activities should not affect the ability of the supervised entities to carry out their tasks independently, when such independence is required by Union law.

70.2. General Approach

70.2.1 Preamble

1475. The competent national authorities play a crucial role in the implementation of AI technology regulations.

70.2.2 Guiding Principles

1476. At local level, regulation is organised as follows:
- at least one market surveillance authority;
- at least one notifying authority.

1477. Note:
- (1) Where there is more than one authority for either category of authority, the Member State concerned must designate a lead authority.

70.3. Market Surveillance Authority

1478. The main elements are as follows:

NO.	THEME	SPECIFICATION
1.	Designation	By each Member State
2.	Number	At least one
3.	Creation	Before 2 August 2025
4.	Nature	Independent authority
5.	Decision	Impartial and without bias

NO.	THEME	SPECIFICATION
6.	Incompatibility	Control by the authority
7.	Organisation	Rules of procedure
8.	Activities	Tasks listed in the instrument of creation Communication of this list, as well as any subsequent changes thereto, to the European Commission
9.	Information	Existence and tasks are made publicly available
10.	Single point of contact	In the case of more than one authority, designation of the market supervisory authority acting as the single point of contact Note: • (1) The European Commission makes the list of the single points of contact publicly available
11.	Resources	Member States shall ensure that the authority is provided with adequate: • technical resources • financial resources • human resources
12.	Competence of personnel	Knowledge of legal requirements Knowledge of standards Cybersecurity Data Fundamental rights Personal data protection Health risks Safety risks AI technologies Data computing
13.	Cybersecurity	Definition of measures appropriate to the situation and to developments in AI technologies
14.	Confidentiality	In accordance with the procedures set out in the AIA (see Art. 78)
15.	Report	First report to the European Commission on 2 August 2025 and once every two years thereafter

70.4. Notifying Authority

1479. The main elements are as follows:

NO.	THEME	SPECIFICATION
1.	Designation	By each Member State
2.	Number	At least one
3.	Creation	Before 2 August 2025
4.	Nature	Independent authority
5.	Decision	Impartial and without bias
6.	Incompatibility	Control by the authority
7.	Organisation	Rules of procedures
8.	Activities	Tasks listed in the instrument of creation Communication of this list, as well as any subsequent changes thereto, to the European Commission
9.	Information	Existence and tasks are made publicly available
10.	Resources	Member States shall ensure that the authority is provided with adequate: • technical resources • financial resources • human resources
11.	Competence of personnel	Knowledge of legal requirements Knowledge of standards Cybersecurity Data Fundamental rights Personal data protection Health risks Safety risks AI technologies Data computing
12.	Cybersecurity	Definition of measures appropriate to the situation and to developments in AI technologies
13.	Confidentiality	In accordance with the procedures set out in the AIA (see Art. 78)
14.	Report	First report to the European Commission on 2 August 2025 and once every two years thereafter

70.5. EU Institutions, Bodies, Offices and Agencies

1480. The European Data Protection Supervisor (EDPS) acts as the competent authority for the supervision of EU institutions, bodies, offices and agencies.

CHAPTER VIII

EU DATABASE OF HIGH-RISK SYSTEMS

1481. Key takeaways: In order to control developments in AI technologies and manage systemic risks, a database of high-risk AI systems is set up and managed by the European Commission.

71 ARTICLE 71. EU DATABASE FOR HIGH-RISK AI SYSTEMS LISTED IN ANNEX III

1.The Commission shall, in collaboration with the Member States, set up and maintain an EU database containing information referred to in paragraphs 2 and 3 of this Article concerning high-risk AI systems referred to in Article 6(2) which are registered in accordance with Articles 49 and 60 and AI systems that are not considered as high-risk pursuant to Article 6(3) and which are registered in accordance with Article 6(4) and Article 49. When setting the functional specifications of such database, the Commission shall consult the relevant experts, and when updating the functional specifications of such database, the Commission shall consult the Board

2. The data listed in Sections A and B of Annex VIII shall be entered into the EU database by the provider or, where applicable, by the authorised representative.

3. The data listed in Section C of Annex VIII shall be entered into the EU database by the deployer who is, or who acts on behalf of, a public authority, agency or body, in accordance with Article 49(3) and (4).

4. With the exception of the section referred to in Article 49(4) and Article 60(4), point (c), the information contained in the EU database registered in accordance with Article 49 shall be accessible and publicly available in a user-friendly manner. The information should be easily navigable and machine-readable. The information registered in accordance with Article 60 shall be accessible only to market surveillance authorities and the Commission, unless the prospective provider or provider has given consent for also making the information accessible the public.

5. The EU database shall contain personal data only in so far as necessary for collecting and processing information in accordance with this Regulation. That information shall include the names and contact details of natural persons who are responsible for registering the system and have the legal authority to represent the provider or the deployer, as applicable.

6. The Commission shall be the controller of the EU database. It shall make available to providers, prospective providers and deployers adequate technical and administrative support. The EU database shall comply with the applicable accessibility requirements.

71.1. Recitals

1482. **(53)** It is also important to clarify that there may be specific cases in which AI systems referred to in pre-defined areas specified in this Regulation do not lead to a significant risk of harm to the legal interests protected under those areas because they do not materially influence the decision-making or do not harm those interests substantially. For the purposes of this Regulation, an AI system that does not materially influence the outcome of decision-making should be understood to be an AI system that does not have an impact on the substance, and thereby the outcome, of decision-making, whether human or automated. An AI system that does not materially influence the outcome of decision-making could include situations in which one or more of the following conditions are fulfilled. The first such condition should be that the AI system is intended to perform a narrow procedural task, such as an AI system that transforms unstructured data into structured data, an AI system that classifies incoming documents into categories or an AI system that is used to detect duplicates among a large number of applications. Those tasks are of such narrow and limited nature that they pose only limited risks which are not increased through the use of an AI system in a context that is listed as a high-risk use in an annex to this Regulation. The second condition should be that the task performed by the AI system is intended to improve the result of a previously completed human activity that may be relevant for the purposes of the high-risk uses listed in an annex to this Regulation. Considering those characteristics, the AI system provides only an additional layer to a human activity with consequently lowered risk. That condition would, for example, apply to AI systems that are intended to improve the language used in previously drafted documents, for example in relation to professional tone, academic style of language or by aligning text to a certain brand messaging. The third condition should be that the AI system is intended to detect decision-making patterns or deviations from prior decision-making patterns. The risk would be lowered because the use of the AI system follows a previously completed human assessment which it is not meant to replace or influence, without proper human review. Such AI systems include for instance those that, given a certain grading pattern of a teacher, can be used to check ex post whether the teacher may have deviated from the grading pattern so as to flag potential inconsistencies or anomalies. The fourth condition should be that the AI system is intended to perform a task that is only preparatory to an assessment relevant for the purposes of the AI systems listed in an annex to this Regulation, thus making the possible impact of the output of the system very low in terms of representing a risk for the assessment to follow. That condition covers, inter alia, smart solutions for file handling, which include various functions from indexing, searching, text and speech processing or linking data to other data sources, or AI systems used for translation of initial documents. In any case, AI systems used in high-risk use-cases listed in an annex to this Regulation should be considered to pose significant risks of harm to the health, safety or fundamental rights if the AI system implies profiling within the meaning of Article 4, point (4) of Regulation (EU) 2016/679 or Article 3, point (4) of Directive (EU) 2016/680 or Article 3, point (5) of Regulation (EU) 2018/1725. To ensure traceability and transparency, a provider who considers that an AI system is not high-risk on the basis of the conditions referred to above should draw up documentation of the assessment before that system is placed on the market or put into service and should provide that documentation to national competent authorities upon request. Such a provider should be obliged to register the AI system in the EU database established under this Regulation. With a view to providing further guidance for the practical implementation of the conditions under which the AI systems listed in an annex to this Regulation are, on an exceptional basis, non-high-risk, the Commission should, after consulting the Board, provide guidelines specifying that practical implementation, completed by a comprehensive list of practical examples of use cases of AI systems that are high-risk and use cases that are not.

1483. (131) In order to facilitate the work of the Commission and the Member States in the AI field as well as to increase the transparency towards the public, providers of high-risk AI systems other than those related to products falling within the scope of relevant existing Union harmonisation legislation, as well as providers who consider that an AI system listed in the high-risk use cases in an annex to this Regulation is not high-risk on the basis of a derogation, should be required to register themselves and information about their AI system in an EU database, to be established and managed by the Commission. Before using an AI system listed in the high-risk use cases in an annex to this Regulation, deployers of high-risk AI systems that are public authorities, agencies or bodies, should register themselves in such database and select the system that they envisage to use. Other deployers should be entitled to do so voluntarily. This section of the EU database should be publicly accessible, free of charge, the information should be easily navigable, understandable and machine-readable. The EU database should also be user-friendly, for example by providing search functionalities, including through keywords, allowing the general public to find relevant information to be submitted upon the registration of high-risk AI systems and on the use case of high-risk AI systems, set out in an annex to this Regulation, to which the high-risk AI systems correspond. Any substantial modification of high-risk AI systems should also be registered in the EU database. For high-risk AI systems in the area of law enforcement, migration, asylum and border control management, the registration obligations should be fulfilled in a secure non-public section of the EU database. Access to the secure non-public section should be strictly limited to the Commission as well as to market surveillance authorities with regard to their national section of that database. High-risk AI systems in the area of critical infrastructure should only be registered at national level. The Commission should be the controller of the EU database, in accordance with Regulation (EU) 2018/1725. In order to ensure the full functionality of the EU database, when deployed, the procedure for setting the database should include the development of functional specifications by the Commission and an independent audit report. The Commission should take into account cybersecurity risks when carrying out its tasks as data controller on the EU database. In order to maximise the availability and use of the EU database by the public, the EU database, including the information made available through it, should comply with requirements under the Directive (EU) 2019/882.

71.2. General Approach

71.2.1 Preamble

1484. The purpose of this database is to group together certain high-risk AI systems in order to promote a policy taking into account the surveillance and development of regulations.

71.2.2 Guiding Principles

1485. The purposes of such a database are:

- to monitor harmonisation processes;
- to improve both technical and legal regulation;
- to define a coordinated risk management policy;
- to be able to intervene in a fast and agile manner in the event of serious or serial risks.

1486. The database is limited to high-risk AI systems listed in Annex III.[1] High-risk AI systems falling under the list of harmonisation legislation[2] are subject to other forms of compilation which enable to achieve the same objectives.[3]

71.2.3 Typology

1487. The systems concerned are the high-risk systems listed in Annex III, which are as follows:

NO.	THEME	SPECIFICATION	REFERENCE
1.	Access to self-employment		AIA, Annex III(4)
2.	Asylum	In so far as use is permitted under relevant Union or national law	AIA, Annex III(7)
3.	Biometrics	In so far as use is permitted under relevant Union or national law	AIA, Annex III(1)
4.	Border control management	In so far as use is permitted under relevant Union or national law	AIA, Annex III(7)
5.	Critical infrastructure	E.g. road traffic, supply of water, gas, heating or electricity	AIA, Annex III(2)
6.	Democracy	Democratic processes	AIA, Annex III(8)
7.	Education		AIA, Annex III(3)
8.	Employment		AIA, Annex III(4)
9.	Essential private services	Access and enjoyment	AIA, Annex III(5)
10.	Essential public benefits	Access and enjoyment	AIA, Annex III(5)
11.	Essential public services	Access and enjoyment	AIA, Annex III(5)
12.	Justice	Administration of justice	AIA, Annex III(8)
13.	Law enforcement	In so far as use is permitted under relevant Union or national law	AIA, Annex III(6)
14.	Migration	In so far as use is permitted under relevant Union or national law	AIA, Annex III(7)

1 AI Act, Art. 6(2).
2 AI Act, Art. 6(1).
3 Machinery Regulation (EU) 2023/1230 of 14 June 2023 concerning the European Injury Database (EU-IDB), Art. 6(5)(d).

NO.	THEME	SPECIFICATION	REFERENCE
15.	Training		AIA, Annex III(3)
16.	Workers' management		AIA, Annex III(4)

1488. The data making up the EU database is submitted by the provider or its authorised representative.

71.3. Composition

1489. It is as follows:

NO.	THEME	SPECIFICATION	RESPONSIBILITY
1.	Identity	Name Address Contact details	Provider Authorised representative
2.	Information is submitted by another person on behalf of the provider	Name Address Contact details	Third party on behalf of the provider
3.	AI system (Identification)	Name References allowing identification and traceability	Provider
4.	AI system (Recipient)	Description of the intended purpose of the AI system and of the components and function	Provider
5.	Functioning	Input data and operating logic	Provider
6.	Market (Country)	List of countries concerned	Provider
7.	Market (Status)	Status: • on the market • in service • recalled	Provider
8.	EU declaration	Copy	Provider
9.	Certificate	Notified body (name, identification number) Certificate: • type • number • expiry date • scanned copy	Provider

NO.	THEME	SPECIFICATION	RESPONSIBILITY
10.	Instructions for use	Exceptions: • law enforcement • migration • asylum • border control management	Provider
11.	Additional information	A URL Note: • (1) this information is optional	Provider
12.	AI system declared not to be high-risk	Information listed in Section B of Annex VIII	Provider
13.	Deployed high-risk AI system	Identification: • name • address • contact details	Deployer
		Information is submitted by another person on behalf of the deployer: • name • address • contact details	Third party on behalf of the deployer
		The URL of the entry of the AI system in the EU database	Deployer
		Fundamental rights impact assessment: • summary of the findings	Deployer
		Personal data Impact assessment • summary	Deployer

CHAPTER IX
POST-MARKET MONITORING, INFORMATION SHARING AND MARKET SURVEILLANCE

1490. Key takeaways: This Chapter mainly concerns:

- the post-market monitoring of AI systems;
- controls;
- associated procedures.

SECTION 1. POST-MARKET MONITORING

72 ARTICLE 72. POST-MARKET MONITORING BY PROVIDERS AND POST-MARKET MONITORING PLAN FOR HIGH-RISK AI SYSTEMS

1. Providers shall establish and document a post-market monitoring system in a manner that is proportionate to the nature of the AI technologies and the risks of the high-risk AI system.

2. The post-market monitoring system shall actively and systematically collect, document and analyse relevant data which may be provided by deployers or which may be collected through other sources on the performance of high-risk AI systems throughout their lifetime, and which allow the provider to evaluate the continuous compliance of AI systems with the requirements set out in Chapter III, Section 2. Where relevant, post-market monitoring shall include an analysis of the interaction with other AI systems. This obligation shall not cover sensitive operational data of deployers which are law-enforcement authorities.

3. The post-market monitoring system shall be based on a post-market monitoring plan. The post-market monitoring plan shall be part of the technical documentation referred to in Annex IV. The Commission shall adopt an implementing act laying down detailed provisions establishing a template for the post-market monitoring plan and the list of elements to be included in the plan by 2 February 2026. That implementing act shall be adopted in accordance with the examination procedure referred to in Article 98(2).

4. For high-risk AI systems covered by the Union harmonisation legislation listed in Section A of Annex I, where a post-market monitoring system and plan are already established under that legislation, in order to ensure consistency, avoid duplications and minimise additional burdens, providers shall have a choice of integrating, as appropriate, the necessary elements described in paragraphs 1, 2 and 3 using the template referred in paragraph 3 into systems and plans already existing under that legislation, provided that it achieves an equivalent level of protection.

The first subparagraph of this paragraph shall also apply to high-risk AI systems referred to in point 5 of Annex III placed on the market or put into service by financial institutions that are subject to requirements under Union financial services law regarding their internal governance, arrangements or processes.

72.1. Recitals

1491. (71) Having comprehensible information on how high-risk AI systems have been developed and how they perform throughout their lifetime is essential to enable traceability of those systems, verify compliance with the requirements under this Regulation, as well as monitoring of their operations and post market monitoring. This requires keeping records and the availability of technical documentation, containing information which is necessary to assess the compliance of the AI system with the relevant requirements and facilitate post market monitoring. Such information should include the general characteristics, capabilities and limitations of the system, algorithms, data, training, testing and validation processes used as well as documentation on the relevant risk-management system and drawn in a clear and comprehensive form. The technical documentation should be kept up to date, appropriately throughout the lifetime of the AI system. Furthermore, high-risk AI systems should technically allow for the automatic recording of events, by means of logs, over the duration of the lifetime of the system.

1492. (81) The provider should establish a sound quality management system, ensure the accomplishment of the required conformity assessment procedure, draw up the relevant documentation and establish a robust post-market monitoring system. Providers of high-risk AI systems that are subject to obligations regarding quality management systems under relevant sectoral Union law should have the possibility to include the elements of the quality management system provided for in this Regulation as part of the existing quality management system provided for in that other sectoral Union law. The complementarity between this Regulation and existing sectoral Union law should also be taken into account in future standardisation activities or guidance adopted by the Commission. Public authorities which put into service high-risk AI systems for their own use may adopt and implement the rules for the quality management system as part of the quality management system adopted at a national or regional level, as appropriate, taking into account the specificities of the sector and the competences and organisation of the public authority concerned.

1493. (114) The providers of general-purpose AI models presenting systemic risks should be subject, in addition to the obligations provided for providers of general-purpose AI models, to obligations aimed at identifying and mitigating those risks and ensuring an adequate level of cybersecurity protection, regardless of whether it is provided as a standalone model or embedded in an AI system or a product. To achieve those objectives, this Regulation should require providers to perform the necessary model evaluations, in particular prior to its first placing on the market, including conducting and documenting adversarial testing of models, also, as appropriate, through internal or independent external testing. In addition, providers of general-purpose AI models with systemic risks should continuously assess and mitigate systemic risks, including for example by putting in place risk-management policies, such as accountability and governance processes, implementing post-market monitoring, taking appropriate measures along the entire model's lifecycle and cooperating with relevant actors along the AI value chain.

1494. (155) In order to ensure that providers of high-risk AI systems can take into account the experience on the use of high-risk AI systems for improving their systems and the design and development process or can take any possible corrective action in a timely manner, all providers should have a post-market monitoring system in place. Where relevant, post-market monitoring should include an analysis of the interaction with other AI systems including other devices and software. Post-market monitoring should not cover sensitive operational data of deployers which are law enforcement authorities. This system is also key to ensure that the possible risks emerging from AI systems which continue to 'learn' after being placed on the market or put into service can be more efficiently and timely addressed. In this context, providers should also be required to have a system in place to report to the relevant authorities any serious incidents resulting from the use of their AI systems, meaning incident or malfunctioning leading to death or serious damage to health, serious and irreversible disruption of the management and operation of critical infrastructure, infringements of obligations under Union law intended to protect fundamental rights or serious damage to property or the environment.

1495. (158) Union financial services law includes internal governance and risk-management rules and requirements which are applicable to regulated financial institutions in the course of provision of those services, including when they make use of AI systems. In order to ensure coherent application and enforcement of the obligations under this Regulation and relevant rules and requirements of the Union financial services legal acts, the competent authorities for the supervision and enforcement of those legal acts, in particular competent authorities as defined in Regulation (EU) No 575/2013 of the European Parliament and of the Council[1] and Directives 2008/48/EC,[2] 2009/138/EC,[3] 2013/36/EU,[4] 2014/17/EU[5] and (EU) 2016/97[6] of the European Parliament and of the Council, should be designated, within their respective competences, as competent authorities for the purpose of supervising the implementation of this Regulation, including for market surveillance activities, as regards AI systems provided or used by regulated and supervised financial institutions unless Member States decide to designate another authority to fulfil these market surveillance tasks. Those competent authorities should have all powers under this Regulation and Regulation (EU) 2019/1020 to enforce the requirements and obligations of this Regulation, including powers to carry our *ex post* market surveillance activities that can be integrated, as appropriate, into their existing supervisory mechanisms and procedures under the relevant Union financial services law. It is appropriate to envisage that, when acting as market surveillance authorities under this Regulation, the national authorities responsible for the supervision of credit institutions regulated under Directive 2013/36/EU, which are participating in the Single Supervisory Mechanism established by Council Regulation (EU) No 1024/2013,[7] should report, without delay, to the European Central Bank any information identified in the course of their market surveillance activities that may be of potential interest for the European Central Bank's prudential supervisory tasks as specified in that Regulation. To further enhance the consistency between this Regulation and the rules applicable to credit institutions

---

1 Regulation (EU) No 575/2013 of the European Parliament and of the Council of 26 June 2013 on prudential requirements for credit institutions and investment firms and amending Regulation (EU) No 648/2012, [2013] OJ L176/1.

2 Directive 2008/48/EC of the European Parliament and of the Council of 23 April 2008 on credit agreements for consumers and repealing Council Directive 87/102/EEC, [2008] OJ L133/66.

3 Directive 2009/138/EC of the European Parliament and of the Council of 25 November 2009 on the taking-up and pursuit of the business of Insurance and Reinsurance (Solvency II), [2009] OJ L335/1.

4 Directive 2013/36/EU of the European Parliament and of the Council of 26 June 2013 on access to the activity of credit institutions and the prudential supervision of credit institutions and investment firms, amending Directive 2002/87/EC and repealing Directives 2006/48/EC and 2006/49/EC, [2013] OJ L176/338.

5 Directive 2014/17/EU of the European Parliament and of the Council of 4 February 2014 on credit agreements for consumers relating to residential immovable property and amending Directives 2008/48/EC and 2013/36/EU and Regulation (EU) No 1093/2010, [2014] OJ L60/34.

6 Directive (EU) 2016/97 of the European Parliament and of the Council of 20 January 2016 on insurance distribution, [2016] OJ L26/19.

7 Council Regulation (EU) No 1024/2013 of 15 October 2013 conferring specific tasks on the European Central Bank concerning policies relating to the prudential supervision of credit institutions, [2013] OJ L287/63.

regulated under Directive 2013/36/EU, it is also appropriate to integrate some of the providers' procedural obligations in relation to risk management, post marketing monitoring and documentation into the existing obligations and procedures under Directive 2013/36/EU. In order to avoid overlaps, limited derogations should also be envisaged in relation to the quality management system of providers and the monitoring obligation placed on deployers of high-risk AI systems to the extent that these apply to credit institutions regulated by Directive 2013/36/EU. The same regime should apply to insurance and re-insurance undertakings and insurance holding companies under Directive 2009/138/EC and the insurance intermediaries under Directive (EU) 2016/97 and other types of financial institutions subject to requirements regarding internal governance, arrangements or processes established pursuant to the relevant Union financial services law to ensure consistency and equal treatment in the financial sector.

72.2. *General Approach*

72.2.1 Preamble

1496. Monitoring is a key requirement for keeping the AI technology market in operational condition and ensure safe and trustworthy dissemination path.

72.2.2 Definition

1497. 'Post-market monitoring system' means 'all activities carried out by providers of AI systems to collect and review experience gained from the use of AI systems they place on the market or put into service for the purpose of identifying any need to immediately apply any necessary corrective or preventive actions'.[8]

72.3. *Classification*

1498. Monitoring includes the following components:

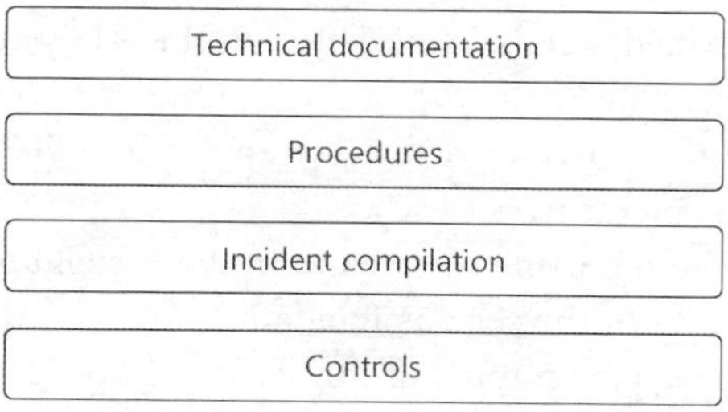

[8] AI Act, Art. 3(25).

72.4. Modalities

1499. Monitoring of high-risk AI systems is based on:

- a system of elements to be monitored;
- procedures for collecting and monitoring usage and incidents;
- consolidation of this documentation within the general technical documentation specific to high-risk AI systems.

72.5. Characteristics

1500. They are as follows:

NO.	THEME	SPECIFICATION
1.	Initialisation	Start of marketing
2.	Monitoring plan	Collection and analysis of relevant data
3.	Duration of monitoring	Lifecycle of high-risk AI systems
4.	Subject-matter of monitoring	Compliance with requirements Management of difficulties

SECTION 2. SHARING OF INFORMATION ON SERIOUS INCIDENTS

73 ARTICLE 73. REPORTING OF SERIOUS INCIDENTS

1. Providers of high-risk AI systems placed on the Union market shall report any serious incident to the market surveillance authorities of the Member States where that incident occurred.

2. The report referred to in paragraph 1 shall be made immediately after the provider has established a causal link between the AI system and the serious incident or the reasonable likelihood of such a link, and, in any event, not later than 15 days after the provider or, where applicable, the deployer, becomes aware of the serious incident.

The period for the reporting referred to in the first subparagraph shall take account of the severity of the serious incident.

3. Notwithstanding paragraph 2 of this Article, in the event of a widespread infringement or a serious incident as defined in Article 3, point (49)(b), the report referred to in paragraph 1 of this Article shall be provided immediately, and not later than two days after the provider or, where applicable, the deployer becomes aware of that incident.

4. Notwithstanding paragraph 2, in the event of the death of a person, the report shall be provided immediately after the provider or the deployer has established, or as soon as it suspects, a causal relationship between the high-risk AI system and the serious incident, but not later than 10 days after the date on which the provider or, where applicable, the deployer becomes aware of the serious incident.

5. Where necessary to ensure timely reporting, the provider or, where applicable, the deployer, may submit an initial report that is incomplete, followed by a complete report.

6. Following the reporting of a serious incident pursuant to paragraph 1, the provider shall, without delay, perform the necessary investigations in relation to the serious incident and the AI system concerned. This shall include a risk assessment of the incident, and corrective action.

The provider shall cooperate with the competent authorities, and where relevant with the notified body concerned, during the investigations referred to in the first subparagraph, and shall not perform any investigation which involves altering the AI system concerned in a way which may affect any subsequent evaluation of the causes of the incident, prior to informing the competent authorities of such action.

7. Upon receiving a notification related to a serious incident referred to in Article 3, point (49)(c), the relevant market surveillance authority shall inform the national public authorities or bodies referred to in Article 77(1). The Commission shall develop dedicated guidance to facilitate compliance with the obligations set out in paragraph 1 of this Article. That guidance shall be issued by 2 August 2025, and shall be assessed regularly.

8. The market surveillance authority shall take appropriate measures, as provided for in Article 19 of Regulation (EU) 2019/1020, within seven days from the date it received the notification referred to in paragraph 1 of this Article, and shall follow the notification procedures as provided in that Regulation.

9. For high-risk AI systems referred to in Annex III that are placed on the market or put into service by providers that are subject to Union legislative instruments laying down reporting obligations equivalent to those set out in this Regulation, the notification of serious incidents shall be limited to those referred to in Article 3, point (49)(c).

10. For high-risk AI systems which are safety components of devices, or are themselves devices, covered by Regulations (EU) 2017/745 and (EU) 2017/746, the notification of serious incidents shall be limited to those referred to in Article 3, point (49)(c) of this Regulation, and shall be made to the national competent authority chosen for that purpose by the Member States where the incident occurred.

11. National competent authorities shall immediately notify the Commission of any serious incident, whether or not they have taken action on it, in accordance with Article 20 of Regulation (EU) 2019/1020.

73.1. Recitals

1501. (115) Providers of general-purpose AI models with systemic risks should assess and mitigate possible systemic risks. If, despite efforts to identify and prevent risks related to a general-purpose AI model that may present systemic risks, the development or use of the model causes a serious incident, the general-purpose AI model provider should without undue delay keep track of the incident and report any relevant information and possible corrective measures to the Commission and national competent authorities. Furthermore, providers should ensure an adequate level of cybersecurity protection for the model and its physical infrastructure, if appropriate, along the entire model lifecycle. Cybersecurity protection related to systemic risks associated with malicious use or attacks should duly consider accidental model leakage, unauthorised releases, circumvention of safety measures, and defence against cyberattacks, unauthorised access or model theft. That protection could be facilitated by securing model weights, algorithms, servers, and data sets, such as through operational security measures for information security, specific cybersecurity policies, adequate technical and established solutions, and cyber and physical access controls, appropriate to the relevant circumstances and the risks involved.

1502. (155) In order to ensure that providers of high-risk AI systems can take into account the experience on the use of high-risk AI systems for improving their systems and the design and development process or can take any possible corrective action in a timely manner, all providers should have a post-market monitoring system in place. Where relevant, post-market monitoring should include an analysis of the interaction with other AI systems including other devices and software. Post-market monitoring should not cover sensitive operational data of deployers which are law enforcement authorities. This system is also key to ensure that the possible risks emerging from AI systems which continue to 'learn' after being placed on the market or put into service can be more efficiently and timely addressed. In this context, providers should also be required to have a system in place to report to the relevant authorities any serious incidents resulting from the use of their AI systems, meaning incident or malfunctioning leading to death or serious damage to health, serious and irreversible disruption of the management and operation of critical infrastructure, infringements of obligations under Union law intended to protect fundamental rights or serious damage to property or the environment.

73.2. *General Approach*

73.2.1 Preamble

1503. Like personal data breaches, serious incidents involving high-risk AI systems must be reported in order to avoid negative effects.

73.2.2 Definition

1504. 'Serious incident' means 'an incident or malfunctioning of an AI system that directly or indirectly leads to any of the following:

(a) the death of a person, or serious harm to a person's health;

(b) a serious and irreversible disruption of the management or operation of critical infrastructure;

(c) the infringement of obligations under Union law intended to protect fundamental rights;

(d) serious harm to property or the environment'.[9]

73.3. *Guiding Principles*

1505. The reporting requirement is organised as follows:

Report

Deadline

Management

Feeback

73.4. *Report*

1506. The characteristics are as follows:

NO.	THEME	SPECIFICATION
1.	Reported items	Serious incidents
2.	Market surveillance authority	Where the incident or violation occurred

[9] AI Act, Art. 3(49).

NO.	THEME	SPECIFICATION
3.	Period	Immediately and, in any event, not later than 15 days
4.	Starting point of the deadline	Establishment of a causal link between the AI system and the incident or the reasonable likelihood of such a link

73.5. Find Out More

73.5.1 Toolbox

1507. The OECD has defined a classification for technology security incidents relating to AI systems: OECD, 'Defining AI incidents and related terms', *OECD Artificial Intelligence Papers,* No. 16, OECD, 6 May 2024.

SECTION 3. ENFORCEMENT

74 ARTICLE 74. MARKET SURVEILLANCE AND CONTROL OF AI SYSTEMS IN THE UNION MARKET

1. Regulation (EU) 2019/1020 shall apply to AI systems covered by this Regulation. For the purposes of the effective enforcement of this Regulation:

(a) any reference to an economic operator under Regulation (EU) 2019/1020 shall be understood as including all operators identified in Article 2(1) of this Regulation;

(b) any reference to a product under Regulation (EU) 2019/1020 shall be understood as including all AI systems falling within the scope of this Regulation.

2. As part of their reporting obligations under Article 34(4) of Regulation (EU) 2019/1020, the market surveillance authorities shall report annually to the Commission and relevant national competition authorities any information identified in the course of market surveillance activities that may be of potential interest for the application of Union law on competition rules. They shall also annually report to the Commission about the use of prohibited practices that occurred during that year and about the measures taken.

3. For high-risk AI systems related to products covered by the Union harmonisation legislation listed in Section A of Annex I, the market surveillance authority for the purposes of this Regulation shall be the authority responsible for market surveillance activities designated under those legal acts.

By derogation from the first subparagraph, and in appropriate circumstances, Member States may designate another relevant authority to act as a market surveillance authority, provided they ensure coordination with the relevant sectoral market surveillance authorities responsible for the enforcement of the Union harmonisation legislation listed in Annex I.

4. The procedures referred to in Articles 79 to 83 of this Regulation shall not apply to AI systems related to products covered by the Union harmonisation legislation listed in section A of Annex I, where such legal acts already provide for procedures ensuring an equivalent level of protection and having the same objective. In such cases, the relevant sectoral procedures shall apply instead.

5. Without prejudice to the powers of market surveillance authorities under Article 14 of Regulation (EU) 2019/1020, for the purpose of ensuring the effective enforcement of this Regulation, market surveillance authorities may exercise the powers referred to in Article 14(4), points (d) and (j), of that Regulation remotely, as appropriate.

6. For high-risk AI systems placed on the market, put into service, or used by financial institutions regulated by Union financial services law, the market surveillance authority for the purposes of this Regulation shall be the relevant national authority responsible for the financial supervision of those institutions under that legislation in so far as the placing on the market, putting into service, or the use of the AI system is in direct connection with the provision of those financial services.

7. By way of derogation from paragraph 6, in appropriate circumstances, and provided that coordination is ensured, another relevant authority may be identified by the Member State as market surveillance authority for the purposes of this Regulation.

National market surveillance authorities supervising regulated credit institutions regulated under Directive 2013/36/EU, which are participating in the Single Supervisory Mechanism established by Regulation (EU) No 1024/2013, should report, without delay, to the European Central Bank any information identified in the course of their market surveillance activities that may be of potential interest for the prudential supervisory tasks of the European Central Bank specified in that Regulation.

8. For high-risk AI systems listed in point 1 of Annex III to this Regulation, in so far as the systems are used for law enforcement purposes, border management and justice and democracy, and for high-risk AI systems listed in points 6, 7 and 8 of Annex III to this Regulation, Member States shall designate as market surveillance authorities for the purposes of this Regulation either the competent data protection supervisory authorities under Regulation (EU) 2016/679 or Directive (EU) 2016/680, or any other authority designated pursuant to the same conditions laid down in Articles 41 to 44 of Directive (EU) 2016/680. Market surveillance activities shall in no way affect the independence of judicial authorities, or otherwise interfere with their activities when acting in their judicial capacity.

9. Where Union institutions, bodies, offices or agencies fall within the scope of this Regulation, the European Data Protection Supervisor shall act as their market surveillance authority, except in relation to the Court of Justice of the European Union acting in its judicial capacity.

10. Member States shall facilitate coordination between market surveillance authorities designated under this Regulation and other relevant national authorities or bodies which supervise the application of Union harmonisation legislation listed in Annex I, or in other Union law, that might be relevant for the high-risk AI systems referred to in Annex III.

11. Market surveillance authorities and the Commission shall be able to propose joint activities, including joint investigations, to be conducted by either market surveillance authorities or market surveillance authorities jointly with the Commission, that have the aim of promoting compliance, identifying non-compliance, raising awareness or providing guidance in relation to this Regulation with respect to specific categories of high-risk AI systems that are found to present a serious risk across two or more Member States in accordance with Article 9 of Regulation (EU) 2019/1020. The AI Office shall provide coordination support for joint investigations.

12. Without prejudice to the powers provided for under Regulation (EU) 2019/1020, and where relevant and limited to what is necessary to fulfil their tasks, the market surveillance authorities shall be granted full access by providers to the documentation as well as the training, validation and testing data sets used for the development of high-risk AI systems, including, where appropriate and subject to security safeguards, through application programming interfaces (API) or other relevant technical means and tools enabling remote access.

13. Market surveillance authorities shall be granted access to the source code of the high-risk AI system upon a reasoned request and only when both of the following conditions are fulfilled:

(a) access to source code is necessary to assess the conformity of a high-risk AI system with the requirements set out in Chapter III, Section 2; and

(b) testing or auditing procedures and verifications based on the data and documentation provided by the provider have been exhausted or proved insufficient.

14. Any information or documentation obtained by market surveillance authorities shall be treated in accordance with the confidentiality obligations set out in Article 78.

74.1. Recitals

1508. **(33)** The use of those systems for the purpose of law enforcement should therefore be prohibited, except in exhaustively listed and narrowly defined situations, where the use is strictly necessary to achieve a substantial public interest, the importance of which outweighs the risks. Those situations involve the search for certain victims of crime including missing persons; certain threats to the life or to the physical safety of natural persons or of a terrorist attack; and the localisation or identification of perpetrators or suspects of the criminal offences listed in an annex to this Regulation, where those criminal offences are punishable in the Member State concerned by a custodial sentence or a detention order for a maximum period of at least four years and as they are defined in the law of that Member State. Such a threshold for the custodial sentence or detention order in accordance with national law contributes to ensuring that the offence should be serious enough to potentially justify the use of 'real-time' remote biometric identification systems. Moreover, the list of criminal offences provided in an annex to this Regulation is based on the 32 criminal offences listed in the Council Framework Decision 2002/584/JHA,[10] taking into account that some of those offences are, in practice, likely to be more relevant than others, in that the recourse to 'real-time' remote biometric identification could, foreseeably, be necessary and proportionate to highly varying degrees for the practical pursuit of the localisation or identification of a perpetrator or suspect of the different criminal offences listed and having regard to the likely differences in the seriousness, probability and scale of the harm or possible negative consequences. An imminent threat to life or the physical safety of natural persons could also result from a serious disruption of critical infrastructure, as defined in Article 2, point (4) of Directive (EU) 2022/2557 of the European Parliament and of the Council,[11] where the disruption or destruction of such critical infrastructure would result in an imminent threat to life or the physical safety of a person, including through serious harm to the provision of basic supplies to the population or to the exercise of the core function of the State. In addition, this Regulation should preserve the ability for law enforcement, border control, immigration or asylum authorities to carry out identity checks in the presence of the person concerned in accordance with the conditions set out in Union and national law for such checks. In particular, law enforcement, border control, immigration or asylum authorities should be able to use information systems, in accordance with Union or national law, to identify persons who, during an identity check, either refuse to be identified or are unable to state or prove their identity, without being required by this Regulation to obtain prior authorisation. This could be, for example, a person involved in a crime, being unwilling, or unable due to an accident or a medical condition, to disclose their identity to law enforcement authorities.

---

10 Council Framework Decision 2002/584/JHA of 13 June 2002 on the European arrest warrant and the surrender procedures between Member States, [2002] OJ L190/1.

11 Directive (EU) 2022/2557 of the European Parliament and of the Council of 14 December 2022 on the resilience of critical entities and repealing Council Directive 2008/114/EC, [2022] OJ L333/164.

1509. **(36)** In order to carry out their tasks in accordance with the requirements set out in this Regulation as well as in national rules, the relevant market surveillance authority and the national data protection authority should be notified of each use of the real-time biometric identification system. Market surveillance authorities and the national data protection authorities that have been notified should submit to the Commission an annual report on the use of real-time biometric identification systems.

1510. **(96)** In order to efficiently ensure that fundamental rights are protected, deployers of high-risk AI systems that are bodies governed by public law, or private entities providing public services and deployers of certain high-risk AI systems listed in an annex to this Regulation, such as banking or insurance entities, should carry out a fundamental rights impact assessment prior to putting it into use. Services important for individuals that are of public nature may also be provided by private entities. Private entities providing such public services are linked to tasks in the public interest such as in the areas of education, healthcare, social services, housing, administration of justice. The aim of the fundamental rights impact assessment is for the deployer to identify the specific risks to the rights of individuals or groups of individuals likely to be affected, identify measures to be taken in the case of a materialisation of those risks. The impact assessment should be performed prior to deploying the high-risk AI system, and should be updated when the deployer considers that any of the relevant factors have changed. The impact assessment should identify the deployer's relevant processes in which the high-risk AI system will be used in line with its intended purpose, and should include a description of the period of time and frequency in which the system is intended to be used as well as of specific categories of natural persons and groups who are likely to be affected in the specific context of use. The assessment should also include the identification of specific risks of harm likely to have an impact on the fundamental rights of those persons or groups. While performing this assessment, the deployer should take into account information relevant to a proper assessment of the impact, including but not limited to the information given by the provider of the high-risk AI system in the instructions for use. In light of the risks identified, deployers should determine measures to be taken in the case of a materialisation of those risks, including for example governance arrangements in that specific context of use, such as arrangements for human oversight according to the instructions of use or, complaint handling and redress procedures, as they could be instrumental in mitigating risks to fundamental rights in concrete use-cases. After performing that impact assessment, the deployer should notify the relevant market surveillance authority. Where appropriate, to collect relevant information necessary to perform the impact assessment, deployers of high-risk AI system, in particular when AI systems are used in the public sector, could involve relevant stakeholders, including the representatives of groups of persons likely to be affected by the AI system, independent experts, and civil society organisations in conducting such impact assessments and designing measures to be taken in the case of materialisation of the risks. The European Artificial Intelligence Office (AI Office) should develop a template for a questionnaire in order to facilitate compliance and reduce the administrative burden for deployers.

1511. **(130)** Under certain conditions, rapid availability of innovative technologies may be crucial for health and safety of persons, the protection of the environment and climate change and for society as a whole. It is thus appropriate that under exceptional reasons of public security or protection of life and health of natural persons, environmental protection and the protection of key industrial and infrastructural assets, market surveillance authorities could authorise the placing on the market or the putting into service of AI systems which have not undergone a conformity assessment. In duly justified situations, as provided for in this Regulation, law enforcement authorities or civil protection authorities may put a specific high-risk AI system into service without the authorisation of the market surveillance authority, provided that such authorisation is requested during or after the use without undue delay.

1512. **(131)** In order to facilitate the work of the Commission and the Member States in the AI field as well as to increase the transparency towards the public, providers of high-risk AI systems other than those related to products falling within the scope of relevant existing Union harmonisation legislation, as well as providers who consider that an AI system listed in the high-risk use cases in an annex to this Regulation is not high-risk on the basis of a derogation, should be required to register themselves and information about their AI system in an EU database, to be established and managed by the Commission. Before using an AI system listed in the high-risk use cases in an annex to this Regulation, deployers of high-risk AI systems that are public authorities, agencies or bodies, should register themselves in such database and select the system that they envisage to use. Other deployers should be entitled to do so voluntarily. This section of the EU database should be publicly accessible, free of charge, the information should be easily navigable, understandable and machine-readable. The EU database should also be user-friendly, for example by providing search functionalities, including through keywords, allowing the general public to find relevant information to be submitted upon the registration of high-risk AI systems and on the use case of high-risk AI systems, set out in an annex to this Regulation, to which the high-risk AI systems correspond. Any substantial modification of high-risk AI systems should also be registered in the EU database. For high-risk AI systems in the area of law enforcement, migration, asylum and border control management, the registration obligations should be fulfilled in a secure non-public section of the EU database. Access to the secure non-public section should be strictly limited to the Commission as well as to market surveillance authorities with regard to their national section of that database. High-risk AI systems in the area of critical infrastructure should only be registered at national level. The Commission should be the controller of the EU database, in accordance with Regulation (EU) 2018/1725. In order to ensure the full functionality of the EU database, when deployed, the procedure for setting the database should include the development of functional specifications by the Commission and an independent audit report. The Commission should take into account cybersecurity risks when carrying out its tasks as data controller on the EU database. In order to maximise the availability and use of the EU database by the public, the EU database, including the information made available through it, should comply with requirements under the Directive (EU) 2019/882.

1513. **(141)** In order to accelerate the process of development and the placing on the market of the high-risk AI systems listed in an annex to this Regulation, it is important that providers or prospective providers of such systems may also benefit from a specific regime for testing those systems in real world conditions, without participating in an AI regulatory sandbox. However, in such cases, taking into account the possible consequences of such testing on individuals, it should be ensured that appropriate and sufficient guarantees and conditions are introduced by this Regulation for providers or prospective providers. Such guarantees should include, inter alia, requesting informed consent of natural persons to participate in testing in real world conditions, with the exception of law enforcement where the seeking of informed consent would prevent the AI system from being tested. Consent of subjects to participate in such testing under this Regulation is distinct from, and without prejudice to, consent of data subjects for the processing of their personal data under the relevant data protection law. It is also important to minimise the risks and enable oversight by competent authorities and therefore require prospective providers to have a real-world testing plan submitted to competent market surveillance authority, register the testing in dedicated sections in the EU database subject to some limited exceptions, set limitations on the period for which the testing can be done and require additional safeguards for persons belonging to certain vulnerable groups, as well as a written agreement defining the roles and responsibilities of prospective providers and deployers and effective oversight by competent personnel involved in the real world testing. Furthermore, it is appropriate to envisage additional safeguards to ensure that the predictions, recommendations or decisions of the AI system can be effectively reversed and disregarded and that personal data is protected and is deleted when the subjects have withdrawn their consent to participate in the testing without prejudice to their rights as data subjects under the Union data protection law. As regards transfer of data, it is also appropriate to envisage that data collected and processed for the purpose of testing in real-world conditions should be transferred to third countries only where appropriate and applicable safeguards under Union law are implemented, in particular in accordance with bases for transfer of personal data under Union law on data protection, while for non-personal data appropriate safeguards are put in place in accordance with Union law, such as Regulations (EU) 2022/868[12] and (EU) 2023/2854[13] of the European Parliament and of the Council.

1514. (149) In order to facilitate a smooth, effective and harmonised implementation of this Regulation a Board should be established. The Board should reflect the various interests of the AI eco-system and be composed of representatives of the Member States. The Board should be responsible for a number of advisory tasks, including issuing opinions, recommendations, advice or contributing to guidance on matters related to the implementation of this Regulation, including on enforcement matters, technical specifications or existing standards regarding the requirements established in this Regulation and providing advice to the Commission and the Member States and their national competent authorities on specific questions related to AI. In order to give some flexibility to Member States in the designation of their representatives in the Board, such representatives may be any persons belonging to public entities who should have the relevant competences and powers to facilitate coordination at national level and contribute to the achievement of the Board's tasks. The Board should establish two standing sub-groups to provide a platform for cooperation and exchange among market surveillance authorities and notifying authorities on issues related, respectively, to market surveillance and notified bodies. The standing subgroup for market surveillance should act as the administrative cooperation group (ADCO) for this Regulation within the meaning of Article 30 of Regulation (EU) 2019/1020. In accordance with Article 33 of that Regulation, the Commission should support the activities of the standing subgroup for market surveillance by undertaking market evaluations or studies, in particular with a view to identifying aspects of this Regulation requiring specific and urgent coordination among market surveillance authorities. The Board may establish other standing or temporary sub-groups as appropriate for the purpose of examining specific issues. The Board should also cooperate, as appropriate, with relevant Union bodies, experts groups and networks active in the context of relevant Union law, including in particular those active under relevant Union law on data, digital products and services.

1515. (153) Member States hold a key role in the application and enforcement of this Regulation. In that respect, each Member State should designate at least one notifying authority and at least one market surveillance authority as national competent authorities for the purpose of supervising the application and implementation of this Regulation. Member States may decide to appoint any

[12] Regulation (EU) 2022/868 of the European Parliament and of the Council of 30 May 2022 on European data governance and amending Regulation (EU) 2018/1724 (Data Governance Act), [2022] OJ L152/1.

[13] Regulation (EU) 2023/2854 of the European Parliament and of the Council of 13 December 2023 on harmonised rules on fair access to and use of data and amending Regulation (EU) 2017/2394 and Directive (EU) 2020/1828 (Data Act), [2023] OJ L, 2023/2854.

kind of public entity to perform the tasks of the national competent authorities within the meaning of this Regulation, in accordance with their specific national organisational characteristics and needs. In order to increase organisation efficiency on the side of Member States and to set a single point of contact vis-à-vis the public and other counterparts at Member State and Union levels, each Member State should designate a market surveillance authority to act as a single point of contact.

1516. (156) In order to ensure an appropriate and effective enforcement of the requirements and obligations set out by this Regulation, which is Union harmonisation legislation, the system of market surveillance and compliance of products established by Regulation (EU) 2019/1020 should apply in its entirety. Market surveillance authorities designated pursuant to this Regulation should have all enforcement powers laid down in this Regulation and in Regulation (EU) 2019/1020 and should exercise their powers and carry out their duties independently, impartially and without bias. Although the majority of AI systems are not subject to specific requirements and obligations under this Regulation, market surveillance authorities may take measures in relation to all AI systems when they present a risk in accordance with this Regulation. Due to the specific nature of Union institutions, agencies and bodies falling within the scope of this Regulation, it is appropriate to designate the European Data Protection Supervisor as a competent market surveillance authority for them. This should be without prejudice to the designation of national competent authorities by the Member States. Market surveillance activities should not affect the ability of the supervised entities to carry out their tasks independently, when such independence is required by Union law.

1517. (158) Union financial services law includes internal governance and risk-management rules and requirements which are applicable to regulated financial institutions in the course of provision of those services, including when they make use of AI systems. In order to ensure coherent application and enforcement of the obligations under this Regulation and relevant rules and requirements of the Union financial services legal acts, the competent authorities for the supervision and enforcement of those legal acts, in particular competent authorities as defined in Regulation (EU) No 575/2013 of the European Parliament and of the Council[14] and Directives 2008/48/EC,[15] 2009/138/EC,[16] 2013/36/EU,[17] 2014/17/

14 Regulation (EU) No 575/2013 of the European Parliament and of the Council of 26 June 2013 on prudential requirements for credit institutions and investment firms and amending Regulation (EU) No 648/2012, [2013] OJ L176/1.

15 Directive 2008/48/EC of the European Parliament and of the Council of 23 April 2008 on credit agreements for consumers and repealing Council Directive 87/102/EEC, [2008] OJ L133/66.

16 Directive 2009/138/EC of the European Parliament and of the Council of 25 November 2009 on the taking-up and pursuit of the business of Insurance and Reinsurance (Solvency II), [2009] OJ L335/1.

17 Directive 2013/36/EU of the European Parliament and of the Council of 26 June 2013 on access to the activity of credit institutions and the prudential supervision of credit institutions and investment firms, amending Directive 2002/87/EC and repealing Directives 2006/48/EC and 2006/49/EC, [2013] OJ L176/338.

EU[18] and (EU) 2016/97[19] of the European Parliament and of the Council, should be designated, within their respective competences, as competent authorities for the purpose of supervising the implementation of this Regulation, including for market surveillance activities, as regards AI systems provided or used by regulated and supervised financial institutions unless Member States decide to designate another authority to fulfil these market surveillance tasks. Those competent authorities should have all powers under this Regulation and Regulation (EU) 2019/1020 to enforce the requirements and obligations of this Regulation, including powers to carry our *ex post* market surveillance activities that can be integrated, as appropriate, into their existing supervisory mechanisms and procedures under the relevant Union financial services law. It is appropriate to envisage that, when acting as market surveillance authorities under this Regulation, the national authorities responsible for the supervision of credit institutions regulated under Directive 2013/36/EU, which are participating in the Single Supervisory Mechanism established by Council Regulation (EU) No 1024/2013,[20] should report, without delay, to the European Central Bank any information identified in the course of their market surveillance activities that may be of potential interest for the European Central Bank's prudential supervisory tasks as specified in that Regulation. To further enhance the consistency between this Regulation and the rules applicable to credit institutions regulated under Directive 2013/36/EU, it is also appropriate to integrate some of the providers' procedural obligations in relation to risk management, post marketing monitoring and documentation into the existing obligations and procedures under Directive 2013/36/EU. In order to avoid overlaps, limited derogations should also be envisaged in relation to the quality management system of providers and the monitoring obligation placed on deployers of high-risk AI systems to the extent that these apply to credit institutions regulated by Directive 2013/36/EU. The same regime should apply to insurance and re-insurance undertakings and insurance holding companies under Directive 2009/138/EC and the insurance intermediaries under Directive (EU) 2016/97 and other types of financial institutions subject to requirements regarding internal governance, arrangements or processes established pursuant to the relevant Union financial services law to ensure consistency and equal treatment in the financial sector.

---

[18] Directive 2014/17/EU of the European Parliament and of the Council of 4 February 2014 on credit agreements for consumers relating to residential immovable property and amending Directives 2008/48/EC and 2013/36/EU and Regulation (EU) No 1093/2010, [2014] OJ L60/34.

[19] Directive (EU) 2016/97 of the European Parliament and of the Council of 20 January 2016 on insurance distribution, [2016] OJ L26/19.

[20] Council Regulation (EU) No 1024/2013 of 15 October 2013 conferring specific tasks on the European Central Bank concerning policies relating to the prudential supervision of credit institutions, [2013] OJ L287/63.

1518. **(159)** Each market surveillance authority for high-risk AI systems in the area of biometrics, as listed in an annex to this Regulation insofar as those systems are used for the purposes of law enforcement, migration, asylum and border control management, or the administration of justice and democratic processes, should have effective investigative and corrective powers, including at least the power to obtain access to all personal data that are being processed and to all information necessary for the performance of its tasks. The market surveillance authorities should be able to exercise their powers by acting with complete independence. Any limitations of their access to sensitive operational data under this Regulation should be without prejudice to the powers conferred to them by Directive (EU) 2016/680. No exclusion on disclosing data to national data protection authorities under this Regulation should affect the current or future powers of those authorities beyond the scope of this Regulation.

1519. **(160)** The market surveillance authorities and the Commission should be able to propose joint activities, including joint investigations, to be conducted by market surveillance authorities or market surveillance authorities jointly with the Commission, that have the aim of promoting compliance, identifying non-compliance, raising awareness and providing guidance in relation to this Regulation with respect to specific categories of high-risk AI systems that are found to present a serious risk across two or more Member States. Joint activities to promote compliance should be carried out in accordance with Article 9 of Regulation (EU) 2019/1020. The AI Office should provide coordination support for joint investigations.

1520. **(161)** It is necessary to clarify the responsibilities and competences at Union and national level as regards AI systems that are built on general-purpose AI models. To avoid overlapping competences, where an AI system is based on a general-purpose AI model and the model and system are provided by the same provider, the supervision should take place at Union level through the AI Office, which should have the powers of a market surveillance authority within the meaning of Regulation (EU) 2019/1020 for this purpose. In all other cases, national market surveillance authorities remain responsible for the supervision of AI systems. However, for general-purpose AI systems that can be used directly by deployers for at least one purpose that is classified as high-risk, market surveillance authorities should cooperate with the AI Office to carry out evaluations of compliance and inform the Board and other market surveillance authorities accordingly. Furthermore, market surveillance authorities should be able to request assistance from the AI Office where the market surveillance authority is unable to conclude an investigation on a high-risk AI system because of its inability to access certain information related to the general-purpose AI model on which the high-risk AI system is built. In such cases, the procedure regarding mutual assistance in cross-border cases in Chapter VI of Regulation (EU) 2019/1020 should apply *mutatis mutandis*.

1521. **(162)** To make best use of the centralised Union expertise and synergies at Union level, the powers of supervision and enforcement of the obligations on providers of general-purpose AI models should be a competence of the Commission. The AI Office should be able to carry out all necessary actions to monitor the effective implementation of this Regulation as regards general-purpose AI models. It should be able to investigate possible infringements of the rules on providers of general-purpose AI models both on its own initiative, following the results of its monitoring activities, or upon request from market surveillance authorities in line with the conditions set out in this Regulation. To support effective monitoring of the AI Office, it should provide for the possibility that downstream providers lodge complaints about possible infringements of the rules on providers of general-purpose AI models and systems.

1522. **(170)** Union and national law already provide effective remedies to natural and legal persons whose rights and freedoms are adversely affected by the use of AI systems. Without prejudice to those remedies, any natural or legal person that has grounds to consider that there has been an infringement of this Regulation should be entitled to lodge a complaint to the relevant market surveillance authority.

74.2. General Approach

74.2.1 Preamble

1523. The control of AI systems is based on the general system of surveillance and control of products within the European Union.

74.2.2 Legal Framework

1524. It is as follows:

- Regulation (EU) 2019/1020 of the European Parliament and of the Council of 20 June 2019 on market surveillance and compliance of products and amending Directive 2004/42/EC and Regulations (EC) No 765/2008 and (EU) No 305/2011 ('MSR');
- Regulation (EU) 2016/679 ('GDPR') and Directive (EU) 2016/680 for AI systems involving personal data ('LED').

74.3. Classification

1525. The AI systems that are subject to surveillance are:
- AI systems;
- high-risk AI systems (Annexes I and III).

1526. Notes:
- (1) General-purpose AI models are subject to specific market surveillance.[21]
- (2) The same applies to general-purpose AI systems.

1527. The table of correspondence between the different regulations is as follows:

NO.	THEME	AIA	MSR (MS&PC)	GDPR
1.	Actors	Operators	Economic operators	Data controllers
2.	Goods	AI system	Product	Processing of personal data
3.	Institution	Market surveillance authority	Market surveillance authority	Data protection authority[22]

74.4. Market Surveillance and Control of AI Systems

74.4.1 Principles

1528. It is carried out in accordance with Regulation (EU) 2019/1020, with the following adjustments:
- a supervised economic operator is an AI system operator, i.e.:
  - o the provider;
  - o manufacturers of products incorporating high-risk AI systems;[23]
  - o the distributor;
  - o the authorised representative;
  - o the user;
  - o third parties who have modified the high-risk AI system;[24]
- a supervised product is 'all AI systems falling within the scope of th[e] Regulation'.

---

[21] See AI Act, Art. 51.

[22] E.g. in France: Commission nationale de l'informatique et des libertés (CNIL).

[23] The relationship with the list of products and services referred to in Annex III of the AI Act.

[24] Modifications described in Annex IV of the AI Act such as:
- intended purpose of the system, the person(s) who developed the system, the date and version of the system;
- how the AI system interacts with, or can be used to interact with, hardware or software that are not part of the AI system itself, where applicable;
- the description of the hardware on which the AI system is intended to run.

74.4.2 Areas

1529. Surveillance and control activities concern:

- the compliance with the requirements to be met by AI systems;
- competition rules.

74.4.3 Cooperation

1530. Communication is organised as follows:

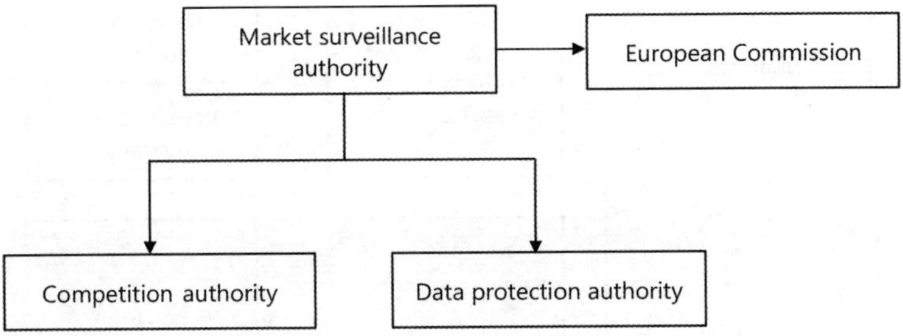

74.4.4 AI Technology and Market Surveillance Authority

1531. Macroscopically, it is organised as follows:

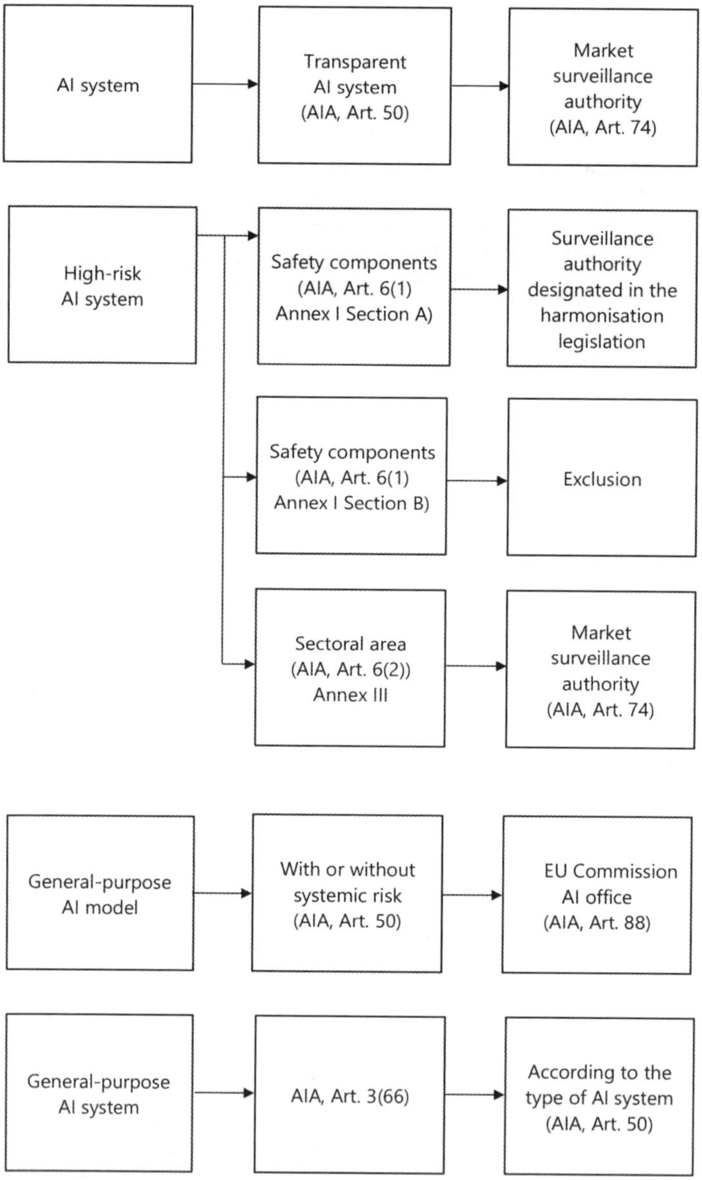

75 ARTICLE 75. MUTUAL ASSISTANCE, MARKET SURVEILLANCE AND CONTROL OF GENERAL-PURPOSE AI SYSTEMS

1. Where an AI system is based on a general-purpose AI model, and the model and the system are developed by the same provider, the AI Office shall have powers to monitor and supervise compliance of that AI system with obligations under this Regulation. To carry out its monitoring and supervision tasks, the AI Office shall have all the powers of a market surveillance authority provided for in this Section and Regulation (EU) 2019/1020.

2. Where the relevant market surveillance authorities have sufficient reason to consider general-purpose AI systems that can be used directly by deployers for at least one purpose that is classified as high-risk pursuant to this Regulation to be non-compliant with the requirements laid down in this Regulation, they shall cooperate with the AI Office to carry out compliance evaluations, and shall inform the Board and other market surveillance authorities accordingly.

3. Where a market surveillance authority is unable to conclude its investigation of the high-risk AI system because of its inability to access certain information related to the general-purpose AI model despite having made all appropriate efforts to obtain that information, it may submit a reasoned request to the AI Office, by which access to that information shall be enforced. In that case, the AI Office shall supply to the applicant authority without delay, and in any event within 30 days, any information that the AI Office considers to be relevant in order to establish whether a high-risk AI system is non-compliant. Market surveillance authorities shall safeguard the confidentiality of the information that they obtain in accordance with Article 78 of this Regulation. The procedure provided for in Chapter VI of Regulation (EU) 2019/1020 shall apply *mutatis mutandis*.

75.1. Recitals

1532. (36) In order to carry out their tasks in accordance with the requirements set out in this Regulation as well as in national rules, the relevant market surveillance authority and the national data protection authority should be notified of each use of the real-time biometric identification system. Market surveillance authorities and the national data protection authorities that have been notified should submit to the Commission an annual report on the use of real-time biometric identification systems.

1533. (96) In order to efficiently ensure that fundamental rights are protected, deployers of high-risk AI systems that are bodies governed by public law, or private entities providing public services and deployers of certain high-risk AI systems listed in an annex to this Regulation, such as banking or insurance entities, should carry out a fundamental rights impact assessment prior to putting it into use. Services important for individuals that are of public nature may also be provided by private entities. Private entities providing such public services are linked to tasks in the public interest such as in the areas of education, healthcare, social services, housing, administration of justice. The aim of the fundamental rights impact assessment is for the deployer to identify the specific risks to the rights of individuals or groups of individuals likely to be affected, identify measures to be taken in the case of a materialisation of those risks. The impact assessment should be performed prior to deploying the high-risk AI system, and should be updated when the deployer considers that any of the relevant factors have changed. The impact assessment should identify the deployer's relevant processes in which the high-risk AI system will be used in line with its intended purpose, and should include a description of the period of time and frequency in which the system is intended to be used as well as of specific categories of natural persons and groups who are likely to be affected in the specific context of use. The assessment should also include the identification of specific risks of harm likely to have an impact on the fundamental rights of those persons or groups. While performing this assessment, the deployer should take into account information relevant to a proper assessment of the impact, including but not limited to the information given by the provider of the high-risk AI system in the instructions for use. In light of the risks identified, deployers should determine measures to be taken in the case of a materialisation of those risks, including for example governance arrangements in that specific context of use, such as arrangements for human oversight according to the instructions of use or, complaint handling and redress procedures, as they could be instrumental in mitigating risks to fundamental rights in concrete use-cases. After performing that impact assessment, the deployer should notify the relevant market surveillance authority. Where appropriate, to collect relevant information necessary to perform the impact assessment, deployers of high-risk AI system, in particular when AI systems are used in the public sector, could involve relevant stakeholders, including the representatives of groups of persons likely to be affected by the AI system, independent experts, and civil society organisations in conducting such impact assessments and designing measures to be taken in the case of materialisation of the risks. The European Artificial Intelligence Office (AI Office) should develop a template for a questionnaire in order to facilitate compliance and reduce the administrative burden for deployers.

1534. **(130)** Under certain conditions, rapid availability of innovative technologies may be crucial for health and safety of persons, the protection of the environment and climate change and for society as a whole. It is thus appropriate that under exceptional reasons of public security or protection of life and health of natural persons, environmental protection and the protection of key industrial and infrastructural assets, market surveillance authorities could authorise the placing on the market or the putting into service of AI systems which have not undergone a conformity assessment. In duly justified situations, as provided for in this Regulation, law enforcement authorities or civil protection authorities may put a specific high-risk AI system into service without the authorisation of the market surveillance authority, provided that such authorisation is requested during or after the use without undue delay.

1535. **(131)** In order to facilitate the work of the Commission and the Member States in the AI field as well as to increase the transparency towards the public, providers of high-risk AI systems other than those related to products falling within the scope of relevant existing Union harmonisation legislation, as well as providers who consider that an AI system listed in the high-risk use cases in an annex to this Regulation is not high-risk on the basis of a derogation, should be required to register themselves and information about their AI system in an EU database, to be established and managed by the Commission. Before using an AI system listed in the high-risk use cases in an annex to this Regulation, deployers of high-risk AI systems that are public authorities, agencies or bodies, should register themselves in such database and select the system that they envisage to use. Other deployers should be entitled to do so voluntarily. This section of the EU database should be publicly accessible, free of charge, the information should be easily navigable, understandable and machine-readable. The EU database should also be user-friendly, for example by providing search functionalities, including through keywords, allowing the general public to find relevant information to be submitted upon the registration of high-risk AI systems and on the use case of high-risk AI systems, set out in an annex to this Regulation, to which the high-risk AI systems correspond. Any substantial modification of high-risk AI systems should also be registered in the EU database. For high-risk AI systems in the area of law enforcement, migration, asylum and border control management, the registration obligations should be fulfilled in a secure non-public section of the EU database. Access to the secure non-public section should be strictly limited to the Commission as well as to market surveillance authorities with regard to their national section of that database. High-risk AI systems in the area of critical infrastructure should only be registered at national level. The Commission should be the controller of the EU database, in accordance with Regulation (EU) 2018/1725. In order to ensure the full functionality of the EU database, when deployed, the procedure for setting the database should include the development of functional specifications by the Commission and an independent audit report. The Commission should take into account cybersecurity risks when carrying out its tasks as data controller on the EU database. In order to maximise the availability and use of the EU database by the public, the EU database, including the information made available through it, should comply with requirements under the Directive (EU) 2019/882.

1536. **(141)** In order to accelerate the process of development and the placing on the market of the high-risk AI systems listed in an annex to this Regulation, it is important that providers or prospective providers of such systems may also benefit from a specific regime for testing those systems in real world conditions, without participating in an AI regulatory sandbox. However, in such cases, taking into account the possible consequences of such testing on individuals, it should be ensured that appropriate and sufficient guarantees and conditions are introduced by this Regulation for providers or prospective providers. Such guarantees should include, inter alia, requesting informed consent of natural persons to participate in testing in real world conditions, with the exception of law enforcement where the seeking of informed consent would prevent the AI system from being tested. Consent of subjects to participate in such testing under this Regulation is distinct from, and without prejudice to, consent of data subjects for the processing of their personal data under the relevant data protection law. It is also important to minimise the risks and enable oversight by competent authorities and therefore require prospective providers to have a real-world testing plan submitted to competent market surveillance authority, register the testing in dedicated sections in the EU database subject to some limited exceptions, set limitations on the period for which the testing can be done and require additional safeguards for persons belonging to certain vulnerable groups, as well as a written agreement defining the roles and responsibilities of prospective providers and deployers and effective oversight by competent personnel involved in the real world testing. Furthermore, it is appropriate to envisage additional safeguards to ensure that the predictions, recommendations or decisions of the AI system can be effectively reversed and disregarded and that personal data is protected and is deleted when the subjects have withdrawn their consent to participate in the testing without prejudice to their rights as data subjects under the Union data protection law. As regards transfer of data, it is also appropriate to envisage that data collected and processed for the purpose of testing in real-world conditions should be transferred to third countries only where appropriate and applicable safeguards under Union law are implemented, in particular in accordance with bases for transfer of personal data under Union law on data protection, while for non-personal data appropriate safeguards are put in place in accordance with Union law, such as Regulations (EU) 2022/868[25] and (EU) 2023/2854[26] of the European Parliament and of the Council.

1537. (149) In order to facilitate a smooth, effective and harmonised implementation of this Regulation a Board should be established. The Board should reflect the various interests of the AI eco-system and be composed of

[25] Regulation (EU) 2022/868 of the European Parliament and of the Council of 30 May 2022 on European data governance and amending Regulation (EU) 2018/1724 (Data Governance Act), [2022] OJ L152/1.

[26] Regulation (EU) 2023/2854 of the European Parliament and of the Council of 13 December 2023 on harmonised rules on fair access to and use of data and amending Regulation (EU) 2017/2394 and Directive (EU) 2020/1828 (Data Act), [2023] OJ L, 2023/2854.

representatives of the Member States. The Board should be responsible for a number of advisory tasks, including issuing opinions, recommendations, advice or contributing to guidance on matters related to the implementation of this Regulation, including on enforcement matters, technical specifications or existing standards regarding the requirements established in this Regulation and providing advice to the Commission and the Member States and their national competent authorities on specific questions related to AI. In order to give some flexibility to Member States in the designation of their representatives in the Board, such representatives may be any persons belonging to public entities who should have the relevant competences and powers to facilitate coordination at national level and contribute to the achievement of the Board's tasks. The Board should establish two standing sub-groups to provide a platform for cooperation and exchange among market surveillance authorities and notifying authorities on issues related, respectively, to market surveillance and notified bodies. The standing subgroup for market surveillance should act as the administrative cooperation group (ADCO) for this Regulation within the meaning of Article 30 of Regulation (EU) 2019/1020. In accordance with Article 33 of that Regulation, the Commission should support the activities of the standing subgroup for market surveillance by undertaking market evaluations or studies, in particular with a view to identifying aspects of this Regulation requiring specific and urgent coordination among market surveillance authorities. The Board may establish other standing or temporary sub-groups as appropriate for the purpose of examining specific issues. The Board should also cooperate, as appropriate, with relevant Union bodies, experts groups and networks active in the context of relevant Union law, including in particular those active under relevant Union law on data, digital products and services.

1538. **(153)** Member States hold a key role in the application and enforcement of this Regulation. In that respect, each Member State should designate at least one notifying authority and at least one market surveillance authority as national competent authorities for the purpose of supervising the application and implementation of this Regulation. Member States may decide to appoint any kind of public entity to perform the tasks of the national competent authorities within the meaning of this Regulation, in accordance with their specific national organisational characteristics and needs. In order to increase organisation efficiency on the side of Member States and to set a single point of contact vis-à-vis the public and other counterparts at Member State and Union levels, each Member State should designate a market surveillance authority to act as a single point of contact.

1539. **(156)** In order to ensure an appropriate and effective enforcement of the requirements and obligations set out by this Regulation, which is Union harmonisation legislation, the system of market surveillance and compliance of products established by Regulation (EU) 2019/1020 should apply in its entirety.

Market surveillance authorities designated pursuant to this Regulation should have all enforcement powers laid down in this Regulation and in Regulation (EU) 2019/1020 and should exercise their powers and carry out their duties independently, impartially and without bias. Although the majority of AI systems are not subject to specific requirements and obligations under this Regulation, market surveillance authorities may take measures in relation to all AI systems when they present a risk in accordance with this Regulation. Due to the specific nature of Union institutions, agencies and bodies falling within the scope of this Regulation, it is appropriate to designate the European Data Protection Supervisor as a competent market surveillance authority for them. This should be without prejudice to the designation of national competent authorities by the Member States. Market surveillance activities should not affect the ability of the supervised entities to carry out their tasks independently, when such independence is required by Union law.

1540. (158) Union financial services law includes internal governance and risk-management rules and requirements which are applicable to regulated financial institutions in the course of provision of those services, including when they make use of AI systems. In order to ensure coherent application and enforcement of the obligations under this Regulation and relevant rules and requirements of the Union financial services legal acts, the competent authorities for the supervision and enforcement of those legal acts, in particular competent authorities as defined in Regulation (EU) No 575/2013 of the European Parliament and of the Council[27] and Directives 2008/48/EC,[28] 2009/138/EC,[29] 2013/36/EU,[30] 2014/17/EU[31] and (EU) 2016/97[32] of the European Parliament and of the Council, should be designated, within their respective competences, as competent authorities for the purpose of supervising the implementation of this Regulation,

---

27 Regulation (EU) No 575/2013 of the European Parliament and of the Council of 26 June 2013 on prudential requirements for credit institutions and investment firms and amending Regulation (EU) No 648/2012, [2013] OJ L176/1.

28 Directive 2008/48/EC of the European Parliament and of the Council of 23 April 2008 on credit agreements for consumers and repealing Council Directive 87/102/EEC, [2008] OJ L133/66.

29 Directive 2009/138/EC of the European Parliament and of the Council of 25 November 2009 on the taking-up and pursuit of the business of Insurance and Reinsurance (Solvency II), [2009] OJ L335/1.

30 Directive 2013/36/EU of the European Parliament and of the Council of 26 June 2013 on access to the activity of credit institutions and the prudential supervision of credit institutions and investment firms, amending Directive 2002/87/EC and repealing Directives 2006/48/EC and 2006/49/EC, [2013] OJ L176/338.

31 Directive 2014/17/EU of the European Parliament and of the Council of 4 February 2014 on credit agreements for consumers relating to residential immovable property and amending Directives 2008/48/EC and 2013/36/EU and Regulation (EU) No 1093/2010, [2014] OJ L60/34.

32 Directive (EU) 2016/97 of the European Parliament and of the Council of 20 January 2016 on insurance distribution, [2016] OJ L26/19.

including for market surveillance activities, as regards AI systems provided or used by regulated and supervised financial institutions unless Member States decide to designate another authority to fulfil these market surveillance tasks. Those competent authorities should have all powers under this Regulation and Regulation (EU) 2019/1020 to enforce the requirements and obligations of this Regulation, including powers to carry our *ex post* market surveillance activities that can be integrated, as appropriate, into their existing supervisory mechanisms and procedures under the relevant Union financial services law. It is appropriate to envisage that, when acting as market surveillance authorities under this Regulation, the national authorities responsible for the supervision of credit institutions regulated under Directive 2013/36/EU, which are participating in the Single Supervisory Mechanism established by Council Regulation (EU) No 1024/2013,[33] should report, without delay, to the European Central Bank any information identified in the course of their market surveillance activities that may be of potential interest for the European Central Bank's prudential supervisory tasks as specified in that Regulation. To further enhance the consistency between this Regulation and the rules applicable to credit institutions regulated under Directive 2013/36/EU, it is also appropriate to integrate some of the providers' procedural obligations in relation to risk management, post marketing monitoring and documentation into the existing obligations and procedures under Directive 2013/36/EU. In order to avoid overlaps, limited derogations should also be envisaged in relation to the quality management system of providers and the monitoring obligation placed on deployers of high-risk AI systems to the extent that these apply to credit institutions regulated by Directive 2013/36/EU. The same regime should apply to insurance and re-insurance undertakings and insurance holding companies under Directive 2009/138/EC and the insurance intermediaries under Directive (EU) 2016/97 and other types of financial institutions subject to requirements regarding internal governance, arrangements or processes established pursuant to the relevant Union financial services law to ensure consistency and equal treatment in the financial sector.

1541. (159) Each market surveillance authority for high-risk AI systems in the area of biometrics, as listed in an annex to this Regulation insofar as those systems are used for the purposes of law enforcement, migration, asylum and border control management, or the administration of justice and democratic processes, should have effective investigative and corrective powers, including at least the power to obtain access to all personal data that are being processed and to all information necessary for the performance of its tasks. The market surveillance authorities should be able to exercise their powers by acting with

---

[33] Council Regulation (EU) No 1024/2013 of 15 October 2013 conferring specific tasks on the European Central Bank concerning policies relating to the prudential supervision of credit institutions, [2013] OJ L287/63.

complete independence. Any limitations of their access to sensitive operational data under this Regulation should be without prejudice to the powers conferred to them by Directive (EU) 2016/680. No exclusion on disclosing data to national data protection authorities under this Regulation should affect the current or future powers of those authorities beyond the scope of this Regulation.

1542. (160) The market surveillance authorities and the Commission should be able to propose joint activities, including joint investigations, to be conducted by market surveillance authorities or market surveillance authorities jointly with the Commission, that have the aim of promoting compliance, identifying non-compliance, raising awareness and providing guidance in relation to this Regulation with respect to specific categories of high-risk AI systems that are found to present a serious risk across two or more Member States. Joint activities to promote compliance should be carried out in accordance with Article 9 of Regulation (EU) 2019/1020. The AI Office should provide coordination support for joint investigations.

1543. (161) It is necessary to clarify the responsibilities and competences at Union and national level as regards AI systems that are built on general-purpose AI models. To avoid overlapping competences, where an AI system is based on a general-purpose AI model and the model and system are provided by the same provider, the supervision should take place at Union level through the AI Office, which should have the powers of a market surveillance authority within the meaning of Regulation (EU) 2019/1020 for this purpose. In all other cases, national market surveillance authorities remain responsible for the supervision of AI systems. However, for general-purpose AI systems that can be used directly by deployers for at least one purpose that is classified as high-risk, market surveillance authorities should cooperate with the AI Office to carry out evaluations of compliance and inform the Board and other market surveillance authorities accordingly. Furthermore, market surveillance authorities should be able to request assistance from the AI Office where the market surveillance authority is unable to conclude an investigation on a high-risk AI system because of its inability to access certain information related to the general-purpose AI model on which the high-risk AI system is built. In such cases, the procedure regarding mutual assistance in cross-border cases in Chapter VI of Regulation (EU) 2019/1020 should apply *mutatis mutandis*.

1544. (162) To make best use of the centralised Union expertise and synergies at Union level, the powers of supervision and enforcement of the obligations on providers of general-purpose AI models should be a competence of the Commission. The AI Office should be able to carry out all necessary actions to monitor the effective implementation of this Regulation as regards general-purpose AI models. It should be able to investigate possible infringements of the rules on providers of general-purpose AI models both on its own initiative, following the results of its monitoring activities, or upon request from market surveillance authorities in line with the conditions set out in this Regulation. To support effective monitoring of the AI Office, it should provide for the possibility that downstream providers lodge complaints about possible infringements of the rules on providers of general-purpose AI models and systems.

1545. (170) Union and national law already provide effective remedies to natural and legal persons whose rights and freedoms are adversely affected by the use of AI systems. Without prejudice to those remedies, any natural or legal person that has grounds to consider that there has been an infringement of this Regulation should be entitled to lodge a complaint to the relevant market surveillance authority.

75.2. General Approach

75.2.1 Preamble

1546. In view of the highly technical nature of general-purpose AI systems, the Regulation entrusts their surveillance and associated control to the AI Office.

75.2.2 Guiding Principles

1547. For general-purpose AI systems and general-purpose AI models, the AI Office carries out:

- control operations;
- investigations at the request of market surveillance authorities.

75.3. Modalities

1548. They are as follows:

NO.	THEME	SPECIFICATION
1.	Actor	Provider of the general-purpose AI model and the general-purpose AI system built on said model
2.	Technology	General-purpose AI model Associated general-purpose AI system
3.	Powers	All the powers of a market surveillance authority
4.	Cooperation	With the market surveillance authority

76 ARTICLE 76. SUPERVISION OF TESTING IN REAL WORLD CONDITIONS BY MARKET SURVEILLANCE AUTHORITIES

1. Market surveillance authorities shall have competences and powers to ensure that testing in real world conditions is in accordance with this Regulation.

2. Where testing in real world conditions is conducted for AI systems that are supervised within an AI regulatory sandbox under Article 58, the market surveillance authorities shall verify the compliance with Article 60 as part of their supervisory role for the AI regulatory sandbox. Those authorities may, as appropriate, allow the testing in real world conditions to be conducted by the provider or prospective provider, in derogation from the conditions set out in Article 60(4), points (f) and (g).

3. Where a market surveillance authority has been informed by the prospective provider, the provider or any third party of a serious incident or has other grounds for considering that the conditions set out in Articles 60 and 61 are not met, it may take either of the following decisions on its territory, as appropriate:

(a) to suspend or terminate the testing in real world conditions;

(b) to require the provider or prospective provider and the deployer or prospective deployer to modify any aspect of the testing in real world conditions.

4. Where a market surveillance authority has taken a decision referred to in paragraph 3 of this Article, or has issued an objection within the meaning of Article 60(4), point (b), the decision or the objection shall indicate the grounds therefor and how the provider or prospective provider can challenge the decision or objection.

5. Where applicable, where a market surveillance authority has taken a decision referred to in paragraph 3, it shall communicate the grounds therefor to the market surveillance authorities of other Member States in which the AI system has been tested in accordance with the testing plan.

76.1. Recitals

1549. (25) This Regulation should support innovation, should respect freedom of science, and should not undermine research and development activity. It is therefore necessary to exclude from its scope AI systems and models specifically developed and put into service for the sole purpose of scientific research and development. Moreover, it is necessary to ensure that this Regulation does not otherwise affect scientific research and development activity on AI systems or models prior to being placed on the market or put into service. As regards product-oriented research, testing and development activity regarding AI systems or models, the provisions of this Regulation should also not apply prior to those systems and models being put into service or placed on the market. That exclusion is without prejudice to the obligation to comply with this Regulation where an AI system falling into the scope of this Regulation is placed on the market or put into service as a result of such research and development activity and to the application of provisions on AI regulatory sandboxes and testing in real world conditions. Furthermore, without prejudice to the exclusion of AI systems specifically developed and put into service for the sole purpose of scientific research and development, any other AI system that may be used for the conduct of any research and development activity should remain subject to the provisions of this Regulation. In any event, any research and development activity should be carried out in accordance with recognised ethical and professional standards for scientific research and should be conducted in accordance with applicable Union law.

1550. (139) The objectives of the AI regulatory sandboxes should be to foster AI innovation by establishing a controlled experimentation and testing environment in the development and pre-marketing phase with a view to ensuring compliance of the innovative AI systems with this Regulation and other relevant Union and national law. Moreover, the AI regulatory sandboxes should aim to enhance legal certainty for innovators and the competent authorities' oversight and understanding of the opportunities, emerging risks and the impacts of AI use, to facilitate regulatory learning for authorities and undertakings, including with a view to future adaptions of the legal framework, to support cooperation and the sharing of best practices with the authorities involved in the AI regulatory sandbox, and to accelerate access to markets, including by removing barriers for SMEs, including start-ups. AI regulatory sandboxes should be widely available throughout the Union, and particular attention should be given to their accessibility for SMEs, including start-ups. The participation in the AI regulatory sandbox should focus on issues that raise legal uncertainty for providers and prospective providers to innovate, experiment with AI in the Union and contribute to evidence-based regulatory learning. The supervision of the AI systems in the AI regulatory sandbox should therefore cover their development, training, testing and validation before the systems are placed on the market or put into service, as well as the notion and occurrence of substantial modification that may require a new conformity assessment procedure. Any significant risks identified during the development and testing of such AI systems should result in adequate mitigation and, failing that, in the suspension of the development and testing process.

1551. Where appropriate, national competent authorities establishing AI regulatory sandboxes should cooperate with other relevant authorities, including those supervising the protection of fundamental rights, and could allow for the involvement of other actors within the AI ecosystem such as national or European standardisation organisations, notified bodies, testing and experimentation facilities, research and experimentation labs, European Digital Innovation Hubs and relevant stakeholder and civil society organisations. To ensure uniform implementation across the Union and economies of scale, it is appropriate to establish common rules for the AI regulatory sandboxes' implementation and a framework for cooperation between the relevant authorities involved in the supervision of the sandboxes. AI regulatory sandboxes established under this Regulation should be without prejudice to other law allowing for the establishment of other sandboxes aiming to ensure compliance with law other than this Regulation. Where appropriate, relevant competent authorities in charge of those other regulatory sandboxes should consider the benefits of using those sandboxes also for the purpose of ensuring compliance of AI systems with this Regulation. Upon agreement between the national competent authorities and the participants in the AI regulatory sandbox, testing in real world conditions may also be operated and supervised in the framework of the AI regulatory sandbox.

1552. (141) In order to accelerate the process of development and the placing on the market of the high-risk AI systems listed in an annex to this Regulation, it is important that providers or prospective providers of such systems may also benefit from a specific regime for testing those systems in real world conditions, without participating in an AI regulatory sandbox. However, in such cases, taking into account the possible consequences of such testing on individuals, it should be ensured that appropriate and sufficient guarantees and conditions are introduced by this Regulation for providers or prospective providers. Such guarantees should include, inter alia, requesting informed consent of natural persons to participate in testing in real world conditions, with the exception of law enforcement where the seeking of informed consent would prevent the AI system from being tested. Consent of subjects to participate in such testing under this Regulation is distinct from, and without prejudice to, consent of data subjects for the processing of their personal data under the relevant data protection law. It is also important to minimise the risks and enable oversight by competent authorities and therefore require prospective providers to have a real-world testing plan submitted to competent market surveillance authority, register the testing in dedicated sections in the EU database subject to some limited exceptions, set limitations on the period for which the testing can be done and require additional safeguards for persons belonging to certain vulnerable groups, as well as a written agreement defining the roles and responsibilities of prospective providers and deployers and effective oversight by competent personnel involved in the real world testing. Furthermore, it is appropriate to envisage additional safeguards to ensure that the predictions, recommendations or decisions of the AI system can be effectively reversed and disregarded and that personal data is protected and is deleted when the subjects have withdrawn their consent to participate in the testing without prejudice to their rights as data subjects under the Union data protection law. As regards transfer of data, it is also appropriate to envisage that data collected and processed for the purpose of testing in real-world conditions should be transferred to third countries only where appropriate and applicable safeguards under Union law are implemented, in particular in accordance with bases for transfer of personal data under Union law on data protection, while for non-personal data appropriate safeguards are put in place in accordance with Union law, such as Regulations (EU) 2022/868[34] and (EU) 2023/2854[35] of the European Parliament and of the Council.

76.2. General Approach

76.2.1 Preamble

1553. The market surveillance authorities are responsible for ensuring that testing in real-world conditions complies with the Regulation.

76.2.2 Guiding Principles

1554. In view of the risks involved, the market surveillance authorities have special powers.

76.3. Modalities

1555. They are as follows:

NO.	THEME	SPECIFICATION
1.	Surveillance	Regulatory sandboxes (AIA, Art. 58)
2.	Authorisation	Derogation from Article 60(4)(f) and (g)[36]
3.	Powers	In case of serious incident: • suspension and termination • modification of testing in real-world conditions

34 Regulation (EU) 2022/868 of the European Parliament and of the Council of 30 May 2022 on European data governance and amending Regulation (EU) 2018/1724 (Data Governance Act), [2022] OJ L152/1.

35 Regulation (EU) 2023/2854 of the European Parliament and of the Council of 13 December 2023 on harmonised rules on fair access to and use of data and amending Regulation (EU) 2017/2394 and Directive (EU) 2020/1828 (Data Act), [2023] OJ L, 2023/2854.

36 AI Act, Art. 60(4)(f) and (g):
(f) the testing in real world conditions does not last longer than necessary to achieve its objectives and in any case not longer than six months, which may be extended for an additional period of six months, subject to prior notification by the provider or prospective provider to the market surveillance authority, accompanied by an explanation of the need for such an extension;
(g) the subjects of the testing in real world conditions who are persons belonging to vulnerable groups due to their age or disability, are appropriately protected.

NO.	THEME	SPECIFICATION
4.	Information	Market surveillance authorities in which testing has been conducted
5.	Remedy	Decisions may be challenged

77 ARTICLE 77. POWERS OF AUTHORITIES PROTECTING FUNDAMENTAL RIGHTS

1. National public authorities or bodies which supervise or enforce the respect of obligations under Union law protecting fundamental rights, including the right to non-discrimination, in relation to the use of high-risk AI systems referred to in Annex III shall have the power to request and access any documentation created or maintained under this Regulation in accessible language and format when access to that documentation is necessary for effectively fulfilling their mandates within the limits of their jurisdiction. The relevant public authority or body shall inform the market surveillance authority of the Member State concerned of any such request.

2. By 2 November 2024, each Member State shall identify the public authorities or bodies referred to in paragraph 1 and make a list of them publicly available. Member States shall notify the list to the Commission and to the other Member States, and shall keep the list up to date.

3. Where the documentation referred to in paragraph 1 is insufficient to ascertain whether an infringement of obligations under Union law protecting fundamental rights has occurred, the public authority or body referred to in paragraph 1 may make a reasoned request to the market surveillance authority, to organise testing of the high-risk AI system through technical means. The market surveillance authority shall organise the testing with the close involvement of the requesting public authority or body within a reasonable time following the request.

4. Any information or documentation obtained by the national public authorities or bodies referred to in paragraph 1 of this Article pursuant to this Article shall be treated in accordance with the confidentiality obligations set out in Article 78.

77.1. Recitals

1556. (8) A Union legal framework laying down harmonised rules on AI is therefore needed to foster the development, use and uptake of AI in the internal market that at the same time meets a high level of protection of public interests, such as health and safety and the protection of fundamental rights, including democracy, the rule of law and environmental protection as recognised and protected by Union law. To achieve that objective, rules regulating the placing on the market, the putting into service and the use of certain AI systems should be laid down, thus ensuring the smooth functioning of the internal market and allowing those systems to benefit from the principle of free movement of goods and services. Those rules should be clear and robust in protecting fundamental rights, supportive of new innovative solutions, enabling a European ecosystem of public and private actors creating AI systems in line with Union values and unlocking the potential of the digital transformation across all regions of the Union. By laying down those rules as well as measures in support of innovation with a particular focus on small and medium enterprises (SMEs), including startups, this Regulation supports the objective of promoting the European human-centric approach to AI and being a global leader in the development of secure, trustworthy and ethical AI as stated by the European Council,[37] and it ensures the protection of ethical principles, as specifically requested by the European Parliament.[38]

1557. (70) In order to protect the right of others from the discrimination that might result from the bias in AI systems, the providers should, exceptionally, to the extent that it is strictly necessary for the purpose of ensuring bias detection and correction in relation to the high-risk AI systems, subject to appropriate safeguards for the fundamental rights and freedoms of natural persons and following the application of all applicable conditions laid down under this Regulation in addition to the conditions laid down in Regulations (EU) 2016/679 and (EU) 2018/1725 and Directive (EU) 2016/680, be able to process also special categories of personal data, as a matter of substantial public interest within the meaning of Article 9(2), point (g) of Regulation (EU) 2016/679 and Article 10(2), point (g) of Regulation (EU) 2018/1725.

1558. (92) This Regulation is without prejudice to obligations for employers to inform or to inform and consult workers or their representatives under Union or national law and practice, including Directive 2002/14/EC of the European Parliament and of the Council (39), on decisions to put into service or use AI systems. It remains necessary to ensure information of workers and their representatives on the planned deployment of high-risk AI systems at the workplace where the conditions for those information or information and consultation obligations in other legal instruments are not fulfilled. Moreover, such information right is ancillary and necessary to the objective of protecting fundamental rights that underlies this Regulation. Therefore, an information

---

37 European Council, Special meeting of the European Council (1 and 2 October 2020) — Conclusions, EUCO 13/20, 2020, p. 6.

38 European Parliament resolution of 20 October 2020 with recommendations to the Commission on a framework of ethical aspects of artificial intelligence, robotics and related technologies, 2020/2012(INL).

requirement to that effect should be laid down in this Regulation, without affecting any existing rights of workers.

1559. (93) Whilst risks related to AI systems can result from the way such systems are designed, risks can as well stem from how such AI systems are used. Deployers of high-risk AI system therefore play a critical role in ensuring that fundamental rights are protected, complementing the obligations of the provider when developing the AI system. Deployers are best placed to understand how the high-risk AI system will be used concretely and can therefore identify potential significant risks that were not foreseen in the development phase, due to a more precise knowledge of the context of use, the persons or groups of persons likely to be affected, including vulnerable groups. Deployers of high-risk AI systems listed in an annex to this Regulation also play a critical role in informing natural persons and should, when they make decisions or assist in making decisions related to natural persons, where applicable, inform the natural persons that they are subject to the use of the high-risk AI system. This information should include the intended purpose and the type of decisions it makes. The deployer should also inform the natural persons about their right to an explanation provided under this Regulation. With regard to high-risk AI systems used for law enforcement purposes, that obligation should be implemented in accordance with Article 13 of Directive (EU) 2016/680.

1560. (96) In order to efficiently ensure that fundamental rights are protected, deployers of high-risk AI systems that are bodies governed by public law, or private entities providing public services and deployers of certain high-risk AI systems listed in an annex to this Regulation, such as banking or insurance entities, should carry out a fundamental rights impact assessment prior to putting it into use. Services important for individuals that are of public nature may also be provided by private entities. Private entities providing such public services are linked to tasks in the public interest such as in the areas of education, healthcare, social services, housing, administration of justice. The aim of the fundamental rights impact assessment is for the deployer to identify the specific risks to the rights of individuals or groups of individuals likely to be affected, identify measures to be taken in the case of a materialisation of those risks. The impact assessment should be performed prior to deploying the high-risk AI system, and should be updated when the deployer considers that any of the relevant factors have changed. The impact assessment should identify the deployer's relevant processes in which the high-risk AI system will be used in line with its intended purpose, and should include a description of the period of time and frequency in which the system is intended to be used as well as of specific categories of natural persons and groups who are likely to be affected in the specific context of use. The assessment should also include the identification of specific risks of harm likely to have an impact on the fundamental rights of those persons or groups. While performing this assessment, the deployer should take into account information relevant to a proper assessment of the impact, including but not limited to the information given by the provider of the high-risk AI system in the instructions for use. In light of the risks identified, deployers should determine measures to be taken in the case of a materialisation of those risks, including for example governance arrangements in that specific context of use, such as arrangements for human oversight according to the instructions of use or, complaint handling and redress procedures, as they could be instrumental in mitigating risks to fundamental rights in concrete use-cases. After performing that impact assessment, the deployer should notify the relevant market surveillance authority. Where appropriate, to collect relevant information necessary to perform the impact assessment, deployers of high-risk AI system, in particular when AI systems are used in the public sector, could involve relevant stakeholders, including the representatives of groups of persons likely to be affected by the AI system, independent experts, and civil society organisations in conducting such impact assessments and designing measures to be taken in the case of materialisation of the risks. The European Artificial Intelligence Office (AI Office) should develop a template for a questionnaire in order to facilitate compliance and reduce the administrative burden for deployers.

1561. (139) The objectives of the AI regulatory sandboxes should be to foster AI innovation by establishing a controlled experimentation and testing environment in the development and pre-marketing phase with a view to ensuring compliance of the innovative AI systems with this Regulation and other relevant Union and national law. Moreover, the AI regulatory sandboxes should aim to enhance legal certainty for innovators and the competent authorities' oversight and understanding of the opportunities, emerging risks and the impacts of AI use, to facilitate regulatory learning for authorities and undertakings, including with a view to future adaptions of the legal framework, to support cooperation and the sharing of best practices with the authorities involved in the AI regulatory sandbox, and to accelerate access to markets, including by removing barriers for SMEs, including start-ups. AI regulatory sandboxes should be widely available throughout the Union, and particular attention should be given to their accessibility for SMEs, including start-ups. The participation in the AI regulatory sandbox should focus on issues that raise legal uncertainty for providers and prospective providers to innovate, experiment with AI in the Union and contribute to evidence-based regulatory learning. The supervision of the AI systems in the AI regulatory sandbox should therefore cover their development, training, testing and validation before the systems are placed on the market or put into service, as well as the notion and occurrence of substantial modification that may require a new conformity assessment procedure. Any significant risks identified during the development and testing of such AI systems should result in adequate mitigation and, failing that, in the suspension of the development and testing process. Where appropriate, national competent authorities establishing AI regulatory sandboxes should cooperate with other relevant authorities, including those supervising the protection of fundamental rights, and could allow for the involvement of other actors within the AI ecosystem such as national or European standardisation organisations, notified bodies, testing and experimentation facilities, research and experimentation labs, European Digital Innovation Hubs and relevant stakeholder and civil society organisations. To ensure uniform implementation across the Union and economies of scale, it is appropriate to establish common rules for the AI regulatory sandboxes' implementation and a framework for cooperation between the relevant authorities involved in the supervision of the sandboxes. AI regulatory sandboxes established under this Regulation should be without prejudice to other law allowing for the establishment of other sandboxes aiming to ensure compliance with law other than this Regulation. Where appropriate, relevant competent authorities in charge of those other regulatory sandboxes should consider the benefits of using those sandboxes also for the purpose of ensuring compliance of AI systems with this Regulation. Upon agreement between the national competent authorities and the participants in the AI regulatory sandbox, testing in real world conditions may also be operated and supervised in the framework of the AI regulatory sandbox.

1562. (157) This Regulation is without prejudice to the competences, tasks, powers and independence of relevant national public authorities or bodies which supervise the application of Union law protecting fundamental rights, including equality bodies and data protection authorities. Where necessary for their mandate, those national public authorities or bodies should also have access to any documentation created under this Regulation. A specific safeguard procedure should be set for ensuring adequate and timely enforcement against AI systems presenting a risk to health, safety and fundamental rights. The procedure for such AI systems presenting a risk should be applied to high-risk AI systems presenting a risk, prohibited systems which have been placed on the market, put into service or used in violation of the prohibited practices laid down in this Regulation and AI systems which have been made available in violation of the transparency requirements laid down in this Regulation and present a risk.

77.2. General Approach

77.2.1 Preamble

1563. A number of authorities are responsible for:

- the protection of personal data;
- the protection of fundamental rights.

1564. AI technologies necessarily have an impact when they use data, particularly for training purposes.

1565. Coordination between authorities is necessary in order to:

- avoid duplication;
- close regulatory loopholes; and
- reduce administrative burdens.

77.2.2 Guiding Principles

1566. In view of the specific nature of AI technologies and their rapid evolution, national market surveillance authorities are competent. They act in coordination with the associated specialised authorities.

77.3. Modalities

NO.	THEME	SPECIFICATION
1.	Bodies	Authority for the protection of personal data Authority for the protection of fundamental rights, including the right to non-discrimination
2.	Areas	Annex III: 1. Biometrics 2. Critical infrastructure 3. Education and vocational training 4. Employment, workers' management and access to self-employment 5. Access to and enjoyment of essential private services and essential public services and benefits 6. Law enforcement, in so far as their use is permitted under relevant Union or national law 7. Migration, asylum and border control management, in so far as their use is permitted under relevant Union or national law 8. Administration of justice and democratic processes
3.	Actors	Provider Authorised representative Importer Distributor Deployer
4.	Activities	Placing on the market or putting into service Regulatory sandboxes Testing in real-world conditions
5.	Powers	Access to technical documentation
6.	Control	Testing organised by the market surveillance authority, with the involvement of the requesting authority, to identify non-compliance
7.	Period	List of activities concerned: • 2 November 2024
8.	Confidentiality	Rules that apply to all activities[39]

[39] AI Act, Art. 78.

78 ARTICLE 78. CONFIDENTIALITY

1. The Commission, market surveillance authorities and notified bodies and any other natural or legal person involved in the application of this Regulation shall, in accordance with Union or national law, respect the confidentiality of information and data obtained in carrying out their tasks and activities in such a manner as to protect, in particular:

(a) the intellectual property rights and confidential business information or trade secrets of a natural or legal person, including source code, except in the cases referred to in Article 5 of Directive (EU) 2016/943 of the European Parliament and of the Council (57);[40]

(b) the effective implementation of this Regulation, in particular for the purposes of inspections, investigations or audits;

(c) public and national security interests;

(d) the conduct of criminal or administrative proceedings;

(e) information classified pursuant to Union or national law.

2. The authorities involved in the application of this Regulation pursuant to paragraph 1 shall request only data that is strictly necessary for the assessment of the risk posed by AI systems and for the exercise of their powers in accordance with this Regulation and with Regulation (EU) 2019/1020. They shall put in place adequate and effective cybersecurity measures to protect the security and confidentiality of the information and data obtained, and shall delete the data collected as soon as it is no longer needed for the purpose for which it was obtained, in accordance with applicable Union or national law.

3. Without prejudice to paragraphs 1 and 2, information exchanged on a confidential basis between the national competent authorities or between national competent authorities and the Commission shall not be disclosed without prior consultation of the originating national competent authority and the deployer when high-risk AI systems referred to in point 1, 6 or 7 of Annex III are used by law enforcement, border control, immigration or asylum authorities and when such disclosure would jeopardise public and national security interests. This exchange of information shall not cover sensitive operational data in relation to the activities of law enforcement, border control, immigration or asylum authorities.

When the law enforcement, immigration or asylum authorities are providers of high-risk AI systems referred to in point 1, 6 or 7 of Annex III, the technical documentation referred to in Annex IV shall remain within the premises of those authorities. Those authorities shall ensure that the market surveillance

---

[40] Directive (EU) 2016/943 of the European Parliament and of the Council of 8 June 2016 on the protection of undisclosed know-how and business information (trade secrets) against their unlawful acquisition, use and disclosure, *OJEU*, L 157, 15 June 2016, p. 1.

authorities referred to in Article 74(8) and (9), as applicable, can, upon request, immediately access the documentation or obtain a copy thereof. Only staff of the market surveillance authority holding the appropriate level of security clearance shall be allowed to access that documentation or any copy thereof.

4. Paragraphs 1, 2 and 3 shall not affect the rights or obligations of the Commission, Member States and their relevant authorities, as well as those of notified bodies, with regard to the exchange of information and the dissemination of warnings, including in the context of cross-border cooperation, nor shall they affect the obligations of the parties concerned to provide information under criminal law of the Member States.

5. The Commission and Member States may exchange, where necessary and in accordance with relevant provisions of international and trade agreements, confidential information with regulatory authorities of third countries with which they have concluded bilateral or multilateral confidentiality arrangements guaranteeing an adequate level of confidentiality.

78.1. Recitals

1567. (10) The fundamental right to the protection of personal data is safeguarded in particular by Regulations (EU) 2016/679[41] and (EU) 2018/1725[42] of the European Parliament and of the Council and Directive (EU) 2016/680 of the European Parliament and of the Council.[43] Directive 2002/58/EC of the European Parliament and of the Council[44] additionally protects private life and the confidentiality of communications, including by way of providing conditions for any storing of personal and non-personal data in, and access from, terminal equipment. Those Union legal acts provide the basis for sustainable and

[41] Regulation (EU) 2016/679 of the European Parliament and of the Council of 27 April 2016 on the protection of natural persons with regard to the processing of personal data and on the free movement of such data, and repealing Directive 95/46/EC (General Data Protection Regulation), [2016] OJ L119/1.

[42] Regulation (EU) 2018/1725 of the European Parliament and of the Council of 23 October 2018 on the protection of natural persons with regard to the processing of personal data by the Union institutions, bodies, offices and agencies and on the free movement of such data, and repealing Regulation (EC) No 45/2001 and Decision No 1247/2002/EC, [2018] OJ L295/39.

[43] Directive (EU) 2016/680 of the European Parliament and of the Council of 27 April 2016 on the protection of natural persons with regard to the processing of personal data by competent authorities for the purposes of the prevention, investigation, detection or prosecution of criminal offences or the execution of criminal penalties, and on the free movement of such data, and repealing Council Framework Decision 2008/977/JHA, [2016] OJ L119/89.

[44] Directive 2002/58/EC of the European Parliament and of the Council of 12 July 2002 concerning the processing of personal data and the protection of privacy in the electronic communications sector (Directive on privacy and electronic communications), [2002] OJ L201/37.

responsible data processing, including where data sets include a mix of personal and non-personal data. This Regulation does not seek to affect the application of existing Union law governing the processing of personal data, including the tasks and powers of the independent supervisory authorities competent to monitor compliance with those instruments. It also does not affect the obligations of providers and deployers of AI systems in their role as data controllers or processors stemming from Union or national law on the protection of personal data in so far as the design, the development or the use of AI systems involves the processing of personal data. It is also appropriate to clarify that data subjects continue to enjoy all the rights and guarantees awarded to them by such Union law, including the rights related to solely automated individual decision-making, including profiling. Harmonised rules for the placing on the market, the putting into service and the use of AI systems established under this Regulation should facilitate the effective implementation and enable the exercise of the data subjects' rights and other remedies guaranteed under Union law on the protection of personal data and of other fundamental rights.

1568. **(151)** To support the implementation and enforcement of this Regulation, in particular the monitoring activities of the AI Office as regards general-purpose AI models, a scientific panel of independent experts should be established. The independent experts constituting the scientific panel should be selected on the basis of up-to-date scientific or technical expertise in the field of AI and should perform their tasks with impartiality, objectivity and ensure the confidentiality of information and data obtained in carrying out their tasks and activities. To allow the reinforcement of national capacities necessary for the effective enforcement of this Regulation, Member States should be able to request support from the pool of experts constituting the scientific panel for their enforcement activities.

1569. **(154)** The national competent authorities should exercise their powers independently, impartially and without bias, so as to safeguard the principles of objectivity of their activities and tasks and to ensure the application and implementation of this Regulation. The members of these authorities should refrain from any action incompatible with their duties and should be subject to confidentiality rules under this Regulation.

1570. **(167)** In order to ensure trustful and constructive cooperation of competent authorities on Union and national level, all parties involved in the application of this Regulation should respect the confidentiality of information and data obtained in carrying out their tasks, in accordance with Union or national law. They should carry out their tasks and activities in such a manner as to protect, in particular, intellectual property rights, confidential business information and trade secrets, the effective implementation of this Regulation, public and national security interests, the integrity of criminal and administrative proceedings, and the integrity of classified information.

78.2. *General Approach*

78.2.1 Preamble

1571. During the declaration, surveillance or control phases, a considerable volume of information must be communicated, in particular by providers and deployers.

1572. In this context, the Regulation provides for the respect of intellectual property rights and trade secrets.

78.2.2 Actors

1573. They are as follows:
- market surveillance authorities;
- notifying authorities;
- notified bodies.

78.3. *Classification*

NO.	THEME	SPECIFICATION
1.	Compliance	Operations by legal or natural persons
2.	Intellectual property	All protected rights
3.	National security	Including public security
4.	Proceedings Classified information	Criminal proceedings Administrative proceedings Union law National law
5.	Source code	Exception: Directive (EU) 2016/943 Art. 5[45]
6.	Trade secret	Know-how

[45] Directive (EU) 2016/943, Art. 5:
'Member States shall ensure that an application for the measures, procedures and remedies provided for in this Directive is dismissed where the alleged acquisition, use or disclosure of the trade secret was carried out in any of the following cases:
(a) for exercising the right to freedom of expression and information as set out in the Charter, including respect for the freedom and pluralism of the media;
(b) for revealing misconduct, wrongdoing or illegal activity, provided that the respondent acted for the purpose of protecting the general public interest;
(c) disclosure by workers to their representatives as part of the legitimate exercise by those representatives of their functions in accordance with Union or national law, provided that such disclosure was necessary for that exercise;
(d) for the purpose of protecting a legitimate interest recognised by Union or national law.'

78.4. *Modalities*

1574. The declaration is implemented according to the following constraints:

NO.	THEME	SPECIFICATION
1.	Data acquisition	Strictly necessary
2.	System	All AI systems
3.	Actors	Provider Authorised representative Importer Distributor Deployer Participants in regulatory sandboxes Subjects of testing in real-world conditions
4.	Activities	Before the placing on the market or before the putting into service
5.	Protection	Cybersecurity measures should be put in place
6.	Deletion of information	At the end of the surveillance or investigation in the absence of prosecution

79 ARTICLE 79. PROCEDURE AT NATIONAL LEVEL FOR DEALING WITH AI SYSTEMS PRESENTING A RISK

1. AI systems presenting a risk shall be understood as a 'product presenting a risk' as defined in Article 3, point 19 of Regulation (EU) 2019/1020, in so far as they present risks to the health or safety, or to fundamental rights, of persons.

2. Where the market surveillance authority of a Member State has sufficient reason to consider an AI system to present a risk as referred to in paragraph 1 of this Article, it shall carry out an evaluation of the AI system concerned in respect of its compliance with all the requirements and obligations laid down in this Regulation. Particular attention shall be given to AI systems presenting a risk to vulnerable groups. Where risks to fundamental rights are identified, the market surveillance authority shall also inform and fully cooperate with the relevant national public authorities or bodies referred to in Article 77(1). The relevant operators shall cooperate as necessary with the market surveillance authority and with the other national public authorities or bodies referred to in Article 77(1).

Where, in the course of that evaluation, the market surveillance authority or, where applicable the market surveillance authority in cooperation with the national public authority referred to in Article 77(1), finds that the AI system does not comply with the requirements and obligations laid down in this Regulation, it shall without undue delay require the relevant operator to take all appropriate corrective actions to bring the AI system into compliance, to withdraw the AI system from the market, or to recall it within a period the market surveillance authority may prescribe, and in any event within the shorter of 15 working days, or as provided for in the relevant Union harmonisation legislation.

The market surveillance authority shall inform the relevant notified body accordingly. Article 18 of Regulation (EU) 2019/1020 shall apply to the measures referred to in the second subparagraph of this paragraph.

3. Where the market surveillance authority considers that the non-compliance is not restricted to its national territory, it shall inform the Commission and the other Member States without undue delay of the results of the evaluation and of the actions which it has required the operator to take.

4. The operator shall ensure that all appropriate corrective action is taken in respect of all the AI systems concerned that it has made available on the Union market.

5. Where the operator of an AI system does not take adequate corrective action within the period referred to in paragraph 2, the market surveillance authority shall take all appropriate provisional measures to prohibit or restrict the AI system's being made available on its national market or put into service, to withdraw the product or the standalone AI system from that market or to recall it. That authority shall without undue delay notify the Commission and the other Member States of those measures.

6. The notification referred to in paragraph 5 shall include all available details, in particular the information necessary for the identification of the non-compliant AI system, the origin of the AI system and the supply chain, the nature of the non-compliance alleged and the risk involved, the nature and duration of the national measures taken and the arguments put forward by the relevant operator. In particular, the market surveillance authorities shall indicate whether the non-compliance is due to one or more of the following:

(a) non-compliance with the prohibition of the AI practices referred to in Article 5;

(b) a failure of a high-risk AI system to meet requirements set out in Chapter III, Section 2;

(c) shortcomings in the harmonised standards or common specifications referred to in Articles 40 and 41 conferring a presumption of conformity;

(d) non-compliance with Article 50.

7. The market surveillance authorities other than the market surveillance authority of the Member State initiating the procedure shall, without undue delay, inform the Commission and the other Member States of any measures adopted and of any additional information at their disposal relating to the non-compliance of the AI system concerned, and, in the event of disagreement with the notified national measure, of their objections.

8. Where, within three months of receipt of the notification referred to in paragraph 5 of this Article, no objection has been raised by either a market surveillance authority of a Member State or by the Commission in respect of a provisional measure taken by a market surveillance authority of another Member State, that measure shall be deemed justified. This shall be without prejudice to the procedural rights of the concerned operator in accordance with Article 18 of Regulation (EU) 2019/1020. The three-month period referred to in this paragraph shall be reduced to 30 days in the event of non-compliance with the prohibition of the AI practices referred to in Article 5 of this Regulation.

9. The market surveillance authorities shall ensure that appropriate restrictive measures are taken in respect of the product or the AI system concerned, such as withdrawal of the product or the AI system from their market, without undue delay.

79.1. Recitals

1575. **(97)** The notion of general-purpose AI models should be clearly defined and set apart from the notion of AI systems to enable legal certainty. The definition should be based on the key functional characteristics of a general-purpose AI model, in particular the generality and the capability to competently perform a wide range of distinct tasks. These models are typically trained on large amounts of data, through various methods, such as self-supervised, unsupervised or reinforcement learning. General-purpose AI models may be placed on the market in various ways, including through libraries, application programming interfaces (APIs), as direct download, or as physical copy. These models may be further modified or fine-tuned into new models. Although AI models are essential components of AI systems, they do not constitute AI systems on their own. AI models require the addition of further components, such as for example a user interface, to become AI systems. AI models are typically integrated into and form part of AI systems. This Regulation provides specific rules for general-purpose AI models and for general-purpose AI models that pose systemic risks, which should apply also when these models are integrated or form part of an AI system. It should be understood that the obligations for the providers of general-purpose AI models should apply once the general-purpose AI models are placed on the market. When the provider of a general-purpose AI model integrates an own model into its own AI system that is made available on the market or put into service, that model should be considered to be placed on the market and, therefore, the obligations in this Regulation for models should continue to apply in addition to those for AI systems. The obligations laid down for models should in any case not apply when an own model is used for purely internal processes that are not essential for providing a product or a service to third parties and the rights of natural persons are not affected. Considering their potential significantly negative effects, the general-purpose AI models with systemic risk should always be subject to the relevant obligations under this Regulation. The definition should not cover AI models used before their placing on the market for the sole purpose of research, development and prototyping activities. This is without prejudice to the obligation to comply with this Regulation when, following such activities, a model is placed on the market.

1576. **(104)** The providers of general-purpose AI models that are released under a free and open-source licence, and whose parameters, including the weights, the information on the model architecture, and the information on model usage, are made publicly available should be subject to exceptions as regards the transparency-related requirements imposed on general-purpose AI models, unless they can be considered to present a systemic risk, in which case the circumstance that the model is transparent and accompanied by an open-source license should not be considered to be a sufficient reason to exclude compliance with the obligations under this Regulation. In any case, given that the release of general-purpose AI models under free and open-source licence does not necessarily reveal substantial information on the data set used for the training or fine-tuning of the model and on how compliance of copyright law was thereby ensured, the exception provided for general-purpose AI models from compliance with the transparency-related requirements should not concern the obligation to produce a summary about the content used for model training and the obligation to put in place a policy to comply with Union copyright law, in particular to identify and comply with the reservation of rights pursuant to Article 4(3) of Directive (EU) 2019/790 of the European Parliament and of the Council.[46]

1577. **(111)** It is appropriate to establish a methodology for the classification of general-purpose AI models as general-purpose AI model with systemic risks. Since systemic risks result from particularly high capabilities, a general-purpose AI model should be considered to present systemic risks if it has high-impact capabilities, evaluated on the basis of appropriate technical tools and methodologies, or significant impact on the internal market due to its reach. High-impact capabilities in general-purpose AI models means capabilities that match or exceed the capabilities recorded in the most advanced general-purpose AI models. The full range of capabilities in a model could be better understood after its placing on the market or when deployers interact with the model. According to the state of the art at the time of entry into force of

---

[46] Directive (EU) 2019/790 of the European Parliament and of the Council of 17 April 2019 on copyright and related rights in the Digital Single Market and amending Directives 96/9/EC and 2001/29/EC, [2019] OJ L130/ 92.

this Regulation, the cumulative amount of computation used for the training of the general-purpose AI model measured in floating point operations is one of the relevant approximations for model capabilities. The cumulative amount of computation used for training includes the computation used across the activities and methods that are intended to enhance the capabilities of the model prior to deployment, such as pre-training, synthetic data generation and fine-tuning. Therefore, an initial threshold of floating point operations should be set, which, if met by a general-purpose AI model, leads to a presumption that the model is a general-purpose AI model with systemic risks. This threshold should be adjusted over time to reflect technological and industrial changes, such as algorithmic improvements or increased hardware efficiency, and should be supplemented with benchmarks and indicators for model capability.

1578. To inform this, the AI Office should engage with the scientific community, industry, civil society and other experts. Thresholds, as well as tools and benchmarks for the assessment of high-impact capabilities, should be strong predictors of generality, its capabilities and associated systemic risk of general-purpose AI models, and could take into account the way the model will be placed on the market or the number of users it may affect. To complement this system, there should be a possibility for the Commission to take individual decisions designating a general-purpose AI model as a general-purpose AI model with systemic risk if it is found that such model has capabilities or an impact equivalent to those captured by the set threshold. That decision should be taken on the basis of an overall assessment of the criteria for the designation of a general-purpose AI model with systemic risk set out in an annex to this Regulation, such as quality or size of the training data set, number of business and end users, its input and output modalities, its level of autonomy and scalability, or the tools it has access to. Upon a reasoned request of a provider whose model has been designated as a general-purpose AI model with systemic risk, the Commission should take the request into account and may decide to reassess whether the general-purpose AI model can still be considered to present systemic risks.

1579. (112) It is also necessary to clarify a procedure for the classification of a general-purpose AI model with systemic risks. A general-purpose AI model that meets the applicable threshold for high-impact capabilities should be presumed to be a general-purpose AI models with systemic risk. The provider should notify the AI Office at the latest two weeks after the requirements are met or it becomes known that a general-purpose AI model will meet the requirements that lead to the presumption. This is especially relevant in relation to the threshold of floating point operations because training of general-purpose AI models takes considerable planning which includes the upfront allocation of compute resources and, therefore, providers of general-purpose AI models are able to know if their model would meet the threshold before the training is completed. In the context of that notification, the provider should be able to demonstrate that, because of its specific characteristics, a general-purpose AI model exceptionally does not present systemic risks, and that it thus should not be classified as a general-purpose AI model with systemic risks. That information is valuable for the AI Office to anticipate the placing on the market of general-purpose AI models with systemic risks and the providers can start to engage with the AI Office early on. That information is especially important with regard to general-purpose AI models that are planned to be released as open-source, given that, after the open-source model release, necessary measures to ensure compliance with the obligations under this Regulation may be more difficult to implement.

1580. **(113)** If the Commission becomes aware of the fact that a general-purpose AI model meets the requirements to classify as a general-purpose AI model with systemic risk, which previously had either not been known or of which the relevant provider has failed to notify the Commission, the Commission should be empowered to designate it so. A system of qualified alerts should ensure that the AI Office is made aware by the scientific panel of general-purpose AI models that should possibly be classified as general-purpose AI models with systemic risk, in addition to the monitoring activities of the AI Office.

1581. **(157)** This Regulation is without prejudice to the competences, tasks, powers and independence of relevant national public authorities or bodies which supervise the application of Union law protecting fundamental rights, including equality bodies and data protection authorities. Where necessary for their mandate, those national public authorities or bodies should also have access to any documentation created under this Regulation. A specific safeguard procedure should be set for ensuring adequate and timely enforcement against AI systems presenting a risk to health, safety and fundamental rights. The procedure for such AI systems presenting a risk should be applied to high-risk AI systems presenting a risk, prohibited systems which have been placed on the market, put into service or used in violation of the prohibited practices laid down in this Regulation and AI systems which have been made available in violation of the transparency requirements laid down in this Regulation and present a risk.

1582. **(160)** The market surveillance authorities and the Commission should be able to propose joint activities, including joint investigations, to be conducted by market surveillance authorities or market surveillance authorities jointly with the Commission, that have the aim of promoting compliance, identifying non-compliance, raising awareness and providing guidance in relation to this Regulation with respect to specific categories of high-risk AI systems that are found to present a serious risk across two or more Member States. Joint activities to promote compliance should be carried out in accordance with Article 9 of Regulation (EU) 2019/1020. The AI Office should provide coordination support for joint investigations.

1583. **(163)** With a view to complementing the governance systems for general-purpose AI models, the scientific panel should support the monitoring activities of the AI Office and may, in certain cases, provide qualified alerts to the AI Office which trigger follow-ups, such as investigations. This should be the case where the scientific panel has reason to suspect that a general-purpose AI model poses a concrete and identifiable risk at Union level. Furthermore, this should be the case where the scientific panel has reason to suspect that a general-purpose AI model meets the criteria that would lead to a classification as general-purpose AI model with systemic risk. To equip the scientific panel with the information necessary for the performance of those tasks, there should be a mechanism whereby the scientific panel can request the Commission to require documentation or information from a provider.

1584. **(173)** In order to ensure that the regulatory framework can be adapted where necessary, the power to adopt acts in accordance with Article 290 TFEU should be delegated to the Commission to amend the conditions under which an AI system is not to be considered to be high-risk, the list of high-risk AI systems, the provisions regarding technical documentation, the content of the EU declaration of conformity the provisions regarding the conformity assessment procedures, the provisions establishing the high-risk AI systems to which the conformity assessment procedure based on assessment of the quality management system and assessment of the technical documentation should apply, the threshold, benchmarks and indicators, including by supplementing those benchmarks and indicators, in the rules for the classification of general-purpose AI models with systemic risk, the criteria for the designation of general-purpose AI models with systemic risk, the technical documentation for providers of general-purpose AI models and the transparency information for providers of general-purpose AI models. It is of particular importance that the Commission carry out appropriate consultations during its preparatory work, including at expert level, and that those consultations be conducted in accordance with the principles laid down in the Interinstitutional Agreement of 13 April 2016 on Better Law-Making.[47] In particular, to ensure equal participation in the preparation of delegated acts, the European Parliament and the Council receive all documents at the same time as Member States' experts, and their experts systematically have access to meetings of Commission expert groups dealing with the preparation of delegated acts.

[47] [2016] OJ L123/1.

79.2. General Approach

79.2.1 Preamble

1585. AI systems presenting a risk are subject to a special procedure.

79.2.2 Definition

1586. Under the Regulation, 'AI systems presenting a risk' shall be understood as 'a "product presenting a risk" as defined in Article 3, point 19 of Regulation (EU) 2019/1020, in so far as they present risks to the health or safety, or to fundamental rights, of persons'.[48]

1587. Under Article 3, point 19 of Regulation (EU) 2019/1020 '"product presenting a risk" means a product having the potential to affect adversely health and safety of persons in general, health and safety in the workplace, protection of consumers, the environment, public security and other public interests, protected by the applicable Union harmonisation legislation, to a degree which goes beyond that considered reasonable and acceptable in relation to its intended purpose or under the normal or reasonably foreseeable conditions of use of the product concerned, including the duration of use and, where applicable, its putting into service, installation and maintenance requirements'.

79.3. Risk Assessment

79.3.1 Initiation of the Procedure

1588. A procedure is initiated by the market surveillance authority if it considers that an AI system presents risks.

79.3.2 Areas

1589. Risks relate in whole or in part to harm to:

- health;
- safety;
- protection of fundamental rights.

---

48 AI Act, Art. 79(1).

79.3.3 Reference Framework

1590. The evaluation is carried out on the basis of 'all the requirements and obligations laid down in th[e] Regulatio'.[49]

79.3.4 Corrective Measures

1591. Depending on the type of risk, the market surveillance authority may prescribe:

- a bringing into compliance;
- a recall; or
- a withdrawal.

1592. This decision must 'state the exact grounds on which it is based'.[50]

79.3.5 Cooperation

1593. In the event of risks affecting several countries, the market surveillance authority must inform the European Commission and the other Member States.

80 ARTICLE 80. PROCEDURE FOR DEALING WITH AI SYSTEMS CLASSIFIED BY THE PROVIDER AS NON-HIGH-RISK IN APPLICATION OF ANNEX III

1. Where a market surveillance authority has sufficient reason to consider that an AI system classified by the provider as non-high-risk pursuant to Article 6(3) is indeed high-risk, the market surveillance authority shall carry out an evaluation of the AI system concerned in respect of its classification as a high-risk AI system based on the conditions set out in Article 6(3) and the Commission guidelines.

2. Where, in the course of that evaluation, the market surveillance authority finds that the AI system concerned is high-risk, it shall without undue delay require the relevant provider to take all necessary actions to bring the AI system into compliance with the requirements and obligations laid down in this Regulation, as well as take appropriate corrective action within a period the market surveillance authority may prescribe.

3. Where the market surveillance authority considers that the use of the AI system concerned is not restricted to its national territory, it shall inform the

---

[49] Ibid.

[50] Regulation (EU) 2019/1020, Art.18.

Commission and the other Member States without undue delay of the results of the evaluation and of the actions which it has required the provider to take.

4. The provider shall ensure that all necessary action is taken to bring the AI system into compliance with the requirements and obligations laid down in this Regulation. Where the provider of an AI system concerned does not bring the AI system into compliance with those requirements and obligations within the period referred to in paragraph 2 of this Article, the provider shall be subject to fines in accordance with Article 99.

5. The provider shall ensure that all appropriate corrective action is taken in respect of all the AI systems concerned that it has made available on the Union market.

6. Where the provider of the AI system concerned does not take adequate corrective action within the period referred to in paragraph 2 of this Article, Article 79(5) to (9) shall apply.

7. Where, in the course of the evaluation pursuant to paragraph 1 of this Article, the market surveillance authority establishes that the AI system was misclassified by the provider as non-high-risk in order to circumvent the application of requirements in Chapter III, Section 2, the provider shall be subject to fines in accordance with Article 99.

8. In exercising their power to monitor the application of this Article, and in accordance with Article 11 of Regulation (EU) 2019/1020, market surveillance authorities may perform appropriate checks, taking into account in particular information stored in the EU database referred to in Article 71 of this Regulation.

80.1. General Approach

80.1.1 Preamble

1594. The provider qualifies, at its own risk, the AI system as high-risk or non-high-risk before it is placed on the market.

80.1.2 Legal Framework

1595. This legal framework concerns:

- the qualification of a high-risk AI system (AIA, Art. 6);
- the registration of an AI system classified as non-high-risk (AIA, Art. 7).

80.1.3 Guiding Principles

1596. In case of doubt, the market surveillance authority may perform checks.

80.2. Modalities

1597. The powers of the market surveillance authority are as follows:

NO.	THEME	SPECIFICATION
1.	Evaluation	Control of requirements
2.	Qualification	High-risk or non-high-risk
3.	Measure	Definition Deadline
4.	Information	National competent authority
5.	Powers	Provisional measures Withdrawal
6.	Refusal	Possible fines
7.	Misclassification	Circumvention of requirements Possible fines
8.	EU database	Access to the EU database

81 ARTICLE 81. UNION SAFEGUARD PROCEDURE

1. Where, within three months of receipt of the notification referred to in Article 79(5), or within 30 days in the case of non-compliance with the prohibition of the AI practices referred to in Article 5, objections are raised by the market surveillance authority of a Member State to a measure taken by another market surveillance authority, or where the Commission considers the measure to be contrary to Union law, the Commission shall without undue delay enter into consultation with the market surveillance authority of the relevant Member State and the operator or operators, and shall evaluate the national measure. On the basis of the results of that evaluation, the Commission shall, within six months, or within 60 days in the case of non-compliance with the prohibition of the AI practices referred to in Article 5, starting from the notification referred to in Article 79(5), decide whether the national measure is justified and shall notify its decision to the market surveillance authority of the Member State concerned. The Commission shall also inform all other market surveillance authorities of its decision.

2. Where the Commission considers the measure taken by the relevant Member State to be justified, all Member States shall ensure that they take appropriate restrictive measures in respect of the AI system concerned, such as requiring the withdrawal of the AI system from their market without undue delay, and shall inform the Commission accordingly. Where the Commission considers the national measure to be unjustified, the Member State concerned shall withdraw the measure and shall inform the Commission accordingly.

3. Where the national measure is considered justified and the non-compliance of the AI system is attributed to shortcomings in the harmonised standards or common specifications referred to in Articles 40 and 41 of this Regulation, the Commission shall apply the procedure provided for in Article 11 of Regulation (EU) No 1025/2012.

81.1. Recitals

1598. (157) This Regulation is without prejudice to the competences, tasks, powers and independence of relevant national public authorities or bodies which supervise the application of Union law protecting fundamental rights, including equality bodies and data protection authorities. Where necessary for their mandate, those national public authorities or bodies should also have access to any documentation created under this Regulation. A specific safeguard procedure should be set for ensuring adequate and timely enforcement against AI systems presenting a risk to health, safety and fundamental rights. The procedure for such AI systems presenting a risk should be applied to high-risk AI systems presenting a risk, prohibited systems which have been placed on the market, put into service or used in violation of the prohibited practices laid down in this Regulation and AI systems which have been made available in violation of the transparency requirements laid down in this Regulation and present a risk.

81.2. General Approach

81.2.1 Preamble

1599. The safeguard procedure ensures general trust in AI technologies within the European Union after a risk assessment.

81.2.2 Consultation

1600. This is organised by the European Commission with all the stakeholders concerned within three months of receipt of a notification under Article 79(5), or within 30 days in the case of non-compliance with the prohibition of the AI practices referred to in Article 5. If there is a consensus, the new risk mitigation requirement should be implemented within six months, or within 60 days in the case of non-compliance with the prohibition of the AI practices referred to in Article 5.

82 ARTICLE 82. COMPLIANT AI SYSTEMS WHICH PRESENT A RISK

1. Where, having performed an evaluation under Article 79, after consulting the relevant national public authority referred to in Article 77(1), the market surveillance authority of a Member State finds that although a high-risk AI system complies with this Regulation, it nevertheless presents a risk to the health or safety of persons, to fundamental rights, or to other aspects of public interest protection, it shall require the relevant operator to take all appropriate measures to ensure that the AI system concerned, when placed on the market or put into service, no longer presents that risk without undue delay, within a period it may prescribe.

2. The provider or other relevant operator shall ensure that corrective action is taken in respect of all the AI systems concerned that it has made available on the Union market within the timeline prescribed by the market surveillance authority of the Member State referred to in paragraph 1.

3. The Member States shall immediately inform the Commission and the other Member States of a finding under paragraph 1. That information shall include all available details, in particular the data necessary for the identification of the AI system concerned, the origin and the supply chain of the AI system, the nature of the risk involved and the nature and duration of the national measures taken.

4. The Commission shall without undue delay enter into consultation with the Member States concerned and the relevant operators, and shall evaluate the national measures taken. On the basis of the results of that evaluation, the Commission shall decide whether the measure is justified and, where necessary, propose other appropriate measures.

5. The Commission shall immediately communicate its decision to the Member States concerned and to the relevant operators. It shall also inform the other Member States.

82.1. Recitals

1601. **(8)** A Union legal framework laying down harmonised rules on AI is therefore needed to foster the development, use and uptake of AI in the internal market that at the same time meets a high level of protection of public interests, such as health and safety and the protection of fundamental rights, including democracy, the rule of law and environmental protection as recognised and protected by Union law. To achieve that objective, rules regulating the placing on the market, the putting into service and the use of certain AI systems should be laid down, thus ensuring the smooth functioning of the internal market and allowing those systems to benefit from the principle of free movement of goods and services. Those rules should be clear and robust in protecting fundamental rights, supportive of new innovative solutions, enabling a European ecosystem of public and private actors creating AI systems in line with Union values and unlocking the potential of the digital transformation across all regions of the Union. By laying down those rules as well as measures in support of innovation with a particular focus on small and medium enterprises (SMEs), including startups, this Regulation supports the objective of promoting the European human-centric approach to AI and being a global leader in the development of secure, trustworthy and ethical AI as stated by the European Council,[51] and it ensures the protection of ethical principles, as specifically requested by the European Parliament.[52]

1602. (58) Another area in which the use of AI systems deserves special consideration is the access to and enjoyment of certain essential private and public services and benefits necessary for people to fully participate in society or to improve one's standard of living. In particular, natural persons applying for or receiving essential public assistance benefits and services from public authorities namely healthcare services, social security benefits, social services providing protection in cases such as maternity, illness, industrial accidents, dependency or old age and loss of employment and social and housing assistance, are typically dependent on those benefits and services and in a vulnerable position in relation to the responsible authorities. If AI systems are used for determining whether such benefits and services should be granted, denied, reduced, revoked or reclaimed by authorities, including whether beneficiaries are legitimately entitled to such benefits or services, those systems may have a significant impact on persons' livelihood and may infringe their fundamental rights, such as the right to social protection, non-discrimination, human dignity or an effective remedy and should therefore be classified as high-risk. Nonetheless, this Regulation should not hamper the development and use of innovative approaches in the public administration, which would stand to benefit from a wider use of compliant and safe AI systems, provided that those systems do not entail a high risk to legal and natural persons. In addition, AI systems used to evaluate the credit score or creditworthiness of natural persons should be classified as high-risk AI systems, since they determine those persons' access to financial resources or essential services such as housing, electricity, and telecommunication services. AI systems used for those purposes may lead to discrimination between persons or groups and may perpetuate historical patterns of discrimination, such as that based on racial or ethnic origins, gender, disabilities, age or sexual orientation, or may create new forms of discriminatory impacts. However, AI systems

[51] European Council, Special meeting of the European Council (1 and 2 October 2020) — Conclusions, EUCO 13/20, 2020, p. 6.

[52] European Parliament resolution of 20 October 2020 with recommendations to the Commission on a framework of ethical aspects of artificial intelligence, robotics and related technologies, 2020/2012(INL).

provided for by Union law for the purpose of detecting fraud in the offering of financial services and for prudential purposes to calculate credit institutions' and insurance undertakings' capital requirements should not be considered to be high-risk under this Regulation. Moreover, AI systems intended to be used for risk assessment and pricing in relation to natural persons for health and life insurance can also have a significant impact on persons' livelihood and if not duly designed, developed and used, can infringe their fundamental rights and can lead to serious consequences for people's life and health, including financial exclusion and discrimination. Finally, AI systems used to evaluate and classify emergency calls by natural persons or to dispatch or establish priority in the dispatching of emergency first response services, including by police, firefighters and medical aid, as well as of emergency healthcare patient triage systems, should also be classified as high-risk since they make decisions in very critical situations for the life and health of persons and their property.

82.2. General Approach

82.2.1 Preamble

1603. Compliance with requirements, harmonised standards or common specifications merely grants a presumption of conformity. Despite this compliance, a market surveillance authority may, after performing an evaluation, still find that an AI system may present risks.

82.2.2 Procedure

1604. It consists of:

- mitigating the risk;
- imposing a recall;
- requiring withdrawal.

82.3. Information

1605. The market surveillance authority informs the European Commission. The latter, after consulting all relevant stakeholders, decides on the measures to be taken. The Commission communicates its decision to:

- the Member States concerned;
- the relevant operators;
- the other Member States.

83 ARTICLE 83. FORMAL NON-COMPLIANCE

1. Where the market surveillance authority of a Member State makes one of the following findings, it shall require the relevant provider to put an end to the non-compliance concerned, within a period it may prescribe:

(a) the CE marking has been affixed in violation of Article 48;

(b) the CE marking has not been affixed;

(c) the EU declaration of conformity referred to in Article 47 has not been drawn up;

(d) the EU declaration of conformity referred to in Article 47 has not been drawn up correctly;

(e) the registration in the EU database referred to in Article 71 has not been carried out;

(f) where applicable, no authorised representative has been appointed;

(g) technical documentation is not available.

2. Where the non-compliance referred to in paragraph 1 persists, the market surveillance authority of the Member State concerned shall take appropriate and proportionate measures to restrict or prohibit the high-risk AI system being made available on the market or to ensure that it is recalled or withdrawn from the market without delay.

83.1. Recitals

1606. (160) The market surveillance authorities and the Commission should be able to propose joint activities, including joint investigations, to be conducted by market surveillance authorities or market surveillance authorities jointly with the Commission, that have the aim of promoting compliance, identifying non-compliance, raising awareness and providing guidance in relation to this Regulation with respect to specific categories of high-risk AI systems that are found to present a serious risk across two or more Member States. Joint activities to promote compliance should be carried out in accordance with Article 9 of Regulation (EU) 2019/1020. The AI Office should provide coordination support for joint investigations.

83.2. General Approach

1607. The elements showing compliance with the Regulation's requirements are essential for the creation and development of AI technology within the European Union.

83.3. Finding

1608. A market surveillance authority may make a finding of non-compliance.

83.4. *Regulation*

1609. Such finding mainly concerns:
- the CE marking;
- the EU declaration of conformity;
- the identification number of the notified body.

1610. If the provider fails to put an end to the non-compliance, the market surveillance authority may decide the following:
- restrictions on marketing conditions;
- prohibition;
- withdrawal.

84 ARTICLE 84. UNION AI TESTING SUPPORT STRUCTURES

1. The Commission shall designate one or more Union AI testing support structures to perform the tasks listed under Article 21(6) of Regulation (EU) 2019/1020 in the area of AI.

2. Without prejudice to the tasks referred to in paragraph 1, Union AI testing support structures shall also provide independent technical or scientific advice at the request of the Board, the Commission, or of market surveillance authorities.

84.1. *Recitals*

1611. (152) In order to support adequate enforcement as regards AI systems and reinforce the capacities of the Member States, Union AI testing support structures should be established and made available to the Member States.

84.2. *General Approach*

84.2.1 Preamble

1612. To optimise procedures and product surveillance within the European Union, an institutional mechanism is established, particularly for testing.

84.2.2 Guiding Principles

1613. The mechanism is as follows:
- EU support structures, designated by the European Commission, perform the following activities within their area of competence:
  - o carry out testing of products at the request of market surveillance authorities, the Union Product Compliance Network or the European Commission;

- o provide independent technical or scientific advice;
- o develop new techniques and methods of analysis.[53]

SECTION 4. REMEDIES

85 ARTICLE 85. RIGHT TO LODGE A COMPLAINT WITH A MARKET SURVEILLANCE AUTHORITY

Without prejudice to other administrative or judicial remedies, any natural or legal person having grounds to consider that there has been an infringement of the provisions of this Regulation may submit complaints to the relevant market surveillance authority.

In accordance with Regulation (EU) 2019/1020, such complaints shall be taken into account for the purpose of conducting market surveillance activities, and shall be handled in line with the dedicated procedures established therefor by the market surveillance authorities.

85.1. Recitals

1614. (162) To make best use of the centralised Union expertise and synergies at Union level, the powers of supervision and enforcement of the obligations on providers of general-purpose AI models should be a competence of the Commission. The AI Office should be able to carry out all necessary actions to monitor the effective implementation of this Regulation as regards general-purpose AI models. It should be able to investigate possible infringements of the rules on providers of general-purpose AI models both on its own initiative, following the results of its monitoring activities, or upon request from market surveillance authorities in line with the conditions set out in this Regulation. To support effective monitoring of the AI Office, it should provide for the possibility that downstream providers lodge complaints about possible infringements of the rules on providers of general-purpose AI models and systems.

1615. (170) Union and national law already provide effective remedies to natural and legal persons whose rights and freedoms are adversely affected by the use of AI systems. Without prejudice to those remedies, any natural or legal person that has grounds to consider that there has been an infringement of this Regulation should be entitled to lodge a complaint to the relevant market surveillance authority.

53 Regulation (EU) 2019/1020 of 20 June 2019, Art. 21(6).

85.2. General Approach

85.2.1 Preamble

1616. Any natural or legal person may submit a complaint with the market surveillance authorities.

85.2.2 Guiding Principles

1617. This specific remedy is without prejudice to any other administrative or judicial remedies.

85.3. Modalities

1618. It is exercised in accordance with the principles defined in Regulation (EU) 2019/1020 of 20 June 2019 on market surveillance and compliance of products and amending Directive 2004/42/EC and Regulations (EC) No 765/2008 and (EU) No 305/2011.[54]

86 ARTICLE 86. RIGHT TO EXPLANATION OF INDIVIDUAL DECISION-MAKING

1. Any affected person subject to a decision which is taken by the deployer on the basis of the output from a high-risk AI system listed in Annex III, with the exception of systems listed under point 2 thereof, and which produces legal effects or similarly significantly affects that person in a way that they consider to have an adverse impact on their health, safety or fundamental rights shall have the right to obtain from the deployer clear and meaningful explanations of the role of the AI system in the decision-making procedure and the main elements of the decision taken.

2. Paragraph 1 shall not apply to the use of AI systems for which exceptions from, or restrictions to, the obligation under that paragraph follow from Union or national law in compliance with Union law.

3. This Article shall apply only to the extent that the right referred to in paragraph 1 is not otherwise provided for under Union law.

[54] Regulation (EU) 2019/1020 of the European Parliament and of the Council of 20 June 2019 on market surveillance and compliance of products and amending Directive 2004/42/EC and Regulations (EC) No 765/2008 and (EU) No 305/2011, [2019] OJ L169/1, amended.

86.1. Recitals

1619. (93) Whilst risks related to AI systems can result from the way such systems are designed, risks can as well stem from how such AI systems are used. Deployers of high-risk AI system therefore play a critical role in ensuring that fundamental rights are protected, complementing the obligations of the provider when developing the AI system. Deployers are best placed to understand how the high-risk AI system will be used concretely and can therefore identify potential significant risks that were not foreseen in the development phase, due to a more precise knowledge of the context of use, the persons or groups of persons likely to be affected, including vulnerable groups. Deployers of high-risk AI systems listed in an annex to this Regulation also play a critical role in informing natural persons and should, when they make decisions or assist in making decisions related to natural persons, where applicable, inform the natural persons that they are subject to the use of the high-risk AI system. This information should include the intended purpose and the type of decisions it makes. The deployer should also inform the natural persons about their right to an explanation provided under this Regulation. With regard to high-risk AI systems used for law enforcement purposes, that obligation should be implemented in accordance with Article 13 of Directive (EU) 2016/680.

1620. (171) Affected persons should have the right to obtain an explanation where a deployer's decision is based mainly upon the output from certain high-risk AI systems that fall within the scope of this Regulation and where that decision produces legal effects or similarly significantly affects those persons in a way that they consider to have an adverse impact on their health, safety or fundamental rights. That explanation should be clear and meaningful and should provide a basis on which the affected persons are able to exercise their rights. The right to obtain an explanation should not apply to the use of AI systems for which exceptions or restrictions follow from Union or national law and should apply only to the extent this right is not already provided for under Union law.

86.2. General Approach

86.2.1 Preamble

1621. The right to understand individual decision-making is expressly and independently provided for in the context of personal data protection.[55]

[55] GDPR (EU) 2016/679, Art. 22.

86.2.2 Guiding Principles

1622. The objective is to extend the rights granted by personal data protection laws to all AI technologies that involve the processing of data related to natural persons in the European Union.

86.3. Characteristics

1623. The exercise of this right to obtain explanations is subject to the following:

NO.	THEME	SPECIFICATION
1.	Individual decision-making	Legal effects Adverse impacts
2.	Harm	Health Safety Fundamental rights
3.	Derogation	Provided for in EU or national law
4.	Application	In the absence of an identical specific right provided for in EU law

86.4. Modalities

1624. It is implemented as follows:

NO.	THEME	SPECIFICATION
1.	Actor	Deployer
2.	Decision-making process	Technical operations and related decisions
3.	Explanations	Clear Meaningful
4.	Form	Written

87 ARTICLE 87. REPORTING OF INFRINGEMENTS AND PROTECTION OF REPORTING PERSONS

Directive (EU) 2019/1937 shall apply to the reporting of infringements of this Regulation and the protection of persons reporting such infringements.

87.1. Recitals

1625. (172) Persons acting as whistleblowers on the infringements of this Regulation should be protected under the Union law. Directive (EU) 2019/1937 of the European Parliament and of the Council[56] should therefore apply to the reporting of infringements of this Regulation and the protection of persons reporting such infringements.

87.2. General Approach

87.2.1 Preamble

1626. The rules applicable to whistleblowers reporting infringements of the AI Act follow the general framework for reporting infringements of EU laws.

87.2.2 Guiding Principles

1627. In the absence of specific rules, whistleblowers are protected as in other situations under EU law and the law of the Member State concerned.

SECTION 5. SUPERVISION, INVESTIGATION, ENFORCEMENT AND MONITORING IN RESPECT OF PROVIDERS OF GENERAL-PURPOSE AI MODELS

88 ARTICLE 88. ENFORCEMENT OF THE OBLIGATIONS OF PROVIDERS OF GENERAL-PURPOSE AI MODELS

1. The Commission shall have exclusive powers to supervise and enforce Chapter V, taking into account the procedural guarantees under Article 94. The Commission shall entrust the implementation of these tasks to the AI Office, without prejudice to the powers of organisation of the Commission and the division of competences between Member States and the Union based on the Treaties.

2. Without prejudice to Article 75(3), market surveillance authorities may request the Commission to exercise the powers laid down in this Section, where that is necessary and proportionate to assist with the fulfilment of their tasks under this Regulation.

[56] Directive (EU) 2019/1937 of the European Parliament and of the Council of 23 October 2019 on the protection of persons who report breaches of Union law, [2019] OJ L305/17.

88.1. General Approach

88.1.1 Preamble

1628. General-purpose AI models, whether or not they pose systemic risk, present serious and real dangers that justify specific powers being granted to the European Commission.

88.1.2 Guiding Principles

1629. The European Commission has exclusive powers of:
- surveillance;
- enforcement.

88.2. Modalities

1630. They are as follows:

NO.	THEME	SPECIFICATION
1.	Body	AI Office
2.	Type	General-purpose AI models without systemic risk General-purpose AI models with systemic risk
3.	Actor	Provider Authorised representative
4.	Activity	Before or after the placing on the market or putting into service
5.	Procedure	All the specific features applicable to this type of model
6.	Initiative	European Commission Market surveillance authority

89 ARTICLE 89. MONITORING ACTIONS

1. For the purpose of carrying out the tasks assigned to it under this Section, the AI Office may take the necessary actions to monitor the effective implementation and compliance with this Regulation by providers of general-purpose AI models, including their adherence to approved codes of practice.

2. Downstream providers shall have the right to lodge a complaint alleging an infringement of this Regulation. A complaint shall be duly reasoned and indicate at least:

(a) the point of contact of the provider of the general-purpose AI model concerned;

(b) a description of the relevant facts, the provisions of this Regulation concerned, and the reason why the downstream provider considers that the provider of the general-purpose AI model concerned infringed this Regulation;

(c) any other information that the downstream provider that sent the request considers relevant, including, where appropriate, information gathered on its own initiative.

89.1. Recitals

1631. (101) Providers of general-purpose AI models have a particular role and responsibility along the AI value chain, as the models they provide may form the basis for a range of downstream systems, often provided by downstream providers that necessitate a good understanding of the models and their capabilities, both to enable the integration of such models into their products, and to fulfil their obligations under this or other regulations. Therefore, proportionate transparency measures should be laid down, including the drawing up and keeping up to date of documentation, and the provision of information on the general-purpose AI model for its usage by the downstream providers. Technical documentation should be prepared and kept up to date by the general-purpose AI model provider for the purpose of making it available, upon request, to the AI Office and the national competent authorities. The minimal set of elements to be included in such documentation should be set out in specific annexes to this Regulation. The Commission should be empowered to amend those annexes by means of delegated acts in light of evolving technological developments.

1632. (162) To make best use of the centralised Union expertise and synergies at Union level, the powers of supervision and enforcement of the obligations on providers of general-purpose AI models should be a competence of the Commission. The AI Office should be able to carry out all necessary actions to monitor the effective implementation of this Regulation as regards general-purpose AI models. It should be able to investigate possible infringements of the rules on providers of general-purpose AI models both on its own initiative, following the results of its monitoring activities, or upon request from market surveillance authorities in line with the conditions set out in this Regulation. To support effective monitoring of the AI Office, it should provide for the possibility that downstream providers lodge complaints about possible infringements of the rules on providers of general-purpose AI models and systems.

89.2. *General Approach*

89.2.1 Preamble

1633. The monitoring actions in respect to general-purpose AI models are carried out by the AI Office on behalf of the European Commission and are implemented during deployment.

1634. They also concern adherence to approved codes of practice.

89.2.2 Guiding Principles

1635. The AI Office is authorised to take all necessary actions to conduct monitoring actions. It may act at the request of:

- the European Commission;
- market surveillance authorities;
- downstream providers.

89.3. *Complaints*

89.3.1 Definition

1636. 'Downstream provider' means 'a provider of an AI system, including a general-purpose AI system, which integrates an AI model, regardless of whether the AI model is provided by themselves and vertically integrated or provided by another entity based on contractual relations'.[57]

89.3.2 Modalities

1637. They are as follows:

NO.	THEME	SPECIFICATION
1.	Theme	Infringement of the AI Act
2.	Technology	General-purpose AI model with or without systemic risk General-purpose AI system
3.	Form	Written
4.	Grounds	Reasoned Detailed

[57] AI Act, Art. 3(68).

NO.	THEME	SPECIFICATION
5.	Complaint	Point of contact of the provider of the technology concerned Description of the relevant facts Description of the obligations involved Any other relevant information

90 ARTICLE 90. ALERTS OF SYSTEMIC RISKS BY THE SCIENTIFIC PANEL

1. The scientific panel may provide a qualified alert to the AI Office where it has reason to suspect that:

(a) a general-purpose AI model poses concrete identifiable risk at Union level; or

(b) a general-purpose AI model meets the conditions referred to in Article 51.

2. Upon such qualified alert, the Commission, through the AI Office and after having informed the Board, may exercise the powers laid down in this Section for the purpose of assessing the matter. The AI Office shall inform the Board of any measure according to Articles 91 to 94.

3. A qualified alert shall be duly reasoned and indicate at least:

(a) the point of contact of the provider of the general-purpose AI model with systemic risk concerned;

(b) a description of the relevant facts and the reasons for the alert by the scientific panel;

(c) any other information that the scientific panel considers to be relevant, including, where appropriate, information gathered on its own initiative.

90.1. Recitals

1638. **(113)** If the Commission becomes aware of the fact that a general-purpose AI model meets the requirements to classify as a general-purpose AI model with systemic risk, which previously had either not been known or of which the relevant provider has failed to notify the Commission, the Commission should be empowered to designate it so. A system of qualified alerts should ensure that the AI Office is made aware by the scientific panel of general-purpose AI models that should possibly be classified as general-purpose AI models with systemic risk, in addition to the monitoring activities of the AI Office.

1639. **(163)** With a view to complementing the governance systems for general-purpose AI models, the scientific panel should support the monitoring activities of the AI Office and may, in certain cases, provide qualified alerts to the AI

Office which trigger follow-ups, such as investigations. This should be the case where the scientific panel has reason to suspect that a general-purpose AI model poses a concrete and identifiable risk at Union level. Furthermore, this should be the case where the scientific panel has reason to suspect that a general-purpose AI model meets the criteria that would lead to a classification as general-purpose AI model with systemic risk. To equip the scientific panel with the information necessary for the performance of those tasks, there should be a mechanism whereby the scientific panel can request the Commission to require documentation or information from a provider.

90.2. General Approach

90.2.1 Preamble

1640. The scientific panel serves as 'the vision' for the future of AI for the European Commission, and particularly for the AI Office.

90.2.2 Guiding Principles

1641. As a true sentinel of the EU, scientists are tasked with alerting the AI Office in the event of a systemic risk related to a general-purpose AI model.

90.3. Modalities

1642. The characteristics of the alerts are as follows:

NO.	THEME	SPECIFICATION
1.	Type	General-purpose AI model with systemic risk
2.	Criterion 1	Concrete identifiable risk at EU level
3.	Criterion 2	General-purpose AI model not classified as presenting systemic risk with such characteristics
4.	Qualification	Alert detailing the reasons for suspecting the existence of such a systemic risk including: • the point of contact of the provider • the relevant facts • other relevant information

91 ARTICLE 91. POWER TO REQUEST DOCUMENTATION AND INFORMATION

1. The Commission may request the provider of the general-purpose AI model concerned to provide the documentation drawn up by the provider in accordance with Articles 53 and 55, or any additional information that is necessary for the purpose of assessing compliance of the provider with this Regulation.

2. Before sending the request for information, the AI Office may initiate a structured dialogue with the provider of the general-purpose AI model.

3. Upon a duly substantiated request from the scientific panel, the Commission may issue a request for information to a provider of a general-purpose AI model, where the access to information is necessary and proportionate for the fulfilment of the tasks of the scientific panel under Article 68(2).

4. The request for information shall state the legal basis and the purpose of the request, specify what information is required, set a period within which the information is to be provided, and indicate the fines provided for in Article 101 for supplying incorrect, incomplete or misleading information.

5. The provider of the general-purpose AI model concerned, or its representative shall supply the information requested. In the case of legal persons, companies or firms, or where the provider has no legal personality, the persons authorised to represent them by law or by their statutes, shall supply the information requested on behalf of the provider of the general-purpose AI model concerned. Lawyers duly authorised to act may supply information on behalf of their clients. The clients shall nevertheless remain fully responsible if the information supplied is incomplete, incorrect or misleading.

91.1. General Approach

91.1.1 Preamble

1643. The hazardous nature of general-purpose AI models with systemic risk requires technological monitoring of both current and future systems.

91.1.2 Guiding Principles

1644. To this end, the AI Office has a special competence to access information related to the general-purpose AI model in order to assess compliance with the Regulation.

91.2. Modalities

1645. They are as follows:

NO.	THEME	SPECIFICATION
1.	Technology	General-purpose AI model
2.	Action	Assessment of the IA model Investigation into the existence of systemic risks at EU level
3.	Expert	Appointment from the experts panel or independent experts
4.	Elements (access)	Technical documentation Through APIs Source code
5.	Grounds	Reasoned request for access with indication of penalties
6.	Cooperation	Prior to access to technical data, a structured dialogue on all aspects of systemic risk assessment and prevention should be organised
7.	Application	Procedure and implementation mechanism are the subject of implementing acts by the European Commission

92 ARTICLE 92. POWER TO CONDUCT EVALUATIONS

1. The AI Office, after consulting the Board, may conduct evaluations of the general-purpose AI model concerned:

(a) to assess compliance of the provider with obligations under this Regulation, where the information gathered pursuant to Article 91 is insufficient; or

(b) to investigate systemic risks at Union level of general-purpose AI models with systemic risk, in particular following a qualified alert from the scientific panel in accordance with Article 90(1), point (a).

2. The Commission may decide to appoint independent experts to carry out evaluations on its behalf, including from the scientific panel established pursuant to Article 68. Independent experts appointed for this task shall meet the criteria outlined in Article 68(2).

3. For the purposes of paragraph 1, the Commission may request access to the general-purpose AI model concerned through APIs or further appropriate technical means and tools, including source code.

4. The request for access shall state the legal basis, the purpose and reasons of the request and set the period within which the access is to be provided, and the fines provided for in Article 101 for failure to provide access.

5. The providers of the general-purpose AI model concerned or its representative shall supply the information requested. In the case of legal persons, companies or firms, or where the provider has no legal personality, the persons authorised to represent them by law or by their statutes, shall provide the access requested on behalf of the provider of the general-purpose AI model concerned.

6. The Commission shall adopt implementing acts setting out the detailed arrangements and the conditions for the evaluations, including the detailed arrangements for involving independent experts, and the procedure for the selection thereof. Those implementing acts shall be adopted in accordance with the examination procedure referred to in Article 98(2).

7. Prior to requesting access to the general-purpose AI model concerned, the AI Office may initiate a structured dialogue with the provider of the general-purpose AI model to gather more information on the internal testing of the model, internal safeguards for preventing systemic risks, and other internal procedures and measures the provider has taken to mitigate such risks.

92.1. Recitals

1646. (161) It is necessary to clarify the responsibilities and competences at Union and national level as regards AI systems that are built on general-purpose AI models. To avoid overlapping competences, where an AI system is based on a general-purpose AI model and the model and system are provided by the same provider, the supervision should take place at Union level through the AI Office, which should have the powers of a market surveillance authority within the meaning of Regulation (EU) 2019/1020 for this purpose. In all other cases, national market surveillance authorities remain responsible for the supervision of AI systems. However, for general-purpose AI systems that can be used directly by deployers for at least one purpose that is classified as high-risk, market surveillance authorities should cooperate with the AI Office to carry out evaluations of compliance and inform the Board and other market surveillance authorities accordingly. Furthermore, market surveillance authorities should be able to request assistance from the AI Office where the market surveillance authority is unable to conclude an investigation on a high-risk AI system because of its inability to access certain information related to the general-purpose AI model on which the high-risk AI system is built. In such cases, the procedure regarding mutual assistance in cross-border cases in Chapter VI of Regulation (EU) 2019/1020 should apply *mutatis mutandis*.

1647. (164) The AI Office should be able to take the necessary actions to monitor the effective implementation of and compliance with the obligations for providers of general-purpose AI models laid down in this Regulation. The AI Office should be able to investigate possible infringements in accordance with the powers provided for in this Regulation, including by requesting documentation and information, by conducting evaluations, as well as by requesting measures from providers of general-purpose AI models. When conducting evaluations, in order to make use of independent expertise, the AI Office should be able to involve independent experts to carry out the evaluations on its behalf. Compliance with the obligations should be enforceable, inter alia, through requests to take appropriate measures, including risk mitigation measures in the case of identified systemic risks as well as restricting the making available on the market, withdrawing or recalling the model. As a safeguard, where needed beyond the procedural rights provided for in this Regulation, providers of general-purpose AI models should have the procedural rights provided for in Article 18 of Regulation (EU) 2019/1020, which should apply *mutatis mutandis*, without prejudice to more specific procedural rights provided for by this Regulation.

92.2. General Approach

92.2.1 Preamble

1648. In coordination with the power to access technical documentation, the AI Office is empowered to conduct evaluations.

92.2.2 Guiding Principles

1649. The evaluations initiated by the AI Office include:

- additional reviews where the documentation received under its right to access technical documentation is insufficient;
- the assessment of systemic risks, either on its own initiative or following an alert from the scientific panel.

92.3. Modalities

1650. They are as follows:

NO.	THEME	SPECIFICATION
1.	Cooperation	Optional organisation of a structured dialogue with the provider
2.	Technology	General-purpose AI model
3.	Prerequisite	Prior consultation of the AI Board
4.	Experts	Scientific panel Independent experts

NO.	THEME	SPECIFICATION
5.	Access	Through APIs Direct access Source code
6.	Grounds	Purpose Reasons Request
7.	Penalties	Application of Article 101

93 ARTICLE 93. POWER TO REQUEST MEASURES

1. Where necessary and appropriate, the Commission may request providers to:

(a) take appropriate measures to comply with the obligations set out in Articles 53 and 54;

(b) implement mitigation measures, where the evaluation carried out in accordance with Article 92 has given rise to serious and substantiated concern of a systemic risk at Union level;

(c) restrict the making available on the market, withdraw or recall the model.

2. Before a measure is requested, the AI Office may initiate a structured dialogue with the provider of the general-purpose AI model.

3. If, during the structured dialogue referred to in paragraph 2, the provider of the general-purpose AI model with systemic risk offers commitments to implement mitigation measures to address a systemic risk at Union level, the Commission may, by decision, make those commitments binding and declare that there are no further grounds for action.

93.1. Recitals

1651. (80) As signatories to the United Nations Convention on the Rights of Persons with Disabilities, the Union and the Member States are legally obliged to protect persons with disabilities from discrimination and promote their equality, to ensure that persons with disabilities have access, on an equal basis with others, to information and communications technologies and systems, and to ensure respect for privacy for persons with disabilities. Given the growing importance and use of AI systems, the application of universal design principles to all new technologies and services should ensure full and equal access for everyone potentially affected by or using AI technologies, including persons with disabilities, in a way that takes full account of their inherent dignity and diversity. It is therefore essential that providers ensure full compliance with accessibility requirements, including Directive (EU) 2016/2102 of the European Parliament and of the Council[58] and Directive (EU) 2019/882. Providers should ensure compliance with these requirements by design. Therefore, the necessary measures should be integrated as much as possible into the design of the high-risk AI system.

1652. (112) It is also necessary to clarify a procedure for the classification of a general-purpose AI model with systemic risks. A general-purpose AI model that meets the applicable threshold for high-impact capabilities should be presumed to be a general-purpose AI models with systemic risk. The provider should notify the AI Office at the latest two weeks after the requirements are met or it becomes known that a general-purpose AI model will meet the requirements that lead to the presumption. This is especially relevant in relation to the threshold of floating point operations because training of general-purpose AI models takes considerable planning which includes the upfront allocation of compute resources and, therefore, providers of general-purpose AI models are able to know if their model would meet the threshold before the training is completed. In the context of that notification, the provider should be able to demonstrate that, because of its specific characteristics, a general-purpose AI model exceptionally does not present systemic risks, and that it thus should not be classified as a general-purpose AI model with systemic risks. That information is valuable for the AI Office to anticipate the placing on the market of general-purpose AI models with systemic risks and the providers can start to engage with the AI Office early on. That information is especially important with regard to general-purpose AI models that are planned to be released as open-source, given that, after the open-source model release, necessary measures to ensure compliance with the obligations under this Regulation may be more difficult to implement.

1653. (162) To make best use of the centralised Union expertise and synergies at Union level, the powers of supervision and enforcement of the obligations on providers of general-purpose AI models should be a competence of the Commission. The AI Office should be able to carry out all necessary actions to monitor the effective implementation of this Regulation as regards general-purpose AI models. It should be able to investigate possible infringements of the rules on providers of general-purpose AI models both on its own initiative, following the results of its monitoring activities, or upon request from market surveillance authorities in line with the conditions set out in this Regulation. To support effective monitoring of the AI Office, it should provide for the possibility

[58] Directive (EU) 2016/2102 of the European Parliament and of the Council of 26 October 2016 on the accessibility of the websites and mobile applications of public sector bodies, [2016] OJ L327/1.

that downstream providers lodge complaints about possible infringements of the rules on providers of general-purpose AI models and systems.

1654. **(164)** The AI Office should be able to take the necessary actions to monitor the effective implementation of and compliance with the obligations for providers of general-purpose AI models laid down in this Regulation. The AI Office should be able to investigate possible infringements in accordance with the powers provided for in this Regulation, including by requesting documentation and information, by conducting evaluations, as well as by requesting measures from providers of general-purpose AI models. When conducting evaluations, in order to make use of independent expertise, the AI Office should be able to involve independent experts to carry out the evaluations on its behalf. Compliance with the obligations should be enforceable, inter alia, through requests to take appropriate measures, including risk mitigation measures in the case of identified systemic risks as well as restricting the making available on the market, withdrawing or recalling the model. As a safeguard, where needed beyond the procedural rights provided for in this Regulation, providers of general-purpose AI models should have the procedural rights provided for in Article 18 of Regulation (EU) 2019/1020, which should apply *mutatis mutandis*, without prejudice to more specific procedural rights provided for by this Regulation.

93.2. General Approach

93.2.1 Preamble

1655. After a structured dialogue[59] with the provider or an evaluation, the European Commission may take action to prevent the occurrence of systemic risks or impose mitigation measures and associated safeguards.

93.2.2 Guiding Principles

1656. As these measures are binding on the provider, there is a safeguard to allow the provider to contest them if the provider believes that the implementation conditions are not being met.

[59] AI Act, Art. 92(7).

93.3. Modalities

1657. They are as follows:

NO.	THEME	SPECIFICATION
1.	Technology	General-purpose AI model with systemic risk
2.	Measures	Compliance Risk mitigation Restrictions on the making available on the market Recall Withdrawal
3.	Procedure	Possibility of initiating a structured dialogue beforehand
4.	Consequences	European Commission decisions are binding notwithstanding possible appeals[1]

94 ARTICLE 94. PROCEDURAL RIGHTS OF ECONOMIC OPERATORS OF THE GENERAL-PURPOSE AI MODEL

Article 18 of Regulation (EU) 2019/1020 shall apply *mutatis mutandis* to the providers of the general-purpose AI model, without prejudice to more specific procedural rights provided for in this Regulation.

94.1. Recitals

1658. (164) The AI Office should be able to take the necessary actions to monitor the effective implementation of and compliance with the obligations for providers of general-purpose AI models laid down in this Regulation. The AI Office should be able to investigate possible infringements in accordance with the powers provided for in this Regulation, including by requesting documentation and information, by conducting evaluations, as well as by requesting measures from providers of general-purpose AI models. When conducting evaluations, in order to make use of independent expertise, the AI Office should be able to involve independent experts to carry out the evaluations on its behalf. Compliance with the obligations should be enforceable, inter alia, through requests to take appropriate measures, including risk mitigation measures in the case of identified systemic risks as well as restricting the making available on the market, withdrawing or recalling the model. As a safeguard, where needed beyond the procedural rights provided for in this Regulation, providers of general-purpose

[1] AI Act, Art. 94.

AI models should have the procedural rights provided for in Article 18 of Regulation (EU) 2019/1020, which should apply *mutatis mutandis*, without prejudice to more specific procedural rights provided for by this Regulation.

94.2. General Approach

94.2.1 Preamble

1659. The objective is to regulate the European Commission's powers to assess general-purpose AI models in case of:

- emergency;
- severity;
- systemic risks.

94.2.2 Guiding Principles

1660. Depending on the situation, the provider must comply with the European Commission's decisions, subject to applicable appeals.

94.3. Modalities

1661. Procedural rights include:

- general procedural rights;
- specific procedural rights provided for by the Regulation.

94.3.1 General Rules

1662. They are as follows:

- 'any measure, decision or order taken or made by market surveillance authorities pursuant to Union harmonisation legislation or this Regulation shall state the exact grounds on which it is based;
- any such measure, decision or order shall be communicated without delay to the relevant economic operator, who shall at the same time be informed of the remedies available to it under the law of the Member State concerned and of the time limits to which those remedies are subject;
- before a measure, decision or order referred to in paragraph 1 is taken or made, the economic operator concerned shall be given the opportunity to be heard within an appropriate period of not less than 10 working days, unless it is not possible to give the economic operator that opportunity because of the urgency of the measure, decision or order, based on health or safety requirements or other grounds relating to the public interests covered by the relevant Union harmonisation legislation.

- if the measure, decision or order is taken or made without the economic operator being given the opportunity to be heard, the economic operator shall be given that opportunity as soon as possible thereafter and that measure, decision or order shall be reviewed promptly by the market surveillance authority'.[2]

2 Regulation (EU) 2019/1020, Art. 18: Procedural rights of economic operators.

CHAPTER X
CODES OF CONDUCT AND GUIDELINES

1663. Key takeaways: This Chapter covers two topics:

- codes of conduct;
- guidelines from the European Commission.

95 ARTICLE 95. CODES OF CONDUCT FOR VOLUNTARY APPLICATION OF SPECIFIC REQUIREMENTS

1. The AI Office and the Member States shall encourage and facilitate the drawing up of codes of conduct, including related governance mechanisms, intended to foster the voluntary application to AI systems, other than high-risk AI systems, of some or all of the requirements set out in Chapter III, Section 2 taking into account the available technical solutions and industry best practices allowing for the application of such requirements.

2. The AI Office and the Member States shall facilitate the drawing up of codes of conduct concerning the voluntary application, including by deployers, of specific requirements to all AI systems, on the basis of clear objectives and key performance indicators to measure the achievement of those objectives, including elements such as, but not limited to:

(a) applicable elements provided for in Union ethical guidelines for trustworthy AI;

(b) assessing and minimising the impact of AI systems on environmental sustainability, including as regards energy-efficient programming and techniques for the efficient design, training and use of AI;

(c) promoting AI literacy, in particular that of persons dealing with the development, operation and use of AI;

(d) facilitating an inclusive and diverse design of AI systems, including through the establishment of inclusive and diverse development teams and the promotion of stakeholders' participation in that process;

(e) assessing and preventing the negative impact of AI systems on vulnerable persons or groups of vulnerable persons, including as regards accessibility for persons with a disability, as well as on gender equality.

3. Codes of conduct may be drawn up by individual providers or deployers of AI systems or by organisations representing them or by both, including with the involvement of any interested stakeholders and their representative organisations, including civil society organisations and academia. Codes of conduct may cover one or more AI systems taking into account the similarity of the intended purpose of the relevant systems.

4. The AI Office and the Member States shall take into account the specific interests and needs of SMEs, including start-ups, when encouraging and facilitating the drawing up of codes of conduct.

95.1. Recitals

1664. (20) In order to obtain the greatest benefits from AI systems while protecting fundamental rights, health and safety and to enable democratic control, AI literacy should equip providers, deployers and affected persons with the necessary notions to make informed decisions regarding AI systems. Those notions may vary with regard to the relevant context and can include understanding the correct application of technical elements during the AI system's development phase, the measures to be applied during its use, the suitable ways in which to interpret the AI system's output, and, in the case of affected persons, the knowledge necessary to understand how decisions taken with the assistance of AI will have an impact on them. In the context of the application this Regulation, AI literacy should provide all relevant actors in the AI value chain with the insights required to ensure the appropriate compliance and its correct enforcement. Furthermore, the wide implementation of AI literacy measures and the introduction of appropriate follow-up actions could contribute to improving working conditions and ultimately sustain the consolidation, and innovation path of trustworthy AI in the Union. The European Artificial Intelligence Board (the 'Board') should support the Commission, to promote AI literacy tools, public awareness and understanding of the benefits, risks, safeguards, rights and obligations in relation to the use of AI systems. In cooperation with the relevant stakeholders, the Commission and the Member States should facilitate the drawing up of voluntary codes of conduct to advance AI literacy among persons dealing with the development, operation and use of AI.

1665. (27) While the risk-based approach is the basis for a proportionate and effective set of binding rules, it is important to recall the 2019 Ethics guidelines for trustworthy AI developed by the independent AI HLEG appointed by the Commission. In those guidelines, the AI HLEG developed seven non-binding ethical principles for AI which are intended to help ensure that AI is trustworthy and ethically sound. The seven principles include human agency and oversight; technical robustness and safety; privacy and data governance; transparency; diversity, non-discrimination and fairness; societal and environmental well-being and accountability. Without prejudice to the legally binding requirements of this Regulation and any other applicable Union law, those guidelines contribute to the design of coherent, trustworthy and human-centric AI, in line with the Charter and with the values on which the Union is founded. According to the guidelines of the AI HLEG, human agency and oversight means that AI systems are developed and used as a tool that serves people, respects human dignity and personal autonomy, and that is functioning in a way that can be appropriately controlled and overseen by humans. Technical robustness and safety means that AI systems are developed and used in a way that allows robustness in the case of problems and resilience against attempts to alter the use or performance of the AI system so as to allow unlawful use by third parties, and minimise unintended harm. Privacy and data governance means that AI systems are developed and used in accordance with privacy and data protection rules, while processing data that meets high standards in terms of quality and integrity. Transparency means that AI systems are developed and used in a way that allows appropriate traceability and explainability, while making humans aware that they communicate or interact with an AI system, as well as duly informing deployers of the capabilities and limitations of that AI system and affected persons about their rights. Diversity, non-discrimination and fairness means that AI systems are developed and used in a way that includes diverse actors and promotes equal access, gender equality and cultural diversity, while avoiding discriminatory impacts and unfair biases that are prohibited by Union or national law. Social and environmental well-being means that AI systems are developed and used in a sustainable and environmentally friendly manner as well as in a way to benefit all human beings, while monitoring and assessing the long-term impacts on the individual, society and democracy. The application of those principles should be translated, when possible, in the design and use of AI models. They should in any case serve as a basis for the drafting of codes of conduct under this Regulation. All stakeholders, including industry, academia, civil society and standardisation organisations, are encouraged to take into account, as appropriate, the ethical principles for the development of voluntary best practices and standards.

1666. (165) The development of AI systems other than high-risk AI systems in accordance with the requirements of this Regulation may lead to a larger uptake of ethical and trustworthy AI in the Union. Providers of AI systems that are not high-risk should be encouraged to create codes of conduct, including related governance mechanisms, intended to foster the voluntary application of some or all of the mandatory requirements applicable to high-risk AI systems, adapted in light of the intended purpose of the systems and the lower risk involved and taking into account the available technical solutions and industry best practices such as model and data cards. Providers and, as appropriate, deployers of all AI systems, high-risk or not, and AI models should also be encouraged to apply on a voluntary basis additional requirements related, for example, to the elements of the Union's Ethics Guidelines for Trustworthy AI, environmental sustainability, AI literacy measures, inclusive and diverse design and development of AI systems, including attention to vulnerable persons and accessibility to persons with disability, stakeholders' participation with the involvement, as appropriate, of relevant stakeholders such as business and civil society organisations, academia, research organisations, trade unions and consumer protection organisations in the design and development of AI systems, and diversity of the development teams, including gender balance. To ensure that the voluntary codes of conduct are effective, they should be based on clear objectives and key performance indicators to measure the achievement of those objectives. They should also be developed in an inclusive way, as appropriate, with the involvement of relevant stakeholders such as business and civil society organisations, academia, research organisations, trade unions and consumer protection organisation. The Commission may develop initiatives, including of a sectoral nature, to facilitate the lowering of technical barriers hindering cross-border exchange of data for AI development, including on data access infrastructure, semantic and technical interoperability of different types of data.

95.2. General Approach

95.2.1 Preamble

1667. Codes of conduct are essential elements of the self-regulation of the AI market by operators.

95.2.2 Guiding Principles

1668. The overall idea is to increase trust in all AI systems by generalising all or part of the requirements imposed on high-risk AI systems.

95.3. Approach

95.3.1 Assessment Policy

1669. The European Commission and Member States must plan for such an objective.

1670. In this case, the European Commission and the AI Board must take into account the specific interests and needs of:

- SME providers;[1]
- start-ups.

[1] Commission Recommendation of 6 May 2003 concerning the definition of micro, small and medium-sized enterprises, [2003] OJ L 124/36.

95.3.2 Characteristics

1671. They are as follows:

NO.	THEME	SPECIFICATION
1.	Initiative	Modality Field Participation
2.	Area	All AI systems
3.	Modalities	Voluntary application
4.	Participation	Operators Any interested stakeholders and their representative organisations
5.	Objectives	In addition to the requirements specific to high-risk AI systems,[2] these include: • environmental sustainability • accessibility for persons with a disability • inclusive design and development • diversity of development teams
6.	Period	Evaluation of the impact of the codes of conduct by the European Commission no later than 2 August 2028 and every three years thereafter

95.4. Find Out More

95.4.1 Toolbox

1672. G7-G20, 'Hiroshima Process International Code of Conduct for Organizations Developing Advanced AI Systems', 30 October 2023.

96 ARTICLE 96. GUIDELINES FROM THE COMMISSION ON THE IMPLEMENTATION OF THIS REGULATION

1. The Commission shall develop guidelines on the practical implementation of this Regulation, and in particular on:

(a) the application of the requirements and obligations referred to in Articles 8 to 15 and in Article 25;

(b) the prohibited practices referred to in Article 5;

[2] AI Act, Chapter III, Section 2, Arts. 8 ff.

(c) the practical implementation of the provisions related to substantial modification;

(d) the practical implementation of transparency obligations laid down in Article 50;

(e) detailed information on the relationship of this Regulation with the Union harmonisation legislation listed in Annex I, as well as with other relevant Union law, including as regards consistency in their enforcement;

(f) the application of the definition of an AI system as set out in Article 3, point (1).

When issuing such guidelines, the Commission shall pay particular attention to the needs of SMEs including start-ups, of local public authorities and of the sectors most likely to be affected by this Regulation.

The guidelines referred to in the first subparagraph of this paragraph shall take due account of the generally acknowledged state of the art on AI, as well as of relevant harmonised standards and common specifications that are referred to in Articles 40 and 41, or of those harmonised standards or technical specifications that are set out pursuant to Union harmonisation law.

2. At the request of the Member States or the AI Office, or on its own initiative, the Commission shall update guidelines previously adopted when deemed necessary.

96.1. Recitals

1673. (7) In order to ensure a consistent and high level of protection of public interests as regards health, safety and fundamental rights, common rules for high-risk AI systems should be established. Those rules should be consistent with the Charter, non-discriminatory and in line with the Union's international trade commitments. They should also take into account the European Declaration on Digital Rights and Principles for the Digital Decade and the Ethics guidelines for trustworthy AI of the High-Level Expert Group on Artificial Intelligence (AI HLEG).

1674. (27) While the risk-based approach is the basis for a proportionate and effective set of binding rules, it is important to recall the 2019 Ethics guidelines for trustworthy AI developed by the independent AI HLEG appointed by the Commission. In those guidelines, the AI HLEG developed seven non-binding ethical principles for AI which are intended to help ensure that AI is trustworthy and ethically sound. The seven principles include human agency and oversight; technical robustness and safety; privacy and data governance; transparency; diversity, non-discrimination and fairness; societal and environmental well-being and accountability. Without prejudice to the legally binding requirements of this Regulation and any other applicable Union law, those guidelines contribute to the design of coherent, trustworthy and human-centric AI, in line with the

Charter and with the values on which the Union is founded. According to the guidelines of the AI HLEG, human agency and oversight means that AI systems are developed and used as a tool that serves people, respects human dignity and personal autonomy, and that is functioning in a way that can be appropriately controlled and overseen by humans. Technical robustness and safety means that AI systems are developed and used in a way that allows robustness in the case of problems and resilience against attempts to alter the use or performance of the AI system so as to allow unlawful use by third parties, and minimise unintended harm. Privacy and data governance means that AI systems are developed and used in accordance with privacy and data protection rules, while processing data that meets high standards in terms of quality and integrity. Transparency means that AI systems are developed and used in a way that allows appropriate traceability and explainability, while making humans aware that they communicate or interact with an AI system, as well as duly informing deployers of the capabilities and limitations of that AI system and affected persons about their rights. Diversity, non-discrimination and fairness means that AI systems are developed and used in a way that includes diverse actors and promotes equal access, gender equality and cultural diversity, while avoiding discriminatory impacts and unfair biases that are prohibited by Union or national law. Social and environmental well-being means that AI systems are developed and used in a sustainable and environmentally friendly manner as well as in a way to benefit all human beings, while monitoring and assessing the long-term impacts on the individual, society and democracy. The application of those principles should be translated, when possible, in the design and use of AI models. They should in any case serve as a basis for the drafting of codes of conduct under this Regulation. All stakeholders, including industry, academia, civil society and standardisation organisations, are encouraged to take into account, as appropriate, the ethical principles for the development of voluntary best practices and standards.

1675. **(53)** It is also important to clarify that there may be specific cases in which AI systems referred to in pre-defined areas specified in this Regulation do not lead to a significant risk of harm to the legal interests protected under those areas because they do not materially influence the decision-making or do not harm those interests substantially. For the purposes of this Regulation, an AI system that does not materially influence the outcome of decision-making should be understood to be an AI system that does not have an impact on the substance, and thereby the outcome, of decision-making, whether human or automated. An AI system that does not materially influence the outcome of decision-making could include situations in which one or more of the following conditions are fulfilled. The first such condition should be that the AI system is intended to perform a narrow procedural task, such as an AI system that transforms unstructured data into structured data, an AI system that classifies incoming documents into categories or an AI system that is used to detect duplicates among a large number of applications. Those tasks are of such narrow and limited nature that they pose only limited risks which are not increased through the use of an AI system in a context that is listed as a high-risk use in an annex to this Regulation. The second condition should be that the task performed by the AI system is intended to improve the result of a previously completed human activity that may be relevant for the purposes of the high-risk uses listed in an annex to this Regulation. Considering those characteristics, the AI system provides only an additional layer to a human activity with consequently lowered risk. That condition would, for example, apply to AI systems that are intended to improve the language used in previously drafted documents, for example in relation to professional tone, academic style of language or by aligning text to a certain brand messaging. The third condition should be that the AI system is intended to detect decision-making patterns or deviations from prior decision-making patterns. The risk would be lowered because the use of the AI system follows a previously completed human assessment which it is not meant to replace or influence, without proper human review. Such AI systems include for instance those that, given a certain grading pattern of a teacher, can be used to check ex post whether the teacher may have deviated from the grading pattern so as to flag potential inconsistencies or anomalies. The fourth condition should be that the AI system is intended to perform a task that is only preparatory to an assessment relevant for the purposes of the AI systems listed in an annex to this Regulation, thus making the possible impact of the output of the system very low in terms of representing a risk for the assessment to follow. That condition covers, inter alia, smart solutions for file handling, which include various functions from indexing, searching, text and speech processing or linking data to other data sources, or AI systems used for translation of initial documents. In any case, AI systems used in high-risk use-cases listed in an annex to this Regulation should be considered to pose significant risks of harm to the health, safety or fundamental rights if the AI system implies profiling within the meaning of Article 4, point (4) of Regulation (EU) 2016/679 or Article 3, point (4) of Directive (EU) 2016/680 or Article 3, point (5) of Regulation (EU) 2018/1725. To ensure traceability and transparency, a provider who considers that an AI system is not high-risk on the basis of the conditions referred to above should draw up documentation of the assessment before that system is placed on the market or put into service and should provide that documentation to national competent authorities upon request. Such a provider should be obliged to register the AI system in the EU database established under this Regulation. With a view to providing further guidance for the practical implementation of the conditions under which the AI systems listed in an annex to this Regulation are, on an exceptional basis, non-high-risk, the Commission should, after consulting the Board, provide guidelines specifying that practical implementation, completed by a comprehensive list of practical examples of use cases of AI systems that are high-risk and use cases that are not.

1676. (146) Moreover, in light of the very small size of some operators and in order to ensure proportionality regarding costs of innovation, it is appropriate to allow microenterprises to fulfil one of the most costly obligations, namely to establish a quality management system, in a simplified manner which would reduce the administrative burden and the costs for those enterprises without affecting the level of protection and the need for compliance with the requirements for high-risk AI systems. The Commission should develop guidelines to specify the elements of the quality management system to be fulfilled in this simplified manner by microenterprises.

1677. **(165)** The development of AI systems other than high-risk AI systems in accordance with the requirements of this Regulation may lead to a larger uptake of ethical and trustworthy AI in the Union. Providers of AI systems that are not high-risk should be encouraged to create codes of conduct, including related governance mechanisms, intended to foster the voluntary application of some or all of the mandatory requirements applicable to high-risk AI systems, adapted in light of the intended purpose of the systems and the lower risk involved and taking into account the available technical solutions and industry best practices such as model and data cards. Providers and, as appropriate, deployers of all AI systems, high-risk or not, and AI models should also be encouraged to apply on a voluntary basis additional requirements related, for example, to the elements of the Union's Ethics Guidelines for Trustworthy AI, environmental sustainability, AI literacy measures, inclusive and diverse design and development of AI systems, including attention to vulnerable persons and accessibility to persons with disability, stakeholders' participation with the involvement, as appropriate, of relevant stakeholders such as business and civil society organisations, academia, research organisations, trade unions and consumer protection organisations in the design and development of AI systems, and diversity of the development teams, including gender balance. To ensure that the voluntary codes of conduct are effective, they should be based on clear objectives and key performance indicators to measure the achievement of those objectives. They should also be developed in an inclusive way, as appropriate, with the involvement of relevant stakeholders such as business and civil society organisations, academia, research organisations, trade unions and consumer protection organisation. The Commission may develop initiatives, including of a sectoral nature, to facilitate the lowering of technical barriers hindering cross-border exchange of data for AI development, including on data access infrastructure, semantic and technical interoperability of different types of data.

96.2. General Approach

1678. The objective is to harmonise the AI technology market within the EU, taking into account

- the rapid technological developments;
- the associated risks.

96.3. Modalities

1679. They are as follows:

NO.	THEME	SPECIFICATION
1.	Area	Definition of AI systems (AIA, Art. 3) Prohibited practices (AIA, Art. 5) High-risk AI systems (AIA, Art. 6) Transparent system (AIA, Art. 50) Application of the definition of an AI system (AIA, Art. 3) Union harmonisation legislation (AIA, Annex I)
2.	Communication	Publication
3.	Particular attention	SMEs and start-ups
4.	Update	At the request of the Member States or the AI Office, or the European Commission on its own initiative

CHAPTER XI
DELEGATION OF POWER AND COMMITTEE PROCEDURE

1680. Key takeaways: The rapid evolution of AI technologies calls for regulatory tools that match this challenge.

1681. This applies to:

- the procedures for exercising delegated acts;
- the assistance of the European Commission by a dedicated committee.

97 ARTICLE 97. EXERCISE OF THE DELEGATION

1. The power to adopt delegated acts is conferred on the Commission subject to the conditions laid down in this Article.

2. The power to adopt delegated acts referred to in Article 6(6) and (7), Article 7(1) and (3), Article 11(3), Article 43(5) and (6), Article 47(5), Article 51(3), Article 52(4) and Article 53(5) and (6) shall be conferred on the Commission for a period of five years from 1 August 2024. The Commission shall draw up a report in respect of the delegation of power not later than nine months before the end of the five-year period. The delegation of power shall be tacitly extended for periods of an identical duration, unless the European Parliament or the Council opposes such extension not later than three months before the end of each period.

3. The delegation of power referred to in Article 6(6) and (7), Article 7(1) and (3), Article 11(3), Article 43(5) and (6), Article 47(5), Article 51(3), Article 52(4) and Article 53(5) and (6) may be revoked at any time by the European Parliament or by the Council. A decision of revocation shall put an end to the delegation of power specified in that decision. It shall take effect the day following that of its publication in the Official Journal of the European Union or at a later date specified therein. It shall not affect the validity of any delegated acts already in force.

4. Before adopting a delegated act, the Commission shall consult experts designated by each Member State in accordance with the principles laid down in the Interinstitutional Agreement of 13 April 2016 on Better Law-Making.

5. As soon as it adopts a delegated act, the Commission shall notify it simultaneously to the European Parliament and to the Council.

6. Any delegated act adopted pursuant to Article 6(6) or (7), Article 7(1) or (3), Article 11(3), Article 43(5) or (6), Article 47(5), Article 51(3), Article 52(4) or Article 53(5) or (6) shall enter into force only if no objection has been expressed by either the European Parliament or the Council within a period of three months of notification of that act to the European Parliament and the Council or if, before the expiry of that period, the European Parliament and the Council have both informed the Commission that they will not object. That period shall be extended by three months at the initiative of the European Parliament or of the Council.

97.1. Recitals

1682. **(49)** As regards high-risk AI systems that are safety components of products or systems, or which are themselves products or systems falling within the scope of Regulation (EC) No 300/2008 of the European Parliament and of the Council,[1] Regulation (EU) No 167/2013 of the European Parliament and of the Council,[2] Regulation (EU) No 168/2013 of the European Parliament and of the Council,[3] Directive 2014/90/EU of the European Parliament and of the Council,[4] Directive (EU) 2016/797 of the European Parliament and of the Council,[5] Regulation (EU) 2018/858 of the European Parliament and of the Council,[6] Regulation (EU) 2018/1139 of the European Parliament and of the Council,[7] and Regulation (EU)

[1] Regulation (EC) No 300/2008 of the European Parliament and of the Council of 11 March 2008 on common rules in the field of civil aviation security and repealing Regulation (EC) No 2320/2002, [2008] OJ L97/72.

[2] Regulation (EU) No 167/2013 of the European Parliament and of the Council of 5 February 2013 on the approval and market surveillance of agricultural and forestry vehicles, [2013] OJ L60/1.

[3] Regulation (EU) No 168/2013 of the European Parliament and of the Council of 15 January 2013 on the approval and market surveillance of two- or three-wheel vehicles and quadricycles, [2013] OJ L60/52.

[4] Directive 2014/90/EU of the European Parliament and of the Council of 23 July 2014 on marine equipment and repealing Council Directive 96/98/EC, [2014] OJ L257/146.

[5] Directive (EU) 2016/797 of the European Parliament and of the Council of 11 May 2016 on the interoperability of the rail system within the European Union, [2016] OJ L138/44.

[6] Regulation (EU) 2018/858 of the European Parliament and of the Council of 30 May 2018 on the approval and market surveillance of motor vehicles and their trailers, and of systems, components and separate technical units intended for such vehicles, amending Regulations (EC) No 715/2007 and (EC) No 595/2009 and repealing Directive 2007/46/EC, [2018] OJ L151/1.

[7] Regulation (EU) 2018/1139 of the European Parliament and of the Council of 4 July 2018 on common rules in the field of civil aviation and establishing a European Union Aviation Safety Agency, and amending Regulations (EC) No 2111/2005, (EC) No 1008/2008, (EU) No 996/2010, (EU) No 376/2014 and Directives 2014/30/EU and 2014/53/EU of the

2019/2144 of the European Parliament and of the Council,[8] it is appropriate to amend those acts to ensure that the Commission takes into account, on the basis of the technical and regulatory specificities of each sector, and without interfering with existing governance, conformity assessment and enforcement mechanisms and authorities established therein, the mandatory requirements for high-risk AI systems laid down in this Regulation when adopting any relevant delegated or implementing acts on the basis of those acts.

1683. (52) As regards stand-alone AI systems, namely high-risk AI systems other than those that are safety components of products, or that are themselves products, it is appropriate to classify them as high-risk if, in light of their intended purpose, they pose a high risk of harm to the health and safety or the fundamental rights of persons, taking into account both the severity of the possible harm and its probability of occurrence and they are used in a number of specifically pre-defined areas specified in this Regulation. The identification of those systems is based on the same methodology and criteria envisaged also for any future amendments of the list of high-risk AI systems that the Commission should be empowered to adopt, via delegated acts, to take into account the rapid pace of technological development, as well as the potential changes in the use of AI systems.

1684. (101) Providers of general-purpose AI models have a particular role and responsibility along the AI value chain, as the models they provide may form the basis for a range of downstream systems, often provided by downstream providers that necessitate a good understanding of the models and their capabilities, both to enable the integration of such models into their products, and to fulfil their obligations under this or other regulations. Therefore, proportionate transparency measures should be laid down, including the drawing up and keeping up to date of documentation, and the provision of information on the general-purpose AI model for its usage by the downstream providers. Technical documentation should be prepared and kept up to date by the general-purpose AI model provider for the purpose of making it available, upon request, to the

---

European Parliament and of the Council, and repealing Regulations (EC) No 552/2004 and (EC) No 216/2008 of the European Parliament and of the Council and Council Regulation (EEC) No 3922/91, [2018] OJ L212/1

8 Regulation (EU) 2019/2144 of the European Parliament and of the Council of 27 November 2019 on type-approval requirements for motor vehicles and their trailers, and systems, components and separate technical units intended for such vehicles, as regards their general safety and the protection of vehicle occupants and vulnerable road users, amending Regulation (EU) 2018/858 of the European Parliament and of the Council and repealing Regulations (EC) No 78/2009, (EC) No 79/2009 and (EC) No 661/2009 of the European Parliament and of the Council and Commission Regulations (EC) No 631/2009, (EU) No 406/2010, (EU) No 672/2010, (EU) No 1003/2010, (EU) No 1005/2010, (EU) No 1008/2010, (EU) No 1009/2010, (EU) No 19/2011, (EU) No 109/2011, (EU) No 458/2011, (EU) No 65/2012, (EU) No 130/2012, (EU) No 347/2012, (EU) No 351/2012, (EU) No 1230/2012 and (EU) 2015/166, [2019] OJ L325/1.

AI Office and the national competent authorities. The minimal set of elements to be included in such documentation should be set out in specific annexes to this Regulation. The Commission should be empowered to amend those annexes by means of delegated acts in light of evolving technological developments.

1685. **(173)** In order to ensure that the regulatory framework can be adapted where necessary, the power to adopt acts in accordance with Article 290 TFEU should be delegated to the Commission to amend the conditions under which an AI system is not to be considered to be high-risk, the list of high-risk AI systems, the provisions regarding technical documentation, the content of the EU declaration of conformity the provisions regarding the conformity assessment procedures, the provisions establishing the high-risk AI systems to which the conformity assessment procedure based on assessment of the quality management system and assessment of the technical documentation should apply, the threshold, benchmarks and indicators, including by supplementing those benchmarks and indicators, in the rules for the classification of general-purpose AI models with systemic risk, the criteria for the designation of general-purpose AI models with systemic risk, the technical documentation for providers of general-purpose AI models and the transparency information for providers of general-purpose AI models. It is of particular importance that the Commission carry out appropriate consultations during its preparatory work, including at expert level, and that those consultations be conducted in accordance with the principles laid down in the Interinstitutional Agreement of 13 April 2016 on Better Law-Making.[9] In particular, to ensure equal participation in the preparation of delegated acts, the European Parliament and the Council receive all documents at the same time as Member States' experts, and their experts systematically have access to meetings of Commission expert groups dealing with the preparation of delegated acts.

1686. **(175)** In order to ensure uniform conditions for the implementation of this Regulation, implementing powers should be conferred on the Commission. Those powers should be exercised in accordance with Regulation (EU) No 182/2011 of the European Parliament and of the Council.[10]

97.2. General Approach

1687. The rapid development of digital technologies, particularly in the field of artificial intelligence, requires a swift adaptation of regulations. This applies to the delegated acts adopted by the European Commission.

---

9 [2016] OJ L123/1.

10 Regulation (EU) No 182/2011 of the European Parliament and of the Council of 16 February 2011 laying down the rules and general principles concerning mechanisms for control by Member States of the Commission's exercise of implementing powers, [2011] OJ L55/13.

1688. These acts aim to regulate the AI technology market by prioritising innovation and protection against risks to:

- health;
- safety;
- fundamental rights.

97.3. Classification

1689. The delegated acts cover the following areas:

NO.	THEME	REFERENCE
1.	**Amendments to Article 6(3)(2) by addition** The Commission is empowered to adopt delegated acts in accordance with Article 97 in order to amend paragraph 3, second subparagraph, of this Article by adding new conditions to those laid down therein, or by modifying them, where there is concrete and reliable evidence of the existence of AI systems that fall under the scope of Annex III, but do not pose a significant risk of harm to the health, safety or fundamental rights of natural persons **Amendments to Article 6(3)(2) by deletion** The Commission shall adopt delegated acts in accordance with Article 97 in order to amend paragraph 3, second subparagraph, of this Article by deleting any of the conditions laid down therein, where there is concrete and reliable evidence that this is necessary to maintain the level of protection of health, safety and fundamental rights provided for by this Regulation	AIA, Art. 6(6) and (7)
2.	**Amendments to Annex III by addition or modification** The Commission is empowered to adopt delegated acts in accordance with Article 97 to amend Annex III by adding or modifying use-cases of high-risk AI systems where both of the following conditions are fulfilled **Amendments to Annex III by removal** The Commission is empowered to adopt delegated acts in accordance with Article 97 to amend the list in Annex III by removing high-risk AI systems where both of the following conditions are fulfilled: (a) the high-risk AI system concerned no longer poses any significant risks to fundamental rights, health or safety, taking into account the criteria listed in paragraph 2 (b) the deletion does not decrease the overall level of protection of health, safety and fundamental rights under Union law	AIA, Art. 7(1) and (3)

NO.	THEME	REFERENCE
3.	**Amendments to Annex IV** The Commission is empowered to adopt delegated acts in accordance with Article 97 in order to amend Annex IV, where necessary, to ensure that, in light of technical progress, the technical documentation provides all the information necessary to assess the compliance of the system with the requirements set out in this Section	AIA, Art. 11(3)
4.	**Amendments to Annex VI and VII** The Commission is empowered to adopt delegated acts in accordance with Article 97 in order to amend Annexes VI and VII by updating them in light of technical progress **Amendments to Article 43(1) and (2)** The Commission is empowered to adopt delegated acts in accordance with Article 97 in order to amend paragraphs 1 and 2 of this Article in order to subject high-risk AI systems referred to in points 2 to 8 of Annex III to the conformity assessment procedure referred to in Annex VII or parts thereof. The Commission shall adopt such delegated acts taking into account the effectiveness of the conformity assessment procedure based on internal control referred to in Annex VI in preventing or minimising the risks to health and safety and protection of fundamental rights posed by such systems, as well as the availability of adequate capacities and resources among notified bodies	AIA, Art. 43(5) and (6)
5.	**Amendments to Annex V** The Commission is empowered to adopt delegated acts in accordance with Article 97 in order to amend Annex V by updating the content of the EU declaration of conformity set out in that Annex, in order to introduce elements that become necessary in light of technical progress.	AIA, Art. 47(5)
6.	**Amendments to Article 51(1) and (2)** The Commission shall adopt delegated acts in accordance with Article 97 to amend the thresholds listed in paragraphs 1 and 2 of this Article, as well as to supplement benchmarks and indicators in light of evolving technological developments, such as algorithmic improvements or increased hardware efficiency, when necessary, for these thresholds to reflect the state of the art	AIA, Art. 51(3)
7.	**Amendments to Annex XIII** The Commission is empowered to adopt delegated acts in accordance with Article 97 in order to amend Annex XIII by specifying and updating the criteria set out in that Annex.	AIA, Art. 52(4)

NO.	THEME	REFERENCE
8.	**Amendments to facilitate compliance with Annex XI** For the purpose of facilitating compliance with Annex XI, in particular points 2 (d) and (e) thereof, the Commission is empowered to adopt delegated acts in accordance with Article 97 to detail measurement and calculation methodologies with a view to allowing for comparable and verifiable documentation. **Amendments to Annex XI and XII** The Commission is empowered to adopt delegated acts in accordance with Article 97(2) to amend Annexes XI and XII in light of evolving technological developments.	AIA, Art. 53(5) and (6)

97.4. Characteristics

1690. They are as follows:

NO.	THEME	SPECIFICATION	COMMENT
1.	Delegation of power	From 1 August 2024	1 August 2024: date of entry into force of the AIA
2.	Duration of the delegation	For a period of five years	From 1 August 2024
3.	Revocation	At any time by the European Parliament or by the Council	Revocation takes effect the day following that of its publication in the *OJEU* or at a later date specified therein. It shall not affect the validity of any delegated acts already in force
4.	Validity	Revocation does not affect the validity of any delegated acts already in force	
5.	Consultation	Experts designated by each Member State	In accordance with the principles laid down in the Interinstitutional Agreement of 13 April 2016 on Better Law-Making[1]
6.	Cooperation	Prior notification to the European Parliament and the Council	Entry into force only if no objection has been expressed within 3 months. That period may be reduced or extended at the initiative of the European Parliament or of the Council
7.	European Commission assistance	A committee is established	Modalities: Regulation (EU) No 182/2011 Art. 5

1 [2016] OJ L123/1.

98 ARTICLE 98. COMMITTEE PROCEDURE

1. The Commission shall be assisted by a committee. That committee shall be a committee within the meaning of Regulation (EU) No 182/2011.

2. Where reference is made to this paragraph, Article 5 of Regulation (EU) No 182/2011 shall apply.

98.1. General Approach

1691. The committee is governed as follows:

> '2. The Commission shall be assisted by a committee composed of representatives of the Member States. The committee shall be chaired by a representative of the Commission. The chair shall not take part in the committee vote.
>
> 3. The chair shall submit to the committee the draft implementing act to be adopted by the Commission.
>
> Except in duly justified cases, the chair shall convene a meeting not less than 14 days from submission of the draft implementing act and of the draft agenda to the committee. The committee shall deliver its opinion on the draft implementing act within a time limit which the chair may lay down according to the urgency of the matter. Time limits shall be proportionate and shall afford committee members early and effective opportunities to examine the draft implementing act and express their views.'[2]

2 Regulation (EU) No 182/2011 of the European Parliament and of the Council of 16 February 2011 laying down the rules and general principles concerning mechanisms for control by Member States of the Commission's exercise of implementing powers, [2011] OJ L55/13–18.

CHAPTER XII
PENALTIES

1692. Key takeaways: The rules on penalty apply to:

- AI systems;
- general-purpose AI models;
- EU institutions when they use AI technologies.

99 ARTICLE 99. PENALTIES

1. In accordance with the terms and conditions laid down in this Regulation, Member States shall lay down the rules on penalties and other enforcement measures, which may also include warnings and non-monetary measures, applicable to infringements of this Regulation by operators, and shall take all measures necessary to ensure that they are properly and effectively implemented, thereby taking into account the guidelines issued by the Commission pursuant to Article 96. The penalties provided for shall be effective, proportionate and dissuasive. They shall take into account the interests of SMEs, including start-ups, and their economic viability.

2. The Member States shall, without delay and at the latest by the date of entry into application, notify the Commission of the rules on penalties and of other enforcement measures referred to in paragraph 1, and shall notify it, without delay, of any subsequent amendment to them.

3. Non-compliance with the prohibition of the AI practices referred to in Article 5 shall be subject to administrative fines of up to EUR 35 000 000 or, if the offender is an undertaking, up to 7% of its total worldwide annual turnover for the preceding financial year, whichever is higher.

4. Non-compliance with any of the following provisions related to operators or notified bodies, other than those laid down in Articles 5, shall be subject to administrative fines of up to EUR 15 000 000 or, if the offender is an undertaking, up to 3% of its total worldwide annual turnover for the preceding financial year, whichever is higher:

(a) obligations of providers pursuant to Article 16;

(b) obligations of authorised representatives pursuant to Article 22;

(c) obligations of importers pursuant to Article 23;

(d) obligations of distributors pursuant to Article 24;

(e) obligations of deployers pursuant to Article 26;

(f) requirements and obligations of notified bodies pursuant to Article 31, Article 33(1), (3) and (4) or Article 34;

(g) transparency obligations for providers and deployers pursuant to Article 50.

5. The supply of incorrect, incomplete or misleading information to notified bodies or national competent authorities in reply to a request shall be subject to administrative fines of up to EUR 7 500 000 or, if the offender is an undertaking, up to 1% of its total worldwide annual turnover for the preceding financial year, whichever is higher.

6. In the case of SMEs, including start-ups, each fine referred to in this Article shall be up to the percentages or amount referred to in paragraphs 3, 4 and 5, whichever thereof is lower.

7. When deciding whether to impose an administrative fine and when deciding on the amount of the administrative fine in each individual case, all relevant circumstances of the specific situation shall be taken into account and, as appropriate, regard shall be given to the following:

(a) the nature, gravity and duration of the infringement and of its consequences, taking into account the purpose of the AI system, as well as, where appropriate, the number of affected persons and the level of damage suffered by them;

(b) whether administrative fines have already been applied by other market surveillance authorities to the same operator for the same infringement;

(c) whether administrative fines have already been applied by other authorities to the same operator for infringements of other Union or national law, when such infringements result from the same activity or omission constituting a relevant infringement of this Regulation;

(d) the size, the annual turnover and market share of the operator committing the infringement;

(e) any other aggravating or mitigating factor applicable to the circumstances of the case, such as financial benefits gained, or losses avoided, directly or indirectly, from the infringement;

(f) the degree of cooperation with the national competent authorities, in order to remedy the infringement and mitigate the possible adverse effects of the infringement;

(g) the degree of responsibility of the operator taking into account the technical and organisational measures implemented by it;

(h) the manner in which the infringement became known to the national competent authorities, in particular whether, and if so to what extent, the operator notified the infringement;

(i) the intentional or negligent character of the infringement;

(j) any action taken by the operator to mitigate the harm suffered by the affected persons.

8. Each Member State shall lay down rules on to what extent administrative fines may be imposed on public authorities and bodies established in that Member State.

9. Depending on the legal system of the Member States, the rules on administrative fines may be applied in such a manner that the fines are imposed by competent national courts or by other bodies, as applicable in those Member States. The application of such rules in those Member States shall have an equivalent effect.

10. The exercise of powers under this Article shall be subject to appropriate procedural safeguards in accordance with Union and national law, including effective judicial remedies and due process.

11. Member States shall, on an annual basis, report to the Commission about the administrative fines they have issued during that year, in accordance with this Article, and about any related litigation or judicial proceedings.

99.1. Recitals

1693. (162) To make best use of the centralised Union expertise and synergies at Union level, the powers of supervision and enforcement of the obligations on providers of general-purpose AI models should be a competence of the Commission. The AI Office should be able to carry out all necessary actions to monitor the effective implementation of this Regulation as regards general-purpose AI models. It should be able to investigate possible infringements of the rules on providers of general-purpose AI models both on its own initiative, following the results of its monitoring activities, or upon request from market surveillance authorities in line with the conditions set out in this Regulation. To support effective monitoring of the AI Office, it should provide for the possibility that downstream providers lodge complaints about possible infringements of the rules on providers of general-purpose AI models and systems.

1694. (168) Compliance with this Regulation should be enforceable by means of the imposition of penalties and other enforcement measures. Member States should take all necessary measures to ensure that the provisions of this Regulation are implemented, including by laying down effective, proportionate and dissuasive penalties for their infringement, and to respect the ne bis in idem principle. In order to strengthen and harmonise administrative penalties for infringement of this Regulation, the upper limits for setting the administrative fines for certain specific infringements should be laid down. When assessing the amount of the fines, Member States should, in each individual case, take into account all relevant circumstances of the specific situation, with due regard in particular to the nature, gravity and duration of the infringement and of its consequences and to the size of the provider, in particular if the provider is an SME, including a start-up. The European Data Protection Supervisor should have the power to impose fines on Union institutions, agencies and bodies falling within the scope of this Regulation.

1695. **(169)** Compliance with the obligations on providers of general-purpose AI models imposed under this Regulation should be enforceable, inter alia, by means of fines. To that end, appropriate levels of fines should also be laid down for infringement of those obligations, including the failure to comply with measures requested by the Commission in accordance with this Regulation, subject to appropriate limitation periods in accordance with the principle of proportionality. All decisions taken by the Commission under this Regulation are subject to review by the Court of Justice of the European Union in accordance with the TFEU, including the unlimited jurisdiction of the Court of Justice with regard to penalties pursuant to Article 261 TFEU.

1696. **(179)** This Regulation should apply from 2 August 2026. However, taking into account the unacceptable risk associated with the use of AI in certain ways, the prohibitions as well as the general provisions of this Regulation should already apply from 2 February 2025. While the full effect of those prohibitions follows with the establishment of the governance and enforcement of this Regulation, anticipating the application of the prohibitions is important to take account of unacceptable risks and to have an effect on other procedures, such as in civil law. Moreover, the infrastructure related to the governance and the conformity assessment system should be operational before 2 August 2026, therefore the provisions on notified bodies and governance structure should apply from 2 August 2025. Given the rapid pace of technological advancements and adoption of general-purpose AI models, obligations for providers of general-purpose AI models should apply from 2 August 2025. Codes of practice should be ready by 2 May 2025 in view of enabling providers to demonstrate compliance on time. The AI Office should ensure that classification rules and procedures are up to date in light of technological developments. In addition, Member States should lay down and notify to the Commission the rules on penalties, including administrative fines, and ensure that they are properly and effectively implemented by the date of application of this Regulation. Therefore the provisions on penalties should apply from 2 August 2025.

99.2. General Approach

99.2.1 Preamble

1697. Maintaining a high level of trust requires the implementation of an administrative penalty mechanism structured around two key aspects:

- the rules on penalty;
- administrative fines.

1698. Note:

- (1) This mechanism is similar to that of the GDPR (Regulation (EU) (2016/679).

99.2.2 Guiding Principles

1699. This new legal framework governs:

- the procedures for determining penalties;
- the scale of fines and their areas of application;
- the application of fines to the public sector at the initiative of Member States.

99.3. Legal Rules

1700. These rules are developed and implemented by Member States, subject to the guiding principles set by the Regulation.

99.3.1 Purpose

1701. The purpose of penalties is to penalise certain infringements of the provisions of the Regulations.

1702. Local legislators must take all measures necessary to ensure that penalties are enforced:

- properly; and
- effectively.

99.3.2 Characteristics

1703. Penalties must, in any event, be:

- effective;
- proportionate;
- dissuasive.

99.4. *Classification*

1704. Penalties are categorised as follows:

<table>
<tr><th>NO.</th><th>THEME</th><th>SPECIFICATION</th><th>PENALTY</th></tr>
<tr><td>1.</td><td>Prohibited practices</td><td>Non-compliance with Article 5</td><td>Administrative fine of up to EUR 35,000,000 or, if the offender is an undertaking, up to 7% of its total worldwide annual turnover for the preceding financial year, whichever is higher</td></tr>
<tr><td>2.</td><td>Providers
Non-compliance</td><td>Article 16:
Obligations of providers of high-risk AI systems</td><td rowspan="7">Administrative fines of up to EUR 15,000,000 or, if the offender is an undertaking, up to 3% of its total worldwide annual turnover for the preceding financial year, whichever is higher</td></tr>
<tr><td>3.</td><td>Authorised representatives
Non-compliance</td><td>Article 22:
Obligations of authorised representatives of providers of high-risk AI systems</td></tr>
<tr><td>4.</td><td>Importers
Non-compliance</td><td>Article 23:
Obligations of importers</td></tr>
<tr><td>5.</td><td>Distributors
Non-compliance</td><td>Article 24:
Obligations of distributors</td></tr>
<tr><td>6.</td><td>Deployers
Non-compliance</td><td>Article 26:
Obligations of deployers of high-risk AI systems</td></tr>
<tr><td>7.</td><td>Providers and deployers
Non-compliance</td><td>Article 50:
Transparency obligations for providers and deployers of certain AI systems</td></tr>
<tr><td>8.</td><td>Notified bodies
Non-compliance</td><td>Article 31:
Requirements relating to notified bodies
Article 33(1), (3) and (4):
Subsidiaries of notified bodies and subcontracting
Article 34:
Operational obligations of notified bodies</td></tr>
<tr><td>9.</td><td>Information supplied to national competent authorities or notified bodies</td><td>Incorrect
Incomplete
Misleading</td><td>Administrative fine of up to EUR 7,500,000 or, if the offender is an undertaking, up to 1% of its total worldwide annual turnover for the preceding financial year, whichever is higher</td></tr>
</table>

99.5. *Personalisation of Penalties*

1705. It is based on the following:

NO.	THEME
1.	Nature of the infringement
2.	Gravity of the infringement
3.	Duration of the infringement
4.	Consequences of the infringement
5.	Previous infringements
6.	Size, annual turnover and market share
7.	Any other aggravating or mitigating factor
8.	Degree of cooperation with the national competent authorities
9.	Degree of responsibility of the operator
10.	Manner in which the infringement became known to the national competent authorities
11.	Intentional or negligent character of the infringement
12.	Mitigation of harm

99.6. *Special Cases*

1706. Administrative fines must take into account the specific interests of:
- SMEs;
- startups; and
- their economic viability.

99.7. *Options*

1707. Member States determine if and to what extent fines may be imposed on:
- public authorities;
- public bodies.

99.8. *Jurisdictions*

1708. Member States decide whether administrative fines are imposed by:
- competent national courts; or
- a specific body.

100 ARTICLE 100. ADMINISTRATIVE FINES ON UNION INSTITUTIONS, BODIES, OFFICES AND AGENCIES

1. The European Data Protection Supervisor may impose administrative fines on Union institutions, bodies, offices and agencies falling within the scope of this Regulation. When deciding whether to impose an administrative fine and when deciding on the amount of the administrative fine in each individual case, all relevant circumstances of the specific situation shall be taken into account and due regard shall be given to the following:

(a) the nature, gravity and duration of the infringement and of its consequences, taking into account the purpose of the AI system concerned, as well as, where appropriate, the number of affected persons and the level of damage suffered by them;

(b) the degree of responsibility of the Union institution, body, office or agency, taking into account technical and organisational measures implemented by them;

(c) any action taken by the Union institution, body, office or agency to mitigate the damage suffered by affected persons;

(d) the degree of cooperation with the European Data Protection Supervisor in order to remedy the infringement and mitigate the possible adverse effects of the infringement, including compliance with any of the measures previously ordered by the European Data Protection Supervisor against the Union institution, body, office or agency concerned with regard to the same subject matter;

(e) any similar previous infringements by the Union institution, body, office or agency;

(f) the manner in which the infringement became known to the European Data Protection Supervisor, in particular whether, and if so to what extent, the Union institution, body, office or agency notified the infringement;

(g) the annual budget of the Union institution, body, office or agency.

2. Non-compliance with the prohibition of the AI practices referred to in Article 5 shall be subject to administrative fines of up to EUR 1 500 000.

3. The non-compliance of the AI system with any requirements or obligations under this Regulation, other than those laid down in Article 5, shall be subject to administrative fines of up to EUR 750 000.

4. Before taking decisions pursuant to this Article, the European Data Protection Supervisor shall give the Union institution, body, office or agency which is the subject of the proceedings conducted by the European Data Protection Supervisor the opportunity of being heard on the matter regarding the possible infringement. The European Data Protection Supervisor shall base his or her decisions only on elements and circumstances on which the parties concerned have been able to comment. Complainants, if any, shall be associated closely with the proceedings.

5. The rights of defence of the parties concerned shall be fully respected in the proceedings. They shall be entitled to have access to the European Data Protection Supervisor's file, subject to the legitimate interest of individuals or undertakings in the protection of their personal data or business secrets.

6. Funds collected by imposition of fines in this Article shall contribute to the general budget of the Union. The fines shall not affect the effective operation of the Union institution, body, office or agency fined.

7. The European Data Protection Supervisor shall, on an annual basis, notify the Commission of the administrative fines it has imposed pursuant to this Article and of any litigation or judicial proceedings it has initiated.

100.1. Recitals

1709. (168) Compliance with this Regulation should be enforceable by means of the imposition of penalties and other enforcement measures. Member States should take all necessary measures to ensure that the provisions of this Regulation are implemented, including by laying down effective, proportionate and dissuasive penalties for their infringement, and to respect the ne bis in idem principle. In order to strengthen and harmonise administrative penalties for infringement of this Regulation, the upper limits for setting the administrative fines for certain specific infringements should be laid down. When assessing the amount of the fines, Member States should, in each individual case, take into account all relevant circumstances of the specific situation, with due regard in particular to the nature, gravity and duration of the infringement and of its consequences and to the size of the provider, in particular if the provider is an SME, including a start-up. The European Data Protection Supervisor should have the power to impose fines on Union institutions, agencies and bodies falling within the scope of this Regulation.

1710. (169) Compliance with the obligations on providers of general-purpose AI models imposed under this Regulation should be enforceable, inter alia, by means of fines. To that end, appropriate levels of fines should also be laid down for infringement of those obligations, including the failure to comply with measures requested by the Commission in accordance with this Regulation, subject to appropriate limitation periods in accordance with the principle of proportionality. All decisions taken by the Commission under this Regulation are subject to review by the Court of Justice of the European Union in accordance with the TFEU, including the unlimited jurisdiction of the Court of Justice with regard to penalties pursuant to Article 261 TFEU.

100.2. General Approach

100.2.1 Preamble

1711. A similar administrative fine system applies to the EU institutions, bodies, offices and agencies.

NO.	THEME	SPECIFICATION	PENALTY
1.	Prohibited practices	Non-compliance with Article 5	Up to EUR 1,500,000
2.	Requirements or obligations under the AIA	Non-compliance other than with Article 5	Up to EUR 750,000

100.2.2 Modalities

1712. They are as follows:

NO.	THEME	SPECIFICATION
1.	Jurisdiction	European Data Protection Supervisor (EDPS)
2.	Assessment of the penalty	Gravity of the infringement Degree of responsibility of the EU body Mitigation of damage Cooperation at the procedural stage Infringement history Manner in which the infringement became known Annual budget of the EU body concerned
3.	Procedure	Adversarial, with respect for the rights of defence
4.	Information	European Commission is informed of the fines imposed and of the proceedings initiated

101 ARTICLE 101. FINES FOR PROVIDERS OF GENERAL-PURPOSE AI MODELS

1. The Commission may impose on providers of general-purpose AI models fines not exceeding 3% of their annual total worldwide turnover in the preceding financial year or EUR 15 000 000, whichever is higher., when the Commission finds that the provider intentionally or negligently:

(a) infringed the relevant provisions of this Regulation;

(b) failed to comply with a request for a document or for information pursuant to Article 91, or supplied incorrect, incomplete or misleading information;

(c) failed to comply with a measure requested under Article 93;

(d) failed to make available to the Commission access to the general-purpose AI model or general-purpose AI model with systemic risk with a view to conducting an evaluation pursuant to Article 92.

In fixing the amount of the fine or periodic penalty payment, regard shall be had to the nature, gravity and duration of the infringement, taking due account of the principles of proportionality and appropriateness. The Commission shall also into account commitments made in accordance with Article 93(3) or made in relevant codes of practice in accordance with Article 56.

2. Before adopting the decision pursuant to paragraph 1, the Commission shall communicate its preliminary findings to the provider of the general-purpose AI model and give it an opportunity to be heard.

3. Fines imposed in accordance with this Article shall be effective, proportionate and dissuasive.

4. Information on fines imposed under this Article shall also be communicated to the Board as appropriate.

5. The Court of Justice of the European Union shall have unlimited jurisdiction to review decisions of the Commission fixing a fine under this Article. It may cancel, reduce or increase the fine imposed.

6. The Commission shall adopt implementing acts containing detailed arrangements and procedural safeguards for proceedings in view of the possible adoption of decisions pursuant to paragraph 1 of this Article. Those implementing acts shall be adopted in accordance with the examination procedure referred to in Article 98(2).

101.1. Recitals

1713. (162) To make best use of the centralised Union expertise and synergies at Union level, the powers of supervision and enforcement of the obligations on providers of general-purpose AI models should be a competence of the Commission. The AI Office should be able to carry out all necessary actions to monitor the effective implementation of this Regulation as regards general-purpose AI models. It should be able to investigate possible infringements of the rules on providers of general-purpose AI models both on its own initiative, following the results of its monitoring activities, or upon request from market surveillance authorities in line with the conditions set out in this Regulation. To support effective monitoring of the AI Office, it should provide for the possibility that downstream providers lodge complaints about possible infringements of the rules on providers of general-purpose AI models and systems.

101.2. General Approach

101.2.1 Preamble

1714. General-purpose AI models are subject to specific regulatory oversight due to their potential risks.

101.2.2 Guiding Principles

1715. The penalties are harsher due to associated risks and consequences.

101.3. Jurisdiction

1716. Unlike AI systems, the power to impose penalties is directly attributed to the European Commission.

101.4. Infringement

1717. The following constitute non-compliance:

NO.	THEME	SPECIFICATION
1.	Obligation	Non-compliance
2.	Information	Failure to supply Incorrect Incomplete Misleading
3.	Special measures	Failure to comply with measures relating to general-purpose AI models with systemic risk (AIA, Art. 93)
4.	Access	Failure to provide access to the general-purpose AI model (AIA, Art. 92)
5.	Form	Implementing acts containing detailed arrangements and procedural safeguards

101.5. Modalities

1718. The fines are fixed based on the following:

NO.	THEME	SPECIFICATION
1.	Infringement	Nature Gravity Duration
2.	Principle	Proportionality Appropriateness
3.	Scope	Effective Proportionate Dissuasive
4.	Mitigating factor	Commitments (AIA, Art. 93(3)) Code of practice (AIA, Art. 56)

1719. Note:

- (1) The same applies to periodic penalty payments.

101.6. Amounts

1720. The European Commission fixes the amount of the fine based on the following:

NO.	THEME	SPECIFICATION
1.	Value	3% of the annual total worldwide turnover or EUR 15,000,000
2.	Threshold	Whichever is higher
3.	Reference	Turnover in the preceding financial year

101.7. Procedure

1721. The rules are as follows:

NO.	THEME	SPECIFICATION
1.	Phase 1	Communication of preliminary findings
2.	Phase 2	Possible hearings
3.	Phase 3	Decisions with or without periodic penalty payments
4.	Phase 4	Appeal to the CJEU Communication of the decision to the AI Board

101.8. Appeals

1722. The Court of Justice of the European Union has unlimited jurisdiction to review decisions of the European Commission fixing a fine.

1723. The CJEU may, regarding the fine imposed:

- reduce it;
- increase it;
- cancel it.

CHAPTER XIII
FINAL PROVISIONS

1724. Key takeaways: The final provisions concern:

- the amendment of a series of regulations for harmonisation purposes;
- the evaluation and review process to take account of AI technological developments;
- the entry into force of the Regulation and its application.

102 ARTICLE 102. AMENDMENT TO REGULATION (EC) NO 300/2008

In Article 4(3) of Regulation (EC) No 300/2008, the following subparagraph is added:

"'When adopting detailed measures related to technical specifications and procedures for approval and use of security equipment concerning Artificial Intelligence systems within the meaning of Regulation (EU) 2024/1689 of the European Parliament and of the Council (*), the requirements set out in Chapter III, Section 2, of that Regulation shall be taken into account.

(*) Regulation (EU) 2024/1689 of the European Parliament and of the Council of 13 June 2024 laying down harmonised rules on artificial intelligence and amending Regulations (EC) No 300/2008, (EU) No 167/2013, (EU) No 168/2013, (EU) 2018/858, (EU) 2018/1139 and (EU) 2019/2144 and Directives 2014/90/EU, (EU) 2016/797 and (EU) 2020/1828 (Artificial Intelligence Act) (OJ L, 2024/1689, 12.07.2024, ELI: http://data.europa.eu/eli/reg/2024/1689/oj).'

102.1. Recitals

1725. (49) As regards high-risk AI systems that are safety components of products or systems, or which are themselves products or systems falling within the scope

of Regulation (EC) No 300/2008 of the European Parliament and of the Council,[1] Regulation (EU) No 167/2013 of the European Parliament and of the Council,[2] Regulation (EU) No 168/2013 of the European Parliament and of the Council,[3] Directive 2014/90/EU of the European Parliament and of the Council,[4] Directive (EU) 2016/797 of the European Parliament and of the Council,[5] Regulation (EU) 2018/858 of the European Parliament and of the Council,[6] Regulation (EU) 2018/1139 of the European Parliament and of the Council,[7] and Regulation (EU) 2019/2144 of the European Parliament and of the Council,[8] it is appropriate to amend those acts to ensure that the Commission takes into account, on the basis of the technical and regulatory specificities of each sector, and without interfering with existing governance, conformity assessment and enforcement mechanisms and authorities established therein, the mandatory requirements for

---

1 Regulation (EC) No 300/2008 of the European Parliament and of the Council of 11 March 2008 on common rules in the field of civil aviation security and repealing Regulation (EC) No 2320/2002, [2008] OJ L97/72.

2 Regulation (EU) No 167/2013 of the European Parliament and of the Council of 5 February 2013 on the approval and market surveillance of agricultural and forestry vehicles, [2013] OJ L60/1.

3 Regulation (EU) No 168/2013 of the European Parliament and of the Council of 15 January 2013 on the approval and market surveillance of two- or three-wheel vehicles and quadricycles, [2013] OJ L60/52.

4 Directive 2014/90/EU of the European Parliament and of the Council of 23 July 2014 on marine equipment and repealing Council Directive 96/98/EC, [2014] OJ L257/146.

5 Directive (EU) 2016/797 of the European Parliament and of the Council of 11 May 2016 on the interoperability of the rail system within the European Union, [2016] OJ L138/44.

6 Regulation (EU) 2018/858 of the European Parliament and of the Council of 30 May 2018 on the approval and market surveillance of motor vehicles and their trailers, and of systems, components and separate technical units intended for such vehicles, amending Regulations (EC) No 715/2007 and (EC) No 595/2009 and repealing Directive 2007/46/EC, [2018] OJ L151/1.

7 Regulation (EU) 2018/1139 of the European Parliament and of the Council of 4 July 2018 on common rules in the field of civil aviation and establishing a European Union Aviation Safety Agency, and amending Regulations (EC) No 2111/2005, (EC) No 1008/2008, (EU) No 996/2010, (EU) No 376/2014 and Directives 2014/30/EU and 2014/53/EU of the European Parliament and of the Council, and repealing Regulations (EC) No 552/2004 and (EC) No 216/2008 of the European Parliament and of the Council and Council Regulation (EEC) No 3922/91, [2018] OJ L212/1.

8 Regulation (EU) 2019/2144 of the European Parliament and of the Council of 27 November 2019 on type-approval requirements for motor vehicles and their trailers, and systems, components and separate technical units intended for such vehicles, as regards their general safety and the protection of vehicle occupants and vulnerable road users, amending Regulation (EU) 2018/858 of the European Parliament and of the Council and repealing Regulations (EC) No 78/2009, (EC) No 79/2009 and (EC) No 661/2009 of the European Parliament and of the Council and Commission Regulations (EC) No 631/2009, (EU) No 406/2010, (EU) No 672/2010, (EU) No 1003/2010, (EU) No 1005/2010, (EU) No 1008/2010, (EU) No 1009/2010, (EU) No 19/2011, (EU) No 109/2011, (EU) No 458/2011, (EU) No 65/2012, (EU) No 130/2012, (EU) No 347/2012, (EU) No 351/2012, (EU) No 1230/2012 and (EU) 2015/166, [2019] OJ L325/1.

high-risk AI systems laid down in this Regulation when adopting any relevant delegated or implementing acts on the basis of those acts.

102.2. General Approach

102.2.1 Preamble

1726. This provision aims to align the horizontal regulation of AI technologies with vertical or sector-specific legislation.

1727. Such legislation is listed in Section B of Annex I for high-risk AI systems. It is excluded from the scope of the Regulation.[9]

102.2.2 Guiding Principles

1728. A uniform EU legislation requires that the European Commission takes into account the provisions related to high-risk AI systems when adopting delegated acts in this sector.

1729. This involves taking into account the following:

NO.	THEME	SPECIFICATION	REFERENCE
1.	Requirement	Compliance with all the requirements of a high-risk AI system	AIA, Art. 8
2.	Risk management	Throughout the entire lifecycle	AIA, Art. 9
3.	Data	Data and data governance	AIA, Art. 10
4.	Documentation	Technical documentation of the high-risk AI system	AIA, Art. 11
5.	Record-keeping	Recording of events (logs)	AIA, Art. 12
6.	Transparency	Information to be provided to deployers	AIA, Art. 13
7.	Human oversight	Decisions by natural persons must prevail, particularly as a last resort	AIA, Art. 14
8.	Resilience	Accuracy, robustness and cybersecurity	AIA, Art. 15

[9] AI Act, Art. 2.

103 ARTICLE 103. AMENDMENT TO REGULATION (EU) NO 167/2013

In Article 17(5) of Regulation (EU) No 167/2013, the following subparagraph is added:

'When adopting delegated acts pursuant to the first subparagraph concerning artificial intelligence systems which are safety components within the meaning of Regulation (EU) 2024/1689 of the European Parliament and of the Council (*), the requirements set out in Chapter III, Section 2, of that Regulation shall be taken into account.

(*) Regulation (EU) 2024/1689 of the European Parliament and of the Council of 13 June 2024 laying down harmonised rules on artificial intelligence and amending Regulations (EC) No 300/2008, (EU) No 167/2013, (EU) No 168/2013, (EU) 2018/858, (EU) 2018/1139 and (EU) 2019/2144 and Directives 2014/90/EU, (EU) 2016/797 and (EU) 2020/1828 (Artificial Intelligence Act) (OJ L, 2024/1689, 12.07.2024, ELI: http://data.europa.eu/eli/reg/2024/1689/oj).'

103.1. Recitals

1730. **(49)** As regards high-risk AI systems that are safety components of products or systems, or which are themselves products or systems falling within the scope of Regulation (EC) No 300/2008 of the European Parliament and of the Council,[10] Regulation (EU) No 167/2013 of the European Parliament and of the Council,[11] Regulation (EU) No 168/2013 of the European Parliament and of the Council,[12] Directive 2014/90/EU of the European Parliament and of the Council,[13] Directive (EU) 2016/797 of the European Parliament and of the Council,[14] Regulation (EU)

---

[10] Regulation (EC) No 300/2008 of the European Parliament and of the Council of 11 March 2008 on common rules in the field of civil aviation security and repealing Regulation (EC) No 2320/2002, [2008] OJ L97/72.

[11] Regulation (EU) No 167/2013 of the European Parliament and of the Council of 5 February 2013 on the approval and market surveillance of agricultural and forestry vehicles, [2013] OJ L60/1.

[12] Regulation (EU) No 168/2013 of the European Parliament and of the Council of 15 January 2013 on the approval and market surveillance of two- or three-wheel vehicles and quadricycles, [2013] OJ L60/52.

[13] Directive 2014/90/EU of the European Parliament and of the Council of 23 July 2014 on marine equipment and repealing Council Directive 96/98/EC, [2014] OJ L257/146.

[14] Directive (EU) 2016/797 of the European Parliament and of the Council of 11 May 2016 on the interoperability of the rail system within the European Union, [2016] OJ L138/44.

2018/858 of the European Parliament and of the Council,[15] Regulation (EU) 2018/1139 of the European Parliament and of the Council,[16] and Regulation (EU) 2019/2144 of the European Parliament and of the Council,[17] it is appropriate to amend those acts to ensure that the Commission takes into account, on the basis of the technical and regulatory specificities of each sector, and without interfering with existing governance, conformity assessment and enforcement mechanisms and authorities established therein, the mandatory requirements for high-risk AI systems laid down in this Regulation when adopting any relevant delegated or implementing acts on the basis of those acts.

103.2. General Approach

103.2.1 Preamble

1731. This provision aims to align the horizontal regulation of AI technologies with vertical or sector-specific legislation.

1732. Such legislation is listed in Section B of Annex I for high-risk AI systems. It is excluded from the scope of the Regulation.[18]

---

[15] Regulation (EU) 2018/858 of the European Parliament and of the Council of 30 May 2018 on the approval and market surveillance of motor vehicles and their trailers, and of systems, components and separate technical units intended for such vehicles, amending Regulations (EC) No 715/2007 and (EC) No 595/2009 and repealing Directive 2007/46/EC, [2018] OJ L151/1.

[16] Regulation (EU) 2018/1139 of the European Parliament and of the Council of 4 July 2018 on common rules in the field of civil aviation and establishing a European Union Aviation Safety Agency, and amending Regulations (EC) No 2111/2005, (EC) No 1008/2008, (EU) No 996/2010, (EU) No 376/2014 and Directives 2014/30/EU and 2014/53/EU of the European Parliament and of the Council, and repealing Regulations (EC) No 552/2004 and (EC) No 216/2008 of the European Parliament and of the Council and Council Regulation (EEC) No 3922/91, [2018] OJ L212/1.

[17] Regulation (EU) 2019/2144 of the European Parliament and of the Council of 27 November 2019 on type-approval requirements for motor vehicles and their trailers, and systems, components and separate technical units intended for such vehicles, as regards their general safety and the protection of vehicle occupants and vulnerable road users, amending Regulation (EU) 2018/858 of the European Parliament and of the Council and repealing Regulations (EC) No 78/2009, (EC) No 79/2009 and (EC) No 661/2009 of the European Parliament and of the Council and Commission Regulations (EC) No 631/2009, (EU) No 406/2010, (EU) No 672/2010, (EU) No 1003/2010, (EU) No 1005/2010, (EU) No 1008/2010, (EU) No 1009/2010, (EU) No 19/2011, (EU) No 109/2011, (EU) No 458/2011, (EU) No 65/2012, (EU) No 130/2012, (EU) No 347/2012, (EU) No 351/2012, (EU) No 1230/2012 and (EU) 2015/166, [2019] OJ L325/1.

[18] AI Act, Art. 2.

103.2.2 Guiding Principles

1733. A uniform EU legislation requires that the European Commission takes into account the provisions related to high-risk AI systems when adopting delegated acts in this sector.

1734. This involves taking into account the following:

NO.	THEME	SPECIFICATION	REFERENCE
1.	Requirement	Compliance with all the requirements of a high-risk AI system	AIA, Art. 8
2.	Risk management	Throughout the entire lifecycle	AIA, Art. 9
3.	Data	Data and data governance	AIA, Art. 10
4.	Documentation	Technical documentation of the high-risk AI system	AIA, Art. 11
5.	Record-keeping	Recording of events (logs)	AIA, Art. 12
6.	Transparency	Information to be provided to deployers	AIA, Art. 13
7.	Human oversight	Decisions by natural persons must prevail, particularly as a last resort	AIA, Art. 14
8.	Resilience	Accuracy, robustness and cybersecurity	AIA, Art. 15

103.3. Structure of the Provisions

103.3.1 Principles

1735. This legislation is listed in in Section B of Annex I for high-risk AI systems: 'List of other Union harmonisation legislation'.

103.3.2 Relationship

1736. The aforementioned requirements may be incorporated into sectoral requirements.[19]

[19] AI Act, Arts. 8–15.

104 ARTICLE 104. AMENDMENT TO REGULATION (EU) NO 168/2013

In Article 22(5) of Regulation (EU) No 168/2013, the following subparagraph is added:

'When adopting delegated acts pursuant to the first subparagraph concerning Artificial Intelligence systems which are safety components within the meaning of Regulation (EU) 2024/1689 of the European Parliament and of the Council (*), the requirements set out in Chapter III, Section 2, of that Regulation shall be taken into account.

(*) Regulation (EU) 2024/1689 of the European Parliament and of the Council of 13 June 2024 laying down harmonised rules on artificial intelligence and amending Regulations (EC) No 300/2008, (EU) No 167/2013, (EU) No 168/2013, (EU) 2018/858, (EU) 2018/1139 and (EU) 2019/2144 and Directives 2014/90/EU, (EU) 2016/797 and (EU) 2020/1828 (Artificial Intelligence Act) (OJ L, 2024/1689, 12.07.2024, ELI: http://data.europa.eu/eli/reg/2024/1689/oj).'

104.1. Recitals

1737. **(49)** As regards high-risk AI systems that are safety components of products or systems, or which are themselves products or systems falling within the scope of Regulation (EC) No 300/2008 of the European Parliament and of the Council,[20] Regulation (EU) No 167/2013 of the European Parliament and of the Council,[21] Regulation (EU) No 168/2013 of the European Parliament and of the Council,[22] Directive 2014/90/EU of the European Parliament and of the Council,[23] Directive (EU) 2016/797 of the European Parliament and of the Council,[24] Regulation (EU) 2018/858 of the European Parliament and of the Council,[25] Regulation (EU)

---

20 Regulation (EC) No 300/2008 of the European Parliament and of the Council of 11 March 2008 on common rules in the field of civil aviation security and repealing Regulation (EC) No 2320/2002, [2008] OJ L97/72.

21 Regulation (EU) No 167/2013 of the European Parliament and of the Council of 5 February 2013 on the approval and market surveillance of agricultural and forestry vehicles, [2013] OJ L60/1.

22 Regulation (EU) No 168/2013 of the European Parliament and of the Council of 15 January 2013 on the approval and market surveillance of two- or three-wheel vehicles and quadricycles, [2013] OJ L60/52.

23 Directive 2014/90/EU of the European Parliament and of the Council of 23 July 2014 on marine equipment and repealing Council Directive 96/98/EC, [2014] OJ L257/146.

24 Directive (EU) 2016/797 of the European Parliament and of the Council of 11 May 2016 on the interoperability of the rail system within the European Union, [2016] OJ L138/44.

25 Regulation (EU) 2018/858 of the European Parliament and of the Council of 30 May 2018 on the approval and market surveillance of motor vehicles and their trailers, and of systems, components and separate technical units intended for such vehicles, amending Regulations (EC) No 715/2007 and (EC) No 595/2009 and repealing Directive 2007/46/EC, [2018] OJ L151/1.

2018/1139 of the European Parliament and of the Council,[26] and Regulation (EU) 2019/2144 of the European Parliament and of the Council,[27] it is appropriate to amend those acts to ensure that the Commission takes into account, on the basis of the technical and regulatory specificities of each sector, and without interfering with existing governance, conformity assessment and enforcement mechanisms and authorities established therein, the mandatory requirements for high-risk AI systems laid down in this Regulation when adopting any relevant delegated or implementing acts on the basis of those acts.

104.2. General Approach

104.2.1 Preamble

1738. This provision aims to align the horizontal regulation of AI technologies with vertical or sector-specific legislation.

1739. Such legislation is listed in Section B of Annex I for high-risk AI systems. It is excluded from the scope of the Regulation.[28]

104.2.2 Guiding Principles

1740. A uniform EU legislation requires that the European Commission takes into account the provisions related to high-risk AI systems when adopting delegated acts in this sector.

---

[26] Regulation (EU) 2018/1139 of the European Parliament and of the Council of 4 July 2018 on common rules in the field of civil aviation and establishing a European Union Aviation Safety Agency, and amending Regulations (EC) No 2111/2005, (EC) No 1008/2008, (EU) No 996/2010, (EU) No 376/2014 and Directives 2014/30/EU and 2014/53/EU of the European Parliament and of the Council, and repealing Regulations (EC) No 552/2004 and (EC) No 216/2008 of the European Parliament and of the Council and Council Regulation (EEC) No 3922/91, [2018] OJ L212/1.

[27] Regulation (EU) 2019/2144 of the European Parliament and of the Council of 27 November 2019 on type-approval requirements for motor vehicles and their trailers, and systems, components and separate technical units intended for such vehicles, as regards their general safety and the protection of vehicle occupants and vulnerable road users, amending Regulation (EU) 2018/858 of the European Parliament and of the Council and repealing Regulations (EC) No 78/2009, (EC) No 79/2009 and (EC) No 661/2009 of the European Parliament and of the Council and Commission Regulations (EC) No 631/2009, (EU) No 406/2010, (EU) No 672/2010, (EU) No 1003/2010, (EU) No 1005/2010, (EU) No 1008/2010, (EU) No 1009/2010, (EU) No 19/2011, (EU) No 109/2011, (EU) No 458/2011, (EU) No 65/2012, (EU) No 130/2012, (EU) No 347/2012, (EU) No 351/2012, (EU) No 1230/2012 and (EU) 2015/166, [2019] OJ L325/1.

[28] AI Act, Art. 2.

1741. This involves taking into account the following:

NO.	THEME	SPECIFICATION	REFERENCE
1.	Requirement	Compliance with all the requirements of a high-risk AI system	AIA, Art. 8
2.	Risk management	Throughout the entire lifecycle	AIA, Art. 9
3.	Data	Data and data governance	AIA, Art. 10
4.	Documentation	Technical documentation of the high-risk AI system	AIA, Art. 11
5.	Record-keeping	Recording of events (logs)	AIA, Art. 12
6.	Transparency	Information to be provided to deployers	AIA, Art. 13
7.	Human oversight	Decisions by natural persons must prevail, particularly as a last resort	AIA, Art. 14
8.	Resilience	Accuracy, robustness and cybersecurity	AIA, Art. 15

105 ARTICLE 105. AMENDMENT TO DIRECTIVE 2014/90/EU

In Article 8 of Directive 2014/90/EU, the following paragraph is added:

'5. For Artificial Intelligence systems which are safety components within the meaning of Regulation (EU) 2024/1689 of the European Parliament and of the Council (*), when carrying out its activities pursuant to paragraph 1 and when adopting technical specifications and testing standards in accordance with paragraphs 2 and 3, the Commission shall take into account the requirements set out in Chapter III, Section 2, of that Regulation.

(*) Regulation (EU) 2024/1689 of the European Parliament and of the Council of 13 June 2024 laying down harmonised rules on artificial intelligence and amending Regulations (EC) No 300/2008, (EU) No 167/2013, (EU) No 168/2013, (EU) 2018/858, (EU) 2018/1139 and (EU) 2019/2144 and Directives 2014/90/EU, (EU) 2016/797 and (EU) 2020/1828 (Artificial Intelligence Act) (OJ L, 2024/1689, 12.07.2024, ELI: http://data.europa.eu/eli/reg/2024/1689/oj).'

105.1. Recitals

1742. **(49)** As regards high-risk AI systems that are safety components of products or systems, or which are themselves products or systems falling within the scope

of Regulation (EC) No 300/2008 of the European Parliament and of the Council,[29] Regulation (EU) No 167/2013 of the European Parliament and of the Council,[30] Regulation (EU) No 168/2013 of the European Parliament and of the Council,[31] Directive 2014/90/EU of the European Parliament and of the Council,[32] Directive (EU) 2016/797 of the European Parliament and of the Council,[33] Regulation (EU) 2018/858 of the European Parliament and of the Council,[34] Regulation (EU) 2018/1139 of the European Parliament and of the Council,[35] and Regulation (EU) 2019/2144 of the European Parliament and of the Council,[36] it is appropriate to amend those acts to ensure that the Commission takes into account, on the basis of the technical and regulatory specificities of each sector, and without interfering with existing governance, conformity assessment and enforcement mechanisms and authorities established therein, the mandatory requirements for

---

29 Regulation (EC) No 300/2008 of the European Parliament and of the Council of 11 March 2008 on common rules in the field of civil aviation security and repealing Regulation (EC) No 2320/2002, [2008] OJ L97/72.

30 Regulation (EU) No 167/2013 of the European Parliament and of the Council of 5 February 2013 on the approval and market surveillance of agricultural and forestry vehicles, [2013] OJ L60/1.

31 Regulation (EU) No 168/2013Regulation (EU) No 168/2013 of the European Parliament and of the Council of 15 January 2013 on the approval and market surveillance of two- or three-wheel vehicles and quadricycles, [2013] OJ L60/52.

32 Directive 2014/90/EU of the European Parliament and of the Council of 23 July 2014 on marine equipment and repealing Council Directive 96/98/EC, [2014] OJ L257/146.

33 Directive (EU) 2016/797Directive (EU) 2016/797 of the European Parliament and of the Council of 11 May 2016 on the interoperability of the rail system within the European Union, [2016] OJ L138/44.

34 Regulation (EU) 2018/858 of the European Parliament and of the Council of 30 May 2018 on the approval and market surveillance of motor vehicles and their trailers, and of systems, components and separate technical units intended for such vehicles, amending Regulations (EC) No 715/2007 and (EC) No 595/2009 and repealing Directive 2007/46/EC, [2018] OJ L151/1.

35 Regulation (EU) 2018/1139 of the European Parliament and of the Council of 4 July 2018 on common rules in the field of civil aviation and establishing a European Union Aviation Safety Agency, and amending Regulations (EC) No 2111/2005, (EC) No 1008/2008, (EU) No 996/2010, (EU) No 376/2014 and Directives 2014/30/EU and 2014/53/EU of the European Parliament and of the Council, and repealing Regulations (EC) No 552/2004 and (EC) No 216/2008 of the European Parliament and of the Council and Council Regulation (EEC) No 3922/91, [2018] OJ L212/1.

36 Regulation (EU) 2019/2144 of the European Parliament and of the Council of 27 November 2019 on type-approval requirements for motor vehicles and their trailers, and systems, components and separate technical units intended for such vehicles, as regards their general safety and the protection of vehicle occupants and vulnerable road users, amending Regulation (EU) 2018/858 of the European Parliament and of the Council and repealing Regulations (EC) No 78/2009, (EC) No 79/2009 and (EC) No 661/2009 of the European Parliament and of the Council and Commission Regulations (EC) No 631/2009, (EU) No 406/2010, (EU) No 672/2010, (EU) No 1003/2010, (EU) No 1005/2010, (EU) No 1008/2010, (EU) No 1009/2010, (EU) No 19/2011, (EU) No 109/2011, (EU) No 458/2011, (EU) No 65/2012, (EU) No 130/2012, (EU) No 347/2012, (EU) No 351/2012, (EU) No 1230/2012 and (EU) 2015/166, [2019] OJ L325/1.

high-risk AI systems laid down in this Regulation when adopting any relevant delegated or implementing acts on the basis of those acts.

105.2. General Approach

105.2.1 Preamble

1743. This provision aims to align the horizontal regulation of AI technologies with vertical or sector-specific legislation.

1744. Such legislation is listed in Section B of Annex I for high-risk AI systems. It is excluded from the scope of the Regulation.[37]

105.2.2 Guiding Principles

1745. A uniform EU legislation requires that the European Commission takes into account the provisions related to high-risk AI systems when adopting delegated acts in this sector.

1746. This involves taking into account the following:

NO.	THEME	SPECIFICATION	REFERENCE
1.	Requirement	Compliance with all the requirements of a high-risk AI system	AIA, Art. 8
2.	Risk management	Throughout the entire lifecycle	AIA, Art. 9
3.	Data	Data and data governance	AIA, Art. 10
4.	Documentation	Technical documentation of the high-risk AI system	AIA, Art. 11
5.	Record-keeping	Recording of events (logs)	AIA, Art. 12
6.	Transparency	Information to be provided to deployers	AIA, Art. 13
7.	Human oversight	Decisions by natural persons must prevail, particularly as a last resort	AIA, Art. 14
8.	Resilience	Accuracy, robustness and cybersecurity	AIA, Art. 15

[37] AI Act, Art. 2.

106 ARTICLE 106. AMENDMENT TO DIRECTIVE (EU) 2016/797

In Article 5 of Directive (EU) 2016/797, the following paragraph is added:

'12. When adopting delegated acts pursuant to paragraph 1 and implementing acts pursuant to paragraph 11 concerning Artificial Intelligence systems which are safety components within the meaning of Regulation (EU) 2024/1689 of the European Parliament and of the Council (*), the requirements set out in Chapter III, Section 2, of that Regulation shall be taken into account.

(*) Regulation (EU) 2024/1689 of the European Parliament and of the Council of 13 June 2024 laying down harmonised rules on artificial intelligence and amending Regulations (EC) No 300/2008, (EU) No 167/2013, (EU) No 168/2013, (EU) 2018/858, (EU) 2018/1139 and (EU) 2019/2144 and Directives 2014/90/EU, (EU) 2016/797 and (EU) 2020/1828 (Artificial Intelligence Act) (OJ L, 2024/1689, 12.07.2024, ELI: http://data.europa.eu/eli/reg/2024/1689/oj).'

106.1. Recitals

1747. (49) As regards high-risk AI systems that are safety components of products or systems, or which are themselves products or systems falling within the scope of Regulation (EC) No 300/2008 of the European Parliament and of the Council,[38] Regulation (EU) No 167/2013 of the European Parliament and of the Council,[39] Regulation (EU) No 168/2013 of the European Parliament and of the Council,[40] Directive 2014/90/EU of the European Parliament and of the Council,[41] Directive (EU) 2016/797 of the European Parliament and of the Council,[42] Regulation (EU) 2018/858 of the European Parliament and of the Council,[43] Regulation (EU)

---

[38] Regulation (EC) No 300/2008 of the European Parliament and of the Council of 11 March 2008 on common rules in the field of civil aviation security and repealing Regulation (EC) No 2320/2002, [2008] OJ L97/72.

[39] Regulation (EU) No 167/2013 of the European Parliament and of the Council of 5 February 2013 on the approval and market surveillance of agricultural and forestry vehicles, [2013] OJ L60/1.

[40] Regulation (EU) No 168/2013 of the European Parliament and of the Council of 15 January 2013 on the approval and market surveillance of two- or three-wheel vehicles and quadricycles, [2013] OJ L60/52.

[41] Directive 2014/90/EU of the European Parliament and of the Council of 23 July 2014 on marine equipment and repealing Council Directive 96/98/EC, [2014] OJ L257/146.

[42] Directive (EU) 2016/797 of the European Parliament and of the Council of 11 May 2016 on the interoperability of the rail system within the European Union, [2016] OJ L138/44.

[43] Regulation (EU) 2018/858 of the European Parliament and of the Council of 30 May 2018 on the approval and market surveillance of motor vehicles and their trailers, and of systems, components and separate technical units intended for such vehicles, amending Regulations (EC) No 715/2007 and (EC) No 595/2009 and repealing Directive 2007/46/EC, [2018] OJ L151/1.

2018/1139 of the European Parliament and of the Council,[44] and Regulation (EU) 2019/2144 of the European Parliament and of the Council,[45] it is appropriate to amend those acts to ensure that the Commission takes into account, on the basis of the technical and regulatory specificities of each sector, and without interfering with existing governance, conformity assessment and enforcement mechanisms and authorities established therein, the mandatory requirements for high-risk AI systems laid down in this Regulation when adopting any relevant delegated or implementing acts on the basis of those acts.

106.2. General Approach

106.2.1 Preamble

1748. This provision aims to align the horizontal regulation of AI technologies with vertical or sector-specific legislation.

1749. Such legislation is listed in Section B of Annex I for high-risk AI systems. It is excluded from the scope of the Regulation.[46]

106.2.2 Guiding Principles

1750. A uniform EU legislation requires that the European Commission takes into account the provisions related to high-risk AI systems when adopting delegated acts in this sector.

---

[44] Regulation (EU) 2018/1139 of the European Parliament and of the Council of 4 July 2018 on common rules in the field of civil aviation and establishing a European Union Aviation Safety Agency, and amending Regulations (EC) No 2111/2005, (EC) No 1008/2008, (EU) No 996/2010, (EU) No 376/2014 and Directives 2014/30/EU and 2014/53/EU of the European Parliament and of the Council, and repealing Regulations (EC) No 552/2004 and (EC) No 216/2008 of the European Parliament and of the Council and Council Regulation (EEC) No 3922/91, [2018] OJ L212/1.

[45] Regulation (EU) 2019/2144 of the European Parliament and of the Council of 27 November 2019 on type-approval requirements for motor vehicles and their trailers, and systems, components and separate technical units intended for such vehicles, as regards their general safety and the protection of vehicle occupants and vulnerable road users, amending Regulation (EU) 2018/858 of the European Parliament and of the Council and repealing Regulations (EC) No 78/2009, (EC) No 79/2009 and (EC) No 661/2009 of the European Parliament and of the Council and Commission Regulations (EC) No 631/2009, (EU) No 406/2010, (EU) No 672/2010, (EU) No 1003/2010, (EU) No 1005/2010, (EU) No 1008/2010, (EU) No 1009/2010, (EU) No 19/2011, (EU) No 109/2011, (EU) No 458/2011, (EU) No 65/2012, (EU) No 130/2012, (EU) No 347/2012, (EU) No 351/2012, (EU) No 1230/2012 and (EU) 2015/166, [2019] OJ L325/1.

[46] AI Act, Art. 2.

1751. This involves taking into account the following:

NO.	THEME	SPECIFICATION	REFERENCE
1.	Requirement	Compliance with all the requirements of a high-risk AI system	AIA, Art. 8
2.	Risk management	Throughout the entire lifecycle	AIA, Art. 9
3.	Data	Data and data governance	AIA, Art. 10
4.	Documentation	Technical documentation of the high-risk AI system	AIA, Art. 11
5.	Record-keeping	Recording of events (logs)	AIA, Art. 12
6.	Transparency	Information to be provided to deployers	AIA, Art. 13
7.	Human oversight	Decisions by natural persons must prevail, particularly as a last resort	AIA, Art. 14
8.	Resilience	Accuracy, robustness and cybersecurity	AIA, Art. 15

107 ARTICLE 107. AMENDMENT TO REGULATION (EU) 2018/858

In Article 5 of Regulation (EU) 2018/858 the following paragraph is added:

'4. When adopting delegated acts pursuant to paragraph 3 concerning Artificial Intelligence systems which are safety components within the meaning of Regulation (EU) 2024/1689 of the European Parliament and of the Council (*), the requirements set out in Chapter III, Section 2, of that Regulation shall be taken into account.

(*) Regulation (EU) 2024/1689 of the European Parliament and of the Council of 13 June 2024 laying down harmonised rules on artificial intelligence and amending Regulations (EC) No 300/2008, (EU) No 167/2013, (EU) No 168/2013, (EU) 2018/858, (EU) 2018/1139 and (EU) 2019/2144 and Directives 2014/90/EU, (EU) 2016/797 and (EU) 2020/1828 (Artificial Intelligence Act) (OJ L, 2024/1689, 12.07.2024, ELI: http://data.europa.eu/eli/reg/2024/1689/oj).'

107.1. Recitals

1752. (49) As regards high-risk AI systems that are safety components of products or systems, or which are themselves products or systems falling within the scope

of Regulation (EC) No 300/2008 of the European Parliament and of the Council,[47] Regulation (EU) No 167/2013 of the European Parliament and of the Council,[48] Regulation (EU) No 168/2013 of the European Parliament and of the Council,[49] Directive 2014/90/EU of the European Parliament and of the Council,[50] Directive (EU) 2016/797 of the European Parliament and of the Council,[51] Regulation (EU) 2018/858 of the European Parliament and of the Council,[52] Regulation (EU) 2018/1139 of the European Parliament and of the Council,[53] and Regulation (EU) 2019/2144 of the European Parliament and of the Council,[54] it is appropriate to amend those acts to ensure that the Commission takes into account, on the basis of the technical and regulatory specificities of each sector, and without interfering with existing governance, conformity assessment and enforcement mechanisms and authorities established therein, the mandatory requirements for

---

47 Regulation (EC) No 300/2008 of the European Parliament and of the Council of 11 March 2008 on common rules in the field of civil aviation security and repealing Regulation (EC) No 2320/2002, [2008] OJ L97/72.

48 Regulation (EU) No 167/2013 of the European Parliament and of the Council of 5 February 2013 on the approval and market surveillance of agricultural and forestry vehicles, [2013] OJ L60/1.

49 Regulation (EU) No 168/2013 of the European Parliament and of the Council of 15 January 2013 on the approval and market surveillance of two- or three-wheel vehicles and quadricycles, [2013] OJ L60/52.

50 Directive 2014/90/EU of the European Parliament and of the Council of 23 July 2014 on marine equipment and repealing Council Directive 96/98/EC, [2014] OJ L257/146.

51 Directive (EU) 2016/797 of the European Parliament and of the Council of 11 May 2016 on the interoperability of the rail system within the European Union, [2016] OJ L138/44.

52 Regulation (EU) 2018/858 of the European Parliament and of the Council of 30 May 2018 on the approval and market surveillance of motor vehicles and their trailers, and of systems, components and separate technical units intended for such vehicles, amending Regulations (EC) No 715/2007 and (EC) No 595/2009 and repealing Directive 2007/46/EC, [2018] OJ L151/1.

53 Regulation (EU) 2018/1139 of the European Parliament and of the Council of 4 July 2018 on common rules in the field of civil aviation and establishing a European Union Aviation Safety Agency, and amending Regulations (EC) No 2111/2005, (EC) No 1008/2008, (EU) No 996/2010, (EU) No 376/2014 and Directives 2014/30/EU and 2014/53/EU of the European Parliament and of the Council, and repealing Regulations (EC) No 552/2004 and (EC) No 216/2008 of the European Parliament and of the Council and Council Regulation (EEC) No 3922/91, [2018] OJ L212/1.

54 Regulation (EU) 2019/2144 of the European Parliament and of the Council of 27 November 2019 on type-approval requirements for motor vehicles and their trailers, and systems, components and separate technical units intended for such vehicles, as regards their general safety and the protection of vehicle occupants and vulnerable road users, amending Regulation (EU) 2018/858 of the European Parliament and of the Council and repealing Regulations (EC) No 78/2009, (EC) No 79/2009 and (EC) No 661/2009 of the European Parliament and of the Council and Commission Regulations (EC) No 631/2009, (EU) No 406/2010, (EU) No 672/2010, (EU) No 1003/2010, (EU) No 1005/2010, (EU) No 1008/2010, (EU) No 1009/2010, (EU) No 19/2011, (EU) No 109/2011, (EU) No 458/2011, (EU) No 65/2012, (EU) No 130/2012, (EU) No 347/2012, (EU) No 351/2012, (EU) No 1230/2012 and (EU) 2015/166, [2019] OJ L325/1.

high-risk AI systems laid down in this Regulation when adopting any relevant delegated or implementing acts on the basis of those acts.

107.2. General Approach

107.2.1 Preamble

1753. This provision aims to align the horizontal regulation of AI technologies with vertical or sector-specific legislation.

1754. Such legislation is listed in Section B of Annex I for high-risk AI systems. It is excluded from the scope of the Regulation.[55]

107.2.2 Guiding Principles

1755. A uniform EU legislation requires that the European Commission takes into account the provisions related to high-risk AI systems when adopting delegated acts in this sector.

1756. This involves taking into account the following:

NO.	THEME	SPECIFICATION	REFERENCE
1.	Requirement	Compliance with all the requirements of a high-risk AI system	AIA, Art. 8
2.	Risk management	Throughout the entire lifecycle	AIA, Art. 9
3.	Data	Data and data governance	AIA, Art. 10
4.	Documentation	Technical documentation of the high-risk AI system	AIA, Art. 11
5.	Record-keeping	Recording of events (logs)	AIA, Art. 12
6.	Transparency	Information to be provided to deployers	AIA, Art. 13
7.	Human oversight	Decisions by natural persons must prevail, particularly as a last resort	AIA, Art. 14
8.	Resilience	Accuracy, robustness and cybersecurity	AIA, Art. 15

[55] AI Act, Art. 2.

108 ARTICLE 108. AMENDMENTS TO REGULATION (EU) 2018/1139

Regulation (EU) 2018/1139 is amended as follows:

(1) in Article 17, the following paragraph is added:

'3. Without prejudice to paragraph 2, when adopting implementing acts pursuant to paragraph 1 concerning Artificial Intelligence systems which are safety components within the meaning of Regulation (EU) 2024/1689 of the European Parliament and of the Council (*), the requirements set out in Chapter III, Section 2, of that Regulation shall be taken into account.

(*) Regulation (EU) 2024/1689 of the European Parliament and of the Council of 13 June 2024 laying down harmonised rules on artificial intelligence and amending Regulations (EC) No 300/2008, (EU) No 167/2013, (EU) No 168/2013, (EU) 2018/858, (EU) 2018/1139 and (EU) 2019/2144 and Directives 2014/90/EU, (EU) 2016/797 and (EU) 2020/1828 (Artificial Intelligence Act) (OJ L, 2024/1689, 12.07.2024, ELI: http://data.europa.eu/eli/reg/2024/1689/oj).';".

(2) in Article 19, the following paragraph is added:

'4. When adopting delegated acts pursuant to paragraphs 1 and 2 concerning Artificial Intelligence systems which are safety components within the meaning of Regulation (EU) 2024/1689, the requirements set out in Chapter III, Section 2, of that Regulation shall be taken into account.';

3) in Article 43, the following paragraph is added:

'4. When adopting implementing acts pursuant to paragraph 1 concerning Artificial Intelligence systems which are safety components within the meaning of Regulation (EU) 2024/1689, the requirements set out in Chapter III, Section 2, of that Regulation shall be taken into account.';

(4) in Article 47, the following paragraph is added:

'3. When adopting delegated acts pursuant to paragraphs 1 and 2 concerning Artificial Intelligence systems which are safety components within the meaning of Regulation (EU) 2024/1689, the requirements set out in Chapter III, Section 2, of that Regulation shall be taken into account.';

(5) in Article 57, the following subparagraph is added:

'When adopting those implementing acts concerning Artificial Intelligence systems which are safety components within the meaning of Regulation (EU) 2024/1689, the requirements set out in Chapter III, Section 2, of that Regulation shall be taken into account.';

(6) in Article 58, the following paragraph is added:

'3. When adopting delegated acts pursuant to paragraphs 1 and 2 concerning Artificial Intelligence systems which are safety components within the meaning of Regulation (EU) 2024/1689, the requirements set out in Chapter III, Section 2, of that Regulation shall be taken into account.'

108.1. Recitals

1757. (49) As regards high-risk AI systems that are safety components of products or systems, or which are themselves products or systems falling within the scope of Regulation (EC) No 300/2008 of the European Parliament and of the Council,[56] Regulation (EU) No 167/2013 of the European Parliament and of the Council,[57] Regulation (EU) No 168/2013 of the European Parliament and of the Council,[58] Directive 2014/90/EU of the European Parliament and of the Council,[59] Directive (EU) 2016/797 of the European Parliament and of the Council,[60] Regulation (EU) 2018/858 of the European Parliament and of the Council,[61] Regulation (EU) 2018/1139 of the European Parliament and of the Council,[62] and Regulation (EU) 2019/2144 of the European Parliament and of the Council,[63] it is appropriate to amend those acts to ensure that the Commission takes into account, on the

---

56 Regulation (EC) No 300/2008 of the European Parliament and of the Council of 11 March 2008 on common rules in the field of civil aviation security and repealing Regulation (EC) No 2320/2002, [2008] OJ L97/72.

57 Regulation (EU) No 167/2013 of the European Parliament and of the Council of 5 February 2013 on the approval and market surveillance of agricultural and forestry vehicles, [2013] OJ L60/1.

58 Regulation (EU) No 168/2013 of the European Parliament and of the Council of 15 January 2013 on the approval and market surveillance of two- or three-wheel vehicles and quadricycles, [2013] OJ L60/52.

59 Directive 2014/90/EU of the European Parliament and of the Council of 23 July 2014 on marine equipment and repealing Council Directive 96/98/EC, [2014] OJ L257/146.

60 Directive (EU) 2016/797 of the European Parliament and of the Council of 11 May 2016 on the interoperability of the rail system within the European Union, [2016] OJ L138/44.

61 Regulation (EU) 2018/858 of the European Parliament and of the Council of 30 May 2018 on the approval and market surveillance of motor vehicles and their trailers, and of systems, components and separate technical units intended for such vehicles, amending Regulations (EC) No 715/2007 and (EC) No 595/2009 and repealing Directive 2007/46/EC, [2018] OJ L151/1.

62 Regulation (EU) 2018/1139 of the European Parliament and of the Council of 4 July 2018 on common rules in the field of civil aviation and establishing a European Union Aviation Safety Agency, and amending Regulations (EC) No 2111/2005, (EC) No 1008/2008, (EU) No 996/2010, (EU) No 376/2014 and Directives 2014/30/EU and 2014/53/EU of the European Parliament and of the Council, and repealing Regulations (EC) No 552/2004 and (EC) No 216/2008 of the European Parliament and of the Council and Council Regulation (EEC) No 3922/91, [2018] OJ L212/1.

63 Regulation (EU) 2019/2144 of the European Parliament and of the Council of 27 November 2019 on type-approval requirements for motor vehicles and their trailers, and systems, components and separate technical units intended for such vehicles, as regards their general safety and the protection of vehicle occupants and vulnerable road users, amending Regulation (EU) 2018/858 of the European Parliament and of the Council and repealing Regulations (EC) No 78/2009, (EC) No 79/2009 and (EC) No 661/2009 of the European Parliament and of the Council and Commission Regulations (EC) No 631/2009, (EU) No 406/2010, (EU) No 672/2010, (EU) No 1003/2010, (EU) No 1005/2010, (EU) No 1008/2010, (EU) No 1009/2010, (EU) No 19/2011, (EU) No 109/2011, (EU) No 458/2011, (EU) No 65/2012, (EU) No 130/2012, (EU) No 347/2012, (EU) No 351/2012, (EU) No 1230/2012 and (EU) 2015/166, [2019] OJ L325/1.

basis of the technical and regulatory specificities of each sector, and without interfering with existing governance, conformity assessment and enforcement mechanisms and authorities established therein, the mandatory requirements for high-risk AI systems laid down in this Regulation when adopting any relevant delegated or implementing acts on the basis of those acts.

108.2. General Approach

108.2.1 Preamble

1758. This provision aims to align the horizontal regulation of AI technologies with vertical or sector-specific legislation.

1759. Such legislation is listed in Section B of Annex I for high-risk AI systems. It is excluded from the scope of the Regulation.[64]

108.2.2 Guiding Principles

1760. A uniform EU legislation requires that the European Commission takes into account the provisions related to high-risk AI systems when adopting delegated acts in this sector.

1761. This involves taking into account the following:

NO.	THEME	SPECIFICATION	REFERENCE
1.	Requirement	Compliance with all the requirements of a high-risk AI system	AIA, Art. 8
2.	Risk management	Throughout the entire lifecycle	AIA, Art. 9
3.	Data	Data and data governance	AIA, Art. 10
4.	Documentation	Technical documentation of the high-risk AI system	AIA, Art. 11
5.	Record-keeping	Recording of events (logs)	AIA, Art. 12
6.	Transparency	Information to be provided to deployers	AIA, Art. 13
7.	Human oversight	Decisions by natural persons must prevail, particularly as a last resort	AIA, Art. 14
8.	Resilience	Accuracy, robustness and cybersecurity	AIA, Art. 15

[64] AI Act, Art. 2.

109 ARTICLE 109. AMENDMENT TO REGULATION (EU) 2019/2144

In Article 11 of Regulation (EU) 2019/2144, the following paragraph is added:

'3. When adopting the implementing acts pursuant to paragraph 2, concerning artificial intelligence systems which are safety components within the meaning of Regulation (EU) 2024/1689 of the European Parliament and of the Council (*), the requirements set out in Chapter III, Section 2, of that Regulation shall be taken into account.

(*) Regulation (EU) 2024/1689 of the European Parliament and of the Council of 13 June 2024 laying down harmonised rules on artificial intelligence and amending Regulations (EC) No 300/2008, (EU) No 167/2013, (EU) No 168/2013, (EU) 2018/858, (EU) 2018/1139 and (EU) 2019/2144 and Directives 2014/90/EU, (EU) 2016/797 and (EU) 2020/1828 (Artificial Intelligence Act) (OJ L, 2024/1689, 12.07.2024, ELI: http://data.europa.eu/eli/reg/2024/1689/oj).'

109.1. Recitals

1762. (49) As regards high-risk AI systems that are safety components of products or systems, or which are themselves products or systems falling within the scope of Regulation (EC) No 300/2008 of the European Parliament and of the Council,[65] Regulation (EU) No 167/2013 of the European Parliament and of the Council,[66] Regulation (EU) No 168/2013 of the European Parliament and of the Council,[67] Directive 2014/90/EU of the European Parliament and of the Council,[68] Directive (EU) 2016/797 of the European Parliament and of the Council,[69] Regulation (EU) 2018/858 of the European Parliament and of the Council,[70] Regulation (EU)

---

[65] Regulation (EC) No 300/2008 of the European Parliament and of the Council of 11 March 2008 on common rules in the field of civil aviation security and repealing Regulation (EC) No 2320/2002, [2008] OJ L97/72.

[66] Regulation (EU) No 167/2013 of the European Parliament and of the Council of 5 February 2013 on the approval and market surveillance of agricultural and forestry vehicles, [2013] OJ L60/1.

[67] Regulation (EU) No 168/2013 of the European Parliament and of the Council of 15 January 2013 on the approval and market surveillance of two- or three-wheel vehicles and quadricycles, [2013] OJ L60/52.

[68] Directive 2014/90/EU of the European Parliament and of the Council of 23 July 2014 on marine equipment and repealing Council Directive 96/98/EC, [2014] OJ L257/146.

[69] Directive (EU) 2016/797 of the European Parliament and of the Council of 11 May 2016 on the interoperability of the rail system within the European Union, [2016] OJ L138/44.

[70] Regulation (EU) 2018/858 of the European Parliament and of the Council of 30May 2018 on the approval and market surveillance of motor vehicles and their trailers, and of systems, components and separate technical units intended for such vehicles, amending Regulations

2018/1139 of the European Parliament and of the Council,[71] and Regulation (EU) 2019/2144 of the European Parliament and of the Council,[72] it is appropriate to amend those acts to ensure that the Commission takes into account, on the basis of the technical and regulatory specificities of each sector, and without interfering with existing governance, conformity assessment and enforcement mechanisms and authorities established therein, the mandatory requirements for high-risk AI systems laid down in this Regulation when adopting any relevant delegated or implementing acts on the basis of those acts.

109.2. General Approach

109.2.1 Preamble

1763. This provision aims to align the horizontal regulation of AI technologies with vertical or sector-specific legislation.

1764. Such legislation is listed in Section B of Annex I for high-risk AI systems. It is excluded from the scope of the Regulation.[73]

109.2.2 Guiding Principles

1765. A uniform EU legislation requires that the European Commission takes into account the provisions related to high-risk AI systems when adopting delegated acts in this sector.

1766. This involves taking into account the following:

(EC) No 715/2007 and (EC) No 595/2009 and repealing Directive 2007/46/EC, [2018] OJ L151/1.

71 Regulation (EU) 2018/1139 of the European Parliament and of the Council of 4 July 2018 on common rules in the field of civil aviation and establishing a European Union Aviation Safety Agency, and amending Regulations (EC) No 2111/2005, (EC) No 1008/2008, (EU) No 996/2010, (EU) No 376/2014 and Directives 2014/30/EU and 2014/53/EU of the European Parliament and of the Council, and repealing Regulations (EC) No 552/2004 and (EC) No 216/2008 of the European Parliament and of the Council and Council Regulation (EEC) No 3922/91, [2018] OJ L212/1.

72 Regulation (EU) 2019/2144 of the European Parliament and of the Council of 27 November 2019 on type-approval requirements for motor vehicles and their trailers, and systems, components and separate technical units intended for such vehicles, as regards their general safety and the protection of vehicle occupants and vulnerable road users, amending Regulation (EU) 2018/858 of the European Parliament and of the Council and repealing Regulations (EC) No 78/2009, (EC) No 79/2009 and (EC) No 661/2009 of the European Parliament and of the Council and Commission Regulations (EC) No 631/2009, (EU) No 406/2010, (EU) No 672/2010, (EU) No 1003/2010, (EU) No 1005/2010, (EU) No 1008/2010, (EU) No 1009/2010, (EU) No 19/2011, (EU) No 109/2011, (EU) No 458/2011, (EU) No 65/2012, (EU) No 130/2012, (EU) No 347/2012, (EU) No 351/2012, (EU) No 1230/2012 and (EU) 2015/166, [2019] OJ L325/1.

73 AI Act, Art. 2.

NO.	THEME	SPECIFICATION	REFERENCE
1.	Requirement	Compliance with all the requirements of a high-risk AI system	AIA, Art. 8
2.	Risk management	Throughout the entire lifecycle	AIA, Art. 9
3.	Data	Data and data governance	AIA, Art. 10
4.	Documentation	Technical documentation of the high-risk AI system	AIA, Art. 11
5.	Record-keeping	Recording of events (logs)	AIA, Art. 12
6.	Transparency	Information to be provided to deployers	AIA, Art. 13
7.	Human oversight	Decisions by natural persons must prevail, particularly as a last resort	AIA, Art. 14
8.	Resilience	Accuracy, robustness and cybersecurity	AIA, Art. 15

110 ARTICLE 110. AMENDMENT TO DIRECTIVE (EU) 2020/1828

In Annex I to Directive (EU) 2020/1828 of the European Parliament and of the Council,[74] the following point is added:

'(68) Regulation (EU) 2024/1689 of the European Parliament and of the Council of 13 June 2024 laying down harmonised rules on artificial intelligence and amending Regulations (EC) No 300/2008, (EU) No 167/2013, (EU) No 168/2013, (EU) 2018/858, (EU) 2018/1139 and (EU) 2019/2144 and Directives 2014/90/EU, (EU) 2016/797 and (EU) 2020/1828 (Artificial Intelligence Act) (OJ L, 2024/1689, 12.07.2024, ELI: http://data.europa.eu/eli/reg/2024/1689/oj).'

110.1. General Approach

110.1.1 Preamble

1767. This provision aims to align the horizontal regulation of AI technologies with vertical or sector-specific legislation.

[74] Directive (EU) 2020/1828 of the European Parliament and of the Council of 25 November 2020 on representative actions for the protection of the collective interests of consumers and repealing Directive 2009/22/EC, [2020] OJ L409/1.

110.1.2 Guiding Principles

1768. A uniform EU legislation requires that the European Commission takes into account the provisions related to high-risk AI systems when adopting delegated acts in this sector.

1769. This involves taking into account the following:

NO.	THEME	SPECIFICATION	REFERENCE
1.	Requirement	Compliance with all the requirements of a high-risk AI system	AIA, Art. 8
2.	Risk management	Throughout the entire lifecycle	AIA, Art. 9
3.	Data	Data and data governance	AIA, Art. 10
4.	Documentation	Technical documentation of the high-risk AI system	AIA, Art. 11
5.	Record-keeping	Recording of events (logs)	AIA, Art. 12
6.	Transparency	Information to be provided to deployers	AIA, Art. 13
7.	Human oversight	Decisions by natural persons must prevail, particularly as a last resort	AIA, Art. 14
8.	Resilience	Accuracy, robustness and cybersecurity	AIA, Art. 15

111 ARTICLE 111. AI SYSTEMS ALREADY PLACED ON THE MARKET OR PUT INTO SERVICE AND GENERAL-PURPOSE AI MODELS ALREADY PLACED ON THE MARKET

1. Without prejudice to the application of Article 5 as referred to in Article 113(3), point (a), AI systems which are components of the large-scale IT systems established by the legal acts listed in Annex X that have been placed on the market or put into service before 2 August 2027 shall be brought into compliance with this Regulation by 31 December 2030.

The requirements laid down in this Regulation shall be taken into account in the evaluation of each large-scale IT system established by the legal acts listed in Annex X to be undertaken as provided for in those legal acts and where those legal acts are replaced or amended.

2. Without prejudice to the application of Article 5 as referred to in Article 113(3), point (a), this Regulation shall apply to operators of high-risk AI systems, other than the systems referred to in paragraph 1 of this Article, that have been placed on the market or put into service before 2 August 2026, only if, as from that date, those systems are subject to significant changes in their designs. In any case, the providers and deployers of high-risk AI systems intended to be used by public authorities shall take the necessary steps to comply with the requirements and obligations of this Regulation by 2 August 2030.

3. Providers of general-purpose AI models that have been placed on the market before 2 August 2025 shall take the necessary steps in order to comply with the obligations laid down in this Regulation by 2 August 2027.

111.1. Recitals

1770. **(84)** To ensure legal certainty, it is necessary to clarify that, under certain specific conditions, any distributor, importer, deployer or other third-party should be considered to be a provider of a high-risk AI system and therefore assume all the relevant obligations. This would be the case if that party puts its name or trademark on a high-risk AI system already placed on the market or put into service, without prejudice to contractual arrangements stipulating that the obligations are allocated otherwise. This would also be the case if that party makes a substantial modification to a high-risk AI system that has already been placed on the market or has already been put into service in a way that it remains a high-risk AI system in accordance with this Regulation, or if it modifies the intended purpose of an AI system, including a general-purpose AI system, which has not been classified as high-risk and has already been placed on the market or put into service, in a way that the AI system becomes a high-risk AI system in accordance with this Regulation. Those provisions should apply without prejudice to more specific provisions established in certain Union harmonisation legislation based on the New Legislative Framework, together with which this Regulation should apply. For example, Article 16(2) of Regulation (EU) 2017/745, establishing that certain changes should not be considered to be modifications of a device that could affect its compliance with the applicable requirements, should continue to apply to high-risk AI systems that are medical devices within the meaning of that Regulation.

111.2. General Approach

1771. Further details can be found in the provisions related to the AI systems concerned.

112 ARTICLE 112. EVALUATION AND REVIEW

1. The Commission shall assess the need for amendment of the list set out in Annex III and of the list of prohibited AI practices laid down in Article 5, once a year following the entry into force of this Regulation, and until the end of the period of the delegation of power laid down in Article 97. The Commission shall submit the findings of that assessment to the European Parliament and the Council.

2. By 2 August 2028 and every four years thereafter, the Commission shall evaluate and report to the European Parliament and to the Council on the following:

(a) the need for amendments extending existing area headings or adding new area headings in Annex III;

(b) amendments to the list of AI systems requiring additional transparency measures in Article 50;

(c) amendments enhancing the effectiveness of the supervision and governance system.

3. By 2 August 2029 and every four years thereafter, the Commission shall submit a report on the evaluation and review of this Regulation to the European Parliament and to the Council. The report shall include an assessment with regard to the structure of enforcement and the possible need for a Union agency to resolve any identified shortcomings. On the basis of the findings, that report shall, where appropriate, be accompanied by a proposal for amendment of this Regulation. The reports shall be made public.

4. The reports referred to in paragraph 2 shall pay specific attention to the following:

(a) the status of the financial, technical and human resources of the national competent authorities in order to effectively perform the tasks assigned to them under this Regulation;

(b) the state of penalties, in particular administrative fines as referred to in Article 99(1), applied by Member States for infringements of this Regulation;

(c) adopted harmonised standards and common specifications developed to support this Regulation;

(d) the number of undertakings that enter the market after the entry into application of this Regulation, and how many of them are SMEs.

5. By 2 August 2028, the Commission shall evaluate the functioning of the AI Office, whether the AI Office has been given sufficient powers and competences to fulfil its tasks, and whether it would be relevant and needed for the proper implementation and enforcement of this Regulation to upgrade the AI Office and its enforcement competences and to increase its resources. The Commission shall submit a report on its evaluation to the European Parliament and to the Council.

6. By 2 August 2028 and every four years thereafter, the Commission shall submit a report on the review of the progress on the development of standardisation deliverables on the energy-efficient development of general-purpose AI models, and asses the need for further measures or actions, including binding measures or actions. The report shall be submitted to the European Parliament and to the Council, and it shall be made public.

7. By 2 August 2028 and every three years thereafter, the Commission shall evaluate the impact and effectiveness of voluntary codes of conduct to foster the application of the requirements set out in Chapter III, Section 2 for AI systems other than high-risk AI systems and possibly other additional requirements for AI systems other than high-risk AI systems, including as regards environmental sustainability.

8. For the purposes of paragraphs 1 to 7, the Board, the Member States and national competent authorities shall provide the Commission with information upon its request and without undue delay.

9. In carrying out the evaluations and reviews referred to in paragraphs 1 to 7, the Commission shall take into account the positions and findings of the Board, of the European Parliament, of the Council, and of other relevant bodies or sources.

10. The Commission shall, if necessary, submit appropriate proposals to amend this Regulation, in particular taking into account developments in technology, the effect of AI systems on health and safety, and on fundamental rights, and in light of the state of progress in the information society.

11. To guide the evaluations and reviews referred to in paragraphs 1 to 7 of this Article, the AI Office shall undertake to develop an objective and participative methodology for the evaluation of risk levels based on the criteria outlined in the relevant Articles and the inclusion of new systems in:

(a) the list set out in Annex III, including the extension of existing area headings or the addition of new area headings in that Annex;

(b) the list of prohibited practices set out in Article 5; and

(c) the list of AI systems requiring additional transparency measures pursuant to Article 50.

12. Any amendment to this Regulation pursuant to paragraph 10, or relevant delegated or implementing acts, which concerns sectoral Union harmonisation legislation listed in Section B of Annex I shall take into account the regulatory specificities of each sector, and the existing governance, conformity assessment and enforcement mechanisms and authorities established therein.

13. By 2 August 2031, the Commission shall carry out an assessment of the enforcement of this Regulation and shall report on it to the European Parliament, the Council and the European Economic and Social Committee, taking into account the first years of application of this Regulation. On the basis of the findings, that report shall, where appropriate, be accompanied by a proposal for amendment of this Regulation with regard to the structure of enforcement and the need for a Union agency to resolve any identified shortcomings.

112.1. General Approach

1772. Further details can be found in the provisions related to the AI systems concerned.

113 ARTICLE 113. ENTRY INTO FORCE AND APPLICATION

This Regulation shall enter into force on the twentieth day following that of its publication in the Official Journal of the European Union.[75]

It shall apply from 2 August 2026.

However:

(a) Chapters I and II shall apply from 2 February 2025;

(b) Chapter III Section 4, Chapter V, Chapter VII and Chapter XII and Article 78 shall apply from 2 August 2025, with the exception of Article 101;

(c) Article 6(1) and the corresponding obligations in this Regulation shall apply from 2 August 2027.

This Regulation shall be binding in its entirety and directly applicable in all Member States.

Done at Brussels, 13 June 2024

113.1. Recitals

1773. (177) In order to ensure legal certainty, ensure an appropriate adaptation period for operators and avoid disruption to the market, including by ensuring continuity of the use of AI systems, it is appropriate that this Regulation applies to the high-risk AI systems that have been placed on the market or put into service before the general date of application thereof, only if, from that date, those systems are subject to significant changes in their design or intended purpose. It is appropriate to clarify that, in this respect, the concept of significant change should be understood as equivalent in substance to the notion of substantial modification, which is used with regard only to high-risk AI systems pursuant to this Regulation. On an exceptional basis and in light of public accountability, operators of AI systems which are components of the large-scale IT systems established by the legal acts listed in an annex to this Regulation and operators of high-risk AI systems that are intended to be used by public authorities should,

[75] I.e. 1 August 2024.

respectively, take the necessary steps to comply with the requirements of this Regulation by end of 2030 and by 2 August 2030.

1774. **(179)** This Regulation should apply from 2 August 2026. However, taking into account the unacceptable risk associated with the use of AI in certain ways, the prohibitions as well as the general provisions of this Regulation should already apply from 2 February 2025. While the full effect of those prohibitions follows with the establishment of the governance and enforcement of this Regulation, anticipating the application of the prohibitions is important to take account of unacceptable risks and to have an effect on other procedures, such as in civil law. Moreover, the infrastructure related to the governance and the conformity assessment system should be operational before 2 August 2026, therefore the provisions on notified bodies and governance structure should apply from 2 August 2025. Given the rapid pace of technological advancements and adoption of general-purpose AI models, obligations for providers of general-purpose AI models should apply from 2 August 2025. Codes of practice should be ready by 2 May 2025 in view of enabling providers to demonstrate compliance on time. The AI Office should ensure that classification rules and procedures are up to date in light of technological developments. In addition, Member States should lay down and notify to the Commission the rules on penalties, including administrative fines, and ensure that they are properly and effectively implemented by the date of application of this Regulation. Therefore the provisions on penalties should apply from 2 August 2025.

113.2. General Approach

113.2.1 Introduction

1775. The Regulation entered into force on 1st August 2024. It applies from 2 August 2026. However, some of its provisions will apply before this date, mainly to:

- protect EU values and minimising risks;
- establish governance at the EU level;
- quickly regulate general-purpose AI models.

113.2.2 Special Cases

1776. The Regulation will apply to high-risk AI systems corresponding to elements or components listed in Annex I from 2 August 2027. They therefore benefit from a one-year grace period.

113.3. Summary Table of Dates

1777. It is as follows:

NO.	THEME	SPECIFICATION	DATE	COMMENT
1.	AI literacy	Art. 4	02.02.2025	AIA, Art. 113(a)
2.	Confidentiality	Art. 78	02.02.2025	AIA, Art. 113(b)
3.	Defence activities	Exclusion	-	AIA, Art. 2
4.	Entry into force of AIA		01.08.2024	AIA, Art. 113
5.	General application of AIA		02.08.2026	AIA, Art. 113
6.	General provisions		02.02.2025	AIA, Art. 113(a) AIA, Chap. I, Arts. 1 to 4
7.	General-purpose AI model		02.08.2025	AIA, Art. 113(b) AIA, Chap. V, Arts. 64 to 70
8.	Governance		02.08.2025	AIA, Art. 113(b) AIA, Chap. VII, Arts. 64 to 70
9.	High-risk AI systems (Annex I)		02.08.2027	AIA, Art. 113(c) AIA, Art. 6(1)
10.	High-risk AI systems (Annex III)		02.08.2026	AIA, Art. 6(2)
11.	High-risk AI systems of public authorities	Placing on the market or putting into service of high-risk AI systems before 02.08.2026	02.08.2030	AIA, Art. 111(2)
12.	Military activities	Exclusion	-	AIA, Art. 2
13.	National competent authorities		02.08.2025	AIA, Art. 113(b)
14.	National security activities	Exclusion	-	AIA, Art. 2
15.	Notified body	See Notifying authorities		
16.	Notifying authorities and notified bodies		02.08.2025	AIA, Art. 113(b) AIA, Chap. III, sec. 4, Arts. 28 to 39

NO.	THEME	SPECIFICATION	DATE	COMMENT
17.	Penalties	General application	02.08.2025	AIA, Art. 113(b) AIA, Chap. XII, Arts. 99 to 101
18.	Penalties for providers of general-purpose AI models		02.08.2026	AIA, Art. 113(b) AIA, Art. 101
19.	Prohibited AI systems	See Prohibited practices		
20.	Prohibited practices	Prohibited AI systems (Art. 5)	02.02.2025	Art. 113(a)
21.	Public authorities referred to in Annex X	Placing on the market or putting into service of high-risk AI systems before 02.08.2027	31.12.2030	AIA, Art. 111(1)
22.	Transparent AI systems		02.08.2026	AIA, Art. 113 AIA, Art. 50

114 THE AI PACT

1778. The European Commission (AI Board) is promoting the AI Pact, to help stakeholders prepare for the implementation of the Regulation. The AI Pact is structured around two pillars:

- Pillar 1: creating a group of organisations that have expressed interest in the AI Pact;
- Pillar 2: encouraging providers and deployers to take proactive measures to comply with the AI Act requirements.[76]

115 CONCLUSION

115.1. Introduction

1779. This EU Regulation is a first step in ushering in the third digital revolution.

1780. A revolution that gives unprecedented access to most human knowledge, past and present, to all internet-connected individuals.

[76] The European AI Strategy is reflected in a European approach based on excellence and trust, embodied in the AI Pact (Communication on Fostering of a European Approach to Artificial Intelligence, April 2024).

115.2. A New Species

1781. Such access to 'world knowledge' signals the emergence of a new human being; this vast ocean of knowledge will exponentially enhance human intelligence's potential, beyond the augmented human.

1782. The assimilation of artificial intelligence will herald a new era.

1783. Far from reducing humans to technological enslavement, this collaboration should pave the way for a humanistic and universal world.

115.3. A Transition Phase

1784. Knowledge for all, in real-time and free of charge, should naturally spread through the principles enshrined in the AI Act, where human primacy and ethical innovation are key.

115.4. A Processor of Universality

1785. Similar to the GDPR, the AI Act establishes the European Union as an ideological pioneer, mandating the development of human-centric AI technologies, where otherness, dignity, and freedom are the key success factors in balancing technological slavery and technological eugenics.

115.5. A New Legal Personality

1786. Ultimately, this path will require recognising legal personality[77] to physical and virtual robots, and to account for the autonomy of AI systems mastered[78] and controlled by humans.[79] A hope.[80]

---

77 A. Bensoussan and J. Bensoussan, *IA robots et droit* ['AI robots and the law'], coll. Théorie et pratique, Bruxelles, Bruylant, 2019, pp. 41 ff.

78 AI Act, Art. 4.

79 AI Act, Art. 14.

80 This is in line with need to align AI with fundamental rights, supplemented by new rights such as:

- the right to human and AI knowledge;
- propriety rights over knowledge;
- the right to privacy and respect for digital avatars;
- the obligation for humanity to fulfil the UN 16 Sustainable Development Goals 16.

ANNEXES TO THE REGULATION

ANNEX I – LIST OF UNION HARMONISATION LEGISLATION

SECTION A. LIST OF UNION HARMONISATION LEGISLATION BASED ON THE NEW LEGISLATIVE FRAMEWORK

1. Directive 2006/42/EC of the European Parliament and of the Council of 17 May 2006 on machinery, and amending Directive 95/16/EC, [2006] OJ L157/24;[1]
2. Directive 2009/48/EC of the European Parliament and of the Council of 18 June 2009 on the safety of toys, [2009] OJ L170/1;
3. Directive 2013/53/EU of the European Parliament and of the Council of 20 November 2013 on recreational craft and personal watercraft and repealing Directive 94/25/EC, [2013] OJ L354/90;
4. Directive 2014/33/EU of the European Parliament and of the Council of 26 February 2014 on the harmonisation of the laws of the Member States relating to lifts and safety components for lifts, [2014] OJ L96/251;
5. Directive 2014/34/EU of the European Parliament and of the Council of 26 February 2014 on the harmonisation of the laws of the Member States relating to equipment and protective systems intended for use in potentially explosive atmospheres, [2014] OJ L96/309;
6. Directive 2014/53/EU of the European Parliament and of the Council of 16 April 2014 on the harmonisation of the laws of the Member States relating to the making available on the market of radio equipment and repealing Directive 1999/5/EC, [2014] OJ L153/62;
7. Directive 2014/68/EU of the European Parliament and of the Council of 15 May 2014 on the harmonisation of the laws of the Member States relating to the making available on the market of pressure equipment, [2014] OJ L189/164;
8. (EU) 2016/424 of the European Parliament and of the Council of 9 March 2016 on cableway installations and repealing Directive 2000/9/EC, [2016] OJ L81/1;
9. Regulation (EU) 2016/425 of the European Parliament and of the Council of 9 March 2016 on personal protective equipment and repealing Council Directive 89/686/EEC, [2016] OJ L81/51;
10. Regulation (EU) 2016/426 of the European Parliament and of the Council of 9 March 2016 on appliances burning gaseous fuels and repealing Directive 2009/142/EC, [2016] OJ L81/99;

---

1 This directive, which is still in force, will gradually be replaced by Regulation (EU) 2023/1230 of the European Parliament and of the Council of 14 June 2023 on machinery and repealing Directive 2006/42/EC of the European Parliament and of the Council and Council Directive 73/361/EEC ([2023] OJ L165/1), which will apply from 14 January 2027.

11. Regulation (EU) 2017/745 of the European Parliament and of the Council of 5 April 2017 on medical devices, amending Directive 2001/83/EC, Regulation (EC) No 178/2002 and Regulation (EC) No 1223/2009 and repealing Council Directives 90/385/EEC and 93/42/EEC, [2017] OJ L117/1;
12. Regulation (EU) 2017/746 of the European Parliament and of the Council of 5 April 2017 on in vitro diagnostic medical devices and repealing Directive 98/79/EC and Commission Decision 2010/227/EU, [2017] OJ L117/176.

SECTION B. LIST OF OTHER UNION HARMONISATION LEGISLATION

13. Regulation (EC) No 300/2008 of the European Parliament and of the Council of 11 March 2008 on common rules in the field of civil aviation security and repealing Regulation (EC) No 2320/2002, [2008] OJ L97/72;
14. Regulation (EU) No 168/2013 of the European Parliament and of the Council of 15 January 2013 on the approval and market surveillance of two- or three-wheel vehicles and quadricycles, [2013] OJ L60/52;
15. Regulation (EU) No 167/2013 of the European Parliament and of the Council of 5 February 2013 on the approval and market surveillance of agricultural and forestry vehicles, [2013] OJ L60/1;
16. Directive 2014/90/EU of the European Parliament and of the Council of 23 July 2014 on marine equipment and repealing Council Directive 96/98/EC, [2014] OJ L257/146;
17. Directive (EU) 2016/797 of the European Parliament and of the Council of 11 May 2016 on the interoperability of the rail system within the European Union, [2016] OJ L138/44;
18. Regulation (EU) 2018/858 of the European Parliament and of the Council of 30 May 2018 on the approval and market surveillance of motor vehicles and their trailers, and of systems, components and separate technical units intended for such vehicles, amending Regulations (EC) No 715/2007 and (EC) No 595/2009 and repealing Directive 2007/46/EC, [2018] OJ L151/1;
19. Regulation (EU) 2019/2144 of the European Parliament and of the Council of 27 November 2019 on type-approval requirements for motor vehicles and their trailers, and systems, components and separate technical units intended for such vehicles, as regards their general safety and the protection of vehicle occupants and vulnerable road users, amending Regulation (EU) 2018/858 of the European Parliament and of the Council and repealing Regulations (EC) No 78/2009, (EC) No 79/2009 and (EC) No 661/2009 of the European Parliament and of the Council and Commission Regulations (EC) No 631/2009, (EU) No 406/2010, (EU) No 672/2010, (EU) No 1003/2010, (EU) No 1005/2010, (EU) No 1008/2010, (EU) No 1009/2010, (EU) No 19/2011, (EU) No 109/2011, (EU) No 458/2011, (EU) No 65/2012, (EU)

No 130/2012, (EU) No 347/2012, (EU) No 351/2012, (EU) No 1230/2012 and (EU) 2015/166, [2019] OJ L325/1;

20. Regulation (EU) 2018/1139 of the European Parliament and of the Council of 4 July 2018 on common rules in the field of civil aviation and establishing a European Union Aviation Safety Agency, and amending Regulations (EC) No 2111/2005, (EC) No 1008/2008, (EU) No 996/2010, (EU) No 376/2014 and Directives 2014/30/EU and 2014/53/EU of the European Parliament and of the Council, and repealing Regulations (EC) No 552/2004 and (EC) No 216/2008 of the European Parliament and of the Council and Council Regulation (EEC) No 3922/91, [2018] OJ L212/1, in so far as the design, production and placing on the market of aircrafts referred to in Article 2(1), points (a) and (b) thereof, where it concerns unmanned aircraft and their engines, propellers, parts and equipment to control them remotely, are concerned.

Notes:

- (1) The legislation listed in Section A complies with the New Legislative Framework.
- (2) The legislation listed in Section B will only need to be brought into compliance after the said legislation is updated.[2]

[2] AI Act, Art. 6(1)(a) and (b).

ANNEX II – LIST OF CRIMINAL OFFENCES REFERRED TO IN ARTICLE 5(1), FIRST SUBPARAGRAPH, POINT (H)(III)

Criminal offences referred to in Article 5(1), first subparagraph, point (h)(iii):

- terrorism,
- trafficking in human beings,
- sexual exploitation of children, and child pornography,
- illicit trafficking in narcotic drugs or psychotropic substances,
- illicit trafficking in weapons, munitions or explosives,
- murder, grievous bodily injury,
- illicit trade in human organs or tissue,
- illicit trafficking in nuclear or radioactive materials,
- kidnapping, illegal restraint or hostage-taking,
- crimes within the jurisdiction of the International Criminal Court,
- unlawful seizure of aircraft or ships,
- rape,
- environmental crime,
- organised or armed robbery,
- sabotage,
- participation in a criminal organisation involved in one or more of the offences listed above.

ANNEX III – HIGH-RISK AI SYSTEMS REFERRED TO IN ARTICLE 6(2)

High-risk AI systems pursuant to Article 6(2) are the AI systems listed in any of the following areas:

1. **Biometrics**, in so far as their use is permitted under relevant Union or national law:
   (a) remote biometric identification systems
   This shall not include AI systems intended to be used for biometric verification the sole purpose of which is to confirm that a specific natural person is the person he or she claims to be;
   (b) AI systems intended to be used for biometric categorisation, according to sensitive or protected attributes or characteristics based on the inference of those attributes or characteristics;
   (c) AI systems intended to be used for emotion recognition.
2. **Critical infrastructure**: AI systems intended to be used as safety components in the management and operation of critical digital infrastructure, road traffic, or in the supply of water, gas, heating or electricity.
3. **Education and vocational training**:
   (a) AI systems intended to be used to determine access or admission or to assign natural persons to educational and vocational training institutions at all levels;
   (b) AI systems intended to be used to evaluate learning outcomes, including when those outcomes are used to steer the learning process of natural persons in educational and vocational training institutions at all levels;
   (c) AI systems intended to be used for the purpose of assessing the appropriate level of education that an individual will receive or will be able to access, in the context of or within educational and vocational training institutions at all levels;
   (d) AI systems intended to be used for monitoring and detecting prohibited behaviour of students during tests in the context of or within educational and vocational training institutions at all levels.
4. **Employment, workers' management and access to self-employment**:
   (a) AI systems intended to be used for the recruitment or selection of natural persons, in particular to place targeted job advertisements, to analyse and filter job applications, and to evaluate candidates;
   (b) AI systems intended to be used to make decisions affecting terms of work-related relationships, the promotion or termination of work-related contractual relationships, to allocate tasks based on individual behaviour or personal traits or characteristics or to monitor and evaluate the performance and behaviour of persons in such relationships.

5. **Access to and enjoyment of essential private services and essential public services and benefits**:
   (a) AI systems intended to be used by public authorities or on behalf of public authorities to evaluate the eligibility of natural persons for essential public assistance benefits and services, including healthcare services, as well as to grant, reduce, revoke, or reclaim such benefits and services;
   (b) AI systems intended to be used to evaluate the creditworthiness of natural persons or establish their credit score, with the exception of AI systems used for the purpose of detecting financial fraud;
   (c) AI systems intended to be used for risk assessment and pricing in relation to natural persons in the case of life and health insurance;
   (d) AI systems intended to evaluate and classify emergency calls by natural persons or to be used to dispatch, or to establish priority in the dispatching of, emergency first response services, including by police, firefighters and medical aid, as well as of emergency healthcare patient triage systems.
6. **Law enforcement**, in so far as their use is permitted under relevant Union or national law:
   (a) AI systems intended to be used by or on behalf of law enforcement authorities, or by Union institutions, bodies, offices or agencies in support of law enforcement authorities or on their behalf to assess the risk of a natural person becoming the victim of criminal offences;
   (b) AI systems intended to be used by or on behalf of law enforcement authorities or by Union institutions, bodies, offices or agencies in support of law enforcement authorities as polygraphs or similar tools;
   (c) AI systems intended to be used by or on behalf of law enforcement authorities, or by Union institutions, bodies, offices or agencies, in support of law enforcement authorities to evaluate the reliability of evidence in the course of the investigation or prosecution of criminal offences;
   (d) AI systems intended to be used by law enforcement authorities or on their behalf or by Union institutions, bodies, offices or agencies in support of law enforcement authorities for assessing the risk of a natural person offending or re-offending not solely on the basis of the profiling of natural persons as referred to in Article 3(4) of Directive (EU) 2016/680, or to assess personality traits and characteristics or past criminal behaviour of natural persons or groups;
   (e) AI systems intended to be used by or on behalf of law enforcement authorities or by Union institutions, bodies, offices or agencies in support of law enforcement authorities for the profiling of natural persons as referred to in Article 3(4) of Directive (EU) 2016/680 in the course of the detection, investigation or prosecution of criminal offences.

7. **Migration, asylum and border control management**, in so far as their use is permitted under relevant Union or national law:
   (a) AI systems intended to be used by or on behalf of competent public authorities or by Union institutions, bodies, offices or agencies as polygraphs or similar tools;
   (b) AI systems intended to be used by or on behalf of competent public authorities or by Union institutions, bodies, offices or agencies to assess a risk, including a security risk, a risk of irregular migration, or a health risk, posed by a natural person who intends to enter or who has entered into the territory of a Member State;
   (c) AI systems intended to be used by or on behalf of competent public authorities or by Union institutions, bodies, offices or agencies to assist competent public authorities for the examination of applications for asylum, visa or residence permits and for associated complaints with regard to the eligibility of the natural persons applying for a status, including related assessments of the reliability of evidence;
   (d) AI systems intended to be used by or on behalf of competent public authorities, or by Union institutions, bodies, offices or agencies, in the context of migration, asylum or border control management, for the purpose of detecting, recognising or identifying natural persons, with the exception of the verification of travel documents.
8. **Administration of justice and democratic processes**:
   (a) AI systems intended to be used by a judicial authority or on their behalf to assist a judicial authority in researching and interpreting facts and the law and in applying the law to a concrete set of facts, or to be used in a similar way in alternative dispute resolution;
   (b) AI systems intended to be used for influencing the outcome of an election or referendum or the voting behaviour of natural persons in the exercise of their vote in elections or referenda. This does not include AI systems to the output of which natural persons are not directly exposed, such as tools used to organise, optimise or structure political campaigns from an administrative or logistical point of view.

ANNEX IV – TECHNICAL DOCUMENTATION REFERRED TO IN ARTICLE 11(1)

The technical documentation referred to in Article 11(1) shall contain at least the following information, as applicable to the relevant AI system:

1. A general description of the AI system including:
   (a) its intended purpose, the name of the provider and the version of the system reflecting its relation to previous versions;
   (b) how the AI system interacts with, or can be used to interact with, hardware or software, including with other AI systems, that are not part of the AI system itself, where applicable;
   (c) the versions of relevant software or firmware, and any requirements related to version updates;
   (d) the description of all the forms in which the AI system is placed on the market or put into service, such as software packages embedded into hardware, downloads, or APIs;
   (e) the description of the hardware on which the AI system is intended to run;
   (f) where the AI system is a component of products, photographs or illustrations showing external features, the marking and internal layout of those products;
   (g) a basic description of the user-interface provided to the deployer;
   (h) instructions for use for the deployer, and a basic description of the user-interface provided to the deployer, where applicable;
2. A detailed description of the elements of the AI system and of the process for its development, including:
   (a) the methods and steps performed for the development of the AI system, including, where relevant, recourse to pre-trained systems or tools provided by third parties and how those were used, integrated or modified by the provider;
   (b) the design specifications of the system, namely the general logic of the AI system and of the algorithms; the key design choices including the rationale and assumptions made, including with regard to persons or groups of persons in respect of who, the system is intended to be used; the main classification choices; what the system is designed to optimise for, and the relevance of the different parameters; the description of the expected output and output quality of the system; the decisions about any possible trade-off made regarding the technical solutions adopted to comply with the requirements set out in Chapter III, Section 2;
   (c) the description of the system architecture explaining how software components build on or feed into each other and integrate into the overall

processing; the computational resources used to develop, train, test and validate the AI system;

(d) where relevant, the data requirements in terms of datasheets describing the training methodologies and techniques and the training data sets used, including a general description of these data sets, information about their provenance, scope and main characteristics; how the data was obtained and selected; labelling procedures (e.g. for supervised learning), data cleaning methodologies (e.g. outliers detection);

(e) assessment of the human oversight measures needed in accordance with Article 14, including an assessment of the technical measures needed to facilitate the interpretation of the outputs of AI systems by the deployers, in accordance with Article 13(3), point (d);

(f) where applicable, a detailed description of pre-determined changes to the AI system and its performance, together with all the relevant information related to the technical solutions adopted to ensure continuous compliance of the AI system with the relevant requirements set out in Chapter III, Section 2;

(g) the validation and testing procedures used, including information about the validation and testing data used and their main characteristics; metrics used to measure accuracy, robustness and compliance with other relevant requirements set out in Chapter III, Section 2, as well as potentially discriminatory impacts; test logs and all test reports dated and signed by the responsible persons, including with regard to pre-determined changes as referred to under point (f);

(h) cybersecurity measures put in place;

3. Detailed information about the monitoring, functioning and control of the AI system, in particular with regard to: its capabilities and limitations in performance, including the degrees of accuracy for specific persons or groups of persons on which the system is intended to be used and the overall expected level of accuracy in relation to its intended purpose; the foreseeable unintended outcomes and sources of risks to health and safety, fundamental rights and discrimination in view of the intended purpose of the AI system; the human oversight measures needed in accordance with Article 14, including the technical measures put in place to facilitate the interpretation of the outputs of AI systems by the deployers; specifications on input data, as appropriate;
4. A description of the appropriateness of the performance metrics for the specific AI system;
5. A detailed description of the risk management system in accordance with Article 9;
6. A description of relevant changes made by the provider to the system through its lifecycle;

7. A list of the harmonised standards applied in full or in part the references of which have been published in the *Official Journal of the European Union*; where no such harmonised standards have been applied, a detailed description of the solutions adopted to meet the requirements set out in Chapter III, Section 2, including a list of other relevant standards and technical specifications applied
8. A copy of the EU declaration of conformity referred to in Article 47;
9. A detailed description of the system in place to evaluate the AI system performance in the post-market phase in accordance with Article 72, including the post-market monitoring plan referred to in Article 72(3).

ANNEX V – EU DECLARATION OF CONFORMITY

The EU declaration of conformity referred to in Article 47, shall contain all of the following information:

1. AI system name and type and any additional unambiguous reference allowing the identification and traceability of the AI system;
2. The name and address of the provider or, where applicable, of their authorised representative;
3. A statement that the EU declaration of conformity referred to in Article 47 is issued under the sole responsibility of the provider;
4. A statement that the AI system is in conformity with this Regulation and, if applicable, with any other relevant Union law that provides for the issuing of the EU declaration of conformity referred to in Article 47;
5. Where an AI system involves the processing of personal data, a statement that that AI system complies with Regulations (EU) 2016/679 and (EU) 2018/1725 and Directive (EU) 2016/680;
6. References to any relevant harmonised standards used or any other common specification in relation to which conformity is declared;
7. Where applicable, the name and identification number of the notified body, a description of the conformity assessment procedure performed, and identification of the certificate issued;
8. The place and date of issue of the declaration, the name and function of the person who signed it, as well as an indication for, or on behalf of whom, that person signed, a signature.

ANNEX VI – CONFORMITY ASSESSMENT PROCEDURE BASED ON INTERNAL CONTROL

1. The conformity assessment procedure based on internal control is the conformity assessment procedure based on points 2, 3 and 44.
2. The provider verifies that the established quality management system is in compliance with the requirements of Article 17.
3. The provider examines the information contained in the technical documentation in order to assess the compliance of the AI system with the relevant essential requirements set out in Chapter III, Section 2.
4. The provider also verifies that the design and development process of the AI system and its post-market monitoring as referred to in Article 72 is consistent with the technical documentation.

ANNEX VII – CONFORMITY BASED ON AN ASSESSMENT OF THE QUALITY MANAGEMENT SYSTEM AND AN ASSESSMENT OF THE TECHNICAL DOCUMENTATION

1. INTRODUCTION

Conformity based on an assessment of the quality management system and an assessment of the technical documentation is the conformity assessment procedure based on points 2 to 5.

2. OVERVIEW

The approved quality management system for the design, development and testing of AI systems pursuant to Article 17 shall be examined in accordance with point 3 and shall be subject to surveillance as specified in point 5. The technical documentation of the AI system shall be examined in accordance with point 4.

3. QUALITY MANAGEMENT SYSTEM

3.1. The application of the provider shall include:

(a) the name and address of the provider and, if the application is lodged by an authorised representative, also their name and address;

(b) the list of AI systems covered under the same quality management system;

(c) the technical documentation for each AI system covered under the same quality management system;

(d) the documentation concerning the quality management system which shall cover all the aspects listed under Article 17;

(e) a description of the procedures in place to ensure that the quality management system remains adequate and effective;

(f) a written declaration that the same application has not been lodged with any other notified body.

3.2. The quality management system shall be assessed by the notified body, which shall determine whether it satisfies the requirements referred to in Article 17.

The decision shall be notified to the provider or its authorised representative.

The notification shall contain the conclusions of the assessment of the quality management system and the reasoned assessment decision.

3.3. The quality management system shall be assessed by the notified body, which shall determine whether it satisfies the requirements referred to in Article 17.

3.4. Any intended change to the approved quality management system or the list of AI systems covered by the latter shall be brought to the attention of the notified body by the provider.

The proposed changes shall be examined by the notified body, which shall decide whether the modified quality management system continues to satisfy the requirements referred to in point 3.2 or whether a reassessment is necessary.

The notified body shall notify the provider of its decision. The notification shall contain the conclusions of the examination of the changes and the reasoned assessment decision.

4. CONTROL OF THE TECHNICAL DOCUMENTATION

4.1. In addition to the application referred to in point 3, an application with a notified body of their choice shall be lodged by the provider for the assessment of the technical documentation relating to the AI system which the provider intends to place on the market or put into service and which is covered by the quality management system referred to under point 3.

4.2. The application shall include:

(g) the name and address of the provider;

(h) a written declaration that the same application has not been lodged with any other notified body;

(i) the technical documentation referred to in Annex IV.

4.3. The technical documentation shall be examined by the notified body. Where relevant, and limited to what is necessary to fulfil its tasks, the notified body shall be granted full access to the training, validation, and testing data sets used, including, where appropriate and subject to security safeguards, through API or other relevant technical means and tools enabling remote access.

4.4. In examining the technical documentation, the notified body may require that the provider supply further evidence or carry out further tests so as to enable a proper assessment of the conformity of the AI system with the requirements set out in Chapter III, Section 2. Where the notified body is not satisfied with the tests carried out by the provider, the notified body shall itself directly carry out adequate tests, as appropriate.

4.5. Where necessary to assess the conformity of the high-risk AI system with the requirements set out in Chapter III, Section 2, after all other reasonable means to verify conformity have been exhausted and have proven to be insufficient, and upon a reasoned request, the notified body shall also be granted access to the training and trained models of the AI system, including its relevant parameters. Such access shall be subject to existing Union law on the protection of intellectual property and trade secrets.

4.6. The decision of the notified body shall be notified to the provider or its authorised representative. The notification shall contain the conclusions of the assessment of the technical documentation and the reasoned assessment decision.

Where the AI system is in conformity with the requirements set out in Chapter III, Section 2, the notified body shall issue a Union technical documentation assessment certificate. The certificate shall indicate the name and address of the provider, the conclusions of the examination, the conditions (if any) for its validity and the data necessary for the identification of the AI system.

The certificate and its annexes shall contain all relevant information to allow the conformity of the AI system to be evaluated, and to allow for control of the AI system while in use, where applicable.

Where the AI system is not in conformity with the requirements set out in Chapter III, Section 2, the notified body shall refuse to issue a Union technical documentation assessment certificate and shall inform the applicant accordingly, giving detailed reasons for its refusal.

Where the AI system does not meet the requirement relating to the data used to train it, re-training of the AI system will be needed prior to the application for a new conformity assessment. In this case, the reasoned assessment decision of the notified body refusing to issue the Union technical documentation assessment certificate shall contain specific considerations on the quality data used to train the AI system, in particular on the reasons for non-compliance.

4.7. Any change to the AI system that could affect the compliance of the AI system with the requirements or its intended purpose shall be assessed by the notified body which issued the Union technical documentation assessment certificate. The provider shall inform such notified body of its intention to introduce any of the abovementioned changes, or if it otherwise becomes aware of the occurrence of such changes. The intended changes shall be assessed by the notified body, which shall decide whether those changes require a new conformity assessment in accordance with Article 43(4) or whether they could be addressed by means of a supplement to the Union technical documentation assessment certificate. In the latter case, the notified body shall assess the changes, notify the provider of its decision and, where the changes are approved, issue to the provider a supplement to the Union technical documentation assessment certificate.

5. SURVEILLANCE OF THE APPROVED QUALITY MANAGEMENT SYSTEM

5.1. The purpose of the surveillance carried out by the notified body referred to in Point 3 is to make sure that the provider duly complies with the terms and conditions of the approved quality management system.

5.2. For assessment purposes, the provider shall allow the notified body to access the premises where the design, development, testing of the AI systems is taking place. The provider shall further share with the notified body all necessary information.

5.3. The notified body shall carry out periodic audits to make sure that the provider maintains and applies the quality management system and shall provide the provider with an audit report. In the context of those audits, the notified body may carry out additional tests of the AI systems for which a Union technical documentation assessment certificate was issued.

ANNEX VIII – INFORMATION TO BE SUBMITTED UPON THE REGISTRATION OF HIGH-RISK AI SYSTEMS IN ACCORDANCE WITH ARTICLE 49

SECTION A – INFORMATION TO BE SUBMITTED BY PROVIDERS OF HIGH-RISK AI SYSTEMS IN ACCORDANCE WITH ARTICLE 49(1)

The following information shall be provided and thereafter kept up to date with regard to high-risk AI systems to be registered in accordance with Article 49(1):

1. The name, address and contact details of the provider;
2. Where submission of information is carried out by another person on behalf of the provider, the name, address and contact details of that person;
3. The name, address and contact details of the authorised representative, where applicable;
4. The AI system trade name and any additional unambiguous reference allowing the identification and traceability of the AI system;
5. A description of the intended purpose of the AI system and of the components and functions supported through this AI system;
6. A basic and concise description of the information used by the system (data, inputs) and its operating logic;
7. The status of the AI system (on the market, or in service; no longer placed on the market/in service, recalled);
8. The type, number and expiry date of the certificate issued by the notified body and the name or identification number of that notified body, where applicable;
9. A scanned copy of the certificate referred to in point 8, where applicable;
10. Any Member States in which the AI system has been placed on the market, put into service or made available in the Union;
11. A copy of the EU declaration of conformity referred to in Article 47;
12. Electronic instructions for use; this information shall not be provided for high-risk AI systems in the areas of law enforcement or migration, asylum and border control management referred to in Annex III, points 1, 6 and 7;
13. A URL for additional information (optional)

SECTION B – INFORMATION TO BE SUBMITTED BY PROVIDERS OF HIGH-RISK AI SYSTEMS IN ACCORDANCE WITH ARTICLE 49(2)

The following information shall be provided and thereafter kept up to date with regard to AI systems to be registered in accordance with Article 49(2):

1. The name, address and contact details of the provider;

2. Where submission of information is carried out by another person on behalf of the provider, the name, address and contact details of that person;
3. The name, address and contact details of the authorised representative, where applicable;
4. The AI system trade name and any additional unambiguous reference allowing the identification and traceability of the AI system;
5. A description of the intended purpose of the AI system;
6. The condition or conditions under Article 6(3) based on which the AI system is considered to be not-high-risk;
7. A short summary of the grounds on which the AI system is considered to be not-high-risk in application of the procedure under Article 6(3);
8. The status of the AI system (on the market, or in service; no longer placed on the market/in service, recalled);
9. Any Member States in which the AI system has been placed on the market, put into service or made available in the Union.

SECTION C – INFORMATION TO BE SUBMITTED BY DEPLOYERS OF HIGH-RISK AI SYSTEMS IN ACCORDANCE WITH ARTICLE 49(3)

The following information shall be provided and thereafter kept up to date with regard to high-risk AI systems to be registered in accordance with Article 49(3):

1. The name, address and contact details of the deployer;
2. The name, address and contact details of the person submitting information on behalf of the deployer;
3. The URL of the entry of the AI system in the EU database by its provider;
4. A summary of the findings of the fundamental rights impact assessment conducted in accordance with Article 27;
5. A summary of the data protection impact assessment carried out in accordance with Article 35 of Regulation (EU) 2016/679 or Article 27 of Directive (EU) 2016/680 as specified in Article 26(8) of this Regulation, where applicable.

ANNEX IX – INFORMATION TO BE SUBMITTED UPON THE REGISTRATION OF HIGH-RISK AI SYSTEMS LISTED IN ANNEX III IN RELATION TO TESTING IN REAL WORLD CONDITIONS IN ACCORDANCE WITH ARTICLE 60

The following information shall be provided and thereafter kept up to date with regard to testing in real world conditions to be registered in accordance with Article 60:

1. A Union-wide unique single identification number of the testing in real world conditions;
2. The name and contact details of the provider or prospective provider and of the deployers involved in the testing in real world conditions;
3. A brief description of the AI system, its intended purpose, and other information necessary for the identification of the system;
4. A summary of the main characteristics of the plan for testing in real world conditions;
5. Information on the suspension or termination of the testing in real world conditions.

ANNEX X – UNION LEGISLATIVE ACTS ON LARGE-SCALE IT SYSTEMS IN THE AREA OF FREEDOM, SECURITY AND JUSTICE

1. SCHENGEN INFORMATION SYSTEM

(a) Regulation (EU) 2018/1860 of the European Parliament and of the Council of 2 November 2018 on the use of the Schengen Information System for the return of illegally staying third-country nationals, [2018] OJ L312/1.

(b) Regulation (EU) 2018/1861 of the European Parliament and of the Council of 28 November 2018 on the establishment, operation and use of the Schengen Information System (SIS) in the field of border checks, and amending the Convention implementing the Schengen Agreement, and amending and repealing Regulation (EC) No 1987/2006, [2018] OJ L312/14.

(c) Regulation (EU) 2018/1862 of the European Parliament and of the Council of 28 November 2018 on the establishment, operation and use of the Schengen Information System (SIS) in the field of police cooperation and judicial cooperation in criminal matters, amending and repealing Council Decision 2007/533/JHA, and repealing Regulation (EC) No 1986/2006 of the European Parliament and of the Council and Commission Decision 2010/261/EU, [2018] OJ L312/56.

2. VISA INFORMATION SYSTEM

(a) Regulation (EU) 2021/1133 of the European Parliament and of the Council of 7 July 2021 amending Regulations (EU) No 603/2013, (EU) 2016/794, (EU) 2018/1862, (EU) 2019/816 and (EU) 2019/818 as regards the establishment of the conditions for accessing other EU information systems for the purposes of the Visa Information System, [2021] OJ L248/1.

(b) Regulation (EU) 2021/1134 of the European Parliament and of the Council of 7 July 2021 amending Regulations (EC) No 767/2008, (EC) No 810/2009, (EU) 2016/399, (EU) 2017/2226, (EU) 2018/1240, (EU) 2018/1860, (EU) 2018/1861, (EU) 2019/817 and (EU) 2019/1896 of the European Parliament and of the Council and repealing Council Decisions 2004/512/EC and 2008/633/JHA, for the purpose of reforming the Visa Information System, [2021] OJ L248/11.

3. EURODAC

Regulation (EU) 2024/1358 of the European Parliament and of the Council of 14 May 2024 on the establishment of 'Eurodac' for the comparison of biometric data in order to effectively apply Regulations (EU) 2024/1315 and (EU) 2024/1350 of the European Parliament and of the Council and Council Directive 2001/55/EC and to identify illegally staying third-country nationals and stateless persons and on requests for the comparison with Eurodac data by Member States' law enforcement authorities and Europol for law enforcement purposes, amending Regulations (EU) 2018/1240 and (EU) 2019/818 of the European Parliament and of the Council and repealing Regulation (EU) No 603/2013 of the European Parliament and of the Council, [2024] OJ L, 2024/1358, ELI: http://data.europa.eu/eli/reg/2024/1358/oj).

4. ENTRY/EXIT SYSTEM

Regulation (EU) 2017/2226 of the European Parliament and of the Council of 30 November 2017 establishing an Entry/Exit System (EES) to register entry and exit data and refusal of entry data of third-country nationals crossing the external borders of the Member States and determining the conditions for access to the EES for law enforcement purposes, and amending the Convention implementing the Schengen Agreement and Regulations (EC) No 767/2008 and (EU) No 1077/2011, [2017] OJ L327/20.

5. EUROPEAN TRAVEL INFORMATION AND AUTHORISATION SYSTEM

(a) Regulation (EU) 2018/1240 of the European Parliament and of the Council of 12 September 2018 establishing a European Travel Information and Authorisation System (ETIAS) and amending Regulations (EU) No 1077/2011, (EU) No 515/2014, (EU) 2016/399, (EU) 2016/1624 and (EU) 2017/2226, [2018] OJ L236/1.

(b) Regulation (EU) 2018/1241 of the European Parliament and of the Council of 12 September 2018 amending Regulation (EU) 2016/794 for the purpose of establishing a European Travel Information and Authorisation System (ETIAS), [2018] OJ L236/72.

6. EUROPEAN CRIMINAL RECORDS INFORMATION SYSTEM ON THIRD-COUNTRY NATIONALS AND STATELESS PERSONS

Regulation (EU) 2019/816 of the European Parliament and of the Council of 17April 2019 establishing a centralised system for the identification of

Member States holding conviction information on third-country nationals and stateless persons (ECRIS-TCN) to supplement the European Criminal Records Information System and amending Regulation (EU) 2018/1726, [2019] OJ L135/1.

7. INTEROPERABILITY

(a) Regulation (EU) 2019/817 of the European Parliament and of the Council of 20 May 2019 on establishing a framework for interoperability between EU information systems in the field of borders and visa and amending Regulations (EC) No 767/2008, (EU) 2016/399, (EU) 2017/2226, (EU) 2018/1240, (EU) 2018/1726 and (EU) 2018/1861 of the European Parliament and of the Council and Council Decisions 2004/512/EC and 2008/633/JHA, [2019] OJ L135/27.

(b) Regulation (EU) 2019/818 of the European Parliament and of the Council of 20 May 2019 on establishing a framework for interoperability between EU information systems in the field of police and judicial cooperation, asylum and migration and amending Regulations (EU) 2018/1726, (EU) 2018/1862 and (EU) 2019/816, [2019] OJ L135/85.

ANNEX XI – TECHNICAL DOCUMENTATION REFERRED TO IN ARTICLE 53(1), POINT (A) – TECHNICAL DOCUMENTATION FOR PROVIDERS OF GENERAL-PURPOSE AI MODELS

SECTION 1 – INFORMATION TO BE PROVIDED BY ALL PROVIDERS OF GENERAL-PURPOSE AI MODELS

The technical documentation referred to in Article 53(1), point (a) shall contain at least the following information as appropriate to the size and risk profile of the model:

1. A general description of the general-purpose AI model including:
   (a) the tasks that the model is intended to perform and the type and nature of AI systems in which it can be integrated;
   (b) the acceptable use policies applicable;
   (c) the date of release and methods of distribution;
   (d) the architecture and number of parameters;
   (e) the modality (e.g. text, image) and format of inputs and outputs;
   (f) the licence.
2. A detailed description of the elements of the model referred to in point 1, and relevant information of the process for the development, including the following elements:
   (a) the technical means (e.g. instructions of use, infrastructure, tools) required for the general-purpose AI model to be integrated in AI systems;
   (b) the design specifications of the model and training process, including training methodologies and techniques, the key design choices including the rationale and assumptions made; what the model is designed to optimise for and the relevance of the different parameters, as applicable;
   (c) information on the data used for training, testing and validation, where applicable, including the type and provenance of data and curation methodologies (e.g. cleaning, filtering, etc.), the number of data points, their scope and main characteristics; how the data was obtained and selected as well as all other measures to detect the unsuitability of data sources and methods to detect identifiable biases, where applicable;
   (d) the computational resources used to train the model (e.g. number of floating point operations), training time, and other relevant details related to the training;
   (e) known or estimated energy consumption of the model.
   With regard to point (e), where the energy consumption of the model is unknown, the energy consumption may be based on information about computational resources used.

SECTION 2 – ADDITIONAL INFORMATION TO BE PROVIDED BY PROVIDERS OF GENERAL-PURPOSE AI MODELS WITH SYSTEMIC RISK

1. A detailed description of the evaluation strategies, including evaluation results, on the basis of available public evaluation protocols and tools or otherwise of other evaluation methodologies. Evaluation strategies shall include evaluation criteria, metrics and the methodology on the identification of limitations.
2. Where applicable, a detailed description of the measures put in place for the purpose of conducting internal and/or external adversarial testing (e.g. red teaming), model adaptations, including alignment and fine-tuning.
3. Where applicable, a detailed description of the system architecture explaining how software components build or feed into each other and integrate into the overall processing.

ANNEX XII – TRANSPARENCY INFORMATION REFERRED TO IN ARTICLE 53(1), POINT (B) – TECHNICAL DOCUMENTATION FOR PROVIDERS OF GENERAL-PURPOSE AI MODELS TO DOWNSTREAM PROVIDERS THAT INTEGRATE THE MODEL INTO THEIR AI SYSTEM

The information referred to in Article 53(1), point (b) shall contain at least the following:

1. A general description of the general-purpose AI model including:
   (a) the tasks that the model is intended to perform and the type and nature of AI systems into which it can be integrated;
   (b) the acceptable use policies applicable;
   (c) the date of release and methods of distribution;
   (d) how the model interacts, or can be used to interact, with hardware or software that is not part of the model itself, where applicable;
   (e) the versions of relevant software related to the use of the general-purpose AI model, where applicable;
   (f) the architecture and number of parameters;
   (g) the modality (e.g. text, image) and format of inputs and outputs;
   (h) the licence for the model.
2. A description of the elements of the model and of the process for its development, including:
   (a) the technical means (e.g. instructions for use, infrastructure, tools) required for the general-purpose AI model to be integrated into AI systems;
   (b) the modality (e.g. text, image, etc.) and format of the inputs and outputs and their maximum size (e.g. context window length, etc.);
   (c) information on the data used for training, testing and validation, where applicable, including the type and provenance of data and curation methodologies.

ANNEX XIII – CRITERIA FOR THE DESIGNATION OF GENERAL-PURPOSE AI MODELS WITH SYSTEMIC RISK REFERRED TO IN ARTICLE 51

For the purpose of determining that a general-purpose AI model has capabilities or an impact equivalent to those set out in Article 51(1), point (a), the Commission shall take into account the following criteria:

(a) the number of parameters of the model;

(b) the quality or size of the data set, for example measured through tokens;

(c) the amount of computation used for training the model, measured in floating point operations or indicated by a combination of other variables such as estimated cost of training, estimated time required for the training, or estimated energy consumption for the training;

(d) the input and output modalities of the model, such as text to text (large language models), text to image, multi-modality, and the state of the art thresholds for determining high-impact capabilities for each modality, and the specific type of inputs and outputs (e.g. biological sequences);

(e) the benchmarks and evaluations of capabilities of the model, including considering the number of tasks without additional training, adaptability to learn new, distinct tasks, its level of autonomy and scalability, the tools it has access to;

(f) whether it has a high impact on the internal market due to its reach, which shall be presumed when it has been made available to at least 10 000 registered business users established in the Union;

(g) the number of registered end-users.

EXPLANATORY MEMORANDUM OF THE EU PROPOSAL FOR AN AI ACT

1. CONTEXT OF THE PROPOSAL

1.1. Reasons for and objectives of the proposal

This explanatory memorandum[3] accompanies the proposal for a Regulation laying down harmonised rules on artificial intelligence (Artificial Intelligence Act). Artificial Intelligence (AI) is a fast evolving family of technologies that can bring a wide array of economic and societal benefits across the entire spectrum of industries and social activities. By improving prediction, optimising operations and resource allocation, and personalising service delivery, the use of artificial intelligence can support socially and environmentally beneficial outcomes and provide key competitive advantages to companies and the European economy. Such action is especially needed in high-impact sectors, including climate change, environment and health, the public sector, finance, mobility, home affairs and agriculture. However, the same elements and techniques that power the socio-economic benefits of AI can also bring about new risks or negative consequences for individuals or the society. In light of the speed of technological change and possible challenges, the EU is committed to strive for a balanced approach. It is in the Union interest to preserve the EU's technological leadership and to ensure that Europeans can benefit from new technologies developed and functioning according to Union values, fundamental rights and principles.

This proposal delivers on the political commitment by President von der Leyen, who announced in her political guidelines for the 2019-2024 Commission 'A Union that strives for more',[4] that the Commission would put forward legislation for a coordinated European approach on the human and ethical implications of AI. Following on that announcement, on 19 February 2020 the Commission published the White Paper on AI - A European approach to excellence and trust[5] The White Paper sets out policy options on how to achieve the twin objective of promoting the uptake of AI and of addressing the

---

3 Proposal for a Regulation of the European Parliament and of the Council laying down harmonised rules on artificial intelligence (Artificial Intelligence Act) and amending certain union legislative acts {SEC(2021) 167 final} - {SWD(2021) 84 final} - {SWD (2021) 85 final}, explanatory memorandum, p. 3, Brussels, 21 April 2021.

4 https://ec.europa.eu/commission/sites/beta-political/files/political-guidelines-next-commission_en.pdf.

5 European Commission, White Paper on Artificial Intelligence 'A European approach to excellence and trust', COM(2020) 65 final, 2020.

risks associated with certain uses of such technology. This proposal aims to implement the second objective for the development of an ecosystem of trust by proposing a legal framework for trustworthy AI. The proposal is based on EU values and fundamental rights and aims to give people and other users the confidence to embrace AI-based solutions, while encouraging businesses to develop them. AI should be a tool for people and be a force for good in society with the ultimate aim of increasing human well-being. Rules for AI available in the Union market or otherwise affecting people in the Union should therefore be human centric, so that people can trust that the technology is used in a way that is safe and compliant with the law, including the respect of fundamental rights. Following the publication of the White Paper, the Commission launched a broad stakeholder consultation, which was met with a great interest by a large number of stakeholders who were largely supportive of regulatory intervention to address the challenges and concerns raised by the increasing use of AI.

The proposal also responds to explicit requests from the European Parliament (EP) and the European Council, which have repeatedly expressed calls for legislative action to ensure a well-functioning internal market for artificial intelligence systems ('AI systems') where both benefits and risks of AI are adequately addressed at Union level. It supports the objective of the Union being a global leader in the development of secure, trustworthy and ethical artificial intelligence as stated by the European Council[6] and ensures the protection of ethical principles as specifically requested by the European Parliament.[7]

In 2017, the European Council called for a 'sense of urgency to address emerging trends' including 'issues such as artificial intelligence …, while at the same time ensuring a high level of data protection, digital rights and ethical standards'.[8] In its 2019 Conclusions on the Coordinated Plan on the development and use of artificial intelligence Made in Europe,[9] the Council further highlighted the importance of ensuring that European citizens' rights are fully respected and called for a review of the existing relevant legislation to make it fit for purpose for the new opportunities and challenges raised by

---

6 European Council, Special meeting of the European Council (1 and 2 October 2020) – Conclusions, EUCO 13/20, 2020, p. 6.

7 European Parliament resolution of 20 October 2020 with recommendations to the Commission on a framework of ethical aspects of artificial intelligence, robotics and related technologies, 2020/2012(INL).

8 European Council, European Council meeting (19 October 2017) – Conclusion EUCO 14/17, 2017, p. 8.

9 Council of the European Union, Artificial intelligence, b) Conclusions on the coordinated plan on artificial intelligence, Adoption, 6177/19, 2019.

AI. The European Council has also called for a clear determination of the AI applications that should be considered high-risk.[10]

The most recent Conclusions from 21 October 2020 further called for addressing the opacity, complexity, bias, a certain degree of unpredictability and partially autonomous behaviour of certain AI systems, to ensure their compatibility with fundamental rights and to facilitate the enforcement of legal rules.[11]

The European Parliament has also undertaken a considerable amount of work in the area of AI. In October 2020, it adopted a number of resolutions related to AI, including on ethics,[12] liability[13] and copyright.[14] In 2021, those were followed by resolutions on AI in criminal matters[15] and in education, culture and the audio-visual sector.[16] The EP Resolution on a Framework of Ethical Aspects of Artificial Intelligence, Robotics and Related Technologies specifically recommends to the Commission to propose legislative action to harness the opportunities and benefits of AI, but also to ensure protection of ethical principles. The resolution includes a text of the legislative proposal for a regulation on ethical principles for the development, deployment and use of AI, robotics and related technologies. In accordance with the political commitment made by President von der Leyen in her Political Guidelines as regards resolutions adopted by the European Parliament under Article 225 TFEU, this proposal takes into account the aforementioned resolution of the European Parliament in full respect of proportionality, subsidiarity and better law making principles.

Against this political context, the Commission puts forward the proposed regulatory framework on Artificial Intelligence with the following specific objectives:

- ensure that AI systems placed on the Union market and used are safe and respect existing law on fundamental rights and Union values;

---

10 European Council, Special meeting of the European Council (1 and 2 October 2020) – Conclusions EUCO 13/20, 2020.

11 Council of the European Union, Presidency conclusions The Charter of Fundamental Rights in the context of Artificial Intelligence and Digital Change, 11481/20, 2020.

12 European Parliament resolution of 20 October 2020 on a framework of ethical aspects of artificial intelligence, robotics and related technologies, 2020/2012(INL).

13 European Parliament resolution of 20 October 2020 on a civil liability regime for artificial intelligence, 2020/2014(INL).

14 European Parliament resolution of 20 October 2020 on intellectual property rights for the development of artificial intelligence technologies, 2020/2015(INI).

15 European Parliament Draft Report, Artificial intelligence in criminal law and its use by the police and judicial authorities in criminal matters, 2020/2016(INI).

16 European Parliament Draft Report, 'Artificial intelligence in education, culture and the audiovisual sector', 2020/2017(INI). In that regard, the Commission has adopted the 'Digital Education Action Plan 2021-2027: Resetting education and training for the digital age, which foresees the development of ethical guidelines in AI and Data usage in education'', Commission Communication COM(2020) 624 final.

- ensure legal certainty to facilitate investment and innovation in AI;
- enhance governance and effective enforcement of existing law on fundamental rights and safety requirements applicable to AI systems;
- facilitate the development of a single market for lawful, safe and trustworthy AI applications and prevent market fragmentation.

To achieve those objectives, this proposal presents a balanced and proportionate horizontal regulatory approach to AI that is limited to the minimum necessary requirements to address the risks and problems linked to AI, without unduly constraining or hindering technological development or otherwise disproportionately increasing the cost of placing AI solutions on the market. The proposal sets a robust and flexible legal framework. On the one hand, it is comprehensive and future-proof in its fundamental regulatory choices, including the principle-based requirements that AI systems should comply with. On the other hand, it puts in place a proportionate regulatory system centred on a well-defined risk-based regulatory approach that does not create unnecessary restrictions to trade, whereby legal intervention is tailored to those concrete situations where there is a justified cause for concern or where such concern can reasonably be anticipated in the near future. At the same time, the legal framework includes flexible mechanisms that enable it to be dynamically adapted as the technology evolves and new concerning situations emerge.

The proposal sets harmonised rules for the development, placement on the market and use of AI systems in the Union following a proportionate risk-based approach. It proposes a single future-proof definition of AI. Certain particularly harmful AI practices are prohibited as contravening Union values, while specific restrictions and safeguards are proposed in relation to certain uses of remote biometric identification systems for the purpose of law enforcement. The proposal lays down a solid risk methodology to define 'high-risk' AI systems that pose significant risks to the health and safety or fundamental rights of persons. Those AI systems will have to comply with a set of horizontal mandatory requirements for trustworthy AI and follow conformity assessment procedures before those systems can be placed on the Union market. Predictable, proportionate and clear obligations are also placed on providers and users of those systems to ensure safety and respect of existing legislation protecting fundamental rights throughout the whole AI systems' lifecycle. For some specific AI systems, only minimum transparency obligations are proposed, in particular when chatbots or 'deep fakes' are used

The proposed rules will be enforced through a governance system at Member States level, building on already existing structures, and a cooperation mechanism at Union level with the establishment of a European Artificial Intelligence Board. Additional measures are also proposed to support innovation, in particular through AI regulatory sandboxes and other measures to reduce the regulatory burden and to support Small and Medium-Sized Enterprises ('SMEs') and start-ups.[17]

1.2. Consistency with existing policy provisions in the policy area

The horizontal nature of the proposal requires full consistency with existing Union legislation applicable to sectors where high-risk AI systems are already used or likely to be used in the near future.

Consistency is also ensured with the EU Charter of Fundamental Rights and the existing secondary Union legislation on data protection, consumer protection, non-discrimination and gender equality. The proposal is without prejudice and complements the General Data Protection Regulation (Regulation (EU) 2016/679) and the Law Enforcement Directive (Directive (EU) 2016/680) with a set of harmonised rules applicable to the design, development and use of certain high-risk AI systems and restrictions on certain uses of remote biometric identification systems. Furthermore, the proposal complements existing Union law on non-discrimination with specific requirements that aim to minimise the risk of algorithmic discrimination, in particular in relation to the design and the quality of data sets used for the development of AI systems complemented with obligations for testing, risk management, documentation and human oversight throughout the AI systems' lifecycle. The proposal is without prejudice to the application of Union competition law.

As regards high-risk AI systems which are safety components of products, this proposal will be integrated into the existing sectoral safety legislation to ensure consistency, avoid duplications and minimise additional burdens. In particular, as regards high-risk AI systems related to products covered by the New Legislative Framework (NLF) legislation (e.g. machinery, medical devices, toys), the requirements for AI systems set out in this proposal will be checked as part of the existing conformity assessment procedures under the relevant NLF legislation. With regard to the interplay of requirements, while the safety risks specific to AI systems are meant to be covered by the requirements of this proposal, NLF legislation aims at ensuring the overall safety of the final product and therefore may contain specific requirements regarding the safe integration of an AI system into the final product. The proposal for a Machinery Regulation, which is adopted on the same day as this proposal fully reflects this approach. As regards high-risk AI systems related to products covered by relevant Old Approach legislation (e.g. aviation, cars), this proposal would not directly apply. However, the ex-ante essential requirements for high-risk

[17] A. Liebl and T. Klein, 'AI Act Impact Survey: Exploring the impact of the AI Act on Startups in Europe', AAI (appliedAI Institute for Europe), 12 December 2022, available at https://aai.frb.io/ [accessed on 8 April 2024].

AI systems set out in this proposal will have to be taken into account when adopting relevant implementing or delegated legislation under those acts.

As regards AI systems provided or used by regulated credit institutions, the authorities responsible for the supervision of the Union's financial services legislation should be designated as competent authorities for supervising the requirements in this proposal to ensure a coherent enforcement of the obligations under this proposal and the Union's financial services legislation where AI systems are to some extent implicitly regulated in relation to the internal governance system of credit institutions. To further enhance consistency, the conformity assessment procedure and some of the providers' procedural obligations under this proposal are integrated into the procedures under Directive 2013/36/EU on access to the activity of credit institutions and the prudential supervision.[18]

This proposal is also consistent with the applicable Union legislation on services, including on intermediary services regulated by the e-Commerce Directive 2000/31/EC[19] and the Commission's recent proposal for the Digital Services Act (DSA).[20]

In relation to AI systems that are components of large-scale IT systems in the Area of Freedom, Security and Justice managed by the European Union Agency for the Operational Management of Large-Scale IT Systems (eu-LISA), the proposal will not apply to those AI systems that have been placed on the market or put into service before one year has elapsed from the date of application of this Regulation, unless the replacement or amendment of those legal acts leads to a significant change in the design or intended purpose of the AI system or AI systems concerned.

1.3. Consistency with other Union policies

The proposal is part of a wider comprehensive package of measures that address problems posed by the development and use of AI, as examined in the White Paper on AI. Consistency and complementarity is therefore ensured with other ongoing or planned initiatives of the Commission that also aim to address those problems, including the revision of sectoral product legislation (e.g. the

[18] Directive 2013/36/EU of the European Parliament and of the Council of 26 June 2013 on access to the activity of credit institutions and the prudential supervision of credit institutions and investment firms, amending Directive 2002/87/EC and repealing Directives 2006/48/EC and 2006/49/EC, [2013] OJ L176/338–436.

[19] Directive 2000/31/EC of the European Parliament and of the Council of 8 June 2000 on certain legal aspects of information society services, in particular electronic commerce, in the Internal Market ('Directive on electronic commerce'), [2000] OJ L178/1–16.

[20] See Proposal for a Regulation of the European Parliament and of the Council on a Single Market for Digital Services (Digital Services Act) and amending Directive 2000/31/EC COM/2020/825 final.

Machinery Directive, the General Product Safety Directive) and initiatives that address liability issues related to new technologies, including AI systems. Those initiatives will build on and complement this proposal in order to bring legal clarity and foster the development of an ecosystem of trust in AI in Europe.

The proposal is also coherent with the Commission's overall digital strategy in its contribution to promoting technology that works for people, one of the three main pillars of the policy orientation and objectives announced in the Communication 'Shaping Europe's digital future'.[21] It lays down a coherent, effective and proportionate framework to ensure AI is developed in ways that respect people's rights and earn their trust, making Europe fit for the digital age and turning the next ten years into the Digital Decade.[22]

Furthermore, the promotion of AI-driven innovation is closely linked to the Data Governance Act,[23] the Open Data Directive[24] and other initiatives under the EU strategy for data,[25] which will establish trusted mechanisms and services for the re-use, sharing and pooling of data that are essential for the development of data-driven AI models of high quality.

The proposal also strengthens significantly the Union's role to help shape global norms and standards and promote trustworthy AI that is consistent with Union values and interests. It provides the Union with a powerful basis to engage further with its external partners, including third countries, and at international fora on issues relating to AI.

2. LEGAL BASIS, SUBSIDIARITY AND PROPORTIONALITY

2.1. Legal basis

The legal basis for the proposal is in the first place Article 114 of the Treaty on the Functioning of the European Union (TFEU), which provides for the adoption of measures to ensure the establishment and functioning of the internal market.

This proposal constitutes a core part of the EU digital single market strategy. The primary objective of this proposal is to ensure the proper functioning of the internal market by setting harmonised rules in particular on the development, placing on the Union market and the use of products and services making use

---

21 Communication from the Commission, Shaping Europe's Digital Future, COM/2020/67 final.

22 2030 Digital Compass: the European way for the Digital Decade.

23 Proposal for a Regulation on European data governance (Data Governance Act) COM/2020/76.

24 Directive (EU) 2019/1024 of the European Parliament and of the Council of 20 June 2019 on open data and the re-use of public sector information, PE/28/2019/REV/1, [2019] OJ L172/56–83.

25 Commission Communication, A European strategy for data COM/2020/66 final.

of AI technologies or provided as stand-alone AI systems. Some Member States are already considering national rules to ensure that AI is safe and is developed and used in compliance with fundamental rights obligations. This will likely lead to two main problems: i) a fragmentation of the internal market on essential elements regarding in particular the requirements for the AI products and services, their marketing, their use, the liability and the supervision by public authorities, and ii) the substantial diminishment of legal certainty for both providers and users of AI systems on how existing and new rules will apply to those systems in the Union. Given the wide circulation of products and services across borders, these two problems can be best solved through EU harmonizing legislation.

Indeed, the proposal defines common mandatory requirements applicable to the design and development of certain AI systems before they are placed on the market that will be further operationalised through harmonised technical standards. The proposal also addresses the situation after AI systems have been placed on the market by harmonising the way in which ex-post controls are conducted.

In addition, considering that this proposal contains certain specific rules on the protection of individuals with regard to the processing of personal data, notably restrictions of the use of AI systems for 'real-time' remote biometric identification in publicly accessible spaces for the purpose of law enforcement, it is appropriate to base this regulation, in as far as those specific rules are concerned, on Article 16 of the TFEU.

2.2. Subsidiarity (for non-exclusive competence)

The nature of AI, which often relies on large and varied datasets and which may be embedded in any product or service circulating freely within the internal market, entails that the objectives of this proposal cannot be effectively achieved by Member States alone. Furthermore, an emerging patchwork of potentially divergent national rules will hamper the seamless circulation of products and services related to AI systems across the EU and will be ineffective in ensuring the safety and protection of fundamental rights and Union values across the different Member States. National approaches in addressing the problems will only create additional legal uncertainty and barriers, and will slow market uptake of AI.

The objectives of this proposal can be better achieved at Union level to avoid a further fragmentation of the Single Market into potentially contradictory national frameworks preventing the free circulation of goods and services embedding AI. A solid European regulatory framework for trustworthy AI will also ensure a level playing field and protect all people, while strengthening Europe's competitiveness and industrial basis in AI. Only common action at

Union level can also protect the Union's digital sovereignty and leverage its tools and regulatory powers to shape global rules and standards.

2.3. *Proportionality*

The proposal builds on existing legal frameworks and is proportionate and necessary to achieve its objectives, since it follows a risk-based approach and imposes regulatory burdens only when an AI system is likely to pose high risks to fundamental rights and safety. For other, non-high-risk AI systems, only very limited transparency obligations are imposed, for example in terms of the provision of information to flag the use of an AI system when interacting with humans. For high-risk AI systems, the requirements of high quality data, documentation and traceability, transparency, human oversight, accuracy and robustness, are strictly necessary to mitigate the risks to fundamental rights and safety posed by AI and that are not covered by other existing legal frameworks. Harmonised standards and supporting guidance and compliance tools will assist providers and users in complying with the requirements laid down by the proposal and minimise their costs. The costs incurred by operators are proportionate to the objectives achieved and the economic and reputational benefits that operators can expect from this proposal

2.4. *Choice of the instrument*

The choice of a regulation as a legal instrument is justified by the need for a uniform application of the new rules, such as definition of AI, the prohibition of certain harmful AI-enabled practices and the classification of certain AI systems. The direct applicability of a Regulation, in accordance with Article 288 TFEU, will reduce legal fragmentation and facilitate the development of a single market for lawful, safe and trustworthy AI systems. It will do so, in particular, by introducing a harmonised set of core requirements with regard to AI systems classified as high-risk and obligations for providers and users of those systems, improving the protection of fundamental rights and providing legal certainty for operators and consumers alike.

At the same time, the provisions of the regulation are not overly prescriptive and leave room for different levels of Member State action for elements that do not undermine the objectives of the initiative, in particular the internal organisation of the market surveillance system and the uptake of measures to foster innovation.

3. RESULTS OF EX-POST EVALUATIONS, STAKEHOLDER CONSULTATIONS AND IMPACT ASSESSMENTS

3.1. Stakeholder consultation

This proposal is the result of extensive consultation with all major stakeholders, in which the general principles and minimum standards for consultation of interested parties by the Commission were applied.

An online public consultation was launched on 19 February 2020 along with the publication of the White Paper on Artificial Intelligence and ran until 14 June 2020. The objective of that consultation was to collect views and opinions on the White Paper. It targeted all interested stakeholders from the public and private sectors, including governments, local authorities, commercial and non-commercial organisations, social partners, experts, academics and citizens. After analysing all the responses received, the Commission published a summary outcome and the individual responses on its website.[26]

In total, 1215 contributions were received, of which 352 were from companies or business organisations/associations, 406 from individuals (92% individuals from EU), 152 on behalf of academic/research institutions, and 73 from public authorities. Civil society's voices were represented by 160 respondents (among which 9 consumers' organisations, 129 non-governmental organisations and 22 trade unions), 72 respondents contributed as 'others'. Of the 352 business and industry representatives, 222 were companies and business representatives, 41.5% of which were micro, small and medium-sized enterprises. The rest were business associations. Overall, 84% of business and industry replies came from the EU-27. Depending on the question, between 81 and 598 of the respondents used the free text option to insert comments. Over 450 position papers were submitted through the EU Survey website, either in addition to questionnaire answers (over 400) or as stand-alone contributions (over 50).

Overall, there is a general agreement amongst stakeholders on a need for action. A large majority of stakeholders agree that legislative gaps exist or that new legislation is needed. However, several stakeholders warn the Commission to avoid duplication, conflicting obligations and overregulation. There were many comments underlining the importance of a technology neutral and proportionate regulatory framework.

Stakeholders mostly requested a narrow, clear and precise definition for AI. Stakeholders also highlighted that besides the clarification of the term of AI, it is important to define 'risk', 'high-risk', 'low-risk', 'remote biometric identification' and 'harm'.

---

26 See all consultation results at: https://ec.europa.eu/digital-single-market/en/news/white-paper-artificial-intelligence-public-consultation-towards-european-approach-excellence.

Most of the respondents are explicitly in favour of the risk-based approach. Using a risk-based framework was considered a better option than blanket regulation of all AI systems. The types of risks and threats should be based on a sector-by-sector and case-by-case approach. Risks also should be calculated taking into account the impact on rights and safety.

Regulatory sandboxes could be very useful for the promotion of AI and are welcomed by certain stakeholders, especially the Business Associations.

Among those who formulated their opinion on the enforcement models, more than 50%, especially from the business associations, were in favour of a combination of an ex-ante risk self-assessment and an ex-post enforcement for high-risk AI systems.

3.2. Collection and use of expertise

The proposal builds on two years of analysis and close involvement of stakeholders, including academics, businesses, social partners, non-governmental organisations, Member States and citizens. The preparatory work started in 2018 with the setting up of a High-Level Expert Group on AI (HLEG) which had an inclusive and broad composition of 52 well-known experts tasked to advise the Commission on the implementation of the Commission's Strategy on Artificial Intelligence. In April 2019, the Commission supported[27] the key requirements set out in the HLEG ethics guidelines for Trustworthy AI,[28] which had been revised to take into account more than 500 submissions from stakeholders. The key requirements reflect a widespread and common approach, as evidenced by a plethora of ethical codes and principles developed by many private and public organisations in Europe and beyond, that AI development and use should be guided by certain essential value-oriented principles. The Assessment List for Trustworthy Artificial Intelligence (ALTAI)[29] made those requirements operational in a piloting process with over 350 organisations.

In addition, the AI Alliance[30] was formed as a platform for approximately 4000 stakeholders to debate the technological and societal implications of AI, culminating in a yearly AI Assembly.

The White Paper on AI further developed this inclusive approach, inciting comments from more than 1250 stakeholders, including over 450 additional

---

27 European Commission, 'Building Trust in Human-Centric Artificial Intelligence', COM(2019) 168.

28 AI HLEG, 'Ethics Guidelines for Trustworthy AI', 2019.

29 HLEG, 'Assessment List for Trustworthy Artificial Intelligence (ALTAI) for self-assessment', 2020.

30 The AI Alliance is a multi-stakeholder forum launched in June 2018. See: https://ec.europa.eu/digital-single-market/en/european-ai-alliance.

position papers. As a result, the Commission published an Inception Impact Assessment, which in turn attracted more than 130 comments.[31] Additional stakeholder workshops and events were also organised the results of which support the analysis in the impact assessment and the policy choices made in this proposal.[32] An external study was also procured to feed into the impact assessment.

3.3. *Impact assessment*

In line with its 'Better Regulation' policy, the Commission conducted an impact assessment for this proposal examined by the Commission's Regulatory Scrutiny Board. A meeting with the Regulatory Scrutiny Board was held on 16 December 2020, which was followed by a negative opinion. After substantial revision of the impact assessment to address the comments and a resubmission of the impact assessment, the Regulatory Scrutiny Board issued a positive opinion on 21 March 2021. The opinions of the Regulatory Scrutiny Board, the recommendations and an explanation of how they have been taken into account are presented in Annex 1 of the impact assessment.

The Commission examined different policy options to achieve the general objective of the proposal, which is to ensure the proper functioning of the single market by creating the conditions for the development and use of trustworthy AI in the Union.

Four policy options of different degrees of regulatory intervention were assessed:

- Option 1: EU legislative instrument setting up a voluntary labelling scheme;
- Option 2: a sectoral, 'ad-hoc' approach;
- Option 3: Horizontal EU legislative instrument following a proportionate risk-based approach;
- Option 3+: Horizontal EU legislative instrument following a proportionate risk-based approach + codes of conduct for non-high-risk AI systems;
- Option 4: Horizontal EU legislative instrument establishing mandatory requirements for all AI systems, irrespective of the risk they pose.

According to the Commission's established methodology, each policy option was evaluated against economic and societal impacts, with a particular focus on impacts on fundamental rights. The preferred option is option 3+, a regulatory framework for high-risk AI systems only, with the possibility for all providers of non-high-risk AI systems to follow a code of conduct. The requirements

[31] European Commission, 'Inception Impact Assessment for a Proposal for a legal act of the European Parliament and the Council laying down requirements for Artificial Intelligence'.

[32] For details of all the consultations that have been carried out see Annex 2 of the impact assessment.

will concern data, documentation and traceability, provision of information and transparency, human oversight and robustness and accuracy and would be mandatory for high-risk AI systems. Companies that introduced codes of conduct for other AI systems would do so voluntarily

The preferred option was considered suitable to address in the most effective way the objectives of this proposal. By requiring a restricted yet effective set of actions from AI developers and users, the preferred option limits the risks of violation of fundamental rights and safety of people and foster effective supervision and enforcement, by targeting the requirements only to systems where there is a high risk that such violations could occur. As a result, that option keeps compliance costs to a minimum, thus avoiding an unnecessary slowing of uptake due to higher prices and compliance costs. In order to address possible disadvantages for SMEs, this option includes several provisions to support their compliance and reduce their costs, including creation of regulatory sandboxes and obligation to consider SMEs interests when setting fees related to conformity assessment.

The preferred option will increase people's trust in AI, companies will gain in legal certainty, and Member States will see no reason to take unilateral action that could fragment the single market. As a result of higher demand due to higher trust, more available offers due to legal certainty, and the absence of obstacles to cross-border movement of AI systems, the single market for AI will likely flourish. The European Union will continue to develop a fast-growing AI ecosystem of innovative services and products embedding AI technology or stand-alone AI systems, resulting in increased digital autonomy.

Businesses or public authorities that develop or use AI applications that constitute a high risk for the safety or fundamental rights of citizens would have to comply with specific requirements and obligations. Compliance with these requirements would imply costs amounting to approximately EUR € 6000 to EUR € 7000 for the supply of an average high-risk AI system of around EUR € 170000 by 2025. For AI users, there would also be the annual cost for the time spent on ensuring human oversight where this is appropriate, depending on the use case. Those have been estimated at approximately EUR € 5000 to EUR € 8000 per year. Verification costs could amount to another EUR € 3000 to EUR € 7500 for suppliers of high-risk AI. Businesses or public authorities that develop or use any AI applications not classified as high risk would only have minimal obligations of information. However, they could choose to join others and together adopt a code of conduct to follow suitable requirements, and to ensure that their AI systems are trustworthy. In such a case, costs would be at most as high as for high-risk AI systems, but most probably lower.

The impacts of the policy options on different categories of stakeholders (economic operators/ business; conformity assessment bodies, standardisation bodies and other public bodies; individuals/citizens; researchers) are explained in detail in Annex 3 of the Impact assessment supporting this proposal.

3.4. *Regulatory fitness and simplification*

This proposal lays down obligation that will apply to providers and users of high-risk AI systems. For providers who develop and place such systems on the Union market, it will create legal certainty and ensure that no obstacle to the cross-border provision of AI-related services and products emerge. For companies using AI, it will promote trust among their customers. For national public administrations, it will promote public trust in the use of AI and strengthen enforcement mechanisms (by introducing a European coordination mechanism, providing for appropriate capacities, and facilitating audits of the AI systems with new requirements for documentation, traceability and transparency). Moreover, the framework will envisage specific measures supporting innovation, including regulatory sandboxes and specific measures supporting small-scale users and providers of high-risk AI systems to comply with the new rules.

The proposal also specifically aims at strengthening Europe's competitiveness and industrial basis in AI. Full consistency is ensured with existing sectoral Union legislation applicable to AI systems (e.g. on products and services) that will bring further clarity and simplify the enforcement of the new rules.

3.5. *Fundamental rights*

The use of AI with its specific characteristics (e.g. opacity, complexity, dependency on data, autonomous behaviour) can adversely affect a number of fundamental rights enshrined in the EU Charter of Fundamental Rights ('the Charter'). This proposal seeks to ensure a high level of protection for those fundamental rights and aims to address various sources of risks through a clearly defined risk-based approach. With a set of requirements for trustworthy AI and proportionate obligations on all value chain participants, the proposal will enhance and promote the protection of the rights protected by the Charter: the right to human dignity (Article 1), respect for private life and protection of personal data (Articles 7 and 8), non-discrimination (Article 21) and equality between women and men (Article 23). It aims to prevent a chilling effect on the rights to freedom of expression (Article 11) and freedom of assembly (Article 12), to ensure protection of the right to an effective remedy and to a fair trial, the rights of defence and the presumption of innocence (Articles 47 and 48), as well as the general principle of good administration. Furthermore, as applicable in certain domains, the proposal will positively affect the rights of a number of special groups, such as the workers' rights to fair and just working conditions (Article 31), a high level of consumer protection (Article 28), the rights of the child (Article 24) and the integration of persons with disabilities (Article 26). The right to a high level of environmental protection and the improvement of the quality of the environment (Article 37) is also relevant, including in relation to the health and safety of people. The obligations for ex ante testing, risk management and human oversight will also facilitate the respect of other fundamental rights by minimising the risk of erroneous or biased AI-assisted decisions in critical areas such as education and training, employment, important services, law enforcement and the judiciary. In case infringements of fundamental rights still happen, effective redress for affected persons will be made possible by ensuring transparency and traceability of the AI systems coupled with strong ex post controls.

This proposal imposes some restrictions on the freedom to conduct business (Article 16) and the freedom of art and science (Article 13) to ensure compliance with overriding reasons of public interest such as health, safety, consumer protection and the protection of other fundamental rights ('responsible innovation') when high-risk AI technology is developed and used. Those restrictions are proportionate and limited to the minimum necessary to prevent and mitigate serious safety risks and likely infringements of fundamental rights.

The increased transparency obligations will also not disproportionately affect the right to protection of intellectual property (Article 17(2)), since they will be limited only to the minimum necessary information for individuals to exercise their right to an effective remedy and to the necessary transparency towards supervision and enforcement authorities, in line with their mandates. Any disclosure of information will be carried out in compliance with relevant legislation in the field, including Directive 2016/943 on the protection of undisclosed know-how and business information (trade secrets) against their unlawful acquisition, use and disclosure. When public authorities and notified bodies need to be given access to confidential information or source code to examine compliance with substantial obligations, they are placed under binding confidentiality obligations.

4. BUDGETARY IMPLICATIONS

Member States will have to designate supervisory authorities in charge of implementing the legislative requirements. Their supervisory function could build on existing arrangements, for example regarding conformity assessment bodies or market surveillance, but would require sufficient technological expertise and human and financial resources. Depending on the pre-existing structure in each Member State, this could amount to 1 to 25 Full Time Equivalents per Member State.

A detailed overview of the costs involved is provided in the 'financial statement' linked to this proposal

5. OTHER ELEMENTS

5.1. Implementation plans and monitoring, evaluation and reporting arrangements

Providing for a robust monitoring and evaluation mechanism is crucial to ensure that the proposal will be effective in achieving its specific objectives. The Commission will be in charge of monitoring the effects of the proposal. It will establish a system for registering stand-alone high-risk AI applications in a public EU-wide database. This registration will also enable competent authorities, users and other interested people to verify if the high-risk AI system complies with the requirements laid down in the proposal and to exercise enhanced oversight over those AI systems posing high risks to fundamental rights. To feed this database, AI providers will be obliged to provide meaningful information about their systems and the conformity assessment carried out on those systems.

Moreover, AI providers will be obliged to inform national competent authorities about serious incidents or malfunctioning that constitute a breach of fundamental rights obligations as soon as they become aware of them, as well as any recalls or withdrawals of AI systems from the market. National competent authorities will then investigate the incidents/or malfunctioning, collect all the necessary information and regularly transmit it to the Commission with adequate metadata. The Commission will complement this information on the incidents by a comprehensive analysis of the overall market for AI.

The Commission will publish a report evaluating and reviewing the proposed AI framework five years following the date on which it becomes applicable.

5.2. Detailed explanation of the specific provisions of the proposal

5.2.1. Scope and definitions (Title I)

Title I defines the subject matter of the regulation and the scope of application of the new rules that cover the placing on the market, putting into service and use of AI systems. It also sets out the definitions used throughout the instrument. The definition of AI system in the legal framework aims to be as technology neutral and future proof as possible, taking into account the fast technological and market developments related to AI. In order to provide the needed legal certainty, Title I is complemented by Annex I, which contains a detailed list of approaches and techniques for the development of AI to be adapted by the Commission in line with new technological developments. Key participants across the AI value chain are also clearly defined such as providers and users of AI systems that cover both public and private operators to ensure a level playing field.

5.2.2. Prohibited artificial intelligence practices (Title II)

Title II establishes a list of prohibited AI. The regulation follows a risk-based approach, differentiating between uses of AI that create (i) an unacceptable risk, (ii) a high risk, and (iii) low or minimal risk. The list of prohibited practices in Title II comprises all those AI systems whose use is considered unacceptable as contravening Union values, for instance by violating fundamental rights. The prohibitions covers practices that have a significant potential to manipulate persons through subliminal techniques beyond their consciousness or exploit vulnerabilities of specific vulnerable groups such as children or persons with disabilities in order to materially distort their behaviour in a manner that is likely to cause them or another person psychological or physical harm. Other manipulative or exploitative practices affecting adults that might be facilitated by AI systems could be covered by the existing data protection, consumer protection and digital service legislation that guarantee that natural persons are properly informed and have free choice not to be subject to profiling or other practices that might affect their behaviour. The proposal also prohibits AI-based social scoring for general purposes done by public authorities. Finally, the use of 'real time' remote biometric identification systems in publicly accessible spaces for the purpose of law enforcement is also prohibited unless certain limited exceptions apply.

5.2.3. High-risk ai systems (Title III)

Title III contains specific rules for AI systems that create a high risk to the health and safety or fundamental rights of natural persons. In line with a risk-based approach, those high-risk AI systems are permitted on the European market subject to compliance with certain mandatory requirements and an ex-ante conformity assessment. The classification of an AI system as high-risk is based on the intended purpose of the AI system, in line with existing product safety legislation. Therefore, the classification as high-risk does not only depend on the function performed by the AI system, but also on the specific purpose and modalities for which that system is used.

Chapter 1 of Title III sets the classification rules and identifies two main categories of high-risk AI systems.

- AI systems intended to be used as safety component of products that are subject to third party ex-ante conformity assessment;
- other stand-alone AI systems with mainly fundamental rights implications that are explicitly listed in Annex III.

This list of high-risk AI systems in Annex III contains a limited number of AI systems whose risks have already materialised or are likely to materialise in the near future. To ensure that the regulation can be adjusted to emerging uses and applications of AI, the Commission may expand the list of high-risk AI systems used within certain pre-defined areas, by applying a set of criteria and risk assessment methodology.

Chapter 2 sets out the legal requirements for high-risk AI systems in relation to data and data governance, documentation and recording keeping, transparency and provision of information to users, human oversight, robustness, accuracy and security. The proposed minimum requirements are already state-of-the-art for many diligent operators and the result of two years of preparatory work, derived from the Ethics Guidelines of the HLEG,[33] piloted by more than 350 organisations.[34] They are also largely consistent with other international recommendations and principles, which ensures that the proposed AI framework is compatible with those adopted by the EU's international trade partners. The precise technical solutions to achieve compliance with those requirements may be provided by standards or by other technical specifications or otherwise be developed in accordance with general engineering or scientific knowledge at the discretion of the provider of the AI system. This flexibility is particularly important, because it allows providers of AI systems to choose the way to meet their requirements, taking into account the state-of-the-art and technological and scientific progress in this field.

Chapter 3 places a clear set of horizontal obligations on providers of high-risk AI systems. Proportionate obligations are also placed on users and other participants across the AI value chain (e.g., importers, distributors, authorized representatives).

Chapter 4 sets the framework for notified bodies to be involved as independent third parties in conformity assessment procedures, while *Chapter 5* explains in detail the conformity assessment procedures to be followed for each type of high-risk AI system. The conformity assessment approach aims to minimise the burden for economic operators as well as for

33 High-Level Expert Group on Artificial Intelligence, Ethics Guidelines for Trustworthy AI, 2019.

34 They were also endorsed by the Commission in its 2019 Communication on human-centric approach to AI.

notified bodies, whose capacity needs to be progressively ramped up over time. AI systems intended to be used as safety components of products that are regulated under the New Legislative Framework legislation (e.g. machinery, toys, medical devices, etc.) will be subject to the same ex-ante and ex-post compliance and enforcement mechanisms of the products of which they are a component. The key difference is that the ex-ante and ex-post mechanisms will ensure compliance not only with the requirements established by sectorial legislation, but also with the requirements established by this regulation

As regards stand-alone high-risk AI systems that are referred to in Annex III, a new compliance and enforcement system will be established. This follows the model of the New Legislative Framework legislation implemented through internal control checks by the providers with the exception of remote biometric identification systems that would be subject to third party conformity assessment. A comprehensive ex-ante conformity assessment through internal checks, combined with a strong ex-post enforcement, could be an effective and reasonable solution for those systems, given the early phase of the regulatory intervention and the fact the AI sector is very innovative and expertise for auditing is only now being accumulated. An assessment through internal checks for 'stand-alone' high-risk AI systems would require a full, effective and properly documented ex ante compliance with all requirements of the regulation and compliance with robust quality and risk management systems and post-market monitoring. After the provider has performed the relevant conformity assessment, it should register those stand-alone high-risk AI systems in an EU database that will be managed by the Commission to increase public transparency and oversight and strengthen ex post supervision by competent authorities. By contrast, for reasons of consistency with the existing product safety legislation, the conformity assessments of AI systems that are safety components of products will follow a system with third party conformity assessment procedures already established under the relevant sectoral product safety legislation. New ex ante re-assessments of the conformity will be needed in case of substantial modifications to the AI systems (and notably changes which go beyond what is pre-determined by the provider in its technical documentation and checked at the moment of the ex-ante conformity assessment).

5.2.4. Transparency obligations for certain ai systems (Title IV)

Title IV concerns certain AI systems to take account of the specific risks of manipulation they pose. Transparency obligations will apply for systems that (i) interact with humans, (ii) are used to detect emotions or determine association with (social) categories based on biometric data, or (iii) generate or manipulate content ('deep fakes'). When persons interact with an AI system or their emotions or characteristics are recognised through automated means, people must be informed of that circumstance. If an AI system is used to generate or manipulate image, audio or video content that appreciably resembles authentic content, there should be an obligation to disclose that the content is generated through automated means, subject to exceptions for legitimate purposes (law enforcement, freedom of expression). This allows persons to make informed choices or step back from a given situation

5.2.5. Measures in support of innovation (Title V)

Title V contributes to the objective to create a legal framework that is innovation-friendly, future-proof and resilient to disruption. To that end, it encourages national competent authorities to set up regulatory sandboxes and sets a basic framework in terms of governance, supervision and liability. AI regulatory sandboxes establish a controlled environment to test innovative technologies for a limited time on the basis of a testing plan agreed with the competent authorities. Title V also contains measures to reduce the regulatory burden on SMEs and start-ups.[35]

5.2.6. Governance and implementation (Titles VI, VII and VII)

Title VI sets up the governance systems at Union and national level. At Union level, the proposal establishes a European Artificial Intelligence Board (the 'Board'), composed of representatives from the Member States and the Commission. The Board will facilitate a smooth, effective and harmonised implementation of this regulation by contributing to the effective cooperation of the national supervisory authorities and the Commission and providing advice and expertise to the Commission. It will also collect and share best practices among the Member States.

At national level, Member States will have to designate one or more national competent authorities and, among them, the national supervisory authority,[36] for the purpose of supervising the application and implementation of the regulation. The European Data Protection Supervisor will act as the competent authority for the supervision of the Union institutions, agencies and bodies when they fall within the scope of this regulation

Title VII aims to facilitate the monitoring work of the Commission and national authorities through the establishment of an EU-wide database for

---

35 A. Liebl and T. Klein, 'AI Act Impact Survey: Exploring the impact of the AI Act on Startups in Europe', AAI (appliedAI Institute for Europe), 12 December 2022, available at https://aai.frb.io/ [accessed on 8 April 2024].

36 This concept, present in Article 59 of the initial 2021 version, no longer exists in the final version of the AI Act.

stand-alone high-risk AI systems with mainly fundamental rights implications. The database will be operated by the Commission and provided with data by the providers of the AI systems, who will be required to register their systems before placing them on the market or otherwise putting them into service.

Title VIII sets out the monitoring and reporting obligations for providers of AI systems with regard to post-market monitoring and reporting and investigating on AI-related incidents and malfunctioning. Market surveillance authorities would also control the market and investigate compliance with the obligations and requirements for all high-risk AI systems already placed on the market. Market surveillance authorities would have all powers under Regulation (EU) 2019/1020 on market surveillance. Ex-post enforcement should ensure that once the AI system has been put on the market, public authorities have the powers and resources to intervene in case AI systems generate unexpected risks, which warrant rapid action. They will also monitor compliance of operators with their relevant obligations under the regulation. The proposal does not foresee the automatic creation of any additional bodies or authorities at Member State level. Member States may therefore appoint (and draw upon the expertise of) existing sectorial authorities, who would be entrusted also with the powers to monitor and enforce the provisions of the regulation.

All this is without prejudice to the existing system and allocation of powers of ex-post enforcement of obligations regarding fundamental rights in the Member States. When necessary for their mandate, existing supervision and enforcement authorities will also have the power to request and access any documentation maintained following this regulation and, where needed, request market surveillance authorities to organise testing of the high-risk AI system through technical mean.

5.2.7. Codes of conduct (Title IX)

Title IX creates a framework for the creation of codes of conduct, which aim to encourage providers of non-high-risk AI systems to apply voluntarily the mandatory requirements for high-risk AI systems (as laid out in Title III). Providers of non-high-risk AI systems may create and implement the codes of conduct themselves. Those codes may also include voluntary commitments related, for example, to environmental sustainability, accessibility for persons with disability, stakeholders' participation in the design and development of AI systems, and diversity of development teams.

5.2.8. Final provisions (Titles X, XI and XII)

Title X emphasizes the obligation of all parties to respect the confidentiality of information and data and sets out rules for the exchange of information obtained during the implementation of the regulation. Title X also includes measures to ensure the effective implementation of the regulation through effective, proportionate, and dissuasive penalties for infringements of the provisions.

Title XI sets out rules for the exercise of delegation and implementing powers. The proposal empowers the Commission to adopt, where appropriate, implementing acts to ensure uniform application of the regulation or delegated acts to update or complement the lists in Annexes I to VII.

Title XII contains an obligation for the Commission to assess regularly the need for an update of Annex III and to prepare regular reports on the evaluation and review of the regulation. It also lays down final provisions, including a differentiated transitional period for the initial date of the applicability of the regulation to facilitate the smooth implementation for all parties concerned.

APPENDICES

APPENDIX A – MAIN ABBREVIATIONS AND ACRONYMS

Abbreviation	Specification
ADCO	Administrative cooperation group
AGI	Artificial general intelligence
AI	Artificial Intelligence
AI Board	European Artificial Intelligence Board https://digital-strategy.ec.europa.eu/en/policies/ai-board
AI HLEG	High-level expert group on artificial intelligence https://digital-strategy.ec.europa.eu/en/policies/expert-group-ai
AI Office	European Artificial Intelligence Office https://digital-strategy.ec.europa.eu/en/policies/ai-office
AIA or AI Act	Artificial Intelligence Act: Regulation (EU) 2024/1689 of the European Parliament and of the Council of 13 June 2024 laying down harmonised rules on artificial intelligence and amending Regulations (EC) No 300/2008, (EU) No 167/2013, (EU) No 168/2013, (EU) 2018/858, (EU) 2018/1139 and (EU) 2019/2144 and Directives 2014/90/EU, (EU) 2016/797 and (EU) 2020/1828
AIaaS	AI as a Service
AIS	Artificial intelligence system
ALARA	As Low As Reasonably Achievable
ANSSI	Agence nationale de la sécurité des systèmes d'information https://www.ssi.gouv.fr/ (French Cybersecurity Agency)
API	Application programming interface
AR	Augmented reality
CELF	Commission d'enrichissement de la langue française (French Language Enrichment Commission)
CEN	European Committee for Standardization https://www.cencenelec.eu/about-cen/
CENELEC	European Committee for Electrotechnical Standardization https://www.cencenelec.eu/
CEPEJ	European Commission for the efficiency of justice https://www.coe.int/en/web/cepej
CERNA	Commission de réflexion sur l'Éthique de la Recherche en sciences et technologies du Numérique d'Allisten https://www.allistene.fr/cerna/ (French Allistene Committee on Research Ethics in Digital Science and Technology)

CES	Consumer Electronics Show https://www.ces.tech
CJEU	Court of Justice of the European Union https://curia.europa.eu
CNIL	Commission nationale de l'informatique et des libertés https://www.cnil.fr (French Data Protection Authority)
CNPEN	Comité national pilote d'éthique du numérique https://www.ccne-ethique.fr/cnpen (French National Pilot Committee on Digital Ethics)
CNRS	Centre national de la recherche scientifique https://www.cnrs.fr (French National Centre for Scientific Research)
CNRTL	Centre national de ressources textuelles et lexicales https://www.cnrtl.fr (French National Center of Textual and Lexical Resources)
CoE	Council of Europe https://www.coe.int
EC	European Commission https://commission.europa.eu
EDPB	European Data Protection Board https://www.edpb.europa.eu
EDPS	European Data Protection Supervisor https://www.edps.europa.eu
EEA	European Economic Area
EESC	European Economic and Social Committee https://www.eesc.europa.eu
ENISA	European Union Agency for Cybersecurity https://www.enisa.europa.eu
ETSI	European Telecommunications Standards Institute https://www.etsi.org
EU	European Union https://european-union.europa.eu
EUCO	Informal name for the European Council https://www.consilium.europa.eu/en/european-council
Eurodac	EU fingerprinting database https://www.edps.europa.eu/data-protection/european-it-systems/eurodac_en
Europol	Agency for Law Enforcement Cooperation https://www.europol.europa.eu
FLOPS	Floating point operations per second

FRA	Agency for Fundamental Rights (Fundamental Rights Agency) https://fra.europa.eu
G7	Group of Seven. G7 is an intergovernmental political and economic forum consisting of seven countries reputed to be the world's leading powers https://g7g20-documents.org/
GDPR	Regulation (EU) 2016/679 of the European Parliament and of the Council of 27 April 2016 on the protection of natural persons with regard to the processing of personal data and on the free movement of such data, and repealing Directive 95/46/EC
GAI or GenAI	Generative artificial intelligence
GAN	Generative adversarial network
GPAI	General-purpose artificial intelligence
HPC	High-Performance Computing
HMI	Human-machine interface
HRI	Human-robot interaction
INRIA	Institut national français de recherche en sciences et technologies du numérique https://www.inria.fr/fr (French National Institute for Research in Digital Science and Technology)
IoT	Internet of Things
ISO	International Organization for Standardization https://www.iso.org/home.html
JORF	Journal officiel de la République française https://www.journal-officiel.gouv.fr/pages/accueil/ (Official Journal of the French Republic)
K-base	Knowledge base
KBS	Knowledge-based system
LLM	Large language model
ML	Machine learning
MS&PC	Market Surveillance and Compliance of Products
MSA	Market Surveillance Authority
MSR	Market Surveillance Regulation: Regulation (EU) 2019/1020 of 20 June 2019 on market surveillance and compliance of products and amending Directive 2004/42/EC and Regulations (EC) No 765/2008 and (EU) No 305/2011
OECD	Organisation for Economic Co-operation and Development https://www.oecd.org/

OJEU	Official Journal of the European Union https://eur-lex.europa.eu/oj/direct-access.html
OQLF	Office québécois de la langue française https://www.oqlf.gouv.qc.ca/ Quebec Office of the French Language
SDGs	Sustainable Development Goals
SIS	Schengen Information System
SMEs	Small and medium enterprises
TEU	Treaty on European Union
TFEU	Treaty on the Functioning of the European Union
UNESCO	United Nations Educational, Scientific and Cultural Organization https://www.unesco.org/en
VR	Virtual reality
WIPO	World Intellectual Property Organization https://www.wipo.int

APPENDIX B – DISTRIBUTION OF RECITALS

RECITALS NO.	UNDER ARTICLES NO.
1.	1.
2.	2
3.	2.
4.	2.
5.	2.
6.	2.
7.	96.
8.	1, 62, 77, 82.
9.	1, 11, 25, 29.
10.	16, 26, 78.
11.	2.
12.	3.
13.	3.
14.	3.
15.	3.
16.	3.
17.	3.
18.	3.
19.	3.
20.	3, 4, 25, 65, 95.
21.	2.
22.	2, 46.
23.	2.
24.	2.
25.	57, 58, 59, 61, 76.

RECITALS NO.	UNDER ARTICLES NO.
26.	5, 13, 16, 50.
27.	13, 14, 15, 40, 50, 95, 96.
28.	5.
29.	5.
30.	5.
31.	5.
32.	15.
33.	5, 14, 26, 74.
34.	27.
35.	3, 5, 26.
36.	3, 5, 26, 74, 75.
37.	3, 5, 26.
38.	3, 5.
39.	3, 5.
40.	2, 3, 5.
41.	2, 3, 5.
42.	5.
43.	5.
44.	5.
45.	5.
46.	6.
47.	6.
48.	7.
49.	2, 43, 97, 102, 103, 104, 105, 106, 107, 108, 109.
50.	43, 46.
51.	6, 43, 46.

RECITALS NO.	UNDER ARTICLES NO.
52.	3, 6, 97.
53.	6, 7, 13, 70, 71, 96.
54.	6.
55.	3.
56.	2.
57.	2.
58.	82.
59.	13, 15, 26, 43, 46.
60.	13, 15.
61.	6.
62.	13.
63.	59.
64.	9, 34.
65.	9.
66.	10, 11, 13, 14, 15, 18.
67.	7, 10, 13.
68.	10, 31.
69.	2.
70.	10, 77.
71.	9, 11, 12, 19, 72.
72.	5, 13, 14, 26, 50.
73.	14, 19, 26.
74.	13, 15, 21.
75.	15.
76.	10, 15.
77.	15, 47.

RECITALS NO.	UNDER ARTICLES NO.
78.	15, 43, 46.
79.	5, 16.
80.	93.
81.	16, 17, 40, 43, 72.
82.	16, 22, 54.
83.	16, 23, 24, 25.
84.	16, 23, 24, 26, 111
85.	16, 25
86.	16, 43.
87.	16.
88.	16, 25.
89.	25.
90.	25.
91.	14, 26.
92.	77.
93.	16, 26, 77, 86.
94.	13, 15.
95.	26.
96.	14, 26, 27, 68, 74, 75, 77.
97.	3, 16, 53, 79.
98.	53.
99.	53.
100.	53.
101.	11, 13, 16, 25, 53, 64, 70, 89, 97.
102.	13, 53.
103.	53.

RECITALS NO.	UNDER ARTICLES NO.
104.	13, 16, 53, 79.
105.	53.
106.	16, 53.
107.	13, 64.
108.	53, 64.
109.	11, 16, 25, 53, 62.
110.	6.
111.	6, 51, 52, 53, 64, 79.
112.	6, 16, 51, 52, 53, 64, 79, 93.
113.	6, 51, 52, 53, 64, 79, 90.
114.	15, 16, 25, 55, 72.
115.	10, 15, 55, 70, 73.
116.	16, 53, 55, 56, 64, 69, 70.
117.	16, 32, 40, 56, 64.
118.	16.
119.	16.
120.	16, 26.
121.	40, 41, 66, 67.
122.	15, 40, 41, 42.
123.	43.
124.	34, 43.
125.	30, 31, 43, 50.
126.	15, 30, 31, 37, 70.
127.	30, 39, 43.
128.	43.
129.	48.

RECITALS NO.	UNDER ARTICLES NO.
130.	74, 75.
131.	12, 13, 15, 26, 49, 71, 74, 75.
132.	13, 50.
133.	3, 5.
134.	5, 13, 26, 50.
135.	13, 25, 50, 56.
136.	16, 26.
137.	13, 26, 50.
138.	57, 58, 59, 70.
139.	43, 57, 58, 59, 62, 70, 76, 77.
140.	57.
141.	26, 57, 60, 61, 74, 75, 76.
142.	57.
143.	26, 43, 57, 58, 59, 62, 66.
144.	1, 62
145.	16, 62.
146.	17, 34, 63, 96.
147.	43.
148.	64, 66, 67, 69.
149.	66, 70, 74, 75.
150.	62, 66, 67.
151.	64, 68, 69, 78.
152.	84.
153.	28, 29, 70, 74, 75.
154.	70, 78.
155.	20, 72, 73.

RECITALS NO.	UNDER ARTICLES NO.
156.	70, 74, 75.
157.	13, 37, 77, 79, 81.
158.	16, 17, 18, 26, 72, 74, 75.
159.	20, 74, 75.
160.	64, 74, 75, 79, 83.
161.	30, 64, 66, 74, 75, 92.
162.	16, 64, 74, 75, 85, 89, 93, 99, 101.
163.	6, 51, 52, 64, 69, 79, 90.
164.	16, 64, 68, 92, 93, 94.
165.	56, 95, 96.
166.	8.
167.	38, 78.
168.	62, 99, 100.
169.	16, 99, 100.
170.	74, 75, 85.
171.	7, 86.
172.	87.
173.	6, 11, 13, 17, 43, 51, 52, 79, 97.
174.	5, 8.
175.	97.
176.	1.
177.	16, 113.
178.	16.
179.	6, 43, 99.
180.	-

APPENDIX C – GLOSSARY

Activation function: function that computes the output value of an artificial neuron based on its input values and its current connection weights.

Note: the output value may be continuous or discrete.[1]

Adaptive learning: learning strategy that consists in adjusting internal knowledge according to advice from an external knowledge source, or transforming newly acquired information according to existing knowledge.[2]

Adaptive neural network: neural network that is able to adjust its performance characteristics according to changes in its environment.[3]

Adaptive resonance theory network (ART network): neural network in which the learning algorithm updates the stored prototypes characterizing categories if the input pattern is sufficiently similar to one of them, or otherwise creates a new category with the input as prototype.

Note: ART networks implement a compromise between plasticity (the ability to learn) and stability (no erasure or corruption of existing knowledge).[4]

Adaptive training: speech training capable of modifying and updating a speech template to improve performance.[5]

Advanced Persistent Threat (APT): a group of cyber attackers with advanced skills and significant resources, capable of carrying out sophisticated cyberattacks, often characterized by a specific set of tools or technique.[6]

Adversarial attack: an adversarial attack aims to send to an AI system one or more malicious requests with the aim of misleading or altering its proper operation.[7]

Adversarial machine learning (AML): machine learning which consists of training a model on a dataset containing misleading or ambiguous data, so that it learns to discern such data.

Note 1: misleading or ambiguous data is often produced by another model.

Note 2: adversarial machine learning is used, for example, to improve the recognition of fake news video, or falsified images and texts.

See also: machine learning, fake news video.[8]

AI: see 'Artificial intelligence'.

AI audio generation: an operation that consists of producing or modifying audio content in response to a prompt, usually using a diffusion model.

Note: Automatic audio generation is used, for example, to compose musical works by imitating a given style or to produce a spoken utterance by imitating a particular voice.

See also: fake news video, prompt, diffusion model.

---

1 ISO 2382:2015, Information technology – Vocabulary, No. 2120683.

2 ISO 2382:2015, Information technology – Vocabulary, No. 2122998.

3 ISO 2382:2015, Information technology – Vocabulary, No. 2120668.

4 ISO 2382:2015, Information technology – Vocabulary, No. 2120665.

5 ISO 2382:2015, Information technology – Vocabulary, No. 2120747.

6 Revue stratégique de cyberdéfense – SGDSN, 12 February 2018, Annex 5 - Glossary.

7 ANSSI, 'Security recommendations for a generative AI system', Guide No. ANSSI-PA-102, 27 September 2024.

8 Commission d'enrichissement de la langue française (CELF) (French Language Enrichment Commission), 'Vocabulaire de l'intelligence artificielle' ['Artificial intelligence vocabulary'], Opinion NOR: CTNR2423171K, *JORF*, n° 0212, 6 September 2024.

Equivalent: audio generative AI.[9]

AI literacy: skills, knowledge and understanding that allow providers, deployers and affected persons, taking into account their respective rights and obligations in the context of Regulation (EU) 2024/1689, to make an informed deployment of AI systems, as well as to gain awareness about the opportunities and risks of AI and possible harm it can cause.[10]

AI model: an AI model refers to a neural network and its parameters (weights, bias).

Note: in a neural network, a weight is a power coefficient of the connection between 2 neurons, which is adjusted throughout the training phase. A bias is a constant linked to a neuron that allows for "compensation" in the calculation of the result.[11]

AI Office: the European Commission's function of contributing to the implementation, monitoring and supervision of AI systems and general-purpose AI models, and AI governance, provided for in Commission Decision of 24 January 2024; references in Regulation (EU) 2024/1689 to the AI Office shall be construed as references to the Commission.[12]

AI practitioners: all individuals or organisations that develop (including research, design or provide data for) deploy (including implement) or use AI systems, excluding those that use AI systems in the capacity of end-user or consumer.[13]

AI regulatory sandbox: a controlled framework set up by a competent authority which offers providers or prospective providers of AI systems the possibility to develop, train, validate and test, where appropriate in real-world conditions, an innovative AI system, pursuant to a sandbox plan for a limited time under regulatory supervision.[14]

AI system impact assessment: formal, documented process by which the impacts on individuals, groups of individuals, or both, and societies are identified, evaluated and addressed by an organization developing, providing or using products or services utilizing artificial intelligence.[15]

AI system's life cycle:

1. AI system lifecycle phases involve:
   - (i) 'design, data and models'; which is a context-dependent sequence encompassing planning and design, data collection and processing, as well as model building;
   - (ii) 'verification and validation';
   - (iii) 'deployment'; and
   - (iv) 'operation and monitoring'.

---

9 COMMISSION D'ENRICHISSEMENT DE LA LANGUE FRANÇAISE (CELF) (French Language Enrichment Commission), 'Vocabulaire de l'intelligence artificielle' ['Artificial intelligence vocabulary'], Opinion NOR: CTNR2423171K, *JORF*, n° 0212, 6 September 2024.

10 Art. 3(56) of the Artificial Intelligence Act (AI Act): Regulation (EU) 2024/1689 of the European Parliament and of the Council of 13 June 2024 laying down harmonised rules on artificial intelligence and amending Regulations (EC) No 300/2008, (EU) No 167/2013, (EU) No 168/2013, (EU) 2018/858, (EU) 2018/1139 and (EU) 2019/2144 and Directives 2014/90/EU, (EU) 2016/797 and (EU) 2020/1828, ([2024] OJ L, 2024/1689, ELI: http://data.europa.eu/eli/reg/2024/1689/oj).

11 ANSSI, 'Security recommendations for a generative AI system', Guide No. ANSSI-PA-102, 27 September 2024.

12 AI Act, Art. 3(47).

13 AI HLEG, 'Ethics guidelines for trustworthy AI', 2019, p. 36.

14 AI Act, Art. 3(55).

15 ISO/IEC 42001:2023, Information technology – Artificial intelligence – Management system, 3.24.

These phases often take place in an iterative manner and are not necessarily sequential. The decision to retire an AI system from operation may occur at any point during the operation and monitoring phase.[16]

2. An AI system's life cycle encompasses its development (including research, design, data provision, and limited trials), deployment (including implementation) and use phase.[17]

Algocracy: a neologism referring to a form of governance that derives its legitimacy from the digital optimisation of social information management, potentially competing with democracy. A prominent example of algocracy would be the establishment of an individual social credit score based on data collected by a digital platform, as currently being experimented with in China.[18]

Algorithm:

1. An algorithm is a method of problem solving through a finite and non-ambiguous series of operations. More specifically, in an artificial intelligence context, it is the series of operations applied to input data to achieve the desired result.[19]
2. A set of symbols and procedures specific to a calculation. By extension, a mechanism that regulates the functioning of organised thought and is explained by representations similar to those used by mathematicians.[20]
3. Finite ordered set of well-defined rules for the solution of a problem.[21]
4. According to Donald Ervin Knuth, a pioneer of modern algorithms, it is 'a finite set of rules that gives a sequence of operations for solving a specific type of problem'. An algorithm has five important features (1) Finiteness ('An algorithm must always terminate after a finite number of steps'), (2) Definiteness ('Each step of an algorithm must be precisely defined; the actions to be carried out must be rigorously and unambiguously specified for each case'), (3) Input ('An algorithm has zero or more inputs: quantities that are given to it initially before the algorithm begins, or dynamically as the algorithm runs. These inputs are taken from specified sets of objects'), (4) Output ('An algorithm has one or more outputs: quantities that have a specified relation to the input'), and (5) Effectiveness ('An algorithm is also generally expected to be effective, in the sense that its operations must all be sufficiently basic that they can in principle be done exactly and in a finite length of time by someone using pencil and paper').[22]

Algorithmic language: artificial language for expressing algorithms.[23]

Alphanumeric data: data represented by letters and digits, possibly together with special characters and the space character.[24]

---

16 OECD Definition, https://oecd.ai/en/ai-principles.

17 AI HLEG, 'Ethics guidelines for trustworthy AI', 2019, p. 36.

18 J. Knight, 'L'algocratie, stade suprême de la bureaucratie?' ['Is algocracy the supreme stage of bureaucracy?'], Blog open-organization.com, 28 February 2018.

19 Glossary of the Montréal Declaration, 2018, https://montrealdeclaration-responsibleai.com/glossaire/.

20 Dictionary of the Centre National de Ressources Textuelles et Lexicales (CNRTL) (French National Center of Textual and Lexical Resources) created by the CNRS, http://www.cnrtl.fr/definition/algorithme.

21 ISO 2382:2015, Information technology – Vocabulary, No. 2121376.

22 D.E. Knuth, *The Art of Computer Programming*, Electronic version by Mathematical Sciences Publishers (MSP), First digital release, December 2013.

23 ISO 2382:2015, Information technology – Vocabulary, No. 2121754.

24 ISO 2382:2015, Information technology – Vocabulary, No. 2121040.

Analytic learning: explanation-based learning. Advanced form of deductive learning in which abstract or structured knowledge is derived from operational knowledge and from domain knowledge.[25]

Analytics (Data analytics): composite concept consisting of data acquisition, data collection, data validation, data processing, including data quantification, data visualization, data documentation and data interpretation.

Note: analytics is used to understand objects or events represented by data, to make predictions for a given situation and to recommend steps to achieve objectives. The insights obtained from analytics are used for various purposes such as decision-making, research, sustainable development, design and planning.[26]

Android: that which has human form. The term is old and much used in science fiction to designate a robot with a human appearance, either as a noun ('an android') or as an adjective ('an android robot'). Today, roboticists prefer the term anthropoid.[27]

Anthropomorphism: attributing characteristics of human behaviour or morphology to other entities such as gods, animals, objects or other phenomena. Essentialism is the attribution to a being or object of its own existence 'in essence', i.e. inherent in the subject in question.[28]

Artificial autonomous agent: software or physical machine capable of calculating decisions, individually, coordinated or not with other agents or with humans, with a view to achieving high-level goals that have been specified for them. Their introduction into fields such as the military, justice, medicine and autonomous transport raises many ethical questions.[29]

Artificial intelligence (AI):

1. Research into ways of endowing computer systems with intellectual capacities comparable to those of human beings.[30]
2. Branch of computer science devoted to developing data processing systems that perform functions normally associated with human intelligence, such as reasoning, learning, and self-improvement.[31]
3. Implementation of a number of techniques designed to enable machines to imitate a real form of intelligence. AI is being implemented in a growing number of fields of application.[32]

---

25 ISO 2382:2015, Information technology – Vocabulary, No. 2123013.

26 ISO/IEC 5259-1:2024, Artificial intelligence – Data quality for analytics and machine learning (ML) – Part 1: Overview, terminology, and examples, 3.12.

27 Futura-Sciences, definitions, https://www.futura-sciences.com/tech/definitions/robotique-androide-8427/.

28 C. de Ganay and D. Gillot, 'Pour une intelligence artificielle maîtrisée, utile et démystifiée' ['For controlled, useful and demystified artificial intelligence'], OPECST Report, n° 4594, *AN*, n° 4594 *Senate* n° 464 of 15 March 2017.

29 ETHICAA, 'Éthique et agents autonomes' ['Ethics and autonomous agents'], a white paper prepared with the support of the Agence Nationale de la Recherche (French National Research Agency) (ANR-13-CORD-0006), July 2018.

30 Dictionary of the Centre National de Ressources Textuelles et Lexicales (CNRTL) (French National Center of Textual and Lexical Resources) created by the CNRS, http://www.cnrtl.fr/lexicographie/intelligence.

31 ISO 2382:2015, Information technology – Vocabulary, No. 2121393.

32 Futura-Sciences, definitions, https://www.futura-sciences.com/tech/definitions/informatique-intelligence-artificielle-555/.

4. The construction of computer programs that engage in tasks that are, for the time being, more satisfactorily performed by human beings, because they require high level mental processes such as: perceptual learning, memory organization and critical reasoning.[33]
5. Artificial intelligence (AI) refers to the series of techniques which allow a machine to simulate human learning, namely to learn, predict, make decisions and perceive its surroundings. In the case of a computing system, artificial intelligence is applied to digital data.[34]
6. Artificial intelligence (AI) is the basis for mimicking human intelligence processes through the creation and application of algorithms built into a dynamic computing environment. Stated simply, AI is trying to make computers think and act like humans. Achieving this end requires three key components: computational systems; data and data management; advanced AI algorithms (code).[35]
7. Theoretical and practical interdisciplinary field concerned with understanding the mechanisms of cognition and reflection, and their imitation by hardware and software devices, for the purpose of assisting or replacing human activities.

   See also: artificial neural network, chatbot, deep learning, machine learning, reinforcement learning, supervised learning, unsupervised learning.[36]

Artificial Intelligence System or AI system (AIS):

1. An AIS is any computing system using artificial intelligence algorithms, whether it's software, a connected object or a robot.[37]
2. Artificial intelligence (AI) systems are software (and possibly also hardware) systems designed by humans[38] that, given a complex goal, act in the physical or digital dimension by perceiving their environment through data acquisition, interpreting the collected structured or unstructured data, reasoning on the knowledge, or processing the information, derived from this data and deciding the best action(s) to take to achieve the given goal. AI systems can either use symbolic rules or learn a numeric model, and they can also adapt their behaviour by analysing how the environment is affected by their previous actions.

   As a scientific discipline, AI includes several approaches and techniques, such as machine learning (of which deep learning and reinforcement learning are specific examples), machine reasoning (which includes planning, scheduling, knowledge representation and reasoning, search, and optimization), and robotics (which includes control, perception, sensors and actuators, as well as the integration of all other techniques into cyber-physical systems).

---

[33] Definition given by one of the pioneers of AI in 1956, Marvin Lee Minsky, See La rédaction Clubic, 'C'est quoi l'intelligence artificielle' ['What's artificial intelligence?'], *Clubic.com*, 16 September 2017.

[34] Glossary of the Montréal Declaration, 2018, https://montrealdeclaration-responsibleai.com/glossaire/.

[35] https://www.netapp.com/fr/artificial-intelligence/what-is-artificial-intelligence/.

[36] Commission d'enrichissement de la langue française (French Language Enrichment Commission), 'Vocabulaire de l'intelligence artificielle' ['Artificial intelligence vocabulary'], Opinion NOR: CTNR1832601K, *JORF*, n° 0285, 9 December 2018.

[37] Glossary of the Montréal Declaration, 2018, https://montrealdeclaration-responsibleai.com/glossaire/.

[38] Humans design AI systems directly, but they may also use AI techniques to optimise their design.

A separate document prepared by the AI HLEG and elaborating on the definition of AI used for the purpose of this document is published in parallel, titled 'A definition of AI: Main capabilities and scientific disciplines'.[39]

3. A machine-based system that is designed to operate with varying levels of autonomy and that may exhibit adaptiveness after deployment, and that, for explicit or implicit objectives, infers, from the input it receives, how to generate outputs such as predictions, content, recommendations, or decisions that can influence physical or virtual environments.[40]
4. An AI system is a machine-based system that, for explicit or implicit objectives, infers, from the input it receives, how to generate outputs such as predictions, content, recommendations, or decisions that can influence physical or virtual environments. Different AI systems vary in their levels of autonomy and adaptiveness after deployment.[41]
5. An AI system encompasses all the technical components of an application based on an AI model: implementation of this AI model, front-end services for users, databases, logging, etc.[42]

Artificial language: language whose rules are explicitly established prior to its use.[43]

Artificial neuron:

1. (neurode) primitive processing element in a neural network, with several inputs and one output, the output value of which is a nonlinear function of a linear combination of the input values with adjustable weighting coefficients.

   Note 1: artificial neurons are modeled according to the functioning of neurons in the nervous system and are interconnected in order to exchange messages.

   Note 2: each artificial neuron is a node of the neural network, that cooperates and communicates with other neurons. A neural network can also have input nodes which are not artificial neurons.[44]
2. (formal neurone) device with several inputs and one output, which simulates certain properties of the biological neuron.

   Note: the output value of the artificial neuron is a non-linear function, generally with a threshold, of a combination of input values whose parameters are adjustable.

   See also: artificial neural network.[45]

Artificial speech: (synthetic speech, artificial voice) speech generated by a functional unit.[46]

Assistance robot:[47]

1. *Physical assistant robot:* personal care robot that physically assists a user to perform required tasks by providing supplementation or augmentation of personal capabilities.[48]

---

39 AI HLEG, 'Ethics guidelines for trustworthy AI', 2019, p. 36.

40 AI Act, Art. 3(1).

41 OECD Definition https://oecd.ai/en/ai-principles.

42 ANSSI, 'Security recommendations for a generative AI system', Guide No. ANSSI-PA-102, 27 September 2024.

43 ISO 2382:2015, Information technology – Vocabulary, No. 2121380.

44 ISO 2382:2015, Information technology – Vocabulary, No. 2120626.

45 Commission d'enrichissement de la langue française (French Language Enrichment Commission), 'Vocabulaire de l'intelligence artificielle' ['Artificial intelligence vocabulary'], Opinion NOR: CTNR1832601K, *JORF*, n° 0285, 9 December 2018.

46 ISO 2382:2015, Information technology – Vocabulary, No. 2120709.

47 ISO 13482:2014: Robots and robotic devices – Safety requirements for personal care robots, 3.18.3, (Expected to be replaced by ISO/DIS 13482).

48 ISO 13482:2014: Robots and robotic devices – Safety requirements for personal care robots, 3.15, (Expected to be replaced by ISO/DIS 13482).

2. *Restraint type physical assistant robot:* physical assistant robot that is fastened to a human during use. Example: this includes wearable suits or non-medical physical assistance exoskeletons.[49]
3. *Restraint-free type physical assistant robot:* physical assistant robot that is not fastened to a human during use.

   Note: this allows free holding/releasing of the robot by the human in order to control or stop the physical assistance. Examples include power assisted devices and/or powered walking aids.[50]

Asynchronous neural network: neural network in which the artificial neurons are not updated simultaneously but, for example, at random or in some organized sequence.[51]

Auditability: auditability refers to the ability of an AI system to undergo the assessment of the system's algorithms, data and design processes. This does not necessarily imply that information about business models and intellectual property related to the AI system must always be openly available. Ensuring traceability and logging mechanisms from the early design phase of the AI system can help enabling the system's auditability.[52]

Augmented reality (AR): augmented reality refers to a virtual interface, in 2D or 3D, which enhances reality by superimposing additional information.[53]

Authorised representative: a natural or legal person located or established in the Union who has received and accepted a written mandate from a provider of an AI system or a general-purpose AI model to, respectively, perform and carry out on its behalf the obligations and procedures established by Regulation (EU) 2024/1689 on artificial Intelligence.[54]

Autonomous vehicle:

1. A vehicle equipped with technologies that facilitate aspects of its operations. Examples range from systems which simply ease the driver's task (such as self-parking) to self-driving vehicles that do not require a driver. This is the difference between automated-driver-assistance systems (ADAS) and the fully autonomous.[55]
2. Vehicle equipped with devices enabling it to perform all or part of the driving tasks. This corresponds to a level of automation according to the SAE classification[56] between level 2 (partial driving automation) and level 5 (full driving automation). A driverless vehicle incorporates devices enabling it to perform all driving tasks with the highest level of automation.[57]

---

49 ISO 13482:2014: Robots and robotic devices – Safety requirements for personal care robots, 3.15.1, (Expected to be replaced by ISO/DIS 13482).

50 ISO 13482:2014: Robots and robotic devices – Safety requirements for personal care robots, 3.15.2, (Expected to be replaced by ISO/DIS 13482).

51 ISO 2382:2015, Information technology – Vocabulary, No. 2120653.

52 AI HLEG, 'Ethics guidelines for trustworthy AI', 2019, p. 36.

53 Futura-Sciences, definitions, https://www.futura-sciences.com/tech/definitions/realite-augmentee-realite-augmentee-3963/.

54 AI Act, Art. 3(5).

55 SAE International. *Taxonomy and definitions for terms related to on-road motor vehicle automated driving systems*, http://standards.sae.org/j3016_201401/ [accessed on 30 March 2018].

56 There are several classifications for vehicle automation levels, including the 5-level nomenclature defined by the American international organisation SAE International: *'Taxonomy and Definitions for Terms Related to Driving Automation Systems for On-Road Motor Vehicles' (J3016_202104, 30 April 2021)*. There are five levels, ranging from Level 1 (Driver Assistance) to Level 5 (Full Driving Automation), https://www.sae.org/standards/content/j3016_202104/.

57 Report to the President of the Republic on Order 2016-1057 of 3 August 2016 concerning the experimentation of driverless vehicles on public roads, *JORF*, 5 August 2016.

Autonomy: ability [of a robot] to perform intended tasks based on current state and sensing, without human intervention.[58]

Backdoor:

1. A backdoor is a Trojan horse hidden in software, an online service or an entire computer system that the user is unaware of.[59]
2. Concealed access, either software or hardware, enabling a malicious user to connect to a machine by stealth. A backdoor can also be the cause of an incorrect protocol implementation.[60]

Bayesian inference: logical approach used to calculate or revise the probability of a hypothesis. This approach is governed by the use of strict rules for combining probabilities, from which Bayes' theorem is derived.[61]

Bayesian network: mathematical tool for probabilistic graphical modelling and data analysis. It is used to represent acquired knowledge (knowledge representation model) or to discover knowledge in a context by analysing data (it is a machine for calculating conditional probabilities), in order to make decisions, diagnose, simulate and control a system.[62]

Belief: (artificial intelligence) statement about an entity of the real or conceptual world, whose validity is measured by a certainty factor.

Note 1: beliefs help derive a conclusion from incomplete knowledge.

Note 2: a belief having a high certainty factor may be considered as a fact.[63]

Bias: bias is an inclination of prejudice towards or against a person, object, or position. Bias can arise in many ways in AI systems. For example, in data-drive AI systems, such as those produced through machine learning, bias in data collection and training can result in an AI system demonstrating bias. In logic-based AI, such as rule-based systems, bias can arise due to how a knowledge engineer might view the rules that apply in a particular setting. Bias can also arise due to online learning and adaptation through interaction. It can also arise through personalisation whereby users are presented with recommendations or information feeds that are tailored to the user's tastes. It does not necessarily relate to human bias or human-driven data collection. It can arise, for example, through the limited contexts in which a system in used, in which case there is no opportunity to generalise it to other contexts. Bias can be good or bad, intentional or unintentional. In certain cases, bias can result in discriminatory and/or unfair outcomes, indicated in this document as unfair bias.[64]

Big data:

1. Extensive datasets – primarily in the data characteristics of volume, variety, velocity, and/or variability – that require a scalable technology for efficient storage, manipulation, management, and analysis.

---

58 ISO 8373:2021, Robotics – Vocabulary, 3.2.

59 Futura-Sciences, definitions, https://www.futura-sciences.com/tech/definitions/informatique-backdoor-2047/.

60 ANSSI, glossary, 'The CyberDic', https://cyber.gouv.fr/en/cyberdico.

61 Dictionnaire de Mathématique élémentaire, http://www.elemathique.com/inference_bayesienne.php.

62 C. de Ganay and D. Gillot, 'Pour une intelligence artificielle maîtrisée, utile et démystifiée' ['For controlled, useful and demystified artificial intelligence'], OPECST Report, n° 4594, *AN*, n° 4594 *Senate* n° 464 of 15 March 2017.

63 ISO 2382:2015, Information technology – Vocabulary, No. 2123792.

64 AI HLEG, 'Ethics guidelines for trustworthy AI', 2019, p. 36.

Note: big data is commonly used in many different ways, for example as the name of the scalable technology used to handle big data extensive datasets.[65]

2. Particularly voluminous sets of digital data produced by the development of new technologies, the storage and exploitation of which require high-performance IT tools.[66]

Biometric categorisation system: an AI system for the purpose of assigning natural persons to specific categories on the basis of their biometric data, unless it is ancillary to another commercial service and strictly necessary for objective technical reasons.[67]

Biometric data: personal data resulting from specific technical processing relating to the physical, physiological or behavioural characteristics of a natural person, such as facial images or dactyloscopic data.[68]

Biometric identification: the automated recognition of physical, physiological, behavioural, or psychological human features for the purpose of establishing the identity of a natural person by comparing biometric data of that individual to biometric data of individuals stored in a database.[69]

Biometric verification: the automated, one-to-one verification, including authentication, of the identity of natural persons by comparing their biometric data to previously provided biometric data.[70]

Bionics: science which aims to improve technology (particularly electronics) by taking advantage of the study of certain biological processes observed in living beings.[71]

Blockchain:

1. A method of recording continuously produced data in the form of blocks linked together in the chronological order of their validation, each block and its sequence being protected against any modification.

   Note: the blockchain is used in particular in the field of cybercurrency, where it fulfils the function of a public register of transactions.[72]

2. A register that can be used to establish traceability for all kinds of products and services. Blockchain can also be used to guarantee the application of smart contracts, programmes that automatically execute the terms of a contract.[73]

Boltzmann machine: totally connected network having both visible neurons and hidden neurons that are cyclically updated according to a probability distribution.

Note 1: during learning, some visible neurons are clamped onto specific states.

---

65 ISO/IEC DIS 20546, Information technology – Big data – Overview and vocabulary, 3.1.2.

66 Conseil d'État, *Puissance publique et plateformes numériques: accompagner l'"uberisation'*, rapport annuel 2017 [Conseil d'État, Annual study, *Public authority and digital platforms: supporting 'uberisation'*].

67 AI Act, Art. 3(40).

68 AI Act, Art. 3(34).

69 AI Act, Art. 3(35).

70 AI Act, Art. 3(36).

71 Dictionary of the Centre National de Ressources Textuelles et Lexicales (CNRTL) (French National Center of Textual and Lexical Resources) created by the CNRS, http://www.cnrtl.fr/lexicographie/bionique.

72 Commission d'enrichissement de la langue française (CELF) (French Language Enrichment Commission), 'Vocabulaire de l'informatique' ['Computer vocabulary'], Opinion NOR: CTNR1713838K, *JORF*, 23 May 2017.

73 Futura-Sciences, definitions, https://www.futura-sciences.com/tech/questions-reponses/internet-revolution-blockchain-definition-fonctionnement-perspectives-7145/.

Note 2: there is some formal equivalence between statistical thermodynamics and the dynamic behaviour of the Boltzmann machine.[74]

Botnet: networks of machines (computers, mobile phones, tablets, etc.) that have been infected by malicious software enabling them to be controlled remotely (these are known as zombie machines).[75]

CE marking: a marking by which a provider indicates that an AI system is in conformity with the requirements set out in Chapter III, Section 2 of Regulation (EU) 2024/1689 on artificial Intelligence and other applicable Union harmonisation legislation providing for its affixing.[76]

CERT (Computer Emergency Response Team): incident response team dedicated to computer security incidents, intended for companies or government departments, but whose information is generally accessible to all.

Certification: (of product or service) activity whereby a body, distinct from the manufacturer, importer, seller, service provider or customer, attests that a product, a service or a combination of products and services complies with the characteristics described in a certification reference document. The certification reference document is a technical document defining the characteristics that a product, a service or a combination of products and services must have, and the procedures for checking compliance with these characteristics. The certification reference document is drawn up by the certification body, which gathers the views of interested parties.[77]

Chatbot:

1. A chatbot, also known as a 'conversational agent', is a computer programme capable of simulating a conversation with one or more humans by voice or text exchange. This tool is now widely used on the Internet by the customer services departments of brands and online retailers, via instant messaging.[78]
2. Software specialising in natural language dialogue with a human, capable in particular of answering questions or triggering the execution of tasks.

   Note 1: a chatbot can be integrated into a terminal or a connected device.

   Note 2: chatbots are used, for example, in sales techniques, search engines and home automation.

   Note 3: the expression 'conversational agent' is also used, but is not recommended.

   See also: agent, machine learning, artificial intelligence.[79]
3. A chatbot is an AI system that can converse with its user in a natural language.[80]

Cobotics: collaborative robotics between robot and human being.

---

[74] ISO 2382:2015, Information technology – Vocabulary, No. 2120664.

[75] Ministère de l'Intérieur, DMISC, *État de la menace liée au numérique en 2018*, [*2018 Digital Threat Landscape*], June 2018.

[76] AI Act, Art. 3(24).

[77] Code de la consommation [French Consumer Code], Art. L. 433-3.

[78] Futura-Sciences, definitions, https://www.futura-sciences.com/tech/definitions/internet-chatbot-15778/.

[79] Commission d'enrichissement de la langue française (French Language Enrichment Commission), 'Vocabulaire de l'intelligence artificielle' ['Artificial intelligence vocabulary'], Opinion NOR: CTNR1832601K, *JORF*, n° 0285, 9 December 2018.

[80] Glossary of the Montréal Declaration, 2018, https://montrealdeclaration-responsibleai.com/glossaire/.

Cognitive: all the functions of the mind (memory, language, decision-making, etc.).[81]

Cognitive modeling: modeling of human perception, action, memory, and reasoning in terms of information processing.[82]

Cognitive science (Cognitivism): interdisciplinary knowledge field, whose stated objective is to discover the representational and computational capacities of the mind and their structural and functional representation in the brain.

Note: cognitive science deals with the symbol-processing nature of cognition and encompasses disciplines as diverse as psychology, computer science, linguistics, anthropology, philosophy, education, mathematics, engineering, physiology, and neuroscience.[83]

Collaborative robot: a robot designed for direct interaction with a human within a defined collaborative workspace.[84]

Collaborative workspace: shared workspace in which the robot and the worker carry out complementary tasks, working on the same part, either simultaneously, in direct collaboration, or alternately, in indirect collaboration.[85]

Common specification: a set of technical specifications as defined in Article 2, point (4) of Regulation (EU) No 1025/2012, providing means to comply with certain requirements established under Regulation (EU) 2024/1689 on artificial intelligence.[86]

Competitive learning: learning in which artificial neurons compete for the right to respond to a given subset of input patterns.

Note: the response of a neuron to an input pattern tends to inhibit other neurons.[87]

Computer-supported collaborative learning: ICT-supported collaborative learning. Activities involving resources, tasks or support systems (human or otherwise), facilitated by Information and Communication Technologies (ICT), that contribute to the effect of collaborative learning.[88]

Concept learning: building a concept representation by applying existing knowledge to new information in order to derive new knowledge and store it for subsequent use.

Note: concept learning may involve an interaction between the version space and the example space of that concept. This interaction may in turn involve reformulation or transformation of initial assertions, experimentation, and selection of tentative examples.[89]

Conceptual schema language: database language, parsable by a computer as well as by a human being, containing all linguistic constructs necessary to express propositions and their manipulation in terms of action descriptions, command conditions, etc.[90]

---

81 Glossary of the Fédération pour la recherche sur le cerveau (FRC) [Federation for Brain Research], http://www.frcneurodon.org/comprendre-le-cerveau/glossaire/.

82 ISO 2382:2015, Information technology – Vocabulary, No. 2123778.

83 ISO 2382:2015, Information technology – Vocabulary, No. 2122976.

84 ISO 10218-2:2011 standard, Robots and robotic devices – Safety requirements for industrial robots – Part 1: Robots. This standard has been withdrawn and replaced by ISO 10218-2:2025 standards Robotics – Safety requirements – Part 1: Industrial robots. However, it should be emphasized that the term 'collaborative robot' is not used in ISO 10218-2:2025.

85 Ministère du travail, *Guide de prévention à destination des fabricants et des utilisateurs pour la mise en œuvre des applications collaboratives robotisées* ['Prevention guide for manufacturers and users of collaborative robotic applications'], 2017.

86 AI Act, Art. 3(28).

87 ISO 2382:2015, Information technology – Vocabulary, No. 2120682.

88 ISO 2382:2015, Information technology – Vocabulary, No. 2178046.

89 ISO 2382:2015, Information technology – Vocabulary, No. 2122972.

90 ISO 2382:2015, Information technology – Vocabulary, No. 2121508.

Conformity: fulfilment of a requirement.[91]

Conformity assessment: the process of demonstrating whether the requirements set out in Chapter III, Section 2 of Regulation (EU) 2024/1689 relating to a high-risk AI system have been fulfilled.[92]

Conformity assessment body: a body that performs third-party conformity assessment activities, including testing, certification and inspection.[93]

Connected autonomous vehicle (CAV): a vehicle that incorporates wireless telecommunications systems enabling it to collect information that it can record, process, use and relay to other vehicles or send to the road infrastructure.[94]

Connected device: electronic equipment that can communicate with a smartphone, tablet, watch, computer or television. It can send and receive information via a wireless link, Bluetooth or Wi-Fi.[95]

Connection weight (Connection strength, Synaptic weight): coefficient that multiplies an input value of an artificial neuron before it is combined with other input values.[96]

Connectionism: (connection science) interdisciplinary approach to artificial intelligence where complex computations are carried out by a network of simple processing elements, each of which is connected to a great number of other elements, and which exchange simple messages, and where parallel processing occurs among a great number of such elements.

Note: connectionism is inspired by the operation of biological neural systems such as the human brain.[97]

Connectionist learning: learning through changes in the connection weights of artificial neurons in a neural network.[98]

Consumer Electronic Show (CES): since 1967, the world's largest trade fair for technological innovations has welcomed thousands of exhibitors from all over the world and hundreds of thousands of professionals. Originally held in New York, it is now held in Las Vegas. CES has been the scene of major announcements that have marked the history of consumer electronics (the video recorder in 1970, the DVD in 1996, high-definition TV in 1998, etc.).[99]

Corrective action: action to eliminate the cause(s) of a nonconformity and to prevent recurrence.[100]

---

91 ISO/IEC 42001:2023, Information technology – Artificial intelligence – Management system, 3.15.

92 AI Act, Art. 3(20).

93 AI Act, Art. 3(21).

94 INRIA, Livre blanc 'Véhicules autonomes et connectés, les défis actuels et les voies de recherche' [White Paper 'Autonomous and Connected Vehicles: Current Challenges and Research Paths'], May 2018.

95 DGCCRF, 'Objets connectés: les risques à connaître', Fiche pratique [Practical information sheet, 'Connected devices: Risks to be aware of'], 14 November 2017.

96 ISO 2382:2015, Information technology – Vocabulary, No. 2120672.

97 ISO 2382:2015, Information technology – Vocabulary, No. 2120620.

98 ISO 2382:2015, Information technology – Vocabulary, No. 2120677.

99 J. Colombain, 'Nouveau monde. Ce qu'il faut savoir à propos du CES 2018 de Las Vegas' ['New world. What you need to know about CES 2018 in Las Vegas'], https://www.francetvinfo.fr/replay-radio/nouveau-monde/nouveau-monde-ce-quil-faut-savoir-a-propos-du-ces-2018-de-las-vegas_2532573.html, 8 January 2018.

100 ISO/IEC 42001:2023, Information technology – Artificial intelligence – Management system, 3.17.

Critical infrastructure: critical infrastructure as defined in Article 2, point (4), of Directive (EU) 2022/2557.[101]

Crowdfunding: coined from crowd and funding. Crowdfunding is a mechanism for raising funds from the general public to finance a creative (music, publishing, film, etc.) or entrepreneurial project. It works most often via the Internet.[102]

Cyber defense: all the technical and nontechnical measures enabling a State to defend its essential information systems in cyberspace.[103]

Cyberbullying: moral or sexual harassment committed by means of an electronic communication network.[104]

Cybercrime:

1. (Cyber crime) Acts that contravene international treaties or national laws, using networks or information systems as a means of committing an offence or crime, or targeting them. Cyber crime does not necessarily use cyberattacks to achieve its ends, for example: telephone or email scams, phishing, FOVI, etc.[105]
2. All criminal offences committed in cyberspace.

   Note: a distinction is made between offences intrinsically linked to new technologies (dissemination of viruses, piracy, illegal copying of software or audiovisual works, etc.) and those for which cyberspace is simply a new place of expression and a new vector of transmission (apology for racism, dissemination of paedophile content, harassment, etc.).[106]

Cybersecurity:

1. The desired state of an information system, enabling it to withstand events originating in cyberspace that could compromise the availability, integrity or confidentiality of the data stored, processed or transmitted, and the related services that these systems offer or make accessible. Cybersecurity calls on information systems security techniques and is based on the fight against cybercrime and the implementation of cyberdefense.[107]
2. Safeguarding of people, society, organizations and nations from cyber risks.

   Note: safeguarding means to keep cyber risk at a tolerable level.[108]

Cyberspace: a communication space formed by the worldwide interconnection of automated digital data processing equipment.[109]

---

101 AI Act, Art. 3(62).

102 Guide du Routard du financement d'entreprise ['Company Financing Rough Guide'], 2016, available for download on the website of the Direction générale des entreprises (DGE) [French Directorate General for Enterprises].

103 ANSSI, glossary, 'The CyberDic', https://cyber.gouv.fr/en/cyberdico.

104 Commission d'enrichissement de la langue française (CELF) (French Language Enrichment Commission), 'Vocabulaire de l'innovation' ['Innovation vocabulary'], Opinion NOR: CTNR1832364K, *JORF*, 7 December 2018.

105 ANSSI, glossary, 'The CyberDic', https://cyber.gouv.fr/en/cyberdico.

106 Commission d'enrichissement de la langue française (CELF) (French Language Enrichment Commission), 'Vocabulaire du droit' ['Legal vocabulary'], Opinion NOR: CTNR1832360K, *JORF*, n° 0283, 7 December 2018.

107 ANSSI, glossary, 'The CyberDic', https://cyber.gouv.fr/en/cyberdico.

108 ISO/IEC 27032:2023, Cybersecurity – Guidelines for Internet security, 3.6.

109 ANSSI, glossary, 'The CyberDic', https://cyber.gouv.fr/en/cyberdico.

Cyberterrorism: all cyber attacks of a terrorist nature that are primarily aimed at a State or group of States, an operator of critical national infrastructures, a company, an institution or a public authority.[110]

Cyborg: Human being with capabilities modified by cybernetic devices (etymologically, the term is a contraction of cybernetic organism). It is used in science fiction to refer to humans enhanced by technology.[111]

Data: re-interpretable representation of information in a formalized manner suitable for communication, interpretation, or processing.

Note: data can be processed by humans or by automatic means.[112]

Data Acquisition and Archiving System (DAAS): DAAS refers to any computing system that can collect and record data. This data is eventually used to train AI systems or as decision-making parameters.[113]

Data mining: data mining also known as Knowledge Discovery in Databases (KDD), aims to extract knowledge from large quantities of data, using automatic or semi-automatic methods.[114]

Data processing: (automatic data processing) systematic performance of operations upon data.

Note 1: example: arithmetic or logic operations upon data, merging or sorting of data, assembling or compiling of programs, or operations on text, such as editing, sorting, merging, storing, retrieving, displaying, or printing.

Note 2: the term data processing must not be used as a synonym for information processing.[115]

Data science: extraction of actionable knowledge from data through a process of discovery, or hypothesis and hypothesis testing.[116]

Database: collection of data organized according to a conceptual structure describing the characteristics of these data and the relationships among their corresponding entities, supporting one or more application areas.[117]

Decision justifiability: an AIS's decision is justified when there exist non-trivial reasons that motivate this decision, and that these reasons can be communicated in natural language.[118]

---

110 Commission d'enrichissement de la langue française (CELF) (French Language Enrichment Commission), 'Vocabulaire du droit' ['Legal vocabulary'], Opinion NOR: CTNR1832360K, *JORF*, n° 0283, 7 December 2018.

111 Futura-Sciences, definitions, https://www.futura-sciences.com/tech/definitions/robotique-cyborg-8458/.

112 ISO/IEC 5259-2:2024 standard, Artificial intelligence – Data quality for analytics and machine learning (ML) – Part 2: Data quality measures, 3.1 [Source:ISO/IEC 2382:2015, 2121272].

113 Glossary of the Montréal Declaration, 2018, https://montrealdeclaration-responsibleai.com/glossaire/.

114 Dictionnaire de Mathématique élémentaire [Dictionary of Elementary Mathematics], http://www.statelem.com/exploration_de_donnees.php.

115 ISO 2382:2015, Information technology – Vocabulary, No. 2121276.

116 ISO/IEC DIS 20546, Information technology – Big data – Overview and vocabulary, 3.1.10.

117 ISO 2382:2015, Information technology – Vocabulary, No. 2121413.

118 Glossary of the Montréal Declaration, 2018, https://montrealdeclaration-responsibleai.com/glossaire/.

Deductive learning: learning by deduction. Learning strategy in which new knowledge is deduced from existing knowledge by means of truth-preserving transformations of assertions.

Note 1: deductive learning generally leads to specialization of existing knowledge.

Note 2: deductive learning includes knowledge reformulation, knowledge compilation, and other truth-preserving transformations.[119]

Deep fake: AI-generated or manipulated image, audio or video content that resembles existing persons, objects, places, entities or events and would falsely appear to a person to be authentic or truthful.[120]

Deep learning:

1. Deep learning is the branch of machine learning that uses artificial neuron networks on many levels. It is the technology behind the latest AI breakthroughs.[121]
2. (Deep structured learning, hierarchical learning) Machine learning that uses an artificial neural network made up of a large number of layers, each of which corresponds to an increasing level of complexity in the processing and interpretation of data.

   Note: deep learning is used in particular for the automatic detection of objects in images and in machine translation.

   See also: artificial neural network, machine learning.[122]
3. A type of artificial intelligence derived from machine learning, where the machine is capable of learning on its own, unlike programming, where it simply executes predetermined rules to the letter.[123]

Delegation: means that permits an object to assign servicing of a message to another object.[124]

Dependency: entity relationship or an attribute relationship that denotes that the existence of one entity or attribute is of interest only if another entity or attribute, respectively, exists.[125]

Deployer: a natural or legal person, public authority, agency or other body using an AI system under its authority except where the AI system is used in the course of a personal non-professional activity.[126]

Design language: specification language with special language constructs and, sometimes, verification protocols, used to develop, analyze, and document the design of hardware or software.[127]

DGCIS: in France, *Direction générale de la compétitivité, de l'industrie et des services,* which became, by decree of 16 September 2014, the DGE.

DGE: in France, *Direction générale des entreprises*, the new name of the DGCIS adopted by decree no. 2014-1048 of 16 September 2014, placed under the authority of the Ministry

---

119 ISO 2382:2015, Information technology – Vocabulary, No. 2123012.

120 AI Act, Art. 3(60).

121 Glossary of the Montréal Declaration, 2018, https://montrealdeclaration-responsibleai.com/glossaire/.

122 Commission d'enrichissement de la langue française (French Language Enrichment Commission), 'Vocabulaire de l'intelligence artificielle' ['Artificial intelligence vocabulary'], Opinion NOR: CTNR1832601K, *JORF*, n° 0285, 9 December 2018.

123 Futura-Sciences, definitions, https://www.futura-sciences.com/tech/definitions/intelligence-artificielle-deep-learning-17262/.

124 ISO 2382:2015, Information technology – Vocabulary, No. 2123792.

125 ISO 2382:2015, Information technology – Vocabulary, No. 2121447.

126 AI Act, Art. 3(4).

127 ISO 2382:2015, Information technology – Vocabulary, No. 2121788.

of the Economy, Industry and Digital. The main mission of this department of the administration is to develop the competitiveness and growth of French businesses and is based around several departments: a general secretariat, the industry department, the digital economy department, the tourism, trade, craft and services department, the competitiveness, innovation and business development department and the territorial, European and international action department.

Diagnostic: pertaining to the detection, analysis, or description of faults, failures, or mistakes.[128]

Diagnostic function: capability of a functional unit to detect problems and to identify the type of error.[129]

Diagnostic program: program that is designed to detect, locate, and describe faults in equipment or errors in programs.[130]

Differential encoding: encoding of a digital data stream in which each element except the first is represented as the difference in value between that element and the previous element.[131]

Differential Manchester encoding: binary phase encoding in which the time interval assigned to each bit is divided in half by a transition and the presence or absence of another transition at the beginning of this time interval determines the value of the bit, i.e. a '0' or a '1', respectively.

Note 1: the transition may occur between two states of a physical variable such as voltage, magnetic polarity, or light intensity.

Note 2: if the physical variable is electrical, this type of encoding is polarity-independent and is free of a DC component.[132]

Diffusion model: generative model obtained by machine learning, during which the statistical noise previously added to the training set data is eliminated and which produces new graphical or audio content.

Note: the prompt given to a model with statistical noise can be an image accompanied by a text specifying, for example, the application of a style or the addition of an element in the composition of the content to be produced.

See also: automatic audio generation, automatic image generation, generative model, machine learning, prompt.

Equivalent: diffusion probabilistic model, latent diffusion model (LDM), score-based generative model.[133]

Digital (adj.): pertaining to data that consist of digits as well as to processes and functional units that use those data.[134]

Digital activity: by digital activity we mean all actions taken by an individual in a digital environment, whether on a computer, a phone or any other connected object.[135]

---

128 ISO 2382:2015, Information technology – Vocabulary, No. 2123046.

129 ISO 2382:2015, Information technology – Vocabulary, No. 2122532.

130 ISO 2382:2015, Information technology – Vocabulary, No. 2122022.

131 ISO 2382:2015, Information technology – Vocabulary, No. 2125957.

132 ISO 2382:2015, Information technology – Vocabulary, No. 2124390.

133 Commission d'enrichissement de la langue française (CELF) (French Language Enrichment Commission), 'Vocabulaire de l'intelligence artificielle' ['Artificial intelligence vocabulary'], Opinion NOR: CTNR2423171K, *JORF*, n° 0212, September 2024.

134 ISO 2382:2015, Information technology – Vocabulary, No. 2121328.

135 Glossary of the Montréal Declaration, 2018, https://montrealdeclaration-responsibleai.com/glossaire/.

Digital commons: digital commons are the applications or data produced by a community. Unlike material goods, they are easily shareable and do not deteriorate when used. Therefore, unlike proprietary software, open-source software – which is often the result of a collaboration between programmers – are considered digital commons since their source code is open and accessible to all.[136]

Digital computer: computer that is controlled by internally stored programs and that is capable of using common storage for all or part of a program and also for all or part of the data necessary for the execution of the programs; executing user-written or user-designated programs; performing user-designated manipulation of digitally represented discrete data, including arithmetic operations and logic operations; and executing programs that modify themselves during their execution.

Note: in English, in information processing, the term computer is often used to refer to a digital computer.[137]

Digital disconnection: digital disconnection refers to an individual's temporary or permanent ceasing of online activity.[138]

Digital literacy:

1. The ability to understand and employ printed information in daily activities, at home, at work and in the community – to achieve one's goals, and to develop one's knowledge and potential.[139]
2. Ability to understand and master the internet, digital tools and information technologies.[140]
3. An individual's digital literacy refers to their ability to access, manage, understand, integrate, communicate, evaluate and create information safely and appropriately through digital tools and networked technologies to participate in economic and social life.[141]

Digital mediation: enabling people to understand and master digital technologies, the issues involved and how they are used, i.e. developing digital literacy for everyone so that they can take action in the digital society. This is achieved by providing qualified, local support to individuals and groups (residents, associations, businesses, pupils, students, parents, professionals, etc.) in lifelong learning situations that facilitate both the appropriation of techniques for using digital tools and the dissemination of the knowledge thus acquired. It therefore serves, in particular, digital inclusion and fosters cooperation useful for achievements and innovations in favour of the common good.[142]

Disruptive innovation: an innovation that fundamentally changes a product or service, a production process, a marketing technique or the way a company is organised.

Note: a disruptive innovation fundamentally transforms a market.

---

136 Glossary of the Montréal Declaration, 2018, https://montrealdeclaration-responsibleai.com/glossaire/.

137 ISO 2382:2015, Information technology – Vocabulary, No. 2121340.

138 Glossary of the Montréal Declaration, 2018, https://montrealdeclaration-responsibleai.com/glossaire/.

139 OECD, 'Literacy in the Information Age', 2000, available at https://doi.org/10.1787/9789264181762-en.

140 Les Cahiers de l'inclusion numérique, 'Digital literacy', *Inclusion Numerique.fr*, Cahier n° 1, 17 November 2014.

141 Glossary of the Montréal Declaration, 2018, https://montrealdeclaration-responsibleai.com/glossaire/.

142 http://www.mediation-numerique.fr.

See also: incremental innovation, innovation pull, innovation push, open innovation, reverse innovation, sustaining innovation.[143]

Distributed data processing: data processing in which the performance of operations is dispersed among the nodes in a computer network.[144]

Note: DDP needs collective cooperation that is achieved by data communication among the nodes.

Distributor: a natural or legal person in the supply chain, other than the provider or the importer, that makes an AI system available on the Union market.[145]

Downstream provider: a provider of an AI system, including a general-purpose AI system, which integrates an AI model, regardless of whether the AI model is provided by themselves and vertically integrated or provided by another entity based on contractual relations.[146]

Drone: remotely piloted aircraft which circulates without a person on board. To be distinguished from the leisure drone 'model aircrafts', which is a remotely piloted aircraft used solely for recreation or competition purposes by a remote pilot, within the pilot's direct line of sight, who is at all times able to directly control its course to avoid obstacles and other aircrafts.[147]

Dynamically programmable connection: neural connection whose connection weight may be modified dynamically.[148]

Emotion recognition system: an AI system for the purpose of identifying or inferring emotions or intentions of natural persons on the basis of their biometric data.[149]

Entity: (databases) any concrete or abstract thing that exists, did exist, or might exist, including associations among these things.

Note 1: examples: a person, an object, an event, an idea, a process, etc.

Note 2: an entity exists whether data about it are available or not.[150]

Ethical AI: ethical AI is used to indicate the development, deployment and use of AI that ensures compliance with ethical norms, including fundamental rights as special moral entitlements, ethical principles and related core values. It is the second of the three core elements necessary for achieving Trustworthy AI.[151]

Ethics:[152]

1. Science that deals with the principles that regulate moral action and conduct.[153]

---

143 Commission d'enrichissement de la langue française (CELF) (French Language Enrichment Commission), 'Vocabulaire de l'innovation' ['Innovation vocabulary'], Opinion NOR: CTNR1832364K, *JORF*, 7 December 2018.

144 ISO 2382:2015, Information technology – Vocabulary, No. 2120540.

145 AI Act, Art. 3(7).

146 AI Act, Art. 3(68).

147 French Order of 11 April 2012 relating to the design of unmanned civil aircraft, the conditions for their use and the skills required of those using them (NOR: DEVA1206042A) (Repealed).

148 ISO 2382:2015, Information technology – Vocabulary, No. 2120673.

149 AI Act, Art. 3(39).

150 ISO 2382:2015, Information technology – Vocabulary, No. 2121433.

151 AI HLEG, 'Ethics guidelines for trustworthy AI', 2019, p. 37.

152 See also 'Ethical AI'.

153 Dictionary of the Centre National de Ressources Textuelles et Lexicales (CNRTL) (French National Center of Textual and Lexical Resources) created by the CNRS, http://www.cnrtl.fr/definition/ethique.

2. Ethics is an academic discipline which is a subfield of philosophy. In general terms, it deals with questions like 'What is a good action?', 'What is the value of a human life?', 'What is justice?', or 'What is the good life?'. In academic ethics, there are four major fields of research:
   (i) meta-ethics, mostly concerning the meaning and reference of normative sentence, and the question how their truth values can be determined (if they have any);
   (ii) normative ethics, the practical means of determining a moral course of action by examining the standards for right and wrong action and assigning a value to specific actions;
   (iii) descriptive ethics, which aims at an empirical investigation of people's moral behaviour and beliefs; and
   (iv) applied ethics, concerning what we are obligated (or permitted) to do in a specific (often historically new) situation or a particular domain of (often historically unprecedented) possibilities for action. Applied ethics deals with real-life situations, where decisions have to be made under time-pressure, and often limited rationality. AI Ethics is generally viewed as an example of applied ethics and focuses on the normative issues raised by the design, development, implementation and use of AI.

   Within ethical discussions, the terms 'moral' and 'ethical' are often used. The term 'moral' refers to the concrete, factual patterns of behaviour, the customs, and conventions that can be found in specific cultures, groups, or individuals at a certain time. The term 'ethical' refers to an evaluative assessment of such concrete actions and behaviours from a systematic, academic perspective.[154]

EuroHPC supercomputer: any computing system fully owned by the Joint Undertaking or co-owned with other Participating States or a consortium of private partners; it can be a classical supercomputer (high-end supercomputer, industrial-grade supercomputer, or mid-range supercomputer), a hybrid classical-quantum computer, a quantum computer or a quantum simulator.[155]

Exascale: a performance level capable of executing ten to the power of eighteen operations per second (or 1 Exaflop).[156]

Exascale supercomputer: a computing system with a performance level capable of executing ten to the power of eighteen operations per second (or 1 Exaflop) supporting applications that deliver high-fidelity solutions in less time and that address problems of greater complexity.[157]

Exoskeleton:

1. A kind of articulated, motorised 'carapace' that a human being can be equipped with.[158]
2. A structure external to the body that allows free or controlled movement with mechanical support to reduce or replace excessive muscular effort.[159]

---

154 AI HLEG, 'Ethics guidelines for trustworthy AI', 2019, p. 37.

155 Regulation EU 2021/1173 of 13 July 2021 on establishing the European High Performance Computing Joint Undertaking and repealing Regulation (EU) 2018/1488, Art. 2(9).

156 Ibid., Art. 2(10).

157 Regulation EU 2018/1488 establishing the European High Performance Computing Joint Undertaking, [2018] OJ L252/1, Art. 2(13). No longer in force. Date of end of validity: 7 August 2021; repealed by Regulation EU 2021/1173 of 13 July 2021.

158 CERNA-ALLISTENE, 'Éthique de la recherche en robotique' ['Ethics of research in robotics'], *November 2014.*

159 POBOT - Sophia-Antipolis Robotics Club, https://pobot.org/.

Expert system: computer system that provides for expertly solving problems in a given field or application area by drawing inferences from a knowledge base developed from human expertise.

Note 1: the term 'expert system' is sometimes used synonymously with 'knowledge-based system', though it is usually taken to emphasize expert knowledge.

Note 2: some expert systems are able to improve their knowledge base and develop new inference rules based on their experience with previous problems.[160]

Fact: (artificial intelligence) statement about an entity of the real or conceptual world, whose validity is generally accepted.

Note: a fact may be viewed as a belief having a high certainty facto.[161]

Feature-based speech recognition: speech recognition achieved by template matching of such distinctive features as pitch, formant frequencies, envelope contours, or noise levels.[162]

Filing system: any structured set of personal data which are accessible according to specific criteria, whether centralised, decentralised or dispersed on a functional or geographical basis.[163]

Filter bubble: the filter bubble (or filtering bubble) expression refers to the 'filtered' information which reaches an individual on the Internet. Various services such as social networks or search engines offer personalized results for their users. This can have the effect of isolating individuals (inside 'bubbles') since they no longer have access to common information.[164]

Fintech: company using innovative and disruptive operational, technological or business models to address existing or emerging issues in the financial services industry.[165]

First-generation language: programming language closely resembling assembly language and very dependent on the machine language of a computer.[166]

Floating-point operation: Any mathematical operation or assignment involving floating-point numbers, which are a subset of the real numbers typically represented on computers by an integer of fixed precision scaled by an integer exponent of a fixed base.[167]

Formal neuron: see 'Artificial neuron'.

Foundation model: the result of machine learning intended to be applied to a task generating data comparable to its training dataset

Note 1: a foundation model is generally obtained by applying supervised learning to a pretrained model.

Note 2: a foundation model is notably used in text generation, image generation and audio generation.

---

160 ISO 2382:2015, Information technology – Vocabulary, No. 2121400.

161 ISO 2382:2015, Information technology – Vocabulary, No. 2123791.

162 ISO 2382:2015, Information technology – Vocabulary, No. 2120761.

163 Regulation (EU) 2016/679 of the European Parliament and of the Council of 27 April 2016 on the protection of natural persons with regard to the processing of personal data and on the free movement of such data, and repealing Directive 95/46/EC (General Data Protection Regulation), [2016] OJ L119/1, Art. 3(6).

164 Glossary of the Montréal Declaration, 2018, https://montrealdeclaration-responsibleai.com/glossaire/.

165 Definition of France FinTech quoted by A. Clot, 'Quel avenir pour la FinTech française' ['What future for French FinTech?'], *Revue Banque & stratégie*, n° 339.

166 ISO 2382:2015, Information technology – Vocabulary, No. 2121759.

167 AI Act, Art. 3(67).

See also: audio generation, image generation, machine learning prompt, pretrained model, supervised learning, text generation, transformer.

Equivalent: deep generative model, generative mode.[168]

French Tech: all those who work in or for French start-ups in France or abroad. Entrepreneurs first and foremost, but also investors, engineers, designers, developers, major groups, associations, the media, public operators, research institutes, etc. who are committed to the growth of start-ups on the one hand and their international reputation on the other.[169]

Generalization: anonymisation techniques that consists of generalizing, or diluting, the attributes of data subjects by modifying the respective scale or order of magnitude (i.e. a region rather than a city, a month rather than a week).[170]

General-purpose AI model: an AI model, including where such an AI model is trained with a large amount of data using self-supervision at scale, that displays significant generality and is capable of competently performing a wide range of distinct tasks regardless of the way the model is placed on the market and that can be integrated into a variety of downstream systems or applications, except AI models that are used for research, development or prototyping activities before they are placed on the market.[171]

General-purpose AI system: an AI system which is based on a general-purpose AI model and which has the capability to serve a variety of purposes, both for direct use as well as for integration in other AI systems.[172]

Generative Adversarial Network (GAN): in a GAN, two antagonist networks are placed in competition to generate an image. They can for example be used to create an image, a recording or a video that appears practically real to a human being.[173]

Generative artificial intelligence or Generative AI (GenAI or GAI):

1. Generative AI is a subsection of artificial intelligence, focused on creating models trained to generate content (text, images, videos, etc.) from a specific corpus of training data.[174]

   Note: generative artificial intelligence is to be distinguished from artificial general intelligence (AGI) or general-purpose artificial intelligence (GPAI).
2. Category of artificial intelligence system using deep neural networks to generate content or control actions using probabilistic methods based on learning data.
3. A branch of artificial intelligence that uses generative models to produce textual, graphic or audiovisual content.

   See also: automatic audio generation, automatic text generation, automatic image generation, artificial intelligence, generative model.[175]

---

168 Commission d'enrichissement de la langue française (CELF) (French Language Enrichment Commission), 'Vocabulaire de l'intelligence artificielle' ['Artificial intelligence vocabulary'], Opinion NOR: CTNR2423171K, *JORF*, n° 0212, 6 September 2024.

169 http://www.lafrenchtech.com/la-french-tech/quest-ce-que-la-french-tech.

170 WP29 Opinion 05/2014 on Anonymisation Techniques, WP216 adopted on 10 April 2014, Annex.

171 AI Act, Art. 3(63).

172 AI Act, Art. 3(66).

173 Glossary of the Montréal Declaration, 2018, https://montrealdeclaration-responsibleai.com/glossaire/.

174 ANSSI, 'Security recommendations for a generative AI system', Guide No. ANSSI-PA-102, 27 September 2024.

175 Commission d'enrichissement de la langue française (CELF) (French Language Enrichment Commission), 'Vocabulaire de l'intelligence artificielle' ['Artificial intelligence vocabulary'], Opinion NOR: CTNR2423171K, *JORF*, n° 0212, 6 September 2024.

Genetic learning: machine learning based on an iterative classification algorithm which selects pairs of classifiers according to strength, and applies genetic operators to the pairs to create offsprings, the strongest of which replace the weakest classifiers in order to generate new, plausible rules when the available rules prove inadequate.

Note: the term 'genetic' comes from the field of natural genetics, where it is linked to heredity, variation of the species, and survival of the fittest.[176]

Governance: human-based system comprising directing, overseeing and accountability.[177]

Hacking:

1. Intentionally accessing a computer system without the authorization of the user or the owner.[178]
2. Gaining unauthorised access to devices by exploiting all the flaws and vulnerabilities of an element or group of elements, whether hardware, network or human.

Harmonised standard: a harmonised standard as defined in Article 2(1), point (c), of Regulation (EU) No 1025/2012.[179]

Hebbian learning: learning that increases the connection weight of a neural connection if the two artificial neurons are activated synchronously and decreases the connection weight if the neurons are activated asynchronously.

Note: in the simplest case, the amount of change of the connection weight is proportional to the product of the two output values.[180]

Heuristic learning: learning strategy developed from results of experimentation, of evaluation, or of trial-and-error methods.[181]

Hidden layer: layer whose artificial neurons do not directly communicate with external systems.[182]

Hidden neuron: artificial neuron that does not directly communicate with external systems.[183]

Hierarchical neural network (hierarchical artificial neural network): neural network consisting of several stages of subnetworks, in which the processing occurs from one stage to the next.[184]

High-end supercomputer: a world-class computing system developed with the most advanced technology available at a given point in time and achieving at least exascale levels of performance or beyond (i.e. post-exascale) for applications addressing problems of greater complexity.[185]

High-impact capabilities: capabilities that match or exceed the capabilities recorded in the most advanced general-purpose AI models.[186]

---

176 ISO 2382:2015, Information technology – Vocabulary, No. 2123021.

177 ISO/IEC 5259-5:2025, Artificial intelligence – Data quality for analytics and machine learning (ML) – Part 5: Data quality governance framework, 3.6 [SOURCE:ISO/IEC 38500:2024, 3.3].

178 ISO/IEC 27032:2023, Cybersecurity – Guidelines for Internet security, 3.9.

179 AI Act, Art. 3(27).

180 ISO 2382:2015, Information technology – Vocabulary, No. 212068.

181 ISO 2382:2015, Information technology – Vocabulary, No. 2122999.

182 ISO 2382:2015, Information technology – Vocabulary, No. 2120639.

183 ISO 2382:2015, Information technology – Vocabulary, No. 2120634.

184 ISO 2382:2015, Information technology – Vocabulary, No. 2120670.

185 Regulation EU 2021/1173 of 13 July 2021 on establishing the European High Performance Computing Joint Undertaking and repealing Regulation (EU) 2018/1488, Art. 2(11).

186 AI Act, Art. 3(64).

High-Performance Computing (HPC): branch of computing that deals with scientific and engineering modelling, and simulation tasks, so demanding that calculations cannot be performed using general-purpose computers. The machines used in HPC are often referred to as supercomputers. The next supercomputing frontier is exascale performance (i.e. at least 10^{18} or 1 billion calculations per second), which is expected to be reached around 2021-2022.[187]

Human-Centric AI: the human-centric approach to AI strives to ensure that human values are central to the way in which AI systems are developed, deployed, used and monitored, by ensuring respect for fundamental rights, including those set out in the Treaties of the European Union and Charter of Fundamental Rights of the European Union, all of which are united by reference to a common foundation rooted in respect for human dignity, in which the human being enjoy a unique and inalienable moral status. This also entails consideration of the natural environment and of other living beings that are part of the human ecosystem, as well as a sustainable approach enabling the flourishing of future generations to come.[188]

Human-machine interface (HMI): tangible or intangible devices that enable interaction between man and machine. The interface can be linked to the transmission of information or a command: this is the case of a computer keyboard or a volume knob. The interface can also be aimed at monitoring the command or its output: on the screen, which enables the machine to communicate with man, the commands entered are displayed as well as an image indicating that the volume has been increased or decreased. The command and its output can be closely linked, as is the case with tactile interfaces.

Human–robot interaction (HRI):

1. Information and action exchanges between human and robot to perform a task by means of a user interface (6.18). Example: exchanges through vocal, visual and tactile means.

   Note: because of possible confusion, it is advisable not to use the abbreviated term 'HRI' for human–robot interface when describing user interface.[189]

2. Action from human to machine or from machine to human: pressing a key on the keyboard, turning the volume control knob or touching the touch screen.

Hyper-connected: a communication capability of transferring data at 10 to the power of twelve bits per second (1 Terabit per second) or beyond.[190]

Image generation: operation that consists of producing or modifying images in response to a prompt, usually using a diffusion model.

Note: automatic image generation can be applied to moving images. This is known as 'automatic video generation'.

See also: fake news video, prompt, diffusion model.

Equivalent: AI image generation, automatic image generation, image2image, image-to-image, text2image, text-to-image.[191]

---

187 European Commission, Memo, MEMO/18/5901, 28 September 2018.

188 AI HLEG, 'Ethics guidelines for trustworthy AI', 2019, p. 37.

189 ISO 8373:2021, Robotics – Vocabulary, 3.15.

190 Regulation EU 2021/117 3 of 13 July 2021 on establishing the European High Performance Computing Joint Undertaking and repealing Regulation (EU) 2018/1488, Art. 2(14).

191 Commission d'enrichissement de la langue française (CELF) (French Language Enrichment Commission), 'Vocabulaire de l'intelligence artificielle' ['Artificial intelligence vocabulary'], Opinion NOR: CTNR2423171K, *JORF*, n° 0212, 6 September 2024.

Importer: a natural or legal person located or established in the Union that places on the market an AI system that bears the name or trademark of a natural or legal person established in a third country.[192]

Incremental innovation: innovation which improves a product or service, a production process, a marketing technique or the way a company is organised without fundamentally changing its characteristics or operation.

See also: disruptive innovation, innovation pull, innovation push, open innovation, reverse innovation, sustaining innovation.[193]

Incremental learning: multistage adaptive learning in which knowledge learned at one stage is transformed in order to accommodate new knowledge provided at subsequent stage.[194]

Independent car (or 'robot car'): motor vehicle equipped with an artificial intelligence system enabling it to be driven without any human intervention (total delegation).

Inductive learning: learning by induction. Learning strategy in which inductions are drawn from supplied knowledge, examples, or observations.[195]

Industrial robot: automatically controlled, reprogrammable multipurpose manipulator(s), programmable in three or more axes, which can be either fixed in place or fixed to a mobile platform for use in automation applications in an industrial environment.

Note 1: the industrial robot includes:

- the manipulator, including robot actuators controlled by the robot control;
- the robot control; and
- the means to teach or program the robot, including any communications interface (hardware and software).

Note 2: this includes any axes that are integrated into the kinematic solution.

Note 3: a mobile robot consists of a mobile platform with an integrated manipulator or robot.[196]

Industrial-grade supercomputer: at least a mid-range supercomputer specifically designed with security, confidentiality and data integrity requirements for industrial users that are more demanding than for a scientific use.[197]

Inference: reasoning by which conclusions are derived from known premises.

Note 1: in artificial intelligence, a premise is either a fact or a rule.

Note 2: the term 'inference' refers both to the process and its result.[198]

Inference engine: component of an expert system that applies principles of reasoning to draw conclusions from representations of information stored in a knowledge base.[199]

Informed consent: a subject's freely given, specific, unambiguous and voluntary expression of his or her willingness to participate in a particular testing in real-world conditions,

---

192 AI Act, Art. 3(6).

193 Commission d'enrichissement de la langue française (CELF) (French Language Enrichment Commission), 'Vocabulaire de l'intelligence artificielle' ['Artificial intelligence vocabulary'], Opinion NOR: CTNR1832364K, *JORF*, n° 0212, 7 December 2018.

194 ISO 2382:2015, Information technology – Vocabulary, No. 2123002.

195 ISO 2382:2015, Information technology – Vocabulary, No. 2123006.

196 ISO 10218-2:2025, Robotics – Safety requirements – Part 2: Industrial robot applications and robot cells, 3.1.1.2.

197 Regulation (EU) 2021/1173 of 13 July 2021 on establishing the European High Performance Computing Joint Undertaking and repealing Regulation (EU) 2018/1488, Art. 2(15).

198 ISO 2382:2015, Information technology – Vocabulary, No. 2123828.

199 ISO 2382:2015, Information technology – Vocabulary, No. 2123868.

after having been informed of all aspects of the testing that are relevant to the subject's decision to participate.[200]

Inheritance: (artificial intelligence) in a hierarchical knowledge representation, default acquisition of class characteristics by one or more of its subclasses.[201]

Input data: data provided to or directly acquired by an AI system on the basis of which the system produces an output.[202]

Input layer: layer whose artificial neurons receive signals from external sources.

Note: by extension, the term 'input layer' is also used for a group of source nodes.[203]

Input neuron: artificial neuron that receives signals from external sources.[204]

Instructions for use: the information provided by the provider to inform the deployer of, in particular, an AI system's intended purpose and proper use.[205]

Integrator: any person who designs, manufactures or assembles robotic systems for a user. The integrator generally assumes the legal status of a manufacturer within the meaning of Directive 2006/42/EC on machinery.[206]

Intelligibility: an AIS is intelligible when a human being with the necessary knowledge can understand its operations, meaning its mathematical model and the processes that determine it.[207]

Intended purpose: the use for which an AI system is intended by the provider, including the specific context and conditions of use, as specified in the information supplied by the provider in the instructions for use, promotional or sales materials and statements, as well as in the technical documentation.[208]

Interactive language: (conversational language) programming language that supports communication between a user and a data processing system in a conversational mode.[209]

Knowledge: (artificial intelligence) collection of facts, events, beliefs, and rules, organized for systematic use.[210]

Knowledge acquisition: process of locating, collecting, and refining knowledge and converting it into a form that can be further processed by a knowledge-based system.

Note: knowledge acquisition via human learning involves a human learner participating in a learning experience. Knowledge acquisition within knowledge engineering typically implies the intervention of a knowledge engineer. Knowledge acquisition is also an important component of machine learning, both with and without human intervention.[211]

---

200 AI Act, Art. 3(59).

201 ISO 2382:2015, Information technology – Vocabulary, No. 2123802.

202 AI Act, Art. 3(33).

203 ISO 2382:2015, Information technology – Vocabulary, No. 2120637.

204 ISO 2382:2015, Information technology – Vocabulary, No. 2120631.

205 AI Act, Art. 3(15).

206 Ministère du travail, *Guide de prévention à destination des fabricants et des utilisateurs pour la mise en œuvre des applications collaboratives robotisées* [*Prevention guide for manufacturers and users of collaborative robotic applications*], 2017.

207 Glossary of the Montréal Declaration, 2018, https://montrealdeclaration-responsibleai.com/glossaire/.

208 AI Act, Art. 3(12).

209 ISO 2382:2015, Information technology – Vocabulary, No. 2121777.

210 ISO 2382:2015, Information technology – Vocabulary, No. 2123771.

211 ISO/IEC 5392:2024, Information technology – Artificial intelligence – Reference architecture of knowledge engineering, 3.19 [SOURCE: adapted from ISO/IEC 2382:2015, 28 January 2009; replace notes].

Knowledge base (K-base): database that contains inference rules and information about human experience and expertise in a domain.

Note: in self-improving systems, the knowledge base additionally contains information resulting from the solution of previously encountered problems.[212]

Knowledge-based system (KBS): information processing system that provides for solving problems in a particular domain or application area by drawing inferences from a knowledge base.

Note 1: the term 'knowledge-based system' is sometimes used synonymously with 'expert system', which is usually restricted to expert knowledge.

Note 2: some knowledge-based systems have learning capabilities.[213]

Knowledge engineer: person who obtains knowledge from a domain expert and other knowledge sources and who organises it as a knowledge base.

Note: see also knowledge engineering.[214]

Knowledge engineering: discipline concerned with acquiring knowledge from domain experts and other knowledge sources and incorporating it into a knowledge base.

Note: the term 'knowledge engineering' sometimes refers particularly to the art of designing, building, and maintaining expert systems and other knowledge-based systems.[215]

Knowledge modelling: process that establishes and maintains the conceptual model for a knowledge base.[216]

Knowledge representation: process or result of encoding and storing knowledge in a knowledge base.[217]

Knowledge source: source of information from which a knowledge base has been created for a specific kind of problem.[218]

Knowledge tree: hierarchical semantic network represented by a tree-like directed graph.[219]

Large Language Model (LLM):

1. A category of generative AI models that can generate text close to natural human language and which are generally trained on a large dataset.[220]
2. Generative model which, from large volumes of textual data, calculates the probabilities of sequences of textual tokens with a view to the automatic generation of text or computer code.

   Note 1: the textual data in the training set of a large language model is generally harvested beforehand from the web and processed by transformers.

   Note 2: large language models are used in particular in chatbot, automatic speech transcription and speech synthesis.

---

212 ISO 2382:2015, Information technology – Vocabulary, No. 2121399 and No. 2123867.

213 ISO 2382:2015, Information technology – Vocabulary, No. 2123773.

214 ISO 2382:2015, Information technology – Vocabulary, No. 2123862.

215 ISO 2382:2015, Information technology – Vocabulary, No. 2123775.

216 ISO/IEC 5392:2024, Information technology – Artificial intelligence – Reference architecture of knowledge engineering, 3.18.

217 ISO 2382:2015, Information technology – Vocabulary, No. 2123776.

218 ISO 2382:2015, Information technology – Vocabulary, No. 123864.

219 ISO 2382:2015, Information technology – Vocabulary, No. 2123801.

220 ANSSI, Security recommendations for a generative AI system, Guide No. ANSSI-PA-102, 27 September 2024.

See also: automatic speech transcription, text generation, chatbot, data harvesting, foundation model, text-to-speech synthesis, text token, transformer.[221]

Law enforcement: activities carried out by law enforcement authorities or on their behalf for the prevention, investigation, detection or prosecution of criminal offences or the execution of criminal penalties, including safeguarding against and preventing threats to public security.[222]

Law enforcement authority:

(a) any public authority competent for the prevention, investigation, detection or prosecution of criminal offences or the execution of criminal penalties, including the safeguarding against and the prevention of threats to public security; or

(b) any other body or entity entrusted by Member State law to exercise public authority and public powers for the purposes of the prevention, investigation, detection or prosecution of criminal offences or the execution of criminal penalties, including the safeguarding against and the prevention of threats to public security.[223]

Layer: (artificial intelligence) in a hierarchically organized neural network, group of artificial neurons whose outputs may connect to neurons in a group toward the output of the network, but not to neurons in a group back toward the input of the network.

Note: artificial neurons of the same layer may have connections among them.[224]

Layered network: neural network whose artificial neurons are hierarchically organized in layers.

Note: a layered network may have a distinct group of source nodes in addition to the layers of artificial neurons.[225]

Learning algorithm: (neural networks) algorithm that adjusts the parameters of a neural network during learning.

Note: in general, a learning algorithm adjusts the connection weights.[226]

Learning strategy: (artificial intelligence) plan for the use of learning techniques prior to their application.[227]

Legal tech: companies using information technology in the field of law in order to offer innovative legal services. These companies have only recently emerged, hence their designation as 'start-ups', so that we also speak of 'legal start-ups'.[228] These companies are start-ups specialised in law. Other terms derived from business sectors have also appeared such as Fintechs for start-ups offering financial services and Medtechs in the medical field.[229]

---

221 Commission d'enrichissement de la langue française (CELF) (French Language Enrichment Commission), 'Vocabulaire de l'intelligence artificielle' ['Artificial intelligence vocabulary'], Opinion NOR: CTNR2423171K, *JORF*, n° 0212, 6 September 2024.

222 AI Act, Art. 3(46).

223 AI Act, Art. 3(45).

224 ISO 2382:2015, Information technology – Vocabulary, No. 2120635.

225 ISO 2382:2015, Information technology – Vocabulary, No. 2120642.

226 ISO 2382:2015, Information technology – Vocabulary, No. 2120676.

227 ISO 2382:2015, Information technology – Vocabulary, No. 2122970.

228 F. G'sell and P.P. Aïdan, 'Le marché français des services juridiques en 2020' ['The French legal services market in 2020'], and T. Wickers, 'Quelques leçons à tirer de l'essor de la legaltech' ['Some lessons to be learned from the rise of legaltech'], *Revue pratique de la prospective et de l'innovation* (RPPI), n° 1, October 2016.

229 Council of Europe, Ethical Charter on the use of artificial intelligence in judicial systems and their environment, CEPEJ (2018)14, 3 December 2018, p. 71.

Machine learning (ML) (Automatic learning):

1. Artificial language composed only of the machine instructions of a specific computer or class of computers.[230]
2. Automatic learning. Process by which a functional unit improves its performance by acquiring new knowledge or skills, or by reorganizing existing knowledge or skills.[231]
3. Machine learning is the branch of artificial intelligence that consists of programing an algorithm so that it can learn by itself. The various techniques can be classified into three major types of machine learning:
   - *in supervised learning*, the artificial intelligence system (AIS) learns to predict a value from entered data. This requires annotated entry-value couples during training. For example, a system can learn to recognize an object featured in a picture;
   - *in unsupervised learning*, AIS learns to find similarities among data that hasn't been annotated, for example in order to divide them into various homogeneous partitions. A system can thereby recognize communities of social media users;
   - *through reinforcement learning*, AIS learns to act on its environment in order to maximize the reward it receives during training. This is the technique through which AIS was able to beat humans in the game of Go or the videogame Dota2.[232]
4. Machine learning is a form of AI that enables a system to learn from data rather than through explicit programming. However, machine learning is not a simple process. Machine learning uses a variety of algorithms that iteratively learn from data to improve, describe data, and predict outcomes.[233]
5. Process by which a functional unit improves its performance by acquiring new knowledge or skills, or by reorganizing existing knowledge or skills.[234]
6. The process by which an algorithm evaluates and improves its performance without the intervention of a programmer, by repeating its execution on data sets until relevant results are obtained on a regular basis.

   Note 1: a machine learning algorithm includes a model whose parameters it modifies, usually with random initial values, according to the results observed.

   Note 2: machine learning is part of artificial intelligence.

   Note 3: machine learning is frequently used for natural language processing and computer vision, or for making diagnoses and predictions.

   See also: unsupervised learning, reinforcement learning, deep learning, supervised learning, chatbot, artificial intelligence, artificial neural network.[235]

Making available on the market: the supply of an AI system or a general-purpose AI model for distribution or use on the Union market in the course of a commercial activity, whether in return for payment or free of charge.[236]

---

230 ISO 2382:2015, Information technology – Vocabulary, No. 2121756.

231 ISO 2382:2015, Information technology – Vocabulary, No. 2123789.

232 Glossary of the Montréal Declaration, 2018, https://montrealdeclaration-responsibleai.com/glossaire/.

233 J. Hurwitz and D. Kirsch, 'Machine Learning For Dummies®', IBM Limited Edition, p. 4.

234 ISO 2382:2015, Information technology – Vocabulary, No. 2123789,

235 Commission d'enrichissement de la langue française (French Language Enrichment Commission), 'Vocabulaire de l'intelligence artificielle' ['Artificial intelligence vocabulary'], Opinion NOR: CTNR1832601K, *JORF*, n° 0285, 9 December 2018.

236 AI Act, Art. 3(10).

Manipulating industrial robot: automatically controlled, reprogrammable, multipurpose, manipulative machine with several degrees of freedom, which may be either fixed in place or mobile for use in industrial automation applications.

Note: the terms 'fixed robot' and 'mobile robot' are sometimes used to refer to manipulating industrial robots.[237]

Manufacturer: person who designs, manufactures new machinery or partly completed machinery covered by Directive 2006/42/EC relating to machinery applies and is responsible for its conformity with a view to its being placed on the market in his own name or trademark for his own use.[238]

Market surveillance authority: the national authority carrying out the activities and taking the measures pursuant to Regulation (EU) 2019/1020.[239]

Mechatronics: an approach aimed at the synergistic integration of mechanics, electronics, automation and information technology in the design and manufacture of a product with a view to increasing and/or optimising its functionality.[240]

Metadata:

1. Data about data or data elements, possibly including their data descriptions, and data about data ownership, access paths, access rights and data volatility.[241]
2. Data that define and describe other data.

Note: In the context of analytics and machine learning, metadata provides information on data items or data records such as their properties, structure, type, context, intended use, ownership, access and volatility.[242]

Microrobotics: an emerging field born from the intersection of robotics and microsystems.[243]

Mid-range supercomputer: a world-class supercomputer with at most one order of magnitude lower performance level than a high-end supercomputer.[244]

Mirror neurons: motor neurons which are activated in the brain of a monkey watching someone perform an action in which these neurons are generally involved. These same neurons are activated (they discharge action potentials) when the organism carries out this action itself.[245]

Mobile robot: robot able to travel under its own control.

Note 1: a mobile robot can be a mobile platform with or without manipulators.

---

237 ISO 2382:2015, Information technology – Vocabulary, No. 2122964.

238 Ministère du travail, *Guide de prévention à destination des fabricants et des utilisateurs pour la mise en œuvre des applications collaboratives robotisées* [*Prevention guide for manufacturers and users of collaborative robotic applications*], 2017.

239 AI Act, Art. 3(26).

240 NF E 01-010 standard, Mécatronique – Vocabulaire ['Mechatronics – Vocabulary'], November 2008.

241 ISO 2382:2015, Information technology – Vocabulary, No. 2121505.

242 ISO/IEC 5259-1:2024, Artificial intelligence – Data quality for analytics and machine learning (ML) – Part 1: Overview, terminology, and examples, 3.23.

243 Futura-Sciences, definitions, https://www.futura-sciences.com/tech/definitions/robotique-microrobotique-4268/.

244 Regulation EU 2021/1173 of 13 July 2021 on establishing the European High Performance Computing Joint Undertaking and repealing Regulation (EU) 2018/1488, Art. 2(18).

245 Futura-Sciences, definitions, https://www.futura-sciences.com/sante/definitions/medecine-neurone-miroir-15890/.

Note 2: in addition to autonomous operation, a mobile robot can have means to be remotely controlled.[246]

Mobile servant robot: personal care robot that is capable of travelling to perform serving tasks in interaction with humans, such as handling objects or exchanging information.[247]

Model card: set of information accompanying a pretrained model and defining the characteristics of its training data set, its parameter settings and the framework for its use.

See also: pretrained model.[248]

Monitored space: space observed by sensors available to the personal care robot (3.13) in which a safety-related object (3.21.1) is detected.[249]

Note 1: monitored space can reach beyond the maximum space (3.18.1) and can be defined by a collection of mobile sensors on the robot and stationary sensors in and outside the maximum space.

Note 2: this space can be static or dynamic depending on the personal care robot and its application.

Multilayered network: layered network having at least two layers.

Note: a multilayered network may have a distinct group of source nodes in addition to the layers of artificial neurons. In this case there is at least one hidden layer.[250]

Nanotechnologies: nanotechnologies and nanoscience are the study, manufacture and manipulation of material structures, devices and systems on a scale of less than about forty nanometres.[251]

National competent authority: a notifying authority or a market surveillance authority; as regards AI systems put into service or used by Union institutions, agencies, offices and bodies, references to national competent authorities or market surveillance authorities in Regulation (EU) 2024/1689 shall be construed as references to the European Data Protection Supervisor.[252]

Network and information system: any electronic communications network within the meaning of the French Post and Electronic Communications Code, any device or any set of interconnected or related devices, one or more of which, in execution of a program, perform automated processing of digital data as well as the digital data themselves, stored, processed, retrieved or transmitted by networks and devices, with a view to their operation, use, protection and maintenance.[253]

Network and information system security: the ability of networks and information systems to withstand, at a given level of confidence, actions that compromise the availability,

---

246 ISO 8373:2021, Robotics – Vocabulary, 4.15.

247 ISO 13482:2014: Robots and robotic devices – Safety requirements for personal care robots, 3.14 (Expected to be replaced by ISO/DIS 13482).

248 Commission d'enrichissement de la langue française (CELF) (French Language Enrichment Commission), 'Vocabulaire de l'intelligence artificielle' ['Artificial intelligence vocabulary'], Opinion NOR: CTNR2423171K, *JORF*, n° 0212, 6 September 2024.

249 ISO 13482:2014: Robots and robotic devices – Safety requirements for personal care robots, 3.18.3 (Expected to be replaced by ISO/DIS 13482).

250 ISO 2382:2015, Information technology – Vocabulary, No. 2120645.

251 Futura-Sciences, definitions, https://www.futura-sciences.com/tech/definitions/technologie-nanotechnologie-4783/.

252 AI Act, Art. 3(48).

253 French Law 2018-133 of 26 February 2018, *JORF*, 27 February 2018.

authenticity, integrity or confidentiality of data stored, transmitted or processed, and the related services that these networks and information systems offer or make accessible.[254]

Neural connection: (neural link, synaptic interconnection, synaptic connection) link between two artificial neurons that is defined by the source neuron, the destination neuron, and a connection weight.

Neural network (neural net, artificial neural network)*:*

1. Network of primitive processing elements connected by weighted links with adjustable weights, in which each element produces a value by applying a nonlinear function to its input values, and transmits it to other elements or presents it as an output value.

   Note 1: whereas some neural networks are intended to simulate the functioning of neurons in the nervous system, most neural networks are used in artificial intelligence as realizations of the connectionist model.

   Note 2: examples of nonlinear functions are a threshold function, a sigmoid function, and a polynomial function.[255]

2. A set of interconnected artificial neurons constituting a computing architecture.

   Synonym: formal neural network, neural network.

   See also: machine learning, supervised learning, artificial neuron.[256]

Neural-network model: abstract model of a neural network that can be simulated in software or implemented as a neurocomputer.[257]

Neurocomputer (Neural computer): special-purpose computer built as a neural network.

Note: the performance usually is measured in connection updates per second.[258]

Neurons: individual units carrying nerve messages through the nervous system. The neuron is the basic working unit of the brain. It is a specialised cell designed to transmit information to other nerve cells, muscle cells and glandular cells.[259]

Neuroscience:

1. All the sciences and disciplines which study the nervous system. The term neuroscience, which has come into widespread use in the last decade, refers to a variety of disciplines united by a common objective: knowledge of the nervous system, how it functions and the phenomena that emerge from this functioning.[260]
2. A multidisciplinary science that brings together researchers from all backgrounds: anatomists, biochemists, pharmacologists, geneticists, molecular biologists, etc. It is organised into eight major identifiable fields: developmental neurobiology, neuroanatomy, molecular and cellular neurobiology, neurochemistry and neuropharmacology, neuroendocrinology, clinical neuroscience, neurophysiology, cognitive science and theoretical neuroscience.[261]

---

254 Ibid.

255 ISO 2382:2015, Information technology – Vocabulary, No. 2120625.

256 Commission d'enrichissement de la langue française (French Language Enrichment Commission), 'Vocabulaire de l'intelligence artificielle' ['Artificial intelligence vocabulary'], Opinion NOR: CTNR1832601K, *JORF*, n° 0285, 9 December 2018.

257 ISO 2382:2015, Information technology – Vocabulary, No. 2120629.

258 ISO 2382:2015, Information technology – Vocabulary, No. 2120627.

259 Glossary of the Fédération pour la recherche sur le cerveau (FRC) [Federation for Brain Research], http://www.frcneurodon.org/comprendre-le-cerveau/glossaire/.

260 Centre National de Ressources Textuelles et Linguistiques (CNRTL), http://www.cnrtl.fr/definition/neurosciences.

261 Fédération pour la recherche sur le cerveau (FRC) [Federation for Brain Research], http://www.frcneurodon.org/comprendre-le-cerveau/a-la-decouverte-du-cerveau/les-neurosciences/.

Neurotransmitters: neurotransmitters are the language of the nervous system, enabling each neuron to communicate with the others.[262]

Nonconformity: non-fulfilment of a requirement.[263]

Nonlayered network: neural network whose artificial neurons are not organized in layers.[264]

Non-destructive testing (NDT): refers to all inspection techniques used to check the integrity of a part, without damaging it, either during production, use or maintenance.[265]

Non-personal data: data other than personal data as defined in Article 4, point (1), of Regulation (EU) 2016/679.[266]

Notified body: a conformity assessment body notified in accordance with Regulation (EU) 2024/1689 and other relevant Union harmonisation legislation.[267]

Notifying authority: the national authority responsible for setting up and carrying out the necessary procedures for the assessment, designation and notification of conformity assessment bodies and for their monitoring.[268]

Object: (artificial intelligence) physical or conceptual entity that may have one or more attributes.

Note: an object is usually associated with other stored objects by means of symbolic inferences or relations.[269]

Open data: open data is digital data that users can access freely. For example, this is the case for most published AI research results.[270]

Open innovation: Innovation process put in place by an organisation, which calls on various external partners, in particular through participative practices and the opening up of data.

Note: External partners may be customers, suppliers or individuals; they may, for example, form groups of product testers or work in collaborative workshops.

See also: collaborative workshop, disruptive innovation, incremental innovation, innovation pull, innovation push, open data, reverse innovation, sustaining innovation.[271]

Operator: A provider, product manufacturer, deployer, authorised representative, importer or distributor.[272]

Output layer: (decision layer) layer whose artificial neurons send signals to an external system.[273]

---

262 Glossary of the Fédération pour la recherche sur le cerveau (FRC) [Federation for Brain Research]: http://www.frcneurodon.org/comprendre-le-cerveau/glossaire/.

263 ISO/IEC 42001:2023, Information technology — Artificial intelligence — Management system, 3.16.

264 ISO 2382:2015, Information technology — Vocabulary, No. 2120643.

265 T. Outrebon, 'L'AFNOR enquête sur l'usine 4.0' ['AFNOR investigates Factory 4.0'], *Informatique News,* 28 December 2015.

266 AI Act, Art. 3(51).

267 AI Act, Art. 3(22).

268 AI Act, Art. 3(19).

269 ISO 2382:2015, Information technology – Vocabulary, No. 2123796.

270 Glossary of the Montréal Declaration, 2018, https://montrealdeclaration-responsibleai.com/glossaire/.

271 Commission d'enrichissement de la langue française (CELF) (French Language Enrichment Commission), 'Vocabulaire de l'innovation' ['Innovation vocabulary'], Opinion NOR: CTNR1832364K, *JORF*, 7 December 2018.

272 AI Act, Art. 3(8).

273 ISO 2382:2015, Information technology – Vocabulary, No. 2120620.

Output neuron: artificial neuron that sends signals to an external system.[274]

Overfitting: (machine learning) creating a model which fits the training data too precisely and fails to generalize on new data.

Note 1: Overfitting can occur because the trained model has learned from non-essential features in the training data (i.e. features that do not generalize to useful outputs), excessive noise in the training data (e.g. excessive number of outliers), a significant mismatch between training data and production data distributions or because the model is too complex for the training data.

Note 2: Overfitting can be identified when there is a significant difference between errors measured on training data and on separate test and validation data. The performance of overfitted models is especially impacted when there is a significant mismatch between training data and production data.[275]

Partially connected network (Diluted network): nonlayered network in which each artificial neuron is not necessarily connected to all the others, or a layered network in which each artificial neuron in a layer is not necessarily connected to all neurons in the adjacent forward layer.[276]

Path dependency: social mechanism through which technological, organizational or institutional decisions, once deemed rational but now subpar, still continue to influence decision-making. A mechanism maintained because of cognitive bias or because change would require too much money or effort. Such is the case for urban road infrastructure when it leads to traffic optimization programs, rather than considering a change to organize transportation with very low carbon emissions. This mechanism must be known when using AI for special projects, as training data in supervised learning can sometimes reinforce old organizational paradigms that are now contested.[277]

Pattern: (artificial intelligence) set of features and their relationships used to recognize an entity within a given context.

Note: these features may include a geometrical shape, a sound, a picture, a signal, or text.[278]

Performance level: the number of floating point operations per second (flops) that a supercomputer can execute.[279]

Performance of an AI system: the ability of an AI system to achieve its intended purpose.[280]

Person carrier robot: personal care robot with the purpose of transporting humans to an intended destination.

Note 1: it might possess a cabin and might be equipped with a seat and/or standing support (or similar).

---

274 ISO 2382:2015, Information technology – Vocabulary, No. 2120632.

275 ISO/IEC 5259-2:2024 standard, Artificial intelligence – Data quality for analytics and machine learning (ML) – Part 2: Data quality measures, 3.21.

276 ISO 2382:2015, Information technology – Vocabulary, No. 2120646.

277 Glossary of the Montréal Declaration, 2018, https://montrealdeclaration-responsibleai.com/glossaire/.

278 ISO 2382:2015, Information technology – Vocabulary, No. 2123798.

279 Regulation EU 2021/1173 of 13 July 2021 on establishing the European High Performance Computing Joint Undertaking and repealing Regulation (EU) 2018/1488, Art. 2(22).

280 AI Act, Art. 3(18).

Note 2: in addition to humans, transportation might include other objects, e.g. pets and property.[281]

Personal care robot: service robot that performs actions contributing directly towards improvement in the quality of life of humans, excluding medical applications.

Note 1: this might include physical contact with the human to perform the task.

Note 2: typical types of personal care robots include: mobile servant robot, physical assistant robot and person carrier robot.[282]

Personal data:

1. Personal data as defined in Article 4, point (1), of Regulation (EU) 2016/679.[283]
2. Personal data are those that help directly or indirectly identify an individual.[284]

Petascale supercomputer: a computing system with a performance level capable of executing ten to the power of fifteen operations per second (or 1 Petaflop).[285]

Pipame: in France, the *Pôle interministériel de prospective et d'anticipation des mutations économiques* (Interministerial centre for forecasting and anticipating economic change) is an interministerial body involving around ten ministries and public bodies (the ministries responsible for industry, ecology, agriculture, health, culture, communication, defence, higher education and research, the *Centre d'analyse stratégique* and Datar). The DGE provides the general secretariat.

Placing on the market: the first making available of an AI system or a general-purpose AI model on the Union market.[286]

Policy: intentions and direction of an organization as formally expressed by its top management.[287]

Post-market monitoring system: all activities carried out by providers of AI systems to collect and review experience gained from the use of AI systems they place on the market or put into service for the purpose of identifying any need to immediately apply any necessary corrective or preventive actions.[288]

Post-remote biometric identification system: a remote biometric identification system other than a real-time remote biometric identification system.[289]

Predictive justice: analysis of large amounts of judicial decisions by artificial intelligence technologies in order to make predictions for the outcome of certain types of specialised disputes (for example, redundancy payments or alimentary pensions). The term 'predictive' used by legal tech companies comes from the branches of science (principally statistics) that make it possible to predict future results through inductive analysis. Judicial

281 ISO 13482:2014, Robots and robotic devices – Safety requirements for personal care, 3.16 (Expected to be replaced by ISO/DIS 13482).

282 ISO 13482:2014, Robots and robotic devices – Safety requirements for personal care, 3.13 (Expected to be replaced by ISO/DIS 13482).

283 AI Act, Art. 3(50).

284 Glossary of the Montréal Declaration, 2018, https://montrealdeclaration-responsibleai.com/glossaire/.

285 Regulation EU 2018/1488 establishing the European High Performance Computing Joint Undertaking, [2018] OJ L252/1, Art. 2(6). No longer in force. Date of end of validity: 7 August 2021; repealed by Regulation EU 2021/1173 of 13 July 2021.

286 AI Act, Art. 3(9).

287 ISO/IEC 42001:2023, Information technology – Artificial intelligence – Management system, 3.5.

288 AI Act, Art. 3(25).

289 AI Act, Art. 3(43).

decisions are processed with a view to detecting correlations between input data (criteria set out in legislation, the acts of the case and the reasoning) and output data (formal judgment such as the compensation amount). Correlations deemed to be relevant make it possible to create models which, when used with new input data (new facts or precisions described as a parameter, such as the duration of the contractual relationship), produce according to their developers a prediction of the decision (for example, the compensation range).[290]

Pretrained model: the result of general-purpose machine learning performed on a large volume of data, which is intended to be reused in a wide variety of tasks, generally following transfer learning.

Note: a pretrained model is accompanied by a model card.

See also: automatic learning, transfer learning, pretrained model instructions.[291]

Privacy: freedom from intrusion into the private life or affairs of an individual when that intrusion results from undue or illegal gathering and use of data about that individual.[292]

Privacy protection: measures taken to ensure privacy.

Note: the measures include data protection and limitations on the gathering, combining, and processing of data about individuals.[293]

Process: set of interrelated or interacting activities that uses or transforms inputs to deliver a result.

Note: whether the result of a process is called an output, a product or a service depends on the context of the reference.[294]

Profiling: profiling as defined in Article 4, point (4), of Regulation (EU) 2016/679.[295]

Prompt: a generative model, generally formulated in natural language, which describes the task to be carried out.

Note: the prompt can take the form of a text to be completed, a question, instructions to be followed when producing the answer, or even one or more examples of expected results.

See also: automatic audio generation, text generation, image generation, large language model, foundation model.[296]

Provider: a natural or legal person, public authority, agency or other body that develops an AI system or a general-purpose AI model or that has an AI system or a general-purpose AI model developed and places it on the market or puts the AI system into service under its own name or trademark, whether for payment or free of charge.[297]

---

290 Council of Europe, European Ethical Charter on the use of artificial intelligence in judicial systems and their environment, CEPEJ (2018)14, 3 December 2018, p. 74.

291 Commission d'enrichissement de la langue française (CELF) (French Language Enrichment Commission), 'Vocabulaire de l'intelligence artificielle' ['Artificial intelligence vocabulary'], Opinion NOR: CTNR2423171K, *JORF*, n° 0212, 6 September 2024.

292 ISO 2382:2015, Information technology – Vocabulary, No. 2126263.

293 ISO 2382:2015, Information technology – Vocabulary, No. 2126377.

294 ISO/IEC 42001:2023, Information technology – Artificial intelligence – Management system, 3.8.

295 AI Act, Art. 3(52).

296 Commission d'enrichissement de la langue française (CELF) (French Language Enrichment Commission), 'Vocabulaire de l'intelligence artificielle' ['Artificial intelligence vocabulary'], Opinion NOR: CTNR2423171K, *JORF*, n° 0212, 6 September 2024.

297 AI Act, Art. 3(3).

Publicly accessible space: any publicly or privately owned physical place accessible to an undetermined number of natural persons, regardless of whether certain conditions for access may apply, and regardless of the potential capacity restrictions.[298]

Putting into service: the supply of an AI system for first use directly to the deployer or for own use in the Union for its intended purpose.[299]

Quantum computer:

1. A computing device that harnesses the laws of quantum mechanics to solve certain particular tasks using therefore fewer computational resources than classical computers.[300]
2. The equivalent of a classical computer, but which performs its calculations by directly using the laws of quantum physics, based on the superposition of quantum states. Whereas a classical computer manipulates bits of information, which are either 0s or 1s, a quantum computer uses qubits (quantum + bit; pronounced (/ˈkjuːbɪt/). A quantum computer can make calculations much faster than a classical computer.[301]

Quantum simulator: a highly controllable quantum device that allows to obtain insights into properties of complex quantum systems or to solve specific computational problems inaccessible to classical computers.[302]

Qubit: (contraction of quantum and bit) quantum state representing the storage unit for quantum information. It consists of a superposition of two basic states, conventionally noted |0> and |1>. A qubit state is made up of a linear quantum superposition of these two states. A qubit memory differs significantly from a classical memory in that a bit can only take the values 0 and 1, and only one at a time. A qubit does not have this restriction.[303]

Query: a query (or prompt) refers to the instruction in text form sent by the user to the AI system.[304]

Randomisation: anonymisation technique that consists of modifying the actual values to prevent linking between the anonymised data and the original values. This goal can be reached through a wide number of methodologies ranging from noise injection to data swapping (permutation).[305]

Randomly connected network: random network neural network whose artificial neurons are connected at random.[306]

---

298 AI Act, Art. 3(44).

299 AI Act, Art. 3(11).

300 Regulation EU 2021/1173 of 13 July 2021 on establishing the European High Performance Computing Joint Undertaking and repealing Regulation (EU) 2018/1488, Art. 2(24).

301 Futura-Sciences, definitions, https://www.futura-sciences.com/sciences/definitions/physique-ordinateur-quantique-4348/.

302 Regulation EU 2021/1173 of 13 July 2021 on establishing the European High Performance Computing Joint Undertaking and repealing Regulation (EU) 2018/1488, Art. 2(25).

303 Futura-Sciences, definitions, https://www.futura-sciences.com/sciences/definitions/physique-qubit-4349/.

304 ANSSI, 'Security recommendations for a generative AI system', Guide No. ANSSI-PA-102, 27 September 2024.

305 WP29 Opinion 05/2014 on Anonymisation Techniques, WP216 adopted on 10 April 2014, Annex.

306 ISO 2382:2015, Information technology – Vocabulary, No. 2120648.

Ransomware: malicious software or virus that blocks access to a system or data and demands payment of a ransom in exchange for restoring it to its original state. There are encrypted versions.[307]

Real-time remote biometric identification system: a remote biometric identification system, whereby the capturing of biometric data, the comparison and the identification all occur without a significant delay, comprising not only instant identification, but also limited short delays in order to avoid circumvention.[308]

Real-world testing plan: a document that describes the objectives, methodology, geographical, population and temporal scope, monitoring, organisation and conduct of testing in real-world conditions.[309]

Reasonably foreseeable misuse: the use of an AI system in a way that is not in accordance with its intended purpose, but which may result from reasonably foreseeable human behaviour or interaction with other systems, including other AI systems.[310]

Rebound effect: the rebound effect is the mechanism through which greater energy efficiency or better environmental performance of goods, equipment and services leads to an increase in use that is more than proportional. For example, screen size increases, the number of electronic devices in a household goes up, and greater distances are travelled by car or plane. The global result is greater pressure on resources and the environment.[311]

Recall of an AI system: any measure aiming to achieve the return to the provider or taking out of service or disabling the use of an AI system made available to deployers.[312]

Recurrent network: neural network in which the connections between artificial neurons form at least one feedback loop.

Note 1: examples: Hopfield network, Boltzmann machine.

Note 2: a nonlayered network is a recurrent network. A layered network is recurrent if there are connections between neurons within a given layer or connections from a given neuron to a neuron in a layer back toward the input.[313]

Red teaming: the practice whereby a 'red team' or independent group challenges an organisation to improve its effectiveness by assuming an adversarial role or point of view. It is particularly used to help identifying and addressing potential security vulnerabilities.[314]

Reinforcement learning: machine learning in which an external programme evaluates the successive results of the algorithm positively or negatively, the accumulation of results enabling the algorithm to improve its performance until it reaches a previously set objective.

Note 1: reinforcement learning is frequently used in robotics.

Note 2: the effectiveness of reinforcement learning has been demonstrated in certain strategic games such as Go.

---

307 Ministère de l'Intérieur, DMISC, *État de la menace liée au numérique en 2018*, ['2018 Digital Threat Landscape'], June 2018.

308 AI Act, Art. 3(42).

309 AI Act, Art. 3(53).

310 AI Act, Art. 3(13).

311 Glossary of the Montréal Declaration, 2018, https://montrealdeclaration-responsibleai.com/glossaire/.

312 AI Act, Art. 3(16).

313 ISO 2382:2015, Information technology – Vocabulary, No. 2120655.

314 AI HLEG, 'Ethics guidelines for trustworthy AI', 2019, p. 37.

See also: machine learning.[315]

Relational database: database in which the data are organized according to a relational model.[316]

Reliability: an AIS is reliable when it performs the task it was designed for, in expected fashion. Reliability is the probability of success that ranges between 51% and 100%, meaning strictly superior to chance. The more a system is reliable, the more its behavior is predictable.[317]

Remote Administration Trojan (RAT): malicious software allowing complete control of the infected machine (or remote administration tool when it is only an administration tool).[318]

Remote biometric identification system: an AI system for the purpose of identifying natural persons, without their active involvement, typically at a distance through the comparison of a person's biometric data with the biometric data contained in a reference database.[319]

Reproducibility: reproducibility describes whether an AI experiment exhibits the same behaviour when repeated under the same conditions.[320]

Restricted space: portion of the maximum space (5.13) restricted by limiting devices (6.21) that establish limits which will not be exceeded.[321]

Note: for mobile platforms, this volume can be limited by special markers on floors and walls, or by software limits defined in the internal map.

Reverse innovation: innovation designed in an emerging or developing country for the local market and then disseminated in developed countries.

Note: reverse innovation generally consists of offering products that are similar to those already available in developed countries, but for example more robust, easier to use and often manufactured at a lower cost.

See also: disruptive innovation, incremental innovation, innovation pull, innovation push, open innovation, sustaining innovation.[322]

Risk:

1. The combination of the probability of an occurrence of harm and the severity of that harm.[323]
2. Effect of uncertainty.

Note 1: an effect is a deviation from the expected – positive or negative.

Note 2: uncertainty is the state, even partial, of deficiency of information related to, understanding or knowledge of, an event, its consequence, or likelihood.

---

315 Commission d'enrichissement de la langue française (French Language Enrichment Commission), 'Vocabulaire de l'intelligence artificielle' ['Artificial intelligence vocabulary'], Opinion NOR: CTNR1832601K, *JORF*, n° 0285, 9 December 2018.

316 ISO 2382:2015, Information technology – Vocabulary, No. 2121470.

317 Glossary of the Montréal Declaration, 2018, https://montrealdeclaration-responsibleai.com/glossaire/.

318 Ministère de l'Intérieur, DMISC, *État de la menace liée au numérique en 2018*, ['2018 Digital Threat Landscape'], June 2018.

319 AI Act, Art. 3(41).

320 AI HLEG, 'Ethics guidelines for trustworthy AI', 2019, p. 37.

321 ISO 8373:2021, Robotics – Vocabulary, 5.14.

322 Commission d'enrichissement de la langue française (CELF) (French Language Enrichment Commission), 'Vocabulaire de l'innovation' ['Innovation vocabulary'], Opinion NOR: CTNR1832364K, *JORF*, 7 December 2018.

323 AI Act, Art. 3(2).

Note 3: risk is often characterized by reference to potential events and consequences, or a combination of these.

Note 4: risk is often expressed in terms of a combination of the consequences of an event (including changes in circumstances) and the associated likelihood (as defined in ISO Guide 73) of occurrence.[324]

Robot:

1. Mechanical device, usually programmable, designed to perform tasks of manipulation or locomotion under automatic control.[325]
2. Czech term derived from robota ('serfdom'), introduced in 1920 by the Czech writer Karel Čapek in the play 'R. U. R. (Rossum's Universal Robots)'; now commonly used to designate:

   (a) Programmed actuated mechanism with a degree of autonomy to perform locomotion, manipulation or positioning.

   Note 1: a robot includes the control system.

   Note 2: examples of mechanical structure of robots are manipulator, mobile platform and wearable robot.[326]

   (b) Actuated mechanism programmable in two or more axes with a degree of autonomy, moving within its environment, to perform intended tasks.

   Note 1: a robot includes the control system and interface of the control system.

   Note 2: the classification of robot into industrial robot or service robot is done according to its intended application.[327]

   (c) Any automatically operated machine that replaces human effort, though it may not resemble human beings in appearance or perform functions in a humanlike manner.[328]

   (d) A device that uses a microprocessor-based automatic control system to perform a specific task for which it has been designed in the industrial, scientific or domestic sectors.[329]

Robo-advisor: online wealth management service that provides portfolio management advice based on an automated algorithm without the use of human financial planners.[330]

Robot system:

1. (Industrial robot system) Industrial robot, end-effector(s)), any end-effector sensors and equipment needed to support the end-effector(s).

   Note: examples of equipment are vision systems, adhesive dispensing, weld control.[331]

---

324 ISO/IEC 42001:2023, Information technology – Artificial intelligence – Management system, 3.7.

325 ISO 2382:2015, Information technology – Vocabulary, No. 122963.

326 ISO 8373:2021, Robotics – Vocabulary, 3.1.

327 ISO 8373:2012, Robots and robotic devices – Vocabulary, 2.6. This standard has been withdrawn and replaced by ISO 8373:2021, Robotics – Vocabulary.

328 Encyclopaedia Britannica, https://www.britannica.com/search?query=robot.

329 Dictionary of the Centre National de Ressources Textuelles et Lexicales (CNRTL) (French National Center of Textual and Lexical Resources) created by the CNRS, http://www.cnrtl.fr/definition/robot.

330 Association française de la gestion financière, *La transformation des sociétés de gestion en "SGP 3.0: Intégrer le digital dans l'ADN de la société de gestion de portefeuille (SGP)* ['The transformation of asset management companies into "SGP 3.0": Integrating digital technology into the DNA of the asset management company'],, Guide, January 2017.

331 ISO 10218-2:2025, Robotics – Safety requirements – Part 1: Industrial robots, 3.1.1.3.

2. (Industrial robot system) System comprising:
   - industrial robot;
   - end-effector(s);
   - any machinery, equipment, devices, external auxiliary axes or sensors supporting the robot performing its task.

   Note: the robot system requirements, including those for controlling hazards, are contained in ISO 10218-2.[332]
3. (Robotic system) Manufacturing cell, including the robot hardware and software, consisting of the manipulator, the power supply, the control system, the end effectors, any equipment with which the robot is interfacing, and any communications interface that is operating and monitoring the robot.[333]

Robotic collaborative application: an application that involves human-robot interaction in a collaborative workspace in direct or indirect collaboration.

Note: this is to be distinguished from work situations in which man and robot capable of collaboration coexist, both working on autonomous tasks in a workshop, an industrial process or a production line.[334]

Robotic collaborative system: a system comprising one or more industrial robots, one or more terminals, and all the mechanisms, equipment, components and sensors required by the robot to perform its task in a collaborative workspace.[335]

Robotic device:

1. Mechanism developed with robotic technology, but not fulfilling all characteristics of a robot. Example: teleoperated remote manipulator, haptic device, end-effector, unpowered exoskeleton).[336]
2. Actuated mechanism fulfilling the characteristics of an industrial robot or a service robot, but lacking either the number of programmable axes or the degree of autonomy. Example: power assist device; teleoperated device; two-axis industrial manipulator.[337]

Robotics:

1. All the subjects involved in understanding the principles and performing the functions that enable a machine to perceive, decide, act and interact in a way that is adapted to its environment and to the tasks for which it has been designed. This ranges from mechanical design to the programming of artificial intelligence techniques and algorithms.[338]
2. (Fundamental terms) techniques involved in designing, building, and using robots or (computer-integrated manufacturing) Branch of engineering involved in designing, building, and using robots.[339]

---

332 ISO 10218-1:2011, Robots and robotic devices – Safety requirements for industrial robots – Part 1: Robots, 3.11. This standard has been withdrawn and replaced by ISO 10218-2:2025, Robotics – Safety requirements – Part 1: Industrial robots, see 'Robot system' 3.1.1.3.

333 ISO 2382:2015, Information technology – Vocabulary, No. 2122965.

334 Ministère du travail, *Guide de prévention à destination des fabricants et des utilisateurs pour la mise en œuvre des applications collaboratives robotisées* ['Prevention guide for manufacturers and users of collaborative robotic applications'], 2017.

335 Ibid.

336 ISO 8373:2021, Robotics – Vocabulary, 3.5.

337 ISO 8373:2012, Robots and robotic devices – Vocabulary, 2.8. This standard has been withdrawn and replaced by ISO 8373:2021, Robotics – Vocabulary.

338 CERNA-ALLISTENE, 'Éthique de la recherche en robotique' ['Ethics of research in robotics'], *November 2014.*

339 ISO 2382:2015, Information technology – Vocabulary, No. 2121394 and No. 2122962.

Robust AI: the robustness of an AI system encompasses both its technical robustness (appropriate in a given context, such as the application domain or life cycle phase) and as well as its robustness from a social perspective (ensuring that the AI system duly takes into account the context and environment in which the system operates). This is crucial to ensure that, even with good intentions, no unintentional harm can occur. Robustness is the third of the three components necessary for achieving Trustworthy AI.[340]

Robustness of an AI system: see 'Robust AI'.

Safeguarded space: space in which the personal care robot initiates a safety-related function if a safety-related object is detected within it.[341]

Note 1: examples of safety-related functions include trajectory changes, speed reduction, protective stop, force limiting.

Note 2: space can be static or dynamic, depending on the personal care robot, its application and its (dynamic) shape.

Safety component: a component of a product or of an AI system which fulfils a safety function for that product or AI system, or the failure or malfunctioning of which endangers the health and safety of persons or property.[342]

Sandbox plan: a document agreed between the participating provider and the competent authority describing the objectives, conditions, timeframe, methodology and requirements for the activities carried out within the sandbox.[343]

Self-learning: learning from an internal knowledge base, or from new input data, without introduction of explicit external knowledge.[344]

Self-organization: capability of an unsupervised learning neural network to adjust its connection weights according to the features found in the input patterns.[345]

Self-organizing network: neural network having a self-organization capability.

Note: a self-organizing network is often designed to emulate the brain cells' ability to organize themselves into behavior or a pattern.[346]

Sensitive operational data: operational data related to activities of prevention, detection, investigation or prosecution of criminal offences, the disclosure of which could jeopardise the integrity of criminal proceedings.[347]

Sensors: a sensor is a device used to measure a physical phenomenon. It supplies a signal – generally an electric current – in relation to the measurement of this phenomenon.[348]

Serious incident: an incident or malfunctioning of an AI system that directly or indirectly leads to any of the following:

(a) the death of a person, or serious harm to a person's health;

(b) a serious and irreversible disruption of the management or operation of critical infrastructure;

---

340 AI HLEG, 'Ethics guidelines for trustworthy AI', 2019, p. 37.

341 ISO 13482:2014: Robots and robotic devices – Safety requirements for personal care robots, 3.18.4 (Expected to be replaced by ISO/DIS 13482).

342 AI Act, Art. 3(14).

343 AI Act, Art. 3(54).

344 ISO 2382:2015, Information technology – Vocabulary, No. 2122968.

345 ISO 2382:2015, Information technology – Vocabulary, No. 2120679.

346 ISO 2382:2015, Information technology – Vocabulary, No. 2120660.

347 AI Act, Art. 3(38).

348 CERNA-ALLISTENE, 'Éthique de la recherche en robotique' ['Ethics of research in robotics'], *November 2014.*

(c) the infringement of obligations under Union law intended to protect fundamental rights;

(d) serious harm to property or the environment.[349]

Service robot: robot in personal use or professional use that performs useful tasks for humans or equipment.

Note 1: tasks in personal use include handling or serving of items, transportation, physical support, providing guidance or information, grooming, cooking and food handling, and cleaning.

Note 2: tasks in professional use include inspection, surveillance, handling of items, person transportation, providing guidance or information, cooking and food handling, and cleaning.[350]

Software engineering:

1. Systematic application of scientific and technological knowledge, methods, and experience to the design, implementation, testing, and documentation of software to optimize its production, support, and quality.[351]
2. All the activities involved in the design and implementation of products and procedures designed to rationalise software production and its monitoring.[352]

Special categories of personal data: the categories of personal data referred to in Article 9(1) of Regulation (EU) 2016/679, Article 10 of Directive (EU) 2016/680 and Article 10(1) of Regulation (EU) 2018/1725.[353]

Specific Absorption Rate (SAR): the specific absorption rate per unit mass of biological tissue, expressed in watts per kg (W/kg). The SAR (n g) corresponds to the specific absorption rate evaluated on n grams of contiguous tissue.[354]

Stakeholders: all those that research, develop, design, deploy or use AI, as well as those that are (directly or indirectly) affected by AI – including but not limited to companies, organisations, researchers, public services, institutions, civil society organisations, governments, regulators, social partners, individuals, citizens, workers and consumers.[355]

State: (artificial intelligence) snapshot description of a problem at one stage of its solution.[356]

Strong environmental sustainability: the notion of strong environmental sustainability goes back to the idea that in order to be sustainable, the rate of natural resource consumption and polluting emissions must be compatible with planetary environmental limits, the rate of resources and ecosystem renewal, and climate stability. Unlike weak sustainability, which requires less effort, strong sustainability does not allow the substitution of the loss of natural resources with artificial capital.[357]

---

349 AI Act, Art. 3(49).

350 ISO 8373:2021, Robotics – Vocabulary, 3.7.

351 ISO 2382:2015, Information technology – Vocabulary, No. 2121370.

352 Futura-Sciences, definitions, https://www.futura-sciences.com/tech/definitions/informatique-genie-logiciel-541/.

353 AI Act, Art. 3(37).

354 CERNA-ALLISTENE, 'Éthique de la recherche en robotique' ['Ethics of research in robotics'], *November 2014.* Anses, 'Avis relatif à l'expertise "Exposition aux radiofréquences et santé des enfants"' ['Opinion on the Expert Appraisal: "Exposure to Radiofrequencies and Child Health"'], collective expert appraisal report, June 2016.

355 AI HLEG, 'Ethics guidelines for trustworthy AI', 2019, pp. 37–38.

356 ISO 2382:2015, Information technology – Vocabulary, No. 2123837.

357 Glossary of the Montréal Declaration, 2018, https://montrealdeclaration-responsibleai.com/glossaire/.

Structured knowledge: knowledge that are organized based on a pre-defined (applicable) set of rules.[358]

Subject: for the purpose of real-world testing, means a natural person who participates in testing in real-world conditions.[359]

Substantial modification: a change to an AI system after its placing on the market or putting into service which is not foreseen or planned in the initial conformity assessment carried out by the provider and as a result of which the compliance of the AI system with the requirements set out in Chapter III, Section 2 of Regulation (EU) 2024/1689 on artificial intelligence is affected or results in a modification to the intended purpose for which the AI system has been assessed.[360]

Supercomputer: any computing system having at least petascale computing performance and procured under Regulation UE 2018/1488 establishing the European High Performance Computing Joint Undertaking.[361]

Supercomputing: computing at performance levels requiring the massive integration of individual computing elements, including quantum components, for solving problems which cannot be handled by standard computing system.[362]

Supervised learning: machine learning in which the algorithm trains itself on a given task using a set of data, each with an annotation indicating the expected result.

Note 1: supervised learning most often uses artificial neural networks.

Note 2: supervised learning is used, for example, for image recognition and machine translation.

See also: machine learning, unsupervised learning, artificial neural network.

Equivalent: supervised training.[363]

Sustainable development: sustainable development refers to the development of human society that is compatible with the capacity of natural systems to offer the necessary resources and services to this society. It is economic and social development that fulfills current needs without compromising the existence of future generations.[364]

Synapse: zone of contact between two neurons, allowing the exchange of information. The first neuron will release the message in the form of chemical molecules which will be picked up by the second and thus propagate the information.[365]

---

358 ISO/IEC 5392:2024, Information technology – Artificial intelligence – Reference architecture of knowledge engineering, 3.13.

359 AI Act, Art. 3(58).

360 AI Act, Art. 3(23).

361 Regulation EU 2018/1488 establishing the European High Performance Computing Joint Undertaking, [2018] OJ L252/1, Art. 2(16). No longer in force Date of end of validity: 7 August 2021; repealed by Regulation EU 2021/1173 of 13 July 2021.

362 Regulation EU 2021/1173 of 13 July 2021 on establishing the European High Performance Computing Joint Undertaking and repealing Regulation (EU) 2018/1488, Art. 2(29).

363 Commission d'enrichissement de la langue française (French Language Enrichment Commission), 'Vocabulaire de l'intelligence artificielle' ['Artificial intelligence vocabulary'], Opinion NOR: CTNR1832601K, *JORF*, n° 0285, 9 December 2018.

364 Glossary of the Montréal Declaration, 2018, https://montrealdeclaration-responsibleai.com/glossaire/.

365 Glossary of the Fédération pour la recherche sur le cerveau (FRC) [Federation for Brain Research], http://www.frcneurodon.org/comprendre-le-cerveau/glossaire/.

Synchronous neural network: neural network in which all artificial neurons are simultaneously updated.[366]

Systemic risk: a risk that is specific to the high-impact capabilities of general-purpose AI models, having a significant impact on the Union market due to their reach, or due to actual or reasonably foreseeable negative effects on public health, safety, public security, fundamental rights, or the society as a whole, that can be propagated at scale across the value chain.[367]

Testing data: data used for providing an independent evaluation of the AI system in order to confirm the expected performance of that system before its placing on the market or putting into service.[368]

Testing in real-world conditions: temporary testing of an AI system for its intended purpose in real-world conditions outside a laboratory or otherwise simulated environment, with a view to gathering reliable and robust data and to assessing and verifying the conformity of the AI system with the requirements of Regulation (EU) 2024/1689 and it does not qualify as placing the AI system on the market or putting it into service within the meaning of Regulation (EU) 2024/1689, provided that all the conditions laid down in Article 57 or 60 are fulfilled.[369]

Text generation: operation by which a large language model, in response to a prompt, automatically produces, modifies or completes texts.

Note 1: automatic generation of text in natural language can be used, for example, to answer a simple question, to produce a summary, a report, a translation, or even a literary work.

Note 2: text generation in programming languages is used in particular for writing or correcting source code.

See also: large language model, prompt.

Equivalent: AI text generation, automatic text generation[370]

Text token: elementary data of a large language model, consisting of a sequence of characters obtained by automatic segmentation of a text.

Note 1: segmentation into text tokens is used both in the machine learning phase and in the processing phase of a prompt.

Note 2: the number of text tokens is used to measure the size of a large language model; it is also used to estimate and invoice the operating cost of large commercial language models.

See also: machine learning, large language model, prompt.[371]

TOR (The onion router): anonymisation system on the Internet based on a succession of bounces via freely accessible servers (called nodes), combined with communication encryption.[372]

---

366 ISO 2382:2015, Information technology – Vocabulary, No. 2120652.

367 AI Act, Art. 3(65).

368 AI Act, Art. 3(32).

369 AI Act, Art. 3(57).

370 Commission d'enrichissement de la langue française (CELF) (French Language Enrichment Commission), 'Vocabulaire de l'intelligence artificielle' ['Artificial intelligence vocabulary'], Opinion NOR: CTNR2423171K, *JORF*, n° 0212, 6 September 2024.

371 Ibid.

372 Ministère de l'Intérieur, DMISC, *État de la menace liée au numérique en 2018*, ['2018 Digital Threat Landscape'], June 2018.

Totally connected network: fully connected nonlayered network in which each artificial neuron is connected to all the others, or a layered network in which each artificial neuron in a layer is connected to all neurons in the adjacent forward layer.[373]

Traceability: the traceability of an AI system refers to the capability to keep track of the system's data, development and deployment processes, typically by means of documented recorded identification.[374]

Training: training is the machine learning process through which AIS build a model from data. The performance of AIS depends on the quality of the model, which itself depends on the quantity and quality of data used during training.[375]

Training data: data used for training an AI system through fitting its learnable parameters.[376]

Transfer learning: automatic learning which consists of subjecting a pretrained model to a new training phase on a reduced volume of data relating to a target domain so that the model thus obtained generates answers relevant to this domain.

Note: transfer learning reduces the time and cost of machine learning in a target domain, particularly when the volume of data available in that domain is low.

See also: machine learning, pretrained model.[377]

Transformer: artificial neural network that performs parallel processing of training data from self-supervised learning in order to develop a generative model.

Note 1: parallel processing makes it possible to speed up learning and thus exploit heterogeneous, unstructured or unstructured data sets at low cost.

Note 2: transformers are used in automatic text generation, automatic image generation and automatic audio generation.

See also: artificial neural network, audio generation, foundation model, image generation, text generation.[378]

Transhumanism:

1. A school of thought which advocates the use of science and modern technology to improve the physical and mental capacities of human beings.
2. A set of techniques and ideas aimed at improving human capacities, whether physical or mental, through the advanced use of nanotechnologies and biotechnologies.[379]
3. The Jesuit researcher and priest Pierre Teilhard de Chardin was one of the first to use the term transhuman, in 1951. Julian Huxley created the concept of transhumanism in 1957. Although the term is a label covering very different movements, it refers to the overcoming of human suffering through scientific discoveries.[380]

---

373 ISO 2382:2015, Information technology – Vocabulary, No. 2120647.

374 AI HLEG, 'Ethics guidelines for trustworthy AI', 2019, p. 38.

375 Glossary of the Montréal Declaration, 2018, https://montrealdeclaration-responsibleai.com/glossaire/.

376 AI Act, Art. 3(29).

377 Commission d'enrichissement de la langue française (CELF) (French Language Enrichment Commission), 'Vocabulaire de l'intelligence artificielle' ['Artificial intelligence vocabulary'], Opinion NOR: CTNR2423171K, *JORF*, n° 0212, 6 September 2024.

378 Ibid.

379 Futura-Sciences, definitions, https://www.futura-sciences.com/tech/definitions/technologie-transhumanisme-16985/.

380 C. de Ganay and D. Gillot, 'Pour une intelligence artificielle maîtrisée, utile et démystifiée' ['For controlled, useful and demystified artificial intelligence'], OPECST Report, n° 4594, *AN*, n° 4594 *Senate* n° 464 of 15 March 2017, p. 203.

Trust:[381] we take the following definition from the literature: 'Trust is viewed as:

1. a set of specific beliefs dealing with benevolence, competence, integrity, and predictability (trusting beliefs);
2. the willingness of one party to depend on another in a risky situation (trusting intention); or
3. the combination of these elements.'[382]

While 'Trust' is usually not a property ascribed to machines, this document aims to stress the importance of being able to trust not only in the fact that AI systems are legally compliant, ethically adherent and robust, but also that such trust can be ascribed to all people and processes involved in the AI system's life cycle.[383]

Trustworthy AI: trustworthy AI has three components:

1. it should be lawful, ensuring compliance with all applicable laws and regulations;
2. it should be ethical, demonstrating respect for, and ensure adherence to, ethical principles and values; and
3. it should be robust, both from a technical and social perspective, since, even with good intentions, AI systems can cause unintentional harm.

Trustworthy AI concerns not only the trustworthiness of the AI system itself but also comprises the trustworthiness of all processes and actors that are part of the system's life cycle.[384]

Unsupervised learning (Data clustering, Unsupervised training): machine learning in which the algorithm uses a set of raw data and obtains a result based on the detection of similarities between some of these data.

Note: unsupervised learning is used, for example, to identify behaviour and recommend purchases.

See also: machine learning, supervised learning.[385]

Validation data: data used for providing an evaluation of the trained AI system and for tuning its non-learnable parameters and its learning process in order, inter alia, to prevent underfitting or overfitting.[386]

Validation data set: a separate data set or part of the training data set, either as a fixed or variable split.[387]

Virtual reality (VR): virtual reality is a technology that immerses people in a digitally created artificial world. It should not be confused with augmented reality (AR). It can be a reproduction of the real world or a completely imaginary universe. The experience is visual, auditory and, in some cases, haptic with the production of feedback effects. When people are equipped with the appropriate interfaces, such as gloves or clothing, they can experience certain sensations linked to touch or certain actions (blow, impact, etc.).[388]

---

381 See also 'Trustworthy AI'.

382 K. Siau and W. Wang, 'Building Trust in Artificial Intelligence, Machine Learning, and Robotics'(2018) 31 *Cutter Business Technology Journal*, pp. 47–53.

383 AI HLEG, 'Ethics guidelines for trustworthy AI', 2019, p. 38.

384 AI HLEG, 'Ethics guidelines for trustworthy AI', 2019, p. 38.

385 Commission d'enrichissement de la langue française (French Language Enrichment Commission), 'Vocabulaire de l'intelligence artificielle' ['Artificial intelligence vocabulary'], Opinion NOR: CTNR1832601K, *JORF*, n° 0285, 9 December 2018.

386 AI Act, Art. 3(30).

387 AI Act, Art. 3(31).

388 Futura-Sciences, definitions, https://www.futura-sciences.com/tech/definitions/technologie-realite-virtuelle-598/.

Voice control system (Voice controller): system in which a speech recognizer issues commands to computer-controlled equipment in response to speech input.

Note: example: a robot that responds to simple voice commands for movement.[389]

VoiceBot: automated relational device based on the same artificial intelligence foundation and equipped with the same capabilities as a chatbot, but for which exchanges are carried out by voice [by telephone or via a smart speaker, editor's note]. Compared with a chatbot, a VoiceBot naturally has to include two complementary layers corresponding to the voice recognition and synthesis stages. Used for customer support, voiceBots can also be seen as an advanced, modern version of interactive voice servers (IVR).[390]

Vulnerable persons and groups: no commonly accepted or widely agreed legal definition of vulnerable persons exists, due to their heterogeneity. What constitutes a vulnerable person or group is often context-specific. Temporary life events (such as childhood or illness), market factors (such as information asymmetry or market power), economic factors (such as poverty), factors linked to one's identity (such as gender, religion or culture) or other factors can play a role. The Charter of Fundamental Rights of the EU encompasses under Article 21 on non-discrimination the following grounds, which can be a reference point amongst others: namely sex, race, colour, ethnic or social origin, genetic features, language, religion or belief, political or any other opinion, membership of a national minority, property, birth, disability, age and sexual orientation. Other articles of law address the rights of specific groups, in addition to those listed above. Any such list is not exhaustive, and may change over time. A vulnerable group is a group of persons who share one or several characteristics of vulnerability.[391]

Whistleblower:

1. (Reporting person) A natural person who reports or publicly discloses information on breaches acquired in the context of his or her work-related activities.[392]
2. A natural person who discloses or reports, in a disinterested manner and in good faith, a crime or misdemeanour, a serious and manifest violation of an international commitment duly ratified or approved by France, a unilateral act of an international organisation taken on the basis of such a commitment, the law or regulations, or a serious threat or harm to the general interest, of which he or she has personal knowledge.[393]

Widespread infringement: any act or omission contrary to Union law protecting the interest of individuals, which:

(a) has harmed or is likely to harm the collective interests of individuals residing in at least two Member States other than the Member State in which:
   (i) the act or omission originated or took place;
   (ii) the provider concerned, or, where applicable, its authorised representative is located or established; or

---

389 ISO 2382:2015, Information technology – Vocabulary, No. 2120769.

390 B. Bathelot, *L'encyclopédie illustrée du marketing* ['The illustrated encyclopaedia of marketing'], updated on 23 May 2018, https://www.definitions-marketing.com/definition/voice-bot/.

391 AI HLEG, 'Ethics guidelines for trustworthy AI', 2019, p. 38.

392 Directive (EU) 2019/1937 of the European Parliament and of the Council of 23 October 2019 on the protection of persons who report breaches of Union law, [2019] OJ L305/17, Art. 5(7).

393 Loi 2016-1691 du 9 décembre 2016 relative à la transparence, à la lutte contre la corruption et à la modernisation de la vie économique [French Law 2016-1691 of 9 December 2016 on transparency, the fight against corruption and the modernisation of economic life], Art. 6.

(iii) the deployer is established, when the infringement is committed by the deployer;

(b) has caused, causes or is likely to cause harm to the collective interests of individuals and has common features, including the same unlawful practice or the same interest being infringed, and is occurring concurrently, committed by the same operator, in at least three Member States.[394]

Withdrawal of an AI system: any measure aiming to prevent an AI system in the supply chain being made available on the market.[395]

394 AI Act, Art. 3(61).

395 AI Act, Art. 3(17).

APPENDIX D – BIBLIOGRAPHY

European Declaration on Digital Rights and Principles for the Digital Decade of 23 January 2023, PUB/2023/89, [2023] OJ C23/1–7, available at: https://eur-lex.europa.eu/legal-content/EN/TXT/?uri=CELEX:32023C0123(01), [accessed on 16 July 2024].

'Status of All 24 Copyright Lawsuits v. AI Companies (Jun.14, 2024): 1st trial in AI cases nears, Thomson Reuters v. ROSS Intelligence', ChatGPT Is Eating the World Report, 14 June 2024, available at: https://chatgptiseatingtheworld.com/2024/06/14/status-of-all-24-copyright-lawsuits-v-ai-companies-jun-14-2026-1st-trial-in-ai-cases-nears-thomson-reuters-v-ross-intelligence/ [accessed on 5 July 2024].

'Artificial Intelligence Sector Study 2022: Research report for the Department for Science, Innovation & Technology (DSIT)', March 2023, 54 p., available at: GOV.UK https://assets.publishing.service.gov.uk/media/641d71e732a8e0000cfa9389/artifical_intelligence_sector_study.pdf [accessed on 5 July 2024].

'L'intelligence artificielle AlphaGo bat une nouvelle fois le champion du monde de go' ['Artificial intelligence AlphaGo beats the world go champion once again'], *Le Monde*, 25 May 2017, available at: https://www.lemonde.fr/pixels/article/2017/05/25/l-intelligence-artificielle-alphago-bat-une-nouvelle-fois-le-champion-du-monde-de-go_5133716_4408996.html [accessed on 16 July 2024, limited access, for subscribers only].

'Paris Pact for People and the Planet', 10 November 2023, available at: https://pactedeparis.org/ [accessed on 5 July 2024].

'Gathering of France's top AI talents', Élysée, Press release, 22 May 2024, available at: https://www.elysee.fr/emmanuel-macron/2024/05/22/rassemblement-des-plus-grands-talents-francais-de-lia (French version, 19 p.) and https://www.elysee.fr/en/emmanuel-macron/2024/05/22/gathering-of-frances-top-ai-talents (English version, 3 p.) [accessed on 5 July 2024].

A

AI HLEG (High-Level Expert Group on Artificial Intelligence), 'Ethics Guidelines for Trustworthy AI', April 2019, 41 p., available at: https://op.europa.eu/fr/publication-detail/-/publication/d3988569-0434-11ea-8c1f-01aa75ed71a1 [accessed on 17 July 2024].

AIA, 'Algorithmic Impact Assessment', v0.10.0, Canada.ca, available at: https://canada-ca.github.io/aia-eia-js/?lang=en [accessed on 30 May 2024, amended on 12 April 2023].

AIA, 'Algorithmic Impact Assessment tool', Canada.ca, available at: https://www.canada.ca/en/government/system/digital-government/digital-government-innovations/responsible-use-ai/algorithmic-impact-assessment.html [accessed on 30 May 2024, amended on 14 May 2024].

Alcaraz, M., 'L'AI Act ouvre la voie à des négociations pour rémunérer les auteurs' ['The AI Act paves the way for negotiations to remunerate authors'], Les *Échos*, 2 February 2024, available at: https://www.lesechos.fr/tech-medias/intelligence-artificielle/lai-act-ouvre-la-voie-a-des-negociations-pour-remunerer-les-auteurs-2073788 [accessed on 10 April 2024, limited access, for subscribers only].

Alcaraz, M., 'La relance de "Plus belle la vie" le pari à 30 millions de TF1' ['The relaunch of "Plus belle la vie", TF1's $30 million gamble'], *Les Échos*, 12 October 2023, available at: https://www.lesechos.fr/tech-medias/medias/la-relance-de-plus-belle-la-vie-le-pari-a-30-millions-de-tf1-1986715 [accessed on 2 May 2024, limited access, for subscribers only].

Alexandre, L. and Babeau, O., 'Anniversaire de ChatGPT: "Le XXIe siècle est né le 30 novembre 2022"' ['ChatGPT anniversary: "The 21st century was born on 30 November 2022"'], *Le Figaro*, 30 November 2023, available at: https://www.lefigaro.fr/vox/societe/

anniversaire-de-chatgpt-le-xxie-siecle-est-ne-le-30-novembre-2022-20231130 [accessed on 15 April 2024, limited access, for subscribers only].

Alexandre, L. and Rameaux, M., 'Des experts tech du monde entier appellent à une pause dans le développement de l'IA. Mais pouvons-nous nous le permettre' ['Tech experts around the world are calling for a pause in the development of AI. But can we afford it?'], *Atlantico.fr*, 31 March 2023, available at: https://atlantico.fr/article/decryptage/des-experts-tech-du-monde-entier-appellent-a-une-pause-dans-le-developpement-de-l-ia-mais-pouvons-nous-nous-le-permettre-entreprises-technologie-innovation-progres-dangers-chatgpt-risques-ia-laurent-alexandre-aurelie-jean-marc-rameaux [accessed on 16 July 2024].

Aghion, P. and Bouverot, A., 'AI: Our Ambition For France', Report by the Artificial Intelligence Commission, 15 March 2024, available in English (127 p.) at https://www.info.gouv.fr/upload/media/content/0001/10/54eefd62c084d66c373a8db1eefaeed88a21b010.pdf and in French (130 p.) at https://www.economie.gouv.fr/files/files/directions_services/cge/commission-IA.pdf [accessed on 3 May 2024].

Anderson, B. and Sutherland, E., 'Collective action for responsible AI in health', *OECD Artificial Intelligence Papers*, No. 10, OECD, 19 January 2024, 41 p., available at: https://www.oecd.org/en/publications/collective-action-for-responsible-ai-in-health_f2050177-en.html or https://doi.org/10.1787/f2050177-en [accessed on 27 June 2024].

ANSSI, 'Security recommendations for a generative AI system', Guide No. ANSSI-PA-102, 29 April 2024, available in English (36 p.) at https://cyber.gouv.fr/sites/default/files/document/security_recommandations_for_a_generative_ai_system.pdf and in French (38 p.) at https://cyber.gouv.fr/sites/default/files/document/Recommandations_de_s%C3%A9curit%C3%A9_pour_un_syst%C3%A8me_d_IA_g%C3%A9n%C3%A9rative.pdf [accessed on 23 July 2024].

Autorité de la concurrence, 'Données, algorithmes et transparence des plateformes: Quels impacts sur la concurrence? Quels enjeux pour la régulation?' (Retour sur les rendez-vous de l'Autorité de la concurrence du 24 nov. 2017) ['Data, algorithms and platform transparency: what impact on competition? What are the issues for regulation?' (A look back at the Autorité de la concurrence's meetings on 24 Nov. 2017], *Dalloz IP/IT*, January 2018 p. 8, available at: https://www.dalloz.fr/documentation/Document?id=DIPIT/CHRON/2018/0029 [accessed on 28 June 2022, limited access, for subscribers only].

B

Baverez, N., 'Géopolitique de l'intelligence artificielle' ['The geopolitics of artificial intelligence'], *Le Figaro*, 2 October 2023, available at: https://www.lefigaro.fr/vox/monde/geopolitique-de-l-intelligence-artificielle-20231001 [accessed on 2 May 2024, limited access, for subscribers only].

Bensamoun, A., 'Report Task Force on the implementation of the European regulation establishing harmonized rules on artificial intelligence ("template")', Conseil supérieur de la propriété littéraire et artistique, Ministère de la culture, 11 December 2024, available in English (47 p.) at https://www.culture.gouv.fr/Media/medias-creation-rapide/cspla_report_ia-template_english_dec._2024.pdf and in French (47 p.) at https://www.culture.gouv.fr/Media/medias-creation-rapide/cspla_rapport_ia_template_dec_.2024.pdf [accessed on 30 December 2024].

Bensoussan, A., 'ChatGPT dans le monde du droit – La cobotique juridique' ['ChatGPT in the Legal World – Legal Cobotics'], Bruxelles, Bruylant, 2024.

Bensoussan, A. and Bensoussan, J., 'Harmoniser les règles civiles de responsabilité en matière d'IA en Europe' ['Harmonising civil liability rules for AI in Europe'], *RLDI*, 2022, n°197, pp. 43–46, available at: www.lesechos.fr [accessed on 19 December 2022, limited access, for subscribers only].

Bensoussan, A. and Bensoussan, J., 'IA robots et droit' ['AI robots and the law'], Théorie et pratique, Bruxelles, Bruylant, July 2019, 632 p.

Bernier, M., 'Cols bleus, blancs roses: serons-nous tous au chômage à cause de l'IA?' ['Blue, pink and white collars: will we all be out of work because of AI?']. *Le Figaro*, 11 August 2023, p. 21, available at: https://www.lefigaro.fr/vox/economie/cols-bleus-blancs-roses-serons-nous-tous-au-chomage-a-cause-de-l-ia-20230810 [accessed on 14 May 2024, limited access, for subscribers only].

Berny, l., '1950 Alan Turing, père de la machine intelligente' ['1950 Alan Turing, father of the intelligent machine'], *Les Échos,* 21 August 2017, available at: https://www.lesechos.fr/2017/08/1950-alan-turing-pere-de-la-machine-intelligente-1116618 [accessed on 26 April 2024, limited access, for subscribers only].

Billion, A., 'L'identité des *a priori* du droit et de l'intelligence artificielle: Étude à partir de l'offre de règlement européen' ['The identity of the a priori of law and artificial intelligence: A study based on the proposal for a European regulation'], Journées d'étude pluridisciplinaire de la jeune recherche, *Revue Lexsociété*, 2023, 12 p., available at: https://hal.science/hal-03983965 n° hal-03983965 [accessed on 3 July 2024].

Borgonovi, F., Calvino, F., Criscuolo, C., Nania, J., Nitschke, J., O'Kane, L., Samek, L. and Seitz H., 'Emerging trends in AI skill demand across 14 OECD countries', *OECD Artificial Intelligence Papers,* No. 2, OECD, 17 October 2023, 64 p., available at: https://www.oecd.org/en/publications/emerging-trends-in-ai-skill-demand-across-14-oecd-countries_7c691b9a-en.html or https://doi.org/10.1787/7c691b9a-en [accessed on 26 June 2024].

Boizard, M., 'La valorisation des données numériques par la protection juridique des algorithmes' ['Enhancing the value of digital data through the legal protection of algorithms'], *Dalloz IP/IT*, February 2018 p. 99, available at: https://www.dalloz.fr/documentation/Document?id=DIPIT/CHRON/2018/0107 [accessed on 28 June 2022, limited access, for subscribers only].

Boué, C-E, 'IA après la tête, les jambes' ['AI after the head, the legs'], *Les Échos*, 27 February 2024, available at: https://www.lesechos.fr/idees-debats/sciences-prospective/ia-apres-la-tete-les-jambes-2078831 [accessed on 11 April 2024, limited access, for subscribers only].

Bradford, A., 'The False Choice Between Digital Regulation and Innovation', (2024) 118(2) *Nw. U. L. Rev.*, available at: https://papers.ssrn.com/sol3/papers.cfm?abstract_id=4753107.

Bretel, A., 'Rapport sur la mise en pratique de la notion de responsabilité de la Déclaration de Montréal: automne 2023' ['Report on the implementation of the concept of responsibility in the Montreal Declaration: fall 2023'], Université de Montréal, 25 March 2024, 16 p., available at: https://declarationmontreal-iaresponsable.com/wp-content/uploads/2024/03/RapportResponsabiliteDDM_A_Bretel-vf-vf.pdf [accessed on 13 May 2024].

Brioscú, A., Lauringson A., Saint-Martin A. and Xenogiani T., 'A new dawn for public employment services', *OECD Artificial Intelligence Papers*, No. 19, OECD, 13 June 2024, 76 p., available at: https://www.oecd.org/en/publications/a-new-dawn-for-public-employment-services_5dc3eb8e-en.html or https://doi.org/10.1787/5dc3eb8e-en [accessed on 27 June 2024].

Butlin, P., Long, R., Elmoznino, E., Bengio, Y., Birch, J., Constant, A., Deane, G., Fleming, S. M., Frith, C., Ji, X., Kanai, R., Klein, C., Lindsay, G., Michel, M., Mudrik, L., Peters, M. A. K., Schwitzgebel, E., Simon, J., and VanRullen, R., 'Consciousness in artificial intelligence: Insights from the science of consciousness', *arXiv* (arXiv:2308.08708) [cs.AI], 2023, available at: http://arxiv.org/abs/2308.08708 [accessed on 7 September 2024].

C

Calvino, F., Criscuolo, C., Dernis, H. and Samek, L., 'What technologies are at the core of AI?', *OECD Artificial Intelligence Papers*, No. 6, OECD, 13 November 2023, 45 p., available at: https://www.oecd.org/en/publications/what-technologies-are-at-the-core-of-ai_32406765-en.html or https://doi.org/10.1787/32406765-en [accessed on 30 May 2024].

Carpentier, L., 'L'IA et la culture: les machines sont-elles nos amies?' ['AI and culture: are machines our friends?'], *Le Monde*, 1 October 2023, p. 26, available at: https://www.lemonde.fr/culture/article/2023/09/30/l-intelligence-artificielle-et-la-culture-les-machines-sont-elles-nos-amies_6191755_3246.html [accessed on 2 May 2024, limited access, for subscribers only].

Causse, H., 'Le droit sous le règne de l'intelligence artificielle: essai' ['Law under the reign of artificial intelligence: an essay'], *Direct droit*, February 2023, 540 p., available at: https://uca.hal.science/hal-03999299v1/document, No. hal-03999299v1. [accessed on 3 July 2024].

Chantepie, G., 'Le droit en algorithmes ou la fin de la norme délibérée?' ['Law in algorithms or the end of the deliberate norm?'], *Dalloz IP/IT*, October 2017, p. 522, available at: https://www.dalloz.fr/documentation/Document?id=DIPIT/CHRON/2017/0385 [accessed on 28 June 2022, limited access, for subscribers only].

Chassagnard-Pinet, S, 'Le e-règlement amiable des différends' ['Electronic amicable dispute resolution'], *Dalloz IP/IT*, October 2017, p. 506, available at: https://www.dalloz.fr/documentation/Document?id=DIPIT/CHRON/2017/0382 [accessed on 28 June 2022, limited access, for subscribers only].

Chassagnard-Pinet, S, 'Les usages des algorithmes en droit: prédire ou dire le droit?' ['The use of algorithms in law: predicting or telling the law?'], *Dalloz IP/IT*, October 2017, p. 495, available at: https://www.dalloz.fr/documentation/Document?id=DIPIT/CHRON/2017/0380 [accessed on 28 June 2022, limited access, for subscribers only].

Chatila, R., Dauchet, M., Devillers, L., Ganascia, J.-G., Grinbaum, A. and Tessier, C., 'Éthique de la recherche en robotique' ['Ethics of research in robotics'], (Report No.°1 of the Research Ethics Board of Allistene, the Digital Sciences and Technologies Alliance), CERNA-ALLISTENE, November 2014, 63 p., available at: http://cerna-ethics-allistene.org/digitalAssets/38/38704_Avis_robotique_livret.pdf [accessed on 6 December 2024].

CIGREF, 'Père d'intelligence artificielle… John McCarthy' ['Father of artificial intelligence... John McCarthy'], 31 May 2014, available at: https://www.cigref.fr/archives/histoire-cigref/blog/pere-d-intelligence-artificielle-john-mccarthy/ [accessed on 26 April 2024].

Clément, M., 'Algorithmes au service du juge administratif: peut-on en rester maître?' ['Algorithms at the service of the administrative judge: can we still control them?'], *AJDA*, 2017, n° 43, p. 2453, available at: https://www.dalloz.fr/documentation/Document?id=AJDA/CHRON/2017/3339 [accessed on 28 June 2022, limited access, for subscribers only].

CNIL, 'IA et libre-arbitre: sommes-nous des moutons numériques?' ['AI and Free Will: Are We Digital Sheep?'], Cahier air2023, 22 April 2024, 38 p., available at: https://www.cnil.fr/sites/cnil/files/2024-04/cahier_air2023.pdf [accessed on 30 May 2024].

Comité national pilote d'éthique du numérique (CNPEN), 'Ethical issues of generative artificial intelligence systems', Opinion No. 7 of 30 June 2023, available in English (24 p.) at https://www.ccne-ethique.fr/sites/default/files/2024-08/CNPEN%20Opinion%207.pdf and in French (28 p.) at https://www.ccne-ethique.fr/sites/default/files/2023-09/CNPEN_avis7_06_09_2023_web-rs2.pdf [accessed on 18 April 2024].

Comité national pilote d'éthique du numérique (CNPEN), 'Enjeux éthiques des technologies de reconnaissance faciale, posturale et comportementale' ['Ethical issues surrounding facial, postural and behavioural recognition technologies'], Opinion No. 8,

20 November 2023, 40 p., available at: https://www.ccne-ethique.fr/sites/default/files/2024-02/CNPEN_AVIS8.pdf [accessed on 17 July 2024].

Conseil d'État, 'Intelligence artificielle et action publique: construire la confiance, servir la performance' ['Artificial intelligence and public action: building trust, serving performance'], Study by the Conseil d'État at the request of the Prime Minister, 31 March 2022, 360 p. (release on 30 August 2022), available at: www.conseil-etat.fr/publications-colloques/etudes or www.conseil-etat.fr/Media/actualites [accessed on 26 June 2024].

Crichton, C., 'Règlement sur l'intelligence artificielle: premiers éléments d'analyse' ['AI Act: Initial points for discussion'], 23 July 2024, available at: https://hal.science/hal-04655310v1, No. hal-04655310 [accessed on 26 September 2024].

D

Déchaux, R., 'Pour une réflexion critique de la régulation éthique et juridique de l'intelligence artificielle' ['A critical reflection on the ethical and legal regulation of artificial intelligence'] (PowerPoint deck), Séminaire critique de l'intelligence artificielle [A critical seminar on artificial intelligence], France. 2022, 33 p., available at: https://amu.hal.science/hal-03815962v1/document, No HAL-03815962 [accessed on 3 July 2024].

Defferrard, F., 'Le pouvoir de *jurisdictio* des algorithmes aux États-Unis: entre fantasme et réalité jurisprudentielle' ['The jurisdictio power of algorithms in the United States: between fantasy and jurisprudential reality'], *Dalloz IP/IT*, 14 December 2017, n° 12, p. 668, available at: https://www.dalloz.fr/documentation/Document?id=DIPIT/CHRON/2017/0455 [accessed on 28 June 2022, limited access, for subscribers only].

Deviller, L., 'Les systèmes d'intelligence artificielle font amplifier les biais de genre dans tous les domaines' ['Artificial intelligence systems amplify gender bias in all fields'], *Le Monde*, 6 June 2023, available at: https://www.lemonde.fr/idees/article/2023/06/06/les-systemes-d-intelligence-artificielle-vont-amplifier-les-biais-de-genre-dans-tous-les-domaines_6176418_3232.html [accessed on 15 May 2024, limited access, for subscribers only].

Dondero, B., 'Justice prédictive: la fin de l'aléa judiciaire?» ["Predictive justice: the end of judicial uncertainty?'], *D.*, 9 March 2017, n° 10, p. 532, available at: https://www.dalloz.fr/documentation/Document?id=RECUEIL/CHRON/2017/0196 [accessed on 28 June 2022, limited access, for subscribers only].

Doré, E., 'Une IA parvient à distinguer le cerveau des hommes et des femmes' ['An AI is able to distinguish between male and female brains'], *Le Figaro*, 26 February 2024, available at: https://www.lefigaro.fr/sciences/une-ia-parvient-a-distinguer-le-cerveau-des-hommes-et-des-femmes-20240226 [accessed on 11 April 2024, limited access, for subscribers only].

Dupré, J. and Lévy Véhel J., 'L'intelligence artificielle au service de la valorisation du patrimoine jurisprudentiel' ['Artificial intelligence to enhance the value of case law heritage'], *Dalloz IP/IT*, October 2017 p. 500, available at: https://www.dalloz.fr/documentation/Document?id=DIPIT/CHRON/2017/0381 [accessed on 28 June 2022, limited access, for subscribers only].

Duranton, S., 'IA générative et productivité: pour le meilleur et pour le pire» ["Generative AI and productivity: for better or for worse'], *Les Échos*, 3 October 2023, p. 10, available at https://www.lesechos.fr/idees-debats/editos-analyses/ia-generative-et-productivite-pour-le-meilleur-et-pour-le-pire-1983814 [accessed on 6 December 2024, limited access, for subscribers only].

E

ENKAOUA, C. 'L'utilisation d'une IA comme ChatGPT ne remplace pas spécialiste; elle complète l'expertise humaine', Entretien avec Alain Bensoussan, avocat au barreau de Paris, spécialiste Droit du numérique et des communications ['The use of an AI like ChatGPT does not replace a specialist; it complements human expertise'. Interview with Alain Bensoussan, lawyer at the Paris Bar, specialist in digital and communications law], *Gaz. Pal.*, 14 November 2023, n° 37, Actualité, p. 7, available at: https://www.gazette-du-palais.fr/article/GPL456b3/ [accessed on 28 June 2024].

ENSER, N., 'L'"Entrée dans le Paradis" du droit d'auteur: pas sans un être humain à l'origine de la création!' ['The "Entry into Paradise" of copyright: Not without a human being at the origin of creation!'] (A comment of US District Court for the District of Columbia, 18 August 2023, *Stephen Thaler v ShiraPerlmutter*), n° 22-1564 (BAH)], *Dalloz Actualité IP/IT et Communication*, 18 September 2023, available at: https://www.dalloz-actualite.fr/print/flash/l-entree-dans-paradis-du-droit-d-auteur-pas-sans-un-etre-humain-l-origine-de-creation [accessed on 2 May 2024, limited access, for subscribers only].

EUROPEAN COMMISSION, 'Communication: The"Blue Guide" on the implementation of EU product rules 2022', [2022] OJ C247/1, 152 p., available at: https://eur-lex.europa.eu/legal-content/EN/TXT/PDF/?uri=CELEX:52022XC0629(04) [accessed on 15 April 2024].

EUROPEAN COMMISSION and DIRECTORATE-GENERAL FOR EDUCATION, YOUTH, SPORT AND CULTURE, 'Ethical guidelines on the use of artificial intelligence (AI) and data in teaching and learning for educators', *Publications Office of the European Union*, September 2022, 40 p., available at: https://data.europa.eu/doi/10.2766/153756.

EUROPEAN COMMISSION and DIRECTORATE-GENERAL FOR RESEARCH AND INNOVATION, 'Successful and Timely Uptake of Artificial Intelligence in Science in the EU', (Scientific Opinion; No. 15): *Publications Office of the European Union*, March 2024, 102 p., available at: https://data.europa.eu/doi/10.2777/46863 or https://op.europa.eu/en/publication-detail/-/publication/d6d8ed54-32a8-11ef-a61b-01aa75ed71a1 [accessed on 6 December 2024].

EUROPEAN COMMISSION and DIRECTORATE-GENERAL FOR RESEARCH AND INNOVATION, 'Living Guidelines on the Responsible use of Generative AI in Research', *Publications Office of the European Union, ERA Forum*, March 2024, 18 p., available at: https://european-research-area.ec.europa.eu/news/living-guidelines-responsible-use-generative-ai-research-published [accessed on 6 May 2024].

F

FABIJAŃSKA, A., RIZZOLI, A., GROTH, P., MARTINKOVÁ, P., OLIVEIRA, A. and YEUNG, K., 'Successful and Timely Uptake of Artificial Intelligence in Science in the EU: Evidence Review Report', SAM Scientific Advice Mechanism Report, 16 April 2024, 128 p., available at: Zenodo https://doi.org/10.5281/zenodo.10977676 [accessed on 6 May 2024].

FERRY, L., 'Avec ChatGPT, allons-nous vers l'IA forte?' ['With ChatGPT, are we moving towards strong AI?'], *Le Figaro*, 22 February 2023, available at: https://www.lefigaro.fr/vox/societe/luc-ferry-avec-chatgpt-allons-nous-vers-l-ia-forte-20230222 [accessed on 22 April 2024, limited access, for subscribers only].

FILIPPUCCI, F., Gal, P., JONA-LASINIO, C., LEANDRO, A. and NICOLETTI, G., 'The impact of Artificial Intelligence on productivity, distribution and growth', *OECD Artificial Intelligence Papers*, No. 15, OECD, 16 April 2024, 64 p., available at: https://www.oecd.org/en/publications/the-impact-of-artificial-intelligence-on-productivity-distribution-and-growth_8d900037-en.html or https://doi.org/10.1787/8d900037-en [accessed on 30 May 2024].

G

G7-G20, 'Hiroshima Process International Code of Conduct for Organizations Developing Advanced AI Systems', 30 October 2023, available at: https://g7g20-documents.org/fileadmin/G7G20_documents/2023/G7/Japan/Leaders/2%20Leaders'%20Annex/Hiroshima%20Process%20International%20Code%20of%20Conduct%20for%20Organizations%20Developing%20Advanced%20AI%20Systems_30102023.pdf and https://digital-strategy.ec.europa.eu/en/library/hiroshima-process-international-code-conduct-advanced-ai-systems [accessed on 28 June 2024].

Ganay, C. de, and Gillot, D., 'Pour une intelligence artificielle maîtrisée, utile et démystifiée' ['For controlled, useful and demystified artificial intelligence'], OPECST Report, n° 4594 *AN* (14th legislature), n° 464 *Sénat* (2016-2017), 15 March 2017, Tome I, 273 p., available at: https://www.senat.fr/rap/r16-464-1/r16-464-11.pdf, Tome II, 275 p., available at: https://www.senat.fr/rap/r16-464-2/r16-464-21.pdf [accessed on 30 May 2024].

Georgieff, A., 'Artificial intelligence and wage inequality', *OECD Artificial Intelligence Papers*, No 13, OECD, 10 April 2024, 37 p., available at: https://www.oecd.org/en/publications/artificial-intelligence-and-wage-inequality_bf98a45c-en.html or https://doi.org/10.1787/bf98a45c-en [accessed on 27 June 2024].

Gervais, D.J., 'Artificial Inventors', *Vanderbilt Law Research Paper*, 5 April 2023, No 23-28, 9 p., available at: SSRN https://ssrn.com/abstract=4410992 or http://dx.doi.org/10.2139/ssrn.4410992 [accessed on 23 July 2024].

Gervais, D.J., 'Pour la cause: la protection par le droit d'auteur des productions des systèmes d'intelligence artificielle' ['For the cause: copyright protection for the products of artificial intelligence systems'], *Les Cahiers de propriété intellectuelle*, January 2023, vol. 35, n° 1, 17 p., available at: https://www.lescpi.ca/articles/volume-35-volume-35-volume-35-numero-1/pour-la-cause-la-protection-par-le-droit-dauteur-des-productions-des-systemes-dintelligence-artificielle/ [accessed on 23 July 2024].

Gervais, D.J., 'The Machine As Author' (2019) 105 *Iowa Law Review*, 2053-2106, *Vanderbilt Law Research Paper*, 25 March 2019, No 19–35, 54 p., available at: SSRN https://ssrn.com/abstract=3359524 [accessed on 23 July 2024].

Godefroy, L., 'La performativité de la justice "prédictive": un pharmakon?' ['The performativity of "predictive" justice: a pharmakon?'], *D.*, 18 October 2018, n° 36, p. 1979, available at: https://www.dalloz.fr/documentation/Document?id=RECUEIL%2FCHRON%2F2018%2F4021&FromId=IPIT_RUB000437_DOC_1 [accessed on 28 June 2022, limited access, for subscribers only].

Godefroy, L., 'Le code algorithmique au service du droit' ['Algorithmic code at the service of the law'], *D.*, April 2018, n° 14, p. 734, available at: https://www.dalloz.fr/lien?famille=revues&dochype=RECUEIL%2FCHRON%2F2018%2F1521 [accessed on 28 June 2022, limited access, for subscribers only].

Grass, E., 'IA le "créa" est mort, vive le créa' ['IA le "créa" is dead, long live le créa'], *Les Échos*, 1 December 2023, available at: https://www.lesechos.fr/idees-debats/editos-analyses/ia-le-crea-est-mort-vive-le-crea-2038517 [accessed on 15 April 2024, limited access, for subscribers only].

Green, A., 'Artificial intelligence and the changing demand for skills in the labour market', *OECD Artificial Intelligence Papers*, No. 14, OECD, 10 April 2024, 55 p., available at: https://www.oecd.org/en/publications/artificial-intelligence-and-the-changing-demand-for-skills-in-the-labour-market_88684e36-en.html or https://doi.org/10.1787/88684e36-en [accessed on 27 June 2024].

Green, A., 'Artificial intelligence and the changing demand for skills in Canada', *OECD Artificial Intelligence Papers*, No. 17, OECD, 30 May 2024, 47 p., available at: https://www.

oecd.org/en/publications/artificial-intelligence-and-the-changing-demand-for-skills-in-canada_1b20cdb6-en.html or https://doi.org/10.1787/1b20cdb6-en [accessed on 27 June 2024].

Guerlin, G., 'Considérations sur les smart contracts' ['Considerations on smart contracts'], *Dalloz IP/IT*, October 2017, p. 512, available at: https://www.dalloz.fr/documentation/Document?id=DIPIT/CHRON/2017/0383 [accessed on 28 June 2022, limited access, for subscribers only].

Guigné, A. de, 'Philippe Aghion: "Pour que la France joue dans la cour des grands, il lui faut massivement investir dans la formation, dans la puissance de calcul, dans l'IA"' ['Philippe Aghion: "For France to play in the big league, it needs to invest massively in training, computing power and AI"'], *Le Figaro*, 2 May 2024, available at: https://www.lefigaro.fr/economie/philippe-aghion-pour-que-la-france-joue-dans-la-cour-des-grands-il-lui-faut-massivement-investir-dans-la-formation-dans-la-puissance-de-calcul-dans-l-ia-20240502 [accessed on 2 May 2024, limited access, for subscribers only].

H-I

Henno, J., 'Calculer plus, mais consommer moins le défi de l'IA' ['Compute more, but consume less – the challenge of AI'], *Les Échos*, 9 April 2024, available at: https://www.lesechos.fr/idees-debats/sciences-prospective/calculer-plus-mais-consommer-moins-le-defi-de-lia-2087662 [accessed on 15 April 2024, limited access, for subscribers only].

Henno, J., '1956: et l'intelligence artificielle devint une science' ['1956: And artificial intelligence became a science'], *Les Échos*, 21 August 2017, available at: https://www.lesechos.fr/2017/08/1956-et-lintelligence-artificielle-devint-une-science-181042 [accessed on 26 April 2024, limited access, for subscribers only].

IBM, 'Everyday ethics for ArtificiaI Intelligence', 11 November 2022, 27 p., available at: https://www.ibm.com/design/ai/ethics/everyday-ethics/ [accessed on 3 May 2024].

Institute for the future, 'The Next Era of Human-Machine Partnerships: Emerging Technologies' Impact on Society & Work in 2030', *Dell Technologies*, 7 May 2017, 23 p., available at: https://www.delltechnologies.com/content/dam/delltechnologies/assets/perspectives/2030/pdf/SR1940_IFTFforDellTechnologies_Human-Machine_070517_readerhigh-res.pdf [accessed on 26 April 2024].

ISED-ISDE, 'Voluntary Code of Conduct on the Responsible Development and Management of Advanced Generative AI Systems', *Innovation, Science and Economic Development Canada*, September 2023, available at: https://ised-isde.canada.ca/site/ised/en/voluntary-code-conduct-responsible-development-and-management-advanced-generative-ai-systems [accessed on 30 May 2024, amended on 28 May 2024].

I-K

Jasor, M., 'L'intelligence artificielle générative, nouvelle alliée des DRH?' ['Is generative artificial intelligence the new ally of HRs?'], *Les Échos*, 5 October 2023 p. 11, www.lesechos.fr/idees-debats/leadership-management/lintelligence-artificielle-generative-nouvelle-alliee-des-drh-1984667 [accessed on 6 December 2024, limited access, for subscribers only].

Jeulin, B., 'Analyse du projet de loi américain sur la divulgation des données d'entraînement des IA génératives' ['Analysis of the US Generative AI Copyright Disclosure Act of 2024'], *Dalloz Actualité IP/IT et Communication*, 27 May 2024, available at: https://www.dalloz-actualite.fr/flash/analyse-du-projet-de-loi-americain-sur-divulgation-des-donnees-d-entrainement-des-ia-generativ [accessed on 27 May 2024, limited access, for subscribers only].

Koenig, G., 'Protéger le droit d'auteur à l'ère de l'IA' ['Protecting copyright in the age of AI'], *Les Échos*, 29 November 2023, available at: https://www.lesechos.fr/idees-debats/

editos-analyses/proteger-le-droit-dauteur-a-lere-de-lia-2037947 [accessed on 15 April 2024, limited access, for subscribers only].

Kwarteng, K. and Dorries, N., 'National AI Strategy', Presented to Parliament, by the Secretary of State for Digital, Culture, Media and Sport, by Command of Her Majesty, (Command Paper; 525), *HM Government*, Version 1.2, September 2021, 35 p., available at: https://assets.publishing.service.gov.uk/media/614db4d1e90e077a2cbdf3c4/National_AI_Strategy_-_PDF_version.pdf [accessed on 27 June 2024].

L

Le Bolzer, J., 'Risques, régulation, éthique: état des lieux des enjeux qui questionnent l'IA' ['Risks, regulation, ethics: an overview of the issues surrounding AI'], *Les Échos*, 12 October 2023, p. 32 (paper), 20 September 2023 (online), available at: https://www.lesechos.fr/thema/articles/risques-regulation-ethique-etat-des-lieux-des-enjeux-qui-questionnent-lia-1979756 [accessed on 2 May 2024, limited access, for subscribers only].

Le Cun, Y., 'Modèles connexionnistes de l'apprentissage' ['Connectionist learning models'], PhD thesis in Computer Science, under the supervision of Maurice Milgram, Université Paris 6, 15 June 1987, 277 p., available at: http://yann.lecun.com/exdb/publis/pdf/lecun-87.pdf [accessed on 30 April 2024].

Legros, C., 'Il me semble indispensable de mettre en avant le principe de précaution' ['I believe it is essential to emphasise the precautionary principle'], Interview with Yoshua Bengio, researcher, *Le Monde*, 29 April 2023, available at: www.scribd.com/document/659195417/2023-04-30-Le-Monde-IA-Bengio-mettre-en-avant-le-principe-de-precaution [accessed on 6 Decembee 2024].

Legros, C., 'L'idée même de vouloir ralentir la recherche sur l'IA s'apparente à un nouvel obscurantisme' ['The very idea of wanting to slow down AI research is akin to a new obscurantism'], Interview with Yann Le Cun, Chief AI Scientist at Meta, *Le Monde*, 29 April 2023, available at: https://www.lemonde.fr/idees/article/2023/04/28/yann-le-cun-directeur-a-meta-l-idee-meme-de-vouloir-ralentir-la-recherche-sur-l-ia-s-apparente-a-un-nouvel-obscurantisme_6171338_3232.html [accessed on 22 April 2024, limited access, for subscribers only].

Legros, C., 'Aujourd'hui, l'intelligence artificielle, c'est le Far West! Nous devons ralentir et réguler' ['Today, AI is the Wild West! We need to slow down and regulate'], Interview with Yoshua Bengio, researcher, *Le Monde*, 28 April 2023, updated on 29 September 2023, available at: https://www.lemonde.fr/idees/article/2023/04/28/yoshua-bengio-chercheur-aujourd-hui-l-intelligence-artificielle-c-est-le-far-west-nous-devons-ralentir-et-reguler_6171336_3232.html [accessed on 22 April 2024, limited access, for subscribers only].

Léna, M., 'Les rapprochements judiciaires' ['Legal reconciliations'], *AJ penal*, 2017, n° 07-08, p. 305, available at: hthttps://www.dalloz.fr/documentation/Document?id=AJPEN/CHRON/2017/0226 [accessed on 28 June 2022, limited access, for subscribers only].

Lestapis, H. de, 'Club Med met l'IA sous bonne surveillance' ['Club Med keeps a close eye on AI'], *Les Échos*, 2 October 2023, available at: https://www.lesechos.fr/thema/articles/club-med-met-lia-sous-bonne-surveillance-1983453 [accessed on 2 May 2024, limited access, for subscribers only].

Levy Provençal, M., 'Le guide de l'IA générative en entreprise' ['Guide to generative AI in the enterprise'], *Brightness*, April 2024, https://www.brightness.fr/actualites/generativeai-fr [accessed on 30 May 2024

Liebl, A. and Klein, T., 'AI Act Impact Survey: Exploring the impact of the AI Act on Startups in Europe', *AAI (appliedAI Institute for Europe)*, 12 December 2022, available at: https://aai.frb.io/assets/files/AI-Act-Impact-Survey_Report_Dec12.2022.pdf [accessed on 8 April 2024].

LINC, 'Sécurité des systèmes d'IA' ['AI system security'], Report from the CNIL's Digital Innovation Lab, *LINC-Cnil*, April 2022, 40 p., available at: https://linc.cnil.fr/sites/linc/files/atoms/files/linc_cnil_dossier-securite-systemes-ia.pdf [accessed on 31 May 2024].

Loignon, S., 'La Sacem exerce son droit d'opposition face aux outils d'intelligence artificielle' ['Sacem exercises its right to object to artificial intelligence tools'], *Les Échos*, 13 October 2023, available at: https://www.lesechos.fr/tech-medias/medias/la-sacem-exerce-son-droit-dopposition-face-aux-outils-dintelligence-artificielle-1986943 accessed on 2 May 2024, limited access, for subscribers only].

Lorenz, P., Perset, K. and Berryhill, J., 'Initial policy considerations for generative artificial intelligence', *OECD Artificial Intelligence Papers*, No. 1, OECD, 18 September 2023, 39 p., available at: https://www.oecd-ilibrary.org/science-and-technology/initial-policy-considerations-for-generative-artificial-intelligence_fae2d1e6-en and https://doi.org/10.1787/fae2d1e6-en [accessed on 30 May 2024].

M-N

Marchand, L., 'Comment ChatGPT s'occupe de planifier votre prochain voyage' ['How ChatGPT takes care of planning your next trip'], *Les Échos*, 27 March 2023, available at: https://www.lesechos.fr/tech-medias/hightech/comment-chatgpt-soccupe-de-planifier-votre-prochain-voyage-1919427 [accessed on 26 April 2024, limited access, for subscribers only].

Marique, E. and Strowel, A., 'Gouverner par la loi ou les algorithms: de la norme générale de comportement au guidage rapproché des conduites' ['Governing by law or algorithms: from general standards of behaviour to close monitoring of conduct'], *Dalloz IP/IT*, October 2017, p. 517, available at: https://www.dalloz.fr/documentation/Document?id=DIPIT/CHRON/2017/0384 [accessed on 28 June 2022, limited access, for subscribers only].

Martin, J-O., 'Laurent Alexandre: "Avec l'IA, la marginalisation de l'espèce humaine est absolument inévitable"' ['Laurent Alexandre: "With AI, the marginalisation of the human species is absolutely inevitable"'], *Le Figaro*, 9 August 2023, available at: https://www.lefigaro.fr/vox/societe/laurent-alexandre-avec-l-ia-la-marginalisation-de-l-espece-humaine-est-absolument-inevitable-20230809 [accessed on 30 April 2024, limited access, for subscribers only].

McFadden, M., Jones, K., Taylor, E. and Osborn, G., 'Harmonising Artificial Intelligence: The Role of Standards in the EU AI Regulation', *Oxford Information Labs* (Working paper 2021.5), Oxford Commission on AI & Good Governance, December 2021, 42 p., available at: https://oxcaigg.oii.ox.ac.uk/wp-content/uploads/sites/11/2021/12/Harmonising-AI-OXIL.pdf [accessed on 26 June 2024].

McSweeny, C., 'Hybrid Intelligence in the Trademark Industry: Combining AI & Human Expertise', CITMA, 21 March 2024 and *Corsearch*, 23 April 2024 available at:https://www.citma.org.uk/resources/hybrid-intelligence-in-the-trade-mark-industry-combining-ai-human-expertise-mb24.html and https://corsearch.com/content-library/blog/hybrid-intelligence-in-the-trademark-industry-combining-ai-human-expertise/ [accessed on 27 June 2024].

Molga, P., 'L'intelligence humaine progresse toujours' ['Human intelligence continues to progress'], *Les Échos*, 23 October 2023, p. 13, available at: https://www.lesechos.fr/idees-debats/sciences-prospective/lintelligence-humaine-progresse-toujours-1988612 [accessed on 14 May 2024, limited access, for subscribers only].

Numeum, 'Behind the codes and the data: A Practical Guide to Ethical AI', version 1, September 2021, 72 p., available in English at https://ai-ethical.com/wp-content/uploads/2022/12/2022-SN-Guide-Methodo-IA-Ethiques-web-version.pdf and in French at https://ai-ethical.com/wp-content/uploads/2021/09/2021-SN-Guide-Me%CC%81thodo-IA-Ethiques-version-web-light.pdf [accessed on 13 May 2024].

O

OECD, 'AI, data governance and privacy', *OECD Artificial Intelligence Papers*, No. 22, OECD, 26 June 2024, 55 p., available at: https://www.oecd.org/en/publications/ai-data-governance-and-privacy_2476b1a4-en.html or https://doi.org/10.1787/2476b1a4-en [accessed on 27 June 2024].

OECD, 'Governing with Artificial Intelligence', *OECD Artificial Intelligence Papers*, No. 20, OECD, 13 June 2024, 32 p., available at: https://www.oecd.org/en/publications/governing-with-artificial-intelligence_26324bc2-en.html or https://doi.org/10.1787/26324bc2-en [accessed on 24 June 2024].

OECD, 'Artificial intelligence, data and competition', *OECD Artificial Intelligence Papers*, No. 18, OECD, 24 May 2024, 60 p., available at: https://www.oecd.org/en/publications/artificial-intelligence-data-and-competition_e7e88884-en.html or https://doi.org/10.1787/e7e88884-en [accessed on 24 June 2024].

OECD, 'Defining AI incidents and related terms', *OECD Artificial Intelligence Papers*, No. 16, OECD, 6 May 2024, 20 p., available at: https://www.oecd.org/en/publications/defining-ai-incidents-and-related-terms_d1a8d965-en.html or https://doi.org/10.1787/d1a8d965-en [accessed on 30 May 2024].

OECD, 'Using AI in the workplace', *OECD Artificial Intelligence Papers*, No. 11, OECD, 15 March 2024, 16 p., available at: https://www.oecd.org/en/publications/using-ai-in-the-workplace_73d417f9-en.html or https://doi.org/10.1787/73d417f9-en [accessed on 27 June 2024].

OECD, 'Explanatory memorandum on the updated OECD definition of an AI system', *OECD Artificial Intelligence Papers*, No. 8, OECD, 5 March 2024, 11 p., available at: https://www.oecd.org/en/publications/explanatory-memorandum-on-the-updated-oecd-definition-of-an-ai-system_623da898-en.html or https://doi.org/10.1787/623da898-en [accessed on 27 June 2024].

OECD, 'Generative artificial intelligence in finance', *OECD Artificial Intelligence Papers*, No. 9, OECD, 15 December 2023, 35 p., available at: https://www.oecd.org/en/publications/generative-artificial-intelligence-in-finance_ac7149cc-en.html or https://doi.org/10.1787/ac7149cc-en [accessed on 30 May 2024].

OECD, 'Common guideposts to promote interoperability in AI risk management', *OECD Artificial Intelligence Papers*, No. 5, OECD, 7 November 2023, 36 p., available at: https://www.oecd.org/en/publications/common-guideposts-to-promote-interoperability-in-ai-risk-management_ba602d18-en.html or https://doi.org/10.1787/ba602d18-en [accessed on 27 June 2024].

OECD, 'Stocktaking for the development of an AI incident definition', *OECD Artificial Intelligence Papers*, No. 4, OECD, 27 October 2023, 36 p., available at: https://www.oecd.org/en/publications/stocktaking-for-the-development-of-an-ai-incident-definition_c323ac71-en.html or https://doi.org/10.1787/c323ac71-en [accessed on 26 June 2024].

OECD, 'The state of implementation of the OECD AI Principles four years on', *OECD Artificial Intelligence Papers*, No. 3, OECD, 27 October 2023, 82 p., available at: https://www.oecd.org/en/publications/the-state-of-implementation-of-the-oecd-ai-principles-four-years-on_835641c9-en.html or https://doi.org/10.1787/835641c9-en [accessed on 26 June 2024].

OECD, 'G7 Hiroshima process on generative artificial intelligence (AI): Towards a G7 common understanding on generative AI', OECD, 7 September 2023, 37 p., available at: https://www.oecd.org/en/publications/g7-hiroshima-process-on-generative-artificial-intelligence-ai_bf3c0c60-en.html or https://doi.org/10.1787/bf3c0c60-en [accessed on 20 September 2023].

OECD, 'OECD Employment Outlook 2023: Artificial Intelligence and the Labour Market', OECD, 11 July 2023, 300 p., available at: https://www.oecd.org/en/publications/oecd-employment-outlook-2023_08785bba-en.html or https://doi.org/10.1787/08785bba-en, [accessed on 20 September 2023, free online reading, access to pdf reserved for purchase).

OECD, 'OECD Framework for the Classification of AI systems', *OECD Digital Economy Papers*, No. 323, OECD, 22 February 2022, 80 p., available at: https://www.oecd.org/en/publications/oecd-framework-for-the-classification-of-ai-systems_cb6d9eca-en.html or https://doi.org/10.1787/cb6d9eca-en [accessed on 30 May 2024].

P-Q

Piquard, A., 'Intelligence artificielle: "Demain, faudra-t-il protéger nos "neuro-droits"?"' ['Artificial intelligence: "Will we need to protect our "neuro-rights" tomorrow?"'], *Le Monde*, 26 October 2023, p. 25, available at: https://www.lemonde.fr/idees/article/2023/10/26/intelligence-artificielle-demain-faudra-t-il-proteger-nos-neuro-droits_6196574_3232.html [accessed on 14 May 2024, limited access, for subscribers only] (Please note: the online version is different from the paper version).

Piquard, A., 'Intelligences artificielles le défi de rendre détectables les contenus générés par des IA' ['Artificial intelligence: The challenge of making AI-generated content detectable'], *Le Monde*, 25 May 2023, available at: https://www.lemonde.fr/economie/article/2023/05/25/le-defi-de-rendre-detectables-les-contenus-generes-par-des-intelligences-artificielles_6174851_3234.html [accessed on 15 April 2024, limited access, for subscribers only] (Please note: as the online version was modified on 29 September 2023, it differs from the paper version).

Pouget, H., 'Standards Setting', EU Artificial Intelligence Act, available at: https://artificialintelligenceact.eu/standard-setting/.

Pouzet, C., 'Les modes de régulation de l'intelligence artificielle par le droit européen: entre droit souple et droit dur' ['How European law regulates artificial intelligence: between soft law and hard law'], Droit Dumas, 2020, p. 104, available at: https://dumas.ccsd.cnrs.fr/dumas-04261774v1/document HAL Id: dumas-04261774. [accessed on 3 July 2024].

Prévost, S. and Royer, E., 'Intelligence artificielle' ['Artificial Intelligence'], Grand angle, Paris, Dalloz, March 2019, ISBN: 978-2-247-19075-1, 351 p.

Prud'homme, B., Régis, C., Farnadi, G., Dreier, V. and Rubel, S., 'Missing links in AI governance', *UNESCO-Mila*, 17 March 2023, ISBN: 978-92-3-100579-4, 362 p., available at: https://unesdoc.unesco.org/ark:/48223/pf0000384787 [accessed on 30 May 2024].

Quinault-Maupoil T., 'Intelligence artificielle le gouvernement lance une vaste expérimentation dans l'administration» ["Artificial intelligence: the government launches a vast experiment in public administration"], *Le Figaro*, 4-5 October 2023, available at: https://www.lefigaro.fr/international/intelligence-artificielle-le-gouvernement-lance-une-vaste-experimentation-dans-l-administration-20231004 [accessed on 30 May 2024, limited access, for subscribers only].

R-S

Racine, J-B., 'La résolution amiable des différends en ligne ou la figure de l'algorithme médiateur' ['The amicable resolution of online disputes or the figure of the mediating algorithm'], *D.* 2018, 13 September 2018, n° 31, p. 1700, available at: https://www.dalloz.

fr/documentation/Document?id=RECUEIL/CHRON/2018/3375 [accessed on 28 June 2022, limited access, for subscribers only].

Rochfeld, J., 'L'encadrement des décisions prises par algorithme' ['How to supervise decisions made by algorithms'], *Dalloz IP/IT*, September 2018, p. 474, available at: https://www.dalloz.fr/documentation/Document?id=DIPIT/CHRON/2018/0439 [accessed on 28 June 2022, limited access, for subscribers only].

Rouvière, F., 'Le raisonnement par algorithmes: le fantasme du juge-robot' ['Algorithmic reasoning: the fantasy of the robot judge'], *RTD civ.*, July 2018, n° 2. p. 530, available at: https://www.dalloz.fr/documentation/Document?id=RTDCIV/CHRON/2018/0214 [accessed on 28 June 2022, limited access, for subscribers only].

Sallé, C., 'Le cri d'alarme des industries culturelles et créatives face aux "boîtes noires" des IA' ['Cultural and creative industries sound the alarm over AI "black boxes"'], *Le Figaro*, 3 October 2023, available at: https://www.lefigaro.fr/medias/le-cri-d-alarme-des-industries-culturelles-et-creatives-face-aux-boites-noires-des-ia-20231003 [accessed on 30 April 2024, limited access, for subscribers only].

Sallé, C., 'Comment l'IA menace l'industrie de la musique' ['How AI threatens the music industry'], *Le Figaro*, 14 April 2023 (digital version), 15-16 April 2023 (paper version), available at: https://www.lefigaro.fr/medias/comment-l-ia-menace-l-industrie-de-la-musique-20230414 [accessed on 22 April 2024, limited access, for subscribers only].

SAM Scientific Advice Mechanism. 'Successful and Timely Uptake of Artificial Intelligence in Science in the EU: Evidence Review Report', 2024, available at: https://doi.org/10.5281/ZENODO.10849580 [accessed on 6 December 2024].

SAPEA (Science Advice for Policy by European Academies), 'Successful and Timely Uptake of Artificial Intelligence in Science in the EU: Evidence Review Report', Berlin: SAPEA (Science Advice for Policy by European Academies), 2024, available at: https://data.europa.eu/doi/10.2777/46863 or https://scientificadvice.eu/advice/artificial-intelligence-in-science/ or https://op.europa.eu/en/publication-detail/-/publication/d6d8ed54-32a8-11ef-a61b-01aa75ed71a1 [accessed on 6 December 2024].

Siau, K. and Wang, W., 'Building Trust in Artificial Intelligence, Machine Learning, and Robotics' (2018) 31 *Cutter Business Technology Journal*, pp. 47–53, available at: https://www.cutter.com/article/building-trust-artificial-intelligence-machine-learning-and-robotics-498981 [accessed on 6 December 2024].

Smith (Herbert Smith Freehills LLP), 'First EU court to consider who holds copyright in AI generated work suggests room for ownership if prompts are sufficiently creative in parallels with a recent Beijing Internet Court decision', *Lexology*, 4 June 2024, available at: https://www.lexology.com/library/detail.aspx?g=a89e4198-119e-476f-95b2-46eaed3de554&utm_source=Lexology+Daily+Newsfeed&utm_mediu%E2%80%A6 [accessed on 27 June 2024].

Schmitt, F., 'L'UE instaure les premières règles au monde contrôlant l'IA' ['The EU introduces the world's first rules controlling AI'], *Les Échos*, 11 December 2023, p. 26, available at: https://www.lesechos.fr/tech-medias/intelligence-artificielle/lue-instaure-les-premieres-regles-au-monde-controlant-lintelligence-artificielle-2040387 [accessed on 14 May 2024, limited access, for subscribers only] (the sub-section 'Des obligations à géométrie variable' ['Variable obligations'], is not in the digital version and only in the paper version).

T-U

Touzet, C., 'Using AI to support people with disability in the labour market', *OECD Artificial Intelligence Papers*, No. 7, OECD, 24 November 2023, 103 p., available at: https://www.oecd.org/en/publications/using-ai-to-support-people-with-disability-in-the-labour-market_008b32b7-en.html or https://doi.org/10.1787/008b32b7-en [accessed on 30 May 2024].

Turing, A.M., 'Computing machinery and intelligence', *Mind*, Oxford University Press, October 1950, vol. 59, No 236, available at: https://academic.oup.com/mind/article/LIX/236/433/986238 and http://www.csee.umbc.edu/courses/471/papers/turing.pdf [accessed on 11 August 2023].

Ugale, G. and Hall, C., 'Generative AI for anti-corruption and integrity in government', *OECD Artificial Intelligence Papers,* No. 12, OECD, 22 March 2024, 50 p., available at: https://www.oecd.org/en/publications/generative-ai-for-anti-corruption-and-integrity-in-government_657a185a-en.html or https://doi.org/10.1787/657a185a-en [accessed on 30 May 2024].

UNESCO, 'Recommendation on the Ethics of Artificial Intelligence', SHS/BIO/REC-AIETHICS/2021, *Unesdoc*, 23 November 2021, 21 p., available at: https://unesdoc.unesco.org/ark:/48223/pf0000380455 [accessed on 30 May 2024].

V-W

Vallet, F., 'Sécurité des systèmes d'IA, les gestes qui sauvent' ['AI system security, a first aid guide'], LINC (CNIL's Digital Innovation Lab), 21 January 2022, available at: https://linc.cnil.fr/securite-des-systemes-dia-les-gestes-qui-sauvent [accessed on 22 July 2024].

Vergara, I., 'Amazon se lance à son tour dans la course à l'IA générative' ['Amazon takes its turn in the generative AI race'], *Le Figaro*, 14 April 2023 (digital version), 15-16 April 2023 (paper version), available at: https://www.lefigaro.fr/secteur/high-tech/amazon-se-lance-a-son-tour-dans-la-course-a-l-intelligence-artificielle-generative-20230414 [accessed on 22 April 2024, limited access, for subscribers only].

Verhagen, A., 'Using AI to manage minimum income benefits and unemployment assistance', *OECD Artificial Intelligence Papers*, No. 21, OECD, 24 June 2024, 54 p., available at: https://www.oecd.org/en/publications/using-ai-to-manage-minimum-income-benefits-and-unemployment-assistance_718c93a1-en.html and https://doi.org/10.1787/718c93a1-en [accessed on 24 June 2024].

Vinzi, V., 'Réinventer le management: l'ère de l'intelligence hybride' ['Reinventing management: the era of hybrid intelligence'], *Les Échos*, 22 January 2024, available at: https://www.lesechos.fr/idees-debats/cercle/opinion-reinventer-le-management-lere-de-lintelligence-hybride-2067738 [accessed on 5 April 2024, limited access, for subscribers only].

Wikipedia contributors, 'Histoire de l'intelligence artificielle' ['History of artificial intelligence'], Wikipedia, Version of 26 March 2024, available at: https://fr.wikipedia.org/w/index.php?title=Histoire_de_l%27intelligence_artificielle&oldid=213702301%20 [accessed on 26 April 2024].

WIPO, 'Getting the innovation ecosystem ready for AI: An IP Policy Toolkit', 5 July 2024, 41 p., available at: https://www.wipo.int/edocs/pubdocs/en/wipo-pub-2003-en-getting-the-innovation-ecosystem-ready-for-ai.pdf [accessed on 5 July 2024].

WIPO, 'China-Based Inventors Filing Most GenAI Patents, WIPO Data Shows', Press release, PR/2024/921, of 3 July 2024, available at: https://www.wipo.int/pressroom/en/articles/2024/article_0009.html [accessed on 5 July 2024].

WIPO, 'Patent Landscape Report - Generative Artificial Intelligence', 2 July 2024, 114 p., available at: https://www.wipo.int/web-publications/patent-landscape-report-generative-artificial-intelligence-genai/assets/62504/Generative%20AI%20-%20PLR%20EN_WEB2.pdf [accessed on 5 July 2024].

WIPO, 'Generative AI: Navigating Intellectual Property', 28 February 2024, 15 p., available at: https://www.wipo.int/export/sites/www/about-ip/en/frontier_technologies/pdf/generative-ai-factsheet.pdf [accessed on 5 July 2024].

WIPO, 'WIPO Conversation – AI Inventions', 22 May 2023, 10 p., available at: https://www.wipo.int/export/sites/www/about-ip/en/frontier_technologies/pdf/wipo-ai-inventions-factsheet.pdf [accessed on 5 July 2024].

WIPO, "What are frontier technologies?", 4 July 2022, 2 p., available at: https://www.wipo.int/export/sites/www/about-ip/en/frontier_technologies/pdf/frontier-tech-6th-factsheet.pdf [accessed on 5 July 2024].

WIPO, "WIPO Technology Trends 2021 - Assistive Technology Executive summary", 2021, 12 p., available at: https://www.wipo.int/edocs/pubdocs/en/wipo_pub_1055_2021_exec_summary.pdf and http://dx.doi.org/10.34667/tind.42922 [accessed on 5 July 2024].

WIPO, "WIPO Technology Trends 2021 - Assistive Technology", 2021, 273 p., available at: https://www.wipo.int/edocs/pubdocs/en/wipo_pub_1055_2021_exec_summary.pdf and http://dx.doi.org/10.34667/tind.42922 [accessed on 5 July 2024].

WIPO, "WIPO Technology Trends 2019 - Artificial Intelligence Executive summary", 2019, 16 p., available at: http://dx.doi.org/10.34667/tind.29086 [accessed on 5 July 2024].

WIPO, "WIPO Technology Trends 2019 - Artificial Intelligence", 2019, 158 p., available at: https://dx.doi.org/10.34667/tind.29084 [accessed on 5 July 2024].

Woitier, C., 'Le Figaro se dote d'une charte sur l'usage de l'IA générative' ['Le Figaro adopts a charter on the use of generative AI'], *Le Figaro*, 13 December 2023, p. 28, available at: https://www.lefigaro.fr/medias/le-figaro-se-dote-d-une-charte-sur-l-usage-de-l-ia-generative-20231212 [accessed on 6 December 2024, limited access, for subscribers only].

Wong, C., 'IA Les ChatGPT du droit se multiplient dans la French Tech' ['IA Legal ChatGPTs are on the rise in French Tech'], *Les Échos*, 9 January 2024, available at: https://www.lesechos.fr/start-up/ecosysteme/ia-les-chatgpt-du-droit-se-multiplient-dans-la-french-tech-2045039 [accessed on 11 April 2024, limited access, for subscribers only].

APPENDIX E – INDEX

The index entries refer to page numbers.

V

W